Birdlife of Houston, Galveston, and the Upper Texas Coast

NUMBER TEN: GULF COAST STUDIES

Sponsored by Texas A&M University—Corpus Christi

John W. Tunnell Jr., General Editor

by TED L. EUBANKS JR.,

ROBERT A. BEHRSTOCK,

and RON J. WEEKS

Foreword by Victor Emanuel

Texas A&M University Press

College Station

Birdlife of Houston, Galveston, and the Upper Texas Coast

Library of Congress Cataloging-in-Publication Data

Eubanks, Ted.
   Birdlife of Houston, Galveston, and the Upper Texas Coast /
by Ted L. Eubanks Jr., Robert A. Behrstock, and Ron J. Weeks;
foreword by Victor Emanuel.
      p. cm.
   Includes bibliographical references and index.
   ISBN-13: 978-1-58544-510-3 (cloth : alk. paper)
   ISBN-10: 1-58544-510-x (cloth : alk. paper)
   1. Birds—Texas—Houston Region.   2. Birds—Texas—Gulf
Coast.   I. Behrstock, Robert A.   II. Weeks, Ron J.   III. Title.
   QL684.T4E93 2006
   598.09764′1411—dc22
                                                    2006006375

CONTENTS

ILLUSTRATIONS

TABLES

FOREWORD

At the age of eight, when I became interested in birds and nature, I was living near downtown Houston. I soon met consummate naturalists such as Joe Heiser and Armand Yramategui. They became my mentors. Over the next thirty years I spent many happy days in the field on the Upper Texas Coast, and I have strong memories of my first fallouts, of sightings of the Eskimo Curlew, and of fine days in the field with friends. I have traveled all over the world and visited all the continents. The Upper Texas Coast remains my favorite place to be out in nature.

When I think of the Texas coast I think of the remarkable abundance and variety of birds. It is especially thrilling and soul satisfying to see any species of native bird in great numbers: a hundred thousand Snow Geese, five thousand American Avocets, one hundred Dickcissels, or one thousand Broad-winged Hawks. These are all wonderful sights, but what especially evokes the Texas coast for me is the variety and numbers of wading birds: herons, egrets, ibis, and spoonbills. A single roadside ditch can be filled with a hundred of these wading birds, each vying for the fish in the receding water. A visit to a rookery is one of the great experiences in nature. I look forward to many more years in the field in the Upper Texas Coast and know that those days will be enhanced by this superb book.

Birders view the publication of a guide to the birds of a distant place as a major event. A book about the birds of the area where you live or an area you like to visit is equally important, if not more so. Such a book, if well done, deepens our appreciation of our birds and our area and connects us even more closely to them. That kind of connection is one of the many rewards of a life spent in nature. *Birdlife of Houston, Galveston, and the Upper Texas Coast* is such a book. It should become an essential part of the library of every birder who lives in this region or who visits it.

I am especially pleased that this book takes a broad view of birds, seeing them as one important part of the natural landscape. They are beautiful and fascinating creatures to be studied and appreciated in their environment. The authors move beyond listing or the chasing of rarities to direct our attention to the lives of birds and the other aspects of the natural world they inhabit. Such a focus can only yield greater rewards to the observer, ensuring that every day spent in nature is an enriching one.

I am also pleased that this book gives due credit to the careful observers of the past, the men and women whose observations over many years provide us with invaluable insight into our region's natural history. This historical perspective enables us to place our own observations in the context of those who came before.

The authors have a wonderful sense of enthusiasm for the Upper Texas Coast. Their accounts are lively, insightful, and delightful. I cannot imagine a better team to write a book on the Upper Texas Coast. Ted Eubanks, Bob Behrstock, and Ron Weeks are superb birders and consummate naturalists. They have tramped through the fields, woodlands, and mudflats of the Upper Texas Coast for many years. No one knows this area better or loves it more. *Birdlife of Houston, Galveston, and the Upper Texas Coast* sets a new standard for what a regional guide can be. No region is more deserving of such a book.

Victor Emanuel
Bolivar Peninsula

Birders have access to many excellent field guides that assist with bird identification. Because of their broad audience and short species accounts, such guides are generally limited to a few illustrations, identification tips, and brief statements concerning the bird's biology and range. As most birders' interests evolve and mature, we require a book that provides additional information about the birds inhabiting our particular corner of the world. Frequently, the book we are looking for has not yet been written.

During the last 30 years the Upper Texas Coast (UTC) has developed a reputation as a world-class venue for traveling birders—avitourists. Each year, especially during spring, thousands of birders from around the world visit this naturalist's Mecca. For many visitors, the UTC's attractiveness stems from the high diversity of large waders, shorebirds, warblers, and sparrows that can be seen during a relatively brief visit. This species diversity is related to many factors, including the region's variety of natural habitats; its position along the migratory routes of both landbirds and waterbirds; agricultural practices that attract and nourish waterfowl and shorebirds; weather patterns that often cause birds to concentrate along the coast; and the warm, insect-rich winters. Additionally, several local environmental organizations administer sanctuaries that provide special opportunities for viewing the local avifauna (appendix 1). The UTC portion of the Great Texas Coastal Birding Trail map series (TPWD 1999) now provides a detailed site template for visiting birders. Once immersed in the trail, many visitors who simply came to bird remain for the prehistoric-looking alligators, prairies blanketed with wildflowers, or cathedral-like forests of longleaf pines that harbor rare orchids and numerous butterflies.

The dollars generated by avitourism represent an important source of local revenue. Nonetheless, the communities of East Texas are players in a tug-of-war between forces that would protect and enhance the environment for people and wildlife, and forces that would dredge, drill, and develop it from horizon to horizon, with no regard for its biological riches. Such development exacerbates the perils that already threaten our birdlife. Migratory birds especially face an array of hazards as they lose their nesting and wintering grounds to timbering, ranching, and residential development, their food base to pesticides, their nest holes to European Starlings, and their offspring to cats and cellular transmission towers.

Readers who were introduced to birding during the last decade may be distressed by some of our discussions. It may be difficult to visualize the immense spring fallouts we discuss, much as we have difficulty envisioning the great herds of bison that once blanketed the prairies. Although quadruple-digit days for any kind of warbler are unlikely to occur again, the UTC still remains one of the finest places in North America to witness the spectacle of migration.

Pulich (1988), Rappole and Blacklock (1985), Seyffert (2001), Wauer (1973), and White (2002) have examined the birds of north-central Texas, the Coastal Bend, the Panhandle, the Big Bend region, and northeast Texas. So far, no single work attempts to summarize what has been discovered during the last 150 years concerning the distribution of birds along the upper coast. *Birdlife of Houston, Galveston and the Upper Texas Coast* was written as a companion to your field guide and binoculars for your visits to Houston, High Island, Galveston, Freeport, or any of the area's other rich and exciting birding spots. We place the birdlife of the region, a seven-county area with a longer bird list than 43 of the 50 states, into a historical and ecological context that begins during precolonial times. We discuss more than 480 kinds of birds including introduced, endangered, extirpated, extinct, and hypothetical species.

The birdlife of any region is in a constant state of flux. Although we base our species accounts on more than a century of sightings, they represent a mere snapshot in biological time. Ranges expand and contract, new species appear, and well-established ones vanish—often in response to habitat changes created by humans. Acknowledging this dynamism is what makes a birder's twentieth visit to the same hedgerow as exciting as the first. We have considered records available to us through the end of 2004, knowing that inevitably, certain accounts will be out of date by the time we go to press. We hope this book is comprehensive enough to serve as a baseline for further inquiries into the birdlife of the Upper Texas Coast.

Previously unpublished information will be of value to local and visiting birders, landowners, gardeners, habitat managers, and indeed any individual with an interest in the region's birdlife. Expanded discussions include extensive documentation of topics such as fallouts (or groundings) of spring migrants, shorebird "big days" and censuses, fall landbird movements, hawk migration, *Empidonax* flycatchers, and wintering hummingbirds. State and federal agency personnel will find information concerning habitat preference, status, and management priorities for sensitive species. Often we discuss plants in relation to birds and their habitats. Common and scientific names of plants we mention are included in appendix 2. Color photographs illustrate typical habitats, significant regional records, and both unusual and characteristic species.

We offer this book to both neophyte and advanced birders, not only to summarize our sightings, or to turn a database into prose, but also to share our passion for the birds of the coast. As did John James Audubon when he visited Galveston and Houston, we too have become infatuated with "the Snipes innumerable, the Blackbirds, the Gallinules, and the Curlews that surround us." For despite all of the alterations that the UTC has suffered since European settlement, there remains a rich and diverse avifauna. We hope we have written this book with a conviction to remain faithful to the innate curiosity, inquisitiveness and *élan* of Audubon and his kind who ventured this path before us. For they derived stimulation and enrichment from the entire tapestry of the natural world, not simply from those few curious anomalies that may only represent slipped stitches. Our aspiration is to lay before you this ornithological mosaic in its entirety, and we hope that you will profit not only from the pattern as it emerges but from each individual tile as it is fitted into position.

ACKNOWLEDGMENTS

Ted Eubanks would like to thank his parents, Ted and Mary, for providing the spark, and his wife, Virginia, for allowing the spark to glow for so many years.

Bob Behrstock is grateful to his parents Jerome and Salli for encouraging his natural history pursuits from early childhood. He also recognizes Ben and Linda Feltner and Mary Ann Chapman, who provided his entrée to East Texas birding and later became his partners in Peregrine Tours.

Ron Weeks would like to thank his wife, Irenna, and his children, Mathias and Ariana, for the time spent away from them while birding and writing about birds. He would also like to recognize his birding mentor in his home state of Montana, the late P. D. Skaar.

Long before we ever considered writing a book about the birds of the UTC, many people shared their time and knowledge with us. During the ensuing years, many more aided our field and library efforts in a variety of ways. We would like to acknowledge the help of many people we have joined in the field, including Ron and Marcia Braun, Charles and Olivia Brower, Mary Ann Chapman, Jane Clayton, Fred Collins, Tom and Sherry Collins, David and Jan Dauphin, Victor Emanuel, Ted Eubanks Sr., T. Ben Feltner and Linda Feltner, David Matson, Jim Morgan, Gretchen Mueller, Will and Jan Risser, and John and Gloria Tveten; and the late birders Margaret Anderson, Charles Clark, George Clayton, Wes Cureton, Emery Froelich, and Paul and Margaret Jones.

This work depends heavily on the many people, too numerous even to begin to mention, who have contributed their sightings to the *Gulf Coast Migrant,* the Clearinghouse section of the *Spoonbill, American Birds,* and *Audubon Field Notes.* To them and to the editors of these publications, we are grateful.

We acknowledge the efforts of the many birders who have compiled annual Christmas Bird Counts organized by the National Audubon Society. We also thank the many skilled leaders who have donated countless hours leading field trips for local bird clubs, including the Ornithology Group of the Outdoor Nature Club of Houston (ONC) and the Houston Audubon Society. Besides supplying our database with records, their actions continue to foster interest in the avifauna of the UTC. Organizations of interest to birders are listed in appendix 1, and we encourage participation in their field trips and support for their environmental activities, upon which the local birdlife depends.

Various individuals provided us with data compilations from which we have drawn, including Ron and Marcia Braun (banding records and various observations), Charles and Olivia Brower (hummingbird banding records), Winnie Burkett and Gail Diane Yavanovich (Bolivar Flats and hawk migration), Fred Collins (waterfowl and shorebirds), Tom and Sherry Collins (Freeport CBC data), T. Ben Feltner and Noel Pettingell (UTC records), Tony and Phyllis Frank (*Spoonbill* records), C. Hacker (band return data), Kevin Karlson (shorebirds), Paula Kennedy (Armand Bayou), Mike Lange (colonial waterbirds), Bob McFarlane (shorebird numbers), Brent Ortego (hummingbirds, eagles, etc.), Dick Payne (avitourism), Dwight Peake (pelagic birds), Frank Peace (hawk migration), Royce Pendergast (far eastern Texas records), Sumita Prasad (various bird records), Cecilia Riley (Henslow's Sparrow, raptor and waterbird counts), David Sarkozi (rail information and local records), Spencer Simon and Jim Neaville (Anahuac and Sea Rim national wildlife refuges), Jim Stevenson (Galveston Island records), Don Verser, Cin-Ty Lee, and Jim Hinson (recent passerine migration records), Matt Wagner (colonial waterbirds), and John and Jana Whittle (far eastern Texas records). Our friend and field companion Jim Morgan helped us on a number of fronts, providing among other things migration dates and sparrow information. We are particularly indebted to Jim for collecting and compiling two decades of fallout censuses and then providing this rare and thus far unpublished data set for our use. Over the years, his census efforts were aided by Fred Collins, Glen Cureton, Penny Cureton, the late Wes Cureton, T. Ben Feltner, Eubanks, and Behrstock.

We are also indebted to Greg Lasley and Chuck Sexton for generously providing several versions of the Texas Bird Records Committee's Review List and to Mark Lockwood for frequently updating us with the committee's latest voting rounds. These data greatly enhance the value of our publication to both the birding and scientific communities.

For no reward other than helping their fellow birders find some of our more exciting avian visitors, Gary Clark, Kathy Adams-Clark, Mike Austin, Peter Gottschling, Susan Ellis, and Lynne Aldrich have donated countless hours operating the UTC's rare bird tape. More recently, Linda Parmer, P. D. Hulce, David Sarkozi, and Sheridan Coffey have made a great deal of UTC bird information available via the listserv Texbirds and their home pages on the World Wide Web. We acknowledge their steadfast efforts with this thankless task.

A number of people shared their hummingbird expertise; many invited us into their yards to observe and photograph. They include Margaret Anderson, Charles and Olivia Brower, Fred Collins, Tom and Sherry Collins, Kim and Kathy Combs, the Paul Fagala family, Fae Humphrey, Gretchen Mueller, Nancy Newfield, Beverly Nuckols, Will and Jan Risser, Steve and Ruth Russell, and Craig Zalk.

Martha Henschen, Maggie Honig, Gretchen Mueller, Katie Northrup, Gloria Saylor, and Doug Williams answered plant questions, provided reference materials, and freely shared their collective botanical wisdom. As this project drew to a close, Judy Boyce provided key back issues of the *Spoonbill*.

Kim Wiar, formerly of the University of Oklahoma Press, encouraged us to produce an early draft of this project. Without her optimism, the project would not have begun. Shannon Davies at Texas A&M University Press exhibited unflagging enthusiasm. She and Jennifer Ann Hobson guided us during the preparation of the text and submission of the final project. To both, our heartfelt thanks. Special thanks to our copyeditor Sally Antrobus. Her patient and thorough editing of our manuscript greatly enhanced the final product. Jon Dunn, Paul Kerlinger, Sumita Prasad, Jim Stevenson, and an anonymous reviewer read part or all of the manuscript. They provided both helpful editorial suggestions and biological perspectives that also greatly enhanced our final product.

Taxonomic and biogeographic expertise was shared by members of the Texas Bird Records Committee (TBRC), including Keith Arnold, John Arvin, and Greg Lasley. Out-of-staters who made helpful suggestions included Giff Beaton, Steve Cardiff and Donna Dittman of Louisiana State University, Paul DeBenedictis, Jon Dunn, Andrew Kratter of Florida Museum of Natural History, and David Sibley.

Our heartfelt thanks to all these people; to anyone we have neglected to mention, our most sincere apologies.

Birdlife of Houston, Galveston, and the Upper Texas Coast

John James Audubon, the fountainhead from whom so much of America's ornithological knowledge flows, visited the Upper Texas Coast (UTC) in 1837. A fledgling republic but a year old, Texas seduced Audubon not only with its promise of wildlife yet unnamed (he did find a new species of rattlesnake) but with its ragtag muster of colonists who had captured the American imagination with their improbable defeat of Santa Ana's numerically stronger Mexican army. Audubon's descriptions of the city of Galveston and the new capital of Houston were singularly unflattering, particularly his brief meeting with Sam Houston, president of the new republic. Yet his infatuation with the birdlife of Galveston Bay and its tributary, Buffalo Bayou, remains vividly etched in his writings. "Ah, my dear friend," he wrote in a letter to Reverend Bachman, "would that you were here just now to see the Snipes innumerable, the Blackbirds, the Gallinules, and the Curlews that surround us; — that you could listen as I do now, to the delightful notes of the Mocking-bird, pouring forth his soul in melody as the glorious orb of day is fast descending towards the western horizon; —that you could gaze on the Great Herons which, after spreading their broad wings, croak aloud as if doubtful regarding the purpose of our visit to these shores!"

In 1938 George Williams remarked that "except for three or four articles recording observations made during a few days of the year, there has been published no survey of bird life along any part of the Texas coast lying north of the Rio Grande Valley." Sixty-five years later, surprisingly few publications have appeared negating Williams's statement. Early publications and papers, including those by John James Audubon (1831–39, 1840–44), Henry Nehrling (1882), John Allen Singley (1893), and George Finlay Simmons (1914), contained simple lists of birds and habitats seen during brief visits to the region. John K. Strecker's (1912) account provided preliminary information on the statewide abundance and seasonal occurrence of Texas birds with limited reference to the UTC. George Williams (1938) supplied the first comprehensive description of the upper coast's waterbirds. This important paper, now largely forgotten, offered insight into the breadth, magnitude, and dynamics of regional waterbird populations and movements. Most significant, Williams's observations now furnish a critical historical perspective for contemporary studies.

Arlie McKay lived in Cove through the early 1970s, working for what was then Humble Oil Company. A "patch birder" who rarely left his neighborhood, he found a number of state and local firsts and regularly communicated with birding luminaries of the time, such as George Williams and Connie Hagar. Arlie recorded his daily sightings on the backs of discarded voting ballots, using a numerical code he created. Although effectively blind in his later years, Arlie identified the area's first Rock Wren by sound (later confirmed by Ben Feltner). He was a mentor and inspiration for many UTC birders, including Ben Feltner, Victor Emanuel, and, in Arlie's last years, Ted Eubanks.

Most subsequent publications remained bound to a traditional checklist format augmented by brief descriptions of expected arrival and departure dates, regional distribution, and general approximations of relative abundance. Among the more contemporary are *The Birds of Galveston Island* (Hall et al. 1959), *Checklist of Birds of the Upper Texas Coast* (Williams 1962), the Texas Ornithological Society's checklists (Arnold and Kutac 1974; TOS 1984, 1995), and the expanded *A Birder's Checklist of the Upper Texas Coast* (Richardson et al. 1998). Of special importance is Harry C. Oberholser's two-volume *The Birdlife of Texas* (1974), edited and to a large extent written by Edward Kincaid. This work presents a wealth of information relating to the distribution, plumage, and biology of Texas birds. When appropriate, we call attention to changes that have occurred along the Upper Texas Coast since its publication.

Other recent works pertaining to East Texas birds include *Birds of Texas: A Field Guide* (Rappole and Blacklock 1994), *Birds of the Texas Coastal Bend* (Rappole and Blacklock 1985), *The Birds of Texas* (Tveten 1993), and *The TOS Handbook of Texas Birds* (Lockwood and Freeman 2004). Note that *Birds of Texas: A Field Guide* includes many records never accepted by the Texas Bird Records Committee, so its coverage of East Texas is quite different than our own. All four texts include bibliographies useful to birders on the Upper Texas Coast.

The *Gulf Coast Migrant,* published by George Williams from 1936 to 1947, and the *Spoonbill,* published from 1950 to the present by the Ornithology Group of the Outdoor Nature Club of Houston, are regional newsletters that contain irregular and often incomplete listings of bird sightings within the general region. When combined, these two periodicals contain over 55 years of accumulated survey data. However, the selective nature (by season, species, and habitat) of the information, and the unwillingness or inability of many observers to provide accurate estimates, makes it difficult to determine trends, distribution, or absolute abundance for most species. Nonetheless, the thousands of sightings reported in these newsletters provide the backbone of *Birdlife of Houston, Galveston, and the Upper Texas Coast.* The regional Audubon Christmas Bird Counts, the Texas seasonal report in *American Birds* magazine, and more recently *Audubon Field Notes,* all published by the National Audubon Society, were of great importance to us, even though affected by the same selective biases. The Texas On-line Clearinghouse, part of David Sarkozi's Web site (Sarkozi 2004) has become a significant (although not always thoroughly documented) collection of Texas bird sightings. Day-to-day sightings and the discussions they generate are available on Texbirds, a University of Houston listserv sponsored by the Texas Audubon Society.

In recent years, journal articles and theses dealing with birds of the UTC and neighboring Louisiana have focused upon the influence of weather on passerine migration, the dynamics of migration at a single site along the coast, stopover ecology of migrating passerines, habitat selection and populations of waterbirds, the biology and status of the endangered Piping Plover, and radar studies documenting movements of raptors and other birds. Dennis (1954) conducted a meteorological analysis of the occurrence of grounded migrants at Smith Point, Chambers County, during the spring of 1951. Hoke (1974) studied migration at a live oak motte at High Island. King (1976) documented an estimated 5,000 dead birds of at least 32 species that washed ashore on Galveston Island on 7 and 8 May 1974. These birds apparently perished in a severe spring storm that struck the UTC on 5 May 1974. Eubanks (1988) furnished details of a massive grounding of migrants along the

UTC during April 1988. Allan Mueller (pers. comm.) compiled an internal report for the U.S. Fish and Wildlife Service inventorying and analyzing the UTC woodlots available to grounded migrants within the coastal "hiatus" (the area of Gulf prairie and marshes, lacking significant woody vegetation, situated between the beach and the inland forests). Moore and colleagues investigated the ecology—for example, habitat selection and suitability, predation, and fat deposition—of migrants at woodlands utilized as stopover points (Moore and Simons 1992; Moore et al. 1992; Moore 2000; Moore and Aborn 2000). Leavens (1979) examined habitat selection in waders on the Bolivar Peninsula. Haig (1987), Haig and Oring (1985, 1988), Nicholls and Baldassarre (1990), and Eubanks (1994) assessed the winter population of the threatened Piping Plover on the UTC. Morrison and Myers (1987) recognized the importance of the region to North American shorebird dynamics, yet gave no data to support the contention. Eubanks and Collins (1993) summarized the historical status and potential for rediscovery of the Eskimo Curlew within the region. Weller (1994) discussed seasonal changes in species diversity within the estuarine wetlands at San Bernard National Wildlife Refuge. Wiedenfeld and Wiedenfeld (1995) documented a massive tornado-related bird kill on 8 April 1993 in Grand Isle, Louisiana. Green et al. (1992) presented extensive data on the trends of various wetland birds associated with Galveston Bay. Lowery (1945), Williams (1945, 1950), and Stevenson (1957) published documents exploring the routes utilized by spring migrants. Their theories of trans- vs. circum-Gulf migration provided a lively dialog that lasted for decades. Gauthreaux (1971) studied and continues to collect radar data on movements of trans-Gulf migrating passerines. Locally, Frank Peace monitored raptor movements along Galveston Bay. Together, their studies are providing insight into the magnitude and timing of spring and fall migrations in which birds pass over the Upper Texas Coast above the limits of conventional optical equipment.

What becomes most apparent from such a review of the literature is that until recently, despite the presence of three major universities within Houston and numerous institutions of higher learning in nearby communities, the academic world has paid surprisingly little attention to one of the most fertile avifaunal regions in the United States.

Ornithological research and observation along the UTC has rested predominantly upon the shoulders of amateurs, birders who have collected and contributed data as the by-product of a hobby. The academic world may quibble with the nature and caliber of the data that have been gathered, and we readily admit that we simply lack sufficient information and corroboration to address each question with equal depth and certainty. Within these pages, however, we believe there resides a wealth of information from which a number of conclusions and opinions can be drawn. We therefore wish to acknowledge the birders and nonprofessional ornithologists who have joined forces with more conventional academic pursuit to advance the study of birds along the UTC, with little reward other than the pleasure derived from watching these remarkable creatures.

Observers such as Audubon, Nehrling, Singley, and Simmons were naturalists in the broadest and most expressive of terms. Their writings are brimful with the natural world; no organism, feathered or otherwise, escaped their gaze. The fact that we have been able, in some small way, to capture a glimpse of the UTC as it existed a century ago is due in large part to the breadth of their vision, the innate curiosity within their souls, and their willingness to transfer these keen observations to the written page. The advent of popular birding and of modern ornithological studies after the end of World War II regrettably frayed the tradition of the field *naturalist*—the common thread that bound Audubon, Nehrling, Simmons, Attwater, Huxley, and Williams. Birding as a hobby and as a sport often cleaves the bird from the bush. The interminable tallies and listings associated with the game of birding are the technical equivalents of a score sheet in a baseball game. No doubt one can follow the general progression of a baseball game from the statistics published in the morning newspaper. Absent from that sterile recounting, however, are the scent of buttered popcorn and roasted peanuts, the anticipation of the first pitch as a slightly off-key national anthem grinds to a finish, and the shouts and ear-splitting whistles that erupt as the home team hero blasts the ball over the center field fence.

Birds offer an open and wonderfully circuitous pathway to the most sensuous and intricate of worlds: nature. We hope to make clear not only what habitats birds use but also that protecting these habitats is crucial if we are to ensure a legacy of birdlife for future generations. We therefore invite birders to enrich the avocation—and everyone's lives—by moving beyond limited listing objectives and by becoming immersed in nature in its most expansive incarnation, like the field naturalists of old.

GEOLOGY, CLIMATE, AND HABITATS

The Upper Texas Coast exists as a discrete entity only in a geopolitical sense, extending from the Sabine River at the Texas-Louisiana border south to the western edge of Brazoria County. As we define it, the region comprises seven counties: Jefferson, Chambers, Galveston, Harris, Waller, Brazoria, and Fort Bend. The area and its major centers of development are depicted on map 1.

Together these counties encompass 6,405 square miles of land. The total area of the UTC (land and water combined) is 7,635 square miles, roughly equivalent to the size of Massachusetts. The region is virtually flat, with little relief between the coast and the most inland counties (for example, Houston lies between approximately 50 and 60 feet above sea level). Only in northwestern Waller County does the landscape slope into rolling hills; and even at its highest point, the UTC ascends to only 249 feet.

GEOLOGY

Perhaps the most noteworthy aspect of the geology of the Upper Texas Coast is how little of it is visible. The ecoregions of the UTC consist of four major habitats that exist at or near sea level (map 2). The surface of the UTC is largely coastal plain. It is inclined toward the Gulf of Mexico at about 5 feet/mile, and with few exceptions exhibits no relief. There are no sea cliffs, offshore stacks, mountains, canyons, or tall riverbanks, and their absence has a profound effect on the types of birds that do and do not occur here.

At and below the surface, most of the UTC is composed of muddy sediments derived from inland mountain ranges that were worn down by the combined forces of wind and water. Over millions of years, rivers, many of which originate far inland, carried this sediment toward the Gulf of Mexico. Approaching the sea, the water's momentum decreased, and its ability to carry suspended loads decreased. Ultimately, the forces of gravity exceeded that of river flow, and silts and sands ended their long journey by settling to the bottom. These sediments built broad deltas that compacted and sank downward, only to be covered and recovered with additional layers of fine particles. In this manner, inch by inch, year by year, the land between Houston and

Table 1. *Area and Elevation of the UTC Counties*

County	Area (mi²)	Minimum Elevation (ft)	Maximum Elevation (ft)
Brazoria	1407	0	146
Chambers	616	2	73
Fort Bend	876	46	127
Galveston	399	0	23
Harris	1734	6	171
Jefferson	937	0	42
Waller	514	110	249

Galveston Island—indeed most of the UTC—was formed. The rich soils that blanket this coastal plain support various agricultural products, but their fine-grained texture, which inhibits drainage, makes them especially suitable for the cultivation of two regionally notable crops: rice and crawfish. In turn, the thousands of seasonally flooded acres devoted to these products, as well as the water that covers them, have become important resources for the region's waterbirds, contributing to the number and diversity of large waders, shorebirds, and waterfowl. These concentrations of birds attract birders, photographers, and hunters who contribute to the region's economy in many ways.

Geologists estimate the sediments along the margin of the UTC to be as much as 50,000 feet thick. The incalculable weight of this sediment layer has impacted even deeper materials. One effect of the coast's own weight is that thick, deeply buried layers of salt, deposited during the drying of an ancient Triassic sea that existed perhaps 200 million years ago, have been compressed and heated (Spearing 1991). In certain places these salt layers were squeezed toward the surface as tall columnar formations known as salt domes. Infrequently, these salt domes proceed upward until they are close enough to the land's surface to raise a dimple. The town of High Island (an island of elevated land surrounded by marsh), complete with stores, homes, roads, a school, and several Houston Audubon Society bird sanctuaries, sits atop such an uplift, although it barely projects from the surrounding coastal marsh and prairie.

Such elevations may seem paltry, but their value to plants, wildlife, and humans is significant. Each additional inch of elevation allows the establishment of more species of plants that cannot tolerate the salty coastal marshes. For example, eastern baccharis, an abundant coastal shrub, can grow on soil only eight inches above the brackish marsh surrounding it. At an elevation of just 14 inches oaks and sweetgum can survive, providing food and shelter for migrating songbirds (Shelford 1963). Besides the commercially valuable deposits of salt and sulfur that are often associated with salt domes, they often displace upward huge accumulations of some of the earth's earlier residents, now modified by pressure, heat, and time, into a product of particular importance to the local economy. Visitors to High Island will have no trouble spotting the numerous pumpers that reach down to tap the pools of oil on and around the salt dome upon which the town sits.

At least four times during the Pleistocene age (roughly the last 1.6 million years), glaciers thousands of feet thick prevented substantial amounts of water from returning to the sea. As ocean levels dropped about 450 feet, rivers seeking sea level eroded deeply into the sediments below, cutting broad valleys such as those of the Trinity and San Jacinto rivers. When the sea was at its lowest point, the edge of the continent was about 50–135 miles seaward of its current location. Beyond those ancient shores, sands carried by steeply flowing rivers were deposited in vast quantities. After the end of the Pleistocene age, and perhaps no more than 5,000–10,000 years ago, melting glacier waters once again flowed seaward, and the oceans rose to meet rivers in their deeply cut beds. Because rivers now flowed through decreased gradients they lost much of their energy, and heavy sands falling out of suspension filled the deep river valleys. Today such sandy deposits are visible in the yet unfilled valleys of the Trinity and San Jacinto rivers. As rising waters covered the mouths of the larger rivers, deep bays were formed, some of which later became partly or wholly isolated from the Gulf.

After the last rise in sea level during the last 5,000–8,000 years, sandy sediments deposited on the sea floor during the Pleistocene and more recent Holocene returned shoreward. These sands, along with minor amounts of recent river sediments, form the building materials of barrier islands and spits. Barrier islands form along "lowland coasts having limited tidal range and relatively low wave energy. They dominate the coastal topography of the northwestern Gulf of Mexico . . . are the most conspicuous coastal feature of Texas . . . and constitute the most important sand beach environment of the region" (Britton and Morton 1989).

Although the formation and maintenance of barrier islands is complex and depends on a variety of oceanic phenomena, the driving force that builds and maintains them is the longshore current that transports sand to the beach. When such sand-bearing currents encounter an obstacle, perhaps a mound of sediment carried shoreward by a hurricane, their sands are deposited against the face of the obstacle. As the obstacle grows, a sand bar forms, encouraging deposition of additional sand and the formation of an island. If currents encounter an obstacle attached to the mainland, such as a headland or a projecting river delta, they may drop their sediments against it, forming a long fingerlike formation called a spit, an example of which is the Bolivar Peninsula. As new islands and spits grow, they often meet and join, forming long, nearly continuous land masses that are broken only where sufficient tidal flows prevent passes from filling in. For approximately 3,000 years, the East and West arms of Galveston Bay have been separated from the Gulf by the UTC's three main barrier island and spit formations: Galveston Island, adjacent Follet's Island, and the Bolivar Peninsula. Sand blowing from the sea side to the bay side of islands and spits broadens them, providing habitat for sand flat and dune plants such as seashore dropseed, gulfdune paspalum, beach evening primrose, beach morning glory, and sea lavender, plants with roots that trap sand grains and stabilize the surface of the beach. Along bay-facing margins that are protected from the more energetic Gulf, fine river sediments settle out. Quickly, salt-tolerant plants such as smooth cordgrass invade and stabilize these sediments, forming extensive marshlands often covered with marshhay cordgrass. As these marshes broaden, plants such as glasswort and saltgrass invade their drier and shallower pans. Below the bay's surface, additional silts are deposited along channel margins and on shallow subtidal flats. These soft bottoms support stands of various "sea grasses" of

Map 1. *Counties, Roads, and Major Population Centers of the UTC.*

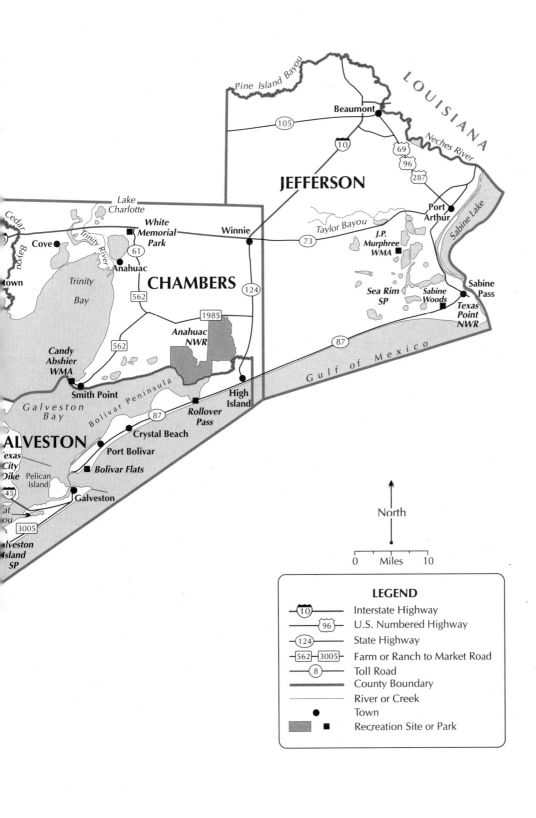

Pine Island Bayou

LOUISIANA

(105)

Beaumont

(10)

JEFFERSON

(69)
(96)
(287)

Neches River

Port
Arthur

Sabine Lake

Lake
Charlotte

White
Memorial
Park

Winnie

(73)

Taylor Bayou

J.P.
Murphree
WMA

Sabine
Pass

Cove

Trinity River

(61)

Anahuac

CHAMBERS

(562)

(124)

Sea Rim
SP

Sabine
Woods

Texas
Point
NWR

Trinity
Bay

(1985)

Anahuac
NWR

(562)

Candy
Abshier
WMA

Smith Point

Bolivar Peninsula

High
Island

(87)

Gulf of Mexico

Galveston
Bay

(87)

Rollover
Pass

Crystal Beach

ALVESTON

Port Bolivar

exas
City
Dike

Bolivar Flats

Pelican
Island

(45)

Galveston

at
ou

(3005)

lveston
sland
SP

North

0   Miles   10

LEGEND

(10) Interstate Highway

(96) U.S. Numbered Highway

(124) State Highway

(562)(3005) Farm or Ranch to Market Road

(8) Toll Road

County Boundary

River or Creek

● Town

■ Recreation Site or Park

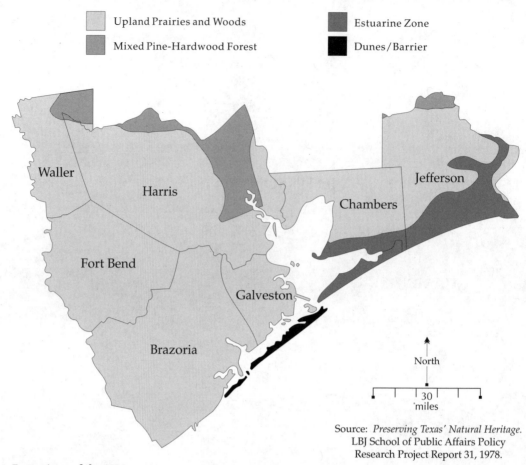

Source: *Preserving Texas' Natural Heritage.*
LBJ School of Public Affairs Policy
Research Project Report 31, 1978.

Legend:
- Upland Prairies and Woods
- Mixed Pine-Hardwood Forest
- Estuarine Zone
- Dunes/Barrier

Map 2. *Ecoregions of the UTC.*

several families (none true grasses), including: widgeon grass, turtle grass and manatee grass. In turn, these plants trap additional silts, helping to stabilize the soft bottom. Species of animals including larvae and juveniles of shrimp, crabs, and many commercially important fishes find protection and nourishment among these plants. Additionally, sea grasses are an important food for several kinds of waterfowl. Unfortunately, most of Galveston Bay's most productive grass flats have disappeared under the blanket of silt thrown up by boating activities such as commercial shipping, shrimp trawling, and pleasure boating, or have been scoured away by the increased flows associated with channel dredging. As we note later, both the loss of these grass beds and the increased particulate load now suspended in the bay's waters have had a profound effect on a number of the region's waterbirds.

Now, as in the distant geological past, the combination of sediments carried seaward by rivers and

Gulf sands carried into bays by tidal flow results in an ever-widening apron of new land that forms along the edge of the continent. Such land, consisting of deposited sediments, forms in a number of ways. At the south end of the Bolivar Peninsula, about 750 acres of mudflats and 550 acres of salt marsh and beach have been added since 1898—when the U.S. Army Corps of Engineers finished the North Jetty of Galveston Bay (Houston Audubon Society data). The jetty, which was built to maintain channel depth at the bay mouth, diverts and slows longshore currents and causes their sediments to fall out of suspension. The combination of silts, sands, and shell gravel comprises Bolivar Flats, now a Houston Audubon Society sanctuary. The flats are recognized as a world-class environment for migrating shorebirds and provide nesting habitat for the threatened Least Tern. On the west end of Galveston Island at San Luis Pass, flats are formed in a different way. There a delta grows, its silts and sands derived from Galveston Bay and the rivers flowing into it. Another kind of flat is formed at sites where certain tidal channels terminate. There, if the scouring forces of tides or currents are weak, sediments are deposited. Over time a delta may emerge from below the surface along such a channel. In Galveston Bay several emergent flood deltas have stabilized into recognizable islands, including Bird, Mud, and Moody's islands.

Not all coastal land, however, is formed through natural processes. The U.S. Army Corps of Engineers is responsible for dredging millions of tons of sediments (as well as snails, clams, crustaceans, and sea grasses) from the main channels of Galveston Bay, the Gulf Intracoastal Waterway, and the Houston Ship Channel. This material, containing petroleum by-products, heavy metals, and the host of toxic organic pollutants that daily find their way into Galveston Bay, is either deposited on land (occasionally resulting in the loss of valuable wetlands) or redistributed in the marine environment, where it then settles out, blocks additional channels, and ensures perpetual job security for the Corps of Engineers. In fairness, not all fill projects are totally disagreeable. In locations around the world, parks and even towns have been created on fill derived from both the land and the sea. Locally, where spoil islands are formed by the dumping of sediments, waterbirds, including pelicans, terns, skimmers, herons, and egrets have profited from the increased availability of nesting habitat. Local fill sites created by human efforts include the east end of Galveston Island and adjacent Pelican Island, the latter recently colonized by returning Brown Pelicans. Dredged sediments, however, are noncompacted masses of loose material that are both difficult and expensive to contain. Often, as soon as these materials are sprayed or bulldozed into place, wind, rain, currents, and tidal action begin to redistribute them throughout the marine environment. Fisher et al. (1973) discuss the detrimental effects of unleashing tons of fine silt on the marine ecosystem: "Perhaps the most serious effect of spoil redistribution is the blanketing of shallow, bay-margin grass flats. Veneering of these areas by barren spoil destroys environments of high organic productivity, affecting the entire ecosystem of the bays and estuaries." Not only do increased sediments in bay waters cover grass flats; they also clog the gills of commercially important filter feeders such as oysters and block light that would otherwise reach through the water column and stimulate plant growth.

No matter how new land is formed, the single most important phenomenon stabilizing it—and the cheapest—is the formation of a mantle of plant life, whether on barrier or emergent islands, deltas, mounds of dumped dredge material, or silty bay edge. Roots of salt marsh and dune vegetation bind fine sediments into a permeable mat that becomes amazingly resistant to the ravages of wind and water. As these plants die and break down, they supply organic matter in a process that changes sand to soil. The resulting humus increases the soil's water-holding capabilities, in turn providing habitat for even more species of plants and animals. Anywhere this armor of protective plants is disrupted—that is, where boat wakes undercut salt marsh bordering the Gulf Intracoastal Waterway or off-road vehicles compact sands and tear away dune vegetation—the unceasing actions of wind and water quickly remove land that took 3,000 years to form. As shoreline development continues, millions of dollars are spent each year repairing damage to the coast, often by installing artificial structures to replicate the action of vegetation that nature supplied for free.

A great deal of fine sediment continues to flow into the Gulf of Mexico, much of it washing seaward during storm-associated high runoffs. Sands and silts from Gulf Coast rivers, including the Mississippi, have filled much of the northern portion of the Gulf, creating a broad and shallow continental shelf. Seaward of Galveston Island and the Bolivar Peninsula, sandy beaches dip below the waves to form the ocean's floor. Near shore, the gradient is about 20–25 feet/mile, lessening to about 1 foot/mile on the broad inner shelf (Fisher et al. 1973). Because the Gulf is shallow, its bottom is rarely far from activities at the water's surface, and wind and waves are constantly lifting sediments off the bottom. Along the UTC, even minor wave action lifts and suspends the very fine sands derived from sediments carried by the Sabine and Mississippi rivers. This accounts for the cloudy or turbid appearance of our nearshore waters. Of interest to us, distribution of seabirds is modified by the clarity, depth, and temperature of the ocean. Most true pelagic birds, those inhabiting the open ocean, avoid these warm, turbid shallows, opting instead for the deep and clear water present beyond the edge of the continental shelf. Unfortunately, the edge of the

Table 2. *Climate of the UTC*

| | County | | | | | | |
	BRA	CHA	FOB	GAL	HAS	JEF	WAR
Jan Min Mean (°F)	42	41	41	48	46	42	38
July Max Mean (°F)	92	91	94	87	93	93	95
Annual Mean (°F)	68	68	69	70	70	69	67
Freeze Days	19	15	16	4	21	18	27
Annual Precipitation (inches)	52.3	51.6	43.9	40.2	42.6	52.8	38.2

shelf lies to the south of the region, so geological processes have rendered the UTC's offshore waters largely unsuitable for storm-petrels, shearwaters, and other true seabirds.

CLIMATE

The climate of the UTC is subtropical-subhumid, with brief, balmy winters followed by extended hot, steamy summers. The mean annual free-air temperature, usually measured as shaded ambient temperature close to the earth's surface, is 69°F (range 67–70°), with a mean winter daily low in January of 44.5°F (range 38–48°) and a mean summer daily high in July of 91.7°F (range 87–95°). Mean annual precipitation varies from a high of 52.8 inches in Jefferson County to a low of 38.2 inches in Waller County. As a general rule the swing in temperature extremes moderates along the coast, and annual rainfall decreases in a north-south and coast-to-inland direction. Elsewhere, such variation in rainfall in a north-south direction is reflected along the length of the Texas coast, with annual precipitation varying from over 50 inches at the Sabine River to less than 20 inches at the Rio Grande in South Texas.

Two principal wind regimes influence the UTC; both significantly affect migrating birds. From March through September, southeastern winds persist. During spring, these southeasterlies provide reliable following winds for migrant birds returning to North America from staging sites in the Yucatán.

From October through April, this southeasterly pattern is broken by short-lived but intense winds originating from the north or northwest. Occasionally, these are true polar fronts. In fall these fronts, with sustained winds of up to 40 knots, furnish the requisite following winds that help to move millions of North American migratory birds in "waves" south

to their wintering grounds. Additionally, these fronts can push several feet of water out of Galveston Bay. Such extreme lowering of the water level exposes vast expanses of normally submerged mud and sand flats to foraging shorebirds. Occasionally, these cold fronts persist until spring. Those that stall along the coast and spawn several days of rainfall (rarely during the last few years) ground thousands of trans-Gulf migrants in woodlands, beaches, and other habitats along the immediate coast.

HABITATS

As defined by its vegetation, the principal biotic region of the UTC is Gulf Prairies and Marshes (Gould 1969), much of which was converted to cropland or urban development; on map 3 the crops, grasslands, and marshes together would make up the Gulf Prairies and Marshes. Interspersed within this generalized habitat are several types of woodland (map 3). Within this region, Gould makes two major divisions: Coastal Prairie and Gulf Coastal Marshlands, stating: "The Coastal Prairie is a nearly level plain less than 150 feet in elevation, dissected by streams flowing into the Gulf. The Coastal Marsh is limited to narrow belts of low wet marsh immediately adjacent to the coast." This belt of coastal marsh, along with the encompassing coastal zone, is characterized by "interconnecting natural waterways, restricted bays, lagoons and estuaries, low to moderate freshwater inflow, long and narrow barrier islands, and an extremely low astronomical tidal range" (Fisher et al. 1972, 1973).

Within the prairie and marsh-dominated coastal hiatus (Lowery 1945), woodlands are restricted to isolated oak-hackberry mottes and narrow strips of riparian bottomland hardwood forests bordering rivers, streams, and bayous. Farther inland, northern Jefferson and Harris counties represent the southern

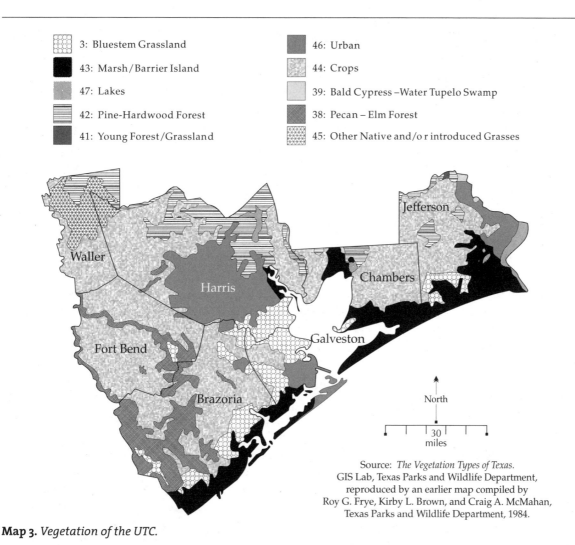

Legend

- 3: Bluestem Grassland
- 43: Marsh/Barrier Island
- 47: Lakes
- 42: Pine-Hardwood Forest
- 41: Young Forest/Grassland
- 46: Urban
- 44: Crops
- 39: Bald Cypress –Water Tupelo Swamp
- 38: Pecan – Elm Forest
- 45: Other Native and/o r introduced Grasses

North

30 miles

Source: *The Vegetation Types of Texas.*
GIS Lab, Texas Parks and Wildlife Department,
reproduced by an earlier map compiled by
Roy G. Frye, Kirby L. Brown, and Craig A. McMahan,
Texas Parks and Wildlife Department, 1984.

Map 3. *Vegetation of the UTC.*

limit of the mixed pine-oak or pine-hardwood forests of the East Texas Pineywoods, and northern Waller County grades into Post Oak Savannah.

Wetlands

Four UTC counties (Jefferson, Chambers, Galveston, and Brazoria) directly border the Gulf of Mexico or Galveston Bay. Their primary maritime habitats are open sand or shell beach, intertidal sand flats, and bayside depositional mixed sand and mudflats that have developed around tidal passes. Along the 125 miles of UTC coastline there are only 6.7 square miles of beach (Fisher et al. 1972, 1973; McGowen et al. 1976). The beaches are relatively narrow, rarely wider than 300 feet from the water's edge to the mean high tide line. Their substrate is terriginous (derived from the land) and/or shell sand, and except in those areas where there is a consistent import of sediments, such

as at tidal passes, they frequently lose their sediments to erosion.

Tides on the UTC are relatively weak. In the Galveston area the Gulf of Mexico exhibits a mean tidal range of only 2.1 feet. National Oceanographic and Atmospheric Administration tidal data from Galveston Bay portray the tidal regime as a mixed, semidiurnal tide with unequal highs and lows. In Galveston Bay, tides cycle every 14 days, with a two-week-period of one high and one low followed by a similar period of two highs and two lows.

The inshore Galveston Bay system is largely dominated by marsh, its primary grass being smooth cordgrass. Beaches are poorly developed along the bay edge, and most shorelines are either erosional escarpment cut into Pleistocene sediment or are covered by coastal marsh (Fisher et al. 1972, 1973). The two major tidal flats on the UTC are Bolivar Flats and the flats at

San Luis Pass. As already noted, Bolivar Flats are depositional sand flats formed where the North Jetty at the mouth of Galveston Bay traps sediments carried by longshore currents. The flats at San Luis Pass are an emergent flood delta deposited at San Luis Pass (the channel between the southwestern tip of Galveston Island and Follet's Island). Less expansive tidal flats have developed (from north to south) at Sabine Pass in Jefferson County; at Rollover Pass near Gilchrist, an emergent flood delta formed after the widening of a pass cut through the Bolivar Peninsula during the 1950s; at Big Reef on the east end of Galveston Island opposite Bolivar Flats; and at San Bernard National Wildlife Refuge, in Brazoria County near the mouth of the San Bernard River.

The Upper Texas Coast prairies and marshes once stretched westward along the coast from the Sabine River and extended as far as 60 miles inland. Now, less than 1 percent of the original grasslands remain, most having been converted to agriculture. The soil underlying much of this prairie is heavy clay, and with irrigation water from wells and rivers it fosters a major rice industry. In addition, an inland rice belt runs east-west through Harris, Waller, Fort Bend, and Brazoria counties. In 1989 some 127,900 acres of rice were planted in the seven UTC counties (U.S. Department of Agriculture 2002). By the year 2002, the cost of growing rice had increased substantially but demand for it had dropped; acreage planted in rice decreased by approximately one half (U.S. Department of Agriculture 2002). Despite five of the UTC counties being among the state's top ten rice producers, birds and birders now have difficulty locating flooded rice fields along the UTC. These paddy fields support immense concentrations of shorebirds, ibis, and waterfowl, particularly during migration and in winter. While at any given moment, any specific acre may host a population of waterbirds, note that this is an ephemeral and unpredictable habitat, for the cultivation of paddy fields is staggered and inconsistent, both seasonally and annually. Furthermore, laser leveling of fields has caused a decrease in the low-lying wet spots available to migrating shorebirds. Ponds maintained by local waterfowl hunters, state or national wildlife refuges maintained for ducks and geese, the shores of variable freshwater impoundments (primarily irrigation ponds), and grazed or mowed pastures with relict depressions provide additional freshwater habitat.

Woodlands

Three distinct forest types are present on the UTC: mixed pine-oak woodlands to the north and east of Houston, riparian bottomland forests that border our rivers and bayous, and remnant canebrakes along the Brazos and San Bernard rivers. Testimony to the fact that woodlands were not extensive along the UTC before the arrival of European settlers, but that wetlands were typical, can be found in the writings of early explorers and ornithologists. In 1845, Carl, Prince of Solms-Braunfels, described the coastal plain along the UTC as varying in "width from thirty to eighty miles. Between the coast and Houston, it is very swampy in some places, so that one can never be too cautious when traveling there" (Weniger 1984). Ferdinand von Roemer, journeying west of Houston apparently during winter, related: "Hardly had we left the city when the flat Houston prairie loomed up as an endless swamp. Large puddles of water followed one another and at several places a large section of land was under water. The long, yellow dry grass and the barren trees added to the drab appearance of the landscape. All of this low coastal region presents a similar picture during this time of year" (Weniger 1984).

In 1839, Benedict noted that the upper San Bernard River had little timber (Weniger 1984). A. A. Parker described the lower Brazos River in 1836: "The river is very crooked, so that it is twice as far from Brazoria to its mouth by water, as it is by land. . . . The river is lined with timber on both sides, about a mile in width; and then, the country is generally an open, level prairie. . . . The timber on the river banks became less, as we descended; and for five miles above the mouth, there is none at all" (Weniger 1984).

Describing Galveston Island in the late 1800s, Singley (1893) remarked: "With the exception of a few live oaks at Lafitte's Grove, fourteen miles down the island (which is said to be a natural grove), there are no trees on the island. Several clumps of a straggling, low growing tree, known locally as 'salt cedar,' have been planted west of the city limits of Galveston, and it was at these clumps that I collected the arboreal species."

The coastal plains and marshes that dominated our region were flat, without trees, and wet throughout much of the year. Yet the riparian woodlands that fringed the rivers, streams, and bayous that traverse the coastal grasslands supported a prolific forest-based birdlife. Besides these isolated ribbons of woods, the great southern evergreen forest of the eastern United States extended west to Houston. The fragmented pine-oak woodlands that dot Houston to the north and east (such as can be seen at the Houston Audubon Society's Edith L. Moore Nature Sanctuary) are remnants of a once great forest that extended unbroken from east of the Appalachians to the confluence of Buffalo and White Oak bayous. On dry soils this forest was dominated by longleaf pine, the oaks suppressed by fires. In wetter areas, beech and magnolia were dominant.

George Finlay Simmons indicated that Buffalo Bayou formed a border between the southern prairies and the northern woodlands. Yet these bands of bottomland hardwood forest, dominated by white oak, sweetgum, sycamore, and magnolia, and in their wettest regions by bald cypress, supported a host of avian species that we see only rarely today, if at all. For example, Nehrling (1882) commented that the Blue-gray Gnatcatcher was "especially abundant on Buffalo Bayou when the magnificent *Magnolia grandiflora* is in bloom. Almost with the agility and grace of a hummingbird, it flies around the showy flowers in pursuit of insects. Nest-building commences early in May. This beautiful domicile is built very high, in small branches of elms, swamp-oaks and other densely leafed forest trees." Habitat alteration has extirpated the Blue-gray Gnatcatcher as a breeder on the UTC. Nehrling considered the Red-cockaded Woodpecker (now absent from the region) "a resident in all of the large pine woods," and he described the now very rare American Swallow-tailed Kite as "a beautiful bird, one of the most characteristic species of this locality; especially abundant in the bottom woods near prairies or fields." These woodlands, particularly the cypress swamps that so characterized the San Jacinto, Trinity, and Sabine river bottoms, were completely timbered in the 1800s. Thousands of acres of these bottomland forests were also sacrificed to timbering, agriculture, pasturage, and eventually to urban development. The mature pine-hardwood forests in the northeastern counties have been harvested and replaced by monoculture pine plantations.

Of tragic consequence to numerous species, the understory thickets that provided nesting habitat for Wood Thrush, Gray Catbird, Kentucky and Swainson's warblers, Yellow-breasted Chat, and other local breeders has been cleared. Nehrling described these thickets and dense underbrush as follows (1882; be cautious of the nomenclature, for Nehrling wrote over a century ago and many of the common and scientific names are archaic): "Thickets of smilax, blackberry bushes, snowball (*Viburnum molle* and *V. dentatum*), *Rhamnus carolinianus*, intermixed with a few larger trees (oaks or elms), which are commonly overgrown by the mustang-grape and the grotesque forms of the supple jack."

Today agencies such as the Texas Forest Service urge landowners who cultivate pine to clear the underbrush; purportedly it competes with the timber as well as increasing the danger of fire. Landowners now harvest their timber at a young age, and the forest remains in a perpetual stage of early successional growth. Therefore many of the remaining pine woodlands on the UTC are relatively young and fragmented. Besides encouraging nest parasitism by Brown-headed Cowbirds, this fragmentation has detrimentally affected breeding populations of many Neotropical migrant species (birds that nest in temperate climes but return to the tropics to winter), particularly deep forest birds such as Wood Thrush, Red-eyed Vireo, and Summer Tanager.

European settlement also brought the clearing of the unique canebrake forests in western Brazoria County. An anonymous visitor described the town of Brazoria in 1831 as follows: "The place for the village had been since cleared of the forest trees which then overspread the country, and at the time of my visit they had been cut away to the distance of half a mile. Beyond that line, every thing was still wild and in the state of nature. The surface is almost entirely level: and such is the want of every species of landmark, that I was informed that the inhabitants could not venture any considerable distance into the woods in a cloudy or misty day for fear lest they should lose their way. The most expert woodsman, it was thought, would find himself at fault for the want of such means as the forest usually affords for determining the points of the compass. What renders the danger still greater, is the frequency of cane brakes, or tracts of land overgrown with the long reeds of which we make fishing poles in the Northern States. These canes there grow in some places among the forest trees, so thick as to render a passage through them inconvenient." These impenetrable canebrakes have long since disappeared, and the birds characteristic of this habitat have diminished as well.

Yet within our transformed woodlands, the basic mechanics of avian biology continue to operate. Many of the species that occur on the UTC are *transient;* that is, they simply pass through the region between their breeding grounds to our north and their wintering grounds in the Neotropics. Most of these species are woodland insectivores, and for them, the conversion of Texas coastal prairie to shrub-invaded grassland and urban woodlot has been potentially beneficial. The continuing destruction of tropical rain forests and the fragmentation of North America woodlands, however, amplifies the importance of the isolated oak and hackberry mottes present within the coastal hiatus, a largely treeless expanse of coastal prairie. While mortality associated with trans-Gulf migration probably had little impact upon the immense Neotropical migrant populations that thrived before European settlement, the dwindling bird populations that remain can ill afford preventable losses.

The *terminal* migrants that depend upon mature bottomland hardwood forests, however, have suffered their declines as a *direct* result of habitat modification. Preservation and restoration of the remnants of this critically endangered forest community are critical if we are to sustain viable populations of many of these avian species. The identification and acquisition of remaining bottomland forests, safeguarding them from further development, are being explored.

Grasslands

Del Weniger, in *The Explorer's Texas*, differentiates the grasslands of Texas based on topography and biotic communities. Grasses are certainly the predominant vegetation type within both plain and prairie, yet according to Weniger, a plain is "a flat expanse which is altogether or practically treeless," and a prairie is "seldom flat or treeless" (1984). These distinctions are crucial when we begin to look at the grasslands of the UTC, for both forms were well represented before the ravages of settlement. Now radically altered, these vanishing grasslands were once reservoirs of great biological diversity. Although largely destroyed, these ecosystems nevertheless still influence the nature and character of the natural world within which we live.

The coastal plains and marshes extended from the coast inland as far as 60–75 miles. Virtually flat, treeless, and wet through most of the year, these plains formed a significant barrier to travelers moving between the coastal ports and the inland centers of commerce. George Finlay Simmons (1914) described Houston and Buffalo Bayou in 1914 as "a coastal prairie region with few farms or ranches; the only timber in this section lies in strips from a quarter to a half mile wide along Buffalo and Bray's Bayous, both of which flow eastward toward Galveston Bay, the latter skirting the city on the south and joining the former a few miles to the east. The remainder of the country is flat, uncultivated prairie, sprinkled with small ponds and grassy marshes." He would later comment that "for weeks after even the slightest shower water stands in the woodlands and on the prairies, making it impossible during the rainy season to leave the graded roads." In contrast to the systematically drained urban habitat that we see today in Houston and surrounding communities, the UTC floated in what seemed to these observers an endless ocean of water and grass.

West of Houston we see progressively more rolling and undulating terrain. Near Katy the coastal plain gives way to prairie, and in that sense the Katy Prairie is aptly named. Originally its soil was mantled with some of the same species that nourished buffalo and formed deep black sods as far north as central Canada. To botanists, their mere mention conveys visions of vast unbroken spaces, of America as it must have looked before Europeans arrived. Its species included little bluestem, big bluestem, broomsedge bluestem, switchgrass, Indiangrass, Florida paspalum, Eastern gamagrass, maidencane, and vinemesquite, some of which may still be found in less disturbed sites. Unlike the featureless coastal plain, however, the grasslands of this prairie contained isolated hummocks or islands of trees and a profusion of forbs. Charles Sealsfield, describing the prairies west of Houston in 1832, wrote: "We distinguished some dark masses, which we afterward discovered to be groups of trees; but to our eyes they looked exactly like islands in a green sea, and we subsequently learned that they were called islands by the people of the country" (Weniger 1984). In addition to the visual relief provided by these mottes, the Katy Prairie was seasonally transformed into a riot of wildflower color. Sealsfield described western Harris or Waller county as follows: "The part of the prairie in which I now found myself presented the appearance of a perfect flowergarden with scarcely a square foot of green to be seen. The most variegated carpet of flowers I have ever beheld lay unrolled before me—red, yellow, violet, blue, every color, every tint was there."

Now, in cultivated sections of the Katy Prairie in Waller and western Harris counties, corn and sorghum are important row crops, and there are significant plantings of soybean and rice. Numerous closely grazed pastures provide excellent habitat for Upland Sandpipers. A significant wintering population of Long-billed Curlews utilizes the area, and it is the only place on the UTC where Mountain Plover occurred with any regularity during the last 25 years.

Yet the foundation upon which both forms of this ecosystem were built is *grass,* and the wildlife that depends upon the grasses has declined in step with the destruction and fragmentation of the habitat. The once predominant coastal prairies are now identified by the Nature Conservancy as one of the most endangered community types within the state and as "imperiled globally." Of the 9 million acres of coastal grasslands that originally occurred undisturbed in what now constitutes Texas, less than 1 percent remains today. Historically these grasslands contained many of the same species that typified the inland prairies, with the addition of silver bluestem, brownseed paspalum, and marshhay cordgrass. Today much of our coastal grassland has been "improved" for livestock grazing with the introduction of a host of African species, including Bermudagrass and its hybrids, weeping lovegrass, Johnsongrass, buffelgrass, and dallisgrass as well as the bahiagrass from Latin America and developed King Ranch bluestem of Eurasian origin.

The primary agents in the destruction of the Texas coastal prairies were agriculture, industrialization, and urbanization. Extensive drainage for agriculture and urban development has diminished the wetland traits of the remaining prairie. With the loss of botanical diversity have come other losses. In 1840 George William Bonnell wrote: "Between Galveston Bay and the Brazos are great quantities of wild game; and on this bayou (Chocolate Bayou) buffaloes are found in considerable abundance." The buffalo has long since been relegated to zoos and private ranches, and Chocolate Bayou now provides cooling waters for an extensive petrochemical complex. Additionally, over the past fifty years vast stretches of coastal

prairie and plain have succeeded to woody shrub through the invasion and proliferation of the exotic Chinese tallow. The elimination of wildfire and the disturbance of these grasslands by grazing have allowed eastern baccharis, a native woody shrub, to dominate many of these prairies. Within the more inland counties, vast stretches of native grassland have been lost to Macartney rose, a non-native, highly invasive shrub that has spread throughout much of the southeastern United States. In the westernmost UTC in Waller County, and in western Brazoria County near Damon, the loamy prairie clays give way to better drained, sandier soils. Here, thickets of huisache flourish, providing wintering habitat for Palm Warbler, Ash-throated Flycatcher, and the eastern subspecies of Bewick's Wren. Unfortunately much of this habitat continues to be cleared and replaced with house trailers surrounded by mowed, lifeless lawns.

Most important, the urbanization of the region and the myriad exotic species introduced around homes for gardens and landscaping have resulted in a discontinuous and chaotic mosaic of alien vegetation. Ominously, all of these factors continue to impact detrimentally the few fragments of coastal grasslands remaining on the UTC.

Attwater's Prairie-Chicken, migrating Eskimo Curlew, and the Texas breeding race of Henslow's Sparrow are examples of birds that have disappeared or are disappearing along with their grassland habitats. Yet grasslands still remain undervalued as a natural resource. Wetlands—at least in theory—had received some protection by law. The interest in protecting coastal woodlands is increasing as a result of the Partners in Flight Initiative, a consortium of multinational governmental and private sector agencies working together to increase populations of Neotropical migrants, in part by acquiring and protecting their habitats. Grassland restoration projects are under way at a few local parks and preserves, but these efforts may be too few and too late for many of these birds. The preservation and restoration of large, undisturbed tracts of coastal plain and prairie, such as those now protected by the recently established Katy Prairie Conservancy, must be undertaken if we are to have any hope of reviving this rich ecosystem and its unique constituents.

Because of the UTC's geological heritage, it lacks many substrate types and elevational features that are known for their special bird assemblages—there are no talus slopes, mesas, volcanic islands, on- or offshore nesting cliffs, brushy slopes, or rain-shadow deserts. The UTC's latitude precludes rain forest, tundra, and ice fields. Indeed, in a global sense, the lack of habitat diversity seems noteworthy. Since European settlement, those habitats that are present have been subjected to pesticides, logging, burning, farming, grazing, dredging, pollution, and siltation or have been buried under asphalt and concrete. Much of the natural vegetation has been removed or modified, and that which remains has suffered the intrusion of a host of exotic species. Farming practices and coastal development have either created or destroyed wetlands. The diking and draining of low-lying areas has changed the salinity and depth of coastal marshes, variously diminishing or improving their availability to birds. Naturally occurring fires have been suppressed, changing the species composition of both prairie and forest plants. Market hunting extinguished the bison and Passenger Pigeon in the region and seriously compromised bird species killed for their plumes; modern hunting as a management practice remains controversial.

Why then, in the face of such apparent ecological adversity and human abuse, does the UTC offer a naturalist so many species of birds to study and enjoy? Among the various factors, we might cite the mild winters that provide arthropod and other invertebrate prey for a wide variety of species. The lack of snow makes seeds and fruit more available to doves, thrushes, waxwings, and finches. Ornamental plantings provide cover and many foods not present historically. Certain shorebirds profit from artificially flooded fields that might otherwise be dry, while other kinds feed in burned fields that might have been brushy. In the cities and suburbs, many species are provided nest sites and supplementary foods by home owners anxious to surround themselves with birds. In less disturbed areas, valuable habitats are being protected and enhanced as new sanctuaries and parks continue to appear across the UTC.

The most important factor influencing the region's avian diversity, however, remains its special position relative to migratory routes and the surrounding avifaunas. Hundreds of thousands of ducks and geese that breed to the north arrive via the Central and Mississippi flyways, either wintering on or passing through the UTC. Each spring and fall, millions of songbirds cross the Gulf of Mexico, many pausing locally for rest, food, and water. Clouds of shorebirds migrating between the pampas of Argentina and Uruguay and the arctic tundra pause to gorge on the UTC's marine and terrestrial invertebrates. Additionally, the area receives migrants, irregularly occurring rarities or vagrants, and very rare accidentals from surrounding zoogeographic regions. Table 3 summarizes the origins of representative birds occurring on the UTC.

The factors that generated a local avifauna of over 480 species would seem to be solidly in place. Until recently, they were anchored to such truisms as: The habitats available to birds are endless and immutable. The migrations of birds are ancient; their return is as guaranteed as the phases of the moon. Climate is predictable; learn to live with it and we have nothing to fear. Resources are infinite; the earth will nourish its own. Two centuries ago, residents on the Upper Texas Coast might have been comfortable with these concepts. Now, each day, homeowners, farmers, conservationists, sportsmen, multinational companies, small businesses, and government realize the fallacy of such perspectives. Sadly, this realization does not always ensure the welfare of birds.

The birdlife of the Texas coast survives both because of and in spite of the actions of the local human population. The U.S. Fish and Wildlife Service designates refuges for migrating waterfowl. At the same time, the goose prairies east and west of Houston disappear a thousand acres at a time under subdivisions. One administration is committed to protecting our coastal wetlands; another decides they should be developed. A thousand bird watchers plant hummingbird gardens, but the woodlands of Waller County are bladed flat for house trailer sites. A stretch of Galveston Island becomes a haven for

Table 3. *Origins of Selected Birds Occurring on the UTC*

Year-round residents	American Oystercatcher, Common Grackle, Seaside Sparrow
Summer visitors	Least Bittern, Least Tern, Purple Gallinule, Acadian Flycatcher
Colonizers from the South	Black-bellied Whistling-Duck, Brown Pelican, Inca Dove, Bronzed Cowbird, Great-tailed Grackle
Colonizers from the Old World	Cattle Egret
Introduced species	Eurasian Collared-Dove, Monk Parakeet, European Starling, Red-vented Bulbul, House Sparrow
Local breeders now possibly extinct	Ivory-billed Woodpecker
Local breeders now extirpated	White-breasted Nuthatch, Henslow's Sparrow
Central/Mississippi Flyway visitors	Snow Goose, Red-breasted Merganser
Northern landbirds wintering annually	Short-eared Owl, Hermit Thrush, White-crowned Sparrow
Annual visitors (western origin)	Cinnamon Teal, Rufous Hummingbird, Vermilion Flycatcher, Bullock's Oriole
Annual visitors (southern origin)	Wood Stork, Groove-billed Ani, Buff-bellied Hummingbird
Eruptive visitors (northern origin)	Red-breasted Nuthatch, Purple Finch, Evening Grosbeak, Rough-legged Hawk
Pelagics of southern origin	Greater Shearwater, Sooty Shearwater
Pelagics of northern origin	Northern Gannet, Long-tailed Jaeger
Migrants utilizing an inland route	Swainson's Hawk, Nashville, Wilson's and Mourning warblers
Trans-Gulf migrants typically utilizing the western Gulf	American Golden-Plover, Hudsonian Godwit, Bay-breasted Warbler, Indigo Bunting
Trans-Gulf migrants uncommon in the western Gulf	Blackpoll, Black-throated Blue, and Cape May warblers, Bobolink
Trans-Gulf migrants rarely in the western Gulf	Connecticut Warbler
Vagrants (Pacific North America)	Wandering Tattler, Surfbird
Vagrants (Neotropical origin)	Blue Bunting, Greenish Elaenia, Green Violet-ear
Vagrants (Old World origin)	Curlew Sandpiper, Lesser Black-backed Gull
Vagrants (Caribbean origin)	Black-whiskered Vireo, Red-billed Tropicbird, Shiny Cowbird
Vagrants (western North America)	Flammulated Owl, Varied Thrush, Cassin's Vireo
Casual Visitors (northern North America)	Purple Sandpiper, Thayer's Gull, Glaucous Gull
Species introduced as game birds	Ring-necked Pheasant

migrating shorebirds while down the road, another home site covers precious habitat.

Bird diversity on the Upper Texas Coast is inextricably linked to habitat diversity. Yes, it is true that there are more kinds of habitat on the UTC than Audubon encountered during the early 1800s (consider Houston—then a treeless marsh), and this increase has undoubtedly benefited many kinds of birds. However, if unbridled development continues, the pendulum will swing in the other direction, and the face of the land will again be simplified. In a worst case scenario, migrating birds will not encounter the landscape of prairie, coastal marsh, and riparian woodlands that Audubon found. Instead, they will look down at a sea of asphalt, ribbons of concrete-lined bayous, and endless fields of roofing shingles. It is becoming more important not to look at birds as a measure of habitat diversity but to look at habitats as a measure of bird diversity.

The eradication of bottomland hardwood forests has doubtless diminished the breeding populations of many Neotropical migrants. Deep forest birds such as Wood Thrush, Red-eyed Vireo, Hooded Warbler, and Summer Tanager have declined in numbers proportionate to the loss of mature bottomland forests. Nehrling (1882) characterized the American Swallow-tailed Kite in Houston as "a beautiful bird, and one of the most characteristic species of this locality. Especially abundant in the bottom woods near prairies or fields." This species has been almost eliminated as a breeding species in Texas, with the remaining scant nesting population limited to the riparian forests bordering the Sabine and Trinity rivers. Swainson's Warbler, a species that nests in bottomlands with a cane and dwarf palmetto understory, has become decidedly rare and restricted. Interestingly, Van Remsen (1986) hypothesized that the eradication of such canebrake habitat in the southeastern United States led to the presumed extinction of Bachman's Warbler. Perhaps the decline of Swainson's Warbler can be attributed to the same habitat alteration. Additional Neotropical species Nehrling found nesting commonly around Houston but no longer breeding in the region include Blue-gray Gnatcatcher, Black-and-white Warbler, and Bell's Vireo, the latter now rare throughout much of its range.

The conversion of coastal prairie to agriculture (particularly rice) and urban sprawl has led to the extirpation of many grassland nesting species. Even as late as 1914 Simmons found Grasshopper Sparrow to be a common nester in the wet grasslands near Houston. Now, except for a rarely reported nest on the Katy Prairie, the species appears only during winter, as does its congener, Henslow's Sparrow. Apparently, the relict local breeding subspecies of Henslow's Sparrow, *Ammodramus henslowii houstonensis,* became extinct more than a decade ago due to the succession of its last remaining grassland to baccharis scrub. Lark Sparrows, which bred commonly in Simmons's time, now nest only exceptionally near Houston and are a decreasing winter resident. Nehrling remarked that Cassin's Sparrow was "a common summer resident on the open grassy prairies." Now, to find the nearest breeding

population, one must travel south to the Coastal Bend. The plight of the Attwater's race of Greater Prairie-Chicken, our most charismatic grassland species, is discussed in more detail in the species accounts.

As detailed previously, little of the original UTC habitat remains unspoiled or unaltered. Yet within this fundamentally transformed region the basic mechanics of avian migration continue to operate. Many of the Neotropical species that occur on the UTC are transient; that is, they simply pass through the region between breeding and wintering grounds. Most of these species are woodland insectivores, and the conversion of Texas coastal prairie to shrub-invaded grassland and urban woodlot has been potentially beneficial. With the continuing destruction of tropical rain forests and eastern North American woodlands, however, the importance of the isolated mottes (usually clumps of trees that dot the prairie) and *cheniers* (the Louisiana French term for oak-covered beach ridges) within the coastal hiatus is amplified. The preservation of the remaining UTC oak-hackberry mottes and the creation of such woodlands on coastal public lands should be given a high priority in the Neotropical Migrant Bird Conservation Program in Texas, as these isolated woodlands act as "migrant traps," attracting birds as they move to or from their wintering grounds in Latin America.

As has also already been noted, the terminal migrants that depend on mature bottomland hardwood forests and coastal grasslands for wintering and breeding have suffered their declines as a direct result of habitat modification. These two vegetation communities are the most endangered on the UTC, and every effort should be made to see that remnants are preserved and restored. For a short time, the Texas Parks and Wildlife Department attempted to restore nearly 600 acres of coastal grasslands in Galveston Island State Park. This program of burning and mowing was designed to eliminate Chinese tallow and baccharis and to return the park to its natural grassland community. Unfortunately, out-of-control fires and concern from the park's neighbors caused cessation of the burning, and mowing has failed to restore the park's grasslands. Similar prairie restoration projects should be initiated on additional coastal public lands, especially those where the public is less likely to hinder aggressive management practices. Remaining bottomland forests should be identified and the prospects for acquisition explored. Examples of mature bottomland forests that should be assessed for acquisition include the cypress swamps that edge North and South Taylor bayous and Lake Charlotte, and the riparian forests bordering the Trinity, San Jacinto, Brazos, and San Bernard rivers.

MIGRATION

The UTC has been referred to as the migration crossroads of North America. Indeed, migratory birds contribute heavily to the UTC's seven-county bird list now approaching 500 species. It is the spectacle of spring migration that attracts most birders to the Upper Texas Coast. The opportunity to see 25 species of warblers before lunch or to study 36 kinds of shorebirds in a day draws birders from across the United States and around the world. Even casual birders return home boasting of 500 Dickcissels sputtering in a salt cedar clump, fields clothed in Yellow Warblers and Indigo Buntings, or the sea of rusty red made up of 10,000 American Avocets glowing in the late afternoon sun.

Birding during fall migration has never been as popular (presumably because of the weather), but the period it covers is more prolonged, providing devotees with many more weekends to sort out plumages, study migration patterns, and search for vagrants blown eastward or westward by the season's ever-changing fronts. Fall migration is not without its spectacles, as the sky is filled with hundreds of thousands of southbound hawks, vultures, Wood Storks, and skein after skein of White-fronted and Snow geese, while ribbons of half a million swallows undulate over the waters of San Luis Pass.

Migration occurs across the entire United States, so what is it that makes the UTC a focal point for the movements of so many kinds of birds? There are numerous answers to this question, as is revealed by examining the UTC's role in the migration patterns of a few of the more obvious groups of birds. Three of the major factors that account for a funneling effect of migrants are the UTC's location near the middle of the North American continent, its proximity to the western Gulf of Mexico, and its location relative to

the Yucatán Peninsula—a major staging area for migrating landbirds.

Each fall, buteos, falcons, accipiters, kites, and other birds of prey abandon the plains, deciduous and boreal forests, and tundra of the midcontinent to make their journey to Middle and South America. Because the thermals that keep migrating raptors and other birds aloft do not form strongly (if at all) over water, migrating raptors avoid long water crossings. Upon encountering the coast of the Gulf of Mexico, they follow its shore westward until they can regain their southbound movement. Smith Point on northeastern Galveston Bay became a popular venue for birders when people realized that this promontory was the spot at which raptors abandoned their coastal flight path to make a short hop across the bay.

Geese and ducks are numerous and important visitors to and through the UTC. Bellrose (1968) developed the concept of migration corridors to compensate for shortcomings associated with migration routes (appropriate only when significant landscape features may be identified) and flyways (too broad, with east-west lateral movements not considered). The western Gulf, roughly from Brownsville to southern Alabama and corresponding to what has been called the Central Flyway, receives geese from at least six migration corridors, five of these associated with Hudson Bay and one with Alaska and the western Canadian Arctic, and receives ducks from perhaps another six corridors, most associated with the prairie regions of the northern United States and southern Canada but also Alaska and parts of western Canada. Many of these migration corridors terminate along the western Gulf. For example, clouds of Snow Geese, the delight of birders and hunters alike, winter on the prairies and marshes of the UTC, while Lesser Scaup and Red-breasted Mergansers congregate on our bays. Other species such as Blue-winged Teal and many White-fronted Geese continue southward along the coast or hop the Gulf, wintering in the fields and marshes of southern Tamaulipas, Veracruz, Tabasco, Chiapas, and the Yucatán.

As spring days lengthen, warblers, vireos, flycatchers, and other insect eaters that winter in the tropics move northward to their nesting grounds across the United States and Canada. While some of these species move northward via an inland land route, such as Mourning, Nashville, and many Wilson's warblers, the majority stage on the Yucatán Peninsula, then fly across the Gulf on a route that takes many of them to the UTC. Strong easterly winds provide the UTC with migrants that are characteristic of the eastern Gulf, such as Blackpoll, Black-throated Blue and Cape May warblers. Westerly frontal systems deliver Townsend's and Hermit warblers, Western Tanagers, and Black-headed Grosbeaks. Again, the presence of the Gulf and the central position of the UTC as well as occasional weather systems are responsible for our springtime songbird diversity.

Shorebirds are better represented on the UTC than perhaps in any other region in North America. They are near and dear to us, and we accord them some detail in the following discussion.

SPRING MIGRATION

The UTC is an excellent place to observe a broad variety of spring migrants—both land- and waterbirds. Most visitors come with the hope of being present during a grounding or fallout of northbound songbirds, species generally referred to as Neotropical migrants. Therefore, a little explanation is in order about the factors that generate fallouts. Birders thus armed may be more likely to encounter a fallout or to understand why there was none. After that, we present some of our own fallout data, commenting on a few of the aspects most interesting to us.

Due to its geographic position relative to Mexico's Yucatán Peninsula and the state of Campeche to its north, the UTC and adjacent western Louisiana are a major departure and arrival point for trans-Gulf Neotropical migrants (Stevenson 1957). Taking advantage of prevailing southeasterly tail winds, vast numbers of spring migrants depart from staging sites along the Yucatán Peninsula and eastern Campeche and are carried to that section of the Gulf Coast between Louisiana and the Texas Coastal Bend. The coastline of the UTC, aligned along a southwest-northeast axis, is exposed to the broadest front of these migrants traversing the Gulf.

As long as the weather remains clear and prevailing winds are conducive to migration, woodlots dotting the prairies and marshes of the coastal hiatus may be nearly devoid of Neotropical migrants, and visiting birders might well concentrate on shorebirds at the rice fields and mudflats. As Lowery (1945) noted, "during clear weather, trans-Gulf spring migrants that do not breed on the Gulf coast . . . proceed inland several hundred miles before coming

down. That stretch of coast which one might suppose to be teeming day after day during the spring with multitudes of migrants which have just completed the over-water passage from Yucatan or Campeche is, in actuality, *during fine weather,* an 'ornithological vacuum' so far as many migrants are concerned." Gauthreaux (1972), monitoring trans-Gulf migration with weather radar, remarked: "In favorable weather (clear to partly cloudy skies and southerly winds), most flocks of trans-Gulf migrants passed over the first coastal woodlands with only a few birds dropping out and alighting; the majority continued farther inland to the first extensive forests."

However, when confronted instead by late spring cold fronts, and the gale-force head winds and drenching precipitation that can accompany them, trans-Gulf migrants by the hundreds of thousands—if not millions—are forced into the Gulf's waters or to ground in isolated oak mottes and cheniers immediately along the coast. In his review of the timing and amount of bird migration in relation to weather, Richardson (1978) summarized a number of researchers' observations of this phenomenon. As he stated in his review: "Most birds land immediately; however, if they encounter a cold front overland north of the Gulf; this can result in large concentrations of grounded birds. When a cold front moves southward into the northern Gulf, trans-Gulf migrants flying north encounter cloud, rain and opposing winds. Although there is apparently considerable mortality, many birds continue northward through the front, and land at the first opportunity; this sometimes results in spectacular concentrations on barrier islands." Gauthreaux (1972) described this phenomenon in coastal Louisiana: "When rain and adverse winds were present over the Gulf, or the Louisiana coast, or both, many more individuals landed in the coastal woodlands. Under these conditions entire flocks often plummeted from great heights into the trees. When viewed through binoculars from one end of a wooded ridge, the migrants looked like large, dark hailstones falling into the trees." Eubanks (1988) described such a grounding he witnessed in the spring of 1987 along the Texas coast:

The warm front moving onshore, with the attendant strong southeasterly (following) winds, created the proximate weather conditions over the Gulf and Yucatán Peninsula that are requisite for an onrushing wave. These onrushing migrants, however, were met in Texas by rainfall associated with an upper level low moving in from the west, and opposing north winds associated with the cold front that developed April 30. . . .

By dawn April 30, every twig, branch and sliver of vegetation along the UTC played host to a passerine (or two, or three. . . .). Flock after flock plummeted out of the leaden sky, each bird making a beeline for the nearest bush or shrub. Two observers on the Bolivar beach counted mixed flocks flying in low off of the Gulf that morning at a rate of 100 birds per minute. Migrants were still arriving at the same pace when the observers finally left for High Island one hour later.

Migrants were not packaged in neat flocks; they swarmed the coast like locusts. Swell after swell of orioles, buntings, grosbeaks, thrushes and warblers broke like an avian tidal wave upon the UTC. As cars whizzed pass on Highway 87, clouds of migrants would erupt in kaleidoscopic cartwheels from the brush along the shoulder. Then, just as quickly, each particle of this fragmented rainbow would settle back into the grass to continue the feeding frenzy. For car after car, truck after truck, eruption after eruption, this amazing cycle continued. The spectacle of April 30 was bare, exposed, glaring and unmistakable.

During these mass spring groundings, the limited oak-hackberry mottes and urban woodlots along the UTC furnish critical habitat for birds requiring essential food and shelter. Although potentially vital for only a few days each season, during periods of inclement weather, these sites (largely absent prior to European settlement) function as crucial lifesavers for tens of thousands of migrants. Indeed, the sheer number of birds converging upon a single motte during these moments is staggering. Eubanks (1988) stated: "Assuming that weather conditions affect each species equally (which is unlikely), a grounding represents a cross-section of migration that has been fixed by weather in place and time."

During the early 1970s, Houston Audubon Society (HAS) recognized the benefit of our few coastal woodlots to the warblers and other Neotropical migrants that rest and feed there after a tiring trans-Gulf flight. In order to protect these habitats, the society

purchased the properties that are now part of the High Island sanctuary complex. Subsequently, organizations including the Texas Ornithological Society, the Nature Conservancy of Texas, Texas Parks and Wildlife Department, Partners in Flight, Amoco, and Phillips Petroleum have helped HAS to acquire, enhance, and protect additional coastal property. These coastal woodlands are of particular importance to threatened species with declining populations or suffering threats from habitat loss or the illegal cage bird trade. During migrations, UTC coastal woodlands offer food and shelter to a number of such threatened birds, including Wood Thrush, Painted Bunting, and Bay-breasted, Prothonotary, Cerulean, Worm-eating, Kentucky, Canada, Golden-winged, and Blue-winged warblers.

Between April 1977 and May 1994, Morgan, Eubanks, Behrstock, and others censused migrants during spring fallouts (table 4). Data from 19 events, each of which generated 1,000 or more individuals, 52,903 birds in all, are presented. Sixty-eight species were enumerated during the censuses; their numbers give a picture of the variety and diversity of Neotropical migrants involved in a major grounding. Other sorts of information may be inferred from the data—for example, which species are consistent trans-Gulf migrants, or how important is the occurrence of species that normally migrate northward via the eastern Gulf?

Fallouts

Sadly, the same conditions that create exceptional birding opportunities along the coast may be responsible for the deaths of millions of migrants, both over water and at the shore. James (1956) documented the death of well over 10,000 warblers and other Neotropical migrants at Padre Island, although the survey suggests that the death toll may have been considerably greater. A sample of 2,421 corpses contained 19 species of warblers and 20 other migrants. Many (perhaps most) of the dead birds had been attracted to light poles and had collided with associated wires.

Recently, Wiedenfeld and Wiedenfeld (1995) documented massive mortality of spring migrants during a tornado and associated storms that struck coastal Louisiana on 8 April 1993. On 10 April 1993, they collected 45 species of birds, nearly all of them Neotropical migrants, totaling an estimated 38,385 individuals, with a high of 4,402 (estimated) per 0.6 miles of

Table 4. *UTC Fallouts by Species and Date, April 1977–May 1997*

Species	TOTAL	TOTAL %	4/16/1977	4/21/1979	4/22/1979	3/28/1980	5/17/1980	5/14/1981	4/21/1982	4/22/1982	4/25/1982	5/7/1982	4/10/1986
Indigo Bunting	9,854	15.768	100	150	3,500	25	140	37	200	1,095	600	65	75
Gray Catbird	5,621	8.994	5	150	300		47	60	500	870	525	650	4
Red-eyed Vireo	3,758	6.013	200	15	5	83	230	65	1	40	55	4	405
Tennessee Warbler	3,092	4.948	200	150	50	4	20	16	35	450	360	15	75
Magnolia Warbler	2,617	4.188		3	2		165	175	2	38	20	795	8
Swainson's Thrush	2,473	3.957	1	50	60		80	100	25	38	255	75	45
Black-and-white Warbler	2,096	3.354	50	35	30	370	17	6	5	77	120	225	
Bay-breasted Warbler	2,058	3.293					200	60	2	1	3	21	
American Redstart	1,850	2.960	10	10	6		225	80	12	16	21	490	
Veery	1,779	2.847	1	3	2		3	22	15	20	400	30	1
Rose-breasted Grosbeak	1,678	2.685	5	30	600	147	2	10	30	80	150	40	30
Hooded Warbler	1,573	2.517	10	85	25			1	20	143	92	16	45
Ovenbird	1,571	2.514		40	5		85	3	5	79	75	57	35
Eastern Kingbird	1,522	2.435	10	50	20	12	58	52	40	40	350	15	8
Scarlet Tanager	1,299	2.079	175	15	30			7	2	63	220	30	30
Ruby-throated Hummingbird	1,260	2.016	50	25	50	15	18	1	110	245	80	1	1
Northern Oriole	1,235	1.976	1	3	200				20	55	80	35	
Orchard Oriole	1,222	1.955	100	30	50	75	1	1	50	125	225	5	
Wood Thrush	1,161	1.858	1	40	30	8	1		15	36	52	47	315
Yellow Warbler	1,150	1.840	10	6	50		6	20	20	50	46	8	1
Summer Tanager	968	1.549	75	25	50	20	2	5	8	40	85	20	80
Common Yellowthroat	948	1.517	20	25	150	800	25	5	50	130	127	49	2
Blue-gray Gnatcatcher	923	1.477		2	1		2	1	4		1	1	15
White-eyed Vireo	910	1.456	20	25	6	315	4		15	53	50	5	16
Eastern Wood-Pewee	837	1.339		10	2	1	85	100	8	15	50	155	1
Northern Parula	757	1.211	2	10		543	2	1	2	7	9	2	40
Blue Grosbeak	745	1.192	20	15	100		1	8	50	160	55	2	
Chestnut-sided Warbler	651	1.042	2	10			7	35			21	79	8
Kentucky Warbler	550	0.880		105	2	4	1	1	2	34	26	7	
Yellow-billed Cuckoo	546	0.874		10	20		90	8	4	10	120	9	
Acadian Flycatcher	525	0.840		1	2		7	14	2	6	25	22	
Yellow-rumped Warbler	507	0.811	1			380							55
Northern Waterthrush	430	0.688	1	21	15		2	15	20	44	40	21	1

Species	Total	%											
Blackburnian Warbler	424	0.678	4	5	1		41	45	1	4	9	11	2
Black-throated Green Warbler	423	0.677	1	6	1		7	30	2	42	4	25	8
Blue-winged Warbler	368	0.589	10	30	3	29	21	10	4	19	39	23	10
Philadelphia Vireo	358	0.573	40	6	2				17	18	3	16	
Worm-eating Warbler	337	0.539	4	40		40		1	1	30	13	1	30
Painted Bunting	335	0.536	1	6	20		8	1	50	65	40		
Gray-cheeked Thrush	297	0.475	4	4			5	5	25	12	107	1	
Yellow-throated Vireo	277	0.443	10	3	3	9		1		8	10	2	35
Scissor-tailed Flycatcher	236	0.378	1	20		2	50	21	10		20	6	2
Prothonotary Warbler	222	0.355		5		11	1		3	12	12		14
Canada Warbler	166	0.266		5			15	115			7	2	
Blackpoll Warbler	143	0.229	20	10					3	4	23		
Empidonax species	130	0.208		5	2		45					45	
Golden-winged Warbler	93	0.149		15				4			4	16	
Cerulean Warbler	79	0.126		15	3				2	2	6		
Great-crested Flycatcher	70	0.112	2	2	2		7	2		1	1		4
Yellow-breasted Chat	53	0.085		8	1				3	1	4		2
Louisiana Waterthrush	46	0.074	1	1	1	6							3
"Traill's" Flycatcher	41	0.066				14							
Yellow-throated Warbler	33	0.053	2	2			16				2		2
Yellow-bellied Flycatcher	31	0.050					2	1					
Warbling Vireo	29	0.046									7	3	1
Chuck-will's-widow	23	0.037							2			2	6
Swainson's Warbler	23	0.037		1			2		2	1	5	1	2
Least Flycatcher	19	0.030								8		1	
Black-billed Cuckoo	18	0.029			2		2	1	1	2	4	1	
Wilson's Warbler	15	0.024	1			1		8					2
Nashville Warbler	10	0.016	1									2	1
Cape May Warbler	9	0.014		1					1				1
Blue-winged x Golden-winged	5	0.008		3	1				1		1		
Olive-sided Flycatcher	4	0.006					2						
Western Kingbird	4	0.006											
Palm Warbler	3	0.005				3							
Black-throated Blue Warbler	2	0.003								1			
Prairie Warbler	2	0.003											
MacGillivray's Warbler	1	0.002											
Total Individuals	**62,495**	**100**	**1161**	**1337**	**5,400**	**2923**	**1750**	**1153**	**1401**	**4,290**	**4659**	**3153**	**1421**

(Continued)

Table 4. (Continued)

Species	5/1/1986	5/7/1987	4/30/1988	4/14/1989	4/15/1989	5/4/1990	5/6/1990	4/20/1991	5/5/1992	5/3/1994	4/6/1996	4/26/1997	5/10/1997
Indigo Bunting	55	125	2,000	220	275	50	40	400	6	143	76	400	77
Gray Catbird	41	295	340	55	15	220	355	350	75	104	1	645	14
Red-eyed Vireo	66	654	285	195	65	16	415	2	36	72	157	565	127
Tennessee Warbler	90	444	390	30	15	30	290	125	125	134	12	29	3
Magnolia Warbler	88	465	180			45	285	5	96	113		46	94
Swainson's Thrush	78	410	325	8	35	75	205	40	280	139	5	56	125
Black-and-white Warbler	95	166	275	55	30	4	110	11	108	96	36	98	32
Bay-breasted Warbler	368	626	130			75	241		75	128		24	104
American Redstart	100	292	225	12	40	20	105	7	62	1	1	26	89
Veery	92	905	135	4	2	2	5		50	25		24	39
Rose-breasted Grosbeak	5	100	240	15	15	80	16	13	12	61	39	151	21
Hooded Warbler	7	80	260	210	130		55	14	1	5		257	1
Ovenbird	118	131	280	16	20	11	50	3	22	49	18	438	16
Eastern Kingbird	50	125	20	45	40	150	6	60	42	35	104	38	81
Scarlet Tanager	25	240	210	55	10	5	6	1	6	19	6	151	15
Ruby-throated Hummingbird	20	175	140	60	40	40	6	40	2	20	6	46	40
Northern Oriole	41	20	430	16	40	50	15	125	1	56	1	46	
Orchard Oriole		50	170	55	65	33	10	75		14	15	42	30
Wood Thrush	1	10	35	55	35	2		2	6	1	85	383	1
Yellow Warbler	25	227	475	1	1	18	75	3	4	49	1	49	5
Summer Tanager	48	30	115	85	40	12	7	6	11	34	72	107	11
Common Yellowthroat	1	14	70	35	130	15	20	9	6	13	22	20	10
Blue-gray Gnatcatcher	2		3	2	40			1		1	48		
White-eyed Vireo	1	84	27	65	42	17	24	6	15	7	69	44	
Eastern Wood-Pewee	24	90	55	5	20	12	15	12	40	45		27	65
Northern Parula		1	3		30	4		7	1	4	2	13	4
Blue Grosbeak		25	100	70	40	10		31		1	3	39	5
Chestnut-sided Warbler	32	141	58	3	4	20	80	12	16	60		56	15
Kentucky Warbler	6	28	33	115	60		1	3		10	22	83	
Yellow-billed Cuckoo	1	70	83	6	3	30	8	3	3	14		37	17
Acadian Flycatcher	15	225	32	12	40	6	6	4	16	2	16	62	10
Yellow-rumped Warbler	1			1	15	2	1	2			49		
Northern Waterthrush	9	22	40	5	4	10	26	2	15	34		67	16
Blackburnian Warbler	41	68	70			3	25	16	18	40	1	7	12
Black-throated Green Warbler	23	95	55	1	1	3	15	13	12	35	1	39	3

Species	1	2	3	4	5	6	7	8	9	10	11	12	13
Blue-winged Warbler	3	2	30	65	45		3	16		5	6	26	
Philadelphia Vireo	28	113	21	70	25	4	40	6	13	20		16	4
Worm-eating Warbler	1	3	12					6			17	8	
Painted Bunting	3		95		30							2	1
Gray-cheeked Thrush	40	33	31	2	2	2		5		3		3	3
Yellow-throated Vireo	4	41	21	45	17	2	8	1	5	9	44	18	
Scissor-tailed Flycatcher		4		1	6		3	2	3	4	1	2	
Prothonotary Warbler		1	3	45	30	14	6	40	12	8	72	1	1
Canada Warbler	3	8	2		1	4		5	1	1		1	
Blackpoll Warbler	35	1	4	2		2	3		1	6		1	
Empidonax species	23	4				10	17		1				13
Golden-winged Warbler	3	5	18	1	2			2		2		3	1
Cerulean Warbler		2	6	3	4			5	5	5	1	7	1
Great-crested Flycatcher	8	12	1		1			6	3	2	1	14	
Yellow-breasted Chat			2	17	9	8	3		8	6	3		1
Louisiana Waterthrush		1		2	3	1	1	2	1	1			
"Traill's" Flycatcher	1	5	30							1	27		
Yellow-throated Warbler		1		1	3					2		1	2
Yellow-bellied Flycatcher	1							1			5		
Warbling Vireo	1	10	1	1	1				1	10		1	
Chuck-will's-widow			1	8	2					2	1		
Swainson's Warbler			2	2		1		1		1			
Least Flycatcher		3			2	2	1			3		1	
Black-billed Cuckoo			2					1		1	1	1	2
Wilson's Warbler		2			1	1	1	1					
Nashville Warbler				4	1	1	1				1	1	1
Cape May Warbler	1	1				5				1			
Blue-winged x Golden-winged													
Olive-sided Flycatcher	1	1											
Western Kingbird													
Palm Warbler						3						1	
Black-throated Blue Warbler								1				1	
Prairie Warbler					1			1				2	
MacGillivray's Warbler						1							
Total Individuals	**1724**	**6684**	**7,570**	**1859**	**1526**	**1129**	**2600**	**1500**	**1216**	**1652**	**1052**	**4222**	**1113**

Observers: J. Morgan, T. Eubanks, R. Behrstock, B. Feltner, F. Collins, G. Cureton, W. Cureton, P. Cureton beach. Because this event occurred during the earlier part of spring migration, their totals reflect a higher percentage of earlier migrants than do our cumulative estimates. Although their numbers suggest massive mortality, during some years these weather phenomena are both often repeated and much more widespread. As with our list, Indigo Bunting, Gray Catbird, and Red-eyed Vireo rank among the top ten species they encountered. A number of generally low-density species, such as Cerulean and Swainson's warblers and Wood Thrush, are of special concern to wildlife managers, and the impact of such natural disasters upon threatened populations must always be taken into account when designing population recovery models.

As Lack (1960) noted: "It is important to distinguish the influence of weather in initiating migration from its influence in making migration conspicuous. As already mentioned, night migrants are precipitated [grounded] by cold fronts and their attendant rain." Therefore the absence of Neotropical migrants within the coastal hiatus is often due to the lack of inclement weather conditions rather than an actual decrease in the numbers of migrants aloft. In this sense, a "silent spring" along the Texas and Louisiana coasts is often due to weather conditions favorable for migrant birds; migrant birders disappointed by an absence of fallouts can take consolation in that knowledge.

FALL MIGRATION

For a variety of reasons, spring migration is more attractive to and better attended by bird watchers. The reasons include the fact that spring's bird movement occurs over a shorter time period, the weather is usually more tolerable, birds are in more colorful breeding plumage and occasionally sing, there are usually fewer bugs, there is a greater chance of a fallout, and many species move north across the western Gulf but south along the eastern Gulf or the Atlantic Coast. Without a doubt, our northbound movement is by far the better known of the two great annual migrations. Nonetheless, during late summer and fall, the UTC serves as a principal staging site for migrants before they continue their southward journey across the Gulf. Fall migration is largely ignored even by local birders, probably because of heat and insects, but it can be extremely rewarding if not quite so colorful and has the added attraction of lasting for several months.

Despite the fact that the southbound migration route of many eastern birds (e.g., Veery, Gray-cheeked and Swainson's thrushes, and Cape May, Kentucky, and Blackpoll warblers) takes them farther east in the fall than on their northbound spring flight, large numbers of Neotropical migrants, including many young of the year, may be observed along the UTC each fall. Some, such as Palm and Black-throated Blue warblers, are actually more likely to be seen during their southbound flights (Dunn and Garrett 1997). Although fall migration is steadier on a day-to-day basis, lacking spring's extreme high highs and low lows, weather patterns during late summer and fall help dictate the likelihood of a good versus a mediocre day of birding. Some knowledge of these patterns will greatly affect success in the field.

Richardson (1978) stated: "Landbirds that fly over the Atlantic from Nova Scotia and New England to the West Indies, and over the Gulf of Mexico from Louisiana [and Texas] to the Yucatán, usually depart in following winds behind powerful cold fronts." As indicated by banding data, many birds stage in woodlands along the coast for days (even weeks) until the north winds of a passing frontal system provide them with the impetus to continue their flights.

Although there is a steady passage of southbound birds through the UTC, the most significant fronts (often not occurring until October) may generate "waves" of migrants as well as sweeping out those lingering on the coast. These waves pass through the UTC during the short period associated with the most dynamic frontal activity. In Texas, the number of birds associated with such waves (as perceived by ground observers) may not approach the masses characteristic of major spring groundings, unlike in Florida, where fall fronts can be far more productive than those of spring (J. Stevenson, pers. comm.).

The data in table 5 are a compilation of a major fall migratory wave associated with the year's first strong northern front on 1 October 1985. The area covered in the survey extended from Sabine Pass to High Island, a distance of less than 30 miles. Although the number of individuals involved pales in comparison to a major spring grounding, the variety of species involved is significant and includes six species of vireos and 25 species of warblers. The Bell's Vireo, Black-throated Gray and Townsend's warblers, and Clay-colored Sparrow suggest a western component to this movement.

Table 5. *Coastal Migrants Censused 1 October 1985, in Taxonomic Order*

Yellow-billed Cuckoo (2)	White-eyed Vireo (40)	Palm Warbler (5)
Chuck-will's-widow (4)	Bell's Vireo (1)	Bay-breasted Warbler (2)
Ruby-throated Hummingbird (225)	Yellow-throated Vireo (1)	Black-and-white Warbler (15)
Eastern Wood-Pewee (5)	Warbling Vireo (1)	American Redstart (15)
Acadian Flycatcher (5)	Philadelphia Vireo (5)	Ovenbird (8)
"Traill's" Flycatcher (2)	Red-eyed Vireo (5)	Northern Waterthrush (10)
Least Flycatcher (2)	Blue-winged Warbler (1)	Common Yellowthroat (75)
Empidonax Flycatchers (10)	Tennessee Warbler (30)	Hooded Warbler (5)
Western Kingbird (1)	Nashville Warbler (15)	Wilson's Warbler (20)
Eastern Kingbird (25)	Northern Parula (40)	Canada Warbler (5)
Scissor-tailed Flycatcher (125)	Yellow Warbler (15)	Yellow-breasted Chat (4)
Tree Swallow (2000)	Chestnut-sided Warbler (2)	Summer Tanager (5)
Cliff Swallow (15)	Magnolia Warbler (15)	Rose-breasted Grosbeak (1)
Barn Swallow (1000)	Black-throated Blue Warbler (1)	Blue Grosbeak (5)
House Wren (15)	Black-throated Gray Warbler (1)	Indigo Bunting (20)
Ruby-crowned Kinglet (15)	Townsend's Warbler (1)	Painted Bunting (5)
Blue-gray Gnatcatcher (100)	Black-throated Green Warbler (5)	Clay-colored Sparrow (1)
Gray Catbird (275)	Blackburnian Warbler (1)	Northern Oriole (1)
Brown Thrasher (550)	Prairie Warbler (1)	

Fall migration is an extended affair, with birds moving from mid-July through Christmas or later. Indeed, the last Turkey Vultures may be moving south as the first Purple Martins are returning from South America. Many of the Neotropical migrants recorded on Christmas Bird Counts (CBCs) are more than likely lingering fall migrants that will continue southward with the onset of the season's first severe weather. Unfortunately, after the thrill of the CBC discovery has faded, few observers attempt to follow up on these lingering migrants. Thus we know little about the importance of UTC woodland habitat to true *wintering* Neotropical migrants. However, a number of species of Neotropical migrants regularly winter in South Texas along the Rio Grande. Therefore we can assume that the UTC is important, if only on a minor scale, to those species for which the northernmost extent of wintering range approaches this region. In addition, species such as Blue-gray Gnatcatcher and Yellow-rumped Warbler are facultative migrants, meaning that their activity hinges upon conditions: their numbers and appearance on the UTC depend on weather to the north, and their duration locally depends upon the severity of our winter season. Previously, thousands of individuals of these two species remained on the UTC during mild winters (Eubanks

data). These days, dozens to hundreds may occur. However, in periods of extreme cold, most individuals vacate the region.

Other noteworthy phenomena are often associated with fall fronts. Strong easterly or northeasterly winds may last for several days (often causing especially high tides) and may blow eastern Gulf migrants to the UTC. These winds produce sightings of species such as Black-throated Blue Warbler and are probably responsible for two of our five Connecticut Warbler records. Conversely, western or northwestern fronts may push birds to the east, displacing them away from the UTC.

Occasionally visible on a grander scale is what is referred to as reverse migration. This behavior is well known on the East Coast and has been observed at several points of land and lakefront hawk watches in the Midwest. During reverse migrations, birds fly in a direction contrary to what would be expected, often in large numbers. Such movement may occur when southbound birds meet an oncoming front that they ride northward. However, not all reverse migrations appear to fit into the same pattern. UTC birds observed migrating northward on October days include Snow and White-fronted geese, American Kestrels, and Killdeer (J. Stevenson, pers. comm.).

A factor in the decrease of locally nesting Neotropical birds is the introduction of exotic species. Such birds compete for resources such as food and nest sites and may spread avian diseases. The well-known European Starling has effectively displaced many native cavity-nesting birds. In much of the country, starlings outnumber Northern Flickers 10:1, posing a significant threat of nest competition (Rich et al. 2004). Other species such as Red-headed Woodpecker and Eastern Bluebird continue to decline as starling populations increase. Nest site competition was exacerbated by continuing deforestation during the last two centuries and the associated loss of natural nesting cavities. Besides starlings, House Sparrows are serious competitors for nest holes, as anyone who maintains a Purple Martin house has witnessed. Other non-natives such as Mute Swan, Ring-necked Pheasant, Rock Pigeon, and Red-vented Bulbul are discussed in the species accounts.

New arrivals on the UTC include several species of purposefully or accidentally released cage birds. Don Verser located Orange Bishop (*Euplectes franciscanus*), an African relative of the House Sparrow, in Houston's Arthur Storey Park at the southeastern corner of the Sam Houston Tollway and Bellaire Boulevard. Perhaps 25–30 were present during late September 2004, as posted on the Texbirds listserv on 28 and 29 September 2004. Nutmeg Mannikin or Spotted Munia (*Lonchura punctulata*) from Asia is a popular cage bird. A small Houston flock was documented with photos received by G. Mueller at Houston Audubon Society. Recently the species was located with Orange Bishops at Arthur Storey Park, making one wonder who left the cage door open.

The advent of a cattle industry in the coastal prairie and the transformation of coastal grasslands to agricultural lands for the cultivation of rice, sorghum, and other crops have fostered an explosion of wintering cowbirds. No doubt, supplemental food in the form of crops, unharvested seed, and cattle feed supplements during UTC winters enhanced population numbers of the native Brown-headed Cowbird and the northward expansion of Bronzed Cowbird, an invader from the south. Parasitism by both of these threatens the nesting success of many native Neotropical species, especially those for which fragmentation of their forest nesting habitats is a problem.

The greatest negative influence upon the UTC's native ecology has been explosive human population growth that began in the mid-1800s. Table 6 dramatically illustrates population change that occurred on the UTC during a single century.

HUMAN POPULATION AND INFLUENCE

The Houston metropolitan region is the most expansive urban-industrial complex in Texas, in both population and land area, and Harris County is the third most populated county in the nation (U.S. Census Bureau 2003). Petroleum refining and petrochemical facilities that have developed along the coast are among the most substantial in the world. Growth in this area is projected to continue at breakneck pace, with Houston's population expected to double early this century. Therefore the detrimental effects upon native ecosystems that are associated with human impacts can be expected to continue to increase in proportion to this continuing population growth.

As a consequence of urbanization and industrialization, the habitats available to birds are now distributed in a patchwork that is very different from what Audubon observed. This mosaic of habitats still contains sufficient habitat and plant diversity to attract a full complement of *species*. However, lacking an unbroken corridor of any single ecological community or the natural gradation between communities, the number of *individuals* of certain species, particularly deep forest and grassland species, has declined. Locally, loss of grasslands continues to

proceed at an astonishing rate. As this is being written (late 2004) another 8,300 acres of west Harris County, including the 2,000-acre Josey Ranch and the 6,000-acre Longenbaugh Ranch, have been sold to for a planned 17,000 home sites.

One special region of the coast that has been heavily impacted by development is Galveston Island. References to the island and its astonishing birdlife pepper this text, involving for example migrating Eskimo Curlews, nesting Black Skimmers, and wintering flocks of Sandhill Cranes. Once a treeless expanse of dunes, marshes, and grasslands ringed by mudflats and sandy beaches, the island now supports a human population of nearly 60,000. As Will Rogers so shrewdly observed, "Acquire land, they aren't making any more of it." Nowhere is this more true than on an island, and Galveston is no exception. Coastal ranches and other private holdings are rapidly being parceled out for residential development. As we write, over 1,200 more subdivision lots are being proposed or actively developed and several condominium towers of up to 15 stories are planned, all in an area that in 1900 was devastated by a hurricane that killed between 6,000 and 12,000 people, at that time the greatest natural disaster to ever hit the United States.

PREDATION AND MORTALITY

Threats to birds vary with the family and habitat considered. For example, migrating shorebirds appear to have a limited set of predators on the UTC.

Table 6. *Population Growth of UTC Counties, 1890–2000*

County	1890	1940	1990	2000	Persons per square mile, 2000
Brazoria	11,506	27,069	191,707	241,767	174
Chambers	2,241	7,511	20,088	26,031	43
Ft. Bend	10,586	32,963	225,421	354,452	405
Galveston	31,476	81,173	217,399	250,158	627
Harris	37,249	528,961	2,818,199	3,400,578	1,967
Jefferson	5,857	145,329	239,397	252,051	279
Waller	10,888	10,280	23,390	32,663	63
Total	109,803	833,286	3,735,601	4,557,700	

Their avian threats include Peregrine Falcon, Merlin, Northern Harrier, and Short-eared Owl. Coyote, gray fox, and bobcat may take others. The greater danger lies in development of their habitat.

On farms, domestic and feral cats and dogs, livestock, and machinery are known to impact nesting species such as Mottled Duck, King Rail, and Eastern Meadowlark.

Automobile strikes are an ongoing and generally underestimated source of mortality. The following are just a few of the species that have been noted as local road kills: Least Bittern, Common Moorhen, Purple Gallinule, King and Clapper rails, Killdeer, Willet, Long-billed Dowitcher, Buff-breasted Sandpiper, Wilson's Snipe, Common Nighthawk, Yellow-billed Cuckoo, Barn Swallow, Yellow Warbler, and Indigo Bunting. During migration the last two species have a strong affinity for open scrubby fields and are occasionally slaughtered in considerable numbers as they fly low across the Bolivar Peninsula's State Highway 87 into extensive stands of willow, baccharis, and rattlebox.

On 16 October 1989, in the wake of the previous day's Hurricane Jerry, Eubanks found the coastal highways littered with the bodies of thousands of dead Chimney Swifts. After similar storms, many observers have found numerous soaked carcasses of large wading birds, including Cattle and Snowy egrets and Tricolored Herons, scattered among the trees of coastal mottes. Dead herons and egrets are also seen tangled in power lines, especially those bordering coastal fresh- and saltwater marshes.

Anyone who has stood outdoors and listened to the chips and call notes of migrating thrushes, Upland Sandpipers, Indigo Buntings, and Dickcissels will appreciate that towers erected for radio, satellite, and cellular telephone communication pose a new and serious threat to migrating birds. Not only do birds strike the towers; they also hit the support wires that radiate out from the structures. These towers are a special threat to night-flying migrants, particularly during foggy or cloudy evenings when their lights may attract and disorient migrants.

Chemicals such as pesticides and herbicides are an ongoing threat to birds of all types, both directly and when their prey base is impacted. A 1971 die-off of waterfowl poisoned by mercury and Dieldrin is mentioned in Oberholser (1974). Apparently these birds were lingerers that failed to migrate before rice farmers sowed their fields, and the birds perished due to fungicides and pesticides used to protect the seed. Over 200 Canada Geese succumbed to Parathion sprayed to control the Russian wheat aphid (Flickinger et al. 1991). In the United States, treating rice seed with mercury is no longer practiced, but many other chemicals are used to control pests.

Finally, cats—both domestic and feral—are known to be great destroyers of birdlife (Seymour 2004). Cats are known to have caused the extinction of certain island birds and mammals, hampered the reintroduction of endangered species, and suppressed populations of grassland songbirds. Studies undertaken by the University of Wisconsin and the U.S. Fish and Wildlife Service Migratory Bird Management Office estimated that in the United States cats might kill from as few as 7.8 million to as many as 100 million birds per year. As Ed Clark, president of the Wildlife Center of Virginia, stated: "The domestic cat's effect on wildlife is toxic. If you let your cat outside, you might as well be pouring poison out your back door. It doesn't matter to a bird if it died from pesticides or a cat. It's still dead" (Ridgley 2003). Anyone whose cat is allowed to run free outdoors is both ignoring and abetting the mortality wreaked by these cunning predators.

ENDANGERED SPECIES

Within modern times, few birds have suffered the catastrophic population decline of the Eskimo Curlew. In North America, only the exterminations of the Carolina Parakeet and Passenger Pigeon parallel the precipitous collapse of this once bountiful prairie shorebird. As recently as 150 years ago, Eskimo Curlews numbered in the millions. During the first half of the twentieth century they plummeted to near oblivion and probable extinction. There are only a few documented occurrences of the species since 1950, and significant debate has been generated by doubts of the curlew's continuing existence. In recognition of the delicate status of this bird, the U.S. Fish and Wildlife Service (USFWS) established an Eskimo Curlew Advisory Group in 1990. Further research may eventually reveal the distinct habitat requirements and migratory distribution of remaining Eskimo Curlews, if indeed any still remain. This information would enhance effective population monitoring during migration. If only someone had studied birds such as the Eskimo Curlew and Attwater's Prairie-Chicken during the 1800s, we would know what is required to save them.

As of May 2004, the Texas Parks and Wildlife Department considered the following UTC residents and visitors as endangered or threatened (names are as listed by TPWD; in some cases these names reflect subspecies or races that occur on the Upper Texas Coast). Endangered: Brown Pelican, Whooping Crane, Northern Aplomado Falcon, American Peregrine Falcon, Attwater's Greater Prairie-Chicken, Eskimo Curlew, Red-cockaded Woodpecker, and Ivory-billed Woodpecker. Threatened: Reddish Egret, White-faced Ibis, Wood Stork, Swallow-tailed Kite, Bald Eagle, White-tailed Hawk, Zone-tailed Hawk, Arctic Peregrine Falcon, Piping Plover, Sooty Tern, Tropical Parula, and Bachman's Sparrow (TPWD 2004a).

The *Partners in Flight North American Landbird Conservation Plan* (Rich et al. 2004) includes 45 Watch List Species that occur on the UTC. Eighteen nest or have nested locally. Those for which immediate conservation action is recommended (increasing the population by 50–100 percent or developing recovery plans) are Red-cockaded Woodpecker, Ivory-billed Woodpecker, Bachman's Sparrow, Henslow's Sparrow, Greater Prairie-Chicken, Swallow-tailed Kite, and Bell's Vireo. Those that are abundant or widespread but declining or threatened and require management (by maintaining or increasing the population) are Swainson's Hawk, Red-headed Woodpecker, Brown-headed Nuthatch, Wood Thrush, Prairie Warbler, Prothonotary Warbler, Worm-eating Warbler, Kentucky Warbler, and Dickcissel. Species that require long-term planning are Swainson's Warbler and Seaside Sparrow. Of these 18 species, only five (Henslow's Sparrow, Greater Prairie-Chicken, Swainson's Hawk, Dickcissel, and Seaside Sparrow) occur in open country. The remaining 13 depend on forests that contain young, mature, old growth, and dead trees. Such pristine and complex forests are a rapidly dwindling resource in East Texas. Only by preserving large tracts that include both old growth timber and surrounding woodlands can we maintain these birds as local nesting species.

FORMAT OF THE SPECIES ACCOUNTS

Common and scientific names and the order of the species accounts conform to the seventh edition of the *A.O.U. Check-list of North American Birds* (American Ornithologists' Union 1998) and recent supplements (Banks et al. 2002, 2004). One exception is the White-chinned Petrel, which occurs in the main body of our list but in the appendix of the *A.O.U. Check-list*.

Each species account begins with a bird's common and scientific name, followed by a one-line summary of its general status on the UTC. Terms used include:

Resident: A species that lives all year on the UTC.
Bi-seasonal migrant: A species that passes through the UTC during spring and fall migration.
Mono-seasonal migrant: A species that passes through the UTC during one season, typically with an elliptical migration pattern such that it occurs only during spring.
Summer terminal migrant: A species that nests on the UTC and winters elsewhere, typically to the south.
Winter terminal migrant: A species that winters on the UTC but nests elsewhere, typically to the north or west.
Vagrant: A term usually applied to rarities visiting from another part of the world or from very different habitat elsewhere in North America.

The words we use most often to express a species' numbers are explained in the list that follows, with illustrative examples. Modifiers such as *very* are used occasionally; these are admittedly subjective. Species with populations that are expanding or contracting, for which there has been a rash of recent records, or that have received renewed interest in field identification are especially difficult to categorize. These include the newest definitions of Canada Goose, Allen's Hummingbird, Couch's and Tropical kingbirds, Brown-crested Flycatcher, Red-vented Bulbul, Cassin's Vireo, and Eastern and Spotted towhees.

Abundant: Species most likely to be encountered and usually in large numbers (Laughing Gull, Great-tailed Grackle, wintering Savannah Sparrow).

Common: Species easily encountered in the proper season but not always in large numbers (Reddish Egret, Horned Lark).
Uncommon: Species that are usually present but may require some searching (Great Horned Owl, wintering Red Knot).
Rare or *Very Rare:* Birds that are infrequently encountered or present in exceptionally small numbers. Either would be extremely difficult to find.
Vagrant is a modifier sometimes used for out-of-range species. These are birds for which we have just a few records and that occur annually or less often. Potentially these could recur with a very low level of regularity (Barrow's Goldeneye, summer American Bittern, Ruff, Curlew Sandpiper).
Accidental: Out-of-range species that are not expected to occur with any regularity, even very rarely (Red-billed Tropicbird, Wandering Tattler, Little Gull, Williamson's Sapsucker, Clark's Nutcracker). This is a subjective category; in many peoples' minds, particularly rare vagrants are considered accidentals, but the small data sets inhibit meaningful distinctions.
Extirpated: Species for which the UTC population has disappeared (White-breasted Nuthatch, Bachman's Sparrow). This is more a more precise term than "locally extinct."
Extinct: Species no longer known to exist anywhere in their historic range (Carolina Parakeet, Passenger Pigeon).
Introduced: Species purposefully released into the wild (Ring-necked Pheasant, European Starling, House Sparrow).
Feral: Species inadvertently introduced into the wild or that have escaped captivity (Mute Swan, Ringed Turtle-Dove).
Hypothetical: Species that possess less than satisfactory documentation (Northern Shrike, Long-billed Thrasher) but are included in the text. We have made some effort not to allow other authors' hypothetical species to persist in this work.

If a species is on the Texas Bird Records Committee (TBRC) Review List, we indicate which records have been accepted, including the date in boldface, location, a county abbreviation, a TBRC number, and if applicable, a Texas Photo Record File (TPRF) number and/or a literature or specimen citation.

For species that are rare in East Texas but not included in the TBRC Review List (e.g., Brant, Red-necked Phalarope, Cassin's Vireo), we often summarize all UTC records at the beginning of the account. Such records may be distinguished from TBRC records because their dates are not boldfaced. These records will be of use to anyone tracking a species for which the range is expanding (e.g., Glossy Ibis, Great Kiskadee). Usually, additional documentation for these records may be found in *American Birds* and *Audubon Field Notes*. For certain rare or very uncommon species, we may present supporting records from surrounding counties such as Colorado or Orange counties. Occasionally we employ the Latin word *fide*, meaning "faith," or in this case "on the faith of," for an undocumented record submitted by a credible observer.

Next is a brief summary of the bird's seasonal status. For mono-seasonal (usually spring only) and bi-seasonal transient migrants, we include multiple earliest and latest spring and/or fall records. As a convention, if we have the data, we include at least three early and late records. For certain species (e.g., Black-throated Gray Warbler) we present additional dates that help establish trends. For others (Canada Goose) we find a single arrival or departure date to be satisfactory in defining a migratory window. Hyphenated dates indicate that an individual or individuals remained between the first and last date. If there are multiple occurrences at an early or late date, we indicate these. Thus (19, 21, 23 x 2 Sep) means

the bird has been encountered once each on 19 and 21 September and twice on 23 September. Between the early and late dates, the main migration window is shown in boldface. This is the period during which the bulk of the population passes through the UTC. For summering and wintering species, we attempt to present the earliest arrival and latest departure dates known to us, and a time period (boldfaced) during which most individuals are present. Occasionally we deviate slightly from this format. In the case of TBRC rarities, we do not present early and late dates unless there are enough records to assess a trend. If a bird is a permanent resident, there are no arrival or departure dates indicated, although we may cite a period when individuals from other regions join the local population.

Next is a brief habitat description that may include a very rare bird's normal range as well as its habitat on the UTC. Last is a discussion of the species as it relates to the UTC. For certain species we discuss factors that are limiting or enhancing a bird's population in other parts of its range. However, most of our discussion deals with a bird while it is present on the UTC. Because of its long-running data set, the Freeport Christmas Bird Count in Brazoria County is often referred to as a yardstick for winter numbers and frequency of occurrence. For some species, we mention vocal or plumage characteristics that aid with identification.

Many of the locations discussed in the text and directions to reach them are found on the *Great Texas Coastal Birding Trail: Upper Texas Coast* map (Texas Parks and Wildlife Department 1999).

In order to save space, months and the counties most commonly mentioned are represented by three-letter abbreviations given in the list that follows. County abbreviations are those used by the TBRC.

ABBREVIATIONS USED IN THE TEXT

*	specimen record
AB	*American Birds*
AFN	*Audubon Field Notes* (later shortened to *Field Notes*)
AMNH	American Museum of Natural History, New York
ANSP	Academy of Natural Science, Philadelphia
A.O.U.	American Ornithologists' Union
Apr	April
Attwater	Attwater Prairie-Chicken National Wildlife Refuge, Colorado County
Aug	August
BRA	Brazoria County
CBC	National Audubon Society Christmas Bird Count
CHA	Chambers County
Co., cos.	county, counties
COL	Colorado County (just west of the UTC)
Dec	December
E	east, eastern
Feb	February
FOB	Fort Bend County
GAL	Galveston County
GCBO	Gulf Coast Bird Observatory
GIW	Gulf Intracoastal Waterway
HAS	Harris County
HL&P	Houston Lighting and Power Company
HMNS	Houston Museum of Natural Science
Is.	island
Jan	January
JEF	Jefferson County
Jul	July
Jun	June
LSUMNS	Louisiana State University Museum of Natural Science (uses the following specimen number prefix)
LSUMZ	Louisiana State University Museum of Zoology
many obs.	seen by many observers
Mar	March
MNH	Museum of Natural History
MOGP	Migration Over the Gulf Project
MON	Montgomery County (just north of the UTC)
MUM	Manchester University Museum, England
N	north, northern
NAB	*North American Birds*

NBS	Neotropical Bird Sanctuary, Quintana, Texas
Nov	November
NWR	National Wildlife Refuge
Oct	October
ORA	Orange County (just east of the UTC)
pers. comm.	personally communicated to us by the observer
pers. obs.	personal observation
S	south, southern
SB	*Spoonbill* (formerly *Gulf Coast Migrant*), published by the Ornithology Group of the Outdoor Nature Club of Houston
SHSU	Sam Houston State University, Huntsville, Texas
Sep	September
SFASU	Stephen F. Austin State University, Nacogdoches, Texas
SP	State Park
TBRC	Texas Bird Records Committee of the Texas Ornithological Society
TBSL	Texas Bird Sounds Library at SHSU
TCWC	Texas Cooperative Wildlife Collection, Texas A&M University, College Station
TCWD	Texas Colonial Waterbird Database
TOS	Texas Ornithological Society
TPRF	Texas Photo Record File, Texas A&M University, Department of Wildlife and Fisheries Sciences, College Station
TPWD	Texas Parks and Wildlife Department
TWRC	Texas Wildlife Rehabilitation Coalition
UMMZ	University of Michigan Museum of Zoology, Ann Arbor
USFWS	U.S. Fish and Wildlife Service
USNM	U.S. National Museum of Natural History, Washington, D.C.
UTA	University of Texas at Austin
UTC	Upper Texas Coast, which for the purposes of this work we define as Brazoria, Chambers, Fort Bend, Galveston, Harris, Jefferson, and Waller counties
VIC	Victoria County (southwest of the UTC)
W	west, western
WAR	Waller County
WMA	Wildlife Management Area
yr	year

Armand Bayou near Clear Lake is one of the few unaltered bayous remaining in the Houston-Galveston area.

An elevated walkway for birders in High Island's Boy Scout Woods passes through the Cathedral, a favorite gathering spot for migrant watchers.

Bolivar Flats and the Galveston shipping lanes constitute an improbable conjunction of nature and industry, yet the flats rank among the most popular shorebird viewing sites in the United States.

Smooth cordgrass (*Spartina alterniflora*), as at Bolivar Flats, is the favorite haunt of Clapper Rails and both Seaside and Nelson's Sharp-tailed sparrows.

Characteristic plant species of brackish marshes are marshhay cordgrass (*Spartina patens*), Gulf cordgrass (*S. spartinae*), and various rushes (*Scirpus* spp.). Birds such as Black Rail prefer this coastal habitat.

The stretch of coast between the Brazos and San Bernard rivers is accreting sediment. Extensive dunes and driftwood at the Brazos River mouth provide shelter for species such as Wilson's and Snowy plovers.

Marshes characterized by cattail (*Typha*), bulrushes (*Scirpus*), rushes (*Juncus*), and reeds (*Phragmites*) attract freshwater bird species such as Least Bittern, Marsh Wren, and Common Yellowthroat.

West Galveston Bay attracts countless loons, waterfowl, gulls, and terns to its rich shallow waters.

The coastal marshes near High Island extend virtually unbroken along the Gulf Intracoastal Waterway northeast to the Sabine River. The absence of trees and shrubs in this coastal "hiatus" concentrates migrants in the few woodlands, such as at High Island and Sabine Woods.

Bushy bluestem (*Andropogon glomeratus*) is one of the dominant grasses on the Katy Prairie and in the region. Bluestem grasslands are important habitats for species such as Grasshopper and LeConte's sparrows.

The Smith family planted the first live oaks (*Quercus virginiana*) at High Island more than a century ago.

Palmetto (*Sabal minor*) swamps are excellent habitat for American Woodcock and breeding Prothonotary and Swainson's warblers.

Longleaf pine (*Pinus palustris*) forest once extended across East Texas from the Sabine River to Houston. Birds such as Red-cockaded Woodpecker, Brown-headed Nuthatch, and Bachman's Sparrow depend on these fire-dependent forests with their open, grassy understory.

Rice stubble as on the Katy Prairie, although an agricultural landscape, is now preferred by waterfowl wintering along the UTC.

Seacoast bluestem (*Schizachyrium scoparium* var. *littoralis*) grasslands once proliferated on Galveston Island; their remnants still attract species such as wintering LeConte's Sparrows.

Taylor Bayou is a finger of East Texas riparian woodland that wends through Chambers County. Its array of nesting warblers includes Prothonotary, Swainson's, and Hooded. Swallow-tailed Kites have nested here in the recent past.

Fish Crows (*Corvus ossifragus*) are often seen coursing along Village Creek, and Yellow-throated Vireos sing from the trees along its banks.

Canada and Cackling geese (*Branta canadensis, B. hutchinsii*) in flight—along the UTC, neither Canada nor Cackling geese are normally seen in concentrations as large as this.

A small duck from the tropics, the Masked Duck (*Nomonyx dominicus*) strays north to the region only rarely, finding refuge in marshes such as Pilant Lake at Brazos Bend State Park. (*Photograph by Mark Lockwood*)

The Attwater's race of Greater Prairie-Chicken (*Tympanuchus cupido attwateri*) was once abundant along the UTC but has been reduced to a heartbreaking handful. (*Photograph by Clifford E. Shackelford*)

(left)
The Neotropic Cormorant (*Phalacrocorax brasilianus*) is the upper coast's breeding cormorant.

(right)
Reddish Egret (*Egretta rufescens*), white morph—along the UTC, the white morph Reddish Egret is far outnumbered by the typical reddish birds.

(below)
Roseate Spoonbills (*Platalea ajaja*) nest in impressive concentrations in the colony at Claybottom Pond, High Island.

Swainson's Hawk (*Buteo swainsoni*) is common during migration in interior agricultural fields, particularly those recently burned or plowed, where it feeds on a variety of prey, including earthworms.

The immature White-tailed Hawk (*Buteo albicaudatus*) is often confused with other species, such as Rough-legged and dark-morph Swainson's hawks.

(left top)
The Crested Caracara (*Caracara cheriway*), increasing in numbers and expanding its range, now extends east to the Louisiana border and coastally to Galveston Island.

(right top)
The Piping Plover (*Charadrius melodus*) is categorized as an endangered or threatened species throughout its range but can be found with relative ease in its prime wintering range along the Texas coast.

(left bottom)
King Rail (*Rallus elegans*), a rustier and more heavily barred freshwater version of Clapper Rail, is declining locally with the loss of freshwater marshes.

The Black-necked Stilt (*Himantopus mexicanus*) is a common nesting shorebird. During the last several years, its winter numbers have increased dramatically.

One of the few photographs of a living Eskimo Curlew (*Numenius borealis*), this rare shot was taken on Galveston Island in 1962. (*Photograph by Don Blietz*)

(top)
A juvenile Short-billed Dowitcher (*Limnodromus griseus*) is readily identifiable by the "tiger striping" on the innermost flight feathers or tertials.

(bottom)
These Laughing Gulls (*Larus atricilla*) were photographed as they followed the Galveston ferry between Galveston Island and the Bolivar Peninsula, a place where many visitors are first exposed to the Texas coast's abundant birdlife.

The Lesser Black-backed Gull (*Larus fuscus*) was once a rare visitor but now occurs in increasing numbers along the UTC.

In addition to nesting on sandy beaches, Least Terns (*Sterna antillarum*) construct their nests on local substrates such as gravel parking lots, gravel roofs, and shell-covered oil-drilling pads.

Black Skimmers (*Rynchops niger*) often struggle to find undisturbed stretches of beach where they can nest.

The Groove-billed Ani (*Crotophaga sulcirostris*) is a tropical cuckoo that wanders northward during winter.

The Burrowing Owl (*Athene cunicularia*) is most often associated with prairie dog colonies in the interior of the state; during winter, a few stray to the coast.

Rufous Hummingbird (*Selasphorus rufus*) is the most common wintering hummingbird on the upper coast. Young birds are the predominant age class.

This Greenish Elaenia (*Myiopagis viridicata*) represents the first and only record of the species for the United States. Discovered by Jim Morgan and Linda Feltner in Boy Scout Woods at High Island, it was subsequently photographed on 20 May 1984.

This Eastern Wood-Pewee (*Contopus virens*) is perched, drenched and exhausted, during a fallout on Galveston Island.

The Alder Flycatcher (*Empidonax alnorum*) has a Downy Woodpecker–like call note that helped to identify this individual. This cryptic species is often found in coastal woodlands (even salt cedars) during early fall.

The Scissor-tailed Flycatcher (*Tyrannus forficatus*) is among the most widely recognized birds in Texas; it is declining rapidly with urbanization.

This Yucatan Vireo (*Vireo magister*) was among the most surprising of species to wander to the UTC (or Texas, for that matter); this first U.S. record was photographed on 28 April 1984 on the Bolivar Peninsula.

The Texas subspecies of Horned Lark (*Eremophila alpestris giraudi*) is the breeding "shore lark" of the Texas coast.

Members of an eastern red-backed form of Bewick's Wren (*Thryomanes bewickii*) winter in small numbers in west Harris and Waller counties. They are often found in huisache stands along with Ash-throated Flycatchers, Blue-gray Gnatcatchers, and Palm Warblers of the eastern subspecies.

The eastern or "Yellow" subspecies of Palm Warbler (*Dendroica palmarum hypochrysea*) winters in small numbers in huisache stands in the western portion of the UTC.

Along the UTC, Nelson's Sharp-tailed Sparrow (*Ammodramus nelsoni*) is found almost exclusively in smooth cordgrass (*Spartina alterniflora*), as seen in this photograph.

Harris's Sparrow (*Zonotrichia querula*), a bird from the northern Great Plains, often winters along the UTC among flocks of White-crowned Sparrows.

Boat-tailed Grackles (*Quiscalus major*) are only infrequently seen inland but are abundant in the coastal marshes.

Bullock's Oriole (*Icterus bullockii*) is one of the Neotropical migrants that occasionally winters in the mature landscapes of older neighborhoods in Houston, Galveston, and other coastal UTC communities. (*Photograph by Robert A. Behrstock*)

Species Accounts

Forty-two species of ducks, geese, and swans have occurred on the UTC's many marine and aquatic habitats, ranking these birds as one of the region's best-represented groups. Although waterfowl are diverse and plentiful during much of the year, only a few are permanent residents. The balance visit from the prairie potholes of the north-central United States and southern Canada to as far north as the tundra around Hudson Bay (the nesting grounds of our Snow and Ross's geese), Alaska, and Baffin Island. Some species are abundant; at UTC reservoirs and harvested rice fields, birds such as Green-winged Teal and Snow Goose appear in the thousands to hundreds of thousands, creating a wildlife spectacle on a par with any in North America. Others such as Barrow's Goldeneye and Long-tailed Duck are great rarities, and their unexpected appearance attracts dedicated birders from throughout the region.

Several factors account for changes in the UTC's waterfowl numbers and diversity; some of these seem to have occurred naturally and others are the result of human activity. On Hudson Bay, Snow Goose populations exploded to the point that their feeding grounds were being destroyed. In response Texas hunters' bag limits were increased to reflect the overpopulation. In Galveston Bay, beds of submerged aquatic vegetation that nourish waterfowl have been lost to dredging and sedimentation. Now, once common diving ducks such as Canvasback and Redhead winter well to the southwest of the UTC. Mottled Duck is another declining species, apparently a victim of changing agricultural practices. At the same time, the tropical Black-bellied Whistling-Duck is extending its range northward from Mexico and the rare Masked Duck has been numerous during several recent years.

Although bird watchers, photographers, and writers appreciate waterfowl with aesthetic values that are often difficult to quantify, there is no ambiguity in the dollar value of the UTC's waterfowl, particularly geese. Late each year hunters from throughout the country visit the UTC (principally W HAS and WAR cos.) and surrounding counties, taking thousands of birds and adding millions of dollars to the economy of East Texas.

Fortunately for both hunters and birders, populations of waterfowl breeding in the northeastern arctic survey area of 1.3 million square miles are among the highest they have been since 1955 when the USFWS began monitoring key nesting areas. Such increases, although dramatic, are not uncommon during dry-wet cycles. According to John Rogers, former acting director of the USFWS, favorable weather conditions following several disastrous drought years as well as restoration of millions of acres of wetlands are responsible for the increases. Various provisions of the Farm Bill and the Clean Water Act and the actions of organizations such as Ducks Unlimited have been responsible for habitat acquisition and protection. The North American Waterfowl Management Plan, an international partnership dedicated to wetland protection, restoration, and enhancement, establishes numerical goals that represent healthy duck populations. After four to five years of wet springs and above-average pond numbers, by 2004 most duck species were above these goals. Hunters' bag limits, currently six ducks per day for the commoner species, have reflected these increases. Note that wintering populations on the UTC vary greatly from year to year depending on weather and the amount of available food. Therefore current statistics may not reflect those presented in the text. Periodic droughts have played a large role in preventing adequate food supplies from developing. The most extreme droughts leave little available marsh habitat for waterfowl.

Fred Collins (pers. comm.) notes an increase in habitat available for waterfowl in N HAS and WAR cos., as new upscale housing developments add landscaped "lakes" used for water detention and amenities such as fountains and domesticated waterfowl. Locally, such ornamental ponds are likely to enhance the spread of aggressive feral species such as Mute Swan. Elsewhere in the country, these ponds attract hundreds of nonmigratory Canada Geese that spread into adjoining neighborhoods and golf courses. Because of its messy droppings, this regal bird is now widely regarded as a nuisance species.

BLACK-BELLIED WHISTLING-DUCK
Dendrocygna autumnalis

Common summer terminal migrant, uncommon and restricted during winter

SUMMER: **Common mid- to late Mar to mid-Nov**

HABITAT: Lakes, ponds, impoundments, rice fields, favors wooded areas when available (for nest sites), although will nest atop rice levees.

DISCUSSION: During the past two decades, few species' ranges have expanded as widely and as rapidly as that of the Black-bellied Whistling-Duck. In the early 1970s the appearance of just one Black-belly sent UTC birders scurrying for their scopes. In those days this duck was included with Green Jay, Plain Chachalaca, and Altamira Oriole as birds one traveled to extreme South Texas to see. Until the mid-1970s it was mainly restricted to its historic U.S. stronghold in the Rio Grande Valley, modestly expanding as a new population center formed in 1958 at Lake Corpus Christi. Bellrose (1976) stated the migrant Texas population occurred regularly only as far north as Refugio Co. and irregularly as far north as FOB, BRA and JEF. Oberholser (1974) considered it a South Texas bird that was "locally scarce to rare on coast from Sinton to Freeport" and only a vagrant in JEF and GAL. In fact, these ducks were first recorded breeding in FOB and just to the west in Austin co. as late as 1975 (AB 30:95). Nonetheless, local residents at the Hale Ranch (now Brazos Bend SP) remarked that this species had been resident on the ranch's lakes for decades.

Since the mid-1970s this species' range has expanded to include wetlands throughout the region (including eastern JEF along the Louisiana border). Black-bellies have nested at McFaddin NWR, JEF, since approximately Jun 1987 (J. Neaville data). Other nesters occurred at the Indian Beach Pond, GAL, on 18 Aug 1989, although they may have bred in that county earlier. Now, during summer, the rice fields of W HAS, WAR, and FOB host hundreds of breeding pairs. Besides nesting on the ground and in tree cavities (often in live oaks when available), they take readily to nest boxes, although five such boxes examined by Behrstock at Attwater one spring morning all contained Barn Owl nestlings. A brood with 11 downy young observed by the Rissers 2 Oct 1994 at Brazos Bend SP agrees with known late breeding dates for the state (Oberholser 1974).

Most whistling-ducks vacate the UTC in late fall, presumably migrating to S Texas and Mexico. Those that linger on the UTC concentrate in large aggregations; winter flocks may exceed 1,000 birds. For example, 1,200 were reported from the Cypress Creek CBC (WAR) 1 Jan 1992. During the winter of 2003, Collins noted a flock of 200–400 Black-bellies that roosted each evening on a lake in N HAS. Apparently these birds abandoned the Katy Prairie for the winter and were spending the day at ponds in an adjacent subdivision.

FULVOUS WHISTLING-DUCK
Dendrocygna bicolor

Common summer terminal migrant, rare winter lingerer

SUMMER: (19 × 2, 22, 25 Feb) **early Mar to mid-Nov** (25–26 Dec; 1, 31 × 2 Jan)

HABITAT: Breeds primarily in inland rice fields, also ponds, lakes, impoundments; at times (early spring) an abundant coastal migrant.

DISCUSSION: Most of North America's Fulvous Whistling-Ducks are concentrated near the Gulf Coast in the rice belt of E Texas and W Louisiana. During spring these birds return from lagoons in E Mexico, and a flood of migrants—occasionally thousands per day—moves NE along the coast. For example, on 18 Apr 1992, Eubanks and Morgan counted 2,500 flying past the beaches of JEF and CHA. The open Gulf is not a barrier to their migration, and streams of migrant whistling-ducks are often seen coursing over the surf with Blue-winged Teal and various waders. For reasons including sightings far offshore and census data from the Lower Texas Coast, McCartney suggests (in Bellrose 1976) that some birds migrate from SE Mexico directly across the Gulf to Louisiana.

Occasionally, moderate numbers of Fulvous-Whistling-Ducks linger into winter, at times turning up on CBCs (e.g., 21 over surf near High Island on 28 Dec 1989 and 21 on 18 Dec 1998 at San Bernard NWR). Bellrose (1976) suggested that few remain after mid-Jan. Although overwintering birds have been documented at San Bernard NWR, his statement has largely held true. Therefore there is about a one-month-long hiatus when "wintering" birds have left and the earliest migrants have yet to arrive in late Feb/early Mar.

The Bird Life of Texas contains a detailed summary of the species' earlier fate in Texas, including a staggering population decrease of more than 90 percent between 1959 and 1960. This collapse occurred when farmers treated rice and rice fields—a preferred habitat of this species—with various pesticides and mercury-containing fungicides. The birds were either poisoned outright or the physiological stress prevented breeding.

This species is one of the most widespread of all ducks. It occurs in N and S America, Africa, Madagascar, India, and Australasia and has been noted on various Caribbean Islands. Kincaid opined that its current range is a collection of now isolated remnants of a huge ancient contiguous distribution. However, the bird is a noted wanderer, and some of its modern distribution may be attributable to recent expansion. Texas birds are known to wander; Bellrose cites an individual banded at the Salton Sea (S California) during Mar of 1956, recovered in Fulshear (FOB) Nov 1957. Kincaid (in Oberholser 1974) suggested that the species' propensity to wander generated a dispersed viable population that allowed it to persist elsewhere during the poisoning and recovery of its Texas haunts.

Lakes at Anahuac and Brazoria NWR, Brazos Bend SP, irrigation and waterfowl impoundments, and areas with rice cultivation are worthwhile places to seek this species. For example, Fred Collins observed 700 in the rice fields of HAS and WAR on 12 May 1992.

GREATER WHITE-FRONTED GOOSE
Anser albifrons

Common winter terminal migrant, common bi-seasonal transient migrant, rare summer lingerer

WINTER: (14, 29 Sep; 4, 10 Oct) **early Oct to late Apr** (25, 27, 30 Apr); wounded birds often linger through summer

HABITAT: Marshy areas, dry and flooded fields (both coastally and inland), rice and corn stubble.

DISCUSSION: Speckle-bellies or Specks (as they are known by local hunters) surf the first frontal systems of fall, a few appearing even while the heat of summer still suffocates the coastal marshes and rice fields. Their eerie, quavering calls are among the first sounds of an impending fall season. Usually, smaller flocks of White-fronts precede the more sizable

gatherings of Snow Geese by several weeks. However, the sudden appearance of these birds, many of which are heading for the lowlands of coastal Tamaulipas, may be no less spectacular than the arrival of our wintering Snow Geese. White-fronted and the Canada-type geese may be difficult to detect as they feed breast high in corn stubble. Often, the only signs of white-fronts are their muted calls and the flashes of white foreheads (their white "front") barely protruding above the corn stalks. The USFWS midwinter surveys of the past ten years suggest that between 100,000 and 200,000 Greater White-fronted Geese winter along the upper coast between Sabine Pass and Corpus Christi. These same surveys indicate that the number of White-fronts wintering in Texas has increased steadily in the last twenty years. Most of these wintering birds are gone by early Mar and only a few remain as late as early Apr. On rare occasions, sick or injured individuals may linger into summer (e.g., one was seen 10 Jun 2001 at McFaddin NWR, JEF).

SNOW GOOSE
Chen caerulescens

Common to abundant winter terminal migrant

WINTER: (4, 6 Oct) **mid-Oct to mid-Mar** (16 May, lingering to 15 Jun); wounded birds remain into summer (i.e., 12 Aug, 3 Sep), only slightly confusing arrival and departure dates

HABITAT: Dry or shallowly flooded fields, lakes or impoundments, rice stubble; occasionally along the coast, but more common inland.

DISCUSSION: Despite Kincaid's statement (in Oberholser 1974)—with apologies to Mae West—that "In the smog-palled, oil- and carbon-blacked Houston–Texas City–Galveston area a really white Snow Goose is nowadays hard to find," by the 1980s the beauty, noise, and sheer numbers of these birds had made them a favorite of birders, nature photographers, and hunters. An early winter's drive through the rice fields or coastal prairies is a visual and auditory celebration, with clouds of Snow Geese at times filling the sky. Once a coastal species wintering in the brackish marshes, on coastal prairies, and on bay waters, Snow Geese shifted inland as rice agriculture converted the interior grasslands to artificial marshes. Birds along the Gulf are Lesser Snow Geese, the more westerly subspecies. A large proportion of these, 10–15 percent, are blue morph birds (formerly Blue Goose, once considered a separate species), which breed mainly N and NE of Hudson Bay (A.O.U. 1983), often in mixed pairs with a white morph mate. As with High Island's migrant songbirds and Rockport's Whooping Cranes, Snow Geese generate considerable revenue through sales of gasoline, motel rooms, restaurant meals, film, and water for flooding impoundments, with the geese also supporting guide and hunting lease fees and sales of arms, ammunition, and hunting licenses. USFWS midwinter waterfowl surveys show that between 500,000 and a million Snow Geese winter along the Texas coast. These same surveys have demonstrated a slow but steady increase the Central Flyway's white goose population.

Despite extensive loss of habitat on the wintering grounds, these numbers provide evidence of the well-publicized population expansion of this species during recent years. Wildlife biologists now consider North America's Snow Goose population to be overabundant. Expanded hunting seasons have been implemented to reduce the harmful effects of the excess birds on their arctic breeding habitat. Most birds vacate the UTC before the end of Mar, but small numbers linger into early Apr with an occasional sick or injured bird staying well into summer.

ROSS'S GOOSE
Chen rossii

Uncommon to common winter terminal migrant

WINTER: (10 Oct) **mid-Oct to mid-Mar** (17, 19 Mar); Apr and May lingerers may represent cripples

HABITAT: Rice fields, marshes, prairie, coastally and inland.

DISCUSSION: Twenty-five years ago UTC birders spent endless hours combing Snow Goose flocks in W HAS Co. for a quick glimpse of a lone Ross's Goose hidden in the crowd. Now wintering flocks containing dozens may be seen annually in the westernmost UTC counties. On 18 Jan 1998, Lockwood and Freeman reported an estimated 1,000 just west of the UTC in Colorado Co. during a winter that produced impressive numbers. Few "light goose" flocks anywhere in our region now lack this species, although (like Snow Goose) it is less common immediately along the coast. TPWD biologists estimated that in the winter

of 1994–95, 53,491 Ross's Geese wintered in coastal zones 1–3 (from Sabine Pass to Lavaca Bay). Therefore patient observers should have little difficulty spotting an occasional Ross's roosting in a field of Snows, or picking one out of a V formation of their appreciably larger cousins. We are aware of several records of the rare dark morph, including two photographed by Eubanks 15 Jan 1993 in WAR and two shot by hunters (*fide* Larry Gore). For trivia buffs: Ross's Goose and Harris' Sparrow, which often inhabits hedgerows on the margins of fields of geese, are two of less than half a dozen birds with breeding range restricted to Canada.

CACKLING GOOSE
Branta hutchinsii

Common, but irregular winter terminal migrant

WINTER: (9 Sep) **early Oct through late Apr** (9 May); these dates do not distinguish Cackling and Canada geese

HABITAT: Interior grasslands and agricultural fields, particularly rice and corn stubble, pastures, inland lakes and reservoirs.

DISCUSSION: Although we recognize fall records from as early as 9 Sep, the bulk of the Cackling and Canada goose migration appears to lag behind the movements of both Snow and Greater White-fronted geese. Significant numbers do not appear until the arrival of the first strong frontal systems in mid- to late Oct. In fact, Cackling Geese appear to linger to the north much later than other species of geese and in mild winters do not occur in large concentrations. This is reflected by USFWS midwinter surveys that range from just a few thousand in some years to over 100,000 in others. Compared with the Snow Goose, Cackling and Canada geese are generally restricted to inland counties, especially WAR, where they are usually seen grazing with White-fronted and other geese.

Recently taxonomists split off four small forms of the Canada Goose and created a new species called Cackling Goose (Banks et al. 2004). These are the northernmost and westernmost nesters of what formerly constituted Canada Goose. Two of these forms winter in our area. Richardson's Cackling Goose (formerly *Branta canadensis hutchinsii*) is the commoner form, constituting the bulk of our Canada-type geese. The TOS checklist (1995) also lists the Taverner's or

Alaskan Cackling Goose (formerly *B. c. taverneri*) that winters on the U.S. West Coast as a rare winter visitor to the Texas coast, and the TBRC News (Lockwood 2004) recognizes specimen evidence from WAR. The following list summarizes the Canada/Cackling Goose complex as presented in *The Birds of North America* (Mowbray et al. 2002):

Canada Goose *Branta canadensis*, large-bodied group, 7 subspecies nesting inland and southerly
B. c. canadensis, Atlantic Canada Goose
B. c. interior, Hudson Bay Canada Goose
B. c. maxima, Giant Canada Goose
B. c. moffitti, Moffitt's or Great Basin Canada Goose
B. c. parvipes, Lesser Canada Goose Goose
B. c. occidentalis, Dusky Canada Goose
B. c. fulva, Vancouver Canada Goose

Cackling Goose *Branta hutchinsii*, small-bodied group, 4 subspecies breeding mainly in tundra
B. h. hutchinsii, Richardson's (or Hutchins's) Cackling Goose
B. h. taverneri, Taverner's (Alaska) Cackling Goose
B. h. minima, Cackling Goose
B. h. leucopareia, Aleutian Cackling Goose

CANADA GOOSE
Branta canadensis

Uncommon to rare and irregular winter terminal migrant

WINTER: (9 Sep) **early Oct through late Apr** (9 May); these dates do not distinguish Cackling and Canada geese
HABITAT: As for the previous species.
DISCUSSION: As a species, Canada Goose now comprises of a group of seven (mostly) large subspecies that were recently separated from Cackling Goose (see preceding account). During winter, *B. c. interior* is an uncommon resident along the coast, *B. c. moffitti* is an uncommon resident on the upper coast, and the smaller *B. c. parvipes* is a rare coastal resident known (at least) from WAR (TOS 1995, Lockwood 2004). Of the geese that are expected to occur on the UTC, Canada Goose is the least common.

The Giant Canada Goose (*B. c. maxima*), four times larger than the local form of Cackling Goose, has not become an established pest on local golf courses and parks as it has in much of the country.

BRANT
Branta bernicla

Accidental winter visitor
Nov 1971 Katy Prairie, FOB (TBRC 1998-43; *TCWC 13337, TPRF 1563)
17–18 Apr 1981 Bolivar Flats, GAL (TPRF 236) (AB 35:841)
Dec 1983 WAR (TBRC 1993-139; TPRF 1175)
13 Dec 1986 High Is., GAL (TBRC 1989-74) (AB 41:301)
8 Jan 1995 Anahuac NWR, CHA (TBRC 1995-9) (AFN 49:166)
21 Feb–5 Mar 1995 near Katy, HAS (TBRC 1995-20) (AFN 49:166, 274)

HABITAT: Seacoast and bays, rarely inland.
DISCUSSION: Both the E and W coast subspecies of Brant (*B. b. bernicla* and *B. b. nigricans* respectively) have been recorded along the UTC, where both are great rarities. The Brant present at Sabine Pass, JEF (AB 35:841), 15 Mar–11 Apr 1981 (record unsubmitted) was possibly the same bird as that confirmed shortly thereafter at Bolivar Flats, since both records represented the Pacific subspecies, *nigricans*. In 1971 an individual of the eastern subspecies *bernicla* was taken on the Katy Prairie, FOB, by K. Girgis of Houston. At the time a TPWD officer advised him of the bird's rarity, but the record was never reported. Fortunately, 26 years later, the mounted specimen was offered to the ornithological community instead of being discarded.

MUTE SWAN
Cygnus olor

Introduced: Feral pairs beginning to breed
19–26 Jan 2003 Anahuac NWR, CHA
20 Sep 2004 Kleb Woods, NW HAS
2004 Successful nesting, NE WAR

HABITAT: Natural and artificial habitats including marshes, ponds, lakes, canals, large ornamental water gardens, and fish ponds.
DISCUSSION: Introduced to the United States in the late 1800s, this attractive, long-lived European

species quickly escaped captivity. It now numbers in the thousands and continues to increase, mainly on the eastern seaboard.

The Mute Swan's threat lies in its preference for feeding on submerged aquatic vegetation used by many species of birds, fishes, and invertebrates, and its tendency to displace other birds including skimmers, terns, and native waterfowl during aggressive encounters. As a result, state and federal agencies along Chesapeake Bay and elsewhere in the East where the species flourishes have developed management plans that include addling (killing) eggs and killing or relocating adults. The former has been shown to have a much smaller effect on population reduction than the latter (Thompson 2003). At the same time, breeders of exotic poultry and ornamental waterfowl continue to provide young swans (cygnets) for private bird collections or for stocking on lakes or ponds.

In Texas, Mute Swan has not yet spread as aggressively as European Starling or Eurasian Collared-Dove. However, small numbers (possibly local escapes) have been observed across the country and as far west as San Francisco Bay (Behrstock observation), so the species' dispersive tendencies should not be underestimated. Pending the establishment of a self-perpetuating population, Mute Swan has not been added to the TBRC's official list of Texas birds and may not be included on an American Birding Association (ABA)-sanctioned State List for Texas.

Recent UTC records include three at Anahuac NWR; five fly-overs (3 adults and 2 immatures) at Kleb Woods Nature Preserve on FM 2920 in NW HAS; and a nest in WAR that produced two cygnets (the latter two records from F. Collins). Increased releases and the greater availability of small, protected lakes in residential and industrial developments are likely to enhance this swan's numbers in East Texas. In our estimation, efforts should be made to prevent the species from becoming established on the UTC.

HABITAT: Open bay waters, large reservoirs and lakes.

DISCUSSION: The Trumpeter Swan, like the Tundra Swan, was once a common winter species along the Texas coast. Now it has been mostly extirpated from its former southern range and rarely drifts farther south than Wyoming and Nebraska. Strecker (1912) considered it a "common winter resident of the coast." Yet most Texans have not been privileged to see this splendid bird firsthand, as wholesale slaughter during the 1800s for both market and pleasure drove it to near extinction. On the UTC, Oberholser reported a specimen collected at High Island 15 Feb 1927—the last record of that era. However, in recent years there have been several sightings of this swan in other regions in Texas. Birds being reestablished in Wisconsin wintered in North Texas in 1989–90, including seven at White Rock Lake, Dallas Co.; Lemon Lake, Dallas Co.; and Plantation Resort, Collins Co. (TPRF 798) (AB 44:290–91). These cygnets originated from Alaskan eggs and were released in Wisconsin on 19 Nov 1989. Elsewhere in Texas, three records of apparently wild birds (of unknown origin) have been accepted by the TBRC: 28 Dec 1989–14 Jan 1990 at Falcon Dam, Starr Co. (TBRC 1990-9; TPRF 936)(AB 44:290); 8 Apr 1993 near Vega, Oldham Co. (TBRC 1996-15); and 7–28 Dec 2000 in northeastern Hemphill Co. (TBRC 2000-141; TPRF 1946). In the winter of 1994–95 birders reported a Trumpeter Swan from Brazoria NWR; however, that record was not sanctioned by the TBRC. The UTC finally got its first TBRC-accepted Trumpeter Swan in 2002 when a nonbanded immature was seen and photographed by many during its 3 Jan–18 Mar stay at Brazoria NWR, BRA.

In the northern states, this species is being introduced in ever-increasing numbers to much of its former range. As reintroduction efforts continue, and the migratory population slowly recovers, we may again see this magnificent swan appear in its former Texas haunts.

TRUMPETER SWAN
(Cygnus buccinator)

Very rare winter terminal migrant, formerly common

3 Jan–18 Mar 2002 Brazoria NWR, BRA (TBRC 2002-7) (NAB 56:139, 193)

TUNDRA SWAN
Olor columbianus

Rare winter terminal migrant

WINTER: (1, 5, 13, 16 Nov) **early Nov to early Mar** (20 Feb; 5, 7 Mar)

HABITAT: Usually occurs on larger lakes and reservoirs.

DISCUSSION: During the 1800s, Tundra (formerly Whistling) Swans blanketed the UTC, particularly Galveston Bay. Audubon noted swans there in the spring of 1837, and Roemer (1849), crossing Galveston Bay near Morgan's Point on 12 Jan 1846, remarked: "In many places the surface of the water was completely blackened by myriads of wild ducks. Whole rows of white swans, resembling silver banks from the distance, clumsy pelicans, geese and various diving birds without number completed the swarms of the feathered denizens." Strecker (1912) stated that Whistling (Tundra) Swan "winters abundantly on Galveston and Corpus Christi bays and at other points along the coast."

Once commonplace, this swan is among our rarest species of waterfowl and sightings have become a less than annual event. This precipitous decline is due to global-level overhunting and local-level loss of habitat. In particular, we note the decline of sea grasses in Galveston Bay during the 1900s, an important food source for grazers such as the Tundra Swan. Whereas this bay once supported vast beds of sea grasses, the only remaining flats in the entire Galveston Bay system are found in Christmas Bay. The most recent reports (which lacked unequivocal documentation ruling out Trumpeter Swan) include 10 flying near Dayton, CHA, on 26 Jan 1998 and two seen from 9 Feb through 22 Mar 2002 on the Katy Prairie. UTC birders should be cautious in identifying adult and immature swans, as the critical field marks are difficult to distinguish on distant birds. Additionally, the likelihood of finding a Trumpeter (see previous species account) may now be equal to or greater than that of finding a Tundra.

WOOD DUCK
Aix sponsa

Uncommon resident, more common winter terminal migrant

HABITAT: Aquatic habitat in or near woods, including ponds, lakes, and bayou margins, cypress-tupelo swamp, hardwood bottomlands; rarely on waterfowl impoundments, and generally absent along the immediate coast.

DISCUSSION: Wood Duck, arguably the most spectacular of North American waterfowl, has survived more than a century of local habitat alteration and degradation. Although no doubt diminished from the numbers that preceded European settlement— Strecker (1912) commented that the Wood Duck was "formerly abundant, now exceedingly rare" in Texas by the early 1900s—it nevertheless remains a significant constituent of the region's mixed riparian forests and cypress swamps.

Wood Ducks have always been in demand for food and trophies and are still being hunted for their attractive plumes, which are incorporated into a variety of trout flies. Additionally, as has been the case with many other species that nest in bottomland hardwood forests, Wood Ducks suffered precipitous declines during the 1800s as old growth trees with suitable nest cavities were logged (first by settlers, then by a burgeoning timber industry). East Texas tree farmers have replaced mixed hardwood forests, which provide acorns and other nuts, with a pine monoculture that is harvested when yet too young to provide nest cavities or much food (Oberholser 1974).

Fortunately, many landowners erect Wood Duck nest boxes to encourage their populations. Lacking gracious hosts, the birds utilize natural cavities, often taking over old nests of Pileated Woodpeckers. Wood Ducks persist even in urban areas such as Houston (despite the conversion of most Houston bayous into concrete drainage ditches). After the young hatch, the females immediately lead them to water, and residents along Buffalo Bayou (in W Houston) have returned home one afternoon to find their backyard swimming pool transformed into a duck nursery.

GADWALL
Anas strepera

Common winter terminal migrant

WINTER: (26 Aug; 4, 11 Sep) **mid-Sep to early May** (8 Jun; Jun–23 July, 10–18 July, these latter records presumably lingering cripples)

HABITAT: Inland lakes and reservoirs, flooded fields, ponds and bayous.

DISCUSSION: Among our dabblers, Gadwall rounds out the top three, trailing Green-winged Teal and trading places with Northern Pintail in relative abundance. Recent USFWS midwinter surveys indicate that about 100,000 to 150,000 winter along the upper coast, and these numbers have been increasing over the past fifty years. Gadwall arrive with the fall fronts (dribbling into our region beginning in Sep) and persist through late spring. Cripples occasionally remain into the early summer. Although most common among the great inland flocks of puddle ducks and geese, Gadwall may appear in appreciable numbers along the coast. For instance, the Freeport CBC reported a high of 10,000 in 1976.

EURASIAN WIGEON
Anas penelope

Very rare vagrant or accidental visitor
14 Apr 1979 Anahuac NWR, CHA (TBRC 1990-51) (AB 33:788)
12 Dec 2000 Peach Point WMA, BRA (TBRC 2001-21; TPRF 1945) (NAB 55:194)

HABITAT: Freshwater lakes, ponds, and reservoirs.
DISCUSSION: The Eurasian Wigeon is regular in the United States along both coasts (and more recently into the interior western states), but any sighting of this species in Texas is exceptional. To date, this Old World species has been documented less than 40 times in Texas, and only twice on the UTC. Additionally, we are aware of four other undocumented reports.

The most recent valid record was a first year male shot at Peach Point WMA. Fortunately, the hunter documented his red-headed wigeon with a disposable camera before having it for dinner. This species should be looked for in flocks of American Wigeon, its close cousin. However, reports of hybrid American-Eurasian Wigeon are also increasing, so any Eurasian-like bird should be carefully described.

AMERICAN WIGEON
Anas americana

Common bi-seasonal transient migrant, common winter terminal migrant

WINTER: (6 Sep) **mid-Sep to mid-May** (1 Jun), **occasionally remaining into the summer months** (13 Jun–10 Jul, 27 Jun; 15, 26, 31 Jul; 5 Aug)
HABITAT: Lakes, ponds, reservoirs, flooded fields, tidal sloughs, occasionally bay and Gulf waters.

DISCUSSION: Strecker (1912) considered the "Baldpate" a "rather common winter resident" in Texas, rejecting Cooke's statement (1888) that it actually bred here. In modern times, American Wigeon has become one of our less common wintering dabblers. The US-FWS surveys tally about 50,000 per year with occasional peaks; for example, 219,605 in 2000. In some winters the marshes of the upper coast contain very few wigeon while the lower coast has above average numbers, indicating that many of the those present here in early fall continue to S Texas and the Laguna Madre to winter. Wigeon are most often found associating with other dabblers, such as Blue-winged Teal, on inland lakes and reservoirs and in flooded rice stubble. As with other ducks, cripples may remain through the summer.

AMERICAN BLACK DUCK
Anas rubripes

Vagrant winter terminal migrant
23 Jan 1916 High Is., GAL (*AMNH 350531)
30 Dec 1972 (2) Sheldon Lake, CHA (*TCWC 13716, 13717)
Dec 1991 Smith Point, CHA (TBRC 1994-15; TPRF 1197)

HABITAT: Ponds, marshes, and impoundments.
DISCUSSION: The status of no species, except perhaps migrant *Empidonax* flycatchers or wintering peeps, has been more confounding and disconcerting than that of the American Black Duck. Few winters pass without a report of this species, yet with only three notable exceptions these records have either been unsubstantiated (mostly unsubmitted) or without sufficient details (and photos or specimens) to rule out Mottled Duck unequivocally. To date, only eight records have been accepted by the TBRC for the entire state.

In recent years the American Black Duck has declined within its eastern U.S. range as a result of increased hybridization (genetic swamping) with the Mallard. Yet even as far back as the early 1900s, Strecker (1912) considered this species to be an "exceedingly rare migrant" in Texas. We are aware of the inherant confusion that lies in separating this species from its carbon copy, the Mottled Duck, individuals of which may be very dark. We are also sensitive to the difficulties associated with procuring documentary photos of these often skittish birds. However, a very few apparently "real" Black Ducks *have* been reported from hunters' check-in stations along the coast (US-FWS, pers. comm.). We consider it possible that the American Black Duck is a very rare, but perhaps annual, visitor to the lakes and marshes of the UTC.

MALLARD
Anas platyrhynchos

Common winter terminal migrant

WINTER: (8, 20 Aug) **mid-Sep to late Apr** (10, 18, 24 May)

HABITAT: Inland lakes, ponds, reservoirs, flooded fields, rarely in coastal waters.

DISCUSSION: The Mallard is the most recognized of North American waterfowl, with a range extending to include all 48 contiguous states, Canada, and Alaska. The species has also been widely domesticated, and the true status of out-of-season individuals (wild, domesticated, or merely lingering cripples) is difficult to determine. Therefore we are skeptical of reports of Mallards oversummering (e.g., mid- to late Jul), since this duck is fairly common in the farm yards and duck ponds of area farmers, ranchers, game clubs, and zoos. Summering Mallards pose a threat to the genetic continuity of the local Mottled Duck population, and releases for put-and-take hunting should be discouraged.

The Mallard is decidedly an inland species in our region, and although usually absent from coastal sites such as Galveston and Bolivar Peninsula, small numbers may appear coastally during late fall fronts (J. Stevenson). Even inland, numbers of wintering Mallards pale in comparison to those of dabblers such as the Green-winged Teal, Northern Pintail, Gadwall, and Northern Shoveler. The USFWS midwinter surveys in 1995 reported only 6,055 Mallards wintering in our region, compared to nearly 130,000 in the Texas Panhandle. The highest total for the Freeport CBC is 950 in 1978, but recent counts have averaged well under 100.

MOTTLED DUCK
Anas fulvigula

Common but decreasing resident

HABITAT: Fresh, brackish, and saltwater marshes; lakes and flooded fields; inland at least to the limits of rice cultivation.

DISCUSSION: The Mottled Duck is one of about six species of ducks known to have nested recently on the UTC (the others being Fulvous Whistling-Duck, Black-bellied Whistling-Duck, Wood Duck, Blue-winged Teal, and Masked Duck). Salt marsh breeders usually construct their nests in cordgrass, while inland breeders utilize prairie or fallow rice fields, generally near ditches or ponds (Bellrose 1976; authors' observations). Pairs, which rather resemble two female Mallards, form early, and by late Feb or Mar females are laying eggs. Some of these early nests are destroyed during spring plowing, but the birds renest readily. Additionally, predation by raccoons, disturbance by cattle and dogs, and flooding of nest sites contribute to the species' unusually low rate of nesting success (Bellrose 1976). Although usually seen in pairs or small family groups, Mottled Ducks muster in late summer. Large flocks (rarely as many as several hundred) may collect in coastal marshes and lakes during this postbreeding season. For example, 400 were noted on 28 Aug 1982 in various UTC locations, and a flock of 100 was present in WAR on 27 Sep 2004. USFWS midwinter surveys in 1995 reported 39,067 Mottled Ducks wintering along the upper coast (Sabine Pass to Lavaca Bay), but their numbers have been in a general decline ever since 1955 when these surveys began. Only once in the last five years have these same Jan surveys counted more than 20,000 Mottled Ducks along the entire Texas coast.

BLUE-WINGED TEAL
Anas discors

Abundant bi-seasonal transient migrant,
uncommon winter terminal migrant,
rare to uncommon summer terminal
migrant

HABITAT: Marshes, irrigation and waterfowl impoundments, flooded ditches.

DISCUSSION: Probably no day passes in our region lacking the presence of Blue-winged Teal. Fall migrants arrive in late Aug, and their numbers swell through late Oct. The first powerful frontal systems in Oct and Nov carry the bulk of the population southward, and winter numbers along the UTC are a shadow of what passes in migration. For example, the USFWS midwinter surveys accounted for only 12,180 in Jan 1995 (compared to the 20,000 that used Attwater NWR alone during late Sep to late Oct 1977). Blue-winged Teal return from their southern haunts in early Mar and remain abundant along our coast until late May or Jun. In wet years hundreds may remain to nest in our region, with Anahuac NWR, West Galveston Is., Brazoria NWR, and San Bernard NWR usually supporting a few breeding pairs even in the driest of years.

CINNAMON TEAL
Anas cyanoptera

Uncommon winter terminal migrant

WINTER: (11, 14 Sep) **late Sep to late Apr** (16, 26, 29 Apr)

HABITAT: Ponds, marshes, and impoundments.

DISCUSSION: With its revealing brick-red plumage signaling its identity, the drake Cinnamon Teal declares rather than whispers its presence. Yet rarely do we see this bird, for among the dabbling ducks this is one of the rarest on the UTC. Virtually absent from the coastal marshes and tidal waters, Cinnamon Teal is typically found with other dabblers congregating in the ponds, puddles, and flooded fields of our inland counties. Warren Lake, Attwater NWR, and Brazos Bend SP are among its preferred haunts. Rarely are flocks seen, and a gathering of more than 10 would be exceptional (although 30 were noted at San Bernard NWR 27 Jan 1990 and 140 were seen 21 Jan 1999 at Attwater NWR). Through much of the year the drake is distinctive and not readily confused with any other duck. However, the females (and post-breeding males) mirror the female Blue-winged Teal with which they frequently associate. Thus wintering numbers of Cinnamon Teal could easily be double those reported. The only summer record is an adult female banded at Anahuac NWR, CHA on 5 Aug 1999.

NORTHERN SHOVELER
Anas clypeata

Common to abundant winter terminal migrant, uncommon summer resident

HABITAT: Inland lakes, reservoirs, flooded fields, ponds, puddles, bayous, and tidal sloughs, occasionally on Gulf and bay waters.

DISCUSSION: Locally, Northern Shoveler, like Blue-winged Teal, is present year-round. It was formerly a common breeder. Audubon noted young on Galveston Is. in late Jun and early Jul 1837, and Strecker (1912) considered it a "common resident, breeding throughout the state" as recently as the early 1900s. Oberholser (1974) reported it nesting in BRA on 30 Jun 1927, the last reported nesting from our region. Northern Shoveler remains a common winter bird; along the coast the USFWS midwinter surveys now report nearly 60,000 annually. This represents a marked increase over the 20,000 birds seen in the same areas 50 years ago.

Northern Shovelers arrive with the early dabblers in late Aug, concentrating in lakes, ponds, flooded fields, and irrigation reservoirs in our inland counties. The species remains relatively common through May, and numbers of nonbreeders may summer (particularly in wet years). Why the Northern Shoveler no longer nests here is a mystery, although we suspect that habitat alteration, particularly in the early half of the twentieth century, led to its extirpation as a breeder.

NORTHERN PINTAIL
Anas acuta

Common winter terminal migrant

WINTER: (11 Aug; 3 Sep) **early Sep to early May** (11 × 2, 12, 15 May)

HABITAT: Fresh and brackish marshes, waterfowl and irrigation impoundments, occasionally on bays and over the Gulf.

DISCUSSION: The Northern Pintail, with a characteristic "sprig" tail adorning the drake, is one of the prized game birds of the UTC. Duck hunters travel to our region from throughout the United States for the opportunity to bag this trophy. Pintail arrive with other dabblers in early fall, riding the first cool waves of the season. Although common on inland lakes and reservoirs, most pintail winter in flooded rice fields and coastal marshes. Tens of thousands may be seen during some winters packed into damp rice and corn stubble fields. Most pintail have departed the UTC by mid-Apr. Those that linger retreat to the area's ponds and lakes as their preferred agricultural fields are drained and plowed. Wounded birds (often flightless) may linger into the summer but rarely survive until the fall. USFWS midwinter surveys indicate that the Northern Pintail is the second most common duck on the UTC, with around 400,000 wintering annually in our region. Central Flyway numbers have seen a slow decline over the years despite periods such as the 1970's, when wintering populations were twice what they are today.

GARGANEY
Anas querquedula

Accidental

17 Apr 1998 Gilchrist, Bolivar Peninsula, GAL (TBRC 1998–93) (AFN 52:355)

HABITAT: A widespread Old World species found from Great Britain to Japan and south to Australia and Africa, Garganey breeds and winters mainly in freshwater habitats, less often in brackish or marine waters (A.O.U. 1983).

DISCUSSION: On 17 Apr 1998, Will Russell observed a male Garganey among a flock of about 25 Blue-winged Teal flying eastward on the Gulf Intracoastal Waterway. The bird was in sight long enough for various wing and facial characteristics to be noted. The two previous records recognized by the TBRC (Kleberg and Presidio cos.) occurred 11 Apr–17 May and 29 Apr–6 May, thus this sighting helps establish a pattern of Apr vagrancy in Texas.

GREEN-WINGED TEAL
Anas crecca carolinensis

Common winter terminal migrant

WINTER: (19, 21 Aug) **late Aug to late May** (29 May), **irregular (nonbreeders) in summer** (30 May–17 July 1999, 24 Jun 1967, 15 Jul 1959)

HABITAT: Waterfowl impoundments, marshes, flooded rice fields, irrigation ponds, bay waters, tidal sloughs; migrants often seen on sand flats (Bolivar Flats) and in nearshore waters.

DISCUSSION: The scarcity of deep, clear-water bays along the UTC limits the numbers of loons, grebes, and diving ducks that winter in our region. A few deeper channels aside, one could walk across most of our bays. However, what the UTC lacks in divers it more than makes up in dabblers, and the most common of the puddle ducks is the Green-winged Teal. During the winter, almost no brackish marsh, tidal slough, or inland rice field is without its compliment of teal, and an evening spent watching the clouds of teal returning to a roost can be awe-inspiring. This species has had some very high wintering totals, such as the 2,126,496 seen during the 1995 midwinter surveys. However, typical numbers are closer to the 300,000 averaged during five recent years. The only duck occurring in similar numbers (according to these surveys) is the Northern Pintail. In 1992 the Cypress Creek CBC tallied 21,188 Green-winged Teal, the North American high count.

Green-winged Teal begin arriving in the late summer, with a scattering of birds on area lakes and ponds through Sep. As the first frontal systems force their way to the UTC, numbers swell, and by mid-Oct virtually no wet spot on the coast is without this species.

We are aware of three UTC sightings of the Old World subspecies *Anas c. crecca* (part of the Common Teal of some authors). Interestingly, two of them were from the same year. Observers participating in the Freeport CBC (BRA) reported a "Common" Teal 26 Dec 1965. One was reported at La Porte (HAS) 5 Feb 1967 and another at Cove (CHA) 2 Mar 1967. We mention this merely to alert observers to the possibility of an occurrence. Drakes of this vagrant form are easily identified, as they exhibit a horizontal white bar through the scapulars instead of a vertical white line at the side of the breast.

CANVASBACK
Aythya valisineria

Uncommon winter terminal migrant

WINTER: (14, 18, 22 Oct) **mid-Oct to late Apr** (26, 29 May; 21 May–2 Jun)

HABITAT: Nearshore ocean waters, large bays and associated estuaries, occasionally lakes and freshwater impoundments.

DISCUSSION: Wintering Canvasbacks congregate where they have access to a large supply of aquatic vegetation, often including American wildcelery (*Vallisneria*), after which they are named. Locally, they are generally uncommon and irregularly distributed. For example, during 2002, eight local CBCs recorded the following numbers: 271 (Sea Rim), 75 (Brazos Bend), 40 (Cypress Creek), 27 (Bolivar), 25 (San Bernard), 18 (Armand Bayou), 8 (Freeport) and 2 (Lake Houston), a far cry from the 5,000 reported at Pleasure Island (JEF) on 20 Jan 1990.

Canvasbacks have always been a favored target of hunters. This selective shooting pressure, combined with droughts, loss of nesting habitat, and lead poisoning, led to a serious drop in their populations. Finally, in 1985 the USFWS stopped the Canvasback hunt. After a decade of aggressive habitat acquisition and management, and some very wet weather, Canvasback (and nearly all other duck) populations are rebounding, and in the fall of 1994 hunting was reinstated along the Atlantic, Mississippi, and Central flyways. The USFWS midwinter survey numbers vary greatly from year to year. An encouraging 25,257 were reported on the upper coast in 1999, but no birds at all were found on this survey during 2000 and 2002 on the entire Texas coast! This seems to indicate variable wintering locations rather than a population decline. We note several summer records (for example 16 May–24 Jul 1959, 24 May–26 Jun 1999, 30 Jul 1960, and 27–28 Aug 1975), which we presume were cripples or birds too weak to migrate.

REDHEAD
Aythya americana

Uncommon winter terminal migrant

WINTER: (13 Oct) **mid-Oct to mid-Apr** (13, 14 × 2, 16, 21 May)

HABITAT: Nearshore waters and bays, occasionally lakes, ponds, and impoundments.

DISCUSSION: Many of the world's Redheads winter in the sea grass beds of the Laguna Madre in S Texas. This duck is always uncommon on the upper coast. In fact, during some years, wintering Redheads are virtually nonexistent in our region. The pooled observations from all local CBCs in these "drought" years may total less than a dozen individuals. For example, in 1995 the USFWS surveys reported 563,761 Redheads wintering along the Texas coast, with only 4,487 of those found between Sabine Pass and Lavaca Bay. In general, the number of Redheads wintering on the Texas coast has slowly declined to about 300,000 birds over the past 50 years. Redheads, like most divers, first arrive after the Sep flush of puddle ducks. Riding the fall frontal systems sweeping south through the Great Plains, Redheads normally do not appear in our region until the heat of summer has finally been banished in Oct. Small flocks (fewer than 100 birds) are still occasionally seen in W Galveston and Christmas bays, where sea grasses (their favored food) maintain a precarious existence. We are aware of several summer records (19 Jun 1998, 28 Jun 1959, 9 Jul 1978, and 24 Aug–1 Sep 1999).

RING-NECKED DUCK
Aythya collaris

Uncommon to locally common winter terminal migrant

WINTER: (1 Sep) **late Oct to mid-Apr** (22, 28 May)

HABITAT: Ponds or impoundments, often with wooded margins.

DISCUSSION: On interior waters, Ring-necked Duck is our most common diver. Unusual in bay and Gulf waters along the coast, at times it is relatively common on inland lakes and ponds such as at Cullinan Park in Sugarland, Elm Lake at Brazos Bend SP, Warren Lake (HAS), and Shoveler Pond at Anahuac NWR. At Hermann Park, Houstonians can usually find a small flock wintering with a few other diving ducks on the lake adjacent to the zoo entrance. The bulk of the state's Ring-necked Ducks winters along the upper coast. In Dec 2002, USFWS surveys counted 7,018 on the Texas coast, with all of these birds recorded in the marshes of the UTC. Ring-necked Ducks begin arriving with the dabbler flocks in Sep, although most do not appear until the arctic fronts in Oct sweep the Plains clean of waterfowl. Birds present 22 Jun 1998 (BRA) and 21 July–4 August (FOB) were likely sick or injured.

GREATER SCAUP
Aythya marila

Uncommon to rare winter terminal migrant

WINTER: (2–3, 5, 6 Nov) **mid-Nov to mid-Mar** (22 × 2, 29–30 Apr; 1 May)

HABITAT: Larger bays and nearshore waters, rarely on fresh water inland.

DISCUSSION: Although not as severe, the identification problems associated with Greater Scaup are reminiscent of those for American Black Duck. Almost identical to the Lesser Scaup (as the Black Duck resembles the Mottled), Greater Scaup is often lost among the immense rafts of its more abundant cousin. Despite many journal and newsletter articles addressing problems of scaup identification, birders rarely make the effort to assign to species each individual scaup seen, except when participating in events such as the annual CBCs. We recommend that flocks of scaup be reported as scaup sp., without a specific designation, unless each bird has been separately identified (a course we also recommend for meadowlarks and dark ibis). In the late 1970s immense numbers of scaup—at times more than 50,000—wintered on the cooling ponds of the HL&P Cedar Bayou power plant near Baytown. By carefully inspecting each flock, birders were able to find significant numbers of wintering Greaters there (approximately 100), perhaps attracted to the mollusks that proliferated in the clear, warm water released by the power plant. Although Greater Scaup occasionally show up at inland sites (for example, at the Hermann Park lakes in Houston), they are best sought on salt water. Occasionally very small flocks of Greater Scaup are present on coastal ponds or close to the beach. More often, they occur among rafts of other divers. Even in preferred habitat, observers may have to go through three or four hundred Lessers to find one Greater Scaup.

LESSER SCAUP
· *Aythya affinis*

Common winter terminal migrant, rare but regular in summer

WINTER: **Late Oct–early May**

HABITAT: Nearshore waters and bays, also lakes and freshwater impoundments.

DISCUSSION: The Lesser Scaup is ever present in our region; at least a few choose to summer in our waters each year. Precise arrival and departure dates are impossible to determine, although the mass of migrants arrives in late Oct and remains through late Apr into early May. During the past 25 years we have witnessed a significant decline in Lesser Scaup along

the UTC. Through the late 1970s, few ducks (and no bay ducks) were as common in our region as Lesser Scaup. Arlie McKay, for example, reported 500,000 at Cove in northwestern CHA on 28 Nov 1962, and Eubanks and David Dauphin counted 50,000 at the HL&P Cedar Bayou cooling ponds near Baytown 5 Feb 1977. In those years rafts of scaup would often blanket W Galveston Bay, extending from near shore into the bay for as far as the eye could see. Earlier, Roemer (1849) commented that in 1846 upper Galveston Bay at Morgan's Point was "completely blackened by myriads of wild ducks." Recent changes in Galveston Bay, including increased turbidity and the loss of sea grass beds, may have displaced these scaup. We note that the USFWS surveys in 1995 accounted for only 33,251 scaup on the upper coast and even fewer, 15,518, on the lower coast. However, in 2002 and 2003 respectively, 104,231 and 228,524 were counted along the Texas coast, suggesting that these birds are either recovering or simply moving around to differing wintering localities.

Small numbers of Lessers are present on the larger waterfowl impoundments and refuge lakes such as those at Anahuac NWR or Brazos Bend SP. A few occur each winter on the lake at Houston's Hermann Park, often allowing close side-by-side comparison with Redheads and Ring-necked Ducks and rarely with Greater Scaup. Huge aggregations are more likely to be encountered through the spotting scope, either in our larger bays or in the Gulf. Lines of scaup are frequently seen skimming over our nearshore waters (especially during rainy weather), and large rafts of these bay ducks are often found along the coast just beyond the surf line. Sea watchers occasionally note large numbers of migrants from wintering grounds to the south; at least 12,000 passed our shores on 26 Mar 1989, although such numbers would be unusual today.

KING EIDER
Somateria spectabilis

Accidental

30 Apr–9 May 1998 Quintana, BRA (TBRC 1998-59) (AFN 52:355 states 9 May, the date indicated by the rehabber. We have changed our record to reflect this and not used the TBRC date of 7 May)

HABITAT: Breeds on tundra adjacent to arctic coastlines; winters in the North Pacific and on the Atlantic seaboard of Canada, sparsely farther south, rarely on the Great Lakes.

DISCUSSION: Birders competing in the second annual Great Texas Birding Classic located the state's first record of this arctic breeder. The bird, a worn subadult male in heavy molt, remained on the beach becoming weaker and weaker until 9 May when it was picked up by a local wildlife rehabilitator. Subsequently it was shipped to Sea World of Ohio, where it fully recovered. About a year later awaiting transfer to the West Coast, it met an untimely death when a mink raided the Sea World complex, killing nearly the entire eider collection of about 50 birds. This individual is illustrated in Lockwood and Freeman (2004, photo 8).

SURF SCOTER
Melanitta perspicillata

Rare and irregular winter terminal migrant

WINTER: (19, 22 Oct) **early Nov to late Apr** (29 May)

HABITAT: Nearshore Gulf waters, rare in upper Galveston Bay (Baytown).

DISCUSSION: The three species of scoters generally avoid Texas, remaining glued to the two seaboards. For example, the USFWS midwinter surveyors reported no scoters in Texas during 1995. When present locally, they are most often seen in nearshore waters along the JEF coastline and Bolivar Peninsula. In some years, rafts may be found south into BRA, and scoters have been seen from the Quintana Jetty on 19 of the 48 Freeport CBCs. In the late 1970s and early 1980s scoters were often found on the HL&P cooling ponds at Cedar Bayou, but not recently. The only recent inland scoter record is one seen 15 Nov 1998 at Danbury, BRA.

Perhaps Surf Scoter is slightly more common than other scoters (or is seen more frequently) in our coastal waters, although the comparison is undermined by the rarity of all scoters in our region. During most winters they are found in rafts of diving ducks along Bolivar Peninsula, in JEF, on W Galveston Is., and into BRA. Surf Scoters have been seen from the Quintana/Surfside jetties on numerous occasions, at times feeding only a few feet from the rocks.

Arlie McKay reported a bird that was shot near Cove, CHA, 11 Nov 1950.

WHITE-WINGED SCOTER
Melanitta fusca

Uncommon to rare and irregular winter terminal migrant

WINTER: (22 Sep; 1, 11, 19 Nov) **early Nov to late Apr** (29 Apr; 8 May; 17 Jun)

HABITAT: Nearshore Gulf waters, rare in upper Galveston Bay (Baytown).

DISCUSSION: The dramatic white wing patches of this species allow for rather distant identification, a welcome aid when trying to call scoters to species as they fly well offshore. A warning, however—Gadwall are often seen offshore in winter as well. White-winged Scoters are often found among flocks of divers (particularly Lesser Scaup and the other two scoters), and a winter's drive along Bolivar Peninsula and JEF will often yield a few individuals of this species. We consider the 22 Sep record anomalous because scoters typically arrive in early Nov (usually as late as Thanksgiving). We are aware of one summer record; on 17 Jun 1977, a bird was in the surf near High Island.

BLACK SCOTER
Melanitta nigra

Rare and irregular winter terminal migrant

WINTER: (6, 9, 11 Nov) **early Nov to late Apr** (21–22 Apr)

HABITAT: Nearshore and (rarely) upper bay waters (Baytown).

DISCUSSION: The Black Scoter, like most of the deepwater divers, arrives after the inland waters to our north have begun to freeze. The Black is less commonly reported here than are other scoters, although this may be a reflection of difficulties in identification and a general disinterest in sea ducks. Furthermore, a dispersed breeding distribution (northern Quebec and Alaska) and their absence from hunters' bags throughout the United States contribute to this species being among the most poorly known ducks in the country. There are years when small mixed flocks of scoters may be seen in nearshore waters between Sabine Pass and Rollover Pass, and from West Galveston Is. to Freeport. Rarely are these flocks found close to shore, and the undulation of Gulf waters submerges the identity of most of these sea ducks. Black Scoters are often best seen when these flocks take flight, however (such as off the end of the Quintana Jetty).

LONG-TAILED DUCK
Clangula hyemalis

Rare winter terminal migrant

WINTER: (12 Nov) **late Nov to mid-Mar** (14 May)
HABITAT: Seacoasts and bays, occasionally on freshwater impoundments adjacent to the coast; very rarely inland.

DISCUSSION: Because most Long-tailed Ducks winter on the Great Lakes and the northern Atlantic seaboard, local sightings are of considerable interest. As would be expected, most of our records are coastal, usually an occasional bird associating with flocks of scaup. However, an inland wanderer was seen during the Cypress Creek CBC 1 Jan 1979. Those that stray here are usually first-winter birds. Eubanks can recall seeing only one adult male (with its characteristic tail streamer) during the past 25 years. Recently there has been an average of two sightings per winter.

Until recently, this species was called Oldsquaw. In 2000 the A.O.U. changed its name to Long-tailed Duck in order to reflect the name long used in Great Britain.

BUFFLEHEAD
Bucephala albeola

Uncommon to common winter terminal migrant

WINTER: (27, 31 Oct; 2, 5 Nov) **early Nov to late Apr** (24, 27, 29 Apr)
HABITAT: Lakes, ponds, waterfowl impoundments, saltwater marshes, less frequently on bay waters.

DISCUSSION: Bufflehead occur in habitats attractive to other ducks, both puddle ducks and divers, although generally in smaller numbers. Unlike many of the divers (particularly the bay ducks), Bufflehead often winter on inland lakes, ponds, and reservoirs. Rarely are they found in large concentrations. The highest Freeport CBC total was 304 in 1981, but the average count is only 25 per year. The USFWS waterfowl surveys in 1995 reported 2,371 Bufflehead from the upper coast and 8,170 on the lower coast.

COMMON GOLDENEYE
Bucephala clangula

Uncommon to rare winter terminal migrant

WINTER: (31 Oct; 4 Nov) **early Nov to late Apr** (20 Apr; 12 May)
HABITAT: Bay and ocean waters, occasional in freshwater impoundments.

DISCUSSION: Goldeneyes arrive with flights of other divers and are rarely seen in good numbers before Thanksgiving. Common Goldeneye are most likely to be seen either just offshore among rafts of scaup and scoters or in the open waters of larger bays. Locally, structures that provide a sheltered channel, such as the Texas City Dike, often attract the few birds present. Offats Bayou with its deep, clear waters often attracts numbers of goldeneyes as well. Although nearly all sightings are from salt water, occasionally the species is found on lakes, water treatment and aquaculture ponds, and waterfowl impoundments. The 1995 USFWS midwinter surveys reported 2,638 Common Goldeneye in Texas, 1,876 of which were found along the upper coast. However, the Freeport count has averaged only eight per year with a high of 67 in 1977.

BARROW'S GOLDENEYE
Bucephala islandica

Very rare or accidental winter terminal migrant
3–31 Dec 1991 La Porte, HAS (TBRC 1991-140; TPRF 1006) (AB 46:287, 882)
Returned 17 Dec 1992–19 Jan 1993 (TBRC 1992-169) (AB 47:274–75, 854)

HABITAT: Locally on freshwater impoundments and adjacent bayous.

DISCUSSION: One of the most startling avian surprises of the 1990s was the 3 Dec 1991 appearance of a drake Barrow's Goldeneye on a settling pond at the Occidental Petroleum Company's OxyChem manufacturing plant in La Porte (HAS). The bird constituted the UTC's first (and Texas' second) record of a species with an Atlantic wintering range only infrequently extending south of New York. Plant personnel responded to the attention and sudden influx of birders by constructing a viewing platform and providing cold drinks, coffee, and souvenir pens for hundreds of appreciative observers. One year later the bird returned for a command performance, remaining from mid-Dec to mid-Jan. Periodically it flew from the property to mingle or roost with numbers of other ducks near the San Jacinto Battleground State Park.

Our practice in this book is not to include records of extreme UTC rarities unless the details were examined by the TBRC. Recently we became aware of an earlier Barrow's Goldeneye record that was never submitted. We present it on the authority of the observers and because it helps establish a date trend. In late 1958, Arlie McKay located a Barrow's Goldeneye near the Baytown Tunnel (CHA/HAS). On 7 Dec 1958, he showed the bird to D. A. Deavers, and to Ben Feltner, who recorded the event in his journal (*fide* Ben Feltner). Coincidentally, the state's first documented Barrow's Goldeneye was also in 1958, one of three birds shot in Hunt Co. on 6 Nov 1958 (Lockwood and Freeman 2004).

HOODED MERGANSER
Lophodytes cucullatus

Uncommon winter terminal migrant

WINTER: (27 Oct; 1 Nov) **early Nov to late Apr** (28 Apr; 16 May)

HABITAT: Ponds or lakes, often but not necessarily with wooded margins; also waterfowl impoundments, occasionally flooded fields or marshes, tidal sloughs, and embayments.

DISCUSSION: Hooded Mergansers are local and rather uncommon UTC winter residents. In recent years, perhaps the most predictable place to observe them has been the ponds around the San Jacinto Battleground State Park, where, for example, 51 were present on 13 Nov 1991. Moderate flocks (10–30) of wintering Hooded Mergansers have also been regular at Barker Reservoir in west Houston (HAS) since 2001 (*fide* Sumita Prasad). Occasionally these ducks feed in the sloughs indenting the bay shores of Galveston Island SP. In previous years Hooded Mergansers wintered in large numbers on Elm Lake at Hale Ranch (now Brazos Bend SP). Unfortunately, the development of the park for recreational purposes appears to have displaced these birds. On 4–5 Mar 1977, a female Hooded Merganser was observed entering a woodpecker cavity along the shores of Elm Lake (AB 31:1159). An inspection of this cavity revealed two merganser eggs that had apparently been

abandoned by the female. Both eggs were infertile, so we hesitate to qualify the Hooded Merganser as a breeder in the UTC. However, merganser eggs were found in Wood Duck boxes in 1999 and 2001 (the latter confirmed as hatching) at Trinity River NWR in nearby Liberty County (*fide* Stuart Marcus).

COMMON MERGANSER
Mergus merganser

Very rare winter terminal migrant

WINTER: (17 Nov) **late Nov to early Mar** (20 Apr)

HABITAT: Large freshwater impoundments, river mouths, bays.

DISCUSSION: Common Mergansers are little more than vagrants on the UTC. Up to several thousand Central Flyway birds winter in Texas, confined mostly to reservoirs in the northern 60 percent of the state (Bellrose 1976). Our database contains only 10 sightings, including specimens from CHA and GAL (Oberholser 1974). We have inland records from the Hermann Park Pond in Houston (which attracts many wintering ducks) and NW HAS. Because of their extreme rarity along the Gulf, we suspect that these records represent a combination of the odd migratory overshoot and frequent misidentifications.

RED-BREASTED MERGANSER
Mergus serrator

Common winter terminal migrant

WINTER: (22, 24 Sep) **early Oct to late May** (10 Jun); occasionally lingers into summer

HABITAT: Locally on bays, river mouths, and nearshore waters, generally shunning fresh water and rare inland (Hermann Park).

DISCUSSION: Flocking Red-breasted Mergansers, our only common "sawbill," confuse CBC participants by appearing then disappearing below the waves in seemingly random combinations and leaving few clues as to how many are actually present. This problem can be particularly vexing at locations such as W Galveston Bay, where rafts of several hundred have occurred. USFWS surveys reported 3,813 "mergansers" (most likely all Red-breasteds) wintering along the upper coast in 1995. The highest Freeport CBC count is 2,054 in 1981, but the average count finds only 117. The largest recent gathering, probably a feeding aggregation, consisted of upward of 1,900 birds found along the Bolivar Peninsula on 7 Jan 2003 (E. Carpenter).

Migrating in flocks of 5 to 15, UTC birds arrive via the Central Flyway, leaving central Canada and crossing the Great Plains (Bellrose 1976). However, the division separating the Central and Mississippi flyways (the latter of which historically hosted more than 10 times as many of these birds as the former) is considered to be Sabine Lake on the JEF-Louisiana border, so population overlap on the wintering grounds is almost certain and would occur here on the UTC. Periodically an individual remains into the summer (19 May–19 Jun 1999, 24 Jun 1978, 18 Jul 1979, 6 Jul 1992). During Apr movements dozens (occasionally more than 100) may be noted along the coast.

MASKED DUCK
Nomonyx dominicus

Rare and irregular visitor, occasional temporary resident

2 Jan 1927 Eagle Nest Lake, BRA (*USNM 300115) (Oberholser 1974)

1 Sep–19 Nov 1967 (4+) Anahuac NWR, CHA (TBRC 1990-52) (AFN 22:65 and cover)

Oct–Dec 1967 near Anahuac NWR, CHA (*TCWC 11150)

16 Oct–16 Nov 1968 Brazoria NWR, BRA (TBRC 1999-51; TPRF 1726) (AFN 22:625)

29 Dec 1977–15 Jan 1978 Anahuac NWR, CHA (TBRC 1990-53)

26 Apr 1989 Brazoria NWR, BRA (TBRC 1989-172) (AB 43:504)

23 Nov 1989 (2) Anahuac NWR, CHA (TBRC 1994-27)

20 Dec 1992–Mar 1993 (1–4) Brazos Bend SP, FOB (TBRC 1993-1; TPRF 1139) (AB 47:275, 843)

2 Feb–26 May 1993 (4–10) McFaddin NWR, JEF (TBRC 1993-88) (AB 47:430)

11 Dec 1993–28 Apr 1994 (2–8) Brazos Bend SP, FOB (TBRC 1994-2; TPRF 1218) (AFN 48:225, 317, 725)

3 Apr 1994 (2) Brazoria NWR, BRA (TBRC 1994-78; TPRF 1323) (AFN 48:317)

19 Nov 1994–15 May 1995 (2–6) Brazos Bend SP, FOB (TBRC 1995-28; TPRF 1324) (AFN 49:69, 166, 275, 696)

18 Dec 1994 Brazoria NWR, BRA (TBRC 1995-15; TPRF 1319) (AFN 49:166, 703)

25 Feb 1995 Anahuac NWR, CHA (TBRC 1995-63; TPRF 1357)

12 Nov 1995–Apr 1996 (2–12) Brazos Bend SP., FOB (TBRC 1996-34) (AFN 50:190, 301)

22 Dec 1996–2 Mar 1997 (1–4) Brazos Bend SP, FOB (TBRC 1997-28; TPRF 1502) (AFN 51:769, 893)

24 April 1997 Galveston Island, Galveston (TBRC 1999-120)

23 Feb–4 Apr 1998 Cullinan Park, FOB (TBRC 1998-30; TPRF 1594) (AFN 52:223, 355)

Additional records from Colorado Co.

11–25 Dec 1993 (1–5) Attwater NWR, COL (TBRC 1994-32; TPRF 1224) (AFN 48:225, 718)

29 Jul–4 Dec 1994 (2–24) Attwater NWR, COL (TBRC 1994-143; TPRF 1302) (AFN 48:961; 49:69, 166)

HABITAT: Coastal and inland lakes, usually with abundant floating vegetation.

DISCUSSION: This tropical species is erratically distributed in the Caribbean and from N Mexico to N Argentina, occasionally nesting in the southeastern United States. As with Least Grebe, the Masked Duck's local presence may reflect the availability of freshwater habitats to the south. Often, this species may be absent from the UTC (and the entire United States) for some years then suddenly stages minor to major invasions. The most spectacular recent influx of these birds occurred during the winter of 1992–93, when more than 140 individuals were documented in Texas. Locally, Masked Ducks appeared at Attwater NWR, Brazos Bend SP, and during the following winter—for the first time—in the Freeport CBC circle. Other UTC sites have included Anahuac NWR, where they have nested, and McFaddin NWR, where they may have nested—they were detected during late May 1993 and Sep 1994 (J. Neaville data). The most recent breeding report is a brood seen at close range by a USFWS biologist at Brazoria NWR on 19 Jun 2001.

Male Masked Ducks in breeding plumage, with a bright blue bill, black and cinnamon plumage, and a discreet black face, present no identification problems. Most sightings, however, are of less distinct individuals. While searching for Masked Ducks, beware of loner Ruddy Ducks, which often utilize similar habitats. On the side of the face, Ruddy Ducks do not have a bold light stripe that is defined by a dark stripe through the eye and another behind the lower base of the bill, as do female and young or nonbreeding male Masked Ducks. Additionally, Ruddies do not have a white patch in their secondaries. If the observer is not sure, the bird is probably a Ruddy. Photographs of Masked Ducks in several plumages, identification and taxonomic notes, and further discussions of the species' habitat requirements, breeding biology, range, and population status may be found in Lockwood (1997).

RUDDY DUCK
Oxyura jamaicensis

Common winter terminal migrant, rare summer terminal migrant

HABITAT: Bay and brackish water, waterfowl and irrigation impoundments, small ponds.

DISCUSSION: Nehrling (1882) remarked that Ruddies were common breeders in the Houston area in the 1880s. By the early 1900s, however, Strecker (1912) commented: "Cooke says that it breeds over much of the Mississippi Valley, from Texas to Minnesota, but I have no record of it breeding in this State." Oberholser (1974) reports breeding from our region—one brood at Anahuac NWR Aug–Sep 1968, and eggs and young in summer 1959 at Jacinto City. Modern observers have rarely commented on nesting, and we suspect that although the Ruddy Duck summers here regularly, most of the breeding season birds are youngsters that have forgone migration.

Ruddy Ducks feed both by diving and by picking near the surface. They take a variety of marine and freshwater plants, eating leaves, stems, seeds, and tubers. They also eat an appreciable amount of animal matter, including clams, snails, fly larvae, and small crustaceans. Because of their generalized food preferences, UTC Ruddies are likely to be seen on a variety of fresh and saline habitats.

Nearly all Central Flyway Ruddies winter in coastal S Texas and on the large lakes of the Mexican plateau. Most Mississippi Flyway birds that winter in Louisiana utilize lakes near the Mississippi River, not straying far west. Thus the UTC lies in a gap between two important wintering areas. The Freeport CBC has a high of 915 in 1964 with an average of 268. Predictable sites include the ponds at the base of the Texas City Dike, Shoveler Pond at Anahuac NWR, and Pilant Lake at Brazos Bend SP, but hundreds to thousands may appear on any impoundment, most often those with emergent vegetation.

Upland Game Birds

The designation *upland game birds* is the hunters' generic term for nonwaterfowl. The taxonomic understanding of this group of "chickenlike" birds has shifted from time to time; older field guides have placed all of them in their own families. As currently recognized by the A.O.U., Ring-necked Pheasant, Greater Prairie-Chicken, and Wild Turkey are members of the family Phasianidae, and Northern Bobwhite belongs to the New World quails, family Odontophoridae. Both families are large, and the former is especially well represented in the Old World, where it contains such familiar birds as peacocks (Indian Peafowl) and Red Junglefowl, precursor to the domestic chicken. Nonetheless, few species occur locally, and were it not for the strident call of the Northern Bobwhite, all might be missed during casual birding.

With its iridescent plumage, long tail, and bright red wattles, the male Ring-necked Pheasant is a dramatic bird. In much of the country it has attained decorative cliché status, adorning calendars, note cards, and placemats, often surrounded by snow. Among hunters, who are responsible for its presence, it symbolizes brisk fall days in the company of well-trained dogs. Various pheasants are numerous in Asia. This one occupies a variety of habitats from central Russia to Japan. Introduced to the UTC as a game bird, it has not fared well on the hot and humid Gulf Coast and, without an intensive reintroduction program, will soon be locally extirpated.

Faring only slightly better is the Attwater's race of Greater Prairie-Chicken, once an abundant bird on the prairies of East Texas. Habitat loss and a string of natural disasters have reduced the wild population to a few dozen. Now its fate hinges on a captive breeding program, but as the UTC's prairies disappear a thousand acres at a time, one wonders if there will be sufficient remaining habitat to sustain an introduced population.

Another low-density bird is the Wild Turkey. Elsewhere in Texas this species may be eerily abundant, and 50 or more may be seen with a single glance. Once locally plentiful, the Wild Turkey was eliminated from the UTC by the early 1940s. Fortunately, turkeys lay large clutches of eggs; if not impacted too heavily by torrential spring rains, raccoons, skunks, bobcats, or various birds of prey, they can quickly build up their numbers. Recent introduction programs have shown promise that Wild Turkeys may once again roam the region's woodlands.

Northern Bobwhite is a bird declining locally. Although it remains plentiful in much of its large range, UTC birds have become scarce. At coastal and inland refuges where shrub- and grasslands are maintained, the birds are still reasonably easy to find, especially in spring when males call their loud *bob-WHITE* from fence posts and tall shrubs.

RING-NECKED PHEASANT
Phasianus colchicus

Introduced, now locally rare and no longer self-perpetuating

HABITAT: Hedgerows, fallow or harvested fields.

DISCUSSION: This attractive Asian species has not fared well along the UTC, and local birders do well even to hear a crowing male, much less see one in the flesh. Thriving populations occur in more northerly latitudes, including the Texas Panhandle, where crisp breezes and a dusting of snow are harbingers of the annual hunt. On the hot, muggy UTC, spring rains flood nests, fire ants rush in to turn hatching chicks to skeletons, and molds, fungi, and parasites plague the adults; despite repeated introductions, the bird has not retained a UTC population. The only recent reports are of one north of Needville (FOB) on 5 Oct 2001 and one female on the Brazos Bend CBC (also FOB) on 22 Dec 2001. Ring-necked Pheasant is the unfortunate product of "put-and-take" game stocking programs and therefore occupies a tenuous place in the inventory of the UTC avifauna.

GREATER PRAIRIE-CHICKEN
Tympanuchus cupido attwateri

Very rare and decreasing resident

HABITAT: Tall grass prairies; coastal and inland.

DISCUSSION: More than a million individuals of the Attwater's race of Greater Prairie-Chicken inhabited the Gulf coastal prairies of Texas and Louisiana at the turn of the twentieth century. For thousands of years the Greater Prairie-Chicken provided people with food, sport, and inspiration, first for the Native Americans whose ceremonial dances mimicked its breeding display and later for the hungry masses of European settlers. Unless we are extremely persistent, careful, and lucky, *Tympanuchus cupido attwateri*, the local race of this species, may soon be represented only by cotton-stuffed study skins in museums, like the extinct Moa of New Zealand, Hawaii's Lesser Koa Finch, and the Great Auk.

The impact of relentless hunting pressure by early European settlers was compounded by habitat losses. Conversion of prairie to agricultural lands (particularly rice cultivation), overgrazing by cattle, then encroaching urbanization, and the recent proliferation of the exotic Chinese tallow have all contributed to the almost total elimination of native coastal grasslands; less than 1 percent of the original grasslands remain. This loss of coastal prairie habitat over the years devastated the once abundant prairie-chickens, just as it devastated the Houston nesting race of Henslow's Sparrow. The result is that the Attwater's race of Greater Prairie-Chicken is now one of the most endangered birds in North America, and the bird struggles to retain an artificial toehold on the UTC. Eubanks last saw prairie-chickens on the Katy Prairie 20 Jan 1977, and a small cluster continued to use the Spaceland Airport (later Houston Gulf Airport, which was closed in Apr 2002) near League City as a booming lek until the early 1980s.

In 1976, over 2,000 of these prairie-chickens survived locally. Sadly, these birds are now outnumbered by Whooping Cranes. The wild population dropped to 456 birds in 1993, 158 in 1994, 68 in 1995, to a low of 42 in 1996. As the prairie-chicken continued its precipitous decline, authorities concluded that only by replenishing protected habitats with captive-bred birds could this species survive in the wild. The Attwater's Prairie-Chicken Recovery Team has established a captive population of birds divided among four conservation and research centers: Houston Zoo, San Antonio Zoo, Fossil Rim Wildlife Center, and Texas A & M University. The program is finally showing welcome if tentative success. The first captive-bred birds were released at Attwater NWR in 1995, followed by releases at the same refuge in 1996 and at both Attwater NWR and the Nature Conservancy's Texas City Prairie Preserve on Galveston Bay in 1997. Bolstered by these introductions, the number of prairie-chickens in the wild increased slightly in 1997 to 58 birds. By 2001, spring lek count figures revealed only 10 males at Attwater and 12 males at Texas City, for an estimated population of 44 birds. However, the 2004 census yielded an estimated 62 birds—40 at Attwater and 22 at Texas City—with five successful clutches located at Attwater.

Clearly, if the bird is to survive, aggressive measures must be taken to acquire and protect remaining habitat. But more important, to reach a projected population of 5,000 birds, habitat must be *recreated* where it once existed. One way to accomplish this is to encourage conservation easements providing landowners with a financial incentive to foster both the bird and its habitat on their own holdings.

WILD TURKEY
Meleagris gallopavo

Rare resident of indeterminate origin, introductions continue

HABITAT: Oak and pecan woodlands and adjacent open land.

DISCUSSION: Turkeys prospered in pre-European Texas, inhabiting dense forests and thickets with abundant mast and berries. Throughout much of the eastern United States, colonists hunted these delectable birds to near extinction, and only in recent years have reintroduction programs restored the Wild Turkey into much of its original range. Nehrling (1882) found it "abundant in all the heavily wooded districts, especially the thick woods with much underbrush near Spring Creek." He continued: "Early in May I have seen the mother bird with about a dozen young ones, but they were so extremely wild that they suddenly disappeared among the almost impenetrable thickets of blackberries and *Smilax*." By 1912 Strecker commented that the Wild Turkey, once abundant in East Texas, was "now rare." By the early 1940s, it had been eliminated from our region; the last sighting was 9 Jul 1942 in Seabrook.

Unfortunately, the Wild Turkey reintroduction programs that have been so successful throughout much of the country (and farther northeast in Texas in particular) have been slow to start on the UTC. Suitable habitat remains, although the dense forests and thickets preferred by this species (such as those in the Big Thicket or close to the Sabine River) continue to be cleared. The few relatively recent sightings we are aware of (7 Feb 1978 FOB, 1 Jan 1987 W HAS, 9 Feb 1992 FOB) may be the product of limited introduction efforts. More encouraging is a reintroduction program begun at Armand Bayou Nature Center in 1994. In that year, 20 Wild Turkeys were released on nature center property, 10 on each side of the bayou. These turkeys apparently survived their transfer from their natal grounds, and breeding has recently been documented. TPWD has reintroduced birds with a few now being seen in northwest BRA where there is (perhaps prematurely) an open season on these birds. We hope that these apparently successful reintroductions will spur others to attempt the same on their lands. For unknown reasons, Wild Turkeys have been slow to reoccupy former territories.

NORTHERN BOBWHITE
Colinus virginianus

Common but decreasing resident

HABITAT: Fields with low brush, tall grass prairie, fallow cultivation, open second growth; occasionally ventures into adjacent residential areas.

DISCUSSION: The Northern Bobwhite, a mainstay of American hunters, both two- and four-legged, is a widespread and durable species. It nests throughout much of the year, eats a wide variety of foods, and is found in nearly all our local habitats except those that are marine or aquatic. During the early 1970s, Kincaid (in Oberholser 1974) considered Bobwhite to be the most successful of Texas' four native quails. Whether they are now losing out to feral cats, overhunting, changing temperatures, recent floods, fire ants, or habitat loss, no one seems to know. Yet everyone agrees that now in the new millennium their numbers are down. However, quail are notorious for their cyclical populations and may someday recover. The Freeport CBC, where managed refuge land produces many of the birds, averaged 178 in the 1970s, 87 in the 1980s, and 80 in the 1990s, with a count high of 556 birds in 1978.

The loons and grebes are two families of diving birds that obtain nearly all of their food below the water's surface. Loons have webbed toes and long, pointed bills. They feed on a variety of fishes captured in underwater pursuit as well as on invertebrates such as crustaceans and aquatic insects. Grebes have variously pointed or rather stubby bills, with which they take a larger percentage of invertebrates as well as some plant matter. Instead of being webbed, the toes of grebes have fleshy flaps referred to as lobes. In both families, the legs are displaced rearward to facilitate diving and swimming underwater, rendering the birds ungainly on land or even incapable of walking.

Most loons and grebes have vexingly similar gray winter plumages the color of dull ocean waters. When breeding, they are some of our most beautiful birds with boldly patterned plumage and, in the case of some grebes, brilliant yellow head plumes.

Three species of loons occur on the UTC, all visitors from the north. For most of their visit they are in winter plumage, but before departing, some individuals have attained their striking breeding plumage. Common Loon is the species most likely to be seen, occurring on bays and nearshore waters. The slightly smaller Pacific Loon has been sighted with increasing regularity, generally on the protected waters of Galveston Bay. Red-throated Loon is a local rarity. We should not let the fact that it was removed from the TBRC review list lull us into a false sense of security. Those familiar with the species have little trouble with its identification, but local birders have few opportunities to practice. Loons' bill sizes overlap and are difficult to judge without direct comparison. Carefully noting head shape and orientation and the distribution of dark on the head and neck allows identification of most individuals.

Six grebes occur locally. Unlike the loons, many species breed throughout the Americas, including the Neotropics and the temperate latitudes of the Southern Hemisphere. Red-necked, Horned, and Eared grebes are visitors from the north. Red-necked is a great rarity. Because of its larger size, it may resemble a miniature loon. Horned and Eared grebes are similar, each with slightly different head and neck pigmentation in winter. Rarely are there more than a few sightings of Horned Grebe during any winter; these birds are usually seen in shallow bay waters or impoundments close to Galveston Bay. Eared Grebes formerly wintered on the UTC in large flocks or "rafts," but their presence now is minimal. Perhaps their numbers have actually declined, or perhaps due to conditions in and around Galveston Bay, they choose to winter elsewhere. In comparison to Horned Grebe, note the Eared's decidedly more spherical body.

The long-necked Western Grebe is the most swanlike of the six. It is a rare visitor, widespread in western North America and common in West Texas. Its look-alike cousin the Clark's Grebe has not yet been recorded locally; based on its abundance in the Trans-Pecos, local records are probably just a matter of time.

Pied-billed Grebe is a familiar species, occurring virtually throughout the United States and from Canada to Argentina. In spring, watch for attentive adults and their striped young on local ponds. This is the grebe most likely to be heard locally; the long song being one of our strange, disembodied marsh noises. Another pond and lake species, the tiny Least Grebe, comes to us by way of Mexico. Locally, it seems to be a rare late summer or fall breeder, taking advantage of seasonal rains.

RED-THROATED LOON
Gavia stellata

Very rare to rare winter terminal migrant
21 Nov 1975–12 Apr 1976 Texas City, GAL (TBRC 1989-47)(AB 30:739)
6 Nov 1976–6 Mar 1977 (1–3) Texas City, GAL (TBRC 1989-48) (AB 31:349)
19 Feb 1978 Texas City, GAL (TBRC 1989-49)
24 Apr 1987 Galveston, GAL (TBRC 1989-69) (AB 41:458, incorrectly listed as 24 March)
27 Apr 1994 Surfside, BRA (TBRC 1995-18; TPRF 1321) (AFN 48:316)
28 Mar 1996 Port Bolivar, GAL (TBRC 1996-82) (AFN 50:301)
19 Apr 1997 near High Island, JEF (TBRC 2000-124)
1 Apr–3 May 1998 Galveston, GAL (TBRC 1998-53; TPRF 1599)(AFN 52:354) Note: additional reports through 9 May

13 Mar 1999 Galveston, GAL (TBRC 1999-27)
Removed from TBRC review list on 17 Aug 2002

Orange County record
01 Mar 1889 ORA (*UMMZ 43763) (Oberholser 1974)

HABITAT: Nearshore Gulf waters; rare (generally during migration) on inland freshwater lakes.

DISCUSSION: The Red-throated Loon is an enigma along the UTC. Although we are aware of nearly 50 published sightings attributed to our seven-county area, only nine were sufficiently detailed to satisfy the demands of the TBRC. Perhaps the considerable variability in bill size of Common Loons, combined with observers confusing loons with cormorants, has led to this surplus of unaccepted records. More unfortunately, many sightings that were likely sound have been rejected by the TBRC due to inadequate descriptions. With that said, we stress that any bird thought to be a Red-throated Loon should be thoroughly documented with detailed field notes including a sketch and, whenever possible, photographs. As with most loons that winter here, Red-throated is most likely to be seen at the Texas City Dike, Offats Bayou in Galveston, and off the Quintana/Surfside jetties.

PACIFIC LOON
Gavia pacifica

Rare winter terminal migrant

WINTER: (19 Nov; 14–15 Dec) **mid-Dec through late Apr** (13, 16, 21 May; 15 May–29 Jun)

HABITAT: Coastal waters, bays, and inlets; exceptionally, inland on lakes.

DISCUSSION: Sight or photo records of basic (nonbreeding) plumaged birds of the Arctic/Pacific Loon complex are often difficult to identify positively to species. Virtually all records of these birds in the lower 48 states are thought to pertain to Pacific Loons. Before the species was removed from the TBRC review list in 1996, that committee voted to list all records as Pacific Loon until an Arctic Loon (*Gavia arctica*) is unequivocally documented for the state. Although the species was rarely reported from and never documented on the UTC until the late 1970s, its recent appearance is more likely due to sharpened observer aptitude than to a shift in the population. Most sightings of Pacific Loon occurred on the

margins of Galveston Bay, with Texas City Dike and Offats Bayou the most predictable locations. Occasionally, a Pacific Loon remains well through the spring and even early summer, sometimes molting into near-alternate plumage. In 1997, two basic plumaged birds were seen at Offats Bayou in Galveston through 15 Jun and one remained until 29 Jun.

COMMON LOON
Gavia immer

Common winter terminal migrant, rare summer lingerer

WINTER: (11 Sep [oversummered?]; 24 Oct) **late Oct through late May** (18 Jun-24 Jul, 20 Jul; 5 Aug)

HABITAT: Nearshore and bay waters, occasionally on larger lakes and reservoirs.

DISCUSSION: Although common when compared to its congeners, the Common Loon is rarely abundant along the coast during winter. Singley (1893) recorded but one sighting from Galveston Bay, Strecker (1912) mentioned only that it wintered on the coast, and Williams (1938) considered it: "rare ... in the Galveston region." Small flocks or rafts may be seen along the Texas City Dike and in Offats Bayou, and we have noted significant concentrations (low 100s) in W Galveston Bay along the GIW. A winter day's drive along our beaches often produces a few loons flying nearshore. The most predictable gathering spot for all the local loons is Offats Bayou, located off 61st Street on Galveston Is. Weeks recorded a flock containing 128 Common Loons, single Red-throated and Pacific loons, and many Eared Grebes there on 1 Apr 1998. The government dredged Offats Bayou to create Shoal Field, once a military air base, and as a result there are numerous deep holes in this inlet where fish congregate during cold snaps (just ask the hundreds of anglers who also gather here during winter). In addition, the water in Offats Bayou is exceptionally clear due to its position relative to Galveston Bay. Fish, clear water, and shelter from occasional storm fronts attract piscivorous species such as loons and grebes. Boat and jet-ski traffic there often pushes loons toward shore where they can be closely observed. A few loons may arrive along the coast in Sep, but not until the beginning of the Oct cold fronts do most of our wintering birds appear. Frequently, Common Loons linger into the early summer, with scattered reports to late Jul. An 11 Sep date may have represented an oversummering bird.

LEAST GREBE
Tachybaptus dominicus

Uncommon to rare late summer and winter visitor, rare breeder

SUMMER: (22 Jul–19 Aug, 25 Aug; 1–2 Sep) into fall
WINTER: (4 Oct) **early Oct through early Apr** (20 May)

HABITAT: Pond to reservoir-sized bodies of fresh water with emergent vegetation, coastal and inland.

DISCUSSION: The Least Grebe is more a nomadic wanderer than a migrant. Its appearance on the UTC may be linked to the diminished availability of fresh water in its breeding areas to the south or to the occasional abundance of inundated habitat on the UTC. In the tropics, the numbers and distribution of this species are known to fluctuate wildly with rainfall. A wet season in S Texas and N Mexico will nurture hundreds of scattered ponds and *resacas* (oxbow lakes), allowing this grebe to stray northward.

Until the latter part of the twentieth century, Least Grebe was considered resident from around Victoria (VIC) south. It has been quite uncommon on the UTC, but recent numbers suggest a true population increase. We now have records for every month and occasional birds remain throughout the year. Locally, this species usually appears singly or in pairs. However, birders participating in the Attwater CBC have found as many as four wintering on Eagle Lake (COL). Least Grebe is known to have bred at Eagle Lake and at Attwater; a dozen or more including half-grown young were present in late Oct 1994 (many obs.).

We have several recent UTC breeding records. An adult incubating two eggs was discovered 1 Sep 1997 by P. Huxford on a small pond in southwest BRA, about a mile east of the Matagorda Co. line. Tom Morris photo-documented this unsuccessful nesting attempt on 7 Sept 1997 (AFN 52:87). Although the species is rare in HAS, Rob Van Zandt saw individuals from 1991 throughout the 1990s on private property just south of the 610 Loop. Nesting evidence was

noted in four years, including the winter of 1997–98, when four young joined their parents. Two adults were seen feeding three juveniles from 22 Jul to 19 Aug 1999 at the Big Pond unit of San Bernard NWR, BRA (Mike Lange and other obs.). The most recent successful nesting efforts were at Lafitte's Cove, GAL, where a pair observed 8 Sep 2002–Jan 2003 hatched four young (subsequently reduced to two); in Brazoria NWR, BRA, where a family group was reported on 29 Mar 2003; and two clutches from Elm Lake, Brazos Bend SP (FOB), discovered on 5 Jun and 20 Aug 2003.

We have winter records from 4 Oct (possibly a lingerer) to a very late departure (if they left at all) of 20 May; most records are Oct–Dec, following late summer rains. A recent winter high of seven birds was noted during Oct 2004 by Whittle at Cattail Marsh (JEF). Birders searching for this species might check San Bernard NWR, Brazoria NWR, Brazos Bend SP, Anahuac NWR, Sheldon Reservoir, inland waterfowl impoundments, and any other shallow natural or artificial lake with emergent and floating vegetation. Its tiny dark bill, dark gray plumage, golden eye, and (in winter) white chin help distinguish Least Grebe from the similar and browner Pied-billed Grebe, with which it often occurs.

PIED-BILLED GREBE
Podilymbus podiceps

Common resident

HABITAT: Almost any natural or impounded body of fresh or brackish water, often but not always with floating and emergent vegetation. Birds seen during late summer and early fall on bay or nearshore waters may represent fall migrants.

DISCUSSION: Probably the most familiar grebe in North America, and the most widespread in the New World, the Pied-billed Grebe dwells in a wide variety of aquatic habitats. It tends to be resident in ice-free regions and migratory where the water freezes over during winter. Almost any freshwater or brackish pond with emergent aquatic vegetation will support a pair of this species, and fall (postbreeding) gatherings of adults and young can exceed 100 individuals (e.g., 130 present in a single pond at Freeport 8 Oct 1998). The Pied-billed Grebe builds a floating platform of rotting vegetation and the female lays her eggs in the center of this mound. The young, sporting zebra stripes and red bridles, cling to their mother's back when alarmed (and young grebes are often alarmed).

HORNED GREBE
Podiceps auritus

Rare winter terminal migrant

WINTER: (1, 10 Oct) **mid Nov to late Mar** (26 Apr; 15 May)

HABITAT: Coastal and inland; fresh- and saltwater ponds and impoundments.

DISCUSSION: Horned Grebe flirts with vagrancy on the UTC; non-CBC reports rarely number more than one or two annually. We suspect the Eared Grebe/Horned Grebe winter identification conundrum results in underreporting of the species. Here at the southern extremity of its Texas wintering range, Horned Grebe cannot be expected with any great certainty. During the late 1970s and the 1980s this species could be seen in large numbers on the HL&P Cedar Bayou cooling ponds in CHA (along with tens of thousands of waterfowl), yet inexplicably these once rich waters have been devoid of waterfowl concentrations during recent years. More recently, Horned Grebe has been found annually on the Houston CBC in Tabbs Bay (*fide* P. D. Hulce). Although at times reported as far inland as W HAS (Warren Lake), this grebe is predominantly seen in Galveston Bay and along the immediate coastline, for example at Sargent Beach southwest of the San Bernard River mouth, on East Beach on Galveston Is., and from the Quintana/Surfside jetties.

RED-NECKED GREBE
Podiceps grisegena

Very rare winter terminal migrant

17 Dec 1978–3 Jan 1979 Freeport, BRA (TBRC 1989-50) (AB 33:295, 588)

19 Dec 1982 Freeport, BRA (TBRC 1991-101) (AB 37:680)

26 Dec 1987 Galveston, GAL (TBRC 1988-297) (AB 42:990)

HABITAT: Nearshore marine waters, bays, river mouths, and coastal freshwater impoundments, rarely inland.

DISCUSSION: Although breeding across much of the northern Great Plains (the origin of many of our waterfowl), the Red-necked Grebe winters almost exclusively in oceanic waters along the Atlantic and Pacific coasts. Texas is situated in the center of the void between these two winter focal points; therefore the species frequents our waters only occasionally. While identification seems a straightforward affair, obtaining certain documentation for Red-necked Grebe in Texas has been a challenge. Indeed, the species has only recently been accepted for inclusion in the official Texas state list. Although the TBRC approved the three sight records we have listed, there is precious little proof of this camera-shy species occurring, and not a single one of our accepted records has been photographed. Four factors contribute to this confusion over the status of the species in the state. First, as already noted, Red-necked Grebes are virtually absent from the entire Gulf Coast; without traveling, UTC birders have little or no opportunity for familiarization. Second, of the 12 or more potential UTC sightings, more than a third have not been submitted for TBRC review. Third, as Kincaid points out (Oberholser 1974), wintering Red-necked Grebes may be present miles offshore or in large bays where they are difficult to spot, much less photograph. Finally, winter birding is a hit-and-miss affair along the UTC, and success may be moderated by tidal cycle, water clarity, wind direction, or ship traffic. The coastal CBCs are anomalous investments of birding time and labor, and not surprisingly all of our accepted records were first reported on CBCs. If birders were willing to perch on the end of the local jetties for hours on end (other than during CBCs), scouring the Gulf for waterbirds, we are certain that reports of Red-necked Grebe, Red-throated Loon, and other vagrants would increase proportionally.

EARED GREBE
Podiceps nigricollis

Formerly common, now uncommon winter terminal migrant

WINTER: (17, 30 Aug, 16 Sep) **late Sep to early Jun** (2, 23, 30 Jun, 10 Jun–19 Jul)

HABITAT: Coastal waters often along jetties, bays, occasionally freshwater impoundments.

DISCUSSION: Typically, Eared Grebes winter in flocks (or "rafts") on larger bodies of water. Previously, large groups could be observed on the UTC along various jetties, in bayous, and along the Texas City Dike. Eared Grebes have declined precipitously along the UTC in recent years, and now they are most often observed as singles or in small groups, especially during early spring fronts. In 2004, the Freeport CBC reported no Eared Grebes for the first time in 40 years. We are unsure whether this downtrend represents a decrease in population or a change in wintering range or is an artifact of observation. At times, immense rafts may still be seen along the JEF coastline and in W Galveston Bay; perhaps these birds simply shifted away from sites frequented by birders. On the other hand, large numbers of grebes have always been seen on W Galveston Bay, and raft sizes there appear to be declining.

In the summer of 1962, Ben Feltner found a nest with three eggs in the vicinity of the Houston Ship Channel near Galena Park (HAS), the only known incidence of breeding on the UTC. During his observations—alone, and with an Ornithology Group field-trip—he observed adults incubating, and covering the nest with vegetation prior to slipping into the water. At the time, other Eared Grebes were present but only one nest was observed (*fide* B. Feltner). On 10 Jun 1999, six Eared Grebes appeared at Freeport, BRA, and two of them lingered until 19 Jul; these birds showed no signs of breeding.

WESTERN GREBE
Aechmophorus occidentalis

Rare winter terminal migrant

WINTER: (12 Sep; 13 Oct) **late Oct to early May** (24 Apr; 6 May)

HABITAT: Bays, bayous, and nearshore waters, brackish impoundments, occasionally inland on freshwater impoundments and reservoirs.

DISCUSSION: Western Grebe appears irregularly along the UTC; most sightings were clustered in the late 1970s and early 1980s. Of our 20+ records, 15 were from the immediate coast (Galveston Is., Bolivar Peninsula, Texas City Dike, W Galveston Bay). Accepted inland reports include sightings at Arcola, Bayshore, and Cedar Bayou. Recent records include two seen at Bolivar Flats 14 Mar 1992, two Western/Clark's seen 25 Dec 1997 during the Sea Rim CBC, and one found 12 Dec 1997 at the end of the Freeport Jetty (Quintana or Surfside not specified). With the recent recognition of the similar Clark's Grebe (*Aechmophorus clarkii*), we alert observers to the possibility that past (and therefore future) sightings of this complex may have involved both *occidentalis* and *clarkii*. Photographs document the presence of *occidentalis* on the UTC, but most previous records lacked specimens, photographs, or details sufficient to determine specific identity. Clark's Grebe has been reported as close to the UTC as McLennan (TOS 1995) and Kleberg counties.

Tubenoses

Tubenoses are small to very large web-footed seabirds united by a gland that excretes excess salt through tubes at the base of the bill. Most are long-winged, riding the ocean's breezes on some of the longest avian migrations. Only a few exhibit colors, but many are strikingly patterned and the whole group is subtly attractive. Their identification, often made from a moving platform, is based upon size, shape, flight characteristics, the distribution of black, gray, brown, or white markings, and occasionally even less obvious characteristics, such as bill shape.

Because of their inaccessibility (most inhabit Southern Ocean waters), the tubenoses are considered by many birders as some of the most desirable of all avian creatures. The most addicted who aggressively pursue them thrive on discomfort, often tempered by a cocktail of motion sickness drugs, and may exhibit several other attributes that stretch the boundaries of normal behavior—even for birders. Despite this enthusiasm, identification and documentation of the UTC's tubenoses (shearwaters, storm-petrels, and a *Procellaria* petrel) remain a challenge for several reasons.

The deep oceanic (pelagic) waters that attract these birds are not found in the shallow northernmost Gulf. Boat trips to offshore waters along more productive parts of the Texas coast are infrequent, and those few are prone to cancellation due to inclement weather. Moreover, oceanic conditions that favor tubenose concentrations may not occur during any particular boat trip. Because storm-petrels and most shearwaters are uncommon or rare, UTC birders (especially those prone to seasickness) have little opportunity to practice identifying them. When a seabird carcass washes up onto the beach, it may be so badly decomposed or gull-scavenged that its discoverer is reticent to carry it to a museum. Finally, the difficulties associated with photographing or obtaining specimens of these birds on the high seas are significant, although video and digital images have recently provided documentation for many seabird records.

The Migration Over the Gulf Project (MOGP) was designed to census landbird numbers and movements over the Gulf of Mexico. As a bonus, it has provided much needed data for species such as shearwaters that are not readily observed from shore and that are seen only infrequently during local boat trips. Begun in 1998, MOGP represents a collaboration between the Louisiana State University Coastal Marine Institute and the U.S. Minerals Management Service, with additional support from seven petroleum companies. Although the project concentrated initially on Louisiana, in the fall of 1999 migration observers were placed on a scattering of offshore oil and gas platforms from Alabama to Texas. Intense field efforts during spring and fall migration periods have generated tens of thousands of sightings previously unavailable to ornithologists. One production rig we refer to is the High Island Rig No. 561 (27°58.40' N, 94°30.00' W). This platform is located 70 miles south of High Island but is in Brazoria County by closest land definition.

The shearwaters are a group of about 22 species of long-winged marine birds. They nest in crevices or burrows on islands and headlands but spend much of the year at sea. When winds are calm, they sit on the water's surface, occasionally forming large, mixed species rafts. More often they are seen skimming low over the waves or making shallow plunges for fish and squid. Many of the species reported off the coasts of North America are long-distance travelers that nest in the Southern Hemisphere. Currently, we recognize

four shearwaters and a closely related *Procellaria* petrel as occurring on the UTC. Of them, the large, pale Cory's Shearwater that nests in the North Atlantic is probably the most likely to be seen locally.

Although widespread and potentially abundant, storm-petrels are small with often inconspicuous field marks that may vary among populations. Locally they pose a special problem. For example, we are aware of four published records of Wilson's Storm-Petrel, *Oceanites oceanicus* (Danforth 1935; Wolfe 1956; Peterson 1960; Oberholser 1974), but to date the only documented Texas record is off Port Aransas. Specimens, unfortunately now lost, would have authenticated their presence. Leach's and Band-rumped storm-petrels are now being observed with some regularity, and additional cruises may yet confirm species such as Wilson's Storm-Petrel.

We hope that one result of this book will be to challenge birders to learn more about the distribution and numbers of tubenoses, especially storm-petrels, that inhabit our offshore waters.

WHITE-CHINNED PETREL
Procellaria aequinoctialis

Accidental
27 Apr 1986 2 miles N of Rollover Pass, GAL (TBRC 1990-129; TPRF 957) (AB 44:1158, 47:384)

HABITAT: Common and widespread in subantarctic waters, circumpolar in the southern oceans from about 55° S to 30° S (Harrison 1983).

DISCUSSION: In spring 1986 a Galveston rehabilitation clinic received an exhausted petrel, first found on the beach near Rollover Pass. Not able to identify the species, a volunteer photographed the bird and then returned to attempts to restore its health. These efforts failed, however, and the bird died. Unaware of the importance of the specimen, the volunteer disposed of the carcass. The remaining documentation, the photographs of the ill bird, were eventually submitted to the TRBC as a possible Sooty Shearwater record. Members of the committee were quick to challenge that identification, and a review of seabird guides determined this wanderer to be the first White-chinned Petrel reported north of the Equator.

Ornithologists have questioned the means by which this vagrant reached the Texas coast, noting that White-chinned Petrels are habitual ship followers and that the bird may have landed onboard and hitchhiked its way across the Pacific Ocean or northward from Cape Horn. We feel it is extremely unlikely that any tubenose followed a ship all the way from Australia to Texas. Additionally, we seriously doubt that one was a ship's passenger all that way, only to die and be discarded just off our beaches. Seabird aficionados will be aware that with increased pelagic coverage, a number of southern ocean seabirds are only now being documented north of the Equator. The record was accepted by the TBRC as the first Texas occurrence. This individual is pictured in Lockwood and Freeman (2004, photo 19).

Note that this species occupies a different location in the *A.O.U. Check-list* (1998). Based upon controversial origin, it is placed in the appendix (Part 1. Species reported from the A.O.U. Check-list area with insufficient evidence for placement on the main list).

CORY'S SHEARWATER
Calonectris diomedea

Uncommon summer visitor or terminal migrant

HABITAT: Nests in the North Atlantic, occurs in pelagic waters off the Atlantic seaboard. In some areas, this species is frequently observed from shore.

DISCUSSION: Previously, this bird was considered rare in offshore Texas waters. More frequent pelagic trips have shown it to be regular in summer and fall. Locally, recognized UTC records are all from the fall of 1999, when this species was noted on 50 occasions from 13 August to 16 Nov at High Island Rig No. 561 (MOGP). Small numbers were seen most days, with a peak count of 26 birds on 5 Nov. This same rig was censused the next spring with no reports of this species. Further exploration of these offshore areas would undoubtedly prove this shearwater to be a regular visitor to the UTC. Records from Apr, Jun, and Oct cited in the UTC checklist were insufficiently documented.

GREATER SHEARWATER
Puffinus gravis

Rare vagrant, status uncertain
4 Nov 1973 Galveston, GAL (*TCWC 9316) (AB 28:76, originally reported as Audubon's Shearwater; Arnold 1975)

20 Apr 1980 High Is., GAL (TBRC 1988-167; TPRF 644) (AB 34:795)

HABITAT: Oceanic waters off the Atlantic seaboard, breeding in southern Atlantic. Rare in western Gulf of Mexico.

DISCUSSION: The potential exists for virtually any pelagic species, particularly those from the Atlantic, to wend their way into the Gulf of Mexico. In the shallow northwestern corner of the Gulf—the true backwaters—these possibilities are scant. As Dwight Peake, Mark Elwonger, Ronnie Carroll, and others have discovered in their recent offshore ventures, pelagic species such as Cory's, Sooty (rare), and Audubon's shearwaters, Band-rumped Storm-Petrel, and Bridled Tern are restricted in the Gulf to deep oceanic waters along and beyond the continental shelf. Sediments from the Mississippi River are carried on longshore currents into the northwest Gulf, and these deposits have extended the shelf away from the UTC. Birders embarking from Galveston and Freeport must travel as far as 125 miles to the SE before reaching deep water (as opposed to 60 miles out of Port Aransas or 40 miles out of Port Isabel). As a result, pelagic birding in Texas is generally restricted to ports S of the UTC (Port O'Connor, Port Aransas, Port Mansfield, Port Isabel), and local reports of these species are largely limited to those stranded after tropical storms. The TBRC presently accepts only 11 records of Greater Shearwater for Texas; both UTC reports were birds discovered grounded on beaches in GAL.

SOOTY SHEARWATER
Puffinus griseus

Rare vagrant, status uncertain
23 Jul 1976 Gilchrist, GAL (*SFASU 2636) (AB 30:976)
26 Dec 1990 Galveston, GAL (TBRC 1991-1) (AB 45:291, 885)
2 Jan 1991 San Luis Pass, BRA (*LSUMNS 151916, TBRC 1991-45; TPRF 988) (*LSUMZ 151916) (AB 45:291)

HABITAT: A visitor from the Southern Hemisphere, found locally in offshore marine waters.

DISCUSSION: Although among the most abundant pelagic species worldwide, the Sooty Shearwater only rarely wanders into the W Gulf of Mexico. Two of the UTC records involved stranded individuals (both preserved as specimens); the third and most surprising was a single bird seen from land on the Galveston CBC. At of the end of 2004, the TBRC had accepted thirteen records. See Greater Shearwater.

AUDUBON'S SHEARWATER
Puffinus lherminieri

Uncommon or rare vagrant, status uncertain
27 May 1929 Sabine Pass, JEF (*USNM 330257)
(Oberholser 1974)
Removed from TBRC review list in 1996
20 Jul 1998 (2) off Freeport, BRA
7 Sep 1999 MOGP High Island Rig, BRA

HABITAT: Offshore marine waters.
DISCUSSION: Hurricane Carla, a devastating tropical storm that careened across Galveston into Houston in 1961, grounded numerous shearwaters as it passed along the UTC. Although details were published in AFN and subsequently in Oberholser (1974), unfortunately no specimens were preserved or photographed. Therefore these records remain unreviewed and unaccepted by the TBRC. Widespread in the tropics, this shearwater nests as close to Texas waters as Bermuda, the West Indies, and islands off the Caribbean coasts of Panama and Venezuela. The Sep 1961 birds associated with Hurricane Carla, and 13 found dead during Sep 1967 in Nueces and Kleberg cos. after Hurricane Beulah, suggest that numbers of these small shearwaters occur in the western Gulf from late spring into fall. A heightened interest in pelagic birds, and the number of boat trips being operated in response to this growing demand, has begun to illuminate what is admittedly a rather murky picture. This species has been reported with regularity farther down the coast off Port O'Connor, with an impressive 206 counted there on 30 Sep 1995. Recent UTC records include four individuals observed with other pelagic species during a 20 Jul 1998 deep water pelagic trip off Freeport, BRA, and one seen 7 Sep 1999 from the High Island Rig No. 561 (MOGP).

LEACH'S STORM-PETREL
Oceanodroma leucorhoa

Rare or rarely observed visitor
23 Jul 1976 Freeport, BRA (*HMNS 13)

6 Jun 1999 off Freeport, BRA (28°08.79′ N, 94° 38.96′ W) (TBRC 1999-67)

HABITAT: Offshore waters.
DISCUSSION: Until recently, Leach's Storm-Petrel was represented by a published but unverified UTC record from 3 Jun 1932 off Galveston (Danforth 1935). In 2000 a specimen, presumably found at Freeport, was located at the Houston Museum of Natural Sciences and verified as this species. The most recent record is from 6 Jun 1999 when one was found along with other pelagics during a fishing and birding trip off Freeport. Texas now has 22 documented records, most from the last ten years. These sightings were made during offshore trips organized by Dwight Peake and Mark Elwonger and originating out of Port O'Connor. The records suggest that this species, although much less common than Band-rumped Storm-Petrel, occurs regularly off the coast from late spring through fall.

BAND-RUMPED STORM-PETREL
Oceanodroma castro

Rare or rarely observed visitor
6 May 1996 San Luis Beach, BRA (TBRC 1996-93)
Removed from TBRC review list in 1996
20 Jul 1998 (9) off Freeport, BRA
6 Jun 1999 (3) off Freeport, BRA
20 Jun 1999 off Freeport, BRA
Early Jun 2001 Seabrook, HAS

HABITAT: Offshore waters.
DISCUSSION: Until recently, UTC reports of Band-rumped Storm-Petrel have been unaccepted, despite the fact that the species has been observed to the south in Texas waters (R. Carroll, D. Peake data). Recent offshore trips have resulted in the species being removed from the TBRC review list. Recently, trips into pelagic waters off the UTC have resulted in sightings of this species. Nine were found at three locations on 20 Jul 1998, three birds were observed at two locations on 6 Jun 1999, and one bird was seen on 20 Jun 1999—all on trips that originated from Freeport, BRA. The most recent UTC record was one found in Seabrook, HAS, during or immediately after the passage of Tropical Storm Allison. The well-meaning finder carried the bird with her wherever she went, fed it cooked rice, and even slept with it at

night! The bird eventually weakened and was turned over to a local wildlife rehabilitator on 6 Jun 2001.

Although the species is typically only a summer visitor to our offshore waters, a bird that was recovered after it struck the mast of a fishing vessel off Port Isabel, Cameron Co., on 27 Feb 2001 indicates that we have much yet to learn about our offshore visitors.

Pelicans and Allies

The order Pelicaniformes consists of six families of freshwater and marine birds, all of which are represented on the UTC. Most of these families are easily recognized, but their relationship to each other may not be so obvious. The order occurs throughout the world, being absent only from extreme polar latitudes, the highest mountains, and the most extensive deserts, all lacking the fish upon which these birds depend.

Although variable in size and proportions, members of the order possess webbed feet, with which all but the water-shunning frigatebirds paddle on the surface or propel themselves underwater. Many species have a prominent gular (throat) pouch that may be inflated with air during displays or filled with water during feeding.

Prey capture modes vary, even among members of the same family. For example, White Pelicans dip fishes from the surface, often in a graceful, coordinated group effort, while Brown Pelicans crash dive from the air, filling their gular pouch with fish and water. The aberrant frigatebirds pirate much of their food from other birds—often their close relatives. Most members of the order simply surface dive for their prey and take it during an underwater chase. Where closely related species nest together (i.e., several boobies on various tropical islands), they segregate by feeding at different distances from shore or specializing on certain types of prey.

Eleven members of the order have been recorded on the UTC. Three (all northern populations of tropical species) nest locally. Accidentals include Red-billed Tropicbird and Red-footed Booby, each represented by a single record.

Although its representatives are infrequently observed along the UTC, the family Sulidae is our largest pelicaniform family and includes the Northern Gannet and three species of boobies. One of them occurs erratically, one is uncommon, and two are great rarities. Boobies nest on tropical islands; the larger gannets seek temperate coasts to breed. They are well known for their comical mating displays and, in the case of several species, colorful feet and other soft parts. Identification of adults is straightforward, but young Northern Gannets and Masked Boobies are confusingly similar, especially when flying by at some distance offshore.

The pelicans and cormorants are each represented by two species; one of each nests locally. White Pelican, one of our largest birds, is a common migrant and winter visitor. It breeds to the north and southwest and is a candidate for a UTC nesting attempt. During migration, huge flocks gracefully swirl over the UTC as the birds fly to and from their wintering sites in eastern and southern Mexico. Unlike the White Pelican, which may occur far inland, Brown Pelican is restricted to the coast. Once eliminated from the UTC, Brown Pelicans have again become common breeders. Line after line of them undulates along the shore, alternating a few leisurely flaps with long buoyant glides.

The two cormorants are black, slim-necked birds that appear rather ducklike on the water. The diminutive Neotropic Cormorant is primarily a summer visitor, but increasing numbers now remain to winter. A decidedly social species, 100 or more may line up side by side along a cable crossing one of Houston's bayous. The larger Double-crested Cormorant may occur virtually anywhere in the country at some stage of the year. It nests on bays and reservoirs both inland and coastally, although not along the UTC. Numbers of them winter locally in freshwater and marine habitats; those present in summer are nonbreeders.

Three more families, all of them tropical, are represented by single species. Each summer, nonbreeding Magnificent Frigatebirds visit Galveston Bay, making their living by scavenging around fishing boats or pirating fishes from terns and other birds that are returning to feed their young at nesting colonies. Magnificent Frigatebird is one of our most graceful and buoyant species. Its unusually long, slender wings, which may span over seven feet, combined with a nearly weightless skeleton, enable it to stay aloft for hours with barely a wing beat.

Red-billed Tropicbird is one of three mostly white, ternlike species that nest on tropical islands. Nonbreeders show up along the eastern coast of North America, but in the Gulf this bird is a vagrant. Adults of all three tropicbirds are graced with long, slender tail streamers and are among our most beautiful birds. Immatures that lack tail streamers must be cautiously diagnosed to distinguish them from the larger terns and from each other.

The Anhinga is one of only four members of its family and the only one found in the New World. Although widespread in the American tropics, in the United States it is largely restricted to the southeastern states. There, it nests along wooded lakeshores, even in city parks, and less often in saline habitats. The Anhinga is popular with birders, as all small bird families seem to be. It is also widely recognized by nonbirders, who are familiar with its snakelike appearance as it swims with its body submerged.

RED-BILLED TROPICBIRD
Phaethon aethereus

Accidental
13 Nov 1985 Houston, HAS (*TCWC 11576) (AB 40:138)

HABITAT: Offshore marine waters, often nesting on islands near shore.

DISCUSSION: On 13 Nov 1985 the state's first Red-billed Tropicbird pitched into a run-of-the-mill Houston suburban yard, lying helpless until noticed by residents. Despite the efforts of rehabilitation experts at the Houston Zoo, it perished on 16 Nov. One would hardly expect to see a tropicbird of any cut in Houston, a city situated some 60 miles inland from the Gulf of Mexico. How did this happen? Many have assumed that the bird originated in the Gulf. The species frequents the offshore waters of the Atlantic, occurring occasionally along the U.S. southern Atlantic coast. However, interior records from the W United States (Zapata Co., Texas, and Arizona, for example) suggest that these birds may be dispersing immatures wandering E from breeding colonies in the Gulf of California and along the Pacific coast of Mexico.

The five most recent Texas records are all from the Gulf: sightings from pelagic trips on 21 Sep 1996, 5 Sep 1998, 18 Jul 2001, and 24 Sep 2004 and one found dead at North Padre Island on 7 Jun 1997. The similar White-tailed Tropicbird does occasionally occur in the western Gulf, although as yet there is no accepted Texas record. Given the difficulty in separating young from each other and from terns, any tropicbird (alive or dead) in the western Gulf warrants close scrutiny supported by a photo or videotape, if possible.

MASKED BOOBY
Sula dactylatra

Uncommon to rare summer terminal migrant, rare winter resident

SUMMER: (15, 22, 31 Mar) **mid-Mar through mid-Oct** (15–16 Nov; 16 Dec)

HABITAT: Islands, oceanic waters, buoys and offshore platforms, occasionally inshore on beaches or artificial structures.

DISCUSSION: Unlike shearwaters and storm-petrels, Masked Booby is one of the few pelagic species that a UTC birder stands a reasonable chance of seeing, albeit it with some persistence.

Although usually encountered well offshore, this booby periodically ventures into coastal waters or roosts on tidal flats such as San Luis Pass or Bolivar Flats. For example, a bird reported 26 June 1994 spent much of the summer perching on the docks at the Coast Guard station near the E end of Galveston Is. During certain summers (for example, 1998), dead or weakened individuals may be common on the beaches, as may have been the case for a 4 Sep 2004 bird at Bolivar Flats. Generally considered a warm-water species, the Masked Booby has nevertheless appeared along the UTC in winter (12 Nov to 27 Feb). A beached adult photographed on 27 Feb 1999 at Surfside, BRA, is the only physically documented winter record from the UTC. We caution observers to distinguish this species carefully from the Northern Gannets with which individuals may fly with during winter.

BROWN BOOBY
Sula leucogaster

Very rare or accidental visitor

25 Jul 1983 GAL (TBRC 1992-156)

31 Mar 1990 (6) Freeport, BRA (TBRC 1990-67)
   (AB 44 : 459)

14 Dec 1996 Galveston, GAL (TBRC 1997-6)

HABITAT: The widespread Brown Booby nests along the coasts of all the continents except Antarctica. In Texas, it may occur over Gulf or inshore waters, often roosting on buoys, offshore platforms, or other artificial structures.

DISCUSSION: Difficulty in separating young Brown and Masked boobies (and perhaps young Northern Gannets) has obscured the status of the Brown Booby in Texas. In addition, most pelagics have been sighted here from land, and the distance from the observer to the observed is often so great as to make detailed views virtually impossible. Brown Booby is occasional in the eastern Gulf (J. Stevenson) and periodic movements into nearshore waters should not be unexpected. The 19 Texas records are distributed as follows: Jan (1), Mar (2), May (1), Jun (1), Jul (2), Aug (5), Sep (3), Oct (2), and Dec (2).

RED-FOOTED BOOBY
Sula sula

Accidental in spring

27 Mar 1983 off Galveston, GAL (TBRC 1988-258; TPRF 758)

HABITAT: Generally found well offshore in clear, warm, marine waters; nests on tropical islands.

DISCUSSION: Of the various members of the family Sulidae that normally occur off the coasts of the Americas, Red-footed Booby is the most highly pelagic. That is, it is the booby most likely to be found very far offshore over deep, blue water. What this behavioral trait means to the booby is a decrease in competition with other more coastal members of its family, in addition to placing it over deep blue water where it finds its flyingfish prey in abundance. What it means to birders is that we should not get our hopes up.

Our sole Red-footed Booby record is not the product of local birding efforts but comes from a seaman off the Galveston coast. The sailor, actively interested in birds, noticed a booby perched upon a mast as his ship neared the Port of Galveston. Photos that he took were sent to the TBRC, and the UTC became the recipient of the only documented record of the species in Texas. Lockwood and Freeman (2004) state that

this same individual was photographed on an oil platform.

NORTHERN GANNET
Morus bassanus

Uncommon winter terminal migrant, rare summer lingerer, occasionally abundant spring transient

WINTER: (4, 29 Aug; 4, 20, 23–24, 24, 30 Sep; 4, 6 Oct) **mid-Oct to late Apr** (10 May; 5 Jun, 13 Jun; 27 Jul)

HABITAT: Northern Gannet nests on headlands and islands along both coasts of the N Atlantic Ocean. It occurs in our nearshore and offshore waters, occasionally by the hundreds.

DISCUSSION: Largest of the New World sulids, and the only one likely to be seen in cold water, this temperate breeder appears regularly (often commonly) along the Texas coast. Usually, first-year birds dominate the flocks alongside the beautiful adults.

Once considered a vagrant, the gannet has had its true coastal status revealed by efforts in recent years to scour nearshore waters for pelagic species. Numbers of gannets may be seen gliding over the Gulf or plunging into shallow waters surprisingly close to the beach. Land-based sightings depend on weather and wind conditions; eastern winds shift the clear water line close to the beach, and gannets often fish along that demarcation between the clear and turbid waters (D. Peake).

This species has been recorded as a migrant or a lingerer during every month of the year. Fall migrants begin to appear in late Oct. In Georgia, gannets are found from 24 Oct to 31 May (G. Beaton), dates slightly offset from our main migration window. Unlike in Georgia, summer lingerers (often moribund birds taken to wildlife rehabbers) are more likely to occur along the UTC. Their summer presence (including a 5 Jun specimen) may simply be the result of longshore currents, as there appears to be no organized movement during those months. Stevenson and Anderson (1994) considered it generally rare to uncommon on the Gulf Coast. For Florida, they present similar dates that have produced both northbound and southbound movements and note that the presence of summer gannets in Florida is "puzzling," as we have found it to be in Texas. Additionally, they provide several Feb, Apr, and May dates for birds flying westward along the Florida Panhandle. These birds could be the source of summer records in the western Gulf.

In some years a significant northeastward migratory movement is witnessed along Galveston Is., the Bolivar Peninsula, and into JEF. In the last two weeks of Mar hundreds (in 1989, thousands) of gannets may be been seen streaming toward the NE; for example, 325 were seen on 26 Mar 1989. Often accompanied by numbers of jaegers, this spring flight is poorly known and understood. The largest UTC CBC tally was 356 birds seen on 19 Dec 1997 at Freeport. We believe such gatherings indicate a more significant wintering population of gannets in the W Gulf than was previously recognized.

AMERICAN WHITE PELICAN
Pelecanus erythrorhynchos

Common winter terminal migrant, common biseasonal transient migrant, uncommon summer nonbreeding lingerer

WINTER: **late Aug to mid-May**

HABITAT: Gulf and bay waters, roosting on spoil islands, sand bars, and intertidal flats in the bay systems, freshwater impoundments, lakes, and reservoirs; frequently seen soaring in regimented formations along the coast.

DISCUSSION: Along the UTC, eight large water birds exhibit white bodies patterned with black flight feathers: Northern Gannet, Wood Stork, Snow Goose, Ross's Goose, White Ibis, American White Pelican, and, rarely, Masked Booby and Whooping Crane. The White Pelican—one of the New World's largest birds—is the only one of these that is likely to be seen floating in large numbers on bay waters. Hundreds congregate at the Bolivar and San Luis Pass flats and on nearby sand bars. Others loaf on spoil islands visible from Rollover Pass and W Galveston Is. (for example, high counts of 1,500 at Bolivar Flats 23 Mar 1993 and 2,268 on 25 Dec 1965 during the Freeport CBC).

Most of the local records pertain to migrants from breeding colonies to the north and northwest, and band returns bear this out. However, the species breeds in small numbers in the northern Laguna Madre and along the Mexican Gulf coast. Thus, a few of our birds may represent northward-dispersing young or adults from nesting efforts to the south or southwest.

Although some American White Pelicans are present in the Galveston Bay complex throughout the summer, we know of no evidence of the species breeding here. As with many of the winter waterbirds that breed to our north, small numbers of adolescents and nonbreeders remain on the UTC through the summer.

BROWN PELICAN
Pelecanus occidentalis

Formerly extirpated, now common resident and reestablished breeder

HABITAT: Occurs on nearshore Gulf waters, Galveston Bay, and estuaries; nests on islands.

DISCUSSION: Ungainly on land, effortless when aloft, and immensely entertaining, the Brown Pelican manifests the essence or soul of the Gulf Coast more recognizably than does any other bird. Communities throughout the Texas coast plaster its image on postcards and placemats, tourism brochures, water towers, city limit signs, motels, and cafés. Although historically abundant along the entire extent of the Texas coast, Brown Pelicans experienced a catastrophic decline in the 1950s. By 1958, they had been eliminated from the UTC, and only scattered birds remained at outposts on the central coast. Galveston Bay colonies that had supported hundreds of nesting pairs were abandoned, and thereafter only a few wanderers were irregularly seen.

Thus the many people who had never seen *one* Brown Pelican on the UTC were hardly prepared for the reappearance of hundreds in the late 1980s. Superficially, this remarkable recovery is attributable to a buildup of populations along the central and southern coast of Texas, and the resultant dispersal of young birds. At a deeper level, their comeback was due to a decrease in egg shell-thinning DDT in the nearshore environment, and an increase in the sensitivity of local residents who had persecuted the birds as competitors for commercially important food fishes. Beginning in 1918, government research (spearheaded by T. Gilbert Pearson, longtime president of the National Association of Audubon Societies), led to education programs that clarified the noncompetitive food habits of the Brown Pelican and its role in the coastal ecosystem. Additionally, the National Audubon Society and USFWS now protect nesting islands used by Brown Pelicans and other potentially low-density waterbirds.

The Brown Pelican's dramatic recovery is perhaps best reflected in colonial waterbird survey data. From a low of six Texas nesting pairs in 1973, its colonies expanded to 3,424 pairs in 2001 (TCWD). During the 1990s Brown Pelicans recolonized Galveston Bay's Little Pelican Island. Five nests were located during 1992, about five in 1993, 125 during 1994 (when a 15 Jul census by Winnie Burkett yielded 82 young of the year and 725 adults and subadults on the island), 200 in 1995, 100 in 1996, 25 in 1997 (and 88 additional nests on the Jig Saw Islands), and more than 329 nests in 1998, when 1,023 chicks were counted on the island. Additional evidence of their buildup was a total of 1,057 individuals observed 27 Dec 1993 during the Galveston CBC, a count that yielded 0–3 birds during much of the 1980s.

Between 2000 and 2004, six Galveston Bay colonies (4 GAL and 2 BRA) were home to a total of 468–1,497 nesting pairs of Brown Pelicans and averaged 877 pairs per year. The largest colonies were on North Deer and Little Pelican islands (TCWD). Thus it would appear that by late 1990s, the UTC's Brown Pelican population had rebounded to more than a self-sustaining level, and it now appears to be limited only by the availability of suitable nesting islands. Nesting pair counts decrease periodically due to predation, a problem endemic to all waterbird colonies on the Texas coast. The presence of six active colonies greatly enhances the likelihood of a successful nesting season somewhere on the bay.

The late Edgar Kincaid remarked that "the picturesque Brown Pelican on its U.S. range soon may be only a memory in the minds of ancient bird watchers . . . [for the] insults have become so great that it has suffered what appears to be an irreversible collapse." We are relieved that Edgar's dire prediction appears to have been premature.

NEOTROPIC CORMORANT
Phalacrocorax brasilianus

Common summer terminal migrant, increasing winter lingerer or visitor

SUMMER: Typically early Mar to late Nov; seasonality appears to be changing and some birds are present all year.

WINTER: Previously, stragglers wintered; now often present in good numbers.

HABITAT: Fresh- and saltwater marshes, bays, less frequently ocean shore and nearshore waters; nests in colonies around large reservoirs and on spoil islands; uncommon inland on lakes and ponds, waterfowl and irrigation reservoirs, and natural and concrete-lined bayous. Usually but not always occurring on smaller bodies of water than Double-cresteds.

DISCUSSION: Neotropic Cormorant (formerly Olivaceous Cormorant), a widespread tropical species, nests in the United States as far north as E Texas and W Louisiana. Although there are a few colonies far to the west, its breeding population is largely restricted to the Gulf Coast. UTC sites include Sidney Island (ORA), Willie Slough Gully (JEF), and Vingt-et-un and North Deer Islands (GAL). At the last site, the Texas Colonial Waterbirds Database reported 304 nests during 2001.

This species has increased in Texas during the past three decades. However, counts of UTC breeding pairs fluctuate greatly. In 1990, the estimated UTC nesting population exceeded 3,300 pairs (M. Lange, pers. comm.) as compared to only 840 in 2001 (TCWD). Neotropics breed in association with other colonial waterbirds, including various herons and egrets. Although the species is present year-round, many individuals vacate the UTC in winter (see next account), becoming commoner and more widespread in Mexico (Howell and Webb 1995). Unlike the similar Double-crested Cormorant, this species is infrequently seen very far inland, although dozens may occur in Houston, where many winter as well. Much of the nesting population seems to move southward, but wintering birds may be encountered along the coast at marinas, jetties, and docks (for example, the pilings at the Galveston ferry landings). Wintering numbers are increasing, as evidenced by the 549 birds counted 20 Dec 1996 on the Freeport CBC. Late summer staging concentrations may comprise hundreds of individuals (241 at Bolivar Flats 29 Aug 1993). If unsure of identification, look for this species' narrow gular patch, outlined in white during the breeding season (but occasionally by Jan), and try to see its feathered lores; the lores of the Double-crested are naked. For the UTC's best views of Neotropic Cormorants, visit Houston Audubon Society's Claybottom Pond rookery at High Island. In Apr 2004, 162 nests were counted there (W. Burkett and others), many not far from the observation platform.

Interestingly, Neotropic Cormorants have also been found nesting in the winter on the UTC and nearby in Matagorda County. On private property during the Mad Island CBC on 15 Dec 2003, nearly 100 Neotropic Cormorants in full breeding plumage were discovered on nests—some feeding chicks, others incubating eggs (*fide* Sumita Prasad). This species also nested at High Island's Claybottom Pond Rookery in the winters of 2002 and 2003 (W. Burkett).

DOUBLE-CRESTED CORMORANT
Phalacrocorax auritus

Common winter terminal migrant, uncommon summer nonbreeder

WINTER: (17, 25, 29 Aug) **mid-Oct to mid-May** (16, 25 Jun)

HABITAT: Freshwater impoundments, fresh and salt marshes, intertidal flats, bay waters and bay edge structures, ocean front and nearshore waters.

DISCUSSION: To the casual observer, there seems always to be an abundance of cormorants along the UTC. In fact, two similarly attired cormorants largely swap places here twice each year. Immense numbers of Double-crested Cormorants arrive on the UTC between Oct and Nov, taking advantage of the cyclical frontal systems that sweep our coast in fall. As the Double-cresteds arrive, many of the diminutive Neotropic Cormorants (which also make the best of the tail winds) depart the UTC for wintering haunts in Mexico. From Mar to May, as the ice melts off their nesting grounds in the northern Great Plains, these Double-cresteds drift back north, only to be replaced by the returning Neotropics. Considered by Strecker (1912) to be at best a "straggler" in Texas at the beginning of the twentieth century, Double-crested Cormorant is now among our most common winter waterbirds, particularly in the eastern half of the state.

The reasons for this population explosion are twofold. First, during the twentieth century, Texas invested considerable resources in developing water supplies. Originally blessed with only two natural freshwater lakes, Texas had increased its number of reservoirs from 11 in 1920 (449,710 acre-feet) to 203 in 1995, impounding 41,822,945 acre-feet (*Texas Almanac* 1996–97). Second, once completed, these

reservoirs were quickly stocked with a variety of game fish to provide opportunities for sport fishing; cormorants have benefited from the new food supply. We are aware of one breeding record near the UTC, a colony near Brown Cedar Cut (Matagorda Bay) in 1926. A few of these birds summer along the UTC (i.e., BRA, CHA, and GAL), with records from 1 Jun to 29 Aug.

ANHINGA
Anhinga anhinga

Common summer terminal migrant, common biseasonal transient migrant, uncommon winter lingerer

SUMMER: (20, 25, 28 Feb) **late Feb to late Nov** (27, 29–30 Dec); scarce and localized in winter; early Feb lingerers nearly overlap with early northbound migrants

HABITAT: Freshwater lakes, swamps, or impoundments with standing water or bordering trees for nesting and roosting; unlike in Florida, largely absent from saltwater habitats.

DISCUSSION: The Anhinga is a habitué of bottomland swamps, sliding through inky, tannin-stained waters in a graceful, serpentine crawl. So snakelike are its actions and the appearance of its head and neck that many local residents insist on referring to this species as the "snakebird."

Although seen away from bottomland forests only in migration, and obscure and secretive even in its preferred habitat, the Anhinga is nevertheless a reasonably common local species. During spring and summer it may be expected at Brazos Bend SP, along Taylor Bayou (CHA), around Lake Charlotte, at High Island and Anahuac NWR, and in the Trinity Delta woodlands. The largest coastal breeding colony is located at the privately owned Harris Reservoir, BRA, where 125 nests were counted in 2001.

During migration, this species wanders far afield. For visiting and resident birders alike, the sight of a huge kettle of Anhingas gliding northward from their winter quarters in Mexico, often in the company of various birds of prey, is an unexpected and astonishing sight. Soaring on stiff wings, with both tail and neck projected to their furthest, migrating Anhingas resemble black paper gliders more than waterbirds.

Few Texas Anhingas nest in coastal colonies. The

majority ventures far inland, breeding in mixed colonies—most often with inland colonial water-birds such as Cattle Egrets and Little Blue Herons. The number of breeding pairs in UTC coastal colonies fluctuates annually, having risen to over 650 pairs in 1987, decreasing to less than 50 in 1990 (M. Lange, pers. comm.), and then increasing to nearly 250 in 2001 (TCWD).

MAGNIFICENT FRIGATEBIRD
Fregata magnificens

Locally common nonbreeding summer visitor, fall lingerer

SPRING–FALL: (9 Mar, 7–8, 12 Apr) **mid-May to early Nov** (11, 14–15, 16, 25 Nov), three winter reports (23, 25, 30 Dec)

HABITAT: Bay and nearshore waters, inland records generally associated with tropical storms including hurricanes.

DISCUSSION: Frigatebirds are the piratic nemesis of terns, boobies, and other tropical seabirds. On the UTC many of the frigatebirds patrol the Royal Tern colonies in Galveston Bay, forcing returning adult terns to drop or disgorge their prey before it can be delivered to the waiting young. Frequently, frigatebirds follow shrimpers and scavenge the "trash" fish and invertebrates discarded as fishermen sort their catch.

Frigatebirds begin to appear on the UTC during mid-May, exceptionally in Mar or early Apr. Nearly all are immatures, identified by a white head and breast. Although a few range east to JEF, their preferred haunts appear to be nearshore waters off Galveston Is. and Galveston Bay as far inland as Baytown. Frigate-birds roost on pilings in Galveston Bay. Some remain on Christmas Bay or to the east near the mouth of Galveston Bay. Others fly each morning across Galveston Is. to the adjacent Gulf waters and back again in evening. Counts of 15 to 20 birds in roost areas are not uncommon. Like many species of raptors, frigatebirds soar on thermals and take flight only after the morning's sun has heated the coastal atmosphere sufficiently to produce these air movements.

Although frigatebirds are usually seen alone or in small gatherings, Galveston Bay along Bolivar Roads may produce several dozen individuals in the heat of summer. Recent single-location counts of 61 leaving a roosting area near Galveston on 12 Jul 2001 and 56 flying between the Quintana and Surfside jetties on 14 Jul 2002 seem to indicate that numbers are increasing. It is not clear whether this is due to an increased prey base at the tern colonies, increased survival at the breeding islands, or a variable even more difficult to measure, such as global warming.

By late Sep most of the birds have disappeared, although some linger into late Oct—40 were counted at Smith Point, CHA, on 12 Oct 1997—and (with increasing frequency) into Nov. Late 2001 was exceptional for lingering birds, with singles reported on 11 Nov (Freeport), 15 Nov (Galveston), and 30 Dec (Beaumont). Records from 7 and 16 Nov 2004, both from the Bolivar ferry, are indicative of this late date trend.

Frigatebirds are among the species most likely to be seen inland after the passing of a tropical storm, occasionally riding the tranquil air in the storm's "eye." For example, several were seen over downtown Houston after the passage of Hurricane Alicia on 22 Aug 1983. Winter and storm-displaced frigatebirds should be carefully scrutinized for the possibility of either Greater Frigatebird (*Fregata minor*) or Lesser Frigatebird (*Fregata ariel*). Oklahoma boasts a specimen record (3 Nov 1975) of the former species! Separation of frigatebird species is treated by Howell (1994).

Large Wading Birds

The UTC is a magnet for large wading birds. The array of habitats available to them includes miles of sandy beaches plus Galveston Bay with its islands, mud- and sandflats, estuaries, and marshes. Farther inland, no bayou, pond, reservoir, or roadside ditch is without its complement of these birds. Twenty-one kinds in five families have reached the UTC, including nearly all the species found in the contiguous 48 states. This impressive tally includes two bitterns, 10 herons and egrets, three ibises, Roseate Spoonbill, two storks,

Greater Flamingo, and two cranes. Only the Old World Little Egret and Common Crane (both North American accidentals) and the Limpkin of the extreme SE United States are missing.

Many of these species feed side by side, decreasing their competition by taking different-sized fishes or shifting their diets to include insects, small mammals, reptiles, and crustaceans. The feeding behavior of such mixed wader assemblages is both complex and dynamic and has long intrigued aquatic ecologists.

Sandhill and Whooping cranes are northern breeders that visit Texas during the winter. Sandhill Cranes may be encountered in vast flocks, often near shallow lakes or rivers where they roost. Whooping Crane is a rarity of global proportions; flyovers may be expected as the birds move to and from their wintering grounds. Rarely, one actually lands on the UTC. American Bittern (probably a very rare local breeder) nests as far north as the fringes of the boreal forest, so it may also be considered a visitor from the north. The tiny Least Bittern is locally common to abundant, especially along the coast, but may be difficult to find in the extensive marshes it inhabits.

A few particularly successful species, including Great and Cattle egrets, Black-crowned Night-Heron, and Glossy Ibis, inhabit wetlands throughout much of the world. However, nearly all the UTC's waders are species characteristic of the American tropics. Several of these (Snowy Egret and Little Blue and Tricolored herons) may be recent pioneers from warmer climes, as is evidenced by the fact that much of their population migrates south each winter.

Most of the large waders nest in extensive marshes or on islands that are difficult (or illegal) to approach. However, visitors to High Island may view Houston Audubon Society's Claybottom Pond rookery via a boardwalk that leads to an observation platform. Here, birders get superb views of nesting waders as they display to each other, build their nests, and raise their young. On 20 Apr 2004, the Claybottom Pond rookery was censused by W. Burkett, J. Garrett and S. Woodward. Although not all of the rookery was accessible, they counted 1,028 nests of eight large waders, the most common being Great and Snowy egrets, Tricolored Heron, and Roseate Spoonbill. One of the highlights of a visit to this rookery is seeing the intense bill, face, and leg colors these birds exhibit at the height of their breeding activities, often for just a few days each year.

AMERICAN BITTERN
Botaurus lentiginosus

Uncommon winter terminal migrant, very rare summer resident

WINTER: (22 Jul; 5 Aug) **early Sep through mid-May** (27 May; 2 Jun)

HABITAT: Freshwater and brackish marshes, impoundments with emergent vegetation, roadside ditches, paddy fields, temporarily flooded wetlands.

DISCUSSION: The American Bittern has bred on the UTC, and nesting was confirmed on Galveston Is. and near Rosenberg (FOB). We recognize summer records for HAS, JEF, and CHA, including recent sightings at McFaddin NWR (S. Simon data) and Anahuac NWR (J. Stevenson). However, most breeding records are weighted toward the first half of the twentieth century (13 Apr 1941 nest with eggs on Galveston Is., 8–11 Apr 1942 nesting near Rosenberg, 26 Jun 1949 summering at Velasco).

Before European settlement, the grasslands of the UTC, riddled with intermittent wetlands that formed in depressions, would have supported a significant population of breeding bitterns. By the end of the 1940s the advent of agriculture, particularly rice farming, had eliminated much of this habitat (good for geese, bad for prairie-chickens and bitterns). However, the spring and summer of 2003 were exceptional in that bitterns summered in sizable numbers at Anahuac NWR, CHA, with an estimate of seven birds on 25 May; breeding was confirmed when Matt Whitbeck captured a juvenile there on 6 Jun. A road-killed bird found near Sabine Woods, JEF, on 20 Jul summered or was an early migrant.

Due to recurrent summer (or late spring?) sightings, it is difficult to present firm early arrival and late departure dates. Records from late Jul and early Aug may be returning birds or may represent postnesting lingerers. By early Sep, this bittern is more frequently encountered, and by early Oct numbers may be seen in late afternoon as they abandon their daytime concealment. During sultry spring evenings, bitterns may be seduced into a few *OOMP, chuck-a-luck* vocalizations, quickly to be joined by a chorus of rails, gallinules, moorhens, and fellow bitterns. Favored observation sites include Shoveler Pond at Anahuac NWR, the margins of ponds at Brazoria NWR, and

Brazos Bend SP; but in reality, any quiet roadside ditch or flooded grassy field may host a bittern or two.

LEAST BITTERN
Ixobrychus exilis

Locally common summer terminal migrant

SUMMER: (28 Feb; 1, 7 Mar) **mid-Mar through early Nov** (17, 21, 27 × 2, 27–28 Dec)

HABITAT: Reed-lined lakes, ponds, and waterways; breeds and forages in both freshwater and estuarine habitats, avoiding marine environments.

DISCUSSION: The tiny Least Bittern, about the size of an American Robin, is one of only two New World members of its far-flung genus. A locally common nester, this dainty wader reaches its greatest abundance in the extensive reed beds near the coast. To obtain extended views of this species, one must find an open foraging area that may also represent the edge of its territory. Favorable search sites supporting multiple pairs include Shoveler Pond at Anahuac NWR, Murphree WMA, State Highway 124 immediately north of the GIW at High Island (early morning being best), Galveston Is. SP, Brazos Bend SP, and the Texas Point, McFaddin, Brazoria, and San Bernard NWRs. At these and similar locations the birds may be seen perched low over the water at the edges of ponds or channels, although they occasionally advance out into the open and forage along the mud, atop water hyacinth, or on piles of dead vegetation.

At first, most people have trouble finding this species because they are searching for a much larger bird. Additionally, not only is this bittern tiny, but its brown, buff, and black tones blend with the dense vertical stems and leaves in which it forages. Once discovered, it usually holds very still (only occasionally freezing in the typical bill-up bittern pose) and becomes nearly imperceptible. To get a sense of the abundance of this otherwise inconspicuous bird, arrive at Shoveler Pond early on a spring morning and listen for its soft *coke-coke-coke* calls.

GREAT BLUE HERON
Ardea herodias

Common resident
23 May–1 June 2004 "Great White" Heron, Texas City, GAL (TBRC 2004-49)

HABITAT: All wetland types, both marine and freshwater, prairie and pastures, often ditches and bayous within towns.

DISCUSSION: Although technically a colonial waterbird (because of its proclivity for nesting in colonies with other herons and egrets), the Great Blue Heron is by nature and disposition among the most solitary, even misanthropic, of our coastal birds. Individuals appear to repel each other, generally tolerating each other only when nesting, roosting, or migrating. Nevertheless this is among our most familiar and widespread waders (albeit in low densities), inhabiting all coastal marine habitats, inland impoundments, flooded cultivation, roadside ditches, and even the concrete-lined "bayous" that drain Houston. Contributing to this success is the species' ability to take an extensive selection of prey, including reptiles, amphibians, smaller birds, insects, a large variety of fishes, crawfish and other crustaceans, and small mammals.

During nesting, Great Blues gather in both inland and coastal rookeries, preferring those sites with emergent woody vegetation since they build rather flimsy nests out of twigs and branches and nest only in the highest trees and shrubs. Approximately 240 pairs nested in UTC coastal colonies in 2001 (TCWD). In 1998, R. Gallaway counted 92 nests on North Deer Island in Galveston Bay. The highest CBC total was of 601 birds counted 16 Dec 1984 at Freeport.

We are aware of two winter records of white morph birds (formerly known as Great White Heron). M. E. Islieb photographed a Jan–Feb 1965 bird, and J. Tveten documented one Jan–Mar 1972 (TPRF 21). Most recently, a Texas City, GAL, bird believed to be a "Great White Heron" was present 23 May–1 Jun 2004. This bird generated much discussion on TexBirds. It was reported as being significantly larger than the typical Great Blues seen with it (per Charles Brower). However, some believed it might simply be an albino Great Blue Heron. The bird's presence came to light at the time of a Greater Flamingo sighting, but Weeks was told that this same heron had been in the area for the past three years! During the early 1980s John C. Dyes photographed a fledgling "Great White Heron" in a nest with two Great Blue Heron parents on North Deer Island, Galveston Bay. Such a mix of nestlings further suggests that "Great White Heron" should be considered a morph rather than a distinct subspecies—as is the case with Reddish Egret.

GREAT EGRET
Ardea alba

Common resident

HABITAT: Nearly any wetland, coastally or inland; occasionally prairie, pastures; prefers still waters.

DISCUSSION: With a local distribution similar to that of the Great Blue Heron, Great Egret differs from its larger cousin in both coloration and a willingness to associate with its kind. As with the previous species (but generally outnumbering it), Great Egrets may by found in nearly any wetland, occasionally stalking drier habitats for reptiles and small mammals. Coastally, sizable flocks are often seen in freshly flooded rice fields or feeding in crawfish ponds in JEF.

Although the population appears to be stable throughout the season, Great Egrets do migrate through the area. They are often seen in Mar and early Apr flying northeast along the coast, presumably returning from Mexico, to breed in colonies farther E along the Gulf. UTC Great Egrets breed in both coastal and inland rookeries, their numbers usually limited within any specific colony. In 2001, approximately 1,450 pairs bred in UTC coastal colonies (TCWD). In 1998, R. Gallaway counted 126 nests on North Deer Island. The highest CBC total is 1,051 counted 20 Dec 1996 at Freeport.

SNOWY EGRET
Egretta thula

Abundant resident, less numerous during winter

HABITAT: Fresh and saltwater marshes, flooded fields and impoundments, beaches and sand- or mudflats, natural and concrete-lined bayous; nesting occurs on bay islands and inland around tree-fringed lakes.

DISCUSSION: During the later part of the nineteenth century and at the beginning of the twentieth, the hats, dresses, and accessories of fashionable ladies were adorned with feathers and other body parts of wading birds. Hardest hit for its lacy nuptial plumes or "aigrettes" was the Snowy Egret. As feather prices skyrocketed, plume hunters opened fire upon entire rookeries of nesting birds, eliminating most of the United States' Snowy Egrets, along with their eggs and young.

Not surprisingly, many people were repulsed by this carnage, including the poet Celia Thaxter, who wrote that a woman wearing avian ornamentation carried "a charnel house of beaks and claws and bones upon her fatuous head" (Kastner 1986). Responding to the slaughter, in 1896 a group of Boston women took up the battle against plume hunters and the millinery industry and formed the Massachusetts Audubon Society. Two years later, newly formed Audubon societies in 15 states coalesced into the National Association of Audubon Societies for the Protection of Wild Birds and Animals, now known as the National Audubon Society.

As the guns were silenced, Texas Snowy Egrets staged a startling comeback. During the 1920s and 1930s, both island and inland colonies prospered. Kincaid (in Oberholser 1974) noted that invading Cattle Egrets, which take insect foods that abound inland, had displaced huge numbers of snowies at inland nesting locations. However, snowies, which take many species of marine prey, have the upper hand at bay island colonies, from which Cattle Egrets have to fly miles to obtain sufficient grasshoppers or other insects to feed their chicks. During 1990 approximately 1,300 pairs of Snowy Egrets bred in UTC coastal colonies (TCWD data). At High Island's Claybottom Pond, now protected by Houston Audubon Society, 109 pairs of snowies nested in 1999 where none had only a couple of years earlier.

For a short time each spring a seemingly endless procession of loose flocks amounting to *thousands* of snowies (often mixed with Little Blue Herons, Green Herons, and a few Tricolored Herons) moves northeast along the Gulf Coast. Those birders lucky enough to witness it are provided with one of our few daytime migration viewing opportunities. Despite the species' huge southbound movements in the fall, moderate numbers remain to winter. During the last 20 years, 200–400 were usually reported at Freeport, with a high of 860 on 18 Dec 1988.

LITTLE BLUE HERON
Egretta caerulea

Common resident, less numerous during winter

HABITAT: Lakes and reservoirs, flooded fields, fresh and saltwater marshes, bayou edges, less frequently on beach and bay margins; nests along pond and lake edge, in freshwater marsh, along forested bayous, and exceptionally in marine sites such as bay islands.

DISCUSSION: Little Blue Heron is primarily a freshwater species; dozens to (rarely) 100 or more may be in view in extensive flooded rice fields. Each summer most retreat from the coast and breed in inland heronries. Thus coastal colonial waterbird surveys often miss the bulk of the Texas breeding population. Approximately 300 pairs were reported for the UTC during the 2001 colonial waterbird surveys (TCWD). During 1998, R. Gallaway counted 35 nests on North Deer Island.

After breeding, adults and young often stage along the coast before migrating south to winter in the mangrove swamps and marshes of Mexico's Gulf Coast. Small numbers do winter, as evidenced by 143 found on 14 Dec 2003 during the Freeport CBC. In spring immense numbers are seen streaming northeastward from Mexico to eastern Gulf colonies—for example, 695 on 26 Mar 1989. Unlike the blue-gray adults, young Little Blues are white. First-year birds winter in low numbers along the coast, and many of these white juveniles are passed off as Snowy Egrets by inexperienced observers. In late winter and early spring, molting Little Blue Herons can appear patchy or calico, exhibiting a mix of adult (blue) and juvenile (white) feathers. The white plumage in the Little Blue is a transient *phase* (soon to be replaced by the blue feathers of the adult), unlike the white *morph* of the Reddish Egret, in which the white is permanent.

TRICOLORED HERON
Egretta tricolor

Locally common resident, less numerous in winter

HABITAT: Occurs on beaches and intertidal flats, marshes, brackish impoundments; only occasionally inland.

DISCUSSION: As a breeding species Tricolored Heron (formerly Louisiana Heron) is largely tied to the beaches, mudflats, bay islands, and saltwater marshes that fringe the UTC. After a postbreeding dispersal a few occur inland, usually on extensive marshes or fields that have been flooded to attract waterfowl. Typically, this species pursues small fishes (usually members of the killifish family known locally as "mud minnows") as well as crustaceans and insects, often hunting in deeper water that is off-limits

to their cousins of shorter stature (Frederick 1997). Although an active feeder, this heron's movements are rarely as prolonged or exaggerated as those of the Reddish Egret, and its unusually slim build, at times bordering on skeletal, lends the species an angularity not exhibited by our other large waders.

The Tricolored Heron is a dominant species in coastal heronries, where colonial waterbird surveys in 2001 tallied over 1,300 pairs (TCWD). As with many of our herons and egrets, the species is migratory, therefore the winter population of Tricoloreds is decidedly diminished from that seen during the summer and fall (Freeport CBC maximum of 206 on 23 Dec 1973). The bulk of the population winters along the southern Gulf, returning with the large migrant heron and ibis flocks in Mar and early Apr; for example, 1,415 were observed 26 Mar 1989.

REDDISH EGRET
Egretta rufescens

Common but localized resident, less numerous in winter

HABITAT: Virtually restricted to beaches and intertidal flats; apparently the few inland records constitute postbreeding wanderers.

DISCUSSION: Attractive, regal, and comical, the Reddish Egret is a sought-after species for the majority of birders visiting from other regions. The U.S. population of Reddish Egret is virtually restricted to the Gulf of Mexico, and the most significant wintering flocks in the New World are found in the Laguna Madre. Unlike most of the region's herons and egrets, which exhibit some flexibility in their habitat preferences, this species is *almost never* seen away from beaches, tidal flats, or shallow lagoonlike impoundments. There it may be seen lurching from side to side like a drunken sailor, popping one wing forward then the other, weaving a bit, listing over while running a few steps, and generally behaving in a less dignified manner than one has come to expect from large waders.

White morph Reddish Egrets are locally uncommon; a full day's birding with a visit to West Galveston (especially San Luis Pass) might produce two or three. A few individuals are pied with some white flight feathers. Most immatures are a readily identifiable grayish pink, but young white morph birds resemble Great Egrets. Reddish Egrets are somewhat less common during the winter when some of the local nesters move south, as do many of our herons and egrets. An examination of the flats at Bolivar or San Luis Pass should produce at least a few lingerers. Locally, birds are known to nest on islands in CHA, GAL, and BRA, typically atop cactus or low shrubbery. Such nests usually contain young by May.

CATTLE EGRET
Bubulcus ibis

Common to abundant resident, less numerous in winter

HABITAT: Prairies and pastures, also fresh- and saltwater marshes; generally absent from mudflats and beaches.

DISCUSSION: The rapid spread of Cattle Egrets throughout the UTC was typical of their whirlwind invasion of the New World, beginning in Surinam late in the nineteenth century. In Texas, the species was first confirmed on Mustang Is. during Nov of 1955 (Oberholser 1974). Locally it was first recorded at Galveston Is. on 26 Mar 1956. By 1958 the birds were nesting locally, and they quickly became a characteristic bird of the region. Information provided by J. J. Ramsey (Oberholser 1974) documents the species' local population explosion. By 1970, at least 24,300 were breeding on the UTC. The Warren Lake rookery (HAS) increased from 250 breeders in 1970 to 3,000 only one year later! During 1970 and 1971, 10,000 birds bred at a heronry near Rosenberg (FOB). Coastal heronries surveyed in 2001 hosted approximately 3,600 pairs (TCWD). The lower numbers may suggest that after its initial population explosion the species is declining to a state of equilibrium.

Cattle Egrets would have been pleased to chase grasshoppers at the feet of the bison that once roamed the tallgrass prairies of the UTC, but unfortunately their paths never crossed. Nowadays, the abundant beef and dairy cattle of the UTC fill the role of the various deer, giraffes, zebras, and other animals that disturb the insects upon which Cattle Egrets feed in the Old World. In Africa and Asia, Cattle Egrets are rarely present in the extraordinary numbers typical of their New World cousins. In part this is because there are more large, terrestrial insect-eating birds such as bustards and hornbills that compete with Cattle

Egrets in the Old World. Additionally, the wide variety of Old World herons, egrets, spoonbills, ibises, cormorants, darters, pelicans, and storks have had millions of years to learn how to hold their own at nesting colonies against the aggressive Cattle Egret. In East Texas our native waders seem less adept at competing for nesting spaces and materials; for example, in 1970, J. J. Ramsey noted that at least 2,000 Snowy Egret nests at the Eagle Lake heronry (COL) had been replaced by Cattle Egret nests.

Locally, Cattle Egrets are numerous throughout the year, more so during spring and fall. During spring migration flocks are often noted returning to East Texas or more northern sites. On 26 Mar 1989, 650 were counted as they flew along the coast with other large wading birds. In the Old World, various populations of Cattle Egrets are sedentary, migratory, or irruptive. This behavioral plasticity is typical of many successful, widespread species that have developed multiple strategies for coping with changes in their environment. Each year, individuals show up far from their homelands; Hancock and Kushlan (1984) suggest that each year there is significant trans-Atlantic migration in both directions.

GREEN HERON
Butorides virescens

Common summer terminal migrant, uncommon winter resident

HABITAT: Nests in woody vegetation along freshwater creeks, sloughs, and bayous and along the margins of inland lakes, irrigation ponds, and reservoirs. Often seen feeding on the edges of bar ditches, streams, and freshwater marshes as well as in natural depressions and pools.

DISCUSSION: The Green Heron is liberally distributed throughout the UTC, yet nowhere would it be classified as common or obvious. With the notable exception of spring, when migrating groups are noted, Green Herons are largely solitary, and rarely do they congregate in what would be classified as a flock. Unless flying, these herons are most frequently seen perched on a limb overhanging a slow-flowing bayou or stream or standing chest-deep in sedges and rushes bordering a freshwater marsh. They feed deliberately, waiting for the intended prey (fish, amphibians, small reptiles, and insects) to venture within striking distance (Hancock and Kushlan 1984). A small group of these herons is resident year-round at the alligator ponds within the Houston Zoo (*fide* Sumita Prasad). In late fall Green Herons largely vacate the UTC, and during particularly harsh winters they may be difficult to find. The highest Freeport CBC count was of 13 birds on 16 Dec 1984. The first migrants are noted in late Mar and early Apr and are often seen flying along the coast in groups, occasionally as many as 25–50 individuals. During the height of their migration Green Herons are often seen perched on buildings and homes along the coast.

Green Heron is one of just a handful of birds known to use tools, baiting the water's surface with insects, feathers, or bits of discarded food remains, then eating the fishes they attract. Jim Stevenson reports seeing a Green Heron that appeared to be using a floating spot of its own excrement as a lure.

BLACK-CROWNED NIGHT-HERON
Nycticorax nycticorax

Common resident

HABITAT: Coastal marshes, sloughs, bayous, and bay edges; also inland in vegetation bordering reservoirs, irrigation ponds, and lakes.

DISCUSSION: Although Black-crowned Night-Herons are present throughout the year, each spring numbers are seen as they fly northeast along the beach. This migration is more likely to be noted in Apr and May, later than that of the Yellow-crowned, suggesting a movement of birds that nest farther north. We lack data that clarify whether UTC wintering birds are northern migrants or lingering local breeders.

On the UTC, Black-crowned Night-Heron is largely a coastal nester, with a few scattered inland colonies near irrigation ponds and reservoirs, including a fair number within the ponds at the Houston Zoo (*fide* Sumita Prasad). The species often nests near breeding colonies of herons, gulls, and terns. Approximately 200 pairs were reported during 2001 colonial waterbird surveys along the UTC (TCWD). These night-herons are renowned predators; during summer they often augment their diets by preying upon young gulls, terns, herons, and waterfowl, including nestlings from their own colonies.

Night-herons emerge at sunset to begin their nocturnal rounds, and the Black-crowned's *kaak-kaak*

call is a common sound around Galveston Bay. However, it is not totally limited to feeding at night and is occasionally seen loafing or roosting around inlets and sloughs during the day. Salt cedar brakes bordering coastal ponds and impoundments are often selected as favored roost sites. The species shows impressive fidelity toward these roosts, often using them for decades.

YELLOW-CROWNED NIGHT-HERON
Nyctanassa violacea

Common summer terminal migrant, northern birds are uncommon winter terminal migrants

SUMMER: **Late Feb/early Mar to early Oct**

HABITAT: Nests in bottomland forest with bald cypress, water oak, southern magnolia, and water tupelo, and occasionally drier forest types; also in residential neighborhoods where tall pines, live oaks, and other trees are used. Feeds on intertidal flats, beaches, rocks, and artificial structures on bay edge and in bayous, wet pastures, roadside ditches, fresh- and saltwater marshes, and wooded swamps. Yellow-crowneds are more likely to roost in saltmarsh than the previous species.

DISCUSSION: Throughout much of the UTC, a familiar sound is the explosive *walk!* voiced by Yellow-crowned Night-Herons as they leave their nests to forage at dusk. However, they also feed during daylight hours, much more so than the Black-crowned Night-Heron.

They are aggressive dispersers and well-known crustacean specialists. This combination of traits has allowed the species to colonize Bermuda, Cuba, the Bahamas, the Socorro Is., the Galapagos, and other outposts, feeding on the abundant land or shore crabs. As the Habitat section suggests, UTC night-herons have access to a wide variety of crustaceans. Along the coast, their diet includes crawfish (mercilessly stalked in wet fields throughout the region), fiddler crabs, blue crabs, and shrimp. Additionally, they prey upon other organisms such as fishes, insects, small birds, leeches, reptiles, and amphibians.

Many Yellow-crowns nest in the settled sections of cities, including Houston and its surrounds. Colonies are loosely scattered through the live oaks of the Rice University campus, pine trees in Bellaire, and many other neighborhoods throughout the seven counties.

This species is highly migratory. It begins to move in late Jul and most have departed the UTC by the arrival of the fall's first frontal systems. The few that linger through winter utilize both coastal and inland habitats; only very infrequently are they seen associating with Black-crowned Night-Herons. The Freeport CBC tallied a high of 252 birds on 20 Dec 1994. Spring migrants returning from Mexico hug the coast, and immense numbers, occasionally 1,000 or more, may be seen streaming northward along with Little Blue Herons, White Ibis, and other large waders. As with the previous species, we are unable to assess what percentage of the wintering birds represents lingering breeders verses migrants from the north or northeast.

WHITE IBIS
Eudocimus albus

Common resident

HABITAT: Understory of flooded bottomland forest, crawfish farms, flooded rice fields, and fresh- and saltwater marshes; irregularly at beaches and tidal flats.

DISCUSSION: Traditionally a resident along the immediate coast, the White Ibis has expanded inland during the past several decades, and flocks are frequently seen over Houston and its surrounds. In particular, young birds often winter in the rice fields of HAS, FOB, and BRA. Immense flocks may be found feeding in the crawfish farms of JEF and CHA, particularly in spring when adults are gathering food for nestlings. During that season hundreds of ibis (and migrating Whimbrels) congregate in the gumbo fields of those counties to gorge upon the numerous crawfish. At sites such as Brazos Bend SP, this species finds all the important food groups in the understory of flooded bottomland forest. White Ibis nest in dense coastal colonies, as do most long-legged waders. Noteworthy aggregations occur in the Trinity River woodlands and on North Deer Island in Galveston Bay. At the latter site, R. Gallaway counted 22,000 nests in 2001.

GLOSSY IBIS
Plegadis falcinellus

Uncommon but increasing visitor, possible breeder

HABITAT: Rice fields, freshwater impoundments with emergent vegetation, occasionally in saltmarsh.

DISCUSSION: Globally, the Glossy Ibis is the most widespread member of its family and the one most likely to disperse. Extremely successful, it is known for being highly nomadic, quickly shifting its nesting sites. During the twentieth century its breeding range changed in many regions (Hancock et al. 1992). Barely known in Texas just ten years ago, this species was a TBRC review species until 1995. It is now rare but regular in small numbers (typically only one or two birds) in the UTC. This situation parallels a current trend in eastern (and very recently western) Mexico, where the Glossy Ibis appears to be pioneering "new" locations, often with White-faced Ibis (Howell 1989; Howell and Behrstock, pers. obs.). It has been documented as breeding in nearby Calhoun County in recent years. Hence birds observed consistently and/or photographed through Jul and Aug during the last several years (many obs.) suggest the presence of a small UTC breeding population. Documenting local reproduction may prove difficult, as the nests are often deeply hidden within reed beds, and the fledglings are eminently confusable with young White-faced Ibis.

Our grasp of the winter status of this species is weak. Given the difficulty of identifying winter *Plegadis*, few birders attempt to sort them out. However, only recently have winter records become annual. Detection of the species in spring may therefore be due more to its easier-to-identify alternate plumage than to any seasonal shift in numbers or distribution.

WHITE-FACED IBIS
Plegadis chihi

Common but possibly declining resident

HABITAT: Flooded fields, freshwater impoundments with emergent vegetation, inland rice fields and crawfish farms; less common in saltmarsh.

DISCUSSION: White-faced Ibis, our common "dark ibis," occasionally reaches triple-digit numbers in the flooded fields of the UTC. In winter these ibis aggregate in sizable flocks, often resembling (and frequently mistaken for) flocks of dark geese as they move between feeding fields. Like the White Ibis, this species has become increasingly common on inland fields during winter, probably because young birds wander widely in late fall. White-faced Ibis nest in coastal colonies, often associating with Tricolored Herons and Reddish Egrets. Participants in colonial waterbird surveys have counted over 1,000 nesting pairs along the UTC. However, numbers vary dramatically from year to year, with only 54 recorded in 2001, when only 149 nests were found along the entire Texas coast (TCWD). The highest CBC count at Freeport was of 2,541 in 1984.

ROSEATE SPOONBILL
Platalea ajaja

Common resident

HABITAT: Fresh and saltmarshes, bay edge, waterfowl and irrigation impoundments and flooded fields, occasionally far inland. Nesting occurs in marshes, on islands (notably at Smith Point, Rollover Pass, and North Deer) and inland lakes (WAL, FOB). Nests are placed in reeds or built upon such plants as huisache, oleander, eastern prickly pear cactus, Chinese tallow, and salt cedar.

DISCUSSION: This species is unique among the world's six spoonbills for its pink (not white or straw-colored) plumage and its New World distribution; it nests from E Texas and Louisiana, S Florida and the Antilles, and the Gulf of California south to eastern Argentina. Based on several distinctions, some taxonomists have placed it in its own genus—*Platalea*. Locally, this rather bizarre-looking yet uncommonly attractive bird is readily encountered from about mid-Apr to mid-Oct. After nesting and during the winter many leave the area, dispersing northward or inland rather than truly migrating. Visiting birders

who have difficulty locating a lingerer should work the roads on West Galveston Is. Larger winter aggregations include Arlie McKay's record of 106 on 31 Jan 1970 at Cove (CHA) and 557 on the 1996 Freeport CBC. Numbers increase from late Feb to Apr, as migrants return to nest.

Data of Oberholser (1974), R. P. Allen (1942), and Hancock and colleagues (1992) document the species' decrease and subsequent increase in the United States. Between 1890 and 1919, after decades of disturbance and collecting by plume hunters, there may have been as few as 20–25 pairs remaining in the entire United States. Allen attributes the spoonbill's decline to disturbance during hunting of egrets and herons (at mixed colonies), rather than to the actual shooting of these birds; their bright pink plumage fades rapidly after death. Nonetheless, some were shot for the millinery business, others for food or for their wings, which were made into fans. During the 1920s, as the tides of fashion and sentiment turned in favor of the spoonbill, it reappeared along the Texas coast, where its numbers grew rapidly. Beginning in 1932, National Audubon Society wardens began to protect nesting islands in Texas, and during May 1968, the Cooperative Fish-eating Bird Survey counted 2,640 on the upper coast alone (Oberholser 1974). Recent data from the Texas Colonial Waterbird Database indicates that the censused nesting population varies greatly from year to year, as evidenced by 1,919 nests in 1989; 405 in 1991; 1,818 in 1996; and then declining again to only 332 nests in 2000. Data from various surveys suggest that Texas nests average about three eggs, from which two young usually fledge.

Storks, Vultures, and Flamingo

JABIRU
Jabiru mycteri

Accidental visitor
26–27 Jul 1973 HAS (*TCWC 9524) (Arnold 1978)

HABITAT: Widespread in the Neotropics and occasionally present by the hundreds on extensive wetlands such as the *llanos* of Venezuela or the *pantanal* of Brazil. Jabirus feed at lake edges, flooded fields,

marshes and mudflats; nesting may occur away from water at drier sites.

DISCUSSION: The closest source of dispersing Jabirus, and most likely the origin of birds found on the UTC or elsewhere in Texas, is the population present in the Mexican state of Campeche, particularly at Laguna de Terminos on the eastern side of the Usumacinta Delta. Birds from that area are well positioned to disperse northward with Wood Storks (see next species account). The timing of the 1973 sighting and of Texas' first substantiated record, initially seen on 11 Aug 1971, and the five subsequent birds, is well within the dispersal dates for Wood Storks. Most Texas Jabirus that occurred to our southwest were on private land. There are two records from Hidalgo Co. and singles from Cameron, Kleberg, Brooks and Nueces cos. (G. Lasley and C. Sexton data). As long as the species prospers in Mexico, further UTC appearances are simply a matter of time. Besides being much larger than Wood Storks, Jabirus show no black in their wings—an excellent field mark to watch for as migrating flocks wheel overhead.

WOOD STORK
Mycteria americana

Irregular but often common postbreeding visitor, rare winter lingerer, formerly bred

VISITOR: (23, 28 Apr; 25 May) **early Jun to late Oct** (2–3, 5, 30 Nov)

HABITAT: Freshwater and brackish marshes, margins of wooded lakeshores; may be seen soaring loosely, not in tight, pelican-like formations.

DISCUSSION: By the early 1900s, Strecker (1912) considered the Wood Stork to be "formerly an abundant species throughout the Eastern and Southeastern sections of the state, still common in some localities." Kincaid (in Oberholser 1974) lists three Texas Wood Stork colonies, all from the UTC (JEF, CHA, and HAS). The last recorded colony, observed from 12 Jun–24 Jul 1960, was present in SW JEF, and consisted of "ca. 50 breeding adults with nests, eggs and young" associating with cormorants, Anhingas, and at least six other species of large waders. Although substantial numbers of these rather unusual looking birds are often present on the UTC, they no longer breed locally.

Most Wood Storks that visit Texas are probably from the great wader colonies of the Usumacinta Delta at the foot of the Yucatán Peninsula. After breeding activities, substantial numbers of these Mexican birds—mostly immatures—drift northward. The timing of this dispersal varies somewhat in relation to the beginning of nesting, which usually occurs during Feb. As the dry season begins in S Mexico, fishes and other aquatic vertebrates are concentrated in any remaining bodies of water, and this abundance of readily available food signals the onset of

nesting (Hancock et al. 1992). From late Jun to mid-Jul, young from this effort appear on our coast, often in the hundreds, many continuing into Louisiana and Arkansas. Occasionally these birds occur at large drying ponds, such as those found at Brazoria NWR. In such muddied pools, they may have the edge over other large waders by locating prey with their bills rather than visually.

Maximum numbers of southbound birds are seen from late Sep to mid-Oct; for example, flocks in the low 100s have been detected crossing Smith Point during fall hawk watches, and 500 were present over the vicinity of Brazos Bend SP (FOB) 16 Oct 1994 (W. and J. Risser data). John Whittle reported an astounding concentration of 5,000 in JEF migrating to the southwest on 29 Sep 1996. This direction would have taken them to the Trinity River bottoms in the general vicinity of Moss Bluff, an area where these storks frequently roost. Also noteworthy were 3,000 that passed the Smith Point Hawk Watch tower on 12 Oct 2004 (Hawk Watch staff).

Records from other months (including a scattering of Apr sightings) may be explained by several phenomena. As always, wintering birds may merely represent lingerers. For example, there are several UTC winter records: 30 Nov 1941, 27 Dec 1941, 2 Jan 1955, 26 Dec 1955, 22 Dec 1966, 14 Jan 1967, 28 Dec 1969, 26 Jan–22 Mar 1975, 16 Jan 1977, and 13 Mar 1992. Hancock et al. (1992) note that a number of smaller colonies have become established in N Georgia and South Carolina, via Florida and S Georgia, and we may be seeing wanderers from these satellite populations. Additionally, after nesting failures during years of unfavorable conditions—too much or too little water—Wood Storks exhibit what Hancock and colleagues refer to as "hardship movements," often appearing in unusual areas where they can obtain sufficient nutrition to survive.

BLACK VULTURE
Coragyps atratus

Locally common resident

HABITAT: Open country, near the coast and inland; roosts in extensive and patchy forest, riparian woodland, and on power transmission pylons. Scavenges at road kills, dumps, and beached carcasses, occasionally in developed areas. Surprisingly absent from much of the immediate coast and beach and no longer present on Galveston Island, but may be common at Surfside (BRA).

DISCUSSION: Until recently the seven New World vultures were usually included in discussions of birds of prey. Although they bear a strong resemblance to the many Old World vultures (close relatives of hawks and eagles), recent genetic and anatomical evidence suggests a closer relation to storks.

Black and Turkey vultures are largely silent, lacking the syrinx (voice box) that is responsible for the endless variety of songs and calls so characteristic of birds. Instead, they communicate with soft grunting noises. Especially on hot days, vultures often appear to have white legs. This is due to the chalky residue that remains when they defecate on their legs—a form of evaporative cooling employed by several other groups of long-legged birds.

Season to season, the UTC's Black Vultures are present in fairly uniform numbers. Certain flocks have permanent roost sites in less disturbed stands of bottomland forest or riparian woodland. The Smith Point Hawk Watch, in operation since 1997, has documented minor fall movements around E Galveston Bay with an eight-year average of 185 birds and a high of 379 in 2001. The daily peak count of 47 birds on 22 Sep 2001 matches the species' typical late Sep/early Oct arrival at Smith Point.

Modern forestry practices that discourage the presence of old trees and thick understory vegetation are detrimental to Black Vultures, which deposit their eggs in stumps and hollow trees (Scott et al. 1977), or on the ground in thickets of various plants. Nehrling (1882), who estimated them to be one-twentieth as common as Turkey Vultures along the UTC, found them nesting on grassy prairies. Singley (1893) noted that they might "occasionally be seen on the [Galveston] beach in company with gulls and terns, clearing up the refuse fish left by the fishermen." Meitzen (1963) reported a Black Vulture nest with two eggs on Pelican Island 27 March 1940. However, we have no evidence that the species has bred on Galveston Island during the past 30 years. In fact, none of the authors has seen a Black Vulture on Galveston Island in the past 25 years. More recently, Eubanks discovered a Black Vulture nesting in roadside debris in WAR. Stevenson reports two recent (2004) nests on buildings, one a greenhouse in Clear Lake.

We presume Black Vultures to be rather common (although low-density) breeders in the riparian woodlands that border our rivers, particularly the Brazos, as well as in the fingers of mixed pine forest that dip into JEF, CHA, and HAS. Sizable Black Vulture roosts may be found in the region, particularly in winter, and in recent years a roost has become established in High Island, probably the most coastal of our Black Vulture congregations. The highest tally on the Freeport CBC was 1,559 in 2000.

TURKEY VULTURE
Cathartes aura

Common resident and bi-seasonal transient migrant

HABITAT: Coastal and inland; open country including beaches, prairie and agricultural lands, not averse to built-up areas; uses a variety of roost sites, including trees and power transmission pylons.

DISCUSSION: The UTC's Turkey (and Black) Vultures exploit a rich and varied smorgasbord of vertebrate carrion, including mammalian, avian, amphibian, and reptilian road kills, as well as dead fish and marine mammals that wash up on the beach. They also profit from carcasses on ranches and trash dumps. Although populations of both local vultures may seem to remain constant throughout the year, the Turkey Vulture is a bird that migrates by the millions through Middle America; however, it does not exhibit major movements through the UTC. The Smith Point Hawk Watch has an eight-year average of 1,573, with a high of 3,091 in 2004. The highest daily total was 591 on 18 Oct 2003. Other more significant flights have been observed inland (4,000 south of Sugarland by Ted Eubanks Sr. and Jr., on 21 Nov 1976). Rarely are winter numbers extreme; however, on 26 Dec 1993, the Brazos Bend CBC tallied 1,981.

The nest sites of Turkey Vulture are varied. They include various structures, caves, cliffs, hollow trees or logs, and the ground—Nehrling (1882) observed them nesting on the largely treeless fringes of the UTC. Prior to the introduction of livestock, trees, and children on Galveston Is., Audubon reported that they nested in clumps of eastern prickly pear cactus. Now, Turkey Vulture has been virtually extirpated from the island; Eubanks recorded only three sightings (including 23 April 1977 and 2 November

1985) during nearly 30 years. Stevenson (living on Galveston Is. for the last eight years) has noted a total of perhaps 15–20, mostly during fall.

GREATER FLAMINGO
Phoenicopterus ruber ruber

Accidental

20–31 May 2004 Texas City Dike, GAL (TBRC 2004-47)

HABITAT: Coastal embayments, mudflats, edges of mangrove swamps, lakes; locally in shallow water, mud, and shell flats along edge of an artificial dike.

DISCUSSION: Greater Flamingo is a known wanderer, occurring with some regularity in southern Florida and the Bahamas. It is abundant in the eastern Yucatán Peninsula, Cuba, and northern South America and is a rare visitor to Texas (A.O.U. 1998). An immature of the Caribbean subspecies made an unprecedented visit to the Texas City Dike, GAL, during late Apr 2004. As this bird had never been observed locally, it was viewed and photographed by hundreds of birders, tourists, and curious locals before it was seen flying away the evening of 31 May. This represents the fifth state record and the first for the UTC.

Raptors

Twenty-five species of diurnal raptors have been recorded in our region. Approximately half of them breed or have bred locally, although few are truly common nesters. The region's importance to different species varies considerably. Some, such as Red-tailed Hawk and Northern Harrier, are scarce breeders yet become abundant and characteristic elements of our winter avifauna. Others, including Crested Caracara and White-tailed Hawk, maintain a minor yet consistent presence throughout the year. Still others, such as Cooper's Hawk and Peregrine Falcon, occur most commonly during migration, with few remaining as sparse winter visitors.

Loss and modification of habitat have impacted the region's birds of prey in a variety of ways. Although the effects are difficult to generalize, they usually seem to be detrimental; only White-tailed Kite seems more numerous in the region as a result, yet it too may be decreasing. Waterfowl impoundments, and the crippled geese they attract, benefit numbers of visiting Bald Eagles, and the vast acreages of fallow fields and rice stubble that carpet much of the UTC provide insects, snakes, and rodents for thousands of wintering hawks. Nonetheless, losses of bottomland forest and woodlots and impacts of pesticides, drainage, increased traffic, and the paving over of thousands of square miles of coastal prairie have directly and indirectly taken their toll on our birds of prey.

From 1991 through 2004, a daily fall hawk count—originally spearheaded by Winnie Burkett and Gail

Diane Yavonovitch and later by Cecilia Riley and Sumita Prasad on behalf of the Gulf Coast Bird Observatory—has been conducted at Candy Abshier WMA at Smith Point on Galveston Bay (CHA, site 049 on the Great Texas Coastal Birding Trail UTC map). Each year, paid counters and volunteers count migrating hawks as they become bottlenecked over Smith Point. Initially the count was conducted from the second or third week of Sep to the second or third week of Oct, enumerating birds of prey as well as other passage migrants. Since 1997 counters have been hired, providing daily coverage from 15 Aug to 15 Nov. The observation tower at Smith Point is open to the public. Birders who want to see migrating hawks (and other species) and learn about raptor identification may wish to visit this tower during the fall.

Count organizers have generously allowed us to draw freely from their data on seasonal totals (table 7), to which we refer in some species accounts. A second tabulation shows the variation in raptors counted over the years; these numbers are more a reflection of weather patterns on migration pathways than of true population fluctuations (table 8).

OSPREY
Pandion haliaetus

Uncommon to locally common winter terminal migrant, rare breeder and summer lingerer

Table 7. *Smith Point Hawk Watch Seasonal Totals, 1997–2004*

Year	1997	1998	1999	2000	2001	2002	2003	2004	Average	Total
Black Vulture	130	105	341	4	**379***	57	96	368	185	1,480
Turkey Vulture	1,225	581	1,295	1,059	2,488	678	2,163	**3,091**	1,573	12,580
Osprey	54	68	54	59	63	48	78	**87**	64	511
Swallow-tailed Kite	40	34	52	46	74	**150**	98	147	80	641
White-tailed Kite	11	25	18	16	**27**	7	18	12	17	134
Mississippi Kite	2,124	2,362	2,975	**4,788**	3,253	3,790	3,809	3,798	3,362	26,899
Bald Eagle	2	0	2	**7**	2	3	2	1	2.4	19
Northern Harrier	445	262	**537**	373	471	144	203	368	350	2,803
Sharp-shinned Hawk	**4,780**	3,231	3,896	1,485	3,878	3,143	1,508	1,923	2,981	23,844
Cooper's Hawk	1,137	1,136	1,197	1,089	**1,281**	1,232	738	1,162	1,122	8,972
Harris's Hawk	0	0	0	0	**2**	0	0	0	0	2
Red-shouldered Hawk	45	36	34	59	54	23	49	**87**	48	387
Broad-winged Hawk	30,417	16,137	34,242	29,956	**103,603**	65,255	21,799	26,028	40,930	327,437
Swainson's Hawk	137	56	129	255	321	168	228	**1,036**	291	2330
White-tailed Hawk	0	1	**2**	0	12	8	**23**	14	8	60
Red-tailed Hawk	**331**	35	204	72	274	44	64	160	148	1184
Ferruginous Hawk	0	0	**2**	0	**2**	1	**2**	1	1	8
Rough-legged Hawk	0	0	2	0	**3**	0	0	0	1	5
Golden Eagle	**3**	0	1	1	0	0	0	0	1	5
Crested Caracara	6	3	4	9	16	7	8	**26**	10	79
American Kestrel	1,297	1,334	1,939	1,310	1,138	**1,947**	816	1,274	1,382	11,055
Merlin	**88**	26	48	43	71	56	79	75	61	486
Peregrine Falcon	65	92	85	79	77	94	88	**129**	89	709
Accipiter species	0	0	113	0	15	18	4	1	25	151
Buteo species	0	0	31	0	4	4	6	5	8	50
Eagle species	0	0	0	0	0	0	3	0	1	3
Falco species	0	0	9	0	1	8	1	3	4	22
Unidentified raptor	656	300	116	38	0	5	1	12	141	1,128
Total	42,993	25,824	47,328	40,748	117,509	76,890	31,884	39,808		

* High counts are boldfaced.

Table 8. *Smith Point Hawk Watch Annual Effort Totals 1997–2004*

Year	Days	Hours	Total Raptors
1997	94	860	42,993
1998	91	677	25,824
1999	92	682	47,328
2000	95	822	40,748
2001	93	745	117,509
2002	91	776	76,890
2003	93	778	31,885
2004	93	796	39,808
Total	742	5,340	422,984

HABITAT: Open coast, bays, and various bodies of fresh water.

DISCUSSION: From roughly early Sep to late May, Ospreys occur with some frequency on the UTC, both along the coast and inland. Most winter Ospreys are encountered near salt water (such as atop power poles on W Galveston Island), on reservoirs near the Gulf, and along Braes Bayou in the city of Houston. The Freeport CBC has averaged 52 over the last ten years, with a high of 74 in 2001. This species becomes increasingly uncommon as one strays from the moderating temperatures of the coast. From about early to late Apr there is a perceptible northward passage. In fall, the first Smith Point census migrants are noted around the last week of Aug; the bulk of the passage occurs from mid-Sep to mid-Oct. Numbers of Smith Point fall migrants have been consistent, averaging 64 per year. The LSU Migration Over the Gulf Project detected Ospreys on 18 Oct 1999 and 10 April 2000 at High Island Rig No. 561, some 70 miles offshore. Despite being established on many islands, Ospreys are rarely seen very far offshore.

Although Ospreys breed on six of the seven continents and on numerous islands, in Texas they are no more than casual nesters. We have a 1925 breeding record from near Port Arthur (JEF); more recently, Ospreys bred on Sam Rayburn Reservoir in NE Texas and on Lake Houston (HAS). Frequently, nonbreeders oversummer, such as along Armand Bayou and at Freeport, making precise arrival and departure dates difficult to establish. As the U.S. Osprey population recovers from its pesticide-induced decline, we in Texas can expect to see more of them nesting on our many and well-stocked lakes and reservoirs.

SWALLOW-TAILED KITE
Elanoides forficatus

Rare (formerly abundant) summer terminal migrant, uncommon bi-seasonal transient migrant

SUMMER: (3–4, 9, 11, 13 Mar) **mid- to late Mar through Sep** (10–11, 3–12 Oct; 19 Nov)

HABITAT: Oberholser (1974) stated that this raptor exhibited its "highest density on coastal prairie and along timbered watercourses." Most recent breeding records are from the bottomland hardwood forests of the Trinity River drainage. Migrants are more widespread, most occurring close to the coast.

DISCUSSION: Nehrling (1882), discussing Swallow-tailed Kite near Houston in the late 1800s, considered it an "abundant summer sojourner from the first part of March to October. A beautiful bird, and one of the most characteristic species of this locality. Especially abundant in the bottom woods near prairies or fields." Once breeding as far north along the Mississippi River as Minnesota, the Swallow-tailed Kite has all but vanished as a breeder from the United States west of the Mississippi. Now it remains reasonably common only along the immediate Gulf coast from central Louisiana to Florida.

This raptor is another species in which the UTC population declined dramatically with the loss of its preferred nesting habitat, typically bottomland forest containing tall bald cypress. Once, when we had an abundance of tall forest adjacent to prairie and freshwater marsh, the Swallow-tailed Kite abounded. The population decline began with the advent of large-scale timbering of old growth forests, and by 1910 the species had been nearly extirpated from Texas. Simmons (1914) considered it as occurring "irregularly during summer" and noted that it had become "very rare." Oberholser reports that the state's last known breeding kites fledged in HAS between 1911 and 1914 (Oberholser 1974).

Recently the species has begun a rather tentative recovery. Nesting was confirmed in nearby Tyler Co. in 1994; in 1996 and 1997 along the Trinity River near

Interstate 10 in CHA (2.5 miles N of the I-10 Trinity River Bridge on the east bank of the Trinity River); and in 1998 at two sites in ORA. The 1998 nests were found as a result of a TPWD program to reward discoverers of confirmed nests. Summering birds have been noted 18 May–17 Jul 1975, five miles N of Rosharon, BRA (TPRF 79); along cypress-lined Taylor Bayou (JEF), where nesting is suspected; and around Elm Lake at Brazos Bend SP (14 May–17 July 1977). In addition there have been persistent reports from the area around Texas Highway 105 north of Vidor (probably 10 miles or so from the confluence of Pine Island Bayou and the Neches River) and from the area of ORA north of I-10 from about Highway 62 east to the Sabine River. These nests may not always be in Texas—in some years they are located on the Louisiana side of the Sabine River (*fide* John Whittle). We can hope that remaining ribbons of riparian habitat, perhaps most importantly in BRA, CHA, and JEF, will continue to support a few pairs of what is currently one of the state's rarest and most spectacular birds of prey.

Although a Swallow-tailed Kite occasionally appears over an inland location such as HAS, most migrants are seen hugging the coast. In spring they are regularly seen floating over isolated coastal woodlands, such as High Island, and also along beaches and the length of Galveston Is., most reports representing solitary birds. The last of the spring migrants pass through in early to mid-May.

Fall counts at Smith Point have revealed a previously unknown UTC passage. These counts averaged 80 per year, showing remarkable increases, with highs of 150 in 2002, and 147 in 2004. On 27 Aug 2004, 48 of these delightful birds were sighted at Smith Point. Because this number of birds is not detected farther south along the coast, we are at a loss to explain their migration route south of the upper coast. Fall migrants pass through from as early as late July to mid-Sep, with highest daily counts from mid- to late Aug. This means that the hawk watch, which starts each year on 15 Aug, misses the earliest part of this passage. Our latest record was observed inside Loop 610 along White Oak Bayou in Houston on 19 Nov 2004 (B. and J. Harwell).

Texas Swallow-tailed Kites are known to feed on many kinds of prey, all affected by herbicides, insecticides, cats, traffic, timbering, and brush clearing.

These include small snakes, frogs, lizards, dragonflies and other large insects, mice, and small birds. To these Nehrling (1882) adds frequent Aug and Sep sightings when numbers fed on "cotton worms" and other insects in cotton fields, an observation supported by other early observers.

WHITE-TAILED KITE
Elanus leucurus

Uncommon but increasing resident

HABITAT: Open savanna and grassland with tall scrub or scattered trees, both coastal and inland.

DISCUSSION: During the twentieth century the White-tailed Kite proliferated, unlike so many other birds of prey. In the late 1800s, Nehrling (1882) considered the species a rarity along the UTC, commenting that "this rare and beautiful bird I have seen several times sailing over cotton fields." Strecker (1912) considered the species a "summer resident of the southern half of the state" but "nowhere abundant." Simmons (1914) and Singley (1893) failed to mention the bird at all. Beginning in the early 1960s, however, this species began a gradual spread along the UTC, particularly along the immediate coast. Observers noted the first GAL breeding kites in 1971 (NW of Hitchcock), and by 1978 this species had become established as a breeder (along Nottingham Ranch Road on W Galveston Is.).

The White-tailed Kite is now a widespread yet low-density breeder throughout the UTC. Therefore we suggest that the increase in White-tailed Kites along the UTC is a legitimate range and population expansion rather than a recent recovery to levels that may have existed in years past. Interestingly, this kite is noticeably more common in winter, when inland breeders apparently work their way to the coastal grasslands. The Freeport count has averaged 27 birds per year over the last 10 years, with an all-time peak count of 76 in 1982. Fall migration is barely noticeable, with the Smith Point Hawk Watch averaging less than 20 per year; some of these may be wintering birds being seen on multiple days. The highest count for a day is only three birds. However, significant fall congregations have been noted (i.e., 20 birds on 12 Aug 1998 at Brazoria NWR, BRA). Recent data from BRA suggest that numbers of this species dropped dramatically between 2002 and 2004 (Weeks). Census data will help determine whether this is simply part of a cycle or a long-term trend.

MISSISSIPPI KITE
Ictinia mississippiensis

Rare summer terminal migrant, common to abundant bi-seasonal migrant, very rare winter lingerer

SUMMER: (13 Mar) **late Mar or early Apr to early Sep** (11, 25 Nov; 12 Dec)

HABITAT: Riparian corridors and mixed pine-hardwood forests during migration; in summer, bottomlands, particularly those dominated by pecan, cottonwood, and sycamore.

DISCUSSION: Mississippi Kite migration is the most blatant, widespread, and leisurely of any UTC raptor's. Unlike most birds of prey, which suddenly appear then just as suddenly depart (accipiters and falcons come to mind), Mississippi Kites enjoy a prolonged and unhurried passage through our area. In season, migrating kettles may be observed almost anywhere. Large numbers occur along the coast, groups of six or more may be seen foraging over busy intersections in Houston or inspecting joggers along the bayous, and in the evening, many conspicuously come to roost in the tall trees of our older neighborhoods.

In early fall, kites may be seen almost daily as they skim the treetops around Houston for dragonflies, cicadas, and lizards. Peak migration extends from late Mar through early May, then again from mid-Aug to early Sep, strongly tapering off then, with only a very few appearing through mid-Oct. On average between 1997 and 2003, the largest migratory push was during the last several days of Aug, with an average of 400 birds per day being tallied on Aug 28.

In the late 1800s, Nehrling (1882) judged this species to be an uncommon breeder, observing nests in pine, pin oak, and sycamore. Strecker (1912) believed the bird resident only in the "extreme southern section" of the state, and Simmons (1914) considered it "very rare" in summer around Houston. In fact, the species' retiring nature may cloud its actual abundance as a breeder. These kites are often seen in and around communities along the Brazos River (Lake Jackson, Richmond, Rosenberg) in summer. In years

past, Mississippi Kites have been seen at Brazos Bend SP in summer as well, soaring over the dead trees in Elm Lake then diving to pluck dragonflies basking on exposed stumps. The species has also been found nesting in recent years along Buffalo Bayou and other area in western HAS. Mississippi Kite is the third most abundant raptor seen during the Smith Point Hawk Watch, averaging 3,300 per year, with a high count of 4,788 in the 2000 fall season; the highest single-day count there was 3,790 seen on 29 Aug 2002. We are aware of a few lingering into late fall, with credible reports from as late as 25 Nov 1950 and 12 Dec 1983.

BALD EAGLE
Haliaeetus leucocephalus

Rare permanent resident, increasingly common winter terminal migrant

HABITAT: Breeds in mature bottomland hardwood forests; winters on lakes, reservoirs, fields; often associating with wintering waterfowl, upon which they scavenge.

DISCUSSION: The saga of the Bald Eagle on the Upper Texas Coast echoes its demise and subsequent recovery throughout the SE United States. Strecker (1912) reported this eagle to be a "resident, locally distributed" in S and E Texas (although the specific counties he mentioned were all south of the UTC). Nehrling (1882) mentioned that the Bald Eagle was "not a common bird" but was "known to breed in certain parts of this region." He also noted that these eagles "build their nests in the tallest trees of the river bottoms." As the floodplain forests were cleared for agriculture, and as the use and variety of pesticides multiplied (affecting the ability of eagles to lay viable eggs), the Bald Eagle all but disappeared from Texas as a breeding species.

Efforts were initiated in 1940 to halt the decline of the Bald Eagle in the United States. The 1940 Bald Eagle Protection Act, the listing of the Bald Eagle as an endangered species in 1967, and the banning of DDT in 1972 stimulated a rebound that is virtually unmatched in endangered species recovery and management. From a low of four nests with two eaglets fledged in 1974, the Texas Bald Eagle breeding population has soared to 110 active nests with 93 eaglets fledged in 2002 (Brent Ortego and Chris Gregory, pers. comm.). In the UTC, 10 active nests produced 17 young in 2002.

Bald Eagles now nest along all the major river systems transecting the UTC, with a significant concentration along the lower reach of the Brazos River. Eggs begin to hatch in mid- to late Jan (eggs reported hatching in BRA 19–20 Jan 1979), and nests with young are seen beginning in early Mar (nest with young S of Richmond 3 Mar 1941). Immature eagles are often seen in late summer loafing around reservoirs near the nest sites (e.g., one immature at Warren Lake 22 Aug 1974).

Although relatively scarce as breeders, Bald Eagles are frequently encountered in our region during winter, arriving in mid- to late Sep. Eagles are especially common around inland rice fields, particularly the Katy Prairie, west of Houston. Favored sites include the Warren Lake vicinity in W HAS and flooded rice stubble and waterfowl impoundments in WAR. At productive sites, several eagles may occur at once, scavenging the carcasses of dead or wounded Snow Geese. However, compared to other areas of the country, the UTC remains eagle-poor. East Galveston Bay migration data (2.4 birds on average during the last eight years) support the contention that if there is a significant coastal movement of this species, it occurs after the end of the hawk watch census period.

NORTHERN HARRIER
Circus cyaneus

Rare (formerly common) or extirpated permanent resident, common winter terminal migrant, common bi-seasonal transient migrant

WINTER: **Late-Sep/early Oct to late Mar**
HABITAT: Marshes, prairies and pastures, fallow fields with low shrubby growth, flooded rice stubble, shores of inland reservoirs and impoundments.

DISCUSSION: The wet Gulf coastal grasslands that once carpeted the UTC were among the preferred Texas habitats of the Northern Harrier. Strecker (1912) considered the species to be "resident, breeding locally." Nehrling (1882) reported the species to be a "common resident in the marshy prairies in the northern part of Harris Co.; also common near the sugar-cane fields on the Brazos." Inevitably, as these grasslands were plowed for agriculture and drained for urban development, the harrier disappeared as a resident. Recent nesting records are scarce; they

include an older record near Dickinson (GAL) and a pair at Galveston Is. SP, where nesting habitat may no longer exist. The birds are also regular in small numbers in summer in BRA, with regular reports from Quintana and from the Brazoria and San Bernard NWRs.

Northern Harrier remains one of our commonest wintering raptors (for example, 327 on the Cypress Creek CBC, 26 Dec 1980), and it is not unusual to see a half dozen or more during a single scan across their open hunting grounds. Sightings of females and immatures predominate in winter, and only a few adult males (if that many) are likely to be noted during a day of birding. Migrants begin arriving in late Aug and early Sep, but small flocks are often seen passing through as late as early Dec. During the past eight years the Smith Point hawk surveys have averaged 350 per year, with a high of 537 in 1999. Most wintering harriers have departed by Apr. Stragglers are difficult to differentiate from rare nesting birds and may be seen well into May, as was a female on 12 May 2001 at High Island (Behrstock).

Besides being a menace to small mammals, reptiles, amphibians, and smaller landbirds, harriers take numbers of shorebirds, both inland and along the coast. Northern Harriers, the "Marsh Hawk" of older field guides, rely not on powerful dives and aerial acrobatics, like the Peregrine Falcon, but on concealment and a stealthy approach. Foraging harriers suddenly pop up from behind a low dike or dune to snatch an unwary snipe or dowitcher (Behrstock obs.).

SHARP-SHINNED HAWK
Accipiter striatus

Uncommon winter terminal migrant, common bi-seasonal transient

WINTER: (5, 7, 17 × 3, 20 Aug) **mid-Sep to mid-May** (14 May; 20 Jun; 6 Jul)
HABITAT: Open areas with tall brush or scattered trees, woodland edge, neighborhoods with mature plantings, hedgerows.

DISCUSSION: As autumn frontal systems finally gather the force to reach the UTC in late Sep, accipiters take advantage of the tail winds and surf to the wintering grounds. Birders congregate at concentration sites or bottlenecks during this period (such as Smith Point) and enjoy the thrill of migrating raptors bulleting by at eye level. As interest in Smith Point has grown, so has the awareness that significant numbers of Sharp-shinned and Cooper's hawks use the Trinity River woodlands as a vector when migrating south. Over the past eight years, the Smith Point fall hawk surveys have annually averaged 2,981 Sharp-shinned Hawks, with a high count of 4,780 in 1997. Many fall days produce in excess of 100 individuals, with most briskly passing westward in ones and twos during the hours just after dawn. During the last week of Sep, average daily counts have approached 140 birds per day. The highest daily count was 616 on 15 Oct 2002, corresponding to a second but usually smaller daily peak 12–15 Oct. Most of the accipiters migrating through Smith Point are immatures.

Spring migration is understated compared to fall. Small flocks of 10 to 15 birds are occasionally seen kettling—that is, rising in tall spirals as they are lifted by the morning's thermals, then peeling off and gliding slowly downward to catch the next thermal. The Sharp-shinned Hawk is a low-density breeder in the Pineywoods, with nesting pairs discovered in recent years in San Augustine and Jasper cos. (Hawk Migration Association). Some of the early fall records may represent birds wandering to the UTC from nearby breeding sites rather than long-distance migrants. The species is widely distributed throughout the UTC during winter. The peak count on the Freeport CBC is only 14 individuals (1988, 1990, and 1991). Residential yards with bird feeders often host a Sharp-shinned or two. This hawk is frequently seen working trees and shrubs bordering open fields, where birds such as the omnipresent Savannah Sparrow are common.

COOPER'S HAWK
Accipiter cooperii

Uncommon winter terminal migrant, common bi-seasonal transient migrant

WINTER: (26, 28 Jul; 4, 7, 13 Aug) **late Aug to late May** (31 May; 5, 16 Jun)

HABITAT: Hedgerows, fallow fields and second growth, residential areas.

DISCUSSION: Cooper's Hawks are more likely to be seen in open country than raiding a neighbor's goldfinch feeder or chicken coop. Frequently, they slice across hedgerows and skim along bar ditches while patrolling for unsuspecting avian prey. These

hawks appear to be as common along the coast as inland in winter, although migrants are more obvious along the immediate coastline. Although less common than the Sharp-shinned Hawk, Cooper's Hawks appear in significant numbers during migration. During the eight years up to 2004, counters reported an annual average of 1,122 Cooper's Hawks at Smith Point, with a maximum of 1,281 in 2001. The highest single-day count was 167 seen on 13 Oct 1998. Daily totals exhibited a distinctly bimodal pattern with peaks occurring during the last week of Aug and in mid-Oct, presumably corresponding to adults and young birds.

Cooper's Hawks were considered by Strecker (1912) to be "resident, breeding locally, principally in the northern and northeastern sections" of Texas. Nehrling (1882) reported the hawk nesting around Houston, and "nests found in April had already half-grown young." Nests found by Nehrling "were similar to crow's nests, built of twigs in the tops of middle-sized trees, and lined with bunches of *Tillandsia*" (Spanish moss). Harassment, loss of habitat, and the widespread use of DDT prompted this hawk's decline in Texas during the first half of the twentieth century. In recent years the bird has experienced a resurgence in Texas, nesting in Waco, San Antonio, and Brackettville. We are aware of no present-day nesting records for the UTC, but an 18 Jun 1988 sighting in WAR may have been a bird nesting locally, as may two birds seen at Humble (HAS) on 7 Aug 2004.

NORTHERN GOSHAWK
Accipiter gentilis

Accidental
12 Jan 1973 Sheldon Reservoir, HAS (TBRC 1989-31) (AB 27:638; Oberholser 1974)

HABITAT: Lowland coniferous forests at high latitudes, mountain coniferous forests at low latitudes; more widespread during migration.

DISCUSSION: The UTC is so far south and east of the lowland range of this large accipiter that a sighting here would almost certainly be a once-in-a-lifetime experience. Such a bird might conceivably show up in extensive pines in the Houston area, forested tracts north of Interstate 10, or at a favorable raptor migration site such as Smith Point. Our one sighting is from Sheldon Reservoir, situated near the southern edge of the Pineywoods.

HARRIS'S HAWK
Parabuteo unicinctus

Rare winter visitor

WINTER: (4–5 Aug; 17, 23 Sep; 2 Oct) **early Oct to mid-Mar** (4 May; 8 Jun)

HABITAT: Harris's Hawk is widely distributed from the savannas, brushland, and cactus deserts of S Texas and Arizona southward to central Argentina and Chile (A.O.U. 1983). Locally, it occurs inland and coastally on agricultural land with fallow fields or low shrubby growth. Scattered trees, fence posts, or telephone poles serve as roosting and hunting perches.

DISCUSSION: Harris's Hawk is a bird of tropical brushlands; its range in the United States is mainly limited to S Texas, New Mexico, and Arizona. It is common in S Texas brush country, normally ranging no closer to the UTC than the central coast, where it breeds in Goliad Co. (Elwonger 1995). However, in the 1990s Harris's Hawk began a northward expansion, and it has become increasingly regular in our area during the winter months. For example, during the 1993–94 CBC season, four UTC counts (Cypress Creek, Houston, San Bernard NWR, and Freeport) yielded a total of five individuals, and to the W, the Attwater CBC logged three more. In Dec 1994, there were at least four birds on the UTC and again others in counties to our west.

Although most Harris's Hawks retreat from the UTC in summer, we recognize an 8 Jun 1989 sighting; an immature photographed at Hermann Park in Houston 4–5 Aug (but possibly present as early as Jun 2004); and an adult photographed at the same location in Nov 2004 (W. Nicholas and S. Prasad). The latter two birds were seen patrolling the cages at the nearby Houston Zoo. Should this northward expansion continue, or should summer birding become more popular, we anticipate increased sightings in our region.

RED-SHOULDERED HAWK
Buteo lineatus

Common resident

HABITAT: Riparian woodlands, pine and mixed pine-oak forests, agricultural land with fallow fields and scattered trees.

DISCUSSION: Although the UTC is blessed with a rich assortment of raptors, casual observers will likely encounter only two of the region's eight recorded buteos. While the Red-tailed Hawk is the common buteo of the grasslands, Red-shouldered Hawk is a forest dweller. It is common in the pine forests of the E UTC as well as in the bottomland forests bordering our major rivers, streams, and bayous, where it shares the forests with species such as Wood Duck, Pileated Woodpecker, and Yellow-throated Vireo.

Red-shouldered Hawks exploit a large prey base, eating snakes, lizards, amphibians, insects, crawfish, rodents, and small birds (and occasionally larger birds: Eubanks saw a Red-shouldered take a Common Moorhen at Brazos Bend SP one evening). Conspicuous raptors, they are not averse to hunting from trees or telephone lines along busy roads, especially those that pass close to remnant stands of bottomland forest. This species is exceptionally vocal and presents a tempting target for harassment by Blue Jays, which have an alarm call remarkably similar to that of the Red-shouldered Hawk, perhaps to draw it away from the jay's nest. Undoubtedly, nestling Blue Jays are a frequent addition to the Red-shouldered's diet. Nest building for this hawk begins in late Dec. Nests may be located 20–60 feet above ground; those we have seen were at the lower end of that range and constructed in the spreading branches of large oaks.

Young Red-shouldereds wander widely, and during winter it is not uncommon to see birds-of-the-year well away for their woodland haunts. The species is infrequently observed in N Mexico, and on the upper Texas coast, near the southern boundary of its range, we experience only a minor fall movement. The Smith Point Hawk Watch averaged 48 per year for the eight years through 2004, with a peak of 87 in 2004; no doubt many of these were local residents and wintering birds. The Freeport CBC averages 78 birds per year, with a peak of 280 in 1984.

BROAD-WINGED HAWK
Buteo platypterus

Rare nester, abundant bi-seasonal transient migrant

SUMMER: (5, 8, 15 × 3 Mar) **late Mar to early Nov** (18, 23, 30 Nov; 15, 17 Dec)

HABITAT: Virtually throughout the UTC during migration, except conspicuously less common immediately along the coast (Galveston Is. and Bolivar Flats); migrant flocks roost in urban woodlots, community parks, residential neighborhoods, coastal mottes, pine and pine-oak forests, and bottomland forests; nesting probable in pine forests of eastern UTC (CHA, JEF).

DISCUSSION: Although infrequently observed, the Broad-winged Hawk is a reasonably common breeding bird of the Pineywoods. Nehrling (1882) remarked that around Houston the bird bred "in the high trees near the rivers and creeks." Historic breeding records include nests near Dickinson (7 Apr 1939, 5 Apr 1940) and Pearland (15–23 Apr 1940, 20 Mar 1941). In recent years John Whittle and others found it summering in our eastern counties. Therefore we suspect that Broad-winged Hawk continues to nest, albeit in low numbers, throughout the pine forests of the E third of our region.

Rare in summer, Broad-winged Hawks reach their zenith in our region during fall migration. A few migrants appear in early to mid-Aug; an adult seen 14 Jul 2000 at High Island is the earliest known migrant (or perhaps just a wanderer). The mass of fall birds passes with the first frontal systems; sizable kettles are usually seen in late Sep. The highest single-day Smith Point counts were approximately 50,000 on 23 Sep 1994 and 25 Sep 2001. The Smith Point Hawk Watch averaged 40,930 per yr over eight years, with a high seasonal total of 103,603 in 2001.

As they approach Smith Point and Trinity Bay from the NE, migrating Broad-wings either cross the bay via the peninsula or move westward along the bay's north shore. Sometimes the extreme altitude of passing birds hampers afternoon observations at Smith Point. However, weather radar monitored by Frank Peace has helped the Smith Point observers confirm both the flight paths and magnitude of these movements. Even more interesting, Peace has recorded large numbers of Broad-wings passing over the region at altitudes too high for the birds to be detected by ground observers. Kettles of migrants often settle into neighborhoods and parks such as Memorial Park in Houston to roost for the evening, and the morning's kettles forming on the first thermals can be breathtaking.

Jim Stevenson witnessed a tragic example of fall Broad-wing migration gone awry. During Sep 2002,

Hurricane Isadore swept through the Gulf of Mexico with sustained winds of 125 mph. As the storm made landfall in W Louisiana, its counterclockwise NE winds encouraged numbers of migrating Broadwings toward Galveston Bay. Normally, Broad-winged Hawks fly to the peninsula at Smith Point then catch a thermal and travel westward across Galveston Bay to the Texas City vicinity. Due to an unfortunate shift in wind direction, many hawks were blown southward across the bay to Galveston Is., not part of their normal migration route. Despite the narrow gap of water, these hawks spent the next several days traveling from one end of the island to the other, searching for a coastline that would provide thermals they could follow to the southwest. Unfortunately, the birds were unwilling to fly into the persistent north wind to make an over-water crossing back to the mainland. Eventually, on 27 and 28 Sep, the Broadwings, mostly juvenile birds, departed southward over the Gulf. Once over water, the birds met not buoying thermals but calm air followed by south winds that drained the birds of any energy reserves they needed to stay aloft. On the morning of 29 Sep, small groups of them began washing up on the beach, talons locked to each other as if each bird tried to ride a fallen comrade before it too succumbed.

Spring migration is often diffuse. Broad-wings are generally scattered across the region, and SE trade winds propel them more successfully over open water crossings. Migrants may linger late into the spring (2 Jun 1999 at Lake Jackson and 10 Jun 1989 near Port Bolivar), their presence overlapping that of the local breeders.

Both Strecker and Nehrling considered Broad-winged Hawk to be a winter resident. Strecker (1912) reported the bird as a "winter resident from the northern border south to the Rio Grande," and Nehrling (1882) stated he found the bird "not uncommon during the winter months" around Houston. Oberholser, however, details only one winter specimen from Texas (12 Dec 1959, San Patricio Co.), and we give credence to only two historic winter records from our region (12 Jan 1962, Sheldon Reservoir, and 6 Feb 1998, Port Bolivar). Broad-winged Hawks may linger late into fall (30 Nov 1986), yet we warn observers that immature Red-shouldereds may closely resemble young Broad-wings (the age class that often delays its southward migration). However, adults seen 15 Dec 2004 during the Galveston CBC and 17 Dec 2004 during the San Bernard NWR CBC (photographed) suggest that count participants need to keep an open mind to the possibility of wintering Broad-wings of any age.

SWAINSON'S HAWK
Buteo swainsoni

Uncommon summer terminal migrant, fairly common bi-seasonal transient migrant

SUMMER: (9, 14, 24–25 Mar) **early Apr to mid-Nov** (26, 29 Nov; 13 Dec)

HABITAT: Prairie and agricultural land.

DISCUSSION: Nehrling (1882) judged Swainson's Hawk as reasonably common during the breeding season, often seen "on the prairies near the woods." As the prairies have been plowed, paved, and invaded by Chinese tallow, Swainson's Hawk has struggled to maintain a breeding presence in our region. Its tenacity is evidenced by one pair that bred for several years in a small sliver of woods at the corner of Kirby and North Braeswood in Houston. When an apartment construction project destroyed the habitat during the nesting season, it appeared that the birds would abandon the area. Happily, they returned the next year to trees across the street, where they nested successfully. Swainson's Hawks have been seen in summer along Interstate 10 (CHA), Interstate 45 between Houston and Galveston (with a nest found recently near Tiki Island), along Texas Highway 288 from Freeport to Houston (BRA), in Freeport, and on the Katy Prairie. During spring 1994, G. D. Yavonovitch and P. Gottschling located six presumed breeding pairs (1 in HAS, 5 in CHA). The expansion seems to be continuing; many birds now breed in BRA.

Swainson's Hawk is an uncommon migrant along the coast, with an average of only 291 seen annually at Smith Point. A peak fall count of 1,036 in 2004 was exceptional. Typically, large flocks are observed farther inland. There, migrating Swainson's Hawks often spend the evening roosting in bare fields, usually settling during the late afternoon. While on the ground, the birds are easily observed, and their light, dark, and immature plumages (held through their first northbound migration) may be studied at leisure.

Nearly all Swainson's Hawks winter in South America. Nevertheless, there are documented winter records in North America. We recognize five from the

UTC: 15–28 Dec 1998 and 22 Jan 1998–7 Feb 1999 (BRA), 31 Dec 1987–29 Feb 1988 (TBRC 1989-55), 2 Feb 1992 (FOB), and an immature photographed by J. Stevenson on 13 Dec 2004 at Anahuac NWR (CHA).

A cautionary note: Dark-morph immature Swainson's Hawks are *easily* confused with immature White-tailed Hawks. The latter's confusing array of dark immature plumages is not dealt with in most field guides, and only infrequently have the two been compared in submitted documentation. Additionally, the flight profile of the White-tailed is very similar to Swainson's. All winter Swainson's Hawk records, and especially immature dark morph records, should be subjected to intense scrutiny.

WHITE-TAILED HAWK
Buteo albicaudatus

Uncommon and local resident

HABITAT: Open country with scattered clumps of trees, or thickets of McCartney rose or huisache; very uncommon along the coast.

DISCUSSION: White-tailed Hawk, like Harris's Hawk, is a raptor of the tropical lowlands. In the United States it is regularly found only in South Texas, where until recently ornithologists believed that its range extended no farther north than the Nueces River. Nehrling, Singley, and Simmons (1892, 1893, 1914) fail to mention the bird from the UTC. Strecker (1912) said it resided "in the Rio Grande Valley" and could be found as far north as Bee and Refugio cos. Kincaid (in Oberholser 1974) notes that "the first habitat" suitable for White-tailed Hawks "can be seen near State Highway 35 in Aransas and Refugio counties." Yet far from being restricted to the brush country of the Rio Grande Valley or the savannas of S Mexico, White-tailed Hawks are becoming increasingly common in the coastal grasslands of the UTC and appear to be spreading eastward. For example, Eubanks observed an immature over High Island in Dec 1993, John Whittle reported an adult circling near High Island on 7 Jan 1995, hawk watchers reported a record 23 from Smith Point in fall 2003, and the species occurred in W Louisiana in early 1997. Locally, nesting has generally been limited to the W and S UTC. For example, nine nests were discovered near Kemah (GAL) in 1941, and the species continues to breed along Galveston Bay (Chocolate Bayou), and in

BRA, FOB, HAS, and WAR. More recently, observers have noted this species at High Island and near Rollover Pass, possibly in response to better field guide coverage of its various and rather different plumages. Despite habitat modifications and efforts to eliminate their hunting perches, several pairs are still resident on and around the Attwater Prairie-Chicken NWR.

Young birds wander widely in winter and are frequently observed hunting alongside Red-tailed Hawks, Northern Harriers, and even Bald Eagles. Prairie burns may attract significant gatherings. For example, J. Morgan reported that a prairie fire within Attwater Prairie-Chicken NWR 5 Feb 1984 eventually attracted 18 White-tailed Hawks. These hawks (as well as numerous Red-tailed Hawks and American Kestrels) preyed upon large insects, particularly grasshoppers fleeing the blaze (SB vol. 33, no. 3). Recent burns were also responsible for a national CBC record 62 White-tailed Hawks on 20 Dec 1996 at San Bernard NWR.

ZONE-TAILED HAWK
Buteo albonotatus

Accidental winter visitor
29 Dec 2003 Houston Heights, HAS (P. D. Hulce)

HABITAT: This southwestern species is a resident of Texas canyons from the Trans-Pecos east to the Hill County and occurs sparingly in the Lower Rio Grande Valley.

DISCUSSION: The only UTC record is an immature spotted 29 Dec 2003 over Houston Heights, HAS. Many would consider this record long overdue, given the species' eastward winter dispersal. On several occasions individuals had been seen just west and north of the UTC. The Attwater Prairie-Chicken NWR CBC in COL and Austin cos. has recorded the species on five of the last nine counts. An adult Zone-tail present at Huntsville SP, Walker Co. (just north of the UTC) 16 Feb 2002 was relocated there the following winter.

RED-TAILED HAWK
Buteo jamaicensis

Uncommon resident, abundant winter terminal migrant

HABITAT: Agricultural land, with utility poles or scattered trees from which to hunt; also lightly urbanized areas where undeveloped land, railroad lines, or power line rights of way serve as foraging areas.

DISCUSSION: Red-tailed Hawk diversity in North America is displayed nowhere more vividly or boldly than on the Katy Prairie of W HAS and WAR, as noted by E. O. Wilson in *The Diversity of Life* (1992). Hawks with a nesting range of hundreds of thousands (millions?) of square miles converge locally to winter in the rodent-rich grasslands W of Houston. Red-tailed Hawk is the region's most common wintering large raptor, abundantly distributed throughout the UTC, and the Katy Prairie is unmatched in its appeal to the broadest spectrum of forms and races. To begin with, the sheer numbers of Red-tails wintering on the Katy Prairie may be staggering (the numbers do tend to fluctuate from year to year). The Cypress Creek CBC, centered in the heart of the Katy Prairie, reported 509 Red-tailed Hawks on 1 Jan 1990, the highest count in the nation that year. Even a relaxed day of birding could easily yield 60 to 100 individuals.

Five general types of Red-tails may be encountered locally, each with dark (melanistic) and pale morphs. Additionally, immature plumages and the odd leucistic or albino bird make the UTC an extraordinary, if not challenging, area to study the species. Besides the typical and numerically dominant eastern form, various western birds occur. These vary from being subtly darker on the underwing and belly to having a strong rufous wash below to being nearly black. Their tails may vary from rosy to deep chestnut. Additionally, three named races are occasionally encountered. The commonest of these is the pale-bellied and rather dark-backed "Fuertes'" Red-tail of the American Southwest. "Krider's" Red-tailed Hawk, a breeder of the northern Great Plains, is one of our rarest wintering raptors, with few occurrences per year. Most of these individuals exhibit a white head, nearly all white tail, and much white in the mantle and wings. However, a few are so ghostly pale that the usually distinctive dark patagial band on the leading edge of the wing may be absent, and identification must be based upon mantle, primary, and tail patterning. Also rare here is the "Harlan's" Hawk (formerly recognized as a separate species) of northern British Columbia and Alaska. Great care must be exercised in separating this black-plumaged race from other very dark western individuals; the fact that

Harlan's Hawks may exhibit three different tail patterns does not help matters. Many of our winter Red-tails are philopatric—that is, they return over and over again to the same wintering sites. Perhaps the most noteworthy example was a Harlan's Hawk that was present for 15 consecutive winters (J. Morgan and Eubanks photos document its distinctive breast markings) on power transmission towers north of Clay Road near Katy, HAS.

Migrant Red-tailed Hawks appear with the first frontal systems of fall and remain in the region into Apr. Fall migration extends well into late Dec and early Jan, and kettles of migrants are often seen during area CBCs. The Smith Point daily high count is 109 on 6 Nov 1997 (the count is typically terminated on 15 Nov). Although occasional along the Bolivar Peninsula and Galveston Is., migrating Red-tails are far less common along the coast than inland and occur less frequently than many of the other coastally migrating raptors. From 1997 to 2004, an average of only 148 per year passed the Smith Point Hawk Watch, with a peak of 331 in 1997. Small numbers of Red-tails remain in the region to breed. Most of the summering birds are found well inland along riparian corridors or in the dwindling woodlands that have so far evaded the developer's bulldozer. They are often seen perched on the tall transmission pylons of power lines crisscrossing the area.

FERRUGINOUS HAWK
Buteo regalis

Rare terminal winter migrant

WINTER: (27 Sep; 5, 13 Oct) **mid-Nov to late Apr** (20 Apr; 5 May)

HABITAT: Usually roosts on fence posts or telephone poles at margins of open fields; recorded most frequently in the open rangelands of the Katy Prairie (where annual); also rare in coastal grassland near the Gulf.

DISCUSSION: The range of this western hawk barely skirts our region, and only on the Katy Prairie is it regular in winter. Although it has been reported close to the coast (i.e., BRA, Galveston Is., Anahuac NWR, and Smith Point), it rarely wanders south or east of Houston. For example, hawk watchers at Smith Point reported only eight between 1997 and 2004, including our rather early 5 Oct 2003 record. As with many of our wintering raptors, Ferruginous Hawk exhibits considerable site fidelity. For example, one adult wintered for over a decade in the same field in WAR, and for several years a dark-morph Ferruginous returned to Colorado Co. near the Attwater Prairie-Chicken NWR. Ferruginous Hawks have been reported from six of 48 Freeport CBCs but none since 1979. Considering the extreme variability of Red-tailed Hawks in our region, it comes as no surprise that local observers at times may struggle with distinguishing this species.

ROUGH-LEGGED HAWK
Buteo lagopus

Very rare winter terminal migrant

WINTER: (16, 22, 26 Oct; 8 Nov) **mid-Nov to early Apr** (1, 19 Apr)

HABITAT: Open fields, exceptionally at urban edge, most sightings in the more inland portions of the UTC.

DISCUSSION: This arctic hawk, our northernmost buteo, strays only casually as far south as the UTC. Normally it ranges no farther S in Central Texas than the zone from Austin east to College Station. Confusion with similar hawks (immature White-tailed, dark western Red-tailed), plus a general lack of local experience with the species has resulted in Rough-legs being consistently misidentified (and therefore overreported) on the UTC and elsewhere in coastal Texas. We have reviewed out-of-season reports from within known nesting territories of White-tailed Hawks (the blackish subadult stages of which are not illustrated in most field guides and roughly resemble the Rough-legged Hawk). We have reviewed "documented" Rough-legged Hawks for which descriptions nicely matched the various races of Red-tailed Hawk (many of these identifications have relied upon only one or two characteristics, often ones shared by these other buteos). We have reviewed descriptions of Rough-legged Hawks that, despite being published month after month in local newsletters, did not preclude the more common species of hawks. We are not being glib; just candid. In our opinion, the Rough-legged Hawk appears along the UTC an average of a few times per decade, and we would expect those appearances to coincide with major invasion years to our north. In addition, Rough-legs, like many wintering raptors, exhibit strong site fidelity and therefore (with the exception of Smith Point Hawk Watch flybys) should be seen repeatedly throughout a season and should be relatively simple to document.

Especially vexing are fall migration hawk watch sightings from the upper coast and the Coastal Bend region to our south. Several factors argue strongly against a correctly identified Rough-legged Hawk in east or southeast Texas. First, wintering Rough-legs do not occur in the northeastern Mexican states of Tamaulipas or Nuevo León, or to their south; the closest records are from western Coahuila, just east of Big Bend (Brewster Co.). Second, these alleged sightings of fall migrant Rough-legs are made weeks before this species moves into the central tier of states and usually before the birds have been recorded in the northernmost states. Last, a number of East Texas reports have been of the extremely rare dark morph of the species, which is readily confused with the much more common dark-morph western Red-tails that visit us or with juvenile White-tailed Hawks. For a Rough-leg to be seen in Texas, it could reasonably be assumed that there are already hundreds to thousands of these birds in the states to our north, with a flood of records in the Texas Panhandle, where they winter (A.O.U. 1998). Thus there is neither historical nor biological explanation for a Rough-leg to be heading down the Gulf Slope during Sep and early Oct.

All caveats and apprehensions aside, we do recognize a number of records of this boreal species from within our region. Accepted records exist for a number of locations, including Brazoria NWR, CHA, W Galveston Is., Bolivar Peninsula, the Katy Prairie, and the Attwater Prairie-Chicken NWR. Beginning in 1976, a Rough-legged Hawk wintered for several years in W Houston near Westheimer and Wilcrest (the bird frequented a remnant piece of prairie that has long since been developed). Greg Lasley's photograph of this species five miles southwest of Sea Rim SP (JEF) 15 Jan 1979 (TPRF 151) probably represents the only documentation for the UTC.

GOLDEN EAGLE
Aquila chrysaetos

Rare winter terminal migrant

WINTER: (10, 19–21 Oct) **late Oct to early Feb** (2, 10 Feb)

HABITAT: Prairie and agricultural land, usually near the coast.

DISCUSSION: The heart of the Golden Eagle's Texas range is distant from the UTC. They breed in our state within two distinct regions—the Texas Panhandle and the Trans-Pecos. In late fall, Golden Eagles occasionally drift toward the UTC. Migrants push slowly south through the Texas Panhandle, young birds deviate east, and every year or two a Golden Eagle materializes within our region. Recent reports include birds at Anahuac NWR, Attwater Prairie-Chicken NWR, Bolivar Peninsula, the Katy Prairie, Brazoria NWR, FOB, and High Island. Often they appear in the general vicinity of flocks of geese and may be seen relatively close to the coast. However, most recent reports are from the inland prairies in W HAS, FOB, and WAR. The exception to this would be birds moving by Smith Point as they head for their wintering areas; five were seen during the hawk watch between 1997 and 2004. We caution observers to take into account the similarity between young Golden and Bald eagles. Immature Bald Eagles are relatively common on the UTC, and their variability leads many observers astray.

CRESTED CARACARA
Caracara cheriway

Uncommon resident, rare transient migrant

HABITAT: Open country with tall brush or scattered trees, often on plowed or recently burned fields, or on roadsides; avoids urbanized areas.

DISCUSSION: Like White-tailed and Harris's hawks, the Crested Caracara is a raptor of tropical scrub and grasslands. This falcon ranges north into the United States only in Florida (with an isolated relict population) and from Louisiana (rarely) and Texas to Arizona. Texas supports the country's largest population, and in recent decades the species has appreciably expanded its range since Arlie McKay first found it nesting at Cove in April 1936.

Along the UTC, caracaras are relatively common within the grasslands of the western cos. (e.g., 46 on the 1986 Attwater CBC just west of the UTC), but they become scarce toward the coast. In recent years, however, caracaras have been regularly reported from High Island, the Bolivar Peninsula, Smith Point, and on Galveston Is., and they may nest at or near all of these sites. The Freeport CBC totals nicely reflect the species' steady UTC increase; totals climbed from four in the 1960s and six in the 1970s to 34 in the 1980s, 82 in the 1990s, and 113 from 2000 to 2003.

Locally, caracaras inhabit grazing land, harvested or fallow rice fields, and mesquite savanna. Nests are usually placed within a prominent tree bordered by grassland, and eggs are laid from early Feb through Apr. Power transmission pylons, telephone poles, and fence posts are favored perches, although the birds are often seen standing on the ground, occasionally in groups, foraging in recently burned or plowed fields. Caracaras take live vertebrate and insect prey, and they relish breaking apart cow pies to get at the dung beetles inside. Stevenson notes that Galveston birds exhibit a fondness for rats and are not likely to be seen scavenging. Elsewhere (and more typically), they are aggressive scavengers. In order to compete with crows, they must be out at or before first light and are often patrolling the roads for carcasses long before the vultures have stirred from their roosts. In flight, the Caracara's shape suggests a raven's, but the bright white patches at all four extremities should eliminate confusion with any corvid or similar-sized bird of prey.

AMERICAN KESTREL
Falco sparverius

Common winter terminal migrant

WINTER: (13, 15 × 2, 16 Aug) **late Aug to late Apr** (22–24 Apr)

HABITAT: Farmland, prairie, railroad and power line rights of way, residential areas; frequently seen gliding among skyscrapers in the center of downtown Houston.

DISCUSSION: In the dead of winter, the "Sparrow Hawk" radiates across our region to occupy virtually every fragment of suitable habitat. While present, these falcons seem to be everywhere, hovering over grasslands, stooping from telephone poles, gliding upon the updrafts between tall buildings, and even snatching goldfinches from backyard bird feeders. The Freeport CBC records an average of 166 annually, with a peak of 383 in 1984. Telephone wires stretched along open fallow fields, rice stubble, and rangelands are perhaps *the* preferred perch from which kestrels compete with Loggerhead Shrikes for insects and small vertebrates.

Although a few early migrants are seen in mid-late Aug, the first frontal systems of fall bring wave after wave of kestrels from the north. Between 1997 and 2004, surveyors at Smith Point reported an average of 1,382 kestrels per season, with a high of 1,947 in 2002. The majority of the birds that passed the platform were females; for example, in 2003 there were 2.2 females per male, with 25 percent of the flybys unsexed (GCBO data). In spring most birds depart by mid-Apr; only a very few linger any later.

This species nests in East Texas in open pine or pine-hardwood stands as far south as that habitat currently extends (generally, Jasper and Newton cos.). Additionally, nesting has been recorded north of Houston in Spring Creek Park (Montgomery Co.) and near Huntsville SP (Walker Co.). According to Cliff Shackelford, kestrels prefer open pine forests that are being managed for Red-cockaded Woodpeckers. Our nesting kestrels represent the "Southeastern" American Kestrel of the subspecies *paulus*. Males of *paulus* are smaller, have very few ventral spots (compared to the migratory subspecies), and can usually be identified in the field. We recognize one summer record from the UTC proper: 20 Jun 1943 at Sheldon Reservoir (not surprisingly, ths was also one of the last areas on the UTC that supported Red-cockaded Woodpeckers).

MERLIN
Falco columbarius

Uncommon bi-seasonal transient migrant, rare winter terminal migrant

WINTER: (11, 21, 23, 25 Aug) **early Sep to late Apr** (2, 5, 9, 15 May)

HABITAT: Coastally at mudflats and wetlands, elsewhere at flooded fields, fallow fields, and pastures; occasionally in residential areas.

DISCUSSION: The Merlin is the most secretive of our falcons, and it is the fortunate observer who is rewarded with prolonged views. The birds occur both inland and coastally and are attracted to concentrations of shorebirds or areas where sparrows and other small birds are abundant. They often expose themselves by perching atop driftwood or small clumps of seaweed along our beaches—what better way to search for a shorebird?—and that is perhaps where they are most likely to be observed.

Merlins appear with the fall raptor push. Usually the earliest birds arrive by the first week of Sep, but a male was present 11 Aug 2004 in Houston's Memorial Park after a freakishly early cold front. During their migration to Mexico and Central and South America, they occasionally linger at coastal flats and work isolated mottes where migrant passerine prey concentrates. Occasionally birds are noted in residential neighborhoods. As might be expected, counts of a falcon that preys on vertebrates ought to be lower than numbers of another that eats abundant insect prey. Not surprisingly, the 1997–2004 Merlin average at Smith Point, 61 per year with a high of 88 in 1997, is only about 4 percent of the average for American Kestrels. Merlins become difficult to find after Mar, but there are a few records of lingering birds as late as mid-May. Small numbers of Merlins winter along the UTC; most hug the immediate coast (including the historical district in Galveston). However, during recent winters, Bear Creek Park (HAS) west of Houston has hosted as many as nine individuals—a surprising concentration. The Freeport CBC averages only two birds per year, with a peak of nine in 2000.

APLOMADO FALCON
Falco femoralis

Rare visitor from nearby reintroduced populations

HABITAT: Native to a remarkable array of habitats, including the yucca grasslands of the American Southwest, dry and seasonally flooded savannas of the tropical lowlands, and the terraced slopes of the high Andes; ranges south to Tierra del Fuego.

DISCUSSION: Once common in the southwestern United States, this falcon has declined for reasons not well understood. It occurred at least as far north as Austin County, documented with a Dec 1900 specimen. Aplomado Falcons were recently reintroduced in the coastal savannas and grasslands of the southern coast of Texas (115 young birds at seven locations by the end of 1999 and most recently in the Trans-Pecos). These reintroductions have created controversy, as the presence of additional birds may have an as yet unknown effect on the few West Texas and New Mexico birds believed to be outliers from the native Mexican population. Considering that some of these birds have been hacked (released) as close as Matagorda Is. (Matagorda Co.), immediately to the

south, it is not surprising that they have strayed northward to the UTC. Recent sightings include one 23 Mar 1997 and two 17 Dec 1999–22 Jan 2000 at San Bernard NWR (BRA), one 7 July 2000 at McFaddin NWR (JEF), and one 4 Dec 2003 on Follett's Is. (GAL).

PEREGRINE FALCON
Falco peregrinus

Rare winter terminal migrant, uncommon bi-seasonal transient migrant

WINTER: (26, 30–31 Jul; 5 Aug) **late Aug to late Apr** (31 May; 1, 5 Jun)

HABITAT: Beaches, mudflats, reservoirs, rice paddies and other wetlands, also prairie, both coastally and inland; may roost and hunt in urban areas (has wintered around buildings in downtown Houston and Galveston and on power poles and water towers along Bolivar Peninsula).

DISCUSSION: The approach of a Peregrine Falcon is often signaled by clouds of shorebirds or waterfowl cartwheeling across the sky to flee the most feared avian predator that visits the UTC. South Texas hosts the largest migrant concentrations of Arctic Peregrines (*F. p. tundrius*), particularly on the expansive sand flats of the Laguna Madre, and numbers of these birds spill through the UTC. Peregrines are the first of their genus to arrive in the fall, with scattered appearances along the immediate coast beginning in late Jul. The bulk of their movement coincides with the first fall frontal systems from late Sep through early Nov. Peregrines may be seen wherever ducks and sandpipers congregate (Anahuac NWR, Bolivar Flats, East Beach, San Luis Pass flats, Brazoria and San Bernard NWRs).

Hawk watchers on Smith Point averaged 89 Peregrines per year between 1997 and 2004, with a high count of 129 in 2004; the highest daily count was an impressive 22 seen on 9 Oct 1994. A few Peregrines remain to winter along the UTC, where most are seen near the immediate coast. The Freeport CBC has averaged four per year during the last 10 years or so, with a peak count of eight in 2003. A few winter in downtown Houston and Galveston, where they swoop down from office buildings and take unsuspecting Rock Pigeons. The last birds depart by late Apr or early May, but a few have lingered through May. Mid-summer records are one stooping on Black-necked

Stilts at Sea Center Texas in Lake Jackson on 26 Jun 1999; one in Galveston on 2 Jul 1933; and one in Cove 15 Jul 1940 (A. McKay). In 1970 the USFWS listed the Arctic Peregrine Falcon as endangered, due to its pesticide-induced decline. With the 1972 banning of organochlorides such as DDT, the protection of nest sites from depredation, and the prohibition of the taking of Peregrines for the sport of falconry, this falcon begin a swift and steady recovery. TPWD considers the American Peregrine Falcon as endangered (TPWD 2004a). In 1984 the USFWS reclassified the Peregrine as threatened due to its improved status, and in 1994 the Peregrine Falcon was removed from the federal endangered species list.

PRAIRIE FALCON
Falco mexicanus

Very rare winter terminal migrant or visitor

WINTER: (28 Sep; 12–13 Oct) **mid-Oct to late Apr** (25, 27, 29 Apr)

HABITAT: Locally on open farmland and prairie with scattered trees or utility poles from which the birds hunt; few coastal records.

DISCUSSION: Prairie Falcon, the large falcon of the western grasslands, is generally restricted to the canyons and cliffs of W Texas. Strecker (1912) believed it to be "resident along the edge of the plains in the Panhandle, on the southern plains, and in the Trans-Pecos region." Although the bird apparently no longer nests in the Panhandle (it formerly did so at Palo Duro Canyon), small numbers continue to breed in the Davis and Chisos mountains. Migrants range through the Panhandle south into the brush country, where hawk watchers at Hazel Bazemore Co. Park in Corpus Christi report one or two every fall. Incredibly, Nehrling (1882) believed the bird to nest around Houston, and he wrote: "This noble bird is resident on the border of woods near prairies." Strecker doubted Nehrling's supposition, and we echo his suspicion. We recognize fewer than 30 records of the species from the past 60 years. Arlie McKay reported the falcon several times from Cove during the 1940s, yet most of the sightings in the past 20 years have been W of Houston. Prairie Falcons were seen repeatedly during the 1980s at Attwater Prairie-Chicken NWR, with the refuge becoming the only reliable spot to see the bird in our region at that time. Most recently Peter Gottschling reported a passing Prairie Falcon near San Leon, 13 Oct 1996 (GAL), and another was seen and photographed by many during its stay on the Katy Prairie (WAR) from 18 Oct 2001 to 7 Feb 2002.

Rails, Gallinules, Coot, and Cranes

What do we know about rails? Along with owls, rails are the most poorly understood and least frequently observed North American birds. Indeed, our two smallest species—Black Rail and Yellow Rail—are consistently on North American birders' lists of most-wanted species. Both occur on the UTC, and Black Rail probably nests locally, but their mere presence does not guarantee an encounter.

Blending in with the reeds and grasses that border ponds, sloughs, and tidal inlets, the UTC's rails mark their presence by sound, not sight. Locally wintering rails call inconsistently, although Virginia calls relatively frequently in response to vocalizing Soras or a hand clap. Tape recordings are a valuable tool both for censusing rails and for coaxing them into the open, but use of recorded calls is discouraged or illegal on our local refuges.

Of the six rails that occur locally, most birders can count on seeing King and Clapper rails and Sora. All are common on the UTC (the first two as breeders), and all are likely to wander into view.

Common Moorhen, Purple Gallinule, and American Coot are another story. All three are large, nest locally, and may be seen during much of the year, often with their youngsters in tow. Only the gaudy Purple Gallinule vacates the UTC, returning each winter to more tropical climes. Coastal refuges such as Anahuac and Brazoria host all nine UTC members of the family Rallidae and are a good place to begin your search.

YELLOW RAIL
Coturnicops noveboracensis

Locally common winter terminal migrant

WINTER: (12, 17 Sep) **late Sep to late Apr**
(1–2 May)

HABITAT: Moist to wet grassy habitats, including coastal prairie and rice cultivation.

DISCUSSION: On the warmest evenings of late spring, a persistent observer may be fortunate enough to hear a Yellow Rail blurt out a few strangled clicks and clatters as a warmup for their performances to come. Yellow Rail, like its close cousin the Black Rail, is the archetypal invisible bird, its presence exposed only when individuals are flushed by the balloon tires of a rice harvester or by a rope tugged across the coastal prairie. For birders, Yellow Rail has long been one of the most sought-after members of the North American avifauna. Until several years ago, Anahuac NWR was *the* site to "get" one, and a birder could stay dry at the same time. Each spring, visitors from around the world rode the "rail buggy," a cart pulled by a tractor rolling on huge low-pressure tires. Buggy riders could see up to several dozen of these diminutive birds as they scurried away from the approaching vehicle.

The buggy is no more (to the great relief of the refuge's nesting Mottled Ducks), but the Yellow Rail still abounds at Anahuac and other coastal refuges, where it is almost certainly the coastal prairie's most common wintering rail. During recent years, most sightings have occurred at Anahuac NWR as birders flushed the rails by dragging a rope across the prairie, all the while swatting mosquitoes and maneuvering over and around uneven ground, hidden water-filled trenches, alligators, and western cottonmouths. According to David Sarkozi, longtime friend of Anahuac NWR, this rail is remarkably common in its proper habitat at the refuge; 29 were banded in the same plot (roughly 1/4 mile square) over one winter with no recaptures. Sarkozi reports that he has personally seen more than a dozen in about two and one half hours of rope dragging. Radio tagging of Yellow Rails by researcher Kelly Mizell indicates that they are territorial in winter, and such high densities indicate an immense Yellow Rail wintering population in the marshes bordering upper Galveston and Trinity bays.

An alternative to plodding through the marshes is to locate a farmer who is harvesting rice in the fall (in any of the UTC cos.) and then stand on the roadside and train binoculars on the area just in front of the machinery. Yellow, Virginia, and King rails and Sora, as well as Le Conte's and Swamp sparrows,

Sedge Wrens, Mottled Ducks and whistling-ducks, bitterns, herons, plenty of meadowlarks, and who knows what else may be seen flushing up from these artificial wetlands. Late harvesting usually takes place from late Sep to early Nov, if conditions are amenable. Numbers of Yellow Rails in rice fields can be prodigious. For example, on 20 Oct 1975, Victor Emanuel reported 31 in a single field in W HAS.

BLACK RAIL
Laterallus jamaicensis

Rare permanent resident, winter status uncertain

HABITAT: Coastally, usually in Gulf cordgrass, also freshwater or saline moist grassy areas; occasionally inland.

DISCUSSION: For many, the very existence of the Black Rail is a matter of repute rather than revelation. Strecker (1912) knew the bird only from the observations of Lloyd, who was aware of it breeding at San Angelo in 1884. Nehrling (1882) reported one taken near Houston 29 Apr 1879. Pope collected a set of six eggs on Bolivar 9 May 1912 (Oberholser 1974). Singley (1893) missed the bird completely during his survey of Galveston Is. Only Simmons (1914) encountered the bird himself. He reported: "On April 21, while beating around in the sedge and tall grass of a tiny marsh about eight miles south of Houston, looking for nests of the Louisiana Clapper Rail, I nearly stepped on a small Rail which I at first took to be an early downy bird of the Clapper variety. However, I soon recognized my mistake and saw that the bird was the rare Black Rail." Truth be told, we know precious little more about this rail's day-to-day livelihood on the UTC today than when field ornithology began in Texas; its foraging and nesting behavior and development of the young are all poorly documented (Kaufman 1996).

Breeding records are clustered in coastal cos. including BRA, GAL, and CHA, where the birds may nest colonially in salt-loving Gulf cordgrass (but perhaps are just concentrated there by the distribution of suitable habitat). The rail's density on the UTC is poorly known, but 10 clutches exposed by a burn and reported 5 June 1969 at Brazoria NWR suggest their true, although possibly sporadic, abundance. During 1983 Eubanks discovered a colony just west of San Luis Pass (BRA); however, these birds seem to have vanished in 1983 in the wake of Hurricane Alicia.

During the 1980s Behrstock participated in perhaps 30 buggy rides at Anahuac NWR, producing a total of no more than six or eight brief sightings of this elusive species. Each year a few lucky observers may see one along coastal roads traversing salt marsh (such as Sportsmen's Road on W Galveston Is.) or scurrying along the edge of the *Spartina* at Bolivar Flats. Typically, Black Rails vocalize in the dead of night during late spring and early summer, yet Eubanks found the birds near San Luis Pass calling throughout the daylight hours. Weeks's experience with spring birds at San Bernard NWR indicates that they are vocal at dawn and dusk (quieting abruptly at sunset). The San Bernard birds are interesting in that they start calling in late Feb and early Mar, only to become quiet or leave the area in Apr. It is quite possible, since these same areas produce birds on the San Bernard CBC, that these rails are visitors, calling on their winter territories before moving to their summer homes. The origins of fall birds such as on 16 Nov 1996 at Anahuac NWR are hard to ascertain; they may be permanent resident UTC birds, returned winter residents, or migrants headed south to winter in Mexican wetlands. It is also possible that UTC breeding birds move southward in winter.

We caution that coastal Northern Mockingbirds are familiar with the Black Rail's distinctive *kicky-DOO* vocalization as well and frequently offer credible imitations. In our experience, occasional observers choose to ignore the many excellent field guide illustrations portraying this tiny, delicately patterned, black-white-and-chestnut bird, settling instead for checking off an all-black downy King or Clapper Rail chick.

CLAPPER RAIL
Rallus longirostris

Locally common resident

HABITAT: Salt marsh at Gulf and bay margins.
DISCUSSION: Seaward edge of coastal wetlands, where it replaces the more familiar and rather similar King Rail. Clappers are sedentary, rarely seen away from smooth cordgrass marsh. Only in brackish marsh, such as along the upper reaches of Galveston Bay, do Kings and Clappers meet. Favorable observation sites for Clappers (and, unfortunately, Clapper-King hybrids) include roads that pass through salt

marsh near Freeport; E and W Galveston Is.; Bolivar Peninsula side roads that run northward toward Galveston Bay; Sea Rim SP; and bay edge at Anahuac NWR. Additionally, birds often venture into the open along margins of cordgrass-covered portions of the Bolivar and San Luis Pass flats, and along W Galveston Bay at Galveston Island SP and Sportsmen's Road. Small concentrations of these birds may be found in these areas, their dusk calling bouts often involving several individuals. The Freeport CBC records an average of 26 with a high of 77 in 1966. Clutches are large (a 10 May Galveston nest contained nine eggs), but gar, raccoons, and large predatory birds such as Great Blue Herons keep the population in check.

Generally, local Clappers exhibit grayer cheeks, more diffuse flank bands, and less chestnut on the breast than do the crisply marked and rather rusty Kings. The centers of the back feathers on both species are dark brown. However, on the Clapper these feathers are fringed in gray, while the King's are bordered with a rich, rusty brown. A proportion of the sightings represents hybrids (although some may be poorly marked youngsters) and must be written off as "Clings."

KING RAIL
Rallus elegans

Common resident, probably a common but cryptic winter terminal migrant

HABITAT: Freshwater or brackish marshes, rice fields, roadside ditches; coastally as well as inland, slightly overlapping but generally replaced by the previous species in tidal salt marsh.
DISCUSSION: Aptly named, the King Rail is big, boisterous, widespread, and not particularly averse to feeding in the open. Aggressive local birders are likely to encounter the species often during the course of a year. Away from intense development, any natural or artificial wetland is likely to harbor breeders. Only in salt marsh is this common species absent, replaced by the similar Clapper. During spring, Kings are often seen skulking through ditches beside quiet farm roads, with strings of downy black chicks awkwardly following their parents in and out of a towering maze of reeds, sedge, or cane. The King's *caak, caak* call is often heard in late evening before sunset, although we confess that we have

difficulty detecting the slight difference between the call of this species and the Clapper—perhaps further evidence of local hybridization.

As agriculture and rains change water use and availability, the distribution of the UTC's nesting King Rail population changes slightly each year. Because of the bird's secretive nature, we have no information on the presumed influx of wintering birds. After nesting, individuals from northern marshes may join our resident birds on the UTC's wetlands. We have nesting records from late Apr and early May with clutches of 8, 9, and 12 eggs. The Freeport CBC averages nine individuals per year, with a high of 49 in 1985.

VIRGINIA RAIL
Rallus limicola

Uncommon winter terminal migrant, rare summer lingerer

WINTER: (26 Aug; 9, 11 Sep) **early Sep to early May** (12, 25 May)

HABITAT: Freshwater marsh, wet prairie, rice fields; coastal and inland.

DISCUSSION: In most years the only indication of the presence of Virginia Rails is during late spring, when the first *kiddik, kiddik* calls begin emanating from the cattail marshes. Most birders see years pass between sightings of this elusive species. This is not necessarily a reflection of their extreme scarcity; rather, they keep a very low profile.

Virginia Rails winter in rice fields, in the reeds bordering irrigation impoundments, and in wet coastal prairie. Locally they appear to be much less common in the most saline coastal environments. The expansive coastal grasslands at Anahuac NWR are particularly suited to this species; a high count of 17 was noted on 12 Nov 1971. Rice harvesters often flush birds during the fall (eight in W HAS 20 Oct 1975). The Freeport CBC averages seven per year with a high of 54 reported in 1981. Perhaps the most interesting UTC record is of a bird that landed on an oil rig 70 miles offshore on 17 Oct 1999 during LSU's Migration Over the Gulf Project (MOGP). Although the species is not known to nest along the UTC, we are aware of two summer reports: 6 Jul 1951 at Smith Point, and 13 Jul–10 Aug 1973 in High Island.

SORA
Porzana carolina

Common winter terminal migrant

WINTER: (10, 13, 25, 29 Jul) **early Aug to early May** (14, 22, 31 May)

HABITAT: Coastally and inland in various wetlands including freshwater marshes, the margins of vegetation-covered ponds, temporary pools, and roadside ditches.

DISCUSSION: The Sora's cascading cackles punctuate spring mornings around our marshes, potholes, and ponds. Unlike our other smaller rails, the Sora is often brazenly exposed as it forages. Gray and plump with a yellowish chicken's beak, Soras tiptoe across pools covered with water hyacinth or water lettuce (such as at Anahuac NWR), inch along the edges of roadside ditches, and snake around rattlebean stalks in coastal pools. Mar–Apr and Oct–Nov have produced the most sightings, probably because of an increase during the migratory period. Our latest spring record of 31 May was from Brazos Bend SP (FOB). In reality, Soras are probably present year-round except in the depths of summer (mid-Jun to early Jul). During fall many migrants pass through the interior rice fields (high count of 117 in W HAS rice fields on 20 Oct 1975). The Freeport CBC reports an average of 11 per year with a high of 69 in 1981.

Two recent mid-Jul records (13 Jul 1996 and 10 Jul 1999) from Anahuac NWR may represent summering birds, but we suspect them to be early fall migrants. Supporting this belief, John Arvin has often observed immature-plumaged birds during Jul in the Lower Grande Valley, with no evidence of local nesting. Soras provide minor sport for Texas hunters; in counties where they may be hunted, the daily bag and possession limit is 25 birds for shotgunners and three per day for falconers.

PURPLE GALLINULE
Porphyrio martinica

Locally common summer terminal migrant, rare winter lingerer

SUMMER: (3, 5, 15, 19 Mar) **early Apr to early Sep** (22 Dec; 8, 18 Jan)

HABITAT: Lakes, ponds, and reservoirs with floating and emergent vegetation.

DISCUSSION: With the exception of the Roseate Spoonbill, no marsh bird on the UTC is as spectacularly adorned as the Purple Gallinule. Its azure head and undersides, chartreuse back, red eye, pale blue forehead, red-and-yellow beak, and banana-yellow legs and feet favor the warblers more than its closest relatives, the dull-colored American Coot and Common Moorhen.

During late spring and summer, this lovely member of the rail family is easily seen on the UTC. Favorable locations include vegetation-covered ponds at Brazos Bend SP and Anahuac NWR. At the latter, a rather late downy chick was noted 18 Sep 2004 (J. Stevenson). The bird's ridiculously long, bright yellow toes distribute its weight, allowing it to walk on the leaves of water lettuce, spatterdock, water lilies, and other aquatic plants, where they forage for seeds and small invertebrates. Unlike the smaller-footed Common Moorhens, or paddle-toed American Coots, Purple Gallinules frequently climb into a willow or a clump of vegetation to feed, a habit aided by their long, slender grasping toes. Tropical in origin, the bulk of the E Texas population migrates south during the winter months; however, we note at least six records of birds that lingered into Dec or Jan. The migration of this gallinule is erratic, almost whimsical, and individuals are likely to appear on a sandy beach or spend an evening high in the shade tree of a suburban yard. A few birds return to the UTC during early to mid-Mar. To ensure sightings, look for them in mid-Apr when they brazenly crisscross the dikes and trails at coastal refuges.

COMMON MOORHEN
Gallinula chloropus

Locally common resident

HABITAT: Freshwater marshes, ponds, lake edge, roadside ditches, artificial impoundments.

DISCUSSION: Along with ratcheting Boat-tailed Grackles and cackling American Coots, the Common Moorhen supplies the cacophonous background music for local marshes and wetlands. The moorhen is capable of emitting a staggering array of atonal squawks and croaks, sounds that, when first heard, are difficult to credit to a bird at all. Of the three locally breeding cootlike species, Common Moorhen is the most cosmopolitan. Unlike its two cousins, it is well distributed in both the New and the Old World. The bird was formerly called Common Gallinule, its current name in North America representing a rare A.O.U. concession to the British (who admit to having moors).

Like a number of other marsh birds, moorhens lay prodigious clutches of eggs, 10–12 being usual but as many as 17 have been recorded (Oberholser 1974). In turn, these young provide nourishment for the area's alligators, bobcats and other mammals, and predatory birds. Multiple broods are raised during the spring and summer, and half-grown young are still present in Oct. During migration, birds from the Midwest pass through our area, some undoubtedly remaining to winter. Moorhens are most common in freshwater marshes near the coast (750 at Anahuac NWR 29 Sep 1984) and relatively rare on the inland ponds and reservoirs W of Houston. The Freeport CBC has averaged 97 per year with a high of 780 in 2001.

AMERICAN COOT
Fulica americana

Common winter terminal migrant, uncommon summer resident

HABITAT: Fresh, brackish, or (rarely) salt water, nesting in most aquatic habitats, including ponds, marshes, artificial impoundments, and bayous.

DISCUSSION: Although the birds are somewhat less common on salt water, no wet spot along our coast is without its compliment of coots. The *poule d'eau* (water chicken or mud hen, generally pronounced "pull-doo"), as it is often called among anglers and duck hunters along the Louisiana border, dominates area ponds, lakes, puddles, marshes, and assorted wetlands during the winter months. Strictly grazers, coots tip, bob, and dive in the water, feeding on aquatic vegetation. Like the moorhen, this large rallid is a permanent local resident, although numbers decline significantly in summer. However, coots are still reasonably easy to find during the breeding season, often accompanied by their outlandish little chicks, which resemble rusty pads of steel wool. Large rafts of coots form at locations offering sufficient aquatic vegetation for nourishment, including Shoveler Pond at Anahuac NWR and some of the waterfowl reservoirs in the W or S portions of the region. In as little as two years, coots, Common

Moorhens, and Purple Gallinules may populate newly created wetlands, including those constructed in north Houston by the Harris County Flood Control District.

The bird is no longer popular as a game species, but Singley (1893) remarked that coots were a "common market species" in Galveston during the late 1800s. Coots in migration do stray, including one that dropped into the reflecting pool at Houston's City Hall 12 Oct 1976. Even the local television stations were impressed by this unusual appearance. Some coots are killed as they mistakenly land on roads that they believe to be bodies of water. Although the birds are relatively scarce in summer, wintering coots occur in large numbers. The Freeport CBC averages 4,768 per year; a high of 25,600 was reported in 1960. Although few consider them a delicacy, Texas hunters are permitted to shoot 15 coots a day. Typically, only the breasts are saved as food.

SANDHILL CRANE
Grus canadensis

Uncommon winter terminal migrant and bi-seasonal transient migrant

WINTER: (13–15 Oct) **mid-Oct to mid-Mar** (17, 21, 29 Apr)

HABITAT: Coastally and inland on prairie and agricultural land; occasionally plowed or shallow flooded fields.

DISCUSSION: Sandhill Crane is one of only two members of its family breeding in the New World. At favorable sites such as the Platte River in Nebraska and Bosque del Apache NWR in New Mexico, Sandhills have become the focus of lucrative ecotourism events attracting thousands of wildlife watchers and photographers. Locally, the sight and sound of even a small flock can be a stirring experience, and it is a simple matter to appreciate why so many cultures associate these beautiful birds (which pair for life and dance when they are courting) with luck, longevity, and fidelity. Although these majestic birds lack the speed of a Wilson's Snipe, or the stealth of a Clapper Rail, licensed Texas hunters may obtain a free permit to kill up to three Sandhills per day for sport and table fare.

Besides being abundant nesters in the far north, Sandhill Cranes have satellite populations that continue to breed in the SE United States and Cuba. Oberholser cites two nineteenth-century records of the Florida Sandhill Crane, *Grus c. pratensis*, nesting along or immediately south of the UTC (1893 in JEF, 1895 in Matagorda Co.). Subsequently this subspecies was extirpated from the region. Birds wintering locally are probably a combination of Western Sandhills, *G. c. tabida*, and Little Brown Sandhills, *G. c. canadensis*. They appear with the crisp breezes of mid- to late Oct, alerting all to their presence with a throaty bugling that is unmistakable among the higher-pitched cries of arriving Snow Geese. Sandhills remain through early Mar, and rare stragglers may linger into Apr. One bird, perhaps sick or crippled, spent most the summer of 1999 on Galveston Is. Often, small flocks of Sandhills are scattered through the goose fields of W HAS and WAR, typically spending the evening on shallow reservoirs. During recent years a flock of up to 200 birds has spent winter days on shortgrass pastures on W Galveston Is. In the evening, they return to the mainland (*fide* J. Stevenson). Although UTC flocks seldom match the huge concentrations in Matagorda, Calhoun, and Jackson cos., 1,426 were tallied 1 Jan 1994 on the Cypress Creek CBC, and 3,721 were counted during the 1989 Freeport CBC.

WHOOPING CRANE
Grus americana

Rare (formerly common) winter terminal migrant and bi-seasonal transient migrant

WINTER: **Late Oct to early Apr**

HABITAT: Coastal wetlands and coastal prairie.

DISCUSSION: No endangered bird in North America has received more public attention than the Whooping Crane, our tallest bird. Both California Condor and Spotted Owl have become popular environmental buzzwords, but these birds are rarely observed by the public. The Bald Eagle has perhaps attracted more fanfare, although here in Texas the Whooping Crane nudges all but the most heinous crimes off the front pages when the birds arrive at Aransas NWR each Oct. Never very common, this species was propelled toward extinction by conversion of marshes and wet prairies to agriculture. By 1937 only two small breeding populations of Whooping Cranes remained, one a sedentary population in

SW Louisiana, and in 1941 only 16 birds migrated to winter on the Aransas NWR.

Sennett (1878), sailing south along the Texas coast from Galveston to Brownsville in 1877, commented that he "saw these noble birds of the prairies feeding in the lagoons . . . and in the wet places around Brownsville, up to about April 1st." Strecker (1912) stated that the Whooping Crane was "formerly an abundant winter resident of Western and Southern Texas," but had become "uncommon in winter." Nehrling (1882) reported that "from November to the end of March these beautiful birds are exceedingly abundant on all the low prairies in the vicinity of Houston." Oberholser (1974) noted the seemingly unlikely evidence of breeding near Eagle Lake (COL), a nest with two eggs, date unknown, cited by Davie (1889). By the 1930s, however, the Whooping Crane population had collapsed, and the final historical sighting on the UTC was on 19 Jan 1936.

Seemingly destined to inch toward extinction, the species has been the focus of conservation efforts over the past 60 years that have finally begun to nudge it toward recovery. In 1937, the Aransas National Wildlife Refuge was established to protect the wintering area of the remaining Whooping Cranes, and in 1967 the Whooping Crane was designated as an endangered species (prior to the Endangered Species Act of 1973). Virtually all the wild birds belong to the only self-sustaining natural wild population,

which has a nesting area located in the Northwest Territories and adjacent portions of Alberta, Canada, primarily within the boundaries of Wood Buffalo National Park. A USFWS news release on 1 Dec 2004 stated that at least 213 Whooping Cranes, including 32 young, returned to winter on the Texas coast. This figure represents a hundred-year high. The USFWS reports that the Aransas–Wood Buffalo population is experiencing an average increase of 4.6 percent per year, and if the average growth rate continues, this population will reach 500 by about 2020.

Fall migration begins in Sep, when Whooping Cranes normally migrate in small flocks of less than 10. They arrive at Aransas NWR between late Oct and mid-Nov, where they will spend about six months. In Apr the birds make the 2,600-mile trip back to Wood Buffalo National Park. Although there are rare reports of sightings of Whoopers migrating over the UTC with Sandhills, we know of only four recent sightings of these endangered cranes spending time here on the ground. During 1986, two Whooping Cranes wintered near San Bernard NWR in BRA, arriving 16 Jan and lingering until 31 Mar (M. Lange). An immature was seen near that same area 22–24 Jan 1998, another was seen from 24 Oct to 7 Feb 1999 near Brazos Bend SP (FOB), and one was photographed on W Galveston Island on 27 Nov 2004. The other recent UTC record is of seven flying over the Katy Prairie (WAR) on 24 Oct 2001.

Shorebirds

Those of us who fell into birds and birding along a coast, any coast, cut our baby teeth on birds of the shore. Gulls, terns, herons, egrets, ducks, pelicans, cormorants, spoonbills, and sandpipers are common if not always readily identified fare for bird-hungry tenderfeet. Coastal birds allow a close approach, offering an easy target for those of us still learning how to focus our binoculars. Just consider how many people have developed an interest in birds after enjoying their presence at close quarters on the beach.

We along the UTC have been gifted with a medley of coastal birds, and for variety, no group eclipses the shorebirds—a portion of the order Charadriiformes that includes the jaegers, gulls, and terns. The plovers, curlews, peeps, and their relatives are the

single most diverse group of birds inhabiting our region. Most of them peak in numbers during late spring, when an incredible 36 species may be seen in a single day (table 9).

Because the UTC's shorebirds seem to arrive together, one might suspect that they share common wintering grounds, but that is hardly the case. Species such as American Avocet may roam no further south than the lagoons of coastal Mexico, while American Golden-Plovers and Buff-breasted and Upland sandpipers winter on the pampas of Argentina. Ruddy Turnstones, Semipalmated Plovers, Short-billed Dowitchers, and Whimbrels head in droves for Latin America, where they are faithful to the continental margins, unlike Least and Spotted sandpipers

Table 9. *Shorebird Migration and Big Days, 1986–1992*

Species	17 Apr 1988	19 Apr 1991	23 Apr 1987	26 Apr 1986	28 Apr 1988	28 Apr 1990	29 Apr 1989	2 May 1992	Total	Avg.	High	Freq.
Black-bellied Plover	210	387	900	342	311	520	448	441	3,559	445	900	8
American Golden-Plover	350	5	470	1,154	183	7	6	15	2,190	274	1,154	8
Snowy Plover	6	12	2	1	1	1		2	25	4	12	7
Wilson's Plover	40	36	3	12	18	12	35	6	162	20	40	8
Semipalmated Plover	400	745	955	817	360	450	647	549	4,923	615	955	8
Piping Plover	25	40	25	35	16	12	38	42	233	29	42	8
Killdeer	200	42	370	23	87	40	61	98	921	115	370	8
American Oystercatcher	1	2	1	2	1	1	3	1	12	2	3	8
Black-necked Stilt	170	110	105	13	130	64	46	180	818	102	180	8
American Avocet	6,000	2,010	16	256	303	150	865	300	9,900	1,238	6,000	8
Greater Yellowlegs	65	207	400	33	270	25	46	137	1,183	148	400	8
Lesser Yellowlegs	700	2,235	2,305	1,313	200	405	815	855	8,828	1,104	2,305	8
Solitary Sandpiper	4	1	1	7	2	4	1	10	30	4	10	8
Willet	410	382	1,002	101	180	150	620	320	3,165	396	1,002	8
Spotted Sandpiper	1	5	10	3	13	12	2	23	69	9	23	8
Upland Sandpiper	4	5	7	62	1	3	1	24	107	13	62	8
Whimbrel	85	40	85	39	149	33	129	1,017	1,577	197	1,017	8
Long-billed Curlew	40	7	8	4	2	1	1	3	66	8	40	8
Hudsonian Godwit	9	1	31	5	1	20	56	74	197	25	74	8

Species	1	2	3	4	5	6	7	8	Total	Mean	Max	No. of censuses
Marbled Godwit	45	1	26	1	5	14	12	6	110	14	45	8
Ruddy Turnstone	140	34	180	193	412	125	995	1,990	4,069	509	1,990	8
Red Knot	40	300	1	14	3	600	600	10	1,568	196	600	8
Sanderling	900	430	595	1,238	701	525	1,900	1,325	7,614	952	1,900	8
Semipalmated Sandpiper	200	2,825	6,411	90	195	950	31	2,332	13,034	1,629	6,411	8
Western Sandpiper	700	846	3,155	231	120	750	275	11	6,088	761	3,155	8
Least Sandpiper	200	601	751	193	190	110	583	850	3,478	435	850	8
White-rumped Sandpiper	8	15	2	99	16	400	114	44	698	87	400	8
Baird's Sandpiper	7	12	1	3	1	6	14	1	45	6	14	8
Pectoral Sandpiper	65	1,453	353	266	1,120	50	1,279	472	5,058	632	1,453	8
Purple Sandpiper				1					1	1	1	1
Dunlin	1,500	4,350	7,170	1,305	1,500	2,800	1,965	6,330	26,920	3,365	7,170	8
Stilt Sandpiper	25	254	250	53	17	350	100	401	1,450	181	401	8
Buff-breasted Sandpiper	6		552	46	362	30	210	65	1,271	182	552	7
Short-billed Dowitcher	500	2,955	245	2,365	181	500	750	440	7,936	992	2,955	8
Long-billed Dowitcher	20,000	2,200	5,150	641	560	6,000	387	5,400	40,338	5,042	20,000	8
Common Snipe	20	2	5	1	7		1		36	6	20	6
Wilson's Phalarope	60	7	2	43	172	3	60	42	389	49	172	8
Total Species	36	36	36	36	36	35	35	35				
Total Individuals	33,136	23,533	30,570	11,004	7,790	15,123	13,096	23,816				

Note: Species are in taxonomic order. Census days are arranged by date and month.

or Greater and Lesser yellowlegs, which occur widely at inland locations. Even within a species there may be considerable variation, as is the case with Red Knot. Some winter along the UTC, but others make a long and perilous flight to the coasts of southern Chile and Argentina (Hayman et al. 1986).

Wherever they arrive from, the UTC's shorebirds are not very difficult to see. But in order to experience this panoply you must first know where to look, and to know where to look you must first consider what makes these birds tick. Ecological differentiation is the necessary condition for coexistence (Hardin 1960): to avoid competition between similar species that coexist in time, such as UTC shorebirds in the spring, there must be a reciprocal separation in space.

At this writing, 88 species of shorebirds have occurred in North America north of Mexico (Clements 2000), and 52 (59 percent) have reached Texas (Lockwood and Freeman 2004). Forty-seven have been recorded locally; only five Texas species (Double-striped Thick-Knee, Collared Plover, Spotted Redshank, Red-necked Stint, and Sharp-tailed Sandpiper) have never been observed on the UTC. Most interesting, 37 species of shorebirds occur on the UTC *annually*.

These 37 species represent only five of the extant shorebird families. Two of these have large constituencies: *Charadrius* plovers with six species, and *Calidris* sandpipers with 11 species. The UTC shorebirds (*Charadrius* and *Calidris* in particular) appear to be a rather homogeneous, closely related group, morphologically similar and at times coexisting both temporally and spatially within a limited geographical range. So how do UTC shorebirds avoid or at least minimize direct competition?

An initial mechanism, or method, by which direct competition is avoided on the UTC is seasonality. By staggering their seasonal occurrence, shorebirds that are morphologically similar minimize competition. The UTC's shorebirds can be segregated into three broad seasonal categories—permanent residents, terminal migrants, and transient migrants (table 10).

Permanent residents are full-time members of the UTC avifauna. These species breed, raise their young, and winter locally. This does not mean, however, that permanent residents are necessarily sedentary or that their populations are stable. Killdeer, for example, are permanent residents of the UTC, yet more northerly migratory populations join our residents in winter

and swell local aggregations far beyond the summer norm. Of the 37 annual UTC shorebirds, only four are permanent residents in the strict sense: Killdeer, American Oystercatcher, Willet, and rarely American Woodcock. We do not include species such as Black-bellied Plover or Sanderling, in which undeveloped gonads may cause them to linger as summer non-breeders. A previous permanent resident, the Northern Jacana, is now extirpated, and Snowy Plover, once extirpated, has become a rare nester again.

Terminal migrants are species for which the UTC serves as a point either of origination or of termination for their migratory journeys. These shorebirds are either local breeders that migrate south (summer terminal migrants) or northern breeders that winter locally (winter terminal migrants). Only two species, Wilson's Plover and Black-necked Stilt, are in the first category, but the stilt's status is changing. In the second category, we have 21 species that are winter terminal migrants, representing the largest single seasonal category on the UTC.

Transient migrants are species that simply pass through the UTC between wintering and breeding areas. These species either appear in both spring and fall (bi-seasonal) or, in a few cases, in the spring only (mono-seasonal). Thirteen species of transient migrants have been reported from the UTC, of which four have elliptical migration patterns and appear exclusively or almost so during spring: American Golden-Plover, Eskimo Curlew, Hudsonian Godwit, and White-rumped Sandpiper. An additional seven species are vagrants that appear inconsistently.

Along with differing migration windows, habitat selection is another mechanism by which UTC shorebirds reduce competition. Habitat selection yields distinct patterns of distribution. These patterns are generated by a combination of factors, including the presence and depth of standing water, moisture content of exposed mud, water salinity (generally correlated with distance inland), vegetation cover, presence and diversity of prey species (a time-related phenomenon), soil density, burning, historical land use (taken on a field-by-field basis), meteorological history of the months preceding spring migration, and probably the presence of migrating birds with similar requirements that, like the hunter's decoy, lure flocks to fields occupied by kindred spirits.

We suggest salinity as a major factor in shorebird habitat partitioning, and therefore we find it helpful

Table 10. *Seasonal Status of Regularly Occurring UTC Shorebirds*

Permanent Residents
1. American Oystercatcher
2. Killdeer
3. Willet
4. Black-necked Stilt*

Summer Terminal Migrants
1. Black-necked Stilt*
2. Wilson's Plover
3. Snowy Plover (rare breeder)

Winter Terminal Migrants
1. American Avocet
2. Black-bellied Plover
3. Semipalmated Plover
4. Snowy Plover
5. Greater Yellowlegs
6. Lesser Yellowlegs
7. Spotted Sandpiper
8. Long-billed Curlew
9. Marbled Godwit
10. Ruddy Turnstone
11. Red Knot
12. Sanderling

13. Western Sandpiper
14. Least Sandpiper
15. Dunlin
16. Short-billed Dowitcher
17. Long-billed Dowitcher
18. Common Snipe
19. American Woodcock

Transient Migrants (bi-seasonal)
1. Solitary Sandpiper
2. Wilson's Phalarope
3. Upland Sandpiper
4. Semipalmated Sandpiper
5. Baird's Sandpiper
6. Pectoral Sandpiper
7. Stilt Sandpiper
8. Buff-breasted Sandpiper

Transient Migrants (mono-seasonal)
1. American Golden-Plover
2. Whimbrel
3. Hudsonian Godwit
4. White-rumped Sandpiper

*In recent years the Black-necked Stilt has become increasingly common in winter immediately along the coast. We suspect that the winter population differs from that which breeds here (most likely from the growing inland breeding population to the north). Without extensive banding, however, the situation remains speculative.

to classify gross UTC shorebird habitats along a salinity gradient (table 11).

Since prey organisms for most shorebirds are invertebrates resident on the surface or in the substrate—and in the case of marine species, prey are often hyperosmotic (saltier than the blood of the predator shorebird)—and water is ingested incidentally as part of the process of prey capture, we believe that the salinity in these habitats in an important factor in the distribution of shorebirds; that is, salinity provides means for spatial separation. Black-bellied Plover and American Golden-Plover, Hudsonian and Marbled godwits, Semipalmated and Western sandpipers, and Short-billed and Long-billed dowitchers are examples of closely related, morphologically similar species that may avoid competition on the UTC by one of the species being saline-tolerant and the other saline-intolerant.

Primary coastal habitats available for saltwater shorebirds are sand and shell beach, sand flat, or mixed sand and mudflat. The 125 linear miles of UTC coastline comprise approximately 6.7 square miles of sand and shell beach (Fisher et al. 1973; McGowen et al. 1976). These beaches are relatively narrow, rarely wider than 300 feet from the water's edge to the mean high tide line. The substrate of UTC beaches is land-derived with smaller amounts of shell sand, except in those areas where there is a consistent import of detrital material (such as tidal passes).

The inshore region of the UTC represents a relatively limited resource for shorebirds. Beaches are poorly developed along the margins of Galveston, Trinity, and associated bays. Most bay shoreline is either erosional escarpment cut into Pleistocene sediment or is covered by coastal marsh (Fisher et al. 1973).

Table 11. *Habitat Partitioning of UTC Shorebirds*

Species	Sandy Beach (Saline)	Broad Intertidal (Saline)	Tidal Slough (Brackish)	Wetland (Fresh)	Grassland (Fresh)	Woodland (Fresh)
Black-bellied Plover	IIIIIIIIIIIIIIIII	IIIIIIIIIIIIIIIII	=======			
Piping Plover	=======	IIIIIIIIIIIIIIIII				
Snowy Plover	=======	IIIIIIIIIIIIIIIII				
Willet	IIIIIIIIIIIIIIIII	IIIIIIIIIIIIIIIII	=======			
Ruddy Turnstone	IIIIIIIIIIIIIIIII	IIIIIIIIIIIIIIIII	=======	....		
Red Knot	IIIIIIIIIIIIIIIII	IIIIIIIIIIIIIIIII				
Sanderling	IIIIIIIIIIIIIIIII	IIIIIIIIIIIIIIIII	=======			
American Oystercatcher	——————	IIIIIIIIIIIIIIIII				
American Avocet	——————	IIIIIIIIIIIIIIIII	=======	——————		
Semipalmated Plover		IIIIIIIIIIIIIIIII	=======	....		
Wilson's Plover	=======	IIIIIIIIIIIIIIIII				
Whimbrel		——————	=======	IIIIIIIIIIIIIIIII	IIIIIIIIIIIIIIIII	
Long-billed Curlew	=======	IIIIIIIIIIIIIIIII	=======	=======	IIIIIIIIIIIIIIIII	
Marbled Godwit		IIIIIIIIIIIIIIIII	=======			
Western Sandpiper	=======	IIIIIIIIIIIIIIIII	=======	=======		
Dunlin	——————	IIIIIIIIIIIIIIIII	=======	=======		
Short-billed Dowitcher		IIIIIIIIIIIIIIIII	=======			
Black-necked Stilt			=======	IIIIIIIIIIIIIIIII		
Killdeer			=======	IIIIIIIIIIIIIIIII	IIIIIIIIIIIIIIIII	
Greater Yellowlegs		——————	=======	IIIIIIIIIIIIIIIII		
Lesser Yellowlegs			=======	IIIIIIIIIIIIIIIII		
Spotted Sandpiper			=======	IIIIIIIIIIIIIIIII		
Wilson's Phalarope		——————	=======	IIIIIIIIIIIIIIIII		
Semipalmated Sandpiper		——————	=======	IIIIIIIIIIIIIIIII		
Least Sandpiper		——————	=======	IIIIIIIIIIIIIIIII		
Baird's Sandpiper	——————	——————		IIIIIIIIIIIIIIIII	IIIIIIIIIIIIIIIII	
Pectoral Sandpiper			——————	IIIIIIIIIIIIIIIII	=======	
Long-billed Dowitcher			——————	IIIIIIIIIIIIIIIII		
American Golden-Plover				IIIIIIIIIIIIIIIII	IIIIIIIIIIIIIIIII	
Solitary Sandpiper				IIIIIIIIIIIIIIIII		
Hudsonian Godwit				IIIIIIIIIIIIIIIII		
White-rumped Sandpiper		——————	=======	IIIIIIIIIIIIIIIII		
Stilt Sandpiper			——————	IIIIIIIIIIIIIIIII		
Common Snipe				IIIIIIIIIIIIIIIII		
Upland Sandpiper				——————	IIIIIIIIIIIIIIIII	
Buff-breasted Sandpiper				=======	IIIIIIIIIIIIIIIII	
American Woodcock						IIIIIIIIIIIIIIIII
Primary habitat	IIIIIIIIIIIIIIIII					
Secondary habitat	=======					
Peripheral habitat	——————					
Migration only	....					

Facing the lack of suitable, accessible foraging substrate along bay margins and the restricted and ephemeral habitats of the open beaches, maritime waders crowd onto the large tidal sand and mudflats. The two major tidal flats on the UTC are Bolivar Flats and the San Luis Pass flats. Bolivar Flats is a depositional sand flat formed by the North Jetty trapping sand carried by longshore currents at the mouth of Galveston Bay, and San Luis Pass flats is an emergent flood delta at San Luis Pass (the channel between the southwestern tip of Galveston Island and Follet's Island). Less expansive tidal sites, from north to south, are at Sabine Pass (JEF), Rollover Pass flats (an emergent flood delta formed by the opening of a fish cut through Bolivar Peninsula near Gilchrist), Big Reef (opposite Bolivar Flats on the east end of Galveston Island) and San Bernard flats (BRA) near the mouth of the San Bernard River.

Freshwater shorebirds rely upon an entirely different assortment of habitats. UTC prairies extend W along the coast from the Sabine River and reach inland 25 to 60 miles. The soil underlying much of this prairie is heavy clay and fosters a major rice industry irrigated with water from wells and rivers. In addition, an inland rice belt runs laterally, E–W, through HAS, WAR, FOB, and BRA. These paddy fields support immense concentrations of migratory shorebirds, particularly in the spring. Ponds maintained for waterfowl by local wildlife refuges, the shores of variable freshwater impoundments (primarily irrigation ponds), and grazed or mowed pastures provide additional freshwater habitat.

BLACK-BELLIED PLOVER
Pluvialis squatarola

Common transient migrant and winter terminal migrant; uncommon summer nonbreeding terminal migrant

WINTER: **Mid-Jul through late May,** nonbreeders present through summer
HABITAT: Widely distributed throughout the coastal zone on sandy beach, sand flat, mixed sand/mudflat and wet shoreline, less commonly on rock jetty, rock groin, and exposed oyster reef. Smaller numbers are present inshore on tidal mudflats and

bay shoreline, in rice fields proximate to the coast, and inland during spring migration.

DISCUSSION: Black-bellied Plovers are solitary or associate in loose flocks of a few individuals on the open beach. Sand and mudflats support larger aggregations, and flocks at prime sites may exceed several hundred individuals (high counts 4,000 on 15 Oct 1988; 1,026 on 27 Apr 1994). Roost sites are usually located adjacent to foraging areas. Spring migration spans Mar through May, with bimodal peaks in early Mar and again in late Apr through mid-May. These peaks, also observed in other spring migrants, may represent an initial massing of locally wintering birds, followed by others that wintered farther south. Fall migration extends from mid-Jul through Nov, peaking in mid-Oct.

The Black-bellied Plover is a maritime species and is found at inland freshwater sites only in migration and relative to a specific location's proximity to the coast. True inland occurrences, such as in W HAS or WAR, are rare; however, the birds occur in small numbers on rice fields near the coast.

Summer nonbreeders, characteristically in basic plumage, are largely restricted to the major sand and mudflats, with smaller numbers scattered along the beaches. Large numbers winter along the UTC coastline. The Galveston CBC, which includes Bolivar Flats, averages about 450 per year, with a peak of 1,151 in 1993.

AMERICAN GOLDEN-PLOVER
Pluvialis dominica

Mostly mono-seasonal: common spring, rare fall transient migrant

SPRING: (17, 23, 25 Feb) **late Feb to late Apr** (13, 18, 28 May)
FALL: (13, 15, 18 Jul) **mid-Jul to late Oct** (26 Sep; 14, 22, 27 Oct; 28 Nov)
HABITAT: Rice fields, shortgrass prairie, pond and lake shores, freshly plowed agricultural land, golf courses (particularly coastal), palustrine wetlands (typically those dominated by woody plants or persistent emergent vegetation—from the Latin *palus* for "marsh"), overgrazed pasture, harvested hayfields, burned rangeland.

DISCUSSION: Breeding on the arctic tundra from Alaska east to Baffin Island, and wintering in the South American grasslands from Bolivia and Brazil S to the pampas of central Argentina, the American Golden-Plover undertakes one of the great annual migratory treks among birds. These plovers are elliptical migrants. In fall they fly E across Canada to New England, then S along the Atlantic Coast to N South America. In spring they return through the Great Plains of the central United States to their arctic breeding areas (this is often called the Great Circle route). Each spring, this plover once swarmed across the prairies of the Great Plains along with Eskimo Curlew, another Great Circle migrant. As the prairies were plowed and hunting pressure increased, their populations plummeted; Singley (1893) remarked that he found the plover to be "much prized as a market bird" in Galveston in 1891. The Eskimo Curlew never recovered, and throughout much of the twentieth century the very existence of this bird has been debatable. The American Golden-Plover, however, rebounded and remains a common to abundant spring migrant that begins arriving the last week of Feb. The height of passage is from late Mar through early Apr, but migration extends in a diminished manner through the end of May. We recognize one midsummer record of an alternate plumage bird seen 17–18 Jun 1999 at Brazoria NWR (BRA), perhaps a sick bird.

Flocks in the rice fields may contain thousands of individuals (e.g., 5,000 on 14 Apr 1979 in CHA). An inland, freshwater species, this bird displays a strong preference for bare, short, or sparsely covered grasslands and fields (Eubanks and Fred Collins), only infrequently occurring on the Gulf's shores. The most disturbed habitats (bare plowed fields) may be used, and like many birds, these plovers occasionally follow tractors. The species is usually absent from saltwater habitats, and most coastal sightings are of flocks flying over the coast from the Gulf of Mexico during migration.

During fall, records are few, scattered, and invariably very close to the Gulf, and in many years they fail to appear at all. A juvenile observed in BRA 26 Sep 2004 represents one of our few recent fall records. An unusual count of 15 seen in the High Island oilfield ponds 7 Oct 1989 represents our highest fall total. On at least two occasions, golden-plovers have lingered into winter. Two were seen at the Texas City Dike 14 Dec 1970–26 Jan 1971, and one appeared on the Freeport CBC 21 Dec 1975.

SNOWY PLOVER
Charadrius alexandrinus

Uncommon winter terminal migrant: previously extirpated but now a rare and local breeder

WINTER: (2, 10, 12, 15 July) **mid-Jul to mid-May** (3, 14, 16 May)

HABITAT: Open sandy beach and tidal sand flats.

DISCUSSION: The Snowy Plover is attracted to the outermost margins of UTC tidal sand flats, where it sweeps its bill through the clouds of brine flies that collect over the damp sand. Unlike our wintering sandpipers, which probe for subsurface prey, Snowy and other plovers pick food from the surface. Snowy Plover may even be seen snapping brine flies from the air.

These plovers roost in the driest dunes, close to tidal flats where they feed, and often escape the wind by tucking themselves into tire tracks left by vehicles. Early writers believed that Snowy Plover nested along the UTC. Strecker (1912) considered it "resident on the Gulf coast from Galveston southward." Williams (1938) reported "downy young were fairly common along the beaches in June." Recent publications continue to treat the species as a local breeder, presumably because of nesting elsewhere along the Gulf Coast. However, it was not until April 2000 when a downy chick was observed at Bolivar Flats (GAL) that any modern nesting evidence was discovered. The next year, on 22 May 2001, Weeks found a dependant youngster at Bryan Beach (BRA). This site had long been suspected to be breeding locale as birds had summered there for some time.

Snowy Plover prefers a relatively unvegetated sandy substrate for its scrape, often nesting in hurricane washover sites along the central and lower coasts. On the UTC our annual rainfall exceeds moisture lost through evaporation and transpiration (the surplus diminishing from north to south), which allows for a profusion of small, well-watered, and therefore well-vegetated dunes (Fisher et al. 1973). As a result, most of the UTC coastal zone offers little in the way of unvegetated nesting habitat for the species. However, additional and largely unexplored breeding habitat is present in the inaccessible stretches of beach between the Brazos and San Bernard rivers and within San Bernard NWR, leaving hope that the Snowy Plover maintains a small breeding population on the UTC.

The first fall migrants begin to filter in during early Jul, and the numbers gradually build to a rather stable winter population of between 100 and 150 individuals (113 on 14 Dec 2001 on San Bernard NWR CBC and 70 on 21 Jan 1988 on Bolivar Flats and San Luis Pass). Spring migration is practically indiscernible, and by late Apr the winter population has faded away. The latest migrant record is a bird seen inland in WAR on 19 Jun 1988.

WILSON'S PLOVER
Charadrius wilsonia

Common summer terminal migrant, uncommon to rare winter resident or winter terminal migrant

SUMMER: (28 Feb; 1–2, 8 Mar) **early Mar to late Sep, a few remaining through winter** (29 Dec; 22 Jan; 2 Feb)

HABITAT: Sandy beach and sand flats, nesting behind the high tide line among coastal grasses or on saltpans vegetated by salt-tolerant plants. Usually found near the abundant fiddler crabs upon which it feeds.

DISCUSSION: Wilson's is our only plover that breeds along the immediate shoreline, and besides Killdeer, one of only two *Charadrius* certain to be nesting on the UTC. Migrants arrive during the first week of Mar, and by mid-Apr territorial birds (with a sharp two-noted call and guttural rolling note) are evident throughout the coastal zone. Pickleweed beds bordering the major tidal flats are prime breeding areas. In late summer, these flats swarm with young Wilson's looking astonishingly like cotton swabs perched on toothpicks.

Although this species is normally the least gregarious of the UTC plovers, during fall large numbers gather at the major sand flats prior to their southbound movements. Their fall staging peaks in late Jul and Aug. High counts noted in the past were 332 at San Luis Pass 9 Aug 1987 and 350 between San Luis Pass and Bolivar Flats on 20 Aug 1988 and again on 30 Jul 1989.

Most of our Wilson's Plovers winter along the Mexican coast. During their travels, they seldom stray more than a mile or two from salt water. In fact, we know of no true inland UTC records. Small numbers, usually less than 10, linger into winter at the major staging sites, particularly Bolivar Flats. The

Galveston CBC, which includes the Bolivar Flats, averages three birds per year, with a high of 20 in 2003. These birds lingered at East Beach and the Bolivar Flats and were seen repeatedly. Because there seems to be a recent trend for more of these birds to winter on the UTC (global warming?), we acknowledge that the earliest and latest dates we give may represent lingering birds, not migrants.

Like other beach-nesting species, Wilson's Plover is under constant threats from predatory birds and from both vehicular and pedestrian traffic. The American Bird Conservancy's Green List cites this plover in its category Species with Restricted Distributions or Low Population Size. Such birds may exhibit stable populations with limited threats but are of concern because of their small global footprint. Birders visiting the local flats can decrease the local vulnerability by giving nesting females wide berth.

SEMIPALMATED PLOVER
Charadrius semipalmatus

Common transient migrant (particularly in spring), uncommon winter terminal migrant, rare summer nonbreeding straggler

WINTER: **Early Jul to mid-May,** with a few remaining through summer; departure and arrival dates obscured by nonbreeding summer lingerers

HABITAT: Sand and mudflats, lagoon shorelines, intertidal wetlands, and rice paddies.

DISCUSSION: Semipalmated Plover seems the archetypal coastal zone plover, ever present in mixed plover flocks on tidal flats during the winter months. During that season it is closely allied with both Snowy and Piping plovers, seeming to prefer a wetter substrate than Snowy and less sandy substrate than Piping. In reality, this distinction is often masked by the seemingly random concentrations of smaller plovers at the major sand flats during peak foraging times. Of the three smaller coastal plovers, Semipalmated is most likely to be observed inland along the bay shores. The Galveston CBC, which includes Bolivar Flats, reports an average of 72 birds with a high of 256 in 1999. During migration this is the only small *Charadrius* regularly taking advantage of the UTC's freshwater wetlands. During late Apr, immense numbers of returning spring migrants concentrate in freshly flooded rice fields. During these periods, single-day counts of several hundred individuals are possible (817 on 26 Apr 1986, 844 in a single pond at Brazoria NWR on 25 Apr 2000, and 955 on 23 Apr 1987). Small numbers of nonbreeders summer at the tidal sand flats. Migrants begin to return in early to mid-Jul and continue to trickle through for several months.

PIPING PLOVER
Charadrius melodus

Uncommon winter terminal migrant, rare summer lingerer

WINTER: (30 Jun, 2, 4 Jul) **early Jul to mid-May** (17 Jun); rarely, a few nonbreeders (floaters that do not return to the nesting sites) remain through summer

HABITAT: Locally, Piping Plover is restricted to the coastal zone where its habitat is similar to that of Semipalmated and Snowy plovers—sandy beach and tidal sand flats.

DISCUSSION: Piping Plover is the poster child for threatened and endangered shorebirds in the United States. Listed as endangered in Canada and on the U.S. Great Lakes, this plover is threatened elsewhere in the United States due to significant population declines (Haig 1992). Piping Plovers breed across three broad geographical fronts: Atlantic Coast beaches, on lake and river shores and islands within the northern Great Plains of the United States and Canada, and along beaches of Lake Superior and Lake Michigan (Haig 1992; Eubanks 1994). According to Haig (1992), declines are "the result of detrimental human activities such as: direct and inadvertent harassment of birds and nests by people, dogs, and vehicles; destruction of beach habitat for development projects; increased predation due to human presence in formerly pristine beach areas; and water level regulation policies that endanger nesting habitat." Fewer than 2,500 breeding pairs remain in the United States and Canada (Haig 1992).

Great Plains plovers, it is now thought, winter primarily along the Gulf of Mexico from W Florida to N Mexico. Recent evidence of this includes 10 banded birds observed 8 Aug 2004 at Bolivar Flats (*fide* John Whittle). At least nine of these were confirmed as belonging to a banding program at Lake Diefenbaker, the largest body of water in southern Saskatchewan. Atlantic Coast plovers are somewhat enigmatic; most researchers now believe they winter along the

Atlantic from South Carolina to Florida and on various islands in the Caribbean (Haig 1992). Texas is a prime wintering state for the species. The 1,905 reported during the 1991 International Piping Plover Survey represented 55 percent of the entire winter survey total, 188 on the UTC alone. The same survey recorded 176 in 1996 and 121 in 2001. Along the UTC, wintering Piping Plovers concentrate at two major and five minor locations. The major sites are Bolivar Flats (75–100 birds) and San Luis Pass (40–60 birds). In addition, both major sites serve as staging areas for large numbers of migrants. From north to south, the five minor wintering sites are Sabine Pass (JEF), the Rollover Pass flats (GAL), Big Reef (E end of Galveston Is.), Wolf Island (between the Brazoria and San Bernard rivers), and the San Bernard flats (BRA). These five sites host approximately 75 to 100 individuals. In addition, a fluctuating number winters on the UTC's open sandy beaches. Finally, unknown numbers winter along the shore of Galveston Bay and its extremities, where the species has been recorded as far inland as upper Trinity Bay at Baytown (HAS) and Cove (CHA).

Piping Plovers arrive on the UTC in mid-Jul (usually around 10 Jul), with significant numbers present by month's end. Surveys in earlier years showed peaks of migrants in mid-Oct, with single-site staging flocks occasionally approaching 300–400 birds. Eubanks recorded a high of 600 at Bolivar Flats on 19 Oct 1980. More recent censuses by W. Burkett and R. McFarlane yielded highs of about 200 individuals—further substantiation for the threatened or endangered status accorded these birds in various states.

By the beginning of Nov, these numbers diminish and stabilize, and the normal wintering population varies little through late Feb. March brings the return of migrant plovers, the movement peaking late in the month. Most have left the UTC by late Apr, and only small numbers linger through May. A few nonbreeders may remain at the major tidal flats through Jun.

KILLDEER
Charadrius vociferus

Common permanent resident, locally abundant winter terminal migrant

HABITAT: Widespread inland in grasslands, pastures, and cultivated fields, on lake and pond shores, and along mowed roadsides. Coastally, they are rare at the uppermost edges of saline sites. Killdeer are tolerant of humans, commonly breeding within the region's cities.

DISCUSSION: Even in the heart of urban Houston the Killdeer's call still echoes through downtown streets each evening, undoubtedly because of their propensity to nest on graveled roofs. Nevertheless, this ubiquitous species exhibits seasonal ebbs and flows and distinct habitat preferences. In general, the Killdeer is a freshwater species, avoiding the major tidal flats and sandy beaches. On the infrequent occasions when individuals are present around saline habitats, such as San Luis Pass or Bolivar Flats, their foraging is usually restricted to dry upland sites. Migrant flocks are frequently seen passing along the coast, and on several fall days we have noticed hundreds, organized in small flocks of 10 to 15 birds, moving laterally along the beach (e.g., on 12 Nov 1994, Behrstock noted three flying over salt water approximately 75 feet offshore at Bolivar Flats).

During winter an influx of northern migrants swells the Killdeer population dramatically; from Dec to Feb single flocks of 1,000 to 2,000 may be recorded in plowed fields. The Freeport CBC records an annual average of 900 with a high of 2,485 in 1975. During nesting season (initiated in early Mar), Killdeer become less gregarious, winter migrants depart, and birds that wintered here or further south disperse throughout the region. Killdeer nest wherever they find a shell or gravel substrate. We have found nests on gravel rooftops, the shoulders of well-traveled roads, shell-covered oil well drilling pads, and even in gravel driveways.

MOUNTAIN PLOVER
Charadrius montanus

Rare winter terminal migrant

WINTER: (26 Nov) **late Nov to early Apr** (20, 23 Mar, 8 Apr)

HABITAT: Bare, plowed agricultural fields with an extremely smooth surface, avoids rough and uneven fields in the early stages of cultivation.

DISCUSSION: The Mountain Plover is a plains shorebird, rarely wandering east to the UTC. Migrant flocks usually pass W of us as they travel between the grasslands of the W Great Plains and their wintering grounds in N Mexico. This shorebird breeds inconsistently in far W Texas (Davis Mountains, Sierra Vieja Mountains), and small groups are occasionally found in winter near Seguin, New Braunfels and Austin. Although the species was once considered to be a regular UTC spring migrant and an individual was photographed on East Beach in Galveston on 10 Nov 2002, we believe most historical records, especially birds reported from the coast, can be discounted due to the similarity between this species and migrant American Golden-Plovers (still a common identification error). Nevertheless, when numbers of this now diminishing shorebird were robust, a certain portion of the population may have drifted farther to the E, though Strecker (1912) makes no mention of this. During the 1980s and 1990s Mountain Plover was discovered wintering in WAR and far W HAS. These plovers arrived around the end of Nov and departed by early Apr. We are aware of very few more recent records; however, given the difficulty of detecting this cryptic and low-density species even in its preferred habitat, estimates of the wintering population are speculative. In all likelihood the total number of wintering birds probably does not exceed a handful of individuals; none has been recorded during recent years.

AMERICAN OYSTERCATCHER
Haematopus palliatus

Uncommon to locally common permanent resident

HABITAT: Spoil islands in the bay, tidal sand and mudflats, sandy beaches, oyster reefs.

DISCUSSION: Although able to consume a variety of prey, UTC American Oystercatchers are restricted to Galveston Bay and its oyster beds. Considered by some merely to represent a well-differentiated form of a widely distributed species, the American Oystercatcher is an exclusively marine bird. It has demonstrated none of the tendencies of its Old World cousin, the Oystercatcher *Haematopus ostralegus,* to exploit interior habitats and differs from it as well in certain plumage characteristics.

Most of the UTC population, no more than 200 individuals, is concentrated in GAL. Apparently these birds are isolated from those of the central and lower Texas coasts. The Galveston CBC averages 36 birds per year, with a high of 139 in 1998. The Freeport CBC suggests some expansion of this species, with no birds being seen until 1987 (except in 1976) but birds seen every year since, with a peak of 21 in 1998. Seasonal fluctuations are attributable to fall stagings of family groups at the major sand flats, where they are easily detected and censused, and to some postbreeding dispersal—for example, they are often seen in late summer at San Luis Pass and Follett's Is.

Oystercatchers nest mainly on spoil islands in the bay, and most of the smaller islands support one breeding pair. Although bivalves are the predominant prey during much of the year, birds staging and roosting on the sand flats also scavenge, often picking at and around fish carcasses. The UTC population appears to have been stable for the past 15 years, but expanding development on barrier islands and increased recreational boat traffic in the adjacent bays may threaten the future of this isolated relict population.

BLACK-NECKED STILT
Himantopus mexicanus

Common summer terminal migrant, uncommon winter resident

SUMMER: **Early Mar to early Oct**
HABITAT: Marshes and sloughs, adjacent pastures and prairies, rice fields.
DISCUSSION: The UTC shorebird palette is limited in its hues, shades of brown and gray being the dominant motif. The Black-necked Stilt stands as a stark exception to this rule. A dramatic black-and-white shorebird, balanced on bubblegum-pink legs, this lively stilt punctuates our marshes with its flair. While nesting, the bird startles at the first sound, noisily hovering over the intruder or attempting to lure the attacker away with an awkward broken-wing display. A common breeding bird along the UTC, it nests in both coastal and inland habitats, always in close proximity to water. In the coastal zone, it nests in brackish marshes bordering sloughs and bays, in coastal prairie that has been burned by ranchers to provide fresh forage for cattle, and in wet meadows. Inland nesting is usually associated with rice fields or reservoirs. This species does not tolerate the high salinities of the open Gulf, and coastal zone occurrences are normally associated with brackish water.

Spring migrants probably begin to arrive the first week of Mar, although the presence of wintering

stilts makes the determination of an exact early arrival date impossible. Numbers increase rapidly through Mar and early Apr. During spring, coastal flocks of 25 to 50 birds arriving from their trans-Gulf migration are common. Summer numbers are stable through Jul, but Aug counts swell dramatically with the development of large staging flocks and the presence of grown young. Numbers decline rapidly through Sep and are greatly reduced by Oct, when the species may be difficult to find. As evidenced by the Freeport CBC numbers, this species has increased as a winter resident during the last several decades (total of 4 in the 1960s, 6 in the 1970s, 74 in the 1980s, 535 in the 1990s, and 410 from 2000 to 2003 alone). Now, many coastal freshwater marshes, such as at Anahuac NWR and the pools at Apffel Park on Galveston's East Beach, contain small wintering flocks. However, even these hardy stilts may leave the region during a rare spell of especially frigid weather.

AMERICAN AVOCET
Recurvirostra americana

Common winter terminal migrant, locally abundant transient migrant (especially spring), rare summer nonbreeder, possibly a former nester

WINTER: **Mid-Jul to early May**
HABITAT: Avocets occur most frequently on the major sand flats and in tidal salt marshes, sloughs, and pools.
DISCUSSION: During his voyage south to the Rio Grande in 1877, G.B. Sennett stopped briefly at Galveston Bay and found staging American Avocets much as they may seen today at Bolivar Flats. He remarked that "at Bolivar Point, on Galveston Bay, March 1st, I found this bird in immense flocks. They were very shy, and it was only by the most careful maneuvering that I could shoot them. They were just casting off their winter plumage" (Sennett 1878). The great wintering flocks of avocets along our coast coalesce to form one of the celebrated wildlife spectacles of our region. With the return during Mar and Apr of birds that winter to our south, immense flocks of 10,000 to 15,000 stage at major sand flats such as Bolivar Flats and San Luis Pass (the 19,000 counted at Bolivar Flats 12 Apr 1980 is still a representative number). There they load up on invertebrates before dispersing to the north and northwest. During high tides, when

these avocet flocks are forced into the shallows, the carpet of black, white, and rust formed by their tightly packed bodies may completely obliterate the shore. Suddenly, in mid-Apr, these flocks vacate the staging sites in dramatic fashion, with 10,000 birds present one day and gone the next.

Small numbers of avocets linger in the coastal zone during summer, particularly at Bolivar Flats. Counts of 300 at Brazoria NWR on 30 May 2001 and 250 in a spoil cell at Bryan Beach on 15 Jun 2003 may represent sizable summer totals, but some of these may have departed after the census. Although Oberholser (1974) noted that the species nests "rarely" on the Upper Texas Coast (a sight record with no specimen), we know of no modern records.

Fall migrants arrive in early Jul (300 adults on Bolivar Flats 17 Jul 1983 and 430 on 21 Jul 2002 at Bryan Beach), their numbers gradually increasing through Nov to a stable Dec through Feb wintering population. The Galveston CBC, which includes Bolivar Flats, averages 1,868 per year, with a high of 6,518 in 1992. Although this is primarily a coastal species, a few birds are also present inland in harvested paddy fields left flooded for waterfowl hunting and on the margins of irrigation reservoirs, temporary pools, and ponds.

NORTHERN JACANA
Jacana spinosa

Extirpated local resident
28 Mar 1972 BRA (TBRC 1989-81)
22 Dec 1972 Maner Lake, BRA (TBRC 1991-103)

HABITAT: Normally from eastern (Tamaulipas) and western Mexico to W Panama and the West Indies, where they inhabit marshes, margins of lakes, and slow-moving waterways with floating vegetation, wet ditches, and occasionally flooded pastures or rice fields.

DISCUSSION: Jacanas are members of a small family of colorful shorebirds. They feed on seeds and small invertebrates, tiptoeing across emergent aquatic vegetation on absurdly elongated toes. The male cares for the young.

Northern Jacanas breed no closer to the UTC than Lake Guerrero in NE Mexico. Those that wander to Texas are usually immatures dispersing northward for the winter. However, for a brief period in the 1970s, the UTC could boast of its own colony of these

tropical shorebirds (in fact, the only breeding jacanas in the United States) when a small localized population, probably totaling no more than 60 individuals, resided at Maner Lake, BRA (Fleetwood 1973). Although the origin of these birds remains unclear, the lake's profusion of water lilies, water hyacinth, and water lettuce supported this colony for well over a decade. The presence of these birds, and their numbers during the late 1960s to late 1970s (representing at least 11 more unsubmitted TBRC records), may be followed in Oberholser (1974) and *American Birds* (vols. 25–32). The combination of a hard freeze during the winter of 1977–78 and the property owners' aggressive program aimed at removing aquatic vegetation eliminated both the preferred habitat and the entire UTC breeding population of these unusual birds. Eubanks's observation of two individuals on 14 Jan 1978 was among the last confirmed sightings at Maner Lake and for the UTC as a whole. The Maner Lake birds could well have been the source for other BRA records, including 30 Dec 1968–9 May 1969 at Brazoria NWR (Oberholser 1974) and 30 Dec 1978–11 Jan 1979, also at Brazoria NWR.

GREATER YELLOWLEGS
Tringa melanoleuca

Common winter terminal migrant, common transient migrant, rare regular summer lingerer

WINTER: (27 Jun, 2, 5 Jul) **early Jul to late May** (24, 28, 31 May)

HABITAT: Freshwater impoundments, rice fields, lake and pond shores, and flooded prairies and pastures; appears to tolerate some salinity, as evidenced by a few individuals that winter at the major sand flats.

DISCUSSION: Greater and Lesser yellowlegs, the two UTC "shanks" (as *Tringas* are called in Great Britain), are among the wintering shorebirds routinely seen in freshwater ponds, waterfowl impoundments, shallow streams, and even Houston's concrete-lined bayous. Occasionally the two species are seen side by side, and the comparison is always instructive. Only along the immediate coast do the two part ways, for some Greaters appear to tolerate salt water: a few winter each year on the major tidal flats. One Greater Yellowlegs banded by Eubanks at San Luis Pass in 1986 returned to the same tidal slough for six consecutive winters. Compared to the numbers that collect in our freshwater wetlands, however, these coastal residents are few and far between. Our largest accumulations of yellowlegs occur in recently flooded rice fields, particularly those where the rice has yet to grow so high as to obscure the soil. Fall migrants appear as early as the last few days of Jun, with bimodal fall movement peaks in Aug and Nov. During the winter this species is typically solitary or loosely grouped in very small flocks. The Freeport CBC has averaged 110 birds per year, with a high of 324 in 1990. Spring migration extends from early Mar through late May, with peak passage the last two weeks of Apr.

Northbound migrants aggregate in large numbers (e.g., 1,000 on 21 Mar 1999 in BRA and 400 on 23 Apr 1987). Small numbers of yellowlegs remain along the UTC in summer; occasionally larger groups linger. In 1999 flocks as large as 150 (20 Jun 1999) were reported in BRA.

Historically, Greater Yellowlegs were harvested by market hunters and sportsmen during seasonal migration, like so many of our shorebirds. Singley (1893) remarked that in 1891 he found Greater Yellowlegs to be "common in the market" in Galveston.

LESSER YELLOWLEGS
Tringa flavipes

Common winter terminal migrant, abundant transient migrant, and rare but regular summer lingerer

WINTER: (27, 29 Jun, 1–2 Jul) **early Jul to late May** (28, 31 May, 4 Jun)

HABITAT: Freshwater impoundments, rice fields, lake and pond shores, and flooded prairies and pastures.

DISCUSSION: In spring passage, waves of migrant Lesser Yellowlegs appear as wisps of smoke drifting northeastward over the shoreline and Galveston Bay. During that period we often see chains of yellowlegs, each link a flock of 25 to 100 birds, flying over the bay for days on end. Lesser Yellowlegs often accumulate in the area's rice fields (e.g., 7,500 along Bolivar Peninsula 14 Apr 1979). This species and Long-billed Dowitchers often dominate local paddy field gatherings.

We suspect that these are but a small fraction of the numbers that fly over the region, for in late Mar and

Apr the call of Lesser Yellowlegs is a prevalent nighttime sound, along with that of Upland Sandpiper. Numbers decrease dramatically after late Apr, and only a few remain by late May.

Small numbers oversummer annually (especially in BRA) in shallow grade freshwater and some brackish ponds. Occasionally larger summering flocks can be found (e.g., 24 at San Bernard NWR, BRA, 14 Jun 2000).

Normal fall arrival begins in earnest during the first week of Jul as birds follow the coast southwestward, peaking in Aug and Nov, like the Greater Yellowlegs. Fall migration numbers are less impressive than spring's, owing to the protracted migratory period. Lesser Yellowlegs winter commonly throughout our region, taking advantage of virtually any available wet spot (drainage ditches, flooded lawns, roadside puddles). The Freeport CBC averages 106 birds per year, with a high of 336 in 1990. Unlike the Greater, however, the Lesser Yellowlegs is exclusively a freshwater species, and observations of Lessers in true marine (as opposed to brackish) habitats are rare.

SOLITARY SANDPIPER
Tringa solitaria

Uncommon bi-seasonal transient migrant, rare but regular winter terminal migrant

SPRING: (1, 8 Mar) **early Mar to late May** (2, 10 Jun)

FALL: (30 Jun, 3, 5 Jul) **mid-Jul to late Oct** (15, 17, 20 Oct)

HABITAT: Freshwater habitats including pools, ditches, marshes, lake edge, and flooded fields.

DISCUSSION: Unlike the annual rush of yellowlegs, the Solitary Sandpiper steals into our midst. Often, the only evidence of its presence is a two-noted whistle heard in the dead of night. The Solitary is, as its name implies, a loner. These sandpipers are ordinarily found along the UTC one bird at a time; 20 birds seen along the coast 20 Jul 1986 represent the most significant count of which we are aware. Spring migrants arrive the first week of Mar, peak in Apr, and pass by early May. Birds heard much later may prove to be Northern Mockingbirds. Fall migrants arrive in mid-Jul, and young of the year trickle through as late as the end of Oct. Very small numbers winter on the UTC, with one or two usually found each season. Locally, this bird is a freshwater obligate, stringently avoiding saline habitats, and preferring roadside ditches, shores of variable ponds and lakes, edges of freshwater marshes, and puddles of rainwater left by spring showers.

WILLET
Catoptrophorus semipalmatus

Common summer terminal migrant (C. s. semipalmatus), common winter terminal migrant (C. s. inornatus)

HABITAT: Sandy beach, mixed sand/mudflats, and lagoon and bay shore; less commonly found foraging on rocky groins and jetties. During migration, often in coastal rice fields; true inland records rare after migration.

DISCUSSION: An observer driving down the coastline in Jun is greeted by a cacophony of calling Willets, each male broadcasting its *pee-willet* call while perched precariously upon a telephone line or fence post. After the Killdeer, Willet is the UTC's most common nesting shorebird. Willets nest abundantly in coastal zone upland sites, building a nest within dense vegetation such as marshhay cordgrass. Our breeding population is the eastern *Catoptrophorus s. semipalmatus.* The western subspecies, *C. s. inornatus,* winters here, apparently replacing the eastern birds. Although many publications refer to the eastern birds as permanent residents, there are no known UTC or eastern U.S. records after Sep (Kevin Karlson, pers. comm.). Eastern birds are browner and smaller than their western counterparts (Sibley 2000).

The Galveston CBC logs an average of 421 Willets annually, with a high of 1,112 in 1989. Spring migration peaks in mid-Apr, and the fall passage has bimodal peaks in Aug and Nov. During spring, migrant Willets spill into rice fields close to the coast (e.g., CHA and BRA). Large gatherings can total hundreds of birds, such as the 1,002 seen 23 Apr 1987 along the coast. Sightings away from the coast are rare and usually occur during fall migration as western birds first arrive along the UTC (however, we suspect a lone Willet seen 19 Jun 1988 in WAR to have been a late spring migrant *C. s. inornatus*). A dyed Willet seen by Eubanks 26 Aug 1990 had been marked and banded that Jul at Quill Lakes, Saskatchewan (*fide* C. Sexton).

WANDERING TATTLER
Heteroscelus incanus

Accidental
23 Apr–8 May 1992 Galveston, GAL (TBRC 1992-64; TPRF 1090) (AB 46:448, 500)

HABITAT: With few exceptions, nonbreeders are found on rocky shorelines.

DISCUSSION: The Wandering Tattler is well named. Its migration takes it from Alaska (and probably Siberia) to such far-flung coasts as Japan, California, Ecuador, the Galapagos, New Zealand, Australia, and many islands in the South Pacific (Hayman et al. 1986). Despite its long and broad flight path, it does not visit the eastern coasts of the Americas. Thus one of the most astonishing records for the UTC (as well as the entire Atlantic Basin) was a Wandering Tattler located by British birders on a rocky groin along the Galveston waterfront. Few local birders investigate these short bits of rocky habitat that define the beaches along the Galveston seawall. However, aside from the Galveston and Quintana/Surfside jetties, they represent some of our few rocky substrates for shorebirds at the Gulf's edge. Subsequently, this bird was photographed in breeding plumage and observed by throngs of grateful birders.

SPOTTED SANDPIPER
Actitis macularia

Uncommon winter terminal migrant

WINTER: (7–8, 10, 12 Jul) **mid-Jul to late May** (24, 26 × 2, 27 May; 6 Jun)

HABITAT: Rocky groins, bulkheads, and jetties, fishing piers and wooden structures along the shore, shorelines of ponds and lakes, the edges of plowed fields with standing water, bar ditches, bayous, and sloughs.

DISCUSSION: Although never common, a few Spotted Sandpipers are present on the UTC for most of the year. In winter the species is primarily solitary. During migration flock sizes rarely exceed four to five individuals, if indeed they can be called flocks, for Spotted Sandpipers in a group segregate so widely that flock structure is nearly indistinguishable. Spotted Sandpiper avoids not only intraspecific but also interspecific contact, only infrequently feeding alongside other shorebirds. Fall migrants return in force in mid-Jul, yet the remaining fall months show little variation in numbers from the normal wintering population. The Freeport CBC averages 16 per year, with a peak of 41 in 2002.

Spring migrants arrive late, and only in May do we see a significant push through our region (e.g., 23 along the coast 2 May 1992). Although Audubon found Spotted Sandpipers nesting along Houston's Buffalo Bayou in the mid-1830s, there is no recent evidence of breeding. We are aware of a summer record—28 Jun 1987.

UPLAND SANDPIPER
Bartramia longicauda

Common transient migrant

SPRING: (4, 13, 15 Mar) **mid-Mar to early May** (16, 20–21 May)

FALL: (28 Jun; 5, 15–16 Jul) **mid-Jul to late Sep** (23, 29 × 2 Sep; 9, 18 Oct)

HABITAT: Widely distributed throughout the grasslands and cultivated fields of the region; overgrazed pasture, harvested hayfields, golf courses, plowed agricultural lands, rice paddies, and even freshly mowed residential lawns.

DISCUSSION: The quavering whistles of Upland Sandpipers fill our nights during the first cool days of autumn. The first significant fronts of the fall season propel thousands of Uplands to the grasslands in South America, and as they pass overhead they mark their presence with their distinctive call. Uplands begin arriving in mid-Jul, although late Aug and early Sep define the period of peak fall movement. However, their fall movement is closely related to the season's first cold fronts to our north (normally early Sep), and passage is often complete by mid-Sep. This is easily demonstrated from counts at the High Island Rig (70 miles offshore) in 1999 when 137 birds were seen or heard on 7 Sep, 85 on 21 Sep, 1 on 29 Sep, 3 on 9 Oct, and 4 on 18 Oct. We are aware of only one record of an Upland remaining into early winter (21 Dec 1982 at Attwater Prairie-Chicken NWR).

In spring this species arrives in early Mar and peaks in early to mid-Apr, with small numbers lingering through mid-May. During spring shorebird surveys (Eubanks and F. Collins), a total of 629

Upland Sandpipers was detected during 108 encounters in 12 habitat types. More than 90 percent were observed 50 or more miles from the coast. Natural habitat (burned prairie) and moderately disturbed habitat (pasture) represented 60 percent of the total, a circumstance almost exactly opposite from that of American Golden-Plover. However, like the American Golden-Plover, Uplands make extensive use of large inland turf farms. Uplands are also found in burned prairie and shortgrass pastures with thick grass up to eight inches in height. Eubanks and Collins observed 247 Upland Sandpipers in pastures with grass that varied from two inches (belly) to eight inches (back) height. While they seemed to prefer pastures without brush or rank weeds, they were tolerant of Plains wild indigo, a plant often prominent in severely overgrazed pastures. During mid- and late afternoon, Uplands were observed in the shade produced by these plants. Although Uplands stringently avoid coastal habitats, one was seen on the beach 5 Sep 1993 (JEF). Hunters at the end of the nineteenth century specifically targeted Uplands for the market; Singley (1893) commented that in 1891 he found Upland Sandpiper to be "common in the market" in Galveston. Alteration of native habitat has apparently diminished the number of Upland Sandpipers breeding in portions of the Great Plains.

ESKIMO CURLEW
Numenius borealis

Largely mono-seasonal: former spring migrant, possibly now extinct

Accepted Texas records

Unknown date unknown Texas location (*AMNH 738187)

1861 unknown Texas location (*MUM B.09395)

23 Apr 1868 Long Point, Washington (*USNM 011118)

8 Mar 1877 N. Padre Is., Nueces (*AMNH 80026) (Oberholser 1974)

19 Mar 1878 Gainesville, Cooke (*Museum of Comparative Zoology, Harvard 171759)

17 Mar 1880 Gainesville, Cooke (*Field Museum of Natural History, Chicago 2143) (Oberholser 1974)

17 Mar 1880 Boerne, Kendall (*Museum of Vertebrate Zoology, Univ. of CA 106841)

19 Mar 1881 Corpus Christi, Nueces (*Topeka MNH 266)

22 or 25 Mar 1889 Brownsville, Cameron (*British MNH 1965-M-2960)

26 Mar 1889 Brownsville, Cameron (*British MNH 1965-M-2961)

27 Mar 1889 Brownsville, Cameron (*British MNH 1891-10-20-1037)

28 Mar 1889 Brownsville, Cameron (*British MNH 1891-10-20-1029)

28 Mar 1889 Brownsville, Cameron (*British MNH 1891-10-20-1031)

28 Mar 1889 Brownsville, Cameron (*British MNH 1891-10-20-1033)

2 Apr 1889 Brownsville, Cameron (*British MNH 1889-10-20-1032)

28 Mar 1890 Brownsville, Cameron (*British MNH 1891-10-20-1034)

13 Mar 1894 Brownsville, Cameron (*Memphis Museum 660)

22 Mar–26 Apr 1959 Galveston Is., GAL (TBRC 2000-125) (Williams 1959; Peterson 1960; Oberholser 1974)

24 Mar–15 Apr 1962 (2) Galveston Is., GAL (TPRF 790) (AB 16 : 431; Oberholser 1974)

Additional UTC unsubmitted records

29 Apr 1945 (2) Galveston Is., GAL (Heiser 1945; Peterson 1960 says 20 Apr, correct date is 29 Apr; Oberholser 1974)

3–6 Apr 1960 Galveston Is., GAL (AFN 14 : 405; Oberholser 1974)

31 Mar–3 Apr 1961 Galveston Is., GAL (Oberholser 1974)

29 Mar 1964 (2) Galveston Is., GAL (AFN 18 : 469)

17 Apr 1987 Sabine Pass, JEF (AB 41 : 459)

HABITAT: Shortgrass prairie, overgrazed, harvested or plowed fields, golf courses, probably lake or pond edge; exceptionally sand flats and sandy beach.

DISCUSSION: Before the undoing of the buffalo herds, the plowing of the Great Plains, and the decimation of some of our most common migratory birds (such as the Passenger Pigeon and Trumpeter Swan) by uncontrolled market hunting, Eskimo Curlew may have been one of the region's most abundant early spring migrants. Even into the twentieth century, Strecker (1912) considered it a "common migrant through extreme eastern section of the State." Since

that time, however, this species has spiraled toward extinction. Recent UTC records that we recognize include Heiser's observation of 2 on Galveston Is. 29 Apr 1945 (Heiser 1945) and a series of records in the late 1950s and early 1960s from W Galveston Is. (Emanuel 1961, 1962; Pettingell 1967). Although an occasional Eskimo Curlew is still reported from the UTC (invariably without documentation), the one record since the 1964 sighting that we consider plausible was of a single, well-described individual observed by John Arvin on 17 Apr 1987 as it flew over Sabine Pass into Louisiana. Note that this would have been at the late end of the historic migration date range.

Martin (1990) adequately summarized historical occurrences in Texas. A review of these data and the inclusion of specimens recently relocated define a migratory window between 7 Mar and 7 May, with an apparent peak between 10 Mar and 5 Apr. Generally, the dates of old specimens cluster in Mar. Three birds collected in West Texas near Fort Stockton on 4 May 1860—now lost, unfortunately for science—would represent the only May specimens from Texas and would have been far west of the species' expected range. An elliptical migrant, this curlew bypassed Texas in the fall.

The curlew's historical center of abundance in Texas apparently extended between the 95th parallel (Galveston Is.) on the east and the 98th (Rio Grande Delta region) on the west. The center point of this region is Lavaca and Matagorda bays. In north Texas, abundance appears to shift somewhat W toward the High Plains.

We know little about the exact habitats preferred by Eskimo Curlews migrating through our region. Based upon anecdotal accounts in the early ornithological literature, conversations with many observers associated with the Galveston sightings, and visits to historical curlew observation sites on Galveston Is., we have developed a rough assessment of the bird's habits. Many historical accounts mention American Golden-Plover (another elliptical migrant) as a cohort species. In fact, a common link between the historical accounts and the Galveston sightings is the consistent presence of American Golden-Plover in the same fields. Therefore we suspect that prior to the general alteration of their habitat, the curlews would have occurred with golden-plovers in prairie burns and "eat-outs" (areas grazed to the ground by bison) on the extensive coastal prairie that dominated the

Upper Texas Coast. In areas subsequently impacted by agriculture (yet prior to their wholesale decline), overgrazed pastures, harvested or burned hayfields, and freshly plowed agricultural lands would have been selected.

WHIMBREL
Numenius phaeopus

Common spring and uncommon fall transient migrant, uncommon winter resident, rare summer nonbreeding straggler

SPRING: (2, 11, 14 Mar) **early Mar to mid-May** (25, 29, 31 May); 10 Jun and 30 Jun records may represent summering birds or late and/or early migrants.

FALL: (1, 4 Jul) **early Jul to late Sep, a few remaining through the winter** (12, 28 Jan, 9 Feb)

HABITAT: Rice fields near the coast (JEF, CHA, BRA), avoiding seemingly identical inland paddy fields in W. HAS, FOB, and WAR; also burned prairie, overgrazed pasture; in fall, the few that appear are usually found on beaches and intertidal sand flats.

DISCUSSION: The Whimbrel is an elliptical migrant that appears on the UTC primarily during spring. Whimbrels arrive in late Mar, peak in late Apr, and remain in small numbers through May. Single compact flocks approaching 100 individuals are not uncommon, and feeding flocks massing in particularly productive fields may total in the thousands (1,017 on 2 May 1992; 1,067 on 9 May 1992; 2,645 on 27 Apr 1994).

Fall migrants arrive by the end of Jun or early Jul, trickling through in small numbers (2 to 5 individuals) through late Sep. Fall arrival is obscured by a few nonbreeders that remain at the major sand flats through the summer months. Wintering birds are rare—only 25 percent of the Galveston counts (all singles) and 20 percent of the Freeport CBCs find the species. The occasional wintering birds are often found among flocks of Long-billed Curlews or on oyster reefs on Galveston Bay (J. Stevenson). Whimbrels congregate in flooded rice fields such as in the gumbo clay soils of our eastern counties, where crawfish are profuse and often harvested. This association is tenuous, however, because if the fields are not plowed periodically, Chinese tallow seedlings may cover them. Along the UTC, crawfish appear to be the Whimbrel's single most important prey item. Laughing Gulls regularly hover over the same paddies and pirate these morsels from the beaks of hungry Whimbrels.

LONG-BILLED CURLEW
Numenius americanus

Common winter terminal migrant, common transient migrant, rare summer nonbreeding resident

WINTER: **early Jul through mid-Apr;** arrival and departure dates obscured by residents

HABITAT: Prairie, plowed cultivated fields, harvested hayfields, mowed turf, golf courses, and to a lesser degree sandy beach and sand flat.

DISCUSSION: Long-billed Curlew contradicts the inclination of so many of our shorebirds to restrict their distribution to either salt or fresh water. Wintering curlews belong to two major categories—large inland flocks using plowed fields and grazed or mowed pasture, and small coastal groups scattered on sand flats and beaches. Those wintering on sand flats feed primarily on small fiddler crabs (*Uca* spp.) that they adroitly extract from sand burrows. Flock and site fidelity appear strong, as same-sized groups may be found at the same wintering locations year after year. We are unsure about the degree to which individual curlews move between inland and coastal habitats and populations. Long-billed Curlews are present year-round, with a few nonbreeders remaining at major sand flats through the summer months. However, their population does exhibit distinct seasonal fluctuations, especially for the inland birds. The first push of fall migrants appears from late Jun through the second week of Jul, followed by a gradual increase through Nov. Peak numbers occur during winter with CBC highs of 717 (in 2001) at Freeport and 218 (in 1989) at Galveston. Numbers decline from Feb through Apr to a summertime low. The species nested on the UTC during the last century; three adults with seven young were seen near Almeda (HAS) 1 Jun 1910, but we are aware of no recent records.

HUDSONIAN GODWIT
Limosa haemastica

Largely mono-seasonal: uncommon to common spring, rare fall transient migrant

SPRING: (10–11, 17 Apr) **mid-Apr through early Jun** (29 May; 2, 10 Jun)

FALL: (15, 19, 26–27 Jul) **mid-Jul through early Nov** (26 Oct; 9–10 Nov)

HABITAT: Rice fields, crawfish ponds, margins of reservoirs, pools and ponds, coastal and inland, rare on coastal sand or mudflats.

DISCUSSION: Of the elliptical migrants that appear along our coast in spring (the others being American Golden-Plover, Whimbrel, and White-rumped Sandpiper), Hudsonian Godwit squeezes through the narrowest of time slots on the return to its breeding grounds in S Alaska and E toward Hudson Bay. The UTC is its center of spring abundance in the United States, extending E to the SW Louisiana prairie and SW to the central Texas coast. Substantial flocks may be found packed into rice fields and crawfish ponds (e.g., 400 in CHA and GAL 12 May 1979; 530 in E WAR 9 May 1987; 685 in CHA rice fields 12 May 1990). In our region the Hudsonian Godwit is a bird of inland freshwater habitats, and we are aware of only two saltwater records (Bolivar and Galveston Is., both during wet cold fronts; J. Stevenson). Indeed, on several occasions we have seen migrating flocks arriving from over the Gulf's open waters, only to continue straight inland to their preferred habitats. En route they must pass over literally tens of thousands of shorebirds feeding just below them on the Bolivar Flats. This species is found almost exclusively in rice paddies (where Marbled Godwits infrequently wander), feeding in areas of deep water from which most of its shorter-legged associates are barred. This godwit has a very narrow migratory window. Migrants begin to appear in mid- to late Apr and peak in mid-May. By early Jun, the movement has been completed.

In fall nearly all Hudsonian Godwits migrate to the southern tip of South America via the E coast of the United States (the Great Circle route), and they are virtually absent from the UTC during that season. However, a few Hudsonians have wandered through our region during the fall. We recognize reports from Jul through Nov, although these comprise only nine records from the past 50 years. One of the state's few documented fall birds was photographed 15 Sep 1991 by Eubanks and Behrstock in an oilfield pond just north of High Island (TPRF 1057). We recognize a single winter record—one injured bird reported by Arlie McKay from Cove 26–27 Dec 1952.

UTC birders should also be on the lookout for Black-tailed Godwit (*Limosa limosa*) and Bar-tailed Godwit (*L. lapponica*). Black-tailed has occurred as close as Vermilion Parish, Louisiana (11–12 May 1994), and the Bar-tailed has been found on the Gulf Coast of Florida (Dittman and Cardiff 2002).

MARBLED GODWIT
Limosa fedoa

Common winter terminal migrant, uncommon summer nonbreeding resident

WINTER: **early Jul through late Apr;** arrival and departure dates obscured by summer nonbreeders

HABITAT: Tidal flats, less frequently sandy beaches, grassy fields, flooded rice paddies; rare inland.

DISCUSSION: Marbled Godwit is our marine counterpart of the Hudsonian Godwit. Its numbers are concentrated at the major sand flats, although during migration a few individuals stray to coastal rice fields where confusion with a dull Hudsonian is possible. The species is nearly absent from true inland locations, although we regularly observe them on Galveston Is. and at Freeport, feeding (often alongside Long-billed Curlews) in wet or dry grassy fields and particularly golf courses, after a late winter or early spring rain. Our largest flocks are primarily in the NE coastal counties, Rollover Pass, the Bolivar Flats, and San Luis Pass (225 at Bolivar Flats 17 Feb 1990).

Marbled Godwit's seasonal pattern is quite typical of those for many marine winter terminal migrants. Peak numbers are observed in spring migration, with a rapid decline in late spring to a few nonbreeding stragglers at the major sand flats. Fall migration is prolonged, with the initial movement in mid-Jul. By early Aug, 100 or more are often present at Bolivar Flats. Numbers build to a peak in Oct, then decline to a relatively stable wintering population from Dec through Feb. The Galveston CBC records an average of 101 birds per year, with a peak of 282 in 1991. The few inland sightings of this godwit have generally occurred during fall migration (i.e., 13–26 Jul 1989 in WAR).

RUDDY TURNSTONE
Arenaria interpres

Common winter terminal migrant, common transient migrant, uncommon nonbreeding summer resident

WINTER: (early Jul) **early Aug–mid-May** (through late May); arrival and departure dates obscured by summering individuals

HABITAT: Sandy beaches, tidal sand and mudflats, rocky breakwaters and jetties; inland during migration in rice paddies and wet plowed fields.

DISCUSSION: For much of the year our beaches and sand flats are visited by these widespread shorebirds. Turnstones often forage in the manner implied by their name, although in our region they are more likely to be seen probing under driftwood, around a discarded beer can, or through the innards of a rotten fish on the beach.

Ruddy Turnstone is characteristic of the marine shorebird guild and, except during migration, is strictly limited to the coastal zone. Typically this species forages on sandy beach, mixed sand and mudflat, and to a lesser degree rock jetties and groins. During migration, however, it may be found throughout rice fields near the coast. The peak spring movement, when birds are most likely to be encountered away from the coast, is during May, about which Williams (1938) commented: "At about mid-May thousands, all in breeding plumage, suddenly appear everywhere near the coast; but within three weeks have disappeared, leaving only a few stragglers." Our high counts (2,540 on 13 May 1989; 2,045 on 9 May 1992; 1,928 on 16 May 1992) mirror Williams's experience. Significant numbers return to the UTC by early Aug, most continuing south. Wintering Ruddy Turnstones are rather uncommon, most concentrating on the major sand flats. The Galveston CBC averages 128 per year, with a high of 499 in 1982.

SURFBIRD
Aphriza virgata

Accidental spring vagrant
16 Mar 1988 W. Galveston Is., GAL (TBRC 1988-222) (AB 42:459)
18–21 Apr 1995 Anahuac NWR, CHA (TBRC 1995-61; TPRF 1356) (AFN 49:275)
6 and 11 Apr 2003 Old Hwy 87, JEF (TBRC 2003-29)

HABITAT: Surfbirds winter on rocky coastlines of the E Pacific Ocean, including some offshore islands, less frequently on sand or gravel beach and saline impoundments.

DISCUSSION: Our coast is bereft of the rocky shores, points, and promontories preferred by shorebirds such as Wandering Tattler, Purple Sandpiper, and Surfbird. The latter is a West Coast species that is almost never seen away from the Pacific. It is, however, highly mobile, and migrates from its arctic breeding grounds as far south as Tierra del Fuego. Surfbirds have strayed to the UTC's salty margin on the three occasions noted, once in Mar and twice in Apr with single records in GAL, CHA, and JEF. Of the eight TBRC-accepted records, seven occurred in Apr; the eighth is the Mar sighting listed here.

RED KNOT
Calidris canutus

Uncommon winter terminal migrant, uncommon transient migrant, rare summer nonbreeding resident

WINTER: (mid-Jul) **late Sep–late Apr** (late May); arrival and departure dates obscured by the presence of summering birds

HABITAT: Intertidal flats and sandy beaches; rarely in coastal rice fields during migration.

DISCUSSION: Known once as the "Robin Snipe" for the same ruddy breeding plumage that gave rise to its present name, the Red Knot is seen along our coast only in late spring and early fall. For much of the year the knot is a decidedly unremarkable, squatty, gray shorebird often seen waddling along the beach at the water's edge.

Although occasionally present in moderately large flocks, Red Knot is among the least common of our regularly occurring marine shorebirds. During the last several years, knot populations have diminished at an alarming rate, a situation attributed to overharvesting of horseshoe crabs (*Limulus polyphemus*) near the Red Knot's Delaware Bay staging areas. After progressing without regulation, this fishery reduced the horseshoe crab population by 75 percent, depriving northbound knots (and other shorebirds) of the energy they derived from eating the crab's eggs. Census data in southern South America revealed a 51 percent decline in knot populations between 2000 and 2002. Populations on Delaware Bay (where 70 percent of North America's Red Knots may occur on one day) decreased 12 percent between 2001 and 2002 (Delaware Riverkeeper Network 2004).

Wintering knots, formerly numbering in the low hundreds but now typically less than 100, are confined to sandy beaches, sand flats, and less commonly rock jetties. During spring migration, the majority is confined as well to the Gulf's sandy margins; however, a few may be seen among the thousands of shorebirds that swarm the coastal rice fields or large rainwater pools. Their spring passage is comparatively significant; single coastal flocks in mid- to late Apr can contain several hundred birds (e.g., 600 on 29 Apr 1989; 725 on 13 May 1989; 600 on 28 Apr 1990), although these numbers may be optimistic by today's standards. A bird seen by several observers at San Luis Pass, GAL, on 26 April 2001 was banded in Patagonia, Argentina, during Mar 1998 at San Antonio Oeste.

Red Knots return southward relatively late; small numbers appear annually in late July with more significant numbers appearing by the third week of Sep. Fall passage culminates in mid-Oct, and during Nov numbers decline steadily to a stable Dec-through-Feb winter population. Small winter flocks, usually containing fewer than 10 individuals, are uncommonly and irregularly distributed along the coastal beaches and flats, often alongside Sanderlings and Ruddy Turnstones. A few Red Knots linger through the summer at the major sand flats; the total summer population was until recently no more than 75 to 100 birds (75 at Bolivar Flats 30 Jun 1984). Presently, summering individuals may total only a dozen birds or fewer, and some summers pass with no reports of the species.

SANDERLING
Calidris alba

Common winter terminal migrant, abundant transient migrant, uncommon summer nonbreeding resident

WINTER: (early Jul) **Aug–mid May** (early Jun); arrival and departure dates obscured by summering birds

HABITAT: Sand beach and mixed sand and mudflats.

DISCUSSION: Most beachgoers are familiar with the Sanderling, the sandpiper that is forever chasing the waves along our beaches. In fact, the Sanderling is our most common open beach shorebird, well known to surf fishermen, sunbathers, and picnickers

who frequent the Gulf's edge. Inland sightings of this shorebird are virtually nonexistent, their distribution being restricted to the marine shore. Here they run back and forth, feeding on tiny shrimplike amphipods that live in the soupy sand at the water's edge, or picking through newly washed-up sargassum seaweed for its bounty of crab, shrimp, and fish larvae.

The Sanderling's spring migration peaks in late Apr and May, by which time many individuals are trimmed in the warm brown hues of their breeding plumage. Migrant flocks are often impressive (8,225 on 16 May 1992; 2,000 on 14 Oct 1978; 1,900 on 29 Apr 1989). Summering groups of nonbreeders may linger (i.e., 100 on 15 Jun 1986 at San Luis Pass). Fall migration is bimodal, with peaks in Aug (adults) and Oct (juveniles). Observers frequently see border skirmishes at the edges of winter territories. Records of marked birds indicate that Sanderlings often defend the same winter feeding territories year after year. Sanderlings are most abundant at those large sand flats that provide roosting sites within close proximity to tidal feeding areas. The largest concentrations are at Bolivar Flats and San Luis Pass, where winter roosts may contain more than 500 individuals.

SEMIPALMATED SANDPIPER
Calidris pusilla

Common transient migrant, more numerous in spring

SPRING: (8, 11 Mar) **mid-Mar through early June** (9, 15, 18–19 Jun)

FALL: (2, 9–10, 13, 15 × 2 Jul) **mid-Jul through late Sep** (29 Sep; 5, 13 Oct)

HABITAT: Primarily freshwater habitats such as ponds, rice fields, margins of reservoirs and lakes, infrequently on beach and sand flats, although occasionally common there.

DISCUSSION: Observers in our region have struggled with the Semipalmated Sandpiper for decades, and no UTC shorebird has been as consistently misidentified or misunderstood. As an example, consider that for years most local observers assumed that Semipalmated Sandpipers wintered along our coast. Strecker (1912) reported that it wintered "regularly on the coast." Oberholser (1974) considered the species to be "very common locally to fairly common along the coast" during that season.

No local CBC before the late 1970s lacked its requisite complement of these sandpipers. Only after Phillips (1975) pointed out the error of our ways did we realize that virtually all of the small, black-legged peeps along our coast in winter were in fact Western Sandpipers. Truth be told, we believe that only within the past decade have we reached a competent understanding of the status and distribution of this shorebird in our region.

On the UTC, Semipalmated Sandpiper is generally found in freshwater habitats. Observations of this species mingling with its close cousins in marine habitats are fewer, although Jim Stevenson notes flocks of them each spring (newly arrived birds?) on brackish pools at Pelican Is. and San Luis Pass. The E end of Galveston Is. has historically provided an opportunity to see this niche partitioning demonstrated in a dramatic fashion. The U.S. Army Corps of Engineers maintains a spoil disposal site near the E end of the island (the San Jacinto Disposal Site), which is only a few hundred yards inland from E Galveston's beach and tidal flats (Big Reef). The disposal site collects fresh rainwater, while the beach and flats on the Gulf of Mexico are saline. During spring, Western Sandpipers may be found at both locations, with the largest concentrations on the flats at Big Reef. Semipalmated Sandpipers, however, are usually found only at the disposal site and do not venture over to Big Reef, even though the habitat there would appear to be suitable. A similar avoidance of saline habitats by Semipalmated Sandpiper has been observed along the central Texas coast (Charles Clark, Rockport, pers. comm.).

The largest concentrations of Semipalmated Sandpipers are found in inland and coastal rice fields (6,411 on 19 Apr 1990; 5,235 on 12 May 1990; 5,201 on 27 Apr 1994). Smaller numbers are also found on the shores of ponds and lakes, along brackish tidal sloughs, and at the edge of freshwater marshes. Spring migrants arrive in mid-Mar; and peak passage occurs during late Apr through mid-May. Small numbers continue to trickle through the area through the first week of Jun and a very few linger into the third week of Jun.

Compared with spring, the volume of fall migration is much diminished. Migrants begin to appear in mid-Jul, with the peak fall passage in late Jul through Aug. Semipalmated Sandpipers remain, albeit in low numbers, through early Oct. We note again, for the record, that we are aware of no evidence of this species remaining along our coast during the winter months.

WESTERN SANDPIPER
Calidris mauri

Common to abundant winter terminal migrant and bi-seasonal migrant

WINTER: **Early Jul to early Jun;** arrival and departure dates obscured by lingerers

HABITAT: Tidal flats, during high tides may feed on sandy beach, freshwater and brackish pools, rice fields, lake edge.

DISCUSSION: Along with Sanderling, Dunlin, and Short-billed Dowitcher, Western Sandpiper is the most common wintering shorebird along our coast and indeed the most abundant *Calidris* in North America. Large concentrations winter at the major tidal sand flats, such as Bolivar, San Luis Pass, and Rollover Pass. Many wintering birds demonstrate strong site fidelity; color-marked individuals return year after year to locations such as Bolivar Flats.

The species is also common inland, where flocks frequent harvested paddy fields, the shores of ponds and lakes, and waterfowl impoundments. Feeding flocks can be significant, both on the tidal flats and in coastal rice fields (6,425 on 21 Jan 1990; 6,000 on 20 Aug 1988; 4,000 on 22 Jan 1989). Inland concentrations are normally a fraction of those on the coast.

Spring migration peaks in mid-Mar; they have diminished by mid-Apr and are largely gone by mid-May. Even during the heat of summer a few non-breeding Westerns may remain along our coast, presumably deferring their northward migration until the next breeding season. Although scarce from mid-May through Jun, during a concerted search at Bolivar Flats virtually any day of the year, you have a chance of seeing this sandpiper, an arctic shorebird that nests no closer to our region than northeastern Alaska.

Fall migrants return in mid-Jul, with bimodal peaks in Aug and Oct. Peak numbers diminish to a stable wintering population Dec through Feb. The Galveston CBC averages 1,953 per year, with a high of 8,373 in 1981. Banding data demonstrate that about 90 percent of the UTC's wintering Westerns are males, the females wintering further south.

Given the short bill length of male Westerns (at times approaching that of a female Semipalmated), it is understandable how many early UTC observers mistakenly reported large numbers of wintering Semipalmated Sandpipers.

LEAST SANDPIPER
Calidris minutilla

Common winter terminal and bi-seasonal migrant, rare summer lingerer

WINTER: (1–2, 4 × 2 Jul) **early Jul through late May** (18 × 2, 19, 22, 24 May)

HABITAT: Inland pond and lake shorelines, rice fields and reservoirs, and inshore on the edge of brackish sloughs and bayous; coastally, on algae-covered rock jetties and in small numbers on the major sand flats, foraging at the edge of salt marsh, and on upland dry mudflats.

DISCUSSION: Least Sandpiper is the smallest of our peeps, and its drab brownish gray feathering (almost identical in color to the surfaces upon which it feeds) combines with its size to create a shorebird that can be remarkably difficult to locate. In fact, this sandpiper's rolling *greet, greet* call often alerts observers to its presence long before the bird itself is actually seen. Least Sandpipers are common wintering shorebirds in freshwater habitats throughout our region but are also seen along the coast, where they forage on jetties and rocky groins. At times they may be seen on tidal flats, where they stay along the dry outer edges or feed on algal mats. The most significant concentrations occur inland and generally during migration (1,075 on 15 Mar 1987; 1,000 on 18 Mar 1979; 1,000 on 19 Aug 1979). This sandpiper's migration to and through the UTC is similar to that of the Western, although it tends to remain later. Spring migration peaks in Mar, with a rapid decline through mid-May. Unlike for Western Sandpiper, we have few summer records for this species (10 June 1989 in CHA; 13 Jun 1999 at San Bernard NWR; 19 June 1988 in WAR, 26 June 1994 at Bolivar Flats; and 21 Jun–1 Jul 1999 at Brazoria NWR). The first fall migrants return the first week of Jul, with an Aug peak followed by a gradual decline in numbers to a stable wintering population Dec through Feb. The Galveston and Freeport CBCs average 243 and 164 birds per year, respectively.

WHITE-RUMPED SANDPIPER
Calidris fuscicollis

Common late spring transient migrant, rare summer straggler, and very rare fall transient migrant

SPRING: (30–31 Mar; 9 Apr) **mid-April through early June** (11, 16–17 Jun; 1–9 Jul)

FALL: (8 Oct; 4, 12 Nov)

HABITAT: Inland rice fields, margins of freshwater impoundments; usually avoid marine habitats, and only occasionally do migrants stray to the major tidal flats, perhaps representing birds that have just crossed the Gulf and have stopped for a breather.

DISCUSSION: Along with Hudsonian Godwit, White-rumped Sandpiper is the latest arriving of the UTC's northbound spring shorebirds. Although we recognize a few Mar records, a more typical arrival date for the species falls in the second or third week of Apr. The bulk of the spring passage occurs in mid-May, and late spring flocks may contain thousands of individuals (11,151 on 12 May 1990 in CHA rice fields; 2,870 on 13 May 1989). Through the first week of Jun, the species continues to be common in inland paddy fields and on the shores of freshwater impoundments. On occasion, flocks of breeding (alternate) plumage birds are seen later in summer, such as 40 on 17 Jun 2002 and 30 on 1 Jul 1999, both at Roger's Pond at Brazoria NWR; this shallow-grade pond concentrates hundreds to thousands of shorebirds when it rapidly dries up in summer. During this same period, the pond and others on the refuge have also consistently attracted (basic) winter plumage birds, 24 Jul 1998, 10–28 Jul 1999, 5 Aug 2000, and 15 Jul 2001; these are presumably "summering" birds as most have an obvious injury to a leg or wing. Few fall records exist; we note one (a juvenile) at Bolivar Flats on 8 Oct 1978, another at Danbury, BRA, on 4 Nov 2003 (J. Stevenson), and at least one more on 12 Nov 1977. Curiously, Strecker (1912) reported this sandpiper to be a "common winter resident on the coast." Oberholser (1974), however, acknowledges only a single specimen from winter (10 Feb 1885 in Calhoun Co.). There is little historic evidence to support Oberholser's record of this rather late migrant: 5 birds seen on the west end of Galveston Is. 5 Feb 1932.

White-rumped and Baird's sandpipers are the only two U.S. peeps in which wing tips extend past the end of the tail. Baird's usually occurs earlier in spring, although the two may overlap. During fall, both are rather uncommon. In spring, note the Baird's tea-colored breast vs. the White-rump's white breast with fine vertical streaks.

BAIRD'S SANDPIPER
Calidris bairdii

Uncommon spring and fall transient migrant

SPRING: (1, 7, 10 Mar) **mid-Mar through mid-May** (22–24, 27–28 May)

FALL: (14–15, 19 Jul) **early August through late Oct** (28, 30 Oct; 5 Nov)

HABITAT: Freshwater habitats including rice fields, grassy areas, occasionally beaches and tidal flats.

DISCUSSION: The Texas migration route of the Baird's Sandpiper lies largely to the W of the UTC. For example, this sandpiper is among the most common migrant shorebirds to frequent the Hornsby Bend water treatment ponds in Austin. In our region, a single day's count in excess of 100 individuals is exceptional. Spring migrants are primarily restricted to freshwater environments, and the largest concentrations are found in inland rice fields. Baird's Sandpiper is also found on grazed or mowed pasture, shortgrass prairie, golf courses, and (uncommonly) the shores of lakes and ponds. Although Baird's Sandpipers arrive in early Mar throughout S Texas (and we do recognize several Mar records from the UTC), in general spring migrants arrive along the UTC the first week of Apr, peaking late in the month. Spring migration extends through mid-May. The species is significantly more common in the spring than during the fall, when it is quite scarce. Fall migrants reach the UTC in early Aug, and young of the year exhibiting boldly scaled backs trickle by through late Oct. Apparently, this sandpiper usually flies non-stop to South America from staging areas in the mid-western United States (Jehl 1979), thereby overflying the UTC in fall. As an example, Eubanks's highest single-day fall count was only 14 adults on the beach at San Luis Pass 25 Aug 1987. Unlike spring migrants, fall Baird's Sandpipers frequent the coastal zone and may be seen feeding among seaweeds deposited on the beach or water hyacinth washed seaward from local rivers or impoundments. During Sep and Oct, birds (mostly juveniles) are found on the major sand flats and sandy beaches. Fall migrants stay on the UTC for an extremely short period, typically only one or two tidal cycles. We recognize a single winter record, an injured bird discovered on the Brazos Bend CBC 26 Dec 1993.

PECTORAL SANDPIPER
Calidris melanotos

Common bi-seasonal transient migrant, rare winter lingerer

SPRING: (14, 16, 21 Feb) **early Mar through late May** (10, 13, 16, 19–22 Jun)

FALL: (27 Jun, 5, 10–16 Jul) **mid-Jul through early Nov** (30 Oct, 10 × 2, 11 Nov)

HABITAT: Freshly flooded rice fields, grazed or flooded pasture, freshly tilled agricultural lands, shores of freshwater lakes and ponds.

DISCUSSION: Pectoral Sandpiper is often eclipsed in numbers by many of the shorebirds that crowd the rice fields. However, few paddies or damp pastures are without this widespread shorebird; and although Lesser Yellowlegs or Long-billed Dowitchers may be more abundant, few migrants are as prevalent within the freshwater guild. Records of the species in saltwater habitats are limited to a few individuals observed during peak migratory movements. Migrants arrive in late Feb, heralding the approach of spring. Pectorals peak during the last two weeks of Apr (1,453 on 23 Apr 1987; 1,120 on 28 Apr 1990; 1,279 on 29 Apr 1989), and linger through early Jun. Three individuals on a pond 19–22 Jun 1988 (WAR) were possibly very early fall migrants but also may have summered (i.e., may have been short-stopped spring migrants). Fall migrants begin returning in mid- to late Jul. Peak passage is during the first two weeks of Aug, but migrants are still present in small numbers through early Nov. Occasionally, Pectoral Sandpipers remain along our coast into early winter (i.e., one on 1 Dec 1991 in JEF, 10 on Galveston Is. 18 Dec 1985, one 19 Dec 2004 on the Freeport CBC, one 21 Dec 1993 in WAR, and one in W HAS 26 Dec 1980). Observers should be aware that Pectorals exhibit extreme sexual dimorphism, and some males may be nearly three inches longer than females. Local birders have mistaken these large males with bright orange to yellow legs and yellow-based bills for Ruffs. The

Pectoral's finely streaked breast, contrasting sharply with its white belly, should rule out its rarer relatives, including Sharp-tailed Sandpiper, only recently recorded in Texas.

PURPLE SANDPIPER
Calidris maritima

Very rare winter terminal migrant

4–5 Dec 1953 Galveston, GAL (TPRF 506) (Peterson 1960; Oberholser 1974)

28 Dec 1968–1 Mar 1969 Freeport, BRA (TPRF 27) (AFN 23: cover, 497)

19–22 Dec 1976 (2) Freeport, BRA (TBRC 1988-252; TPRF 704) (AB 31:349, 771)

12 Nov 1977–14 Jan 1978 Freeport, BRA (TBRC 1988-251; TPRF 686) (AB 32:228, 374)

21 Dec 1980–Feb 1981 Freeport, BRA (TBRC 1988-250; TPRF 687) (AB 35:639)

17 Dec 1989–mid Apr 1990 Freeport, BRA (TBRC 1990-8; TPRF 856) (AB 44:291–92, 461, 877)

16 Dec 1990–25 Apr 1991 (1–2) Freeport, BRA (TBRC 1990-154; TPRF 947) (AB 45:291, 470, 884)

20 Dec 1992 Freeport, BRA (TBRC 1993-11) (AB 47:851)

19 Dec 1993 Freeport, BRA (TBRC 1994-43)

29 Nov 2002–3 May 2003 Quintana, BRA (TBRC 2002-119; TPRF 2080)

29 Apr 2003–4 May 2003 Port Bolivar, GAL (TBRC 2003-37)

HABITAT: Virtually restricted to the area's few rock groins and jetties.

DISCUSSION: Wintering primarily on rocky shorelines along the Atlantic Coast (regularly south only to the Carolinas), Purple Sandpiper occurs as a sporadic visitor to Texas. Completely lacking a natural rocky coastline, our state would seem to be less hospitable than most. However, the relatively recent construction of rock groins, jetties, and breakwaters along our coast now allows wayward Purple Sandpipers to sustain themselves here for the winter season. Most recent UTC records are limited to the jetties that protect the harbor entrance at Freeport (BRA). The arrival dates of these birds are misleading, for most have been found during the Freeport CBC, about the only time during the year that this jetty is regularly inspected. We suspect that Purple Sandpipers arrive in our region as early as mid-Nov (12 Nov 1977) and linger as late as early May (3 May 2003). It is also possible that the Freeport records (accounting for eight of the 14 accepted state records) represent a mere five or six total individuals returning year after year.

DUNLIN
Calidris alpina

Common to abundant winter resident and transient migrant, rare nonbreeding summer resident

WINTER: (28–29 Sep; 8 Oct) **late Sep through late May** (5–7, 10 Jun)

HABITAT: Intertidal flats, bay shoreline; less common in rice fields.

DISCUSSION: Dunlin is one of our latest-arriving wintering shorebirds; only Mountain Plover, Purple Sandpiper, and American Woodcock appear later. A few Dunlin straggle to the coast in late Sep, but normally, significant numbers do not appear until the cold snaps of Oct. Observers have often reported this shorebird much earlier in the fall, due, we believe, to a confusion between Dunlin and female Western Sandpipers (which have a decurved bill that may seem as long), wading Stilt Sandpipers, or a handful of oversummering Dunlin.

Once it has arrived, however, Dunlin is the most abundant saltwater shorebird on the UTC. In fact, based upon our spring shorebird counts, Dunlin is the most abundant shorebird in our region in absolute numbers, whatever the habitat. It is generously distributed throughout the coastal zone, the largest concentrations occurring predictably at the major tidal flats. The Galveston CBC (which includes Bolivar Flats) averages 1,120 per year, with a high of 3,158 in 1980. Significant numbers are also found inshore along bay shorelines. Although highest numbers occur along the coast, the Dunlin, along with the Western Sandpiper, is rather adaptable in its habitat requirements, utilizing inland fresh water as well. Spring migration occurs Mar through May, and by late May the species has largely vacated the UTC. Spring staging flocks, both coastal and inland, can be staggering (e.g., 32,385 on 27 Apr 1994; 7,900 on 16 May 1992; 7,170 on 19 Apr 1991).

Oversummering Dunlin are rare but regular; recent records include individuals on 21 Jun 1986;

29 June 1991; 25 Jun–3 Jul 1994 (breeding plumage); 4 Jul 1999 (3 birds, 2 in breeding plumage); 9–28 Jul 1999 (winter plumage); 10 and 23 Jul 1994 (winter plumage); 9 Aug 1992; and 29 Aug 2000 (molting from breeding plumage).

CURLEW SANDPIPER
Calidris ferruginea

Very rare spring–early summer transient migrant
28 Apr–8 May 1984 Crystal Beach, GAL (TPRF 314) (AB 38 : 933)
24 Jun–7 Jul 1994 Bolivar Flats, GAL (TBRC 1994-120; TPRF 1274) (AFN 48 : 962)
24 Nov 1994 JEF (TBRC 1994-186) (AFN 49 : 69)
30 Apr–2 May 1997 Galveston, GAL (TBRC 1997-80; TPRF 1625) (AFN 51 : 894)

HABITAT: Locally on mudflats and shallow freshwater impoundments; elsewhere, various freshwater habitats; also muddy seacoast and brackish impoundments.

DISCUSSION: Of the world's shorebirds, Curlew Sandpiper is among the most likely to roam. Breeding in a limited region in central Siberia (rarely in Alaska), this shorebird undertakes a monumental long-distance migration south to Africa, India, and Australasia. From these migratory pathways this sandpiper frequently strays, appearing unexpectedly in the most unlikely of places. Vagrants have appeared throughout much of the New World, including both coasts of the United States and many inland states. Most of the nine Curlew Sandpipers recorded in Texas are spring migrants returning north; only three appeared during fall.

The first UTC (and Texas) Curlew Sandpiper drifted to Crystal Beach on the Bolivar Peninsula. Discovered by Lars Jonsson on 28 Apr 1984, it remained through 8 May. The bird frequented a shallow freshwater pond several hundred yards inland from the Gulf. It arrived in mottled prenuptial plumage; during its stay the gray feather edges on its belly rapidly wore away, revealing its brilliant cinnamon breeding plumage. On 24 Jun 1994, Winnie Burkett discovered another in winter (basic) plumage at the Bolivar Flats. This sandpiper, the second to occur in our region, foraged on intertidal mudflats, where it associated with Western Sandpipers and a late Dunlin.

STILT SANDPIPER
Calidris himantopus

Common bi-seasonal transient migrant, rare winter terminal migrant and summer lingerer

SPRING: (1, 8, 11 Mar) **early Mar through late May** (2–3, 16, 21, 22 Jun)
FALL: (27, 29 Jun; 1–4; 6–7 Jul) **early Jul through late Oct;** departure dates obscured by winter lingerers
HABITAT: Flooded paddy fields, shallow impoundments, variable pools and ponds, and natural rainwater-filled depressions.

DISCUSSION: With a little perseverance (particularly when working to tease a few basic plumage stilts out of a sea of winter dowitchers), a Stilt Sandpiper may be found along our coast during virtually any week of the year. Stilt Sandpipers begin arriving in early Mar. Spring passage peaks in early May, and large numbers remain through the third week of the month. As with many freshwater shorebirds, this species lingers into summer only rarely (four in breeding plumage on 16 Jun 2002 at Brazoria NWR; 21 Jun 1972 at High Island; 22 Jun 1987 at Anahuac NWR). Our late Jun dates of lingerers approach our early fall arrival dates within five days, and we cannot be certain which way some of these birds were headed.

Fall migration is an extended exercise; birds arrive in early Jul, peak in Aug, and linger through late Oct. Barring particularly frigid weather, this species winters in small numbers along the coast (more commonly in S Texas). We recognize winter records through Feb (16 Feb 1992, 17 Feb 1980, 28 Feb 1963), and we have no doubt that this species is present in our region in low numbers throughout most of the winter months. A flock of 88 present 15–20 Feb 2002 in a spoil cell near Freeport represents an exceptionally large winter concentration. The Freeport CBC tallied this species on only 14 of 48 counts, with a high of 36 in 1991.

Stilt Sandpipers feed with a dowitcher-like sewing machine motion in significantly deeper water than do their fellow freshwater migrants (with the exception of Hudsonian Godwit), and are therefore often found in the deeper ponds and pools not exploited by other shorebirds. Migrant flocks may at times be sizable (3,005 on 12 May 1990; 750 on 31 Jul 1989).

BUFF-BREASTED SANDPIPER
Tryngites subruficollis

Common spring, uncommon fall transient migrant

SPRING: (7, 14, 18 Mar) **mid-Mar through late May** (18–19 May; 3 Jun)

FALL: (4, 20, 24, 31 Jul) **late Jul to late Sep** (14, 24 Oct)

HABITAT: Freshly tilled fields, recently flooded rice paddies, dry pastures, golf courses, inland ponds; uncommonly on the Gulf's shores.

DISCUSSION: Buff-breasted Sandpiper is more commonplace in our region than was supposed by many early observers, although Singley (1893) judged them "the most abundant of the sandpiper found in the market" in Galveston in 1891. Perhaps in the past, their cryptic plumage caused them to be overlooked by birders. We recognize the difficulty in detecting a species that, like Upland Sandpiper, Sprague's Pipit, and Eastern Meadowlark, is rendered virtually invisible against a variegated palette of dry grass stems. Additionally, the soil of many of our inland counties is the same buffy color as this sandpiper, and large numbers feeding in freshly plowed fields may blend in perfectly.

Buff-breasted Sandpiper is most effectively seen during late spring, against an unbroken carpet of brilliant green rice sprouts. Here males experiencing the season's first rush of raging hormones face off belly to belly, elevating their wings to expose the snow-white linings (a breeding display rarely seen by those who do not venture to the High Arctic). Buffies begin to arrive the third week of Mar and peak during the last week of Apr and the first week of May. The last migrants are usually encountered in mid-May.

In fall the species returns by the end of Jul, passing in small numbers through the end of Sep. A flock of twelve on the shore of a small irrigation pond 19–22 June 1988 in WAR may have summered locally, being later than our latest spring record by two weeks and earlier than our earliest fall record by a similar period. This sighting most likely represents one of the few Jun records outside Canada or Alaska. However, another one was observed 4–20 Jul 1989, also in WAR. This bird, with an injured leg, may represent a lingering spring migrant that was unable to continue northward. During shorebird surveys, Eubanks and F. Collins detected Buff-breasted Sandpipers in nine habitat types, where a total of 586 individuals were located during 33 encounters. They were most common more than 50 miles inland in HAS and WAR. Forty miles from the coast (WAR), they are present on turf farms. Nearer to the coast, in CHA and Matagorda cos., they were found consistently but never in large numbers. These data suggest that migrating Buff-breasteds are more apt to utilize inland areas for staging. Other observers found concentrations of Buff-breasteds in coastal rice fields, including several flocks in BRA and Matagorda cos., and just over 500 birds were counted in CHA in mid-Apr 1998 (Behrstock). Although this species is not a "beach bird," we have a few fall records from that habitat, including 2 at Bolivar Flats 19 Sep 1992; 18 E of High Island 5 Sep 1993 (Behrstock photos), and a juvenile on the beach near Sabine Pass 14 Oct 1978.

RUFF
Philomachus pugnax

Very rare bi-seasonal transient migrant
29 Mar–1 Apr 1981 Galveston, GAL (TBRC 1989-118)
11 Apr 1981 High Is., GAL (TBRC 1988-78)
12–14 May 1984 Crystal Beach, GAL (TBRC 1988-226; TPRF 667) (AB 38:933)
7 Sep 1989 High Island, GAL (TBRC 1989-201) (AB 44:123)
18–21 Apr 1993 CHA (TBRC 1993-86; TPRF 1158) (AB 47:431)
21 Apr 1994 near Anahuac NWR, CHA (TBRC 1994-88) (AFN 48:317)
28 Apr 2001 Brazoria NWR, BRA (TBRC 2001-91) (TPRF 1984)
19 Apr 2003 CHA (TBRC 2003-34)
17 Apr 2002 CHA (TBRC 2002-85)
19 Apr 2003 CHA (TBRC 2003-34)

HABITAT: Breeds from the British Isles eastward across northern Europe and Asia, rarely to Alaska. Locally, occurs at muddy sites with standing water, either fresh (rice paddies or marsh edge) or saline (shallow coastal embayments).

DISCUSSION: Ruff is an Old World shorebird, breeding consistently no closer to Texas than E Siberia or perhaps Scandinavia. British and European birds migrate via W Europe to their wintering grounds in Africa; more easterly breeders winter in southern Asia, Asia Minor, Australia, and on several island groups (A.O.U. 1998). Much like Curlew Sandpiper, Ruff has a penchant for wandering, and the species has been seen throughout the New World—along both coasts of the United States and in Mexico, Guatemala, Panama, and Peru.

There is a considerable size difference between males and females. What makes this species especially impressive are the elongated feathered neck ruffs and ear tufts and the array of colors exhibited by breeding plumage males. Unfortunately, these distinctive breeding males have yet to be seen in our region; local birders see only the rather drab females (once known as reeves) or males in basic plumage. This has presented us with a conundrum. Of the 32 published sightings from the UTC, to date only nine have been reviewed and accepted by the TBRC. Observers have consistently confused migrating Pectoral Sandpipers with Ruffs; the two may occur together in rice fields or at pond edges. Both are of similar configuration and may exhibit brightly colored legs and bills, but they differ in plumage details. Many local birders have not carefully and cautiously worked through this identification challenge, and their sightings have been rejected by TBRC reviewers.

SHORT-BILLED DOWITCHER
Limnodromus griseus

Common winter terminal migrant, common transient migrant, uncommon nonbreeding summer lingerer

WINTER: **Early Jul through late May;** arrival and departure dates obscured by summer lingerers

HABITAT: Coastal mudflats, tidal sloughs and bayous, rarely and briefly (during migration) in coastal rice fields and wet pastures.

DISCUSSION: The two dowitchers extend our opportunity to delve into habitat partitioning by salinity. Structurally equivalent, they are so similar that while in basic (nonbreeding) plumage, their call is about the only certain means of separating the two. Short-billed Dowitcher, however, is a bird of the coast. Wintering flocks gather on the major tidal flats, with a few spreading around the bay margins. Although they mix with Long-billed Dowitchers in brackish marshes, the most substantial concentrations remain immediately along the coast.

During spring migration, Short-billed Dowitchers bleed into coastal paddy fields, particularly those near the Gulf. But even during migration they are absent from freshwater habitats farther inland, such as the rice fields of W HAS and WAR. During spring, migrants often gather in substantial flocks (2,955 on 23 Apr 1987; 2,365 on 26 Apr 1986). Migrants arrive in early Mar; their passage continues through late May. Numbers of Short-billed Dowitchers remain on the tidal flats through summer, and flocks of 50 to 75 may be encountered on the local flats. Occasionally, brackish ponds near the coast harbor large numbers in winter (basic) plumage (240 on 1 Jul 1999 at Brazoria NWR).

Fall migrants begin arriving in early to mid-Jul; the height of migratory passage is in Aug and Sep, but many remain to winter. The Galveston and Freeport CBCs average 292 and 202 per year, respectively. Color banding has demonstrated that the birds show considerable wintering site fidelity, certain marked birds returning annually to the Bolivar Flats.

LONG-BILLED DOWITCHER
Limnodromus scolopaceus

Common winter terminal migrant, abundant transient migrant, rare nonbreeding summer lingerer

WINTER: (9, 13, 15 × 2 Jul) **early Jul through late May** (28–29, 31 × 2 May)

HABITAT: Rice and flooded tilled fields, margins of impoundments, reservoirs, and ponds.

DISCUSSION: Long-billed Dowitcher replaces Short-billed in freshwater wetlands. The Short-billed does occur in some numbers in coastal rice fields during migration, but the Long-billed is essentially absent from marine habitats. For example, in the years that Eubanks banded shorebirds at Bolivar Flats, a Long-billed Dowitcher was never captured, although Short-bills were frequently netted. Within its chosen habitats, this dowitcher is an extraordinarily abundant shorebird. Migrant flocks cover the rice fields, and single-day counts exceeding 20,000 individuals are possible (20,000 in CHA rice fields 14 Apr 1979; 20,000 in BRA and CHA rice fields 17 Apr 1988). Spring migrants begin arriving in mid-Mar, with peak passage in mid-Apr. Numbers decline rapidly after the third week of Apr, and the birds become scarce by mid-May. Unlike Short-billed Dowitcher, its marine counterpart, this freshwater species lingers only rarely through summer. Fall migrants return the third week of Jul, and fall migration, while only a shadow of the spring's, peaks in mid-Oct. Smaller numbers overwinter; the Freeport and Galveston CBCs average 115 and 111 per year, respectively, however, many CBC dowitchers are not identified to species.

WILSON'S SNIPE
Gallinago delicata

Common winter terminal migrant

WINTER: (25–26 Aug; 3 Sep) **early Sep through late Apr** (29 Apr; 1, 5 May)
SUMMER: (19 Jun)
HABITAT: Rice fields and irrigated agricultural land, harvested paddy fields (left flooded for waterfowl hunting), freshwater marsh, muddy fields, roadside ditches, margins of reservoirs, ponds, and pools.
DISCUSSION: On the UTC, Wilson's Snipe (formerly Common Snipe) is a freshwater obligate. Although the birds are occasionally present in the emergent vegetation of brackish pools along the coast, we have yet to record them in a truly marine environment.

Snipe arrive from late Aug to mid-Sep, but large concentrations are not present until mid-Oct. In favorable habitats such as muddy fields in WAR, moderate numbers may be present (400 in WAR 18 Oct 1987; 400 in WAR 17 Nov 1987). However, given the secretive nature of this bird, its cryptic coloration, and its uncanny ability to disappear completely in two-inch-tall rice stubble, we admit that thousands could easily winter in the rice fields and inland marshes of our region. The Freeport CBC averages 87 per year, with a high of 333 in 1975. Migratory peaks are not readily discernible, and given the wide availability of suitable habitat, the winter population is more or less stable. This species is a winter terminal migrant; relatively few continue to wintering grounds farther southwest. Snipe begin to depart in early Apr, with very small numbers remaining into the first week of May. We have a single summer record: Bob Honig saw and heard one 19 Jun 2003 on the Katy Prairie Conservancy, WAR.

Snipe and American Woodcock are the only shorebirds legally hunted in Texas. Currently, hunters may take eight snipe per day. In the past, the total kill of snipe and other lightly hunted migratory species was not rigorously monitored. Beginning in Oct 1997, Texas hunters joined sportsmen in 21 other states participating in the Harvest Information Program (HIP), in which hunters are asked to estimate their take of snipe and American Woodcock; King, Clapper, Virginia, and Sora rails; and Common Moorhens and Purple Gallinules (Sasser 1997). This program is also expected to clarify the annual take of various doves. After answering a few short questions, licensed hunters are eligible for a free permit entitling them to a three-bird daily bag limit of Sandhill Cranes.

AMERICAN WOODCOCK
Scolopax minor

Uncommon winter terminal migrant, rare early summer breeder

WINTER: (2 × 2, 3, 11 Aug) **late Oct through mid-Mar** (29 Apr; 6, 10 May)
HABITAT: Riparian woodlands bordering creeks and streams, bottomland forest, swamps.
DISCUSSION: American Woodcock is unique among UTC shorebirds in its preference for woodland habitats. The species is never abundant, and most winters pass with only a handful of sightings. Woodcock are most common in the riparian woodlands that border the creeks and streams in inland counties such as HAS and WAR. They are extremely rare along the coast; Eubanks recorded woodcock at Galveston Is. on only one occasion (a single individual in a small isolated woodlot on 9 Dec 1984). The woodlands included within the Freeport CBC circle do regularly hold the species, with an average of seven per year found on that count and a peak of 39 in 1977. Woodcock roost in leaf litter during daylight hours, streaming out into bordering agricultural fields to feed at dusk. They arrive on the UTC quite late in the fall (late Oct and early Nov), rarely being observed before Dec. However, the arrival and departure dates of this bird are complicated by the presence of a local (NE Texas) breeding population. A few woodcock appear in early Aug, birds we suspect to be local breeders dispersing from NE Texas. The main woodcock flight of birds that breed well to our north does not appear until Oct. Woodcock often linger through mid-Mar, and many of these late individuals engage in flight displays and songs. We do recognize reports from late Apr and early May, birds we suspect are northern breeders that have delayed their return (since birds in E Texas begin courtship as early as late Jan). Two birds Weeks found displaying in Lake Jackson (BRA) 31 Jan–5 Feb 2001 may have represented breeding

birds; however, no nest was found. The woodcock has been confirmed as breeding in our region on several occasions. Oberholser (1974) reports that J. J. Carroll discovered a nest with eggs near Fauna at the southern end of Sheldon Reservoir (HAS) 17 Mar 1926. Eubanks found a woodcock with young in N HAS 15 Mar 1977. Julie A. Robinson and Glenn Aumann are responsible for our most recent breeding record of Woodcock. These researchers discovered a nest with two eggs 6 Feb 1997 at the University of Houston Coastal Center (west of La Marque and north of Hitchcock, GAL). By 9 Feb the nest contained four eggs, but on 20 Feb the observers found the nest depredated (Robinson and Aumann 1997). In addition, there are several summer records that probably indicate nesting. For several years in the mid-1980s woodcock displayed in the Houston Arboretum, occasionally lingering into Jul. Arlie McKay reported summer birds in Jun from Cove (26 Jun 1936, 22 Jun 1947), and Wes Cureton reported scaring one up along White Oak Bayou (HAS) 1 Jul 1985.

In 1997 the USFWS expressed concern over the decline in the woodcock population and implemented restrictive hunting regulations. According to the USFWS, woodcock numbers have experienced long-term declines throughout the bird's range, their breeding populations having fallen 52 percent in the Eastern Region since 1968. In the Central Region, breeding populations have declined 39 percent since 1968. Currently, Texas hunters' daily bag limit is three; previously it was five.

WILSON'S PHALAROPE
Phalaropus tricolor

Common transient migrant, rare winter terminal migrant

SPRING: (4, 9, 16 Mar) **early Mar through late May** (22, 24, 27–30 May; 8 Jun)

FALL: (1, 4, 11, 15–16 Jul) **mid-Jul through early Oct** (departure and arrival dates obscured by lingerers)

HABITAT: Flooded rice fields, freshwater impoundments, rarely on sandy beach and tidal flat.

DISCUSSION: Of the three species of phalaropes, Wilson's is the only one appearing regularly along our coast. We encounter most of our phalaropes in rice fields during the spring, when dozens may be seen scattered among the teeming masses of migrant shorebirds. Spring migrants arrive in late Mar, but they are not common until the end of Apr (i.e., 329 at Brazoria NWR on 25 Apr 2000). Small numbers are present through mid-May. A few nonbreeders may remain through summer (25 Jun 1936; 21 Jun 1972; 28 Jun 1978; 17 Jun 2002).

Fall migrants arrive in mid-Jul, peak in late Aug, and remain in small numbers through late Sep. In fall, large feeding flocks are occasionally present on area ponds and reservoirs (800 in a pond near the E end of Galveston 28 Aug 1982 and 510 in another at Freeport 21 Aug 1999). Although these phalaropes winter regularly in S Texas, the UTC is too far north to encounter them. Rarely, they remain through early winter. There are HAS records as late as 4 Jan 1976 and 12 Jan 1992. Sightings at Danbury (BRA) and West Galveston, both on 26 Feb, may represent early migrants.

RED-NECKED PHALAROPE
Phalaropus lobatus

Very rare transient migrant
4 Oct 1959 Baytown Tunnel, HAS
29 Apr 1979 NE Brazoria, BRA
5 Nov 1980 Brazoria NWR, BRA
4 Sep–17 Oct 1982 East Galveston, GAL
18 May 1985 East Galveston, GAL
20 Sep 1986 San Luis Pass, GAL (photographed)
5–7 Oct 1986 High Island oil fields, GAL
30 Apr 1988 Galveston Island, GAL
15–27 Sep 1999 Freeport, BRA (photographed)
3 Sep 2000 near Bolivar Flats, GAL
26 Sep 2004 Bryan Beach, BRA

HABITAT: Coastal ponds and reservoirs, tidal flats.

DISCUSSION: During its nonbreeding season, Red-necked (formerly Northern) Phalarope is primarily a pelagic species and is never common anywhere in Texas. The occurrence of this species on the UTC is especially irregular and unpredictable, and the authors have observed it here only three times. On 4 Sep 1982, Behrstock and J. Morgan discovered one associating with approximately 800 Wilson's Phalaropes at the U.S. Army Corps of Engineers dredge fill site at E Galveston Is., and Eubanks relocated—apparently— this same individual 14 Sep. Additionally, Eubanks photographed a single Red-necked in a small pool at San Luis Pass 20 Sep 1986. Weeks found one among hundreds of Wilson's in a pond along the Freeport

Storm Levee on 15 Sep 1999; this bird remained until 29 Sep. In addition to our own sightings, we recognize seven more records of this species from the UTC. Although it is not a TBRC review species, these ten records are summarized here. Seven of the ten occurred during fall migration.

RED PHALAROPE
Phalaropus fulicarius

Accidental spring transient migrant
20 Apr 1984 Bolivar Flats, GAL (TPRF 318) (AB 38 : 933)
21 Apr 1999 San Luis Pass, GAL (TBRC 1999-40)

DISCUSSION: Like the previous species, Red Phalarope is pelagic during the nonbreeding season. Most Texas records are from the interior of the state (at least 26 as of 2004); locally, this shorebird has been well documented only twice. We note reports on at least three other occasions, but those sightings were not reviewed by the TBRC. One of these unsubmitted records was a winter (basic) plumage bird seen from the Quintana/Surfside jetties by Will Russell on 22 Dec 1974 (AB 29 : 490).

Jaegers, Gulls, Terns, and Skimmer

Because of its location, the UTC hosts an especially rich diversity of members of the family Laridae: jaegers, gulls, terns, and the Black Skimmer. Thirty-two species in four subfamilies have been recorded, slightly less than one-third of the entire family.

The origin of the UTC's larids is an interesting study in zoogeography. A few of the local species are found around the world, either associating with the continental margins (Gull-billed and Caspian terns) or fanning out over the high seas (jaegers, Sooty Tern). Several, including Pomarine Jaeger, Black-legged Kittiwake, Sabine's Gull, and Arctic Tern, nest in the Arctic, migrating south across the world's oceans to the Northern or Northern and Southern hemispheres. Broadly speaking, most of our gulls (i.e., Glaucous, Thayer's, Mew, Little, Sabine's) come to us from high latitudes and most of the terns and the Black Skimmer from the warmer tropical or subtropical shores, but there are exceptions.

The three jaegers, all arctic nesters, winter at sea, occasionally appearing in our nearshore waters or on land. Most sightings are made as observers scan the Gulf for birds scavenging around fishing boats. Identifying adult jaegers is usually not a problem, but immatures and badly worn individuals can be extremely perplexing and have been the subject of many articles in the popular and technical literature.

Of the UTC's 16 gull species, only one, the abundant and charismatic Laughing Gull, nests locally. It and other species such as Ring-billed, Herring, and Great Black-backed gulls have profited from their association with humans and our abundant refuse. Neither Franklin's nor California gull is a bird of the Arctic; both nest on fresh or saline waters in the interior of the continent, often in huge colonies. Two rarely observed UTC gulls come to us from southern waters: Yellow-footed Gull, which (along with the locally rare Elegant Tern) has its stronghold in the Gulf of California, and Kelp Gull, a widespread bird of Southern Hemisphere seacoasts that has recently nested on islands off Louisiana.

Barring some of the smaller species, most of our gulls mature in three or four years. Each year's plumage is slightly to significantly different from that of the previous year. Add seasonal differences, feather wear, and hybrids to the mix, and it is easy to see why gulls are some of the most difficult birds to identify despite their size and approachability. Even common species may present identification problems, especially when they appear in unusual places. New birders do well to concentrate on the adults; however, most soon wind up tackling the more confusing younger birds. Dramatic improvements in optics and field guides have revealed confusing species such as gulls to a new generation of birders, and no doubt our knowledge of this fascinating group along the UTC is destined to grow more precise in future years.

The UTC's 12 terns, six of which nest locally, are a delightful assemblage of mainly coastal species.

Although a few are pelagic and infrequently seen, most can be studied at leisure on the local beaches or at sand flats such as Bolivar or San Luis Pass. A day's birding during the latter part of Apr will usually produce seven species, all in readily identifiable plumage. Two are marsh birds: Black and Gull-billed terns. Black Terns may be numerous on the beaches and flats at the Gulf's edge, but the Gull-billed Tern is an insect feeder, more likely to be seen a little inland.

Few people have trouble identifying the Black Skimmer, a locally common UTC breeder rendered virtually unmistakable by its strikingly contrasting black and white plumage and asymmetrical, scissorlike red bill. The brown juveniles look like large, dark terns, but their bill shape gives them away. Recently used UTC nesting sites include flats near San Luis Pass, islands in Galveston Bay, and Freeport's well-known colony in a Dow Chemical parking lot, which the birds have used since 1968.

Skimmers belong to a small subfamily of three tropical species. Like most terns—to which they are closely related—skimmers feed on fish, but instead of diving for their prey, they snatch it from the surface during long, low, graceful flights. Most skimmers occur along the coast, but they may wander far inland, often roosting on sand bars.

POMARINE JAEGER
Stercorarius pomarinus

Uncommon to rare winter terminal migrant, uncommon transient migrant

WINTER: (23 Jul; 22 Sep) **early Sep through late Mar** (21, 26 Apr; 4, 11 May; 10 Jun)

HABITAT: Open Gulf and inshore waters.

DISCUSSION: Jaegers are birds of the open sea, and only occasionally do they venture close enough to the coast to be detected by land-based observers. Unlike on the lower coast (Port Aransas, Port O'Connor, Port Isabel), we have yet to organize consistent offshore boat trips that would help us determine the exact status of this species or the other pelagic birds that occur in adjacent Gulf waters. We are dependent, therefore, on the relatively few occasions when these birds are grounded (particularly in the summer months) or when birds veer close enough to the

coast to be identified. Recent pelagic trips out of Port O'Connor have detected Pomarine Jaegers offshore as early as 26 Jul, and we suspect that migrant jaegers begin to arrive in late Jul and early Aug (we are unsure whether our 26 Jul bird at Bolivar Flats recently migrated or oversummered). Pomarine Jaegers appear to be most common Nov through Mar (Peake and Elwonger 1996) and are seen sporadically throughout the winter months. Jaegers frequent tidal passes and ship channels (e.g., the Galveston and Surfside/Quintana jetties), drifting near shore when the blue water line shifts toward the beach or when attracted by fishing activities. During such periods we may see several jaegers working the gull and tern flocks that concentrate over the clear water or following shrimp boats to harass the gulls and terns until they disgorge their catch (usually a small fish thrown overboard as the catch is sorted). Onshore observers scanning flocks of birds following shrimp trawlers have a good opportunity to observe these birds; in this manner, at least 15 were seen from shore along the Bolivar Peninsula on 27 Feb 1998.

Louisiana State University's Migration Over the Gulf Project (MOGP) recorded the species from the High Island Rig (70 miles offshore) between 26 Sep and 17 Nov 1999 when the study ended for the season. High counts were noted in mid-Nov with 20 Pomarine (plus 14 unidentified) jaegers on 14 Nov, 100 unidentified jaegers on 16 Nov, and 33 Pomarine on 17 Nov. The same rig recorded 10 Pomarines on 28 Mar 2000 and another on 4 May 2000. The spring report matches onshore reports from the late 1980s and early 1990s, when Eubanks and Behrstock noticed a significant migratory movement of seabirds in Mar. During that period thousands of gulls, terns, herons, egrets, Northern Gannets, and jaegers moved northeast in our nearshore waters (3 Pomarine, 9 Parasitic, 7 jaeger species during the 26 Mar 1989 migratory movement).

Evidence suggests that some nonbreeding jaegers remain on the wintering grounds through the summer months. In Europe, for example, "non-breeders remain widely scattered over the North Atlantic in summer, some staying in winter quarters" (Cramp 1983). Summer sightings from our coast suggest that, as in the North Atlantic, some nonbreeding jaegers remain in the Gulf. Occasionally a summering Pomarine Jaeger remains around one of the major tidal flats. As Cramp noted, "wearing and bleaching may create amazing variations" among immature jaegers as summer approaches. These jaegers normally spend several weeks here completing their molt (e.g., 31 May through 2 Aug 1986 at San Luis Pass). One noted 10–18 Jun 1998 at the mouth of the San Bernard River, BRA, may represent the same situation.

PARASITIC JAEGER
Stercorarius parasiticus

Rare winter terminal migrant, rare transient migrant

WINTER: (19 Aug; 10 Sep) **early Sep through late Mar** (23, 26 Apr; 16 May)

HABITAT: Open Gulf and inshore waters.

DISCUSSION: Based upon our limited knowledge, the Parasitic Jaeger appears to mirror the Pomarine along our coast, although in significantly lower numbers. Based upon his extensive experience in pelagic waters of the Gulf, Dwight Peake (pers. comm.) comments: "Parasitic Jaeger shows its distribution in pelagic waters much different from the Pomarine. Of several thousand jaeger sightings, fewer than 10 are of Parasitic. It does seem to be more common nearshore, but in my experience it is usually less common than Pomarine." We suspect that this jaeger arrives in late Jul and early Aug, with the primary push occurring in late Sep and early Oct. Parasitics remain in offshore waters through late Apr, although most have departed by Mar. We recognize a number of summer records, including three adults off of San Luis Pass 21 Jun 1961. An adult seen off the Quintana Jetty 19 Jul 1992 may have been an early fall migrant or a nonbreeder that remained in the Gulf through the summer months. Recent reports of birds seen from shore number about one per year, but this is largely a function of the number of observation hours.

LONG-TAILED JAEGER
Stercorarius longicaudus

Accidental visitor
27–30 Nov 1971 Gilchrist, GAL (TPRF 26)
    (AB 26: 87)

HABITAT: Open Gulf waters.

DISCUSSION: Although we admit that data are scarce, the Long-tailed appears to be the one jaeger

virtually absent from the Gulf in winter. Peake and Elwonger (1996) considered it "rare in spring and fall," although we note accepted Texas records indicating that the bird appears predominantly in late summer and fall (6, 8, 12–14, 17 Jun; 16, 26, 31 Aug; 30 Aug–2 Sep; 4–8, 5, 30 Sep; 2 Oct; 31 Oct–5 Nov; 3, 5, 27–30 Nov; 20 Feb). Only one of the Texas records is from the immediate coast, an immature found on the tidal flats at Rollover Pass, GAL, 27–30 Nov 1971. Given the difficulty in identifying jaegers, particularly those on the wing, we suspect that this species ventures to our state more frequently than these few records indicate, and late fall trips offshore will undoubtedly add to the number of sightings.

LAUGHING GULL
Larus atricilla

Abundant resident, common winter terminal migrant

HABITAT: Ocean, bays, beaches and mudflats, coastal rice fields, coastal freshwater impoundments, occasionally well inland.

DISCUSSION: We will not hazard a guess as to how many people have been ushered into the world of birds by throwing scraps of picnic lunches to Laughing Gulls begging at the stern of the Bolivar ferry. No gull is as familiar along our coast, appearing on numerous souvenirs from postcards to potholders. We photograph them begging for corn chips, hundreds scavenge around shrimp trawlers and fish docks, and at times prodigious flocks enliven our coastal tidal flats.

Laughing Gulls nest in immense colonies on coastal spoil islands, particularly Pelican Island off Galveston. Colonial waterbird data document over 22,000 breeding pairs recorded along the UTC in 2001, with about 6,000 breeding pairs each in the Pelican Island and North Deer Island colonies. After nesting, these gulls gather on the major tidal flats, and roosting flocks in late summer can be spectacular (68,000 counted by W. Burkett at Bolivar Flats 20 Aug 1993). Eubanks, Fred Collins, Keith Arnold, and others banded young Laughing Gulls in the Pelican Island colony for many years, and Eubanks's data demonstrate the migratory nature of this species. Band returns suggest that young UTC Laughing Gulls migrate S across the Gulf of Mexico in fall, rounding

Table 12. *Galveston Bay Laughing Gull Band Return Data*

Date Banded	Date Reencountered	Location Reencountered
27 Jun 1981	17 Oct 1981	Cow Bayou, Texas
27 Jun 1981	9 Jan 1983	93 miles W of Champerico, Guatemala
27 Jun 1981	25 Apr 1984	Galveston Island, Texas
27 Jun 1981	9 Aug 1988	Near Ixchel, Guatemala
3 Jul 1981	14 Jan 1982	Quepos, Costa Rica
3 Jul 1981	13 Nov 1983	Villa Morelos, Nayarit, Mexico
3 Jul 1981	19 May 1984	Aldama, Tamaulipas, Mexico
3 Jul 1981	6 Dec 1982	Puerto Vallarta, Jalisco, Mexico
3 Jul 1981	9 Feb 1982	Santo Tomás de Castilla, Guatemala
3 Jul 1981	9 Feb 1982	Port of Puntarenas, Costa Rica
3 Jul 1981	26 Aug 1987	San Luis Pass, Texas
3 Jul 1981	9 Sep 1985	18 miles S of Anahuac, Texas
2 Jul 1983	8 Mar 1984	Achotines, Panama
2 Jul 1983	2 Apr 1984	Champerico, Guatemala
1 Jul 1984	5 Nov 1985	Oaxaca, Mexico
1 Jul 1984	5 Jan 1986	Barrio La Esperanza, Guatemala
1 Jul 1984	6 Jan 1986	Crystal Beach, Texas
1 Jul 1984	14 Apr 1989	Bolivar Peninsula, Texas

the Yucatán Peninsula and entering the Golfo de Honduras. From there, they cross Central America to the Pacific Coast. Support for this notion may be found in the banding return data (table 12). We have received a return from Puerto Barrios, which is located on the Caribbean side of Guatemala within the Golfo de Honduras. Directly across Guatemala from Puerto Barrios, there have been two returns from Champerico, situated on the Pacific Ocean. Although these data are limited, we suggest this to be one of the routes by which Laughing Gulls cross from the Caribbean to the Pacific. Once across, they disperse widely along the Pacific Coast (south to Panama, north to Nayarit, Mexico). Incredibly, one individual strayed as far as the Marquesas, one of the five island groups of French Polynesia (C. Hacker data).

Laughing Gulls breed in their third summer, and young birds apparently do not return to the Texas coast until that time; note in the table the 19 May 1984 return from Aldama, Tamaulipas, Mexico. This gull, banded as a hatchling in 1981, may have been returning to the Texas coast to breed in its third year.

Laughing Gulls are primarily coastal birds, ventur-

ing inland only along the major rivers and bayous (such as Buffalo Bayou). Frequently they spread inland to feed in the coastal rice fields, particularly in spring. During this season they are often seen harassing Whimbrels, forcing them to disgorge prey (almost always a just-captured crawfish). The gulls also harass Brown Pelicans, sometimes riding on a pelican's back while waiting for it to make one slip and release part of its catch. A pelican defends against this pirating by holding its bill underwater until it has maneuvered the fish well into its gullet.

FRANKLIN'S GULL
Larus pipixcan

Uncommon bi-seasonal transient migrant, rare winter terminal migrant

SPRING: (6, 9 Mar) **early Mar to late May** (26 May; 15 Jun)

FALL: (22, 24 Sep) **early Oct to late Nov;** departure dates obscured by winter lingerers

HABITAT: Nests in large colonies on shallow prairie lakes. Most winter along the Pacific Coast of South

America, crossing the Isthmus of Tehuantepec to the Atlantic Coast as they migrate northward (Howell and Webb 1995). Locally on coastal tidal flats, rice fields, and impoundments.

DISCUSSION: To birders who have observed flock after flock of Franklin's Gulls passing northward over the King Ranch (Kenedy Co.), or inland of Corpus Christi (Nueces Co.), their relative absence along the UTC may seem curious. However, this dainty gull is decidedly noncoastal during migration, and large numbers are more likely to be seen well inland, as they have a nearly statewide migration path. Nonetheless, a few Franklin's Gulls do appear along the coast, usually at sites that attract other roosting or bathing gulls and terns: the Bolivar Flats, Texas City Dike, San Luis Pass, Quintana/Surfside jetties, or the large, temporary, and (usually) freshwater lake between High Island and the Gulf of Mexico. Each year a few Franklin's Gulls linger into winter; they have been found on just 11 of 48 Freeport counts (high of 12 in 1959) and 2 of 25 Galveston CBCs. Most lingerers leave by the end of Dec, but we recognize winter dates as late as 16 Feb 1978. Note that shorter-legged Franklin's Gulls may be missed among flocks of roosting gulls. Watch for their rounded pigeonlike heads and short bills. In flight, note the white band that isolates the wing tip of adults (unlike in the Laughing Gull).

LITTLE GULL
Larus minutus

Accidental winter terminal migrant

7–20 Apr 1984 Galveston Is., GAL (TPRF 511) (AB 38: 933)

9 Feb 1986 San Luis Pass, GAL/BRA (TBRC 1992-144) (AB 40: 301)

8–20 Apr 2001 Beaumont, JEF (TBRC 2001-72) (TPRF 1905)

27–29 Apr 2003 Beaumont, JEF (TBRC 2003-48)

6–18 Jan 2005 Quintana Jetty, BRA (seen and photographed by many obs.; TBRC 2005-39)

HABITAT: Open Gulf and bay waters.

DISCUSSION: The morning of 7 Apr 1984 Eubanks sat down to have breakfast on the deck of his home overlooking W Galveston Bay. A raft of Eared Grebes gathered nearby, accompanied by a small group of Bonaparte's Gulls. As the grebes plunged to feed, the gulls would dabble in the water over the submerged raft. Eubanks finally decided to focus a scope on this gathering, soon spotting the first Little Gull for the UTC (and only the third for the state).

The Little Gull is an Old World species, having only recently colonized North America. Of the 37 records for Texas as of 2004, 34 occurred after the 1984 Galveston sightings. During the 1990s Texas birders began to survey inland lakes and reservoirs regularly, particularly those in NE and far W Texas. As a result, species such as Little, Black-headed, and Mew gulls are being found with increasing regularity. Nearly all the Texas Little Gull records occurred during winter; however, three of the five local records are from Apr.

On 6 Jan 2005, a Little Gull in first winter plumage was located at the Quintana Jetty. It was observed both on the water, where it fed with Bonaparte's Gulls, and roosting on land in a mixed gull flock. Weeks, Will and Jan Risser, and others obtained unambiguous photos from as little as three feet away.

BONAPARTE'S GULL
Larus philadelphia

Common winter terminal migrant

WINTER: (13–14, 25 Oct) **mid-Nov through mid-April** (27 Apr, 1, 20 May)

HABITAT: Gulf and bay waters, roosts on beach and tidal flats; less common on local inland lakes and reservoirs.

DISCUSSION: Bonaparte's is the most diminutive of our regularly occurring gulls, seeming more like a tern than gull as it feeds along our beaches. Hovering over the white water, pattering over the foam, these gulls appear to be walking on the sea as they dart and tumble among the waves. At times, the swash zone may be alive with them, each line of breaking waves forcing dozens to hundreds into the air.

Bonaparte's Gulls arrive with the cold of winter and are usually not seen in numbers until Nov, Dec, or even early Jan. The Galveston and Freeport CBCs average 232 and 161 birds per year, respectively, with peaks counts of about 1,000 birds. Occasionally they pass through in late spring, by which time many have molted into their immaculate black-headed breeding plumage.

Most of our Bonaparte's Gulls are beach birds, and significant roosting flocks gather at the tidal flats (2,100 seen by W. Burkett at Bolivar Flats 23 Mar 1993). Frequently, they follow barges coursing the GIW, and many disperse rather widely throughout Galveston Bay (Baytown, Kemah, Seabrook). Only small numbers occur on the upper coast's inland lakes, although elsewhere in the state, dam spillways often attract large flocks. On three occasions Bonaparte's Gull has been found during summer: 27 Jul 1996 at Pleasure Island, JEF (juvenile), 9 Aug 1992 at Bolivar Flats, and 16–22 Aug 1976 at the Texas City Dike (photographed by Eubanks).

UTC birders should be on the lookout for the Old World counterpart of Bonaparte's Gull, the Black-headed Gull (*Larus ridibundus*). There are now more than 20 Texas records, most coming from inland reservoirs but one accepted Texas record from Baffin Bay in Kleberg Co. on the central coast. Black-headed Gull has both a different wing pattern and a differently shaped hood than those of Bonaparte's Gull.

MEW GULL
Larus canus

Accidental winter terminal migrant
23 Jan 2001 Galveston, GAL (TBRC 2001-19)

HABITAT: Winters on open coastal beaches, tidal flats, and bays, less frequently at inland sites.
DISCUSSION: Although liberal in its choices of habitats throughout its range, the Mew Gull has been recorded on the UTC beaches only once. This species nests both inland and coastally in western Canada and Alaska, utilizing lakes, streams, and other wetlands. Its global range is circumpolar; many records from North America's eastern seaboard pertain to the Old World form referred to as Common Gull.

Most of the 25 Texas Mew Gull sightings have occurred at interior lakes and landfills, and future UTC birders may find the same as greater attention is paid to these habitats. Among roosting gulls, note its diminutive size—it is the smallest of the white-headed gulls—and its tiny yellow bill, both useful departures for a more thorough diagnosis. Lockwood and Freeman (2004) note the dramatic increase in

Texas sightings after 1995 but could not differentiate observer bias from true population increase.

RING-BILLED GULL
Larus delawarensis

Common to abundant winter terminal migrant, uncommon summer lingerer

WINTER: **Late Aug or Sep through late May;** arrival and departure dates obscured by lingerers
HABITAT: Open Gulf and bay waters, tidal flats, sandy beach, inland lakes and reservoirs.
DISCUSSION: Although in absolute numbers the Laughing Gull eclipses all gulls along our coast, Ring-billed Gull is the most pervasive. Unlike Laughing and Herring gulls, it is not restricted to the Gulf's salty margins. Lines of these gulls are seen each winter's morning flying inland along the Gulf Freeway toward Houston from their roost sites along the shore. No UTC mall or shopping center is without a troupe of these gulls searching the parking lots for scraps.

Ring-billed Gulls begin to arrive along our coast in late Aug, although most wait until the cold fronts of late Sep provide the north winds that facilitate an easy flight. Wintering numbers are significant, the Galveston and Freeport CBCs averaging 2,841 and 1,577 per year, respectively, with highs of over 6,000. Most remain until May, and small numbers stay along the immediate coast through summer.

CALIFORNIA GULL
Larus californicus

Rare winter terminal migrant

WINTER: (26–28 Oct) **early Nov through mid-April** (1, 4, 6 May)
HABITAT: Gulf and bay waters, roosting on beach and tidal flats.
DISCUSSION: California Gull, widespread in the western United States and western Canada, occasionally strays E to Texas. For decades it went largely unrecorded in the state. Now the availability of improved field guides and Web pages that discuss the identification of gulls and their plumage variations, combined with improved optics and photographic

equipment, permit birders to attempt identifications that would have been unheard of 30 years ago. These advances, along with an increased interest in ferreting out rare birds, allow birders to detect more and more of these unusual gulls buried in the immense flocks that winter along our coast. For example, the TBRC accepts only one record prior to 1979, when the first UTC bird was photo-documented on 28 Oct at Texas City, GAL. The species was removed from the review list in 1999, as it now averages over the review maximum of five records per year. During most winters they are rare but regular on the UTC. The best locations to search for them are East Beach and along Galveston Island west to San Luis Pass. The winter of 2000–2001 produced exceptional numbers and as many as ten individuals were seen.

HERRING GULL
Larus argentatus

Common winter terminal migrant, uncommon summer lingerer

WINTER: **Mid-Sep through late May;** arrival and departure dates obscured by lingerers

HABITAT: Open Gulf and bay waters, beaches, tidal flats; uncommon inland.

DISCUSSION: Among our four common winter gulls (Laughing, Bonaparte's, Ring-billed, and Herring), the Herring Gull stands out for size alone. Most of our wintering Herrings are immatures, and these giant brown-and-gray gulls dominate any flock with which they happen to be consorting, both in size and in aggressiveness. These young birds are incredibly variable, exhibiting a broad sweep of browns, blacks, and grays. Herrings range from sooty gray, almost charcoal, to the lightest tan or even "washed-out" white. Just as we recommend that birders adopt the Red-tailed Hawk as the standard for measuring buteos (bigger than, lighter than, wings more pointed than), we suggest the same approach for gulls using the Herring Gull as a yardstick. Young Herrings often remain around the tidal flats during summer, and the combination of salt spray and summer sun may leave their feathers bleached and worn. Periodically we hear of a Glaucous Gull report from Jul or Aug. We simply advise all to remember that in late spring and summer there are numbers of all-white gulls along our coast, virtually all Herring Gulls. Even the most

bleached Herring Gull is likely to have some remnant of dark pigment in its primaries. Winter numbers are smaller than those of Ring-bills, and Herrings are more likely to be found immediately along the coast. Averages of 559 and 221 birds per year are found on the Galveston and Freeport CBCs, respectively.

THAYER'S GULL
Larus thayeri

Very rare winter terminal migrant

WINTER: (5, 8 × 2, 13 Nov) to (16, 21, 24 Apr)
HABITAT: Gulf and bay waters, roosting on beach and tidal flats.

DISCUSSION: Until recently, ornithologists considered Thayer's Gull to be part of the Herring Gull complex. Now, many believe it to be conspecific with the Iceland Gull. For the moment, American ornithologists still recognize Thayer's Gull as a separate species, one that presents a formidable identification obstacle for local observers. Because Thayer's Gull was removed from the TBRC review list in Jun of 2004, we summarize our more than 20 records. Fourteen of them were accepted by the TBRC prior to delisting, 10 are documented in the Texas Photo Record File (TPRF), and at least two are supported by specimens.

Seventeen Thayer's Gulls were found in GAL, mainly at San Luis Pass, East Beach, Bolivar, or along the coast between Bolivar and High Island. Two records are from BRA at Surfside and Freeport, and two are from coastal JEF. About half of these pertain to birds that appeared during spring; 10 are Nov–Dec records; and there are singles from Jan and Feb. As is the case for Glaucous Gull (see species account), we are intrigued by the appearance of spring birds and struggle to understand just where they might be during the prior winter months. Both Thayer's and Glaucous gulls are quite unusual in Mexico; that seems an unlikely source. Elsewhere on the Gulf Coast is a possibility—perhaps even on the Gulf's waters east of the UTC. Or perhaps they congregate farther north in the Great Plains around open lakes and reservoirs that eventually freeze up in late winter.

However they arrive, and wherever they might have been, most of our recent Thayer's Gulls have been found along the beach between Bolivar and Sabine Pass, particularly the stretch from High Island east into JEF. This section of the Texas coast veers to the east, and one hypothesis suggests that gulls migrating north along the coast are presented with a choice. Either they continue north, beginning an overland flight to the Great Lakes (the most likely choice for Thayer's), or they turn to the east to continue along the Gulf into Louisiana. Much like the Sharp-shinned Hawks and other raptors that migrate down the Trinity River to Smith Point, this forced reorientation apparently delays many of these gulls. This bottleneck effect becomes apparent in late spring, and during the weeks between early Apr and early May, thousands of gulls and terns, including unusual species such as Thayer's, Lesser Black-backed, and Glaucous, may be found along this beach. A second hypothesis proposes that gulls and terns remain near these beaches where food may be more abundant. The most recent UTC record was found not far from the beach at a drive-in in Galveston, where the first-winter bird was sampling the cuisine.

LESSER BLACK-BACKED GULL
Larus fuscus

Rare winter terminal migrant, very rare summer visitor

WINTER: (18 Aug, 28 Aug–11 Sep; 5 Sep, 12 Sep; 6, 15, 21 Oct) **early Nov through mid-Apr** (21, 23–26 Apr)
SUMMER: (10 Jul–11 Sep [possibly two birds]; 18 Aug)
HABITAT: Beaches and tidal flats; no accepted inland records.
DISCUSSION: Surprisingly, although the Great Black-backed Gull is an abundant breeding bird in E North America, there are more UTC records of its Old World relative, the Lesser Black-backed Gull. Indeed, on 1 Nov 1997, the TBRC removed Lesser Black-backed Gull from its review list. This species is now seen quite regularly, and as many as four individuals have occurred on a few occasions.

Most if not all UTC records of Lesser Black-backeds pertain to the pale subspecies *L. f. graellsii*, the breeding race of Iceland (from which most eastern U.S. records may originate) and much of Europe. However, we are aware of at least two UTC reports of Lesser Black-backed Gulls that suggest one of the two darker races—either *fuscus*, which has not been successfully documented in the United States (*fide* Jon Dunn), or *intermedius*, which is extremely rare in

the United States—both of which have mantle and wing coloration similar to that of Great Black-backed Gull and Kelp Gull. These birds are usually found in the flocks of roosting gulls that gather at the major tidal flats. San Luis Pass, East Beach, and Bolivar Flats are far and away our most productive gull sites, related, we believe, to their positions at points of major tidal exchange. The constituents of these flocks change *daily*, as gulls pass in and out of the bay systems. Typically, these birds arrive in Nov, but they have been found as early as 10 Jul (Bolivar Flats, GAL); this exceptionally early bird was joined by another first-year bird in Aug, and one of them stayed until 11 Sep 2004 (C. Lee). A second basic (winter) plumage bird was photographed on Follett's Island, BRA, on 18 Aug 1999. Like Glaucous and Thayer's gulls, spring Lesser Black-backeds have been seen along the coast between Bolivar Flats and Sabine Pass.

Discussions of this species' identification, taxonomy, distribution, and migratory behavior, including an in-depth treatment of New World records, are found in *Birding* (Post and Lewis 1995a, 1995b).

YELLOW-FOOTED GULL
Larus livens

Hypothetical summer visitor
9 Jul 1998 near Surfside, BRA (TBRC 1998-141; TPRF 1743)

HABITAT: This dark-backed gull nests on islands in the Gulf of California (Sea of Cortez), often in the immediate company of Royal and Elegant terns. After the breeding season, many disperse northward to southern California, especially to the Salton Sea. Unlike most other large gulls, it reaches sexual maturity in only three years.
DISCUSSION: The only Texas record of Yellow-footed Gull was found by Weeks at Follett's Island, BRA, on 9 Jul 1998. This second-summer bird was documented with 25 photographs, roosting on the beach and in flight. The timing of this sighting matches the species' usual northward dispersal into southern California. This record represents the farthest east the species has been reported and the first record for Texas (Weeks and Patten 2000).

In 2006 the TBRC voted to not accept this record, based on a detailed comparison of photos of the BRA bird with members of a hybrid Kelp X Herring Gull population nesting on the Chandeleur Islands off Louisiana. Such hybrids were discussed by Dittmann and Cardiff (2005) and in litt. to the TBRC. Based on their re-evaluation of seven characteristics discussed by Weeks and Patten, plus two additional physical traits and plumage sequence, we cannot rule out the possibility of a hybrid and deem this species hypothetical on the UTC.

GLAUCOUS GULL
Larus hyperboreus

Rare winter terminal migrant

WINTER: (28 Sep; 16, 25 Nov) **early Dec through mid Apr** (29 Apr; 1, 12 May)

HABITAT: Gulf and bay waters, roosting on beach and tidal flats.

DISCUSSION: Glaucous Gull is the first "rare" gull encountered by most UTC observers. It became common enough in Texas that on 1 Nov 1997, the TBRC removed the species from its review list. We are aware of slightly over 40 UTC records, which represent about 50 percent of the occurrences for the state.

Larger than a Herring Gull and usually ghostly white (virtually all of our birds are in first- or second-winter plumage), a Glaucous Gull on the beach is hard to miss. Although it is a bird of the winter, note that most of our Glaucous Gulls arrive in Mar and Apr. We are stumped as to where these birds might be during the early winter, but we doubt that an immaculate white gull as large as a terrier could be overlooked in the months preceding their spring appearance. Glaucous Gulls are frequently found along the beaches or among flocks of gulls at the major tidal flats. We alert observers to the many bleached Herring Gulls that superficially resemble this species, particularly in late spring. Pay special attention to the bird's primaries.

GREAT BLACK-BACKED GULL
Larus marinus

Rare winter terminal migrant

24 Mar–23 Jul 1974 Bolivar Flats, GAL (TPRF 249) (AB 28: 662, 924)

22 Nov 1980–16 Apr 1981 Kemah/Seabrook, GAL/HAS (TPRF 230) (AB 35: 202, 841)

returning fall **1981–28 Apr 1982** (AB 36: 310, 872)

returning **22 Dec 1982** (AB 37: 671)

returning fall **1983–Apr 1984** (AB 38: 222, 335, 701, 933)

returning **4 Nov 1984–winter 1984–85** (AB 39: 76, 694)

8 Feb 1981 Galveston, GAL (TBRC 1989-111)

24 Jan 1984 GAL (AB 38: 355) (TBRC 1989-65)

27 Apr 1986 JEF (TBRC 1988-11) (AB 40: 496)

18 Dec 1989 San Luis Pass, GAL (TBRC 1990-12; TPRF 845) (AB 44: 292)

1 Feb 1990 Bolivar Flats, GAL (TBRC 1990–69)

28 Dec 1993 Galveston, GAL (TBRC 1994-64) (AFN 48: 226)

20 Mar 1994 Sea Rim SP, JEF (TBRC 1994-53) (AFN 48: 317)

4 Feb–10 Aug 1996 Galveston, GAL (TBRC 1996-10) (AFN 50: 190, 302)

22 Nov 1996 Galveston, GAL (TBRC 1996-169)

18 Apr–1 May 1998 Bolivar Flats, GAL (TBRC 1998-111)

22 Dec 1997–15 Mar 1998 Bolivar Flats, GAL (TBRC 1998-14; TPRF 1796)

31 Jan 2004 GAL (TBRC 2004-10)

31 Jan 2004 East Beach, GAL (TBRC 2004-10)

HABITAT: Open coastal beaches, tidal flats, & bays.

DISCUSSION: For many years the only coal-black-backed gull seen along the UTC would be assumed to be this species. However, with the recent arrival of Kelp Gull, such an assumption has become less certain. The Great Black-backed Gull is an abundant breeder along the Atlantic Coast, regularly wintering south to Florida. Recent range expansions have marched this bird W into the Gulf of Mexico, although it remains relatively rare in Louisiana. In the past decade it has become nearly an annual visitor on our coast; both adults and immatures having appeared. They arrive in winter (often late winter) when more northerly waters freeze, forcing many gulls southward. Individuals have twice lingered into summer. A first-year bird with an injured leg remained on Bolivar Flats into August 1996. About one-half of the state records have occurred on the UTC.

KELP GULL
Larus dominicanus

Accidental winter terminal migrant

15 Jan–5 Apr 1996 Galveston, GAL (TBRC 1996-17; TPRF 1393) (AFN 50: 190, 302) returning 30 Nov 1996–21 Apr 1997 (TBRC 1996-180; TPRF 1523) (AFN 51: 515, 769, 894)

HABITAT: Coasts and islands, occasionally far inland, typically at 6° to 65° S (Harrison 1983), but recently found nesting in SW Ecuador at 2°15′ S (Haase 1996); rare but breeding in the W Atlantic Basin.

DISCUSSION: A large, cosmopolitan, coastal species of the Southern Hemisphere, Kelp Gull has only recently been found north of the Equator. Cautious observers have noted Galveston's East Beach is close to international shipping lanes (a favorite target of those questioning the validity of vagrant birds), and Kelp Gulls have been guests at certain wild animal amusement parks. Nonetheless, since the summer of 1989, ornithologists in Louisiana have been observing a small population present on the Chandeleur Islands in the northern Gulf. Incongruously, these birds have been hybridizing with Herring Gulls, another species that as a nester is foreign to the Gulf's warm waters (R. D. Purrington in litt., Dittman and Cardiff 1998). Kelp Gulls have also been observed in several years since 1991, and possibly as early as 1987, in the Rio Lagartos–Las Coloradas vicinity at the N end of the Yucatán Peninsula (Howell et al. 1993).

Located by P. D. Hulce on 15 Jan 1996 at the E end of Galveston Island, and subsequently identified by Jon Dunn and Behrstock, the state's first Kelp Gull was observed by perhaps as many as 1,200 birders (D. Peake estimate); over 840 birders signed a guest register organized by Fae Humphrey and the late Martha Micks. On 19 Apr, the last day the bird was seen in Texas, Dale Zimmerman photographed it east of Galveston between High Island and Sabine Pass.

On 1 Dec. 1996, the same or another Kelp Gull appeared at E Galveston Island. Neither bird exhibited obvious signs of being part of a hybrid swarm. The Kelp Gull was recently added to the A.O.U.'s *Check-list of North American Birds* (Banks et al. 2002).

SABINE'S GULL
Xema sabini

Very rare fall migrant
25 Oct 1964 Off Galveston, GAL (TPRF 109) (AFN 19: 58; Oberholser 1974)

HABITAT: Pelagic waters, uncommon inshore, rare transient migrant on inland lakes.

DISCUSSION: Sabine's is among the most pelagic of the gulls; away from its arctic nesting grounds it is rarely seen onshore and then usually during fall migration. During winter, these gulls congregate at cold-water upwellings south of the Equator, rarely straying to the Gulf of Mexico. Most of the more than 60 Texas records consist of young birds migrating south across the interior of the state. Only once has this gull been documented along the UTC, a single bird seen off Galveston by participants on an early pelagic birding trip. We believe that Sabine's Gulls are more likely to appear in our area on inland lakes and reservoirs from late Sep through Oct, the period when these gulls appear almost annually elsewhere in Texas. However, beach runners should also remain alert to the possibility of encountering the species, as North Padre Island fishing and nature guide Billy Sandifer has encountered Sabine's Gulls along that beach on at least five occasions.

The origin and pronunciation of this bird's name are a source of confusion for Texas birders. The name has nothing to do with the Sabine River (pronounced "sahbeen") or the Spanish word *sabino* for the bald cypress tree; instead it refers to Sir Edward Sabine (pronounced "saybin"), British astronomer, physicist, and polar explorer (1770–1837), after whom the bird was named by his brother Joseph.

BLACK-LEGGED KITTIWAKE
Rissa tridactyla

Rare winter terminal migrant
1 Feb 1970 Bolivar Flats, GAL (TPRF 324)
23 Dec 1973 Freeport, BRA (TBRC 1990-131) (AB 28: 454)
14 Jan–28 Feb 1977 Texas City, GAL (AB 31: 350) (Eubanks 1977)
27–29 Nov 1981 (3) GAL (TBRC 1992-142) (AB 36: 196)
20 Apr 1985 JEF (TBRC 1990-137; TPRF 955) (AB 39: 324)
21 Dec 1986 Freeport, BRA (TBRC 1992-101) (AB 41: 1103)
4–18 Jan 1987 Texas City, GAL (TBRC 1991-117)
29 Mar–16 Apr 1988 Rollover Pass, GAL (TBRC 1990-125; TPRF 956) (AB 42: 459)

17 Dec 1989 Freeport, BRA (TBRC 1990-104) (AB 44: 877)

25 Apr 1990 High Is., GAL (TBRC 1990-116) (AB 44: 461)

29 Nov 1990 Galveston, GAL (TBRC 1990-162)

16 Dec 1990 Freeport, BRA (TBRC 1990-160) (AB 45: 884)

7–8 Dec 1990 Galveston, GAL (TBRC 1993-32)

28 Apr 1991 Bolivar Flats, GAL (TBRC 1991-60) (AB 45: 471)

15 Dec 1991 Freeport, BRA (TBRC 1992-5) (AB 46: 880)

22 Dec 1991 Rollover Pass, GAL (TBRC 1991-148) (AB 46: 870)

20 Dec 1992 Freeport, BRA (TBRC 1993-10) (AB 47: 851)

24–25 Apr 1993 JEF (TBRC 1993-68; TPRF 1151) (AB 47: 431)

10 Sep 1995 Rollover Pass, GAL (TBRC 1995-117) (AFN 50: 80)

8 Jan 1996 Galveston, GAL (TBRC 1996-96) (AFN 50: 972)

10 Feb 1996 Galveston, GAL (TBRC 1996-18) (AFN 50: 191)

21–22 Dec 1996 Surfside, BRA (TBRC 1996-178) (AFN 51: 514) (FN 51: 770)

25 Apr 1997 GAL (TBRC 1997-111) (AFN 51: 894)

7 Nov 1998 Quintana, BRA (TBRC 1998-142)

HABITAT: Circumpolar, breeding colonies occur on islands and rocky headlands, most birds wintering at sea well north of the Gulf of Mexico; locally, beaches and tidal flats, bays, impoundments near the Gulf.

DISCUSSION: Black-legged Kittiwakes are among our most confiding gulls, often found around boat docks, fishing piers, or on the decks of docked shrimp boats. Invariably, we see young birds, the age class that appears along our coast. Usually they may be closely approached, allowing views that test the close focus capabilities of binoculars. Although Black-legged Kittiwakes have been recorded well inland (e.g., Warren Lake in W HAS), the typical UTC sighting consists of a single bird occurring along or very close to the coast (especially at the Quintana/Surfside jetties), with or close to Laughing Gulls.

Kittiwakes arrive in late Nov (the 10 Sep 1995 record from Rollover Pass is extraordinarily early), remaining through Apr. Although they are still considered a rar-

ity, during the past decade, appearances have become practically an annual event. The increase in fall records from Texas reservoirs resulted in the species' Nov 1999 removal from the TBRC review list.

GULL-BILLED TERN
Sterna nilotica

Common summer terminal migrant, uncommon winter terminal migrant

HABITAT: Breeds throughout the tropics and warmer temperate regions; inhabits salt- and fresh-water marshes, shallow fresh to extremely salty impoundments, flooded and freshly tilled fields, and coastal prairie; pairs or small colonies nest in salt marsh, on islands, and on uplands of sandy beaches, often with other terns and Black Skimmers.

DISCUSSION: With its short, thick bill, short tail, and very different feeding habits, Gull-billed Tern is different enough from other terns in its anatomy and biology to have been placed in its own genus, *Gelochelidon* (which translates to "laughing swallow").

Terns are generally a gregarious lot, feeding together over water and roosting on beaches in large mixed flocks. The Gull-billed Tern, however, is rarely seen roosting in numbers and very infrequently on the beach. It feeds more over marshes and agricultural fields, frequently taking insects in the air rather than fish from the water.

During spring, Gull-billeds are commonly seen near the coast at freshly flooded rice fields, often roosting on low earthen dikes. Other predictable sites are salt marshes near the bay edge at Anahuac NWR and San Luis Pass, where the birds' grayer backs help differentiate them from other local terns. Their diet includes grasshoppers, locusts, dragonflies, beetles, moths, crabs, shrimp, various aquatic insects, and frogs but rather few fish (Oberholser 1974).

Locally, Gull-billed Terns usually nest in association with Black Skimmers and a few Least Terns. For many years they nested at Galveston Island SP, where they colonized the highest point of land adjacent to Galveston Bay. The largest and most consistent UTC nesting locale is the Black Skimmer lot at Dow Chemical in Freeport, where 72 of the 193 UTC nests were found in 2001 (Texas Colonial Waterbird Database). Smaller numbers of Gull-billed Terns nesting in association with Black Skimmers have been noted on rooftops in Galveston (Smalley et al. 1991). Texas egg dates span mid-Apr to mid-Jul (Oberholser 1974). Small numbers overwinter in the coastal marshes of the UTC; the Freeport CBC averages 12 birds per year, with a high of 45 in 1988.

CASPIAN TERN
Sterna caspia

Common bi-seasonal transient and winter terminal migrant, uncommon breeder

HABITAT: Beaches, sandbars and spoil islands, intertidal flats; occasionally on inland lakes.

DISCUSSION: Caspian is the largest tern in the New World, about an inch longer than the Royals with which it frequently roosts, and much bulkier. Numbers of these powerful fliers fluctuate greatly as migrants from inland colonies in Canada and the northern tier of states (and possibly Atlantic Coast breeding sites), pass through our area. The highest fall count recorded locally is 209 at Bolivar Flats 19 Sep 1994 (W. Burkett). These migrants numerically dominate our few pairs of local breeders. The local breeding population has fluctuated between 50 to 125 breeding pairs in recent years, with 56 pairs detected along the UTC in 2001 (TCWD). Winter populations are modest, with average annual CBC counts of 79 and 63 birds from Freeport and Galveston, respectively.

A certain portion of the birding population is unable to perceive the difference in color between the red of a Caspian's thick carrot-shaped bill and the orange of a Royal Tern's decidedly thinner bill. For those still learning the terns, and for whenever direct size comparison is not possible, remember that the distribution of black (as the field guides generally illustrate) is of value in distinguishing these species. From below, Caspians exhibit quite sooty primaries compared to the Royal's very white under wing. Additionally, Caspian is the only North American tern that retains its black cap throughout the year, and even molting and juvenile birds show a darkly speckled forecrown. The easiest way to identify the species is to learn the adults' loud grating *kraaaa* call, which often announces their presence. Caspians are much more likely than Royals to be seen feeding in inshore waters.

ROYAL TERN
Sterna maxima

Abundant summer terminal migrant and bi-seasonal transient migrant, common winter terminal migrant; possibly some are resident

HABITAT: Beaches, flats, sand bars and spoil islands; unlikely inland except after hurricanes.

DISCUSSION: The sheer biomass of Royal Terns present along our beaches and around the various bays places them among the most familiar members of their family, along with Laughing Gulls and perhaps Forster's Terns. It is difficult to assess what percentage of our local breeders (if any) are resident year-round. Band returns indicate that UTC nesters move east to other Gulf Coast states at least as far as Florida, and also to Cuba (C. Hacker).

Normally, Royals as well as Sandwich and Least terns, Black Skimmers, and Magnificent Frigatebirds are associated with the marine environment; however, after hurricanes, these birds and other marine species often end up far inland, where they lend an unusual ambiance to the rice paddies of western HAS and WAR. Royal Terns breed in immense colonies on spoil islands in our bays. Breeding totals have been as high as 18,000 pairs (1995), although 4,713 pairs in 2001 was more typical (TCWD).

After fledging, adults and young rest on tidal flats such as at Bolivar and San Luis Pass. There, during late summer and fall, flocks grow to immense proportions by Aug (W. Burkett counted 15,700 at Bolivar Flats 4 Oct 1993).

Smaller numbers overwinter; the Galveston and Freeport CBCs average 219 and 113, respectively. Usually, the Royal's orange or yellow-orange bill, along with its smaller size and white under wings, distinguish it throughout the year from Caspian Terns with which it may occur. Additionally, unlike Caspians, winter Royals sport a mostly white crown. Note: Royals with deep red bills were photographed 25 April 1992 along the beach near High Island (Millington and Reid 1995), and small numbers of such birds have been observed and photographed in GAL (J. Stevenson).

ELEGANT TERN
Sterna elegans

Accidental fall visitor
4–18 Nov 2001 Galveston, GAL (TBRC 2001-134)

HABITAT: Breeds on rocky islands such as Isla Raza in the central Gulf of California, competing for nesting space with Royal Terns and Heermann's Gulls. Additional (and recently pioneered) colonies are now present in S California. Outside the nesting season, occurs on beaches, tidal flats, sand bars, and spoil islands.

DISCUSSION: On 4 Nov 2001, David Sibley—in town for a book signing—spotted an Elegant Tern in a gull and tern flock at East Beach in Galveston. Over the next two weeks, this touched off a series of sightings of what may have been as many as three birds. Much debate centered around the possibility of one or more of the birds being a Cayenne Tern, a South American subspecies of Sandwich Tern with features similar to those of an Elegant Tern.

At present, the TBRC has formally accepted only one individual seen in the Galveston area. This record follows a series of sightings in Florida over the past few years, including an apparent breeding attempt with a Sandwich Tern. Along the W Coast of the United States, large numbers of Elegant Terns and Brown Pelicans move northward after their nesting season (a trait they share with Wood Storks and Magnificent Frigatebirds), remaining in nearshore waters throughout summer and early fall. Thus the timing of these sightings, if not their location, is not without some biological basis.

SANDWICH TERN
Sterna sandvicensis

Common summer terminal migrant, uncommon winter resident

HABITAT: Beaches, tidal flats, sand bars, and spoil islands.

DISCUSSION: Sandwich is one of several locally nesting terns, including Gull-billed and Caspian, which breed in both the Old World and New. Unlike the other two species, which nest circumglobally (and often far inland), Sandwich has a more restricted distribution and is almost always found along seacoasts, where it feeds in deeper water than either Gull-billed or Caspian. Breeding numbers vary greatly from year to year; 2,332 pairs were noted in 2001 (TCWD). These terns are normally found in mixed gull and tern flocks around the tidal flats and on the beaches. Staging flocks in summer can be significant (6,000 at Bolivar Flats 11 Jul 1993, W. Burkett). Sandwich Tern is migratory, and most leave our coast by Nov. However, a few remain along the coast through the winter months, particularly around the tidal flats. The Galveston and Freeport CBCs average five and two birds per year, respectively, with a high of 32 reported at Galveston in 2001. They return to our region in Mar, when hundreds of paired Sandwich Terns may be seen courting along our beaches.

COMMON TERN
Sterna hirundo

Abundant bi-seasonal transient migrant, uncommon summer nonbreeding terminal migrant, rare winter terminal migrant or lingerer

HABITAT: Beaches, tidal flats, sand bars, and spoil islands.

DISCUSSION: Common Terns are present along our coast throughout the year, although their population dynamics are remarkably convoluted. During migration they are abundant along our beaches and on the major tidal flats. Arriving in late Mar, and apparently peaking in Apr and early May (7,500 along Bolivar Peninsula 28 Apr 1983), significant numbers are present through May. The species was once a local breeder; H. E. Dresser commented that he found Common Terns nesting "abundantly" around Galveston Bay 1–3 Jun 1864 (Oberholser 1974). Bent (1921) refers to three small colonies with eggs near Cedar Lake 17 May 1923, and J. Heiser found nests with eggs on Bird Island 15 Jun 1930. For over 60 years, however, Common Tern has not bred on the UTC. In Louisiana, Lowery (1974) noted a nest on the Chandeleur Islands and later the presence of adults with young in 1973. The state's second nest, found on the Chandeleurs in the spring of 1997, was almost certainly washed away as a storm passed directly over it (D. Dittman data).

Common Terns remain along our coast through most of the summer, at times gathering in significant numbers (225 on East Beach 2 Jul 1989). Although many of the Commons present here in late May are adults in prime breeding plumage, most of the summer birds are second-year individuals in basic (winter) plumage. We believe that as Common Terns migrate north from their wintering grounds, many young nonbreeders "short-stop" their journey at the northern edge of the wintering range. After lingering in our region through most of the summer, many of these young Commons migrate south (soon to be followed by the adults). For a few weeks, between the early Aug departure of the young and the Sep return of migrant adults, we experience a hiatus when very few Common Terns are present on our beaches. After returning in Sep, the adult terns remain along the coast well into Dec. The peak of the fall movement occurs in Sep and Oct (1,500 at Bolivar Flats 15 Oct 1988; 1,000 at San Luis Pass 8 Oct 1989). Numbers drop appreciably toward Christmas; the Galveston and Freeport CBCs average 23 and 14 birds per year, respectively. Few are seen between the New Year and their return in Mar or Apr. Unlike Forster's Terns, which occasionally range well inland, Common Terns are restricted to the immediate coast. Therefore any small tern seen over one of our inland lakes in winter is virtually certain to be a Forster's.

FORSTER'S TERN
Sterna forsteri

Common bi-seasonal transient and terminal winter migrant, uncommon summer terminal migrant

HABITAT: Open Gulf and bay waters, tidal flats and beaches, regularly venturing inland along our major rivers and bayous, nesting in colonies on bay spoil islands and isolated points of land; in winter and during migration, occasionally seen on inland lakes and reservoirs.

DISCUSSION: Of the often confusing medium-sized terns (Common, Forster's, Roseate, and Arctic), Forster's and Common are characteristic local species. Forster's is present in considerable numbers for much of the year, especially near its nesting islands in Galveston Bay. Common may be more numerous on the beaches or on the flats, notably during late spring and fall. During winter, the black "earmuffs" and frosty white primaries of Forster's Terns serve to distinguish them from similar Common Terns. Large

numbers may be seen at this time, with both the Freeport and the Galveston CBCs averaging around 1,000 birds per count.

Breeding birds exhibit an orange bill (not red, like the Common's bill) and legs. These terns are ever present within the coastal zone, becoming less consistent away from the Gulf. Colonial waterbird surveys indicated that in 2001, over 2,237 pairs bred along the UTC. Especially during the cooler months, Forster's Terns stay out over the Gulf waters for hours on end, typically closer to shore than feeding Common Terns. To get an accurate sense of their abundance, an observer needs to scan well out from the beach and count the thousands of Forster's Terns that will only come ashore to roost in the evening.

LEAST TERN
Sterna antillarum

Locally common to abundant summer terminal migrant, common bi-seasonal migrant, rare winter lingerer

SPRING/SUMMER: (25 Feb [photo]; 5, 11 Mar) **mid-Mar through early Oct** (8, 11, 15 Oct)

HABITAT: Beaches, bay edge, intertidal flats, islands, nearshore waters; nesting on shell drilling pads, abandoned roads, parking lots, gravel rooftops.

DISCUSSION: Least Tern is North America's smallest tern. Local nesters represent the subspecies *S. a. antillarum,* although we presume that the few birds migrating through the inland counties are the Interior Least Tern *S. a. athalassos* (e.g., 2 in WAR 14 Aug 1988; 1 on Warren Lake HAS 2 Aug 1989). Although our breeding birds are not as threatened as their inland cousins, all coastal populations have been seriously impacted by recreation, traffic, erosion of nesting islands, and residential development. For example, 1,600 pairs were displaced due to the construction of Tiki Island Village (a residential development adjacent to the causeway connecting E Galveston Island with the mainland). Previously, Galveston Bay supported many more of these birds, with a peak in 1974 of 2,035 pairs. Two years later, only 62 pairs were present, and 1981 saw a low of 49 pairs. Currently, Galveston Bay supports a few hundred pairs (422 pairs in the entire UTC in 2001, according to colonial waterbird surveys), about 40 percent of the state's total population. Galveston Bay provides at least 45 nesting sites, such as spoil islands and shell reefs, although only 2 to 13 are utilized during any single year (Burkett 1994). Most birds begin to arrive in mid- to late Mar and are on eggs by early Apr.

At sites such as Houston Audubon Society's Bolivar Flats Shorebird Sanctuary, Least Terns are protected from beach traffic (but not high water or predators such as coyotes), and the now substantial colonies there exhibit mixed success. Nesting birds place their two or three eggs in a scrape on sand, mud, or shell rubble, often just above the tide line. Frequently, rains and high tides flood nests that are too close to the water's edge, but the birds are persistent renesters. Along Galveston's Port Industrial Boulevard, Least Terns with small fishes in their bills may be seen landing on various flat rooftops. There, well above the threat of high water, they nest and rear their young. Least Terns stage on the major tidal flats after nesting (3,000 at San Luis Pass 25 Aug 1990; 2,000 at San Luis Pass 24 Aug 1986), and most are gone by mid-Oct. A few have remained into Dec (25 Dec 1966 and 20 Dec 1992 at Freeport), but this one of the terns least expected to appear here during the winter months. One photographed 25 Feb 1998 at Galveston appears to be an exceptionally early migrant.

BRIDLED TERN
Sterna anaethetus

Occasional summer visitor
17 Sep 1988 Bolivar Flats, GAL (TBRC 1988-299; *SFASU 3088; TPRF 746) (AB 43: 129)
25 Sep 1988 (25 birds) off Freeport, BRA (TBRC 1988-246) (AB 43: 129)
1 May 1993 (25 birds) off Galveston, GAL (TBRC 1993-93)
Removed from TBRC review list on 1 Nov 1997
6 Jun 1999 30 miles off Freeport, BRA
    (P. Hockey)
19 Aug, 6–7 Sep 1999 MOGP High Island Rig, BRA
    (C. Cox)
30 Apr 2001 off Freeport, BRA (J. Stevenson)
HABITAT: Deep blue ocean water, generally beyond the edge of the Continental Shelf; nests on tropical islands, occasionally within sight of land.

DISCUSSION: Besides the first three records listed above, Oberholser (1974) includes details of three sight records in or seaward of Galveston Bay (the species was hypothetical for Texas when the book was published): single birds 10 and 13 Sep 1961, and five 25 miles offshore 16 May 1971. Additionally, Fred Collins reported an individual 17 Aug 1990 60–70 miles SE of Galveston. Although we have shied away from hypothetical records, the dates of all sightings, whether confirmed or not, suggest a summer presence worthy of attention. The group of five birds reported offshore on 16 May was in the vicinity of a windrow of *Sargassum* seaweed, typical for this species. As with the storm-petrels, our knowledge of Bridled Tern suffers from the combination of a lack of offshore observations coupled with the very shallow nature of the NW Gulf, rendering it unattractive to blue water seabirds. On the state's central coast, the edge of the continental shelf and the beginning of deep blue ocean water may be encountered about 50 miles offshore. There, during May, Jun, and Sep trips, the species regularly occurs in two-digit figures (D. Peake, R. Carroll data). Because of its abundance along other portions of the Texas coast, on 1 Nov 1997, the TBRC removed this species from its review list.

SOOTY TERN
Sterna fuscata

Occasional visitor, formerly nested

HABITAT: Offshore pelagic waters; rarely near shore.

DISCUSSION: Sooty Tern, like Bridled Tern, is a bird of deep blue water, occurring only rarely near shore. The species is an occasional UTC nester: 5 May 1939 Pelican Island, 13–25 May 1940 Pelican Island (nests with eggs 15 May), 15 May 1941 Pelican Island; 27 Jul 1947 Galveston. Since the 1940s, sightings suggestive of nearby nesting include 4 Jun 1983 on Redfish Is., Galveston Bay; 6 Jul 1996 at Bolivar Flats; 20 Apr and 2 May 1998, both from the Bolivar ferry; and 6 Jun 1998 at the San Luis Pass Black Skimmer colony. Sooty Terns regularly breed along the central Texas coast; nesting populations may yet reestablish themselves locally.

Pelagic trips out of Freeport recorded 60 individuals on 20 Jul 1998 and one on 6 Jun 1999. This species was also noted from the Migration Over the Gulf Project (MOGP) High Island Rig on 4 dates from 19 Aug to 23 Sep 1999. These records suggest that the species is regular offshore in summer. However, most of our onshore Sooty Terns appear in the fall, usually associated with tropical weather systems that force them to shore. These fall records include 10 Sep 1961 La Porte, 13 Sep 1961 Cove (both 1961 records were related to Hurricane Carla); 5 Sep 1973 Bacliff, GAL (injured bird captured, originally banded in the Dry Tortugas); 15 Sep 1974 at Bolivar (a dead bird on the beach); 12 Sep 1998 at Armand Bayou Nature Center, HAS; and 16 Sep 1998 and 30 Aug 2003 at Anahuac NWR. The 1998 birds were associated with Tropical Storm Frances; it also deposited Sooties on Indian Beach, W Galveston Is. (J. Stevenson) and grounded one in Sargent (just outside the UTC in Matagorda Co.). On 15 Sep 1998, the Sargent bird was turned over to local wildlife rehabilitators and its band revealed that it was 21 years old!

BLACK TERN
Chlidonias niger

Common bi-seasonal transient migrant and nonbreeding summer visitor

SUMMER: (6, 11, 16 Mar) **early to mid-Apr through late Oct** (25, 31 Oct, 5, 6–12, 15 Nov)

HABITAT: Open Gulf waters, beaches, tidal flats, bay edge, often seen in migration over inland agricultural fields, lakes, ponds, and reservoirs.

DISCUSSION: Unlike most of our terns that inhabit the immediate coast, Black Tern is a bird of inland marshes and wetlands. Nonetheless, many of the first spring arrivals are noted at coastal sites such as Bolivar Flats and San Luis Pass. Here, their pale gray plumage distinguishes them from the Common and Forster's terns with which they roost. Like the Gull-billed Tern, Blacks eats some fish but subsists largely on insects taken in the air, off vegetation, or picked from the water's surface. In this sense, it is also similar to Franklin's Gull, another species that breeds away from the coast. Black Terns begin to arrive along the UTC in early to mid-Mar and continue to pass through until late May. Significant numbers of nonbreeders linger, along with Common Terns, through summer.

Black Terns migrate S though the interior of the United States and winter off both coasts of South America, from Panama south to Peru and Surinam

(A.O.U. 1998). As they move southward they stage along our coast in staggering numbers, especially at San Luis Pass. For example, Singley (1893) reported: "A millinery hunter came in with several hundred of this Tern that had been shot on the island [Galveston] near San Luis Pass." Black Terns still stage at San Luis Pass in monumental numbers, for example 10,000 on 24 Aug 1986, 8,000 on 3 Sep 1988, and 8,000 again on 25 Aug 1990. Arriving in Aug, migrant Black Terns stage for only a brief period before continuing south. Departing our coast, they migrate over the Gulf, and boat trips in late Sep and early Oct often encounter thousands. The bird is a great rarity during winter (we are aware of records as late as 25 Feb) and is not expected during the coldest months.

BLACK NODDY
Anous minutus

Accidental spring vagrant
15 Apr and 1 May 1998 Rollover Pass and Bolivar Flats, GAL (TBRC 1998-63) (AFN 52: 356)

HABITAT: Circumtropical in offshore waters. A few (apparently nonbreeders) summer on the Dry Tortugas, Florida. The closest nearshore records are from Nueces Co., Texas, and Cancun, Quintana Roo, Mexico; closest nesting population probably on islands off Belize (A.O.U. 1998).

DISCUSSION: On 15 Apr 1998, the UTC's first Black Noddy was found by Mark Johnston, who was at the end of Yacht Basin Road just west of Rollover Pass along with Jon Dunn, Stu Tingley, Behrstock, and some thirty grateful birding tour participants. From 5:15 to 5:40 P.M., the bird was seen continuously as it flew over the Gulf Intracoastal Waterway, occasionally venturing barely inland over the adjacent salt marsh. Al Viola and two British tour participants secured documentary photos and video. About ten minutes later, Tingley, Dunn and others saw the bird flying over the parking lot at the Rollover Pass cut and then out to sea. The bird appeared during a period of warm, dry days with south winds.

On 1 May the same bird (judging from the wear pattern of the upper wing coverts) was located at the Bolivar Flats by several teams participating in the Great Texas Birding Classic. Subsequently, a who's-who of North American birders submitted written documentation. Ned Brinkley, Tony Leukering, Dorothy Metzler, Don Richardson, and others obtained photos. A number of local observers identified the bird as a Brown Noddy—perhaps not surprising, considering the Black Noddy's extreme rarity in the United States. The only other Texas records were photographed 22 June 1975 on North Padre Is., Nueces Co., and 27 Jul 1998, San Jose Is., Aransas Co.

BLACK SKIMMER
Rynchops niger

Locally common resident

HABITAT: Bay waters and tidal flats, Gulf beach margins, nearshore waters, river mouths, sloughs and saline impoundments; nesting on beach uplands, spoil islands, parking lots, and rooftops.

DISCUSSION: At first glance, the Black Skimmer seems a bit ungainly and oddly constructed, as if put together from ill-fitting spare parts. Yet its shocking orange-and-black asymmetrical bill is an extraordinary tool for snatching small fishes from just below the water's surface. Unfortunately, loss of nesting habitat, disturbance of beach colonies, and erosion of nesting islands have resulted in our local skimmer population dipping well below historic figures. For example, the construction of Tiki Island Village permanently displaced 1,200 nesting pairs. Galveston Bay's Redfish Is. historically hosted 14 species of nesting waterbirds, including skimmers, but subsidence and erosion eventually forced the skimmers to abandon it in 1991 (Burkett 1994). Additionally, beach-nesting birds frequently experience setbacks when flood tides cover eggs and chicks. At unprotected colonies, careless or uninformed drivers crush eggs and young, and they also scare adults away from nests, leaving the exposed nestlings to bake in the sun or be eaten by the constantly patrolling Laughing Gulls. Such disturbance by beachgoers may explain the loss of 125 pairs that nested at the east end of Galveston Is. adjacent to what is now Apffel Park. Where birds have attempted to colonize, pedestrian and vehicular barriers have been responsible for greatly increased nesting success of Black Skimmers and other birds with which they nest, such as Least Terns (B. MacFarlane, pers. comm.). Several colonies now exist on flat rooftops (Smalley et al. 1991), but the young are prone to panicking, often plunging to their death on the sidewalks below.

Until recently, one of the two main UTC skimmer colonies was at San Luis Pass (GAL). There, with a little help from Houston Audubon Society and the USFWS, approximately 400 pairs reared over 370 chicks in 1994. Subsequently, this colony disbanded, perhaps because of disturbance, and the birds now nest on islands in the Bay (W. Burkett data). The largest UTC skimmer colony is in Freeport (BRA). There, about 700 pairs nest in a protected parking lot owned by Dow Chemical.

In 2001, 2,118 pairs of skimmers nested along our coast (TCWD data). Young skimmers, which hatch with stubby, symmetrical bills, quickly leave the nest scrape and are shaded from the merciless summer sun by beach plants or a parent's wing. After a few weeks, the rotund downy young attain the size of a grapefruit. By then, the lower mandible has elongated perceptibly. Feathering out quickly, most chicks fledge between mid-Jul and early Aug. By early Sep, the colonies are empty. Then the fully formed brown young may be seen sunning on the beaches or squealing for their parents and begging for a meal. In winter the birds are very local, concentrating at the large sand flats such as Bolivar Flats. The Galveston CBC records an average of 1,181 birds annually, but despite the nesting colony, the nearby Freeport CBC often misses them.

Pigeons and Doves

Pigeons and doves are members of the family Columbidae, one of the world's largest, most widespread, and most successful groups of birds. To a large extent, they owe this success to an anatomical adaptation. Unlike the young of other birds, which are fed fruit or insects, nestlings of pigeons and doves are fed "pigeon milk," a substance formed by cells lining the parents' digestive tract. And unlike certain shorebirds, flycatchers, and seedeaters, among which reproduction depends upon a few seasonal food items being available during a short period of favorable weather, doves may breed whenever suitable weather coincides with an abundance of any food that nourishes the adults. Locally, people who put out seed for their neighborhood birds provide much of this food. In certain parts of the UTC, a well-provisioned feeding table may attract up to half a dozen species of doves and pigeons.

Most of the UTC columbids are locally or seasonally common. Only Band-tailed Pigeon, a western species also found in the mountains of NE Mexico, is a great rarity. The Passenger Pigeon ranged as far south as GAL before it became extinct due to hunting. It last occurred there in 1900, about the time it disappeared from most of the United States.

ROCK PIGEON
Columba livia

Abundant introduced resident

HABITAT: Rural and urban areas, generally associating with and profiting from human activity.

DISCUSSION: The Rock Pigeon (formerly Rock Dove), an Old World species known to all of us simply as the pigeon, now occurs in a feral state throughout the Western Hemisphere (A.O.U. 1983). Locally, it nests on a variety of natural and artificial structures including buildings, bridges, and towers as well as in nest boxes provided by pigeon admirers. This is one of the few UTC species that may nest during all months of the year. The Rock Pigeon is remarkably adept at exploiting a variety of food sources; a small sample of its feeding sites includes railroad sidings, farmyards, backyard bird feeders, park benches, dumpsters, and gutters. Although common wherever people have provided the necessary shelter and food (even if only a highway overpass and stale popcorn), Rock Pigeons are generally absent from the few remaining wild lands along the UTC. This can be clearly seen in comparing the CBC numbers from the adjacent Freeport and San Bernard count circles. The largely developed Freeport circle averages 300 birds per year, compared to the undeveloped San Bernard circle, which averages just 22 per year.

BAND-TAILED PIGEON
Patagioenas fasciata

Accidental Visitor
25 Oct 1980 Bolivar Peninsula, GAL
2 Jun 2004 Mont Belvieu, CHA

HABITAT: Mountain forests throughout much of the western United States, including West Texas. Frequently descends to sea level when fruit (cherries, elderberries, etc.) is abundant. Flocks often visit feeders, individuals literally standing atop one another as they consume a prodigious amount of seed (Behrstock).

DISCUSSION: Typically, U.S. Band-tailed Pigeons wander no closer to the UTC than the Davis and Chisos mountains of West Texas. However, the species is a common resident in the Sierra Madre de Oriental south of Monterrey, Nuevo León, so a vagrant to our region may have originated in Mexico. We recognize two UTC records: an individual was seen in Johnson Woods on the Bolivar Peninsula, GAL, 25 Oct 1980 by B. Whitney, B. Barth, and B. Scott, and one was photographed at Mont Belvieu, CHA, on the unlikely date of 2 Jun 2004, by B. Peacock.

RINGED TURTLE-DOVE
Streptopelia risoria

Introduced resident, locally common

HABITAT: Older neighborhoods with tall shade trees.

DISCUSSION: A familiar bird on parts of the UTC, the introduced Ringed Turtle-Dove has bred locally for decades. It is found in many neighborhoods with mature shade plantings, although some populations occur in more rural parts of the region. These ghostly pale doves are easily located where they occur, perching conspicuously on wires and often coming to feeders with other members of their family.

Apparently, there are no naturally occurring wild populations of Ringed Turtle-Dove; all are escapes or the offspring of escapes derived from selective breeding of the African Collared-Dove (*S. roseogrisea*). Because of their questionable roots, in 1992 the American Birding Association removed this species from its official list of "countable" North American birds.

Where feral populations occur (e.g., Bellaire), they are decidedly sedentary, at best slowly spreading, unlike the superficially similar Eurasian Collared-Dove.

EURASIAN COLLARED-DOVE
Streptopelia decaocto

Locally common and increasing local resident

HABITAT: Urban woodlots, landscaped yards.

DISCUSSION: Eurasian Collared-Dove, a widespread and aggressive Old World species, is currently spreading westward throughout much of the country from its historic U.S. stronghold in southern Florida. Although often confused with Ringed Turtle-Dove (*Streptopelia risoria*), Collared-Dove can easily be separated by its voice, overall darker coloration, gray undertail coverts, contrasting dark primaries, and the dark band on the base of the underside of the tail (DeBenedictis 1994; Craves 2000; Sibley 2000). The two species hybridize, so beware of intermediate birds. After an avalanche of UTC records, first from coastal sites then from large mixed inland dove roosts, this bird now draws little attention. During late April 1986, Jon Dunn and others observed a possible pioneer along the seawall at the extreme eastern end of Galveston Island. The spread of this species may initially have been aided by the escape of captive birds in BRA and possibly elsewhere. But the recent explosion across the country has made such "introductions" moot. Sizable populations now exist in Freeport, Galveston and Houston, and this species is well established and flourishing on the UTC and throughout the rest of the state. The highest CBC total to date is 243 at Galveston in 2002.

WHITE-WINGED DOVE
Zenaida asiatica asiatica

Locally common and increasing resident

HABITAT: Urban and residential areas, usually with mature shade trees; not present in extensive stands of mixed conifer or bottomland hardwood forests. Pecan trees in urban and suburban neighborhoods seem to be preferred for roosting. Flocks are often attracted to feeders and are capable of consuming a serious amount of birdseed.

DISCUSSION: Until recently, White-winged Dove was largely restricted to the southern tip of Texas. Strecker (1912) considered it a "very abundant resident of the Lower Rio Grande counties." This being a migratory species, virtually all Texas White-wings left the state in winter, forming huge wintering flocks in Mexico.

The UTC's first White-winged Doves arrived with the help of humans. TPWD officials released White-winged Doves in Galveston in the 1950s, and for many years birders traveled to the county courthouse in the city of Galveston to see their White-winged Dove for the year. Infrequently, birds would appear along the coast (High Island, Freeport); most observers assumed that these doves had dispersed from the original flock in Galveston.

During the last two decades, however, White-winged Dove has undergone a Texas range expansion similar to the Inca Dove's. White-winged Doves are now resident throughout much of East and Central Texas and have become increasingly common residents in parts of Houston (where they appeared as early as 1988). These newly arrived White-wings appear to be less apt to migrate in winter, when large gatherings coalesce in urban neighborhoods. Additionally, flocks of as many as 2,000 have been seen migrating west along the UTC coast during summer and in spring; others have been detected offshore on boats and oil rigs. These do not appear to be daily feeding movements, as seen in the Austin and San Antonio areas. Even though some areas such as Freeport have yet to be populated by breeding birds, we suspect that (as with Inca Dove) it is only a matter of time before White-winged Dove becomes a common resident throughout the urban UTC.

MOURNING DOVE
Zenaida macroura carolinensis

Common resident and bi-seasonal migrant

HABITAT: Rural and urban areas, overgrown fields and light woodland, often at roadsides and in hedgerows, common in residential neighborhoods where it is attracted to feeders.

DISCUSSION: The Mourning Dove is a familiar bird throughout the UTC. Its soothing cooing is one of the region's most familiar bird sounds and one of few heard throughout the year.

During the milder coastal winters, when seeds and fruits linger on native and introduced plants (and backyard birders scatter tons of seed), Mourning Doves continue to nest and produce offspring. Indeed, this species is one of the very few birds capable of nesting on the UTC throughout the year.

Kincaid (in Oberholser 1974) went to great lengths to convince us that Mourning Doves, which breed in every Texas county, are capable of thriving and reproducing in just about every habitat, elevation, and climatic regime the state offers. This is fortunate, because during the 2001–2002 hunting season, Texas hunters bagged nearly 4.5 million of these 4.5-ounce evolutionary wonders; almost 318,000 of which were taken in the Gulf Prairie ecological region (TPWD Small Game Harvest Survey Results 2001–2002). Along with hunting, other causes of significant mortality listed by Kincaid include "automobiles, utility wires, poisoned grain, bad weather, [and] disease." At the onset of colder weather, often mid-Oct, many Mourning Doves move southward. Then, large feeding congregations and communal roosts are often observed, and hundreds may share a roadside telephone wire. The Freeport CBC averages 666 per year, with a high of 2,044 in 1996.

PASSENGER PIGEON
Ectopistes migratorius

Previously common to abundant winter terminal migrant, now extinct.

HABITAT: Woodlands of E North America; now extinct.

DISCUSSION: This abundant pigeon was one of the first North American birds to become extinct after European settlement. Legendary flocks were said to darken the sky as they passed by for several hours. As railroads facilitated the shipping of perishable goods, hunters shot millions of Passenger Pigeons to provide meat for the cities of the eastern seaboard. Astonishingly, the population, said to total billions of birds, was totally wiped out.

Formerly, this pigeon occurred S to GAL. The last Texas report was in 1900 and pertained to birds seen on upper Galveston Bay (Oberholser 1974). Nehrling (1882) remarked that the Passenger Pigeon was occasionally common during migration: "In September and October 1881, I saw immense numbers in the post oak woods, where they were feeding on acorns." The species was declared extinct when the last captive died in 1914.

INCA DOVE
Columbina inca

Locally common resident

HABITAT: Urban and rural residential areas, farms, parks, scrubby woodland edge.

DISCUSSION: Inca Dove is a southern species that has extended its range northward during the past century. It was once limited to South Texas, but Strecker (1912) noted the appearance of Inca Dove in Waco by 1904–1905 and in San Antonio, Austin, and Bryan in the next few years; however, it did not reach the UTC until nearly half a century later. The first Incas were recorded locally by S. Williams in Angleton (BRA) on 1 May 1955 (AFN 9:343) and in Houston on 11 Apr 1956. By the early 1970s, they occupied most urban areas in the region, including Baytown, High Island, and Freeport. The Inca is now a common member of the UTC's bird feeder assemblage, and 20 or more may congregate in favorable urban yards. Inca Doves are rarely found away from human habitations; even in open agricultural areas, they are usually restricted to areas around barns, livestock enclosures, and houses.

Although it is superficially similar to both Mourning Dove and Common Ground-Dove, note the Inca's uniformly scaled plumage and the white-edged tail. Incas are often first detected by the rattling sound made by their wings as they flush. The oft-repeated, mournful two-note call has been rendered as *cold coke* and *no hope*.

COMMON GROUND-DOVE
Columbina passerina passerina

Uncommon to common winter terminal migrant and recent summer resident

WINTER: (28–29, 31 Jul; 11 Aug) **late Aug to early May** (2 × 2, 7, 10, 15 May)

HABITAT: Pastures or prairie with scattered shrubs such as huisache, hollies, MacCartney rose, or low-growing oaks; also hedgerows, woodland edge, occasionally coastal salt cedars.

DISCUSSION: Unlike the aggressive Inca Dove, which has conquered our residential communities, the diminutive Common Ground-Dove shuns settled areas, preferring wilder countryside. An oft-repeated *huh wuh . . . huh wuh* may betray one sitting unnoticed on a huisache or wild persimmon branch. Usually, these birds occur as widely spaced individuals or in small groups; a CBC in suitable habitat might scrape up a few dozen; Freeport tallied 49 in 1972.

During fall migration, ground-doves are often found in salt cedar thickets and brushy hedgerows along the immediate coast (e.g., 6 in a salt cedar stand in JEF, 18 Oct 1989). However, most of our overwintering records are from inland areas such as W HAS, FOB, and WAR. Common Ground-Dove's speckled breast, pink-based bill, and short dark tail distinguish it from similar local species.

Apparently, ground-doves once nested on the UTC; Oberholser (1974) referred to confirmed breeding records from HAS and JEF. There were no recent summer sightings of apparent breeding birds until Weeks found singing birds 30 Jun–12 Aug 2001 at San Bernard NWR, BRA. Birds were found again in the same areas in 2002, indicating that this species may have extended its range eastward to the UTC. Other summer records from recent years include 13 Jul 1996 in CHA and three in WAR on 7 Jul 2001.

Parakeets

Parrots are found throughout the New World tropics, occurring locally into temperate climes. Native populations are found as close to the United States as Cuba and extreme northern Mexico. Although certain species (including the now extinct Carolina Parakeet) have made temporarily successful forays north of the border, the family's presence in the United States is now attributable largely to human intervention. Various tropical species—clearly escapes from the cage bird trade—have become numerous in warmer regions such as S Florida and S California. Although they provide a splash of color and a novel element to the avifauna, many compete for nest holes with native birds such as woodpeckers. Two Mexican species have become abundant in S Texas, although their origin is mired in controversy. On the UTC, the somberly colored Monk Parakeet of temperate South America has become numerous.

MONK PARAKEET
Myiopsitta monachus

Introduced resident, local but increasing

HABITAT: Urban and rural areas, frequently along railroad and power line rights-of-way, where they nest on towers; also nests in large palms; occasionally present at feeders.

DISCUSSION: Monk Parakeet is resident from southern Brazil, Paraguay, and central Bolivia to southern Argentina (A.O.U. 1983), where it inhabits temperate regions. Although a member of a largely tropical family, it is at home in cooler climes, nesting successfully at least as far north as the Chicago lakefront, where winter temperatures frequently drop to −20°F.

Flocks of several to 25 or more can be encountered in Houston and its surrounding communities, occasionally well away from the city. As in other parts of the country where they are successfully established, their bulky haystacklike stick nests are placed in trees and upon such structures as water towers, light poles, and towers supporting power lines. Despite Reliant Energy's efforts to remove them, tower nests may be seen in Houston at dozens of locations as well as on many of the electrical substations. The Kemah–San Leon–Texas City area hosts a relatively large population.

Monk Parakeets are noisy and where present are easily encountered; chattering roosting flocks may be heard and seen as they come to nests during the winter months. Some birds may become habituated to platform feeders, where they relish white sunflower and black oil seed (B. Strickland). So far, they constitute a novel and largely harmless addition to our avifauna.

CAROLINA PARAKEET
Conuropsis carolinensis

Previous visitor (?), now extinct

HABITAT: Bottomland forests.
DISCUSSION: Carolina Parakeet may have occurred on the UTC. Based upon Hagar and Packard (1952) and Oberholser (1974), the TOS (1995) states that Carolina Parakeet was resident in the NE corner of Texas in the Red River Valley, wandering irregularly during fall and winter to JEF and other E counties. The A.O.U. (1983, p. 268), however, finds the "Texas records doubtful."

Cuckoos

The five cuckoos that inhabit the UTC provide birders with a hint of the diversity exhibited by this large and widespread family. Our local species range from wholly black to attractively patterned; some even possess colorful accents of bare facial skin. They take prey from the size of a caterpillar to snakes or small birds. None of the local cuckoos is a nest parasite, a trait common to many species in both the New World and the Old. Nor do any of our cuckoos utter the repeated *Coo' coo* phrase delivered by the Common Cuckoo and mimicked hourly by innumerable clocks.

Yellow-billed, Black-billed, and Mangrove cuckoos are long, slender, superficially similar birds that skulk in woodlands during the nesting season. Yellow-billed Cuckoo, often referred to as Rain Crow, nests locally; its long series of cackling notes is often considered a portent of upcoming precipitation. Black-billed Cuckoo is a rather uncommon visitor during migration, often appearing in very open habitats where it is readily viewed. The Mangrove Cuckoo, a rare visitor, shares the Yellow-billed's yellow lower mandible but exhibits a more richly colored chest.

The loose-jointed Groove-billed Ani is one of several large, all-black cuckoos with heavy bills, long, expressive tails, and decidedly floppy movements. It occurs here during fall and winter after a certain portion of the nesting population disperses northward. Anis often associate with livestock, pulling ticks off horses and cattle, but will happily walk alongside a lawn mower, collecting insects that are discharged with the grass clippings.

Unlike most of its cousins, the Greater Roadrunner is not a woodland skulker and is usually seen in the open. Although it is encountered on the UTC only rarely, it is probably one of our most widely recognized birds because of its cartoon fame. Much of the roadrunner's diet consists of snakes and lizards, but individuals prey upon a variety of birds from hummingbirds to fledgling quail and eat foods containing meat that are offered by humans. Although they spend most of their time on the ground, roadrunners nest in trees, often singing from elevated branches.

BLACK-BILLED CUCKOO
Coccyzus erythropthalmus

Uncommon spring, rare fall transient migrant

SPRING: (5, 9 Apr) **mid-Apr to late May** (29 May; 6–7 Jun)
FALL: (22, 26 Jul) **late Jul to early Oct** (15, 21–22 Oct; 6, 8, 12 Nov)
HABITAT: Margin and interior of coastal mottes, where they range from high canopy to (more characteristically) the forest floor, and occasionally inland woodlots; often in more open habitat, including thickets of rattlebox or willows bordering ponds.
DISCUSSION: The inert, noiseless type that shuns conspicuous activity, this cuckoo generally avoids open-country exhibitionism. However, during the mad rush of spring migration, this skulker dares exposure, occurring in hedgerows, scrub, and even perched along barbed wire fences. Although these cuckoos are rarely present in large numbers, as many as 45 have been seen on a single day (5 May 1973). Rare in fall, most sightings are of single individuals seen from Aug through mid-Oct. The peak fall movement occurs during late Aug (eight sightings in one year between 12 and 16 Aug). Although we have no true winter records, the species has lingered as late as 12 Nov.

Recently, a museum specimen secured in Texas was identified as the migratory Dark-billed Cuckoo (*C. melacoryphus*) of South America. Because of its superficial resemblance to Black-billed Cuckoo, all birds seen during the later part of the year should be carefully scrutinized. For an illustration, see Hilty and Brown (1986).

YELLOW-BILLED CUCKOO
Coccyzus americanus americanus

Common summer terminal migrant and bi-seasonal transient migrant, rare winter lingerer

SUMMER: (17, 19 Mar) **early Apr through late Oct** (30 Oct; 2, 5, 15 Nov)

HABITAT: Broadleaf woodland, second growth and hedgerows, riparian corridors, and well-wooded neighborhoods.

DISCUSSION: The Yellow-billed Cuckoo has declined in parts of our country, particularly in southwestern riparian woodlands, yet the species remains a fairly common breeder in most of the UTC hardwood forests. Nehrling (1882) remarked that the bird bred "abundantly in the thickets on the edges of woods, and is in this part of our country a very unsuspicious bird, as it is not only often seen in gardens, but sometimes breeds in them, in pomegranate bushes, in *Banksia* and Cherokee-rose thickets, etc." Cuckoos arrive along our coast rather late in the spring, and significant numbers are often not noted until well into May. Coastal migrants may occasionally surface in impressive numbers; for example, 220 on 10 May 1976 (J. Stevenson) and 120 were observed 25 Apr 1982. Vocalizing breeders are well distributed by late May; bottomland forests supporting the highest densities are those where pecans predominate.

Yellow-billed Cuckoos occasionally linger into winter; we note a 14 Feb record, and one—a vocalizing bird in a known territory—remained in Galveston through 29 Feb, if it ever left at all. The Freeport CBC has reported them four times (1970, 1975, 1982, and 2002). The most recent winter record is one that lingered along Cocklebur Slough at San Bernard NWR from 21 Nov to 18 Dec 1998. We offer a note of caution: any winter cuckoo is noteworthy; and given the fact that Mangrove Cuckoo has wandered to the UTC in winter (see next account), out-of-season birds should be closely examined and well documented.

MANGROVE CUCKOO
Coccyzus minor continentalis

Rare visitor

30 Dec 1964 Galveston, GAL (TBRC 1988-45) (Oberholser 1974)

30 Dec 1981–13 Jan 1982 Bolivar Pen, GAL (TPRF 257) (AB 36:310) (Gallucci and Morgan 1987)

04 May 1987 White Oak Bayou, Houston, HAS (TBRC 1988-88)

11 May 1997 Quintana, BRA (TBRC 1997–90; TPRF 1665) (AFN 51:894)

HABITAT: Coastal and inland thickets.

DISCUSSION: Since Frank M. Chapman instigated annual Christmas bird censuses at the turn of the twentieth century, literally thousands of early-winter avian rarities and distributional anomalies have been discovered and documented. Indeed, for many participants, searching for rarities has become a special joy of the season. Upholding this tradition, birders participating in the 1964 Galveston CBC discovered the UTC's (and the state's) first Mangrove Cuckoo (Oberholser 1974). After locating the bird, Pat and Jim Ellis were unsure of their identification. Halting their day's birding activities, they sped to the Rosenberg Library to find a field guide that might contain an illustration of the Mangrove Cuckoo; yes, they were successful.

Nearly two decades passed before another Mangrove Cuckoo was seen on our coast. This second bird, the state's first thoroughly documented Mangrove Cuckoo, was discovered simultaneously and exactly 17 years later by Iowa birder Eugene Armstrong and a group of birding tourists from Arkansas. The Arkansans, while waiting on Bolivar Peninsula for the Galveston ferry crossing, noticed a Mangrove Cuckoo foraging in a thicket near their cars. For the next two weeks the bird remained in an overgrazed marshy pasture vegetated with rattlebox, mesquite, oleander, baccharis, and various grasses (Gallucci and Morgan 1987).

Subsequent records include one in Houston and, most recently, from the coast: on 11 May 1997, M. Gray and D. Verser discovered and photographed a Mangrove Cuckoo along the road to Bryan Beach during a large fallout that included an estimated more than 100 cuckoos.

In Mexico and Central America, this species is frequently observed well inland (Behrstock, pers. obs.)

so the Houston record, while unusual, is not without precedent. Most birds observed along the Gulf Coast have been identified as the richly colored subspecies *C. m. continentalis*, which breeds in eastern Mexico.

GREATER ROADRUNNER
Geococcyx californianus

Probable extirpated resident, now a rare visitor
1980 near Alief, HAS
11 Oct 1981 W HAS
18 Dec 1983 Freeport, BRA
1 Dec 1985 W HAS
14 Dec 1986 N HAS
11–15 Apr 1987 Alvin, BRA
2 Jan 1988 N HAS
20 Jan 1990 WAR
19 Jan 1992 WAR
9 Apr 1992 CHA
1 Sep 2004 Kleb Woods, N HAS

HABITAT: To the southwest and west, roadrunners live in a variety of drier habitats, including mesquite brush and tall cactus desert. Locally, their easternmost population occurs in mixed pine forest, less-disturbed agricultural land, and around extensive thickets of plants such as huisache. In all cases, its distribution appears to be linked to dry, sandy habitats favorable to snakes and lizards, upon which they feed.

DISCUSSION: The range of the Greater Roadrunner (known in South Texas as *El Paisano*) rims the landward side of the Upper Texas Coast region. This charismatic cuckoo breeds in pine forests just east of the UTC, where its mournful cooing mingles incongruously with the rising *zee-zee-zee* of Prairie Warblers and the sweet minor key trills of Bachman's Sparrows. To the west of the UTC, roadrunners occur as close as Austin and Colorado cos., where the bird has been seen consistently at Attwater NWR and near Bellville. Roadrunners are abundant in South Texas brush country as well, and their range extends as far north as Matagorda County. Yet curiously, the Greater Roadrunner is virtually absent from the UTC. Williams noted that the first UTC sighting did not occur until 1956, and we recognize only a scattering of records since that initial report. Apparently, a very few birds still inhabit northern HAS, where they have been seen just south of Tomball (E. Carpenter) and on FM 2920 between Spring and Tomball (G. Clark). The most recent published sighting was 1 Sep 2004 at Kleb Woods in NW HAS, where Fred Collins notes that two to three pairs may be in residence and are seen daily in warm weather.

GROOVE-BILLED ANI
Crotophaga sulcirostris sulcirostris

Uncommon and irregular winter visitor

WINTER: (6, 20, 23–24 Aug) **mid-Sep to mid- to late Apr** (26 Apr; 1, 4 May)
HABITAT: Coastal thickets of baccharis, willows, oleander, salt cedar; inland in various shrubs, along fence rows, occasionally residential plantings.
DISCUSSION: The Groove-billed Ani is a South Texas specialty, occurring nowhere else in the United States as a breeding species. After nesting in brush country to the south, a certain portion of the population disperses north and northeastward, some birds ranging as far as Louisiana and even Florida. This dispersal typically occurs in mid-September, as evidenced by recent arrival dates of 19 Sep 1999, 17 Sep 2000, 22 Sep 2001, 14 Sep 2002. After a flurry of sightings in Sep, the birds become much less common. Along our coast, Groove-billed Ani is at best an irregular winter visitor. It occurs perhaps most consistently at coastal sites from High Island (rarely farther east) to West Galveston Is., and southwest along the coast. The Freeport CBC found this species on 32 of 46 counts, with an amazing peak of 46 birds in 1972.

During late spring any lingering birds return south; one seen 20 Jul 1960 at Sheldon Reservoir (HAS) and another seen 15 Jul 2001 at Anahuac NWR may represent our only summer records. Occasionally, anis veer inland to suburban gardens or along fence lines in agricultural land. Even when present, their small flocks are often difficult to see as they pass much of the day concealed in dense vegetation. A nearby Northern Mockingbird that has added the visitor's sweet call to its repertoire often reveals their presence. Occasionally the true ani persona may be appreciated, as when a squealing gang of them crosses the road exhibiting their typical follow-the-leader flight, propelled by alternating series of quick flaps and glides and furious pumps of their loosely jointed tails.

Lacking reasonable documentation, the closely related Smooth-billed Ani (*C. ani*) is not accepted by the TBRC (TOS 1995; Lockwood and Freeman 2004). Oberholser (1974) lists it as hypothetical for Texas; of four possible records, two are from the UTC. Observers should be aware that young Groove-billeds may not show the obvious bill striations exhibited by adults.

Owls

The UTC does not support a great diversity of owls. Eight kinds have been recorded, only half of which currently nest in the region. Fortunately, our four resident species are reasonably easy to see.

In the agricultural tracts that fringe the UTC, the ghostly white Barn Owl is readily encountered, usually as it hunts small mammals from a utility wire just after dark. During daylight hours birders often flush Barn Owls from their roosts, and they may be chased from hiding by mobbing flocks of crows or jays.

The large and noisy Barred Owl and the diminutive Eastern Screech-Owl are perhaps the next most easily encountered species. Barred Owl inhabits the region's forests but persists locally within wooded city limits. An imitation of its call often gets a response, even in daylight, and may also attract a Red-shouldered Hawk, Pileated Woodpecker, or flock of scolding Blue Jays.

The Eastern Screech-Owl flourishes in forests and older residential neighborhoods that provide food and nest sites. It is sufficiently widespread that its whinnying song is familiar to nonbirders throughout much of the UTC. During spring, males may perch some distance from the female's nest hole, becoming the frequent targets of roving flocks of small songbirds that harass these owls mercilessly. Birders attuned to such mobbing flocks will see their share of small owls and an occasional snake. Imitating the screech-owl's trill can attract a wide variety of birds, including woodpeckers, flycatchers, vireos, various sparrows, and at times even hummingbirds.

Great Horned Owl, the last resident species, occurs spottily in both large and smaller woodland tracts. Nesting pairs are often staked out, they or their parents having inhabited the same parcel for decades.

Two species, Long-eared and Short-eared owls, are visitors from the north. As is the case for many birds that live in higher latitudes, their winter movements are irruptive rather than strictly migratory; locally, their presence and abundance are unpredictable. Short-eared Owl is most often seen at dusk or dawn flapping over coastal prairies or saltmarsh edge. The less common Long-eared Owl is more of a forest dweller, occurring in tall thickets, conifers, woodlands, and neighborhoods with large trees.

The tiny Flammulated Owl is the New World's only migratory member of the screech-owl clan. Occasionally, moderate numbers of migrants are encountered in Texas far from the western mountains in which they breed. Locally, this owl is a rare visitor, but trends of occurrence suggest that it may be more regular than has been presumed.

Previously, Burrowing Owl (or tunnel owl, as it is sometimes called), nested on the UTC. In other parts of its range, including West Texas and the Texas Panhandle, populations of this delightful bird have plummeted owing to the merciless persecution of the prairie dogs that dig its nesting tunnels. Presumably its absence from our region is related to agricultural practices. The species has a propensity to disperse, or wander, occasionally showing up on ships at sea. Current records pertain to nonbreeders, presumably, from the west or north.

BARN OWL
Tyto alba pratincola

Locally common to uncommon resident

HABITAT: Both inland and along the coast in mottes and other groves of trees, windbreaks, dense tangles of vegetation, buildings, abandoned barns, and a variety of other structures.

DISCUSSION: Suburban sprawl reduced suitable open habitat in our region for this ghostly predator, yet the Barn Owl remains fairly common in the coastal grasslands and interior agricultural fields. Perhaps these owls have even profited in some areas from the presence of abandoned buildings and rodent infestations.

The Barn Owl's success may also be credited to its flexible nest site requirements and its ability to adjust its foraging strategy as its prey population changes. An inspection of Barn Owl pellets at Brazos Bend SP revealed that they consumed prey as large as swamp rabbits and hispid cotton rats and as small as shrews and goldfinches. On the UTC, Barn Owls nest in barns, silos, churches, grain storage and drying facilities, warehouses, deer blinds, whistling-duck nest boxes, hollow trees, and probably cavities in the banks of rivers and bayous; Nehrling (1882) discovered the nest of a Barn Owl 6 May 1881 in a high bank of a gully near Spring Creek.

The Barn Owl usually hunts alone over prairie, fallow and active agricultural land, marsh, and residential areas, generally avoiding the most extensive tracts of heavy forest. Winter roosts may contain dozens of individuals; one pine grove in W HAS contained over 40 Barn Owls (although a pair of Great Horned Owls displaced them in short order). The Freeport CBC averages four per year, with peaks of 11 in 1978 and 1983. The Mad Island CBC conducted just S of the UTC often records the country's highest totals, averaging over 50 per year.

FLAMMULATED OWL
Otus flammeolus

Accidental or very rare fall visitor
3 Nov 1977 Gulf of Mexico, GAL (AB 31:187)
11 Nov 1989 Galveston, GAL (SB 38, no. 12; TPRF 1560)
25 Oct 2001 offshore rig located 27°17′ N, 94°34′ W, BRA (photo)

HABITAT: Flammulated Owl breeds in montane pine forest from British Columbia to S Mexico (including W Texas), wintering as far south as Guatemala and El Salvador.

DISCUSSION: The migratory habit of this little owl is unique among New World screech-owls. Along with its slow song and certain anatomical characteristics, this propensity to migrate allies it with the large assemblage of Old World scops owls (genus *Otus*), and it is now considered the only New World member of that genus. Even within its main range this tiny traveler's movements are rarely documented, so the three local records simply defied prediction.

Brent Ortego spotted the first UTC Flammulated Owl 3 Nov 1977 about 75 miles SE of Galveston on an oil rig in the Gulf of Mexico (AB 31:187). The second sighting occurred at one of Galveston Island's tiny oceanfront pocket parks, where on 11 Nov 1989, caretakers found one in an exhausted condition. It was photographed by Greg Lasley (TPRF 1560) and then turned over to rehabbers at the TWRC to be fattened up prior to release. The latest UTC record was one recovered 25 Oct 2001 from the Ocean Star Rig No. 167 (BRA by closest land point definition). Other marine Flammulateds (one off Port O'Connor, Calhoun Co., 10 Oct 1999, and another offshore in Louisiana, 11 Oct 1999) and an inland record from Wharton (Wharton Co.) on 5 Nov 2000 suggest that the species may be a regular but rarely detected late fall migrant.

Another small migratory owl that is possible on the UTC is Northern Saw-whet Owl (*Aegolius acadicus*). Texas records are most numerous in the Trans-Pecos and the Panhandle. However, it has occurred as close as Liberty County immediately east of HAS.

EASTERN SCREECH-OWL
Megascops asio

Locally common resident

HABITAT: Extensively wooded areas, rural woodlots, residential communities with large trees such as live oaks; occasionally roosts in buildings.

DISCUSSION: Unlike many of the resident species that declined after European settlement, Eastern Screech-Owl benefited from the widespread alteration of the landscape. Except along the raw fringes of urban development, cities such as Houston and Beaumont are heavily planted with live oak, sweetgum, southern magnolia, sugar hackberry, pines, and other landscape trees, native and exotic. Both unkempt and manicured urban woodlots now replace the screech-owl-free prairies and marshes of presettlement days. This continuum of large mature trees, interspersed with mowed lawns where the birds can hunt, provides excellent if modified habitat for this bird. Eastern Screech-Owl is the only small owl that breeds on the UTC. Few residential neighborhoods are without them, and in the older sections of our communities where shade trees have matured, screech-owls reach a density approaching one pair per city block. Only in the isolated mottes immediately along the coast is the species absent; it is rare in the Brazosport area (possibly due to the very high density of Barred Owls, which prey upon screech-owls), and the Freeport CBC now struggles to record it. During the evening, these birds often lurk in the shadows near streetlights, which attract large insects, or hunt where domestic garbage or the day's offering of birdseed provides forage for mice and other small mammals. Many people who enjoy listening to the sweet whinny of courting owls in the early spring, and again as dispersing birds set up new territories during late summer and fall, erect nest boxes to augment the supply of natural nesting cavities. Indeed, Gehlbach (1994) argues that the modified habitats of the suburbs provide a wealth of nesting cavities, abundant small vertebrate prey, warmer microhabitats, and a cleared understory that is good for hunting but bad for predators (except cats). With these advantages, suburban Eastern Screech-Owls exhibit a reproductive advantage over their cousins living in more pristine habitats.

One of the general characteristics distinguishing Eastern from Western Screech-Owl (*Megascops kennicottii*) is the presence of the Eastern's red-plumaged version. The percentage of red morphs in a population (versus intermediate or gray) varies geographically. Some subspecies have virtually none, others more than 50 percent. Along the UTC, red birds are considerably less common; very rusty birds are infrequently observed here. We have seen a number of (apparently) mixed birds in which plumage was washed with red, giving them a decidedly brown appearance. The TOS checklist (1995) suggests that the state's easternmost birds belong to the small subspecies *M. a. floridanus*. Marshall (1967 and pers. comm.) suggests that UTC birds exist west of *floridanus* and just east of the slightly larger *hasbroucki*, a common Texas Hill Country bird. Along the southern Mississippi River Valley, birds exhibit a mixture of traits of *floridanus* and the *asio*, and our larger UTC birds may belong to this racially mixed population.

Because of certain vocal, behavioral, and anatomical differences, König and colleagues (1999) elevated the New World screech-owls, except Flammulated, to the genus *Megascops*, formerly a subgenus that contained these birds (see Flammulated Owl account).

GREAT HORNED OWL
Bubo virginianus virginianus

Uncommon resident

HABITAT: A variety of forest types, including bottomland hardwoods, mixed pine-hardwoods, mature plantings of pine and live oak; also in older residential tracts with mature shade trees.

DISCUSSION: In the New World, the remarkably successful Great Horned Owl has the largest breeding range of any member of its family. Besides the physiological advantages attributable to its large size (especially in high latitudes and altitudes), its broad distribution derives from its ability to find food and shelter in a great variety of habitats, including: stunted spruces of the northern forests, woodlots dotting the dry grasslands of South America, stunted forests in the high Andes, and the bottomland hardwoods on the UTC.

By Dec, this owl's pleasant territorial hooting announces the beginning of its nesting season. Night-roaming native mammals as well as cats and small dogs are reminded by this calling to maintain a low profile for the next several months, lest they find themselves high in the forest canopy confronting a nest full of snapping beaks. When nest sites are available, Great Horned Owls are common in open grasslands and agricultural tracts, and they are frequently seen perched atop telephone poles and silos. In the wettest bottomland forests of the UTC, the Great Horned Owl is often replaced by the Barred Owl, both of which will eat their smaller cousins, such as Eastern Screech-Owl. The Freeport CBC averages 10 Great Horned Owls per year and located a high of 30 in 1988.

BURROWING OWL
Athene cunicularia hypugaea

Rare winter terminal migrant, apparently extirpated breeder

WINTER: (30 Sep, 11 Oct) **early Oct to late Mar** (15 Mar, 24 Apr)

HABITAT: Sandy prairie, agricultural land, beaches, rock jetties.

DISCUSSION: Burrowing Owl is one of the most widespread New World owls, in terms of both latitude and altitude. This species wanders widely, frequently alighting on ships at sea or appearing coastally on rocky jetties and seawalls. Apparently, disjunct populations in Florida resulted from the Wisconsin Glaciation, which split the range of many wide-ranging species. Island populations in the Caribbean attest to its dispersive nature.

Nehrling (1882) reported this owl as "every year increasing" around Houston, breeding in burrows made in better-drained prairies and uncultivated fields. He cites nesting in the burrows of the "salamander," a species of pocket gopher (Shelford 1963) represented locally by the plains pocket gopher (*Geomys bursarius;* Davis 1974). This mammal is known to provide burrows for Florida populations (J. Stevenson). Burrows dug by the nine-banded armadillo (*Dasypus novemcinctus*) would likely provide suitable nest sites as well. Our most recent breeding records are from 1940 and 1953. Now, this species is only an occasional winter visitor to the region, and many winters pass without a single sighting. The most recent records include singles at Smith Point, CHA, on 7 Dec 2000 (a tagged Canadian bird located by transmitter); near Brazos Bend SP, FOB, on 23 Dec 2000; at San Leon, GAL, on 4 Jan 2001, and Bryan Beach, BRA, from 3 Dec 2004 to 8 Jan 2005 (R. and K. Lookingbill, W. and J. Risser). The Freeport CBC recorded this species on only four of its 48 counts (1961, 1979, 1987, and 1993).

BARRED OWL
Strix varia georgica

Locally common resident

HABITAT: Bottomland cypress forest, mixed pine forest, live oak woodland; occasionally in extensive mature residential plantings. Forages in more open habitats such as agricultural land, fallow fields, and the margins of roads. Considered by some to be a nighttime equivalent of the Red-shouldered Hawk.

DISCUSSION: The *Who COOKS for you? Who COOKS for you allllllllll* of the Barred Owl still rings from UTC forests, especially along cypress-lined bayous and from dense stands of moss-draped live oaks. During nesting, their bizarre cackles, howls, screeches, and sputters disrupt the nighttime stillness that blankets our forests. Local populations plummeted with the original timbering of extensive stands of bottomland hardwoods, but the owl survives and even thrives in pine, oak, and mixed-species forests.

Barred Owls usually nest in hollow trees or cavities left by falling dead branches, but they are not averse to wooden boxes or the old nests of squirrels, crows, or raptors (Scott et al. 1977). Typically they forage in forests with an open understory and in adjacent openings where they put themselves in harm's way (unfortunately, road-killed birds are common); they are often encountered with Barn Owls, hunting on agricultural land hundreds of feet from the nearest woods. Suggested locations for finding and hearing Barred Owls include Taylor Bayou (JEF), and Brazos Bend SP (FOB), but they occur within the Houston area and in many wooded communities. These owls are especially common in the Brazos River bottomlands; the Freeport CBC averages 24 birds per year, with a high of 51 in 1987.

LONG-EARED OWL
Asio otus wilsonianus

Rare winter terminal migrant

WINTER: (3, 21 Nov; 6 Dec) **late Nov to early Mar** (10, 19 Mar)

HABITAT: Stands of conifers, residential shade trees.

DISCUSSION: Simmons (1914) remarked that he had the "pleasure of examining an odoriferous specimen of this bird shot March 19 in the deep woods on Buffalo Bayou a few miles west of the city." He noted that this bird (or *avicide,* as he termed it) represented only his second record for the region. Our files contain less than a dozen reports from the 1950s through the very early 1980s. Virtually all previous sightings concerned birds that were present in mature pine-oak forests (Cove, Baytown, Houston, and its surrounding communities). Although many of these neighborhoods are being torn down and rebuilt, suitable roosting habitat continues to exist, at least for the odd migrant. Since the early 1990s, Long-eared Owl has been encountered only very rarely. The most recent records are of one seen (and later heard) 2 Feb 1999 in NW Houston (R. Alderson), one photographed in salt cedars at Quintana, BRA, 3 Nov 1999, and another found near Jones Creek, BRA, during the Freeport CBC on 17 Dec 2000.

SHORT-EARED OWL
Asio flammeus flammeus

Uncommon winter terminal migrant

WINTER: (10, 31 Oct) **mid-Oct to mid-Apr** (21, 27 Apr)

HABITAT: Locally in marsh, prairie, and agricultural lands, both coastally and inland.

DISCUSSION: As with many northern owls, Short-eareds are often irruptive rather than strictly migratory. Small but predictable numbers appear annually on the UTC, where they tend to be dawn and dusk hunters. Early birders, or those lingering in the field until late afternoon, have an excellent chance of seeing one. Favored areas include Anahuac and Brazoria NWRs, marshes and coastal prairies on Galveston Island, and marshes near Freeport and adjacent to Bolivar Flats.

Well inland, the species may be seen in fallow fields, extensive stretches of prairie, rice stubble, or similar habitats. Short-eared Owls often hunt close to the ground in the manner of Northern Harriers, with which they occasionally squabble. The owl's floppier flight, rounder wings, and black "wrist" patches should preclude confusion. The Freeport CBC found the species on 41 of 48 counts, averaging four per year, with a peak of 23 in 1970. Three summer reports from the UTC are supported by convincingly written descriptions but no physical documentation: 26 May 2003 at Brazoria NWR, 5 Jul 1999 along old Highway 87 in JEF, and 25 Jul 2003 at San Bernard NWR.

Nighthawks and Nightjars

The ancient Greeks believed these birds could suck milk from goats, hence their family name Caprimulgidae, or goatsuckers. The other commonly applied name—nightjar—is derived from their churring or jarring nocturnal calls.

The four local goatsuckers are gray or brown, soft-plumaged birds that perch by standing horizontally on tiny feet. Individuals appear to have a small beak, but when the mouth is open, the gape extends from one side of the head to the other, forming a huge trap that engulfs a variety of flying insects. Most species feed on moths, beetles, and flies, but the large Chuck-will's-widow can swallow bats and smaller birds.

The family is loosely divided into two groups: the nighthawks (strictly New World birds) and all the other genera, each with two representatives on the UTC. Members of both have intricately patterned plumage that blends into leaf litter, tree bark, or sun-dappled gravel. Nighthawk plumage is especially variable, and a number of regional populations or races have been described on the basis of color differences. The longer-winged nighthawks have smaller eyes (because they feed when there is still some light—at dusk or on cloudy days) and very short rictal bristles on the margin of the bill. They often forage in flocks and remain aloft in sustained feeding flights, like swallows.

The remaining nightjars take prey in a flycatcher-like manner, flying up from the ground or a branch to engulf a targeted prey item and then often returning to the same perch. Because they feed after night falls, they have large eyes and long, sensitive, hairlike rictal bristles that form an insect-catching basket around the open mouth. Their shorter wings are designed for brief, powerful sallies and maneuverability among branches. Although they may be locally common, the other nightjars do not feed in flocks. Members of both groups have species- and sex-specific patterns in their wings or tail as well as distinctive calls with which the males communicate in the dark. The non-nighthawk genera are especially vocal during moonlit nights and may call incessantly throughout the entire evening.

Lesser and Common nighthawks nest on open ground or rooftops and are the goatsuckers most likely to be encountered by birders. Unlike the other local species, nighthawks are barred below and have long, pointed wings. The two nighthawks may be separated by wing pattern—often difficult to appreciate in roosting birds—and voice. Residents of East Texas often refer to Common Nighthawk as "bull bat," alluding to the roar made by the wings of displaying males.

Chuck-will's-widow and Whip-poor-will are two of the many nightjars with names that are onomatopoeic; that is, the names mimic the sound and rhythm of their song. Although the former is larger, usually redder, and has a different tail pattern, isolated birds may present a challenge. Both species occur in the coastal migrant traps and, especially Chuck-will's-widow, at inland sites. UTC residents can become temporary insomniacs when a migrating "chuck" calls loudly all through a moonlit night. Chuck-will's-widows nest very close to the UTC, and small numbers may still breed locally. Whip-poor-wills are more common during fall. They are infrequently seen, but the number of road kills suggests that many sneak through. Both species have been negatively impacted by forest destruction. However, when woodlands are allowed to regenerate, they may again become locally common.

LESSER NIGHTHAWK
Chordeiles acutipennis texensis

Uncommon fall visitor lingering rarely into winter; rare spring visitor and possible breeder

SPRING: (29–30 Mar; 8, 11 × 2, 17 Apr) **mid-Apr to mid-Jun** (9, 19 Jun)

FALL: (9, 29 Aug) **late Aug to late Oct** (27 Oct; 9, 28 Nov)

HABITAT: Beach, sandy prairie, coastal marsh, occasionally inland sites.

DISCUSSION: Assessing the true status of Lesser Nighthawk has presented us with a conundrum. The "Texas" Nighthawk, as the Lesser was known, is easily confused with the abundant Common Nighthawk. Many of the records we have reviewed failed to rule out female Common Nighthawks, which tend to be smaller and browner than males.

Lesser Nighthawks nest as near to the UTC as the central coast (Lake Corpus Christi, for example), yet despite highly suggestive reports from Galveston Island, we have no irrefutable evidence of local nesting. The birds that breed in South Texas retreat into central Mexico south to northern South America in the winter, and therefore we suspect that this bird appears along our coast only as a migrant. Our meager (and rather confusing) data suggest that Lesser Nighthawk disperses northward into our region in late summer and early fall, as a number of tropical species tend to do, with a few remaining along the coast into winter (i.e., 26 Dec 1982 in Galveston).

A few of the birds returning to South Texas in spring may overshoot, explaining their presence along our coast. One such individual was photographed on 23 Apr 1997 after being stunned in a vehicular collision near San Bernard NWR, BRA. Although a few Lesser Nighthawks have been reported at inland locations, most sightings are from Quintana northeast along the coast to JEF.

COMMON NIGHTHAWK
Chordeiles minor

Common summer terminal migrant, rarely lingering to/through winter

SUMMER: (3–4, 14 Mar) **mid-Apr to late Oct** (29 Oct; 24 Nov)

HABITAT: Beach, coastal and inland prairie, cities, often nesting on rooftops.

DISCUSSION: On most spring or summer evenings, the Common Nighthawk's loud *peent* is as characteristic a sound in our sultry region as the omnipresent drone of air conditioners. Another species that has adopted the philosophy "If you can't beat 'em, join 'em," these birds nest commonly on tar-and-gravel roofs in both rural and deep urban areas throughout the UTC. Profiting from the bright city lights that attract clouds of night-flying insects, several to occasionally 12 or more may be seen foraging around well-lit highway billboards. Besides utilizing roof tops, they nest in sparsely vegetated sandy areas behind beaches, on abandoned oilfield pads, and on the shoulders of shell or gravel roads.

During late Mar and Apr, Common Nighthawks begin to return from their wintering grounds in central South America. Although we recognize several Mar records, most do not arrive along the UTC until mid-Apr (in fact, our late Feb and early Mar records may represent wintering birds). Although this is not considered a fallout species, a migratory wave may deposit prodigious numbers on telephone wires and fence posts along the coast. For example, on 12 May 1979, 500 appeared in flocks of 15–25 as they migrated over the Bolivar Peninsula. The species is rare in winter, but a very few linger into Dec (or later) most years; the Freeport CBC has detected individuals on just three of its 48 counts. Jan and Feb reports, including multiples at the Houston Arboretum (*fide* B. and

M. Honig), are probably birds that remained through unusually warm winters.

Common Nighthawk has experienced small to significant declines throughout much of its range. Poulin and colleagues (1996) attribute this decline to factors such as pesticides depressing the bird's prey base and a change from graveled to smooth roofs. At least two subspecies occur on the UTC; *C. m. chapmani* breeds in our region, and *C. m. minor* is known to migrate through East Texas (TOS 1995). Birders along the UTC should be alerted to the potential occurrence of the Antillean Nighthawk (*Chordeiles gundlachii*). This Caribbean species breeds in south Florida and has wandered as close to the UTC as Louisiana. Local birders should learn its distinctive, insectlike *piddy dick* call and keep an ear cocked.

CHUCK-WILL'S-WIDOW
Caprimulgus carolinensis

Common spring and fall transient migrant; rare (perhaps extirpated) summer breeder, rare winter lingerer

SPRING: (5, 10, 17 Mar) **mid-Mar to mid-May** (8, 19 May)
FALL: (26, 31 Jul) **mid-Aug to mid-Oct** (26 Oct; 14 Nov; 14, 16–17, 19–20 Dec; 26 Jan)
HABITAT: Coastal woodlands, well-vegetated residential areas; mixed pine-oak forest.
DISCUSSION: Nehrling (1882) found Chuck-will's-widow "common during breeding season in dry woods, with much undergrowth . . . near Spring Creek they are common, but not in the wet wooded tracts near Houston." As the fingers of Pineywoods that extend south into the UTC were timbered, this goatsucker—like the Red-cockaded Woodpecker, Brown-headed Nuthatch, and Bachman's Sparrow—retreated northward into the remaining East Texas forests. The most recent summer sightings are 40 years old (18 Jun 1960 near Sheldon, 29 Jun 1961 in Cove) and are from locations consisting of undisturbed mixed pine and oak woodlands that have now been significantly altered. At present it appears as though Chuck-will's-widow is an extirpated nesting bird on the UTC; however, it remains a common transient, possibly to an as yet undiscovered population in the Big Thicket.

During migration, it is most often chanced upon in coastal woodlands, roosting in the leaf litter or on a low branch. Numbers of them pass through inland sites as well, where they are often detected by their persistent calling. Occasionally they can be seen during the evening hawking insects over coastal marshes and grasslands or residential neighborhoods. Their large size, more thickset appearance, and shorter flights help distinguish them from Common Nighthawks or bats. On several occasions this species has been found during winter in coastal woodlands. Most of these individuals likely represent fall migrants lingering into mild early winters. For instance, a bird seen 16 Dec 1998 (Eubanks) in Sabine Woods (JEF) did not remain until Christmas. Thus birds found during the Freeport CBC in 1998, 1999, and 2000 (M. Austin) are noteworthy.

WHIP-POOR-WILL
Caprimulgus vociferus vociferus

Rare spring, uncommon fall migrant, rare winter lingerer

SPRING: (5, 12, 18 Mar) **mid-Mar to late Apr** (23–24 Apr; 11 May)
FALL: (20 Aug; 3, 16 Sep) **late Aug to early Nov** (3–4, 11 Nov)
HABITAT: See Chuck-will's-widow.
DISCUSSION: Never common on the UTC, "whips" are most often recorded during fall. Live Whip-poor-wills are infrequently observed along the UTC. However, each year numerous birds are found after they have been stunned or killed by slamming into an automobile or colliding with a building—bittersweet evidence of a rather significant migratory movement.

On 29 Jan 1978, Eubanks discovered a torpid Whip-poor-will at High Island the morning after a particularly cold night. After being warmed by the heater as it sat in a box in the front seat of his truck, the bird regained its senses and began to fly wildly around the cab. Once released, the bird returned to the woods, where it might have remained for the rest of the winter. Although there are many late fall–winter sightings, the only Freeport CBC record is one encountered on 20 Dec 1987.

Observers should be aware of the possibility of finding a migrant Common Poorwill (*Phalaenoptilus nuttallii*) on the UTC. We are aware of one undocumented report of this small goatsucker from the UTC—one vocalizing bird heard in west Houston by Bob and Mary Ann Moore 11 Apr 1987. This species has been reported as close as Goliad Co. (TOS 1995). Unlike Whip-poor-will's, a resting Common Poorwill's tail extends only barely, if at all, past the wing tips.

Swifts

WHITE-COLLARED SWIFT
Streptoprocne zonaris

Accidental winter visitor
20 Dec 1987 Freeport, BRA (TBRC 1988-144; TPRF 555) (AB 42:289, 988; Eubanks and Morgan 1989)

HABITAT: Abundant and widely distributed in Latin America, including northeastern Mexico and some Caribbean islands. Occasionally at sea level, mainly in foothills and mountains, occurring in both wet and dry habitats.

DISCUSSION: White-collared Swift is extremely rare north of Mexico; of the handful of U.S. records (California, Florida, and Texas), four are from Texas. The one UTC record represents a bird photographed repeatedly by Morgan and Eubanks during the 1987 Freeport CBC. Documentary photos were obtained during a stop-and-go chase as the bird flew northeastward along the Gulf in the direction of Galveston. Until one was photographed at Brownsville (Cameron Co.) on 18 May 1997, this was the only live White-collared Swift physically documented in the United States.

CHIMNEY SWIFT
Chaetura pelagica

Common to abundant summer terminal migrant, common bi-seasonal transient migrant

SUMMER: (9, 11, 14 Mar) **mid-Mar to late Oct** (5, 11 Nov; 6 Dec)
HABITAT: Urban and suburban areas, nesting in uncapped chimneys, also wooded areas with hollow trees; utilizes other artificial structures—wells, silos, and specially constructed nest towers.

DISCUSSION: A bird that profited from human presence, the Chimney Swift is common in many parts of the UTC that were once covered with prairie or marsh and thus devoid of nesting cavities. Now, above vast sterile subdivisions where Greater Prairie-Chickens once crooned their eerie notes on breeding leks, and Henslow's Sparrows *tsilicked* through the evening, scores of Chimney Swifts twitter from street to identical street, competing with Purple Martins for the flying insects that mosquito-fogging trucks have failed to kill. Because Chimney Swifts are capable of devouring prodigious numbers of insects, including at least some mosquitoes, they are worth encouraging in any neighborhood. Unfortunately, designers of modern homes often specify chimneys with vented caps, which prevent the birds from entering to nest. For this reason, TPWD and the Driftwood Wildlife Association (Paul and Georgean Kyle) provide plans for structures that attract and house these valuable birds, in much the same manner as other concerned groups provide additional nesting or roosting sites for bats, Purple Martins, and Eastern Bluebirds.

Chimney Swifts may arrive on the UTC in early Mar but do not become common until about the third week of the month. Simmons (1914) reported spring arrivals in Houston ranging from 24 to 30 Mar. Reports of "small swifts" in Feb most likely refer to wintering rather than migrating birds.

Swifts are abundant through the summer, and fall migrants may stage in large numbers (i.e., 1,750 over rice fields in W HAS 26 Sep 1982). Fall gatherings of Chimney Swifts are vulnerable to late summer inclement weather along the coast. Eubanks found thousands of dead swifts on West Galveston Island after the passage of Hurricane Jerry 15–16 Oct 1989.

Chimney Swifts may linger late into the fall (through Thanksgiving), and there are records from

Jan and Feb, including 8 Feb 1954 in Freeport and 19 Feb 1954 in Houston. The Freeport CBC also recorded an unidentified swift on 19 Dec 1993. We note, however, that George Lowery and his students once found wintering Vaux's Swifts, *Chaetura vauxii*, around the LSU campus in Baton Rouge, so any winter *Chaetura* along our coast should best be considered *Chaetura* species until more certain identification can be made.

Hummingbirds

Admiring the bejeweled iridescence of a hummingbird spinning in reverse or hovering in midair lures many a novice into the great pastime of birding. Some observers are content simply to hang feeders, sit back in recliners, and allow the hummers to work their magic. The more botanically inclined (and those most intense about this hummer quest) often invest copious time and money in cultivating native and introduced plants with blossoms that attract and nourish their feathered guests.

Yards well attended by hummers can become social focal points, and when a rarity appears, it is often looked upon as a great source of pride and achievement. CBC participants in the Freeport area have made a science of scouring their neighborhoods for hummers (an impressive 12 species have been documented in the city of Lake Jackson alone), and much of what we know concerning the winter distribution of hummingbirds along the UTC has been gleaned from their data. Table 13 presents numbers extracted from *American Birds* and *Audubon Field Notes* and presents the species and numbers of hummingbirds that were sighted during 30 Freeport CBCs.

Ruby-throated Hummingbird, the principal breeding species of the eastern United States, makes up the mass of the UTC's migratory hummer movement. However, no less than 11 other members of the family have been confirmed in the region, many appearing with predictable regularity. Sightings of the less common species usually occur during winter, most appearing in yards that provide a combination of feeders and flowers. Unfortunately, despite the phenomenon having been recognized and documented more than two decades ago, most currently available guides to eastern birds give little if any indication of the presence of western species wintering in the Southeast. However, statistics presented in recent CBC issues of *American Birds* and *Audubon Field Notes* indicate that high counts for as many as four

Table 13. *Freeport Christmas Bird Count Hummingbird Totals, 1975–2004*

Species	Avg.	Yrs. Seen	High	Total
Rufous Hummingbird	7	30	28	223
Ruby-throated Hummingbird	2	28	5	54
Black-chinned Hummingbird	2	26	7	63
Broad-tailed Hummingbird	1	25	4	41
Buff-bellied Hummingbird	2	23	6	58
Anna's Hummingbird	1	19	7	34
Hummingbird species	1	13	6	32
Selasphorus species	2	9	11	45
Archilochus species	1	8	5	21
Calliope Hummingbird	0	4	2	5
Blue-throated Hummingbird	0	1	1	1
Total Hummingbirds	19			577

western species occurred in southeastern Texas and Louisiana.

Questions worth pondering that relate to the historic abundance of hummers wintering along the UTC, and indeed the entire Gulf Coast, include:

• When prairie and marsh dominated the region, and urban woodlots full of nectar-bearing ornamental plantings were nonexistent, did hummingbirds pass through on their journeys to Middle America without lingering?

- Prior to the increased interest in birding and the proliferation of feeders, did hummingbirds winter largely unnoticed on the UTC?
- In response to the greater availability of feeders and food-bearing plants, has there been an actual increase in wintering hummingbirds; that is, have hummers modified their wintering strategies accordingly (as we have witnessed with geese being "short-stopped" in northern states), or are there just more birders finding them?
- Rather than assuming that wintering hummingbirds such as Rufous or Broad-tailed have paused en route from their northwestern U.S. breeding sites to the tropics, could some of these species or individuals actually have moved northward out of the Mexican highlands instead?

Hill and colleagues (1998) summarized eastern U.S. Rufous Hummingbird records from much of the twentieth century, shedding light on some of these questions. First detected on the eastern seaboard in 1909, wintering Rufous Hummingbirds have continued to increase dramatically in number to the present. Although the number of people in the Southeast who are now attracting hummingbirds has expanded, and our ability to identify a Rufous Hummingbird has improved, we consider the upswing in records (up to several hundred per year in some southeastern states) too great to be merely the result of improved detection; we consider it a true population increase. Other species of hummingbirds handled by banders in the Southeast have not been detected in similarly rising numbers, suggesting that the increase is peculiar to (or at least most pronounced for) Rufous Hummingbird.

Several possible scenarios have been suggested for the increase in wintering Rufous Hummingbirds in the Southeast. One involves increased survival of migrants that fly east instead of south in the fall, this survival initiating a shift in the gene pool causing more birds to fly eastward. Thus, Rufous Hummingbird would be profiting from a rapid evolutionary change in its migratory behavior, as was documented with the Blackcap (*Silvia atricapilla*) in Europe. Another hypothesis: Rufous Hummingbirds that fly to traditional wintering areas in Mexico find habitat destruction and increased competition for blossoms.

Some might wander northward to the SE United States, where they enjoy minimal competition. The six- to eight-week gap between when the bulk of Rufous Hummingbirds leave the western United States and when they appear in the Southeast may be explained by birds migrating into and then wandering out of Mexico.

As mentioned earlier, well-planted gardens are especially attractive to migrating and wintering hummingbirds. A sampling of plants that are proven hummer attractors on the UTC includes the native Texas mallow or Turk's cap, giant Turk's cap from Mexico, shrimp plant (perhaps the favorite), cigar plant, coral vine (or queen's wreath), various coral beans (*Erythrina* spp.), firebush or firecracker bush (*Hamelia*), tropical or scarlet sage and many other species of *Salvia,* eastern redbud, cardinal flower, and trumpetvine. A list of everyone's favorites would be several times longer. If seeds or cuttings cannot be obtained from friends, most are readily available from local nurseries.

We would like to call attention to the identification problems posed by many hummingbird species, particularly for females and immatures, and we especially caution the attempted identification of many winter *Archilochus* and *Selasphorus*. The data presented here are, for the most part, based upon sight records and are therefore subject to the errors intrinsic to such identifications. However, we have scrutinized the literature and have attempted to cite only those records that we feel represent correct identifications.

Recently, Charles Brower of West Columbia, Kay and Robert Lookingbill of Lake Jackson, Brent Ortego of Raisin, and Sumita Prasad and Craig Zalk of Houston have begun to band UTC hummers (as have Nancy Newfield in Louisiana and Bob Sargent in the Southeast), further clarifying the true status of wintering birds. Through these efforts, we now know that a large percentage of them are first-year birds. Table 14 presents data on eight species of hummingbirds identified in hand by Brower during recent banding activities. By far the bulk of the birds he banded were Black-chinned and Rufous hummingbirds.

New and seasoned birders have an opportunity to immerse themselves in hummingbird viewing, talks, and banding demonstrations at the Xtreme Hum-

Table 14. *UTC Winter Hummingbird Banding Totals, 2001–2002 and 2002–2003*

Species	Number of Males	Number of Females	Total
Black-chinned Hummingbird			
2001–2002	15	21	36
2002–2003	3	12	15
Rufous Hummingbird			
2001–2002	17	18	35
2002–2003	18	16	34
Ruby-throated Hummingbird			
2001–2002	4	2	6
2002–2003	5	4	9
Allen's Hummingbird			
2001–2002	3	0	3
2002–2003	1	2	3
Buff-bellied Hummingbird			
2001–2002	0	3	3
2002–2003	1	0	1
Calliope Hummingbird			
2001–2002	1	1	2
2002–2003	1	0	1
Broad-tailed Hummingbird			
2001–2002	2	0	2
Costa's Hummingbird			
2001–2002	1	0	1

Note: Hummingbirds listed in this table were banded by Charles Brower. About 75% of all birds banded had hatched the previous summer.

mingbird Xtravaganza sponsored by the Gulf Coast Bird Observatory in Lake Jackson. Watch for this event during mid-Sep.

GREEN VIOLET-EAR
Colibri thalassinus

Accidental visitor

26 May–19 Jun 1981 Lake Jackson, BRA (TPRF 248) (AB 35:841)

HABITAT: Breeds in mountains from central Mexico to northern Argentina; locally, has occurred in well-planted gardens with feeders.

DISCUSSION: Green Violet-ear may not breed as close to our borders as other tropical accidentals such as Plain-capped Starthroat, Bahama Woodstar, or Cinnamon, Berylline, and White-eared hummingbirds. Nonetheless, it is one of the commonest tropical vagrant hummers that appear in the United States. Early Texas records did not always involve hummingbird feeders, but most subsequent sightings have been at sugar water bottles and/or in well-planted gardens. Like many montane tropical hummingbirds, this species is an altitudinal migrant, nesting during the height of the flowering season in mixed coniferous forests, then descending and dispersing. Although it is a UTC accidental, the number of accepted Texas sightings, largely in the Hill Country, has grown to 41 (including a 14–17 Jul 1994 individual photographed just a few miles N in Montgomery Co.). Owing to the propensity of the species (or perhaps only of a certain geographical population) to venture northward, and the large number of feeders now luring hummers, we see no reason why it should not continue to appear here.

BROAD-BILLED HUMMINGBIRD
Cynanthus latirostris magicus

Very rare visitor

6 Aug–15 Sep 1984 Beaumont, JEF (TPRF 337) (AB 39:76)

28 Sep 1993 HAS (TBRC 1993–136)

9 Nov 1998, 30 Jan–25 Feb 1999 Lake Jackson, BRA (TBRC 1999-15); original Nov sighting not recognized by TBRC

3 Nov 2001–18 Feb 2002 Houston, HAS (TBRC 2001-0143); reportedly present as early as mid-Oct

31 Oct–Dec 2004 NW Houston, HAS (S. Gross, M. Reid photo) (TBRC no longer considers this a Review Species)

HABITAT: Usually in drier habitats including low open woods and thorn forest, oak woodland, sparsely vegetated desert, and residential areas in the southwestern U.S.; locally at well-planted residences.

DISCUSSION: Broad-billed Hummingbird is a rare summer resident in West Texas (TOS 1995). It breeds as far eastward as New Mexico, wintering rarely in S Texas. However, it is a fairly common resident in the Sierra Madre Oriental just south of Monterrey, Mexico (less than 150 miles south of Brownsville). Thus it is likely that Broad-billed Hummingbirds appearing along the coast in East Texas may have originated from the southwest rather than the west.

This hummingbird has been recorded at least five times on the UTC and is rare enough that observers should carefully document and verify additional sightings. Colorful males are distinctive; females resemble a faded female White-eared Hummingbird (*Hylocharis leucotis*), which is even less likely to occur, although increasing in West Texas and not without precedent in the Gulf states. The Lake Jackson individual was an immature male. The subsequent two Houston records were adult males.

BUFF-BELLIED HUMMINGBIRD
Amazilia yucatanensis chalconota

Uncommon and irregular winter visitor, very rare summer straggler

WINTER: (14, 17 Aug; 1, 3, 16, 22 Sep) **late Sep through early May** (12, 17–28 May)

HABITAT: Well-planted gardens, usually with Turk's cap and shrimp plant, occasionally with sugar water feeders; also in woodlots with shrubbery such as salt cedar and lantana, immediately bordering the coast.

DISCUSSION: Buff-bellied Hummingbird is an uncommon and inconsistent winter bird on the UTC. A tropical species locally common in the Lower Rio Grande Valley north to Matagorda Co., it exhibits a northward postbreeding dispersal, as do some other tropical species, such as Brown Pelican, Wood Stork, and Groove-billed Ani. Historically, Oberholser (1974) considered the Buff-bellied Hummingbird a vagrant not only in Orange Co., immediately northeast of the UTC, but also in Corpus Christi, where it is fairly regular and breeds north at least to Victoria Co. It now occurs annually in Louisiana, wandering as far eastward as Florida.

During the last several decades, most of the Buff-bellies reported along the UTC were seen near the coast or on the margins of the Galveston Bay complex. CBC data also suggest that they are more common immediately along the coast, often in well-planted yards with feeders. The Freeport CBC found this species on 25 of 48 counts, including seven recent winters in a row, with a high of six in 2001. We have fewer records of Buff-bellied Hummingbird in the (potentially) drier and cooler inland portions of the region and away from the moderating influence of the warm Gulf waters.

Early fall records include an individual on Galveston Island 1 Sep 1993 and one photographed at a feeder with Ruby-throated Hummingbirds on 22 Sep 1992 in Cove (CHA) at the yard of P. and T. Fagala. In recent years, a pattern of even earlier dates has emerged in the yard of Denis James in Lake Jackson, BRA (14 Aug 2000, 17 Aug 2001, and 2 Sep 2002). This yard and others nearby have hosted many late spring (May) records, including a female that lingered until 5 Jul 2002. These occurrences may be a harbinger of local breeding during coming years. Recently, summering birds have been documented in nearby Washington and Austin cos., suggesting a more widespread range expansion.

Buff-bellies resemble both the tropical Rufous-tailed Hummingbird (*A. tzacatl*), which has never been confirmed in Texas, and the Berylline Hummingbird (*A. beryllina*), a rarity in the American Southwest. For distinguishing characteristics, see Howell and Webb (1995) or Williamson (2001). Arriving young Buff-bellies may be largely gray below; their large size, bill and tail color, scattered green feathers in the gorget, and calls distinguish them from more regularly occurring species.

VIOLET-CROWNED HUMMINGBIRD
Amazilia violiceps

Accidental late winter/early spring
2 Mar 1998 Lake Jackson, BRA (TBRC 1998-40) (AFN 52:356)

HABITAT: Dry foothills from southeastern Arizona and southwestern New Mexico south through much of western Mexico.

DISCUSSION: The only UTC record of this southwestern vagrant is one identified by Joyce Wheeler of Lake Jackson and later photographed by Tom and Sherry Collins. Unfortunately, this bird spent only one morning in the yard, disappointing many who hoped to glimpse a great Texas rarity. The other four accepted Texas records are all from the Rio Grande Valley, ranging from Weslaco (east of McAllen) to El Paso. Be warned: some Violet-crowneds are very dull, showing little color in either the cap or the bill.

BLUE-THROATED HUMMINGBIRD
Lampornis clemenciae clemenciae

Very rare vagrant
9 Sep 1982 Houston, HAS
29 Apr 1989 Sea Rim SP, JEF
17 Dec 1989 Lake Jackson, BRA
18–21 Nov 2002 Mont Belvieu, HAS

HABITAT: Pine-oak woodlands in canyons of the Southwest.

DISCUSSION: This large western hummer breeds sparingly in the Chisos Mountains of Texas as well as in New Mexico, Arizona, and south at least to Oaxaca, Mexico. Rarely, it appears in other parts of Texas, including the Rio Grande Valley and along the Gulf Coast. The TBRC has not considered our few UTC records, as the species is not on its review list. Oberholser (1974) lists a Houston sighting from 18 to 20 Aug 1968, yet without corroborative documentation we are hesitant to include this record.

On 17 Dec 1989 the temperature hovered just above freezing during the Freeport CBC (not every Freeport CBC is conducted in shirtsleeves). Notwithstanding the frigid temperatures, a Blue-throated Hummingbird, having materialized about two weeks earlier at feeders in at least two different Lake Jackson yards, faithfully appeared and become one of the few winter records of this species for Texas.

RUBY-THROATED HUMMINGBIRD
Archilochus colubris

Common to abundant bi-seasonal transient migrant, uncommon summer terminal migrant, rare winter lingerer

SUMMER: (23 × 2, 24 Feb; 2, 4 × 2, 6 Mar) **early Mar to late Oct**; lingering winter birds obscure departure dates

HABITAT: Woodland, hedgerows, residential areas with ornamental plantings and sugar water feeders; breeds in dense woodlands near water. Of the two UTC nests we have located, one (CHA) was built on the lower branches of a southern magnolia, the other (HAS) on a small limb of a green ash hanging out over a creek.

DISCUSSION: The UTC is blessed with a spectacular passage of Ruby-throats, the common breeding hummingbird of eastern North America. Each spring and fall, countless numbers of these glittering sprites defy our perceptions of the laws of both physics and logic by flying nonstop across the Gulf of Mexico. During spring migration, swarms of them may be seen around sugar water feeders, ornamental plantings, or the weedy Japanese honeysuckle vines that have become naturalized throughout the area. During our censused fallouts this species was the 14th-most common bird, constituting 2 percent of the total.

Once the hordes of migrants have passed, the Ruby-throated Hummingbird becomes a scarce summer resident, and most observers will not see another until postbreeders start drifting south. Well-sited feeders should host a few by early Aug, and by early to mid-Sep, a dozen or more may be present. Late fall departure dates (and certainly many of our winter records) have been clouded by the simultaneous arrival of similar-appearing female and immature male Black-chinned (and other) hummingbirds.

Ruby-throats may remain along our coast through winter (when usually less common than Rufous and Black-chinneds). During the winter of 2001–2002, five of the 58 hummingbirds banded by Brower in BRA were Ruby-throats. In addition, an immature male photographed by Eubanks 15 Dec 1990 at Sea Isle on west Galveston Island attained definitive plumage before it departed the following spring. Presumably the same male overwintered again the following year. A bird observed 1–29 Feb 1992 (T. and P. Frank) likely wintered, and Behrstock photographed males in Bellaire during two winters in the mid-1990s. Additionally, two wintering Ruby-throats, one a second-year male and the other an adult female, were banded at Russ Pitman Park in Bellaire (HAS) Feb 2004 (S. Prasad).

Unusually plumaged birds occur on occasion: a pale, off-white individual was observed in Crosby, HAS, 16–21 Sep 1994 (B. Nuckols, Behrstock photos); a pied adult male was present in Jersey Village, HAS, 9–15 Sep 1995 (K. and K. Combs, Behrstock photos), and another pale bird was present at the Echols residence in Richmond, FOB, 9–13 Oct 2002 (S. Prasad photos). Virtually all albino or leucistic Ruby-throats handled by banders are first-year birds (Bob and Martha Sargent data), so the pied adult male at Jersey Village is noteworthy.

BLACK-CHINNED HUMMINGBIRD
Archilochus alexandri

Uncommon winter terminal migrant

WINTER: (13, 15–26, 19–22 Aug; 7–10 Sep) **early Sep to early Apr** (24, 26 Apr)

HABITAT: Upland and riparian woodlands, scrub, dry canyons, residential areas; associated locally with hummingbird feeders and well-planted yards, seen only rarely "in the wild."

DISCUSSION: Black-chinned Hummingbird may be seen throughout much of Texas, breeding as near to the UTC as the Hill Country and the Coastal Bend. In West Texas the winter temperature fluctuations are greater than along our coast, and the well-drained, often nutrient-poor soils to our west support different and less luxuriant vegetation. The mild winters, dense evergreen vegetation, and abundant flowering plants along the UTC are ideal for this species, and it should come as no great surprise that each year "lingering Ruby-throats" remain through the winter, only to molt into Black-chinneds. Ornithologists investigating migration have determined that, weather permitting, males of certain hummingbirds (and other birds as well) migrate only a short distance, presumably so as to be able to return quickly in spring to begin territorial defense. By making a short flight to the Gulf Coast, male Black-chinneds can utilize well-planted gardens and a huge number of feeders, augmented by the insects that survive the Gulf Coast's mild winters. During the winters of 2001–2002 and 2002–2003, a majority of the hummingbirds banded by Charles Brower in BRA were Black-chinneds. However, of those 24, only eight were males, suggesting that coastward movement has a survival value for females as well. Other banders in the Southeast have established that large numbers of Black-chinneds of both sexes winter along the Gulf Coast.

Definitive arrival and departure dates are difficult to determine for three reasons. First, Black-chinned can easily slip in unnoticed among the hordes of departing Ruby-throats. Second, the birds are often ignored until their purple gorget feathers start to emerge, and by then most observers cannot remember when they arrived. Third, female Black-chinneds may never be identified as such.

Bird banders' literature addresses the points involved in differentiating in-hand females and subadult males of Black-chinneds and Ruby-throats. These problems are not thoroughly addressed by most field guides. Only recently has birders' literature focused on the fine points of the separation (Howell and Webb 1995; Williamson 2001). Superficially, note the Black-chinned's longer bill and its habit of furiously pumping its tail up and down as it hovers at feeders, a behavior rarely shared by Ruby-throats.

ANNA'S HUMMINGBIRD
Calypte anna

Rare winter terminal migrant

WINTER: (21, 24 Sep) **early Oct through early Mar** (13, 16 Mar)

HABITAT: Feeders and gardens with plantings for hummingbirds.

DISCUSSION: Anna's is another species that winters in association with feeders and gardens. Occasionally, males appear with a glittering red gorget and crown. Others may approach that condition before departing. Although not impossible to identify, some females certainly pass as lingering "green jobs," in part because most field guides do not alert unwary readers to the potential winter presence of the species along the Gulf. Many guides still maintain that Anna's is a sedentary species, rarely drifting eastward from the west coast or southern Arizona. Anna's is the only U.S. hummingbird that sings, and its vocalizations are often heard throughout the winter.

UTC birders should also be aware of the potential for Costa's Hummingbird (*Calypte costae*). On 17 Dec 2001 during the Mad Island CBC in nearby Matagorda Co., Brower discovered (and later banded) a young male Costa's at a feeder in the town of Matagorda.

CALLIOPE HUMMINGBIRD
Stellula calliope

Rare winter terminal migrant and bi-seasonal transient

WINTER: (11–12, 24, 28 Sep) **early Oct through early Mar** (30 Mar; 1 Apr)

HABITAT: Calliope breeds in the western mountains of Canada and the United States and in extreme northwestern Mexico. Most winter farther south in Mexico, often at low elevations. Locally, it occurs at feeders in well-planted yards.

DISCUSSION: Calliope Hummingbird, the tiniest breeding bird north of Mexico, only recently began to appear in the Southeast with any consistency. Oberholser (1974) fails to mention it as either a winter bird in Texas or a seasonal visitor to the eastern half of our state. Now known to range as far eastward as the Gulf states, the Calliope has wandered as far afield as New Jersey. This species tends to get "pushed around" by other birds and is often seen only briefly at feeders. Although the male is distinctive, the females and young are quite nondescript and may be overlooked among the crowds of *Selasphorus* battling around the feeders. Recent advances in field guides and increasing banding efforts have led to the realization that this western species is a rare but regular winter visitor to the UTC and the rest of the Gulf Coast; at least 24 were identified in Louisiana during the winter of 2001–2002. One of the longest remaining and best documented Texas individuals, a female, spent seven weeks in Lake Jackson (BRA) from late Jan to late Mar 1988. A banded adult male present at a Houston feeder 7–13 Jan 2002 was found to be the same bird that had been banded and recaptured several times at Raisin (Victoria Co.) during the previous two years.

BROAD-TAILED HUMMINGBIRD
Selasphorus platycercus platycercus

Uncommon winter terminal migrant

WINTER: (1, 9, 17, 27 Sep; 4 Oct) **early Oct through early Apr** (14, 18, 26 Apr)

HABITAT: Well-planted gardens, usually with hummingbird-attracting flowers and feeders.

DISCUSSION: As observers in the Southeast become aware that several western hummingbirds may occur there, the instances of Broad-tailed Hummingbird being reported have increased proportionately. Most of the Broad-taileds that appear along the Gulf are young birds, and without close examination, they may be written off as Rufous Hummingbirds.

Certainly more Broad-taileds are seen than are identified, perhaps because the rufous at the base of the tail (a defining field mark if seen well) is a rather obscure trait. In addition, most field guides do not adequately discuss the species' winter distribution along the Gulf. In truth, this hummingbird is emerging as an annual, low-density UTC species. The Freeport CBC recorded it on 25 of 48 counts, with a high of 4 in 1993. On rare occasions several are present in one yard, and that may account for the male's U-shaped courtship flights that we occasionally see (Behrstock, pers. obs.). In the Freeport–Lake Jackson vicinity, Broad-taileds tend to show up late in the year, sometimes lingering into Apr. Depending on their mood, birds may give various calls; most often heard is a frequently uttered *seek* note—higher-pitched than that of a Rufous. Unfortunately, the characteristic trill produced by the male's specially shaped outer primaries is only rarely, if ever, heard locally.

RUFOUS HUMMINGBIRD
Selasphorus rufus

Uncommon to common fall transient migrant and winter terminal migrant

WINTER: (20, 24 × 2, 25 Jul) **late Jul through early Apr** (1, 6, 13 Apr; 1 May)

HABITAT: Suitably planted gardens, especially those with sugar water feeders.

DISCUSSION: Many southbound Rufous Hummingbirds enter Mexico via the mountains of West Texas, but a fair number stream eastward, spreading across the Gulf Coast. We know little about the routes they take, if indeed they are routes and not just a barely synchronized easterly drift. Theories include an eastward movement along the Rio Grande; spreading to the Gulf and then northward along it after actually reaching the mountains of northern Mexico; and taking a direct route from the Rockies to the Gulf (although the paucity of Great Plains sightings in early fall would seem to dispel this notion). In truth, no one knows the route by which these western jewels reach the Gulf states. We only know that each year they return.

Adult male Rufous Hummingbirds arrive first, a few appearing as early as late Jul. Some years, during late Jul or early Aug, it seems everyone has a Rufous or two at feeders. These early migrants usually linger a few days or weeks, occasionally piling up in favored yards from late Sep to mid-Oct, then disappear, presumably to the east or south. The next wave of birds consists of immatures, which are then followed by females (Hill et al. 1998). Early birds that do remain are joined by the major push of Rufous arriving in late Oct and early Nov. Freeport counts and banding data (tables 13 and 14) suggest that Rufous is our most common wintering western hummer. During some years, the number of birds wintering inland tends to bear this out; during other years, inland Black-chinneds may outnumber the Rufous.

One of the smallest yet most belligerent and territorial of the North American hummers, a Rufous will sit next to a sugar water bottle, guarding it for virtually the entire winter. To diminish confrontations, additional feeders or a well-planted garden will give other hummers a chance to feed without being under the threat of constant bombardment.

Although many of our early arrivals are easily identified adult males, some show up with a few red feathers on the lower margin of the gorget and varying amounts of rufous and green on the back. Only later in late winter or early spring do they attain their brilliant rufous adult plumage. Uniformly green-backed birds arriving with a cluster of red feathers in the center of a largely white throat are likely females (Stiles 1972), but beware of female Broad-taileds that have more uniformly green tails. Individuals of both sexes photographed during late summer exhibited heavy wing molt that appeared complete by early Oct. Tail and body molt continue through winter and into spring. During their spring departure, some males already possessing fully developed red throats were in heavy gorget molt with numerous feather sheaths visible. A bird's entire feather renewal may take eight months or more. As a rule, the feathers of the gorget (interramal and malar feathering) are the last to be replaced during molt, presumably because their display value is minimal on the wintering grounds. However, the flashing throats of wintering males (and even females) are anything but minimal, often allowing one to locate the birds easily as they perch amid verdant foliage or engage in aerial combat.

ALLEN'S HUMMINGBIRD
Selasphorus sasin sasin

Rare or very uncommon winter terminal migrant

1 Mar 1976 Houston, HAS (*TCWC 9945) (AB 30:741; Beavers 1977); Newfield (1985) speculated that this specimen exhibited hybrid characteristics with *S. rufous*

7 Nov 1987–6 Mar 1988 Freeport, BRA (TBRC 1988–215; TPRF 865) (AB 42:289, 457)

11 Jan 1993 Houston, HAS (TBRC 1993–69) (AB 47:276)

15–23 Feb 1999 HAS (TBRC 1999–123)

18 Dec 2001–17 Feb 2002 HAS (TBRC 2002–95)

19 Jan–16 Feb 2002 West Columbia, BRA (TBRC 2002–27)

25 Jan 2002 Lake Jackson, BRA (TBRC 2002–28)

27 Jan 2002 Lake Jackson, BRA (TBRC 2002–30)

18 Oct 2002 near Sweeney, BRA (TBRC 2002–114, TCWC 13910)

30 Jan 2004 West Columbia, BRA (TBRC 2004–13)

Oct 2003–15 Feb 2004 north Houston, HAS (TBRC 2004–17) (banded)

14 Feb 2004 Lake Jackson, BRA (TBRC 2004–30)

5 Mar 2004 Angleton, BRA (banded)

FALL: (18–22 Oct; 7 Nov; 28 Dec) to SPRING: (27 Feb; 1, 6 Mar)

HABITAT: Hummingbird feeders and well-planted gardens.

DISCUSSION: Besides the records mentioned, we are aware of at least 17 other sightings of probable Allen's Hummingbirds. Because of the increase in confirmed records, in Jun 2004, Allen's Hummingbird was removed from the TBRC review list, and the committee is now willing to accept sight records of well-documented males. Nonetheless, heed their warning: "It is likely that the vast majority of the adult male sight records are in fact Allen's, however, at our present state of knowledge it will take hand-held measurements of tail feathers to have a record accepted. Courtship flight of this species is also distinctive, however it is doubtful this would be observed in Texas." Fortunately, due to the recent efforts of numerous banders in the Southeast (most notably Nancy Newfield and Bob Sargent) and Texas (Brent Ortego, Glenn Schwartz, Kay and Robert Lookingbill, Sumita Prasad, Craig Zalk, and Charles Brower), we now know that Allen's Hummingbirds are annual in small numbers all along the Texas coast and at various inland sites. At least six Allen's were banded along the Texas coast during the winter of 2001–2002, and several the next winter. Limited data suggest a Rufous to Allen's ratio of about 7:1 (Brent Ortego, pers. comm.).

Kingfishers

RINGED KINGFISHER
Ceryle torquata torquata

Rare visitor
21 Oct–9 Dec 1989 Brazos Bend SP, FOB
9 Dec 1989 Anahuac NWR, CHA
31 Oct–5 Nov 1998 Brazos Bend SP, FOB

HABITAT: Margins of natural and artificial lakes and ponds, banks of large rivers, infrequently smaller wooded creeks; nest burrows are excavated in riverbanks, road cuts, and hillsides.

DISCUSSION: Ringed Kingfisher is widespread in the Neotropics, where it occurs in a variety of habitats on both still and flowing waters. There have been at least three recent sightings of this wide-ranging, powerful flier, the largest of the six New World kingfishers. Two of these occurred, almost exactly nine years apart, at Brazos Bend SP (FOB). The individual located 9 Dec 1989 near the entrance to Anahuac NWR (J. Parmeter) was present on the same day as another at Brazos Bend.

Ringed Kingfisher is a fairly common resident in the Rio Grande Valley and has been recorded with increasing frequency (including nesting evidence) to our west in the Hill Country. It should come as no surprise that a large, aggressive fish-eating bird would expand northward into a warm state that provides thousands of large and small impoundments, many of which are stocked with fish, and that also has irrigation canals and roadside ditches. As with Least Grebe, Masked Duck, and Northern Jacana, records of tropical waterbirds outside their normal range may reflect the abundance of suitable aquatic habitat that is currently available. Birders often locate the Ringed Kingfisher by ear; listen for its loud, evenly spaced, gracklelike *chak'... chak'* calls. As the bird flies overhead, the uniformly dark reddish underparts should be easy to observe.

BELTED KINGFISHER
Ceryle alcyon alcyon

Common winter terminal migrant, uncommon to rare during the breeding season (early May to mid-Sep)

HABITAT: Any body of water that supports small fish, including bay edge, fresh and saline channels and impoundments, marshes, roadside ditches, and even Houston's concrete-lined bayous.

DISCUSSION: Presumably Belted Kingfisher was once abundant on the UTC, given our once endless miles of winding bayous, slow-flowing streams, and backwaters. Now that many of the waterways have been straightened, channelized, and paved, these kingfishers find few steep riverbanks where they may burrow and build their nests. Historically, Belted Kingfisher has nested along the Brazos and Trinity rivers, at Brazos Bend SP, and on the Bolivar Peninsula (nest building 29 Mar 1940), but there are few recent records. Their population swells in the winter; many a roadside bar ditch, stream, and shallow pool has a patrolling Belted Kingfisher during the colder months. Marshes and swamps along the coast attract the highest numbers. During the coldest winters when the shallow, open waters of the inland counties freeze (if only for a few days), most kingfishers retreat toward the Gulf, swelling the coastal populations even further. The Freeport CBC averages 67 per year, with a high of 119 in 1984.

GREEN KINGFISHER
Chloroceryle americana

Accidental or very rare visitor

HABITAT: This widespread Neotropical species is found along clear streams and lake or pond edges with adequate overhanging vegetation. It is the second smallest of the six New World kingfishers.

DISCUSSION: The UTC's first Green Kingfisher was seen 7 Apr 2001 by canoeist Scott Gleason. He discovered it on Cypress Creek near the Mercer Arboretum in Humble, HAS. The next month, he relocated it and obtained photos that documented a female. Apparently two Green Kingfishers were present that summer on Cypress Creek (*fide* Eric Carpenter). During 2002, Gleason again observed a Green Kingfisher at the same locale. This stretch of Cypress Creek is a shallow, clear-water stream that offers ideal Green Kingfisher habitat. Other reports near the UTC, including one in Liberty Co. on 23 Nov 2002, suggest that additional records should be expected in the coming years.

Woodpeckers

The woodpeckers are an easily recognized and often colorful group of small to large insect-eating birds. Characteristically, they have a sharp bill designed for chiseling both food and nest cavities from dead or dying trees. This feeding habit requires a host of body modifications, including specialized feet, tongue, nostrils, and tail feathers and the musculature necessary to beat their heads against trees and other woody plants day in and day out.

Woodpeckers provide a great service to other cavity nesters. Frequently, birds such as Wood Ducks, owls, chickadees, *Myiarchus* flycatchers, and Prothonotary Warblers nest in woodpecker holes after the original inhabitants abandon them.

Fourteen kinds of woodpeckers are known from the UTC. Four are vagrants from the west or southwest and have been detected only once or twice. Some of our local woodpeckers, including Red-bellied and Downy, are numerous and may be encountered with little effort. Others, such as the diminutive Red-cockaded and the gaudy Red-headed, have fallen prey to greedy or unmanaged forest practices and large-scale clearing for development. Formerly common locally, these species now barely survive.

The magnificent Ivory-billed Woodpecker once inhabited our forests. Now, after decades of searching and the suggestion that at least one male maintained a precarious foothold in Arkansas, there is no firm evidence the species persists. Nearly as large, the Pileated Woodpecker is still locally common, as it is in much of the United States. The Northern Flicker, formerly considered two species, occurs on the UTC as two distinctive forms, each representing a different geographic region.

Although local birders undoubtedly appreciate our woodpeckers, visitors from countries with a long history of habitat management prize them. In England, for example, many forests have been subjected to nearly a thousand years of aggressive management. Such forests are kept in a youthful state that lacks the abundance of dead trees into which woodpeckers excavate their nest holes. Therefore, a successful morning's birding in East Texas may produce as many kinds of woodpeckers as a birder may reasonably expect to see during a lifetime afield in Great Britain and neighboring Europe.

Dying or dead trees provide more than just nesting cavities for these birds. Woodpeckers consume many species of insects, including the grubs and adults of beetles that live in decaying wood. Cutting old growth trees and tidying up the understory by removing fallen trunks deprives these birds of a large measure of their diet.

Contrary to the image provided by television cartoons, not all woodpeckers are especially vocal. Males define their domains to females or other males by drumming on tree trunks, although a metal chimney flu may also be used to broadcast a message far and wide. Especially favored drumming sites are hollow branches, yet another resource associated with dead or dying trees. Advanced birders find and identify the various woodpeckers by learning the unique rolls and syncopated taps that the males beat out as an expression of their territoriality.

RED-HEADED WOODPECKER
Melanerpes erythrocephalus erythrocephalus

Local resident in serious decline, irruptive transient and uncommon terminal migrant

HABITAT: Open areas with snags including cutover, burned, or herbicide-sprayed mixed pine and hardwood forest, roadsides, old orchards and pasture edge; nesting in various dead trees, including sycamore, magnolia, and water oak; avoids closed-canopy forest.

DISCUSSION: Although Nehrling (1882) found it to be the "most abundant of its family in and near Houston; breeding commonly," this attractive woodpecker now barely hangs on in isolated pockets around Houston and areas to the east, such as near White Memorial Park (CHA). Unfortunately, clearcutting of forests, their replacement with young trees, and the removal of snags for disease control, to minimize accident risks, or because they are an "eyesore" have nearly extirpated local Red-headed Woodpeckers. Additionally, this cavity nester must now compete with the non-native European Starling for the few remaining nesting trees. Selective logging and the thoughtful practice of leaving dead trees standing for nesting purposes would greatly encourage populations of this species.

Red-headed Woodpecker is migratory; in most years one or two young birds wend their way to the coast (where they are largely absent as nesters). Occasionally they appear along the Gulf in impressive numbers. Eubanks recalls a late fall on Galveston Island when dozens of Red-headed Woodpeckers were present, a few even feeding on the trunks of palm trees and on telephone poles. Such fall occurrences of multiple birds have not been reported in recent years. Although annual for many years, this species was missed entirely on eight of the last ten Freeport CBCs.

ACORN WOODPECKER
Melanerpes formicivorus formicivorus

Accidental winter visitor
7 Jan–24 Feb 1968 Bear Creek Park, HAS

HABITAT: One of the most widespread New World woodpeckers, occurring in lowland and montane oak-dominated habitats from Oregon south to northern Colombia.

DISCUSSION: Acorn Woodpecker is a montane species; its nearest resident populations are located in the mountains of West Texas and the Sierra Madre Oriental of NE Mexico. Occasionally they wander; there are E Texas reports from Aransas, Bastrop, and Hays cos. (TOS 1995). The errant HAS Acorn Woodpecker visited Bear Creek Park west of Houston from early Jan to late Feb 1968. This county park is

partially forested in pine (a western finger of the East Texas pine forests), and there are numbers of large water oaks and sycamores along the banks of Bear Creek. Acorn Woodpeckers drill holes in pines, oaks, and other trees (often substituting a telephone pole or the siding on a house), into which they stuff acorns for future consumption. Presumably all of the right ingredients—acorns, dead pine trees, one lost woodpecker—were present to produce this remarkable record.

GOLDEN-FRONTED WOODPECKER
Melanerpes aurifrons aurifrons

Accidental winter visitor
26 Dec 1993–15 Jan 1994 Brazos Bend SP, FOB

HABITAT: Usually drier areas with live oaks, mesquites, and other larger trees or columnar cactus, in which they nest.

DISCUSSION: Golden-fronted Woodpecker replaces the Red-bellied to our southwest; its range extending from Calhoun, Jackson, and Victoria cos. south, while the Red-bellied is present in the remaining riparian woodlands from the Mission River (and rarely to the Nueces River) northward (Rappole and Blacklock 1985). Although the TOS (1995) mentions Golden-fronted Woodpecker as a vagrant in BRA, FOB, and HAS cos., we recognize but one UTC record with substantiation that definitively rules out Red-bellied. A Golden-fronted Woodpecker was present 26 Dec 1993 to 15 Jan 1994 at Brazos Bend SP (FOB). Photos demonstrate its diagnostic head and tail markings (P. D. Hulce).

RED-BELLIED WOODPECKER
Melanerpes carolinus

Common resident

HABITAT: Deciduous and mixed woodlands, residential areas with mature trees.

DISCUSSION: Because it is noisy, widespread throughout older neighborhoods, and given to visiting feeders for sliced citrus fruit, suet, and sunflower seeds, the Red-bellied is one of the most widely recognized UTC woodpeckers. Along with the aforementioned foods, its UTC diet would include insects such as ants and beetles, berries of dogwood and poison ivy, and acorns (Scott et al. 1977). Generally, Red-bellieds nest in a dead branch of a living tree; such holes also provide roosting sites during the winter. Two subspecies occur on the UTC; *M. c. harpaceus* nests locally, and *M. c. zebra* is a winter visitor (TOS 1995). Although common throughout the wooded UTC, this woodpecker—like most of our resident eastern woodpeckers—is absent from the coastal hiatus. However, a few scattered individuals have been seen in High Island and Sabine Woods. The small resident population that established a toehold in Galveston may no longer exist. The Freeport CBC, which includes the Brazos River bottomlands, averages 133 per year, with a peak of 271 in 2003.

WILLIAMSON'S SAPSUCKER
Sphyrapicus thyroideus nataliae

Accidental winter visitor
18 Oct 1975 High Island, GAL
19 Dec 1982 Freeport, BRA

HABITAT: Usually breeds in montane forests with pine and fir, winters in lowlands; occurring from British Columbia to about central Mexico.

DISCUSSION: Williamson's Sapsucker, like its Red-naped cousin, is a western woodpecker that appears rarely in East Texas. Williamson's usually winters no closer to the UTC than the Davis Mountains of West Texas, although on occasion it has wandered as near as the Texas Hill Country. We are aware of only two UTC records, both coastal. The first for our region was present 18 Oct 1975 at High Island (GAL). Another was reported on the Freeport CBC (BRA) 19 Dec 1992.

YELLOW-BELLIED SAPSUCKER
Sphyrapicus varius

Common winter terminal migrant

WINTER: (13, 17 Sep) **late Sep to early May** (2–3, 9, 16 May)

HABITAT: Various wooded situations and residential plantings; occasionally at feeders.

DISCUSSION: How common and widespread the retiring Yellow-bellied Sapsucker is locally becomes apparent as soon as one makes the connection between this species and the rows of holes drilled into tree trunks. Although this woodpecker drills into a variety of hardwoods, we have noticed a distinct preference for sugar hackberry. Besides actually lapping at the sap that collects in these holes, the sapsucker also eats ants and other insects attracted to the sugary liquid. Fruits of blackberry, Virginia creeper, and flowering dogwood are also consumed (Scott et al. 1977). Sapsucker wells provide a seductive feeding medium for numbers of insects; a variety of other birds, including warblers and hummingbirds, take advantage of these winter soup kitchens. Although the species is rather solitary and rarely seen even with other sapsuckers, an individual or two may join a mixed winter feeding flock of insectivores, when their presence is often first signaled by their rather catbirdlike *mew* call. The Freeport CBC averages 89 birds per year with a high of 216 in 1972. We note a summer record 1–31 Jul 1961 in Cove (CHA).

RED-NAPED SAPSUCKER
Sphyrapicus nuchalis

Accidental winter visitor
15–16 Mar 1996 High Island, GAL
19 Dec 1999 Oyster Creek, BRA

HABITAT: Woodlands, isolated oak mottes.

DISCUSSION: Scientists now have a number of advanced tools to aid in determining the relationships between species. As a result, since about 1980, the ornithological tide has turned from "lumping" to "splitting" as evidence (often biochemical) is found to separate similar-appearing birds that were once classified as a single species. Where this will end is unknown, but we suspect that the number of "new" species extracted from the old will continue to grow for the foreseeable future, and the legions of birders who keep life lists hope so too. The Yellow-bellied Sapsucker was recently divided into three species: Yellow-bellied, Red-naped, and Red-breasted. Both Red-naped and Red-breasted are western species; Yellow-bellied is the only one that occurs here with any frequency. The first UTC report of a Red-naped Sapsucker was a male that frequented High Island in Mar 1996. The second was another male videotaped on 19 Dec 1999 near Oyster Creek during the Freeport CBC (Ron and Marcia Braun and others). Observers should be cautious in identifying this species, carefully noting the throat pattern, as some Yellow-bellied Sapsuckers may show red on the nape.

LADDER-BACKED WOODPECKER
Picoides scalaris symplectus

Rare resident, uncommon to rare winter visitor

HABITAT: Widespread, ranging from S California and Nevada to NE Nicaragua (A.O.U. 1983), inhabiting tall brush such as mesquite and huisache (often with cactus), orchards and open parklike woodland, and occasionally residential plantings. In denser forest, may be replaced by Downy Woodpecker.

DISCUSSION: Ladder-backed Woodpecker is one of two woodpeckers inhabiting the mesquite brushland to our southwest and west, including much of the Texas Hill Country; the other is the Golden-fronted. Ladder-backs are regularly seen near Victoria, and their range extends north well into Matagorda Co. Although formerly more widespread and found all the way east to Houston, Ladder-backs are now mainly limited to the narrow band of mesquite-huisache woodlands that crosses far western WAR (extending into parts of Austin and Colorado cos.). In WAR the number of sightings, including one on 4 Jul 1989, suggests that the species is a rare breeder, barely penetrating the western portion of the region. During the winter of 2002, Weeks found an apparent range extension near Damon, west BRA: four birds were located on 23 Feb, and what probably represented lingerers from this group were seen and heard there during the summer. Others found on 21 Jun 2003 along Davis Estates Road, FOB, and 18 Dec 2004 along Beard Road, FOB, were likely part of this same eastward-moving group of birds.

During winter Ladder-backs are somewhat more common, although they are rarely seen away from the drier western and southwestern portions of the UTC. Recent records near the coast include Houston, Galveston, and Freeport (recorded four times on Freeport CBCs). The sharp *peek* call of the Ladder-back, often followed by a dry rattle, is huskier than a Downy's call.

DOWNY WOODPECKER
Picoides pubescens

Common resident

HABITAT: Light woodland, second growth, hedgerows, residential neighborhoods.

DISCUSSION: Downy Woodpeckers are common and well-known UTC residents, frequently attracted to yards with mature vegetation and to bird feeders. They nest in fairly open woodland or artificial approximations, such as orchards, and in older neighborhoods that provide dead trees or live trees with dead branches. Learning this bird's high-pitched *peek* contact note and sweet kingfisher-like rattle helps differentiate it from the locally rare Hairy Woodpecker, which has a lower-pitched *pick* delivery. During winter, mixed foraging flocks often include one or two individuals. The Freeport CBC averages 46 per year and tallied a high of 151 in 1987.

Downy Woodpecker (and Carolina Chickadee) reappeared on Galveston Is. following a Sep 2002 tropical storm. Counterclockwise north winds seem to have blown these birds from nearby forests on the mainland to the island (*fide* J. Stevenson).

HAIRY WOODPECKER
Picoides villosus auduboni

Presumably extirpated resident, rare winter terminal migrant

HABITAT: Many types of open woodlands, both deciduous and coniferous; residential areas, orchards, parklike areas with scattered trees, swamps, and in Latin America, pine-oak and montane evergreen forests (A.O.U. 1998).

DISCUSSION: Hairy Woodpecker has the largest range of any New World member of its family, inhabiting forests from central Alaska to W Panama. It breeds in much of NE Texas and as close as the Big Creek Scenic Area (San Jacinto Co.) about 60 miles north of Houston. It is locally extirpated, no longer nesting on the UTC, and is now little more than a winter rarity. Its frequency of occurrence has dropped dramatically; since 1991 there have been no sightings during the Freeport CBC, where it had previously been tallied in 25 different years. Now, most winters pass without so much as a single record. Single birds seen during the past several years include Cypress, HAS, on 10 May 2003; Spring, HAS, on 14 Nov 2004 (D. MacSorley), and near the mouth of the San Bernard River on 17 Dec 2004, during the San Bernard CBC (S. Almoney).

RED-COCKADED WOODPECKER
Picoides borealis borealis

Formerly a locally common resident; now extirpated

HABITAT: Red-cockaded Woodpecker is listed as endangered at both the state and federal levels. Breeding birds depend on open stands of mature, fire-adapted pines, such as shortleaf, slash, loblolly, and longleaf. These pines are adapted to periodic fires that keep the stands open and discourage hardwoods from filling in the gaps. Additionally, nest trees are infected with the fungus that causes pine red-heart disease (*Phellinus pini*). The birds forage in pine and mixed pine-hardwood forests that may contain common bald cypress or other trees, orchards, and even cornfields (Winkler et al. 1995).

DISCUSSION: Red-cockaded Woodpecker disappeared, as had the Ivory-billed Woodpecker before it, as a result of the clear-cutting of the mature softwood forests that extended into the eastern portion of the region. This species exhibits the unfortunate trait of nesting in diseased live trees—the bane of modern forestry managers. Generally, pines are not infected with red-heart disease until they are mature. Today's shareholder-oriented tree harvesting schedules (still reeling economically from the ravages of 150 years of unbridled clear-cutting with no consideration for either the human or wildlife populations of the twenty-first century), dictate the removal of trees as they become mature, and sometimes before that. Thus, as the trees best suited for nesting are removed, the woodpecker's populations disappear.

It has been estimated that a family group (clan) of 3–4 Red-cockaded Woodpeckers requires 143–225 acres and that a healthy population of the birds requires 61,750 acres or more (Winkler et al. 1995). Other factors affecting the bird's decline include loss of habitat to commercial development and the resulting fragmentation of the forest; fire control measures that encourage an increase in the height and number of oaks and other understory species, making the forest unsuitable for this woodpecker; competition with Red-bellied and Red-headed woodpeckers for existing nest holes; tree loss from hurricane or tornado damage; and death of trees from bark-beetle infestations.

Today's colonies are found in protected sites including military bases, state forests and national wildlife refuges, and property set aside by a handful of particularly enlightened timber companies. Trees with active nests are readily identified by their extensive smooth areas cleared of bark and by trails of resin running from small holes drilled near the nest entrance. Inducing the flow of sticky resin and removing bark to make the trunk smooth may prevent some snake predation.

Typically, nest holes are not excavated near lateral branches that could act as perches for predators. Food does not appear to be a limiting factor in the species' distribution, as the birds take a large variety of terrestrial and adult aquatic insects, spiders and other arthropods, nuts, pine seeds, and various fruits. The species is still locally common to the north and east of the region. Visiting birders find the most accessible and predictable birds at Jones State Forest (about 45 minutes north of Houston's George Bush Intercontinental Airport), where several colonies have been encouraged. Nest trees there are marked with bands of paint, and the nest holes may be reinforced with metal edging to prevent use by larger species. During winter, these woodpeckers may join mixed bird flocks. At no time of the year are they likely to be seen very far from their colonies.

NORTHERN "YELLOW-SHAFTED" FLICKER
Colaptes auratus auratus

Common winter terminal migrant; rare breeder

WINTER: (12, 13 Sep; 1 Oct) **mid-Oct to early Apr** (2 Jun)

HABITAT: Small woodlots to extensive forest, wooded neighborhoods, open habitat with widely scattered trees; often seen feeding on the ground.

DISCUSSION: Once known as Yellow-shafted Flicker, this colorful bird is familiar throughout the eastern United States. It has a number of local names; perhaps the best known is yellowhammer, its nickname in Alabama, where it is the state bird. Apparently, two races of Northern Flicker occur on the UTC. The expected form is *C. a. auratus,* an uncommon breeder in East Texas and a common migrant and winter resident. The race *C. a. borealis* is known to winter in East Texas (TOS 1995). It is a very rare local breeder, known to have nested during the summer of 2000 in CHA and HAS.

The arrival of flickers usually coincides with the year's early cool fronts, not much before mid-Oct.

They become common by Nov; many are reported from woodlands on UTC area CBCs. The Freeport CBC reported a record 473 in 1980. However, flickers seem to be less common and somewhat irruptive these days. Their scarcity may be due to a combination of habitat loss and nest site competition with European Starlings or may be an indication that global warming permits them to winter farther north.

NORTHERN "RED-SHAFTED" FLICKER
Colaptes auratus collaris

Rare winter terminal migrant

HABITAT: Overgrown fields, second growth, light woodland, residential areas.

DISCUSSION: A breeder in western North America, including West Texas, and south into the mountains of Middle America, the "Red-shafted" form of Northern Flicker is a rare and infrequently reported visitor to the UTC. The Freeport CBC has recorded it in five years, with a high of five in 1980 (the same year that a high of the "Yellow-shafted" form was recorded). Despite its striking reddish orange wing linings, local birders may not always attempt to separate it from Yellow-shafted Flicker, given its subspecific status.

PILEATED WOODPECKER
Dryocopus pileatus pileatus

Locally common resident

HABITAT: Various forest types including bottomland hardwoods, pine or mixed pine, live oak, and post oaks; occasionally in orchards or well-vegetated neighborhoods with mature trees; ventures into second growth.

DISCUSSION: Pileated Woodpecker is likely the largest remaining woodpecker north of Mexico. Logging, real estate development, and the clearing of trees for disease control have heavily impacted the forests that originally supported this spectacular bird. Nonetheless, it is still surprisingly common on the UTC, breeding within the city of Houston and well-vegetated neighboring communities. This impressive bird may be found in mixed pine-oak woodlands of our eastern counties and the dense riparian habitat bordering our rivers and bayous. Evidence of its presence may include its loud knocking and flickerlike calls, as well as its large, rectangular of squarish nest hole entrances. Occasionally the Freeport CBC leads the country in the number of Pileateds reported; the count averages 43 per year, but a high of 103 was tallied in 1985. As with many of our resident eastern forest birds, Pileated Woodpecker is nearly absent from the coastal zone. One seen 17 Apr 1999 at Quintana, BRA, was a notable exception.

IVORY-BILLED WOODPECKER
Campephilus principalis

Previously an uncommon and local permanent resident; now extirpated

Although the TBRC does not accept UTC sight records, there are eggs and specimen records from nearby Jasper and Liberty cos. to as far as the NW corner of the Texas Panhandle. We note UTC records listed by Oberholser (1974), none submitted to the TBRC. In the nineteenth century several specimens now lost were taken by J. J. Audubon in Apr or May 1837 on Buffalo Bayou, HAS and FOB, and there are records in May 1864, BRA, and 1880–81 on Spring Creek, HAS. For the first half of the twentieth century we have five records: Jun 1913, Spring Creek, HAS; 29 May 1927, BRA; 19 May 1937, Neches River, JEF-ORA co. line; 1938, ORA; and 1938, Bunn Bluff, JEF. Oberholser gives one more record, 1960–63 between the Trinity and Neches rivers, county unknown.

HABITAT: Formerly local in extensive stands of mature pine forest with dying or dead trees, SW along the coast to the Brazos River and inland to the Trinity River bottomlands (TOS 1995).

DISCUSSION: Hopes that a remnant population of Ivory-billed Woodpeckers might exist were shattered in the mid-1990s with the publication of a three-year survey that failed to locate any surviving birds in Cuba (Lammertink 1995). Nonetheless, reports continued to emanate (via returning birdwatchers), suggesting that a few individuals may still persist in mature forest at the eastern end of the island. Lacking any confirmed report of an Ivory-bill for more than 60 years, most ornithologists considered it extinct in the southeastern United States. Therefore, when Gene Sparling of Hot Springs, Arkansas, reported a male Ivory-billed Woodpecker on 11 Feb 2004, the rediscovery spread not only glee but a true sense of astonishment throughout the birding world.

Efforts to locate additional individuals with a flotilla of canoeing birders and sophisticated electronic listening devices continue at and around Arkansas' Cache River National Wildlife Refuge, the site of the bird's discovery. So far, these have been unsuccessful.

The TOS (1995) mentions unsubstantiated sightings from 1967 and 1972 for the Neches and Trinity River bottomlands. The lack of recordings or photos and confusion with the widespread and relatively similar Pileated Woodpecker have hindered attempts to confirm recent records.

Flycatchers

One of every 18 bird species known from the UTC is a flycatcher, a member of the huge and often confusing Neotropical family Tyrannidae. Of the 27 kinds reported locally, seven are breeders. Despite its usually warm winters and persistent insect populations, the UTC is not tropical enough to support a year-round population of flycatchers. Only the Great Kiskadee—a very recent invader from the south—is likely to remain through the winter. The balance of our nesting flycatchers, especially Scissor-tailed Flycatcher and Western Kingbird, may linger a little but none can really be expected well past the Christmas Bird Counts. During winter, the UTC's nesting flycatchers abandon the region and are replaced by a hardier group of visitors, including: Eastern, Say's, and (rarely) Black phoebes, and Ash-throated, Brown-crested, Vermilion, and (rarely) Least flycatchers.

Flycatchers that visit the UTC represent a number of habitats and geographic regions. These include boreal forest, thorn scrub and Tamaulipan woodland, montane sycamore-lined canyons, tropical savannas and marshes, and eastern deciduous forest. The seasonal appearance and numbers of many species are predictable; habitually, they concentrate at sites such as the coastal migrant traps at High Island or Quintana. Others appear as rare individuals, perched on a fence wire miles from any regularly visited site. Discovering such a wanderer and photographing it is an unforgettable highlight for any birder.

GREENISH ELAENIA
Myiopagis viridicata

Accidental visitor
20–23 May 1984 High Is., GAL (TBRC 1988-289; TPRF 330) (AB 38:934; Morgan and Feltner 1985)

HABITAT: Tropical lowlands and foothills from N Mexico to N Argentina; vocal differences suggest more than one species may be involved.

DISCUSSION: The single U.S. occurrence of this sedentary, phlegmatic flycatcher defies logical explanation, being perhaps best relegated to the *miracle* category of unusual bird records. In trying to explain its presence, the usual cast of suspects—cage bird, disoriented migrant, and ship-assisted visitor—do not seem to apply. Nonetheless, on 20 May 1984, a Greenish Elaenia was discovered foraging in the understory of High Island's Louis P. Smith Audubon Sanctuary (Boy Scout Woods), a coastal sugar hackberry motte. The bird was netted, measured, photographed, and—much to the consternation of certain members of the museum community—released unharmed. During the next several days many local birders, joined by others from around the country, were able to study this unique and cooperative bird at close range.

OLIVE-SIDED FLYCATCHER
Contopus cooperi

Uncommon spring, common fall transient migrant

SPRING: (16, 26 Apr) **late Apr to late May** (31 May; 5, 11 Jun)

FALL: (24, 29 Jul; 7, 10 Aug) **mid-Aug through late Oct** (6 × 2, 11 Nov)

HABITAT: Woodland edge; feeds from exposed perches over open fields and grasslands adjacent to woodlands.

DISCUSSION: During spring, Olive-sided Flycatcher migrates north into the United States and Canada via the Mexican mainland. This species is not a regular trans-Gulf migrant; only four were seen among 62,495 migrants censused during spring fall-outs. Thus its true numbers cannot be assessed during visits to the UTC's usual coastal migrant traps.

Fall migration of this species eclipses the spring movement in both absolute numbers and duration of the passage; for example, on 19 Aug 1978, a high count of 41 was tallied in GAL and CHA. Eubanks's personal spring high count for Olive-sided Flycatchers along the UTC was 17 on 16 May 1983. Stevenson suggests the lower spring totals are representative of a smaller population of birds that nests to our northeast, while the larger fall totals correspond to birds drifting southeastward from more expansive nesting grounds to our northwest. The southward movement, as with many of the flycatchers, is focused between mid-Aug and early Sep, when multiple birds can be seen during the sultry days of late summer. Because fall migrants are more common on the UTC, a certain percentage of those birds may actually traverse the Gulf on the way to their wintering grounds.

Olive-sided Flycatcher winters only casually in the United States, where a few are known from California (A.O.U. 1998). The bulk of the population travels south to the mountains of South America—although a smaller percentage winters in Middle America. Thus a record from 27 Dec 1941 at Sheldon, HAS (S. Williams) is exceptional. We warn of the similarity of this species to both Eastern and Western Wood-Pewee and of the need to note very carefully the flight behavior, plumage, and proportions of out-of-season birds.

WESTERN WOOD-PEWEE
Contopus sordidulus

Rare bi-seasonal vagrant
25 Oct 1981 Johnson's Woods, Bolivar Peninsula, GAL
28 Apr 1984 High Island, GAL
16 Sep 1984 High Island, GAL
6–8 Oct 2000 Quintana, BRA
27–29 Sep 2000 W Galveston Is., GAL
15 Oct 2001 W Galveston Is., GAL
7 Apr 2004 W Galveston Is., GAL

HABITAT: Various woodlands, including riparian, evergreen oak, and mixed deciduous-conifer. Occurs from sea level to montane elevations.

DISCUSSION: This western species is a rarely detected migrant on the UTC. Because of its similarity to Eastern Wood-Pewee, determination of its identity should be based upon its vocalizations. Five records pertain to fall migrants, while only two are spring records. To date, all reports have been from coastal BRA and GAL, but this may simply be a reflection of where birders concentrate.

EASTERN WOOD-PEWEE
Contopus virens

Common bi-seasonal transient, uncommon summer terminal migrant; rare winter terminal migrant

SUMMER: (24–25 Mar; 5 Apr) **mid-Apr to late Oct** (3, 17–28 Nov)

HABITAT: Woodlands, coastal mottes, residential areas with mature trees.

DISCUSSION: The first northbound Eastern Wood-Pewees return by late Mar or early Apr. They are common by the third week of Apr, passing through the local migrant traps into late May. Migrants can be numerous; about 1,000 were seen on 3 May 1973 between High Island (GAL) and Sabine Pass (JEF). Unfortunately, these days, such numbers would be highly unlikely. Few birds remain, and this woodland flycatcher is little more than a low-density summer resident over much of the UTC. Furthermore, during recent years, it appears to have suffered a major decline. Fall migrants begin to arrive in mid- to late Aug and may remain until late Oct.

Eastern Wood-Pewee has been reported twice from the Freeport CBC (1966 and 1973) and from High Island on 23 Dec 1973. Any winter reports should be carefully documented due to the species' rarity then and its similarity to phoebes and other flycatchers, especially Westyern Wood-Peewee.

Empidonax Flycatchers
Many birders consider *Empidonax* flycatchers the genus most difficult to identify among all North American birds. Even bird banders who handle migrants are stumped by certain individuals. Often, species such as Willow and Alder flycatchers, both of which migrate through the UTC, may only be safely identified by their vocalizations. Techniques for distinguishing these species in the field have progressed appreciably during the past three decades, yet the art of field identification remains at best imperfect. Because of the debatable nature of *Empidonax*

Table 15. Empidonax *Flycatchers Found on the UTC during the Labor Day Weekend 2–4 September 1989*

Species	Sep 2	Sep 3	Sep 4
Yellow-bellied	2	2	2
Acadian	4	2	3
"Traill's"	13	6	6
Alder	3	0	0
Least	10	6	9
Empid. species	4	0	2

identification, and sometimes heated disagreement, the data in the following species descriptions are mainly restricted to our own records (largely Eubanks's), which represent either banded birds or, in the case of the "Traill's" complex, vocalizing birds. Discussions are supplemented with additional banding data from C. Brower and M. Ealy in BRA.

With the exception of the locally breeding Acadian Flycatcher, *Empidonax* are transient migrants. Except for nesting Acadians and a few early Leasts, *Empidonax* do not appear on the UTC until the first of May. Their spring migratory window is narrow; most birds pass through during the last three weeks of May.

The fall movement is extended and substantial; birds first appear in Jul, occasionally lingering (as may Least Flycatcher) through winter. The zenith of fall *Empidonax* migration is from mid-Aug through the Labor Day weekend, and although the heat is taxing, the reward in the number and variety of species present is worth the cost in sweat. Table 15 presents *Empidonax* flycatchers seen on the UTC during the Labor Day Weekend 2–4 Sep 1989.

YELLOW-BELLIED FLYCATCHER
Empidonax flaviventris

Uncommon spring, common fall transient migrant

SPRING: (24–25; 28 Apr) **late April to late May** (28–29 May; 4, 6 Jun)

FALL: (24 Jul; 2, 4–5, 6 × 2 Aug) **early Aug to early Oct** (26, 29 × 2 Oct; 1, 2 Nov)

HABITAT: Interior parks and woodlands, coastal mottes, less frequently in scrub.

DISCUSSION: Yellow-bellied Flycatcher is one of the latest spring migrants passing through the UTC

and may be missed until a week into May. Like Acadian Flycatcher, Yellow-bellied is most likely to be encountered in the shaded interior of coastal mottes and woodlots, but wooded inland parks such as Houston Audubon's Edith L. Moore Nature Sanctuary in west Houston or Russ Pittman Park in Bellaire attract their share. Besides its late appearance, its yellow eye-ring, breast, and wing bars aid identification, but prepared birders will locate it by its voice.

Individuals are more often heard than seen; during fall migration, their peweelike *chewee* is often heard along the coast. During both north- and southbound migration, significant numbers can be seen in coastal migrant traps. For example, 17 were counted at Quintana on 17 May 2001, and 14 were tallied at the same location on 15 Aug 2001. An anomalous pair of Yellow-bellieds lingered at Brazos Bend SP from 29 May through 4 Jun 1978. One of these birds vocalized and defended a territory, yet no firm evidence of breeding (however unlikely) surfaced. The only report of a winter bird was from Bear Creek Park on 29 Nov 2001, made by observers familiar with the bird in the northeast. Unfortunately, the written details did not totally eliminate Cordilleran or Pacific-slope flycatchers; members of this species pair were found in two other UTC locations that same fall/winter.

ACADIAN FLYCATCHER
Empidonax virescens

Common summer terminal migrant

SUMMER: (21 Mar; 4–5 Apr) **early Apr to late Oct** (18–19 Oct; 1 Nov)

HABITAT: Moist bottomland or riparian forest.

DISCUSSION: The only *Empid* that breeds on the UTC, Acadians arrive in early spring, occasionally delivering their explosive two-note song as they pass through coastal woodlands, shady parks, and gardens en route to their nearby breeding grounds. At times they are common in the migrant traps; Eubanks and others tallied 225 on 7 May 1987.

Acadians are particularly common along river corridors throughout the UTC. Their explosive two-syllable *peet-za* song is one of the most familiar vocalizations in the local bottomlands. This species molts prior to migration, and early fall birds exhibit buffy wing bars and a bright yellow belly.

ALDER FLYCATCHER
Empidonax alnorum

Occasional spring, common fall migrant

SPRING: (19, 25 May: both confirmed by vocalizations)

FALL: (8–10, 12 Aug) **late Aug to mid-Sep** (9, 13 Sep; 4 Dec)

HABITAT: Coastal mottes and scrub, dense forests of the northeast UTC.

DISCUSSION: The difficulty in separating this bird from Willow Flycatcher clouds the actual UTC status of both species. Even banders are encouraged not to band birds of this species pair without obtaining vocal confirmation. Thanks to advice given to us by Steve Cardiff of LSU, as well as the consistent observations of birders at key points along the coast, UTC Alder Flycatchers are no longer quite the enigma they once were. Only a few Alders pass through during mid-May; as is the case with most *Empids*, their spring migration is late and brief. In fall, Alders arrive during mid-Aug. Willow and Alder flycatchers can be fairly common until about Labor Day (when Least is the most abundant UTC *Empid*). During Aug, Alder may vocalize and even sing as it passes through the UTC, especially at sites where multiple birds are present. Although we have heard no vocalizing Alder later than 9 Sep and the latest banding records are from 13 Sep, evidence from Louisiana suggests that the species may remain as late as the end of Sep. One was seen and heard on W Galveston Island by an experienced observer familiar with the species on the incredibly late date of 4 Dec 2000. The relative abundance of Willow and Alder flycatchers is a subject of much conjecture and debate. Eubanks, with a focus along the coast north of Galveston Island, found that of the two "Traill's-type" flycatchers that migrate through the region, Alder appears to be by far the most numerous. Jim Stevenson, focused on Galveston Island, considered Willow to be predominant. We raise the possibility that both are correct. It may be that Alder is a more common migrant through the dense forests and mottes of north GAL and JEF counties, a pattern that would correspond with Cardiff's observations in Cameron Parish (pers. comm.). Willow, however, may be the more common migrant from Galveston Island south, consistent with other observations from the Coastal Bend.

WILLOW FLYCATCHER
Empidonax traillii

Rare spring, occasional fall transient migrant

SPRING: Single vocalizing birds 19 May and 6 Jun

FALL: (16, 24–25 Jul) **late Jul to mid-Aug** (18 Aug; 24–25 Sep; 16 Oct)

HABITAT: Coastal xeric scrub, willow groves.

DISCUSSION: The Willow Flycatcher's local status continues to be confused, and we offer dates with some apprehension. Willow's spring migration appears to mirror Alder's; both pass through in small numbers during mid-May. In fall, however, Willow arrives in advance of Alder and has departed by Labor Day. The dates we provide represent vocalizing birds; the three from 16 Jul 1984 were banded and photographed as well.

"TRAILL'S" FLYCATCHER
Empidonax traillii/alnorum

Occasional spring, common early fall transient migrant

SPRING: (17, 25, 28 Apr) **late Apr to late May** (19, 25 × 2 May)

FALL: (16 Jul; 5 Aug) **late Jul to late mid-Sep** (16, 21, 29–30 Oct)

HABITAT: Coastal scrub and woodland.

DISCUSSION: Since most migrating *Empids* are silent, the majority of Willow/Alder flycatchers cannot be positively identified. As Steve Cardiff (pers. comm.) remarked, "it is more or less impossible to differentiate between specimens of Alder and 'eastern Willows,' much less identify even some of them in the field based on plumage alone." Therefore silent Willow/Alder flycatchers must be recorded simply as "Traill's Flycatcher," and the data we present refer to this group of unidentified Willow/Alder flycatchers.

LEAST FLYCATCHER
Empidonax minimus

Occasional spring, common fall transient migrant; rare winter terminal migrant

SPRING: (4, 10, 14–15 Apr) **mid-Apr to mid-May** (19, 22, 25 × 2 May; 1 Jun)

FALL: (15 × 3, 16, 20 Jul) **late Jul to late Oct** (25 Oct; 9, 17 Nov)

HABITAT: Coastal scrub and mottes; feeds near the ground along the edge of coastal woodlands, also in rattlebox, baccharis, and even open grasslands.

DISCUSSION: Although uncommon during spring, Least Flycatcher is the most regularly seen fall UTC *Empid*. Leasts begin their southward migration surprisingly early. For example, Eubanks saw the species outside Monterrey, Mexico, as early as 8 Jul. From mid-Jul through Oct they occur in a broad range of coastal habitats, although they prefer edge and open scrub and avoid the interior of the major coastal mottes. Eubanks and colleagues found 48 on 1 Sep 1990. Some winters, a few Leasts linger through the CBC period and longer unless pushed south by a severe cold front. During mild winters a few may remain until spring, accounting for a number of Mar sightings. For example, a Least discovered in WAR on 1 Jan 1987 could be found in the same small yaupon grove through 12 Mar. Some woodlots host Leasts in consecutive years, and we assume that those present in the same woodlots for more than one winter represent returning individuals. The Freeport CBC recorded Leasts in nine of 48 years. "*Empidonax* species" (Least being the most likely of the genus because it winters fairly far north) was reported in 30 of those years.

PACIFIC-SLOPE/CORDILLERAN FLYCATCHER
Empidonax difficilis/occidentalis

Rare fall (and winter?) terminal migrant
27 Sep 1996 Anahuac NWR, CHA
22–24 Nov 2001 W. Galveston Island, GAL
22 Dec 2001 CR42 near Brazos Bend SP, BRA

HABITAT: These two difficult-to-identify species nest (in aggregate) from Alaska to S Mexico in coastal and montane pine-oak and humid coniferous forests and second-growth woodland. Both winter (in aggregate) in a wide variety of lowland to montane evergreen or deciduous forest types (A.O.U. 1998).

DISCUSSION: On 22 Nov 2001, a very yellow *Empidonax* was found in a small woodlot on W Galveston Is. Over the next two days the bird was seen and heard by several experienced observers. Exactly one month later a very yellow *Empidonax* was attracted to a screech-owl tape during the Brazos Bend SP CBC.

Because this bird was silent, it could not be identified beyond the *difficilis/occidentalis* species pair. The only other UTC report was a bird heard by Austin at Anahuac NWR on 27 Sep 1996. Cordilleran (pronounced "kor-dee-*yair*-an") Flycatcher nests in W Texas, and Pacific-slope Flycatcher is a casual migrant as far as S Louisiana and accidental even farther east (A.O.U. 1998). Their call notes are sufficiently similar for people who do not hear them frequently to be unlikely to differentiate them. Conclusive identification of either on the UTC should be based upon recordings and/or in-hand measurements.

BLACK PHOEBE
Sayornis nigricans semiatra

Very rare winter terminal migrant
31 Oct 1958–1 Feb 1959 Galveston, GAL
7 Nov 1959–6 Mar 1960 Galveston, GAL
28 Jan–19 Mar 1978 Brazos Bend SP, FOB
31 Jan–21 Feb 2004 Bellaire, HAS

HABITAT: Often found along streams; may nest under eaves, bridges, or other artificial structures in close proximity to humans; during winter dispersal, usually closely associated with water.

DISCUSSION: This western species regularly breeds as close as the southwestern Hill Country, occurring as far eastward as Castroville (just west of San Antonio). During winter, Texas breeders may disperse to the south and east. In recent winters the species has been reported with regularity in the Rio Grande Valley, where it occasionally summers. Only rarely does it occur as far east as the UTC.

EASTERN PHOEBE
Sayornis phoebe

Common winter terminal migrant

WINTER: (14–15, 20, 22 Aug) **late Sep to late Mar** (13, 16, 28–30 Apr; 6 May)

HABITAT: Brushy fields, open marshes, riparian vegetation.

DISCUSSION: Eastern Phoebe is one of the UTC's most common and widespread winter visitors. It is easily found in a variety of habitats, often perching conspicuously and calling out its presence. Typically, birds arrive in late Sep and early Oct, later building to peak wintering numbers. The Freeport CBC averages 340 per year, with a noteworthy high of 1,246 in 2000. Most depart for the breeding grounds by late Mar; rarely they linger into late Apr and May. Oberholser (1974) indicates that breeding occurred in BRA, but there is no recent evidence to suggest this is still the case. The most recent summer record was one seen 11 Jun 1985 in NW HAS by S. Williams. The closest breeding populations are in the Hill Country and north of the UTC in East Texas.

SAY'S PHOEBE
Sayornis saya saya

Rare winter terminal migrant

WINTER: (9, 17, 21, 24 Sep) **late Sep to early Mar** (6 Mar)

HABITAT: Sea level to at least lower montane elevations, inhabiting grazed land, scrubby woodland, open brushy fields.

DISCUSSION: This widespread western flycatcher breeds as close to the UTC as the eastern Trans-Pecos region of West Texas. In winter, it can regularly be found east and south of its breeding range; however, only rarely is it found as far east as the UTC. These winter wanderers appear as early as Sep. Many are never seen a second time, but some overwinter. The majority has left for the breeding grounds by Mar. The Freeport CBC recorded singles of this species on eight of 46 counts.

VERMILION FLYCATCHER
Pyrocephalus rubinus mexicanus

Uncommon winter terminal migrant

WINTER: (14, 19, 22 Aug; 1–2 Sep) **mid-Sep to mid-Mar** (5, 11 Mar; 27 Apr; 12 Jun)

HABITAT: Rattlebox and similar open, low vegetation, often in and around temporary pools and lakes; migrants frequent low foliage, fences, and utility lines along the coast.

DISCUSSION: The UTC's mild, insect-rich winters attract migrants from the north, southwest, and west. By Oct or Nov each year, a small but predictable influx of Vermilion Flycatchers arrives, each brightening the edge of a UTC pond or fence line. Frequently

visited sites include Brazos Bend SP, Brazoria NWR, and waterfowl impoundments in W HAS. The Freeport CBC averages 12 per year, with a high of 26 in 1994. Rarely, they are found during spring migration; sightings are usually at open coastal habitats, including Quintana, Galveston, and the grazed prairies behind the beach east of High Island.

ASH-THROATED FLYCATCHER
Myiarchus cinerascens cinerascens

Locally uncommon winter terminal migrant

WINTER: (12, 19 Jul; 14, 24 Aug) **early Sep to late Mar** (28–29 Apr; 1, 8 May)

HABITAT: Thickets of huisache and rattlebox, occasionally in riparian areas as well; primarily in WAR, rare but regular elsewhere within the region.

DISCUSSION: Ash-throated Flycatcher has been reported at Cove (CHA), Houston, and a number of UTC migrant traps, including Freeport, High Island, West Galveston, and the salt cedars along the beach east of High Island. However, it is most predictably observed in WAR. There, isolated groves of huisache—an *Acacia* elsewhere widespread—lend a decidedly western air and create a tall brush habitat that attracts this species, occasionally in numbers. It is also regular in winter in BRA at the southwestern edge of the UTC. There, the San Bernard CBC found the species in each of the last nine years, with a high of 16 in 2004, suggesting that it may be increasing locally. Not far from there, the Freeport CBC located it in 15 of the last 16 years, with a peak of seven in 1991. Ash-throated is the *Myiarchus* most likely to be encountered in winter, but it must be carefully separated from Brown-crested Flycatcher, as that species has also been detected with increasing frequency during recent years.

GREAT CRESTED FLYCATCHER
Myiarchus crinitus boreus

Uncommon summer terminal migrant

SUMMER: (9, 13–14, 14 Mar) **late Mar to early Nov** (5, 7, 15, 28 Nov)

HABITAT: Bottomland hardwood forest, mixed pine-hardwood forest, residential areas with tall mature trees.

DISCUSSION: Great Crested Flycatcher is the only *Myiarchus* breeding along the UTC. It was once quite common, but recent destruction of mature woodlands has decreased the local population. It is still a common migrant throughout the region, especially in the woodlots immediately along the coast. Spring migrants begin to appear in mid- (rarely) to late Mar; some are still moving through in mid-May.

Fall migrants can be found in UTC migrant traps as early as mid-Aug and rarely as late as Nov. This species very rarely lingers into the winter months; there are reports from 5 Jan 1974 at High Island and 18 Jan 1999 along County Road 18 in BRA. There were reports on the Freeport CBC in 1968 and 1969. Winter reports should be treated with caution due to the similarity of both Ash-throated and Brown-crested flycatchers—an often under-appreciated winter identification challenge. During late spring, birds identified as Great Cresteds should be thoroughly studied and their bill colors carefully noted in order to eliminate a possible Brown-crested Flycatcher.

BROWN-CRESTED FLYCATCHER
Myiarchus tyrannulus cooperi

Uncommon winter, rare summer visitor
30 Dec–18 Jan 1966 Cove, CHA
3 Nov 1985 Galveston Island SP, GAL
30 Mar 1987 Sea Isle, GAL
15 Dec 1991 Freeport, BRA
17 Dec 1997 San Bernard NWR, BRA
11 Jan–28 Jan 1998 (2) San Bernard NWR, BRA
6 Jun 1998 Quintana, BRA
15 Nov 1998 Quintana NBS, BRA
6 Dec 1998–14 Apr 1999 San Bernard NWR, BRA
23–27 Feb 2001 CR 24A, BRA
14 Dec 2001 San Bernard NWR, BRA
9–12 Sep 2004 W Galveston Is., GAL

HABITAT: Locally, in oak mottes, light woodland, scrub, usually along the coast. Elsewhere, widespread in various types of tropical woodland, scrub, mangroves, etc., from S Texas to SE California and south to N Argentina.

DISCUSSION: This large tropical flycatcher has been observed locally at least 12 times. We note single records for summer and fall, but most reports come from BRA (especially San Bernard NWR) during the winter. In South Texas, it shares the same trees with Great Kiskadee, and one might expect the Kiskadee to have a similar pattern of winter dispersal. In fact, over half of the 15 UTC Kiskadee records are from spring, whereas most Brown-cresteds show up during winter. Lacking specimen records, it is difficult to assess whether UTC birds originate in the Rio Grande Valley, Arizona, or SE California or belong to one of the South American populations. Due to its bill size, Kenn Kaufman and Rick Bowers suspected a Mexican origin for a bird videotaped by Weeks at San Bernard NWR. Calling birds offer a loud, rather flat *whit* that is not as sweet as the strident note of Great Crested, nor does it possess the rolling quality of the Ash-throated's call. Silent birds are most likely to be confused with Ash-throated Flycatcher. Noting the tail pattern from below is the best way to separate the species; Brown-cresteds lack the (adult) Ash-throated's dark tail tips.

Observers along the UTC should be aware that the pool of potential *Myiarchus* species is not limited to Great Crested, Brown-crested, and Ash-throated. A number of tropical species—for example, La Sagra's (*M. sagrae*), Nutting's (*M. nuttingi*), and Dusky-capped (*M. tuberculifer*) flycatchers—may someday occur on the UTC. Any out-of-season *Myiarchus* should be carefully documented.

GREAT KISKADEE
Pitangus sulphuratus texensis

Rare visitor, mainly along the coast; rare summer terminal migrant, rare resident inland and coastally
14–17 Apr 1976 High Island, GAL (TPRF 115) (AB 30:864)
29–30 Apr 1977 High Island, GAL (AB 31:1022)
13 Apr 1979 High Island, GAL (AB 33:788)
21 Dec 1980 Freeport, BRA
22 Apr 1983 Sabine Woods, JEF
7 May 1989 High Island, GAL
10 Apr 1993 Anahuac NWR, CHA
18 Dec 1994 Freeport, BRA
10 Feb 1998 Houston, HAS
14 Feb 1998 Sharp Road near Katy-Hockley cutoff, HAS
16 Jan 1999 HAS
17 Apr 1999 San Bernard NWR, BRA
26 Apr 2000 SH 124 and FM 1985, CHA
25 May 2001 San Luis Pass, GAL

30 May 2001–18 Dec 2004 Baytown, CHA:
    successful breeding documented
28 Sep 2002 Smith Point, CHA
1 Nov 2003 Katy Prairie, WAR: same bird as next
    record?
8 Jan–16 Mar 2004 Katy Prairie, HAS; two birds,
    nest building observed
3 May 2004 Sabine Woods, JEF
26 May 2004 1 mi W of SH 124 and 5 mi. S of
    Winnie, CHA
27 Jul 2004 Port Arthur, JEF: three birds
14 Aug–30 Sep 2004 Sabine Woods, JEF
30 Oct 2004 San Bernard NWR, BRA

HABITAT: In South Texas, this tropical flycatcher
nests in woodland edge, riparian corridors, savanna
with scattered trees, in towns, and on power transmission substations in agricultural land. Farther
south, found also in marshes and mangroves. Locally,
occurs in coastal mottes and along fence lines near
the beach, rarely inland in agricultural areas.

DISCUSSION: Kiskadees are wanderers, not migrants in the classic sense. They occur irregularly in
other parts of Texas and in several southern states.

Rarely do we present a list of records for a bird
that now nests on the UTC. However, the above dates
provide an historical perspective for this species' recent influx into the region. Most of our sightings are
from the coastal counties, but there are records, including nesting pairs, from HAS and WAR.

Previously, breeding birds could be expected northeast along the Gulf as far as Refugio and Aransas cos.
Indeed, breeding was not even suspected on the UTC
until two birds were found near Baytown, CHA, on 30
May 2001. One year later (1 Jun 2002) David Dauphin
found two adults with two young at the Baytown site,
so that the UTC's first breeding pair was confirmed.
Subsequently, these birds have been present at
least through mid-Aug 2004. On 16 Mar 2004, F.
Collins observed two birds nest building on the Katy
Prairie (WAR), but the success of the nest was not
reported.

Behrstock (2000) correlated the northward range
expansion of several tropical dragonflies with an increase in winter mean low temperatures recorded
in Houston. Warmer winters may increase prey availability for insect-eating birds, as both larval and
adult insects should exhibit increased survival with
elevated temperatures. Writers on both sides of the

Atlantic have commented on similar northward
extensions of various insects, possibly the result of
global warming. Thus Great Kiskadees may be experiencing a northward shift in their range in response
to increased availability of insects during the winter
months.

SULPHUR-BELLIED FLYCATCHER
Myiodynastes luteiventris

Very rare vagrant
2 Sep 1965 Anahuac NWR, CHA (TBRC 1989-30)
    (AFN 20:71)
7–10 May 1983 Bolivar Peninsula, GAL (TBRC
    1988-80; TPRF 596) (AB 37:890)
22 May 1999 Galveston Is., GAL (TBRC 1999-52;
    TPRF 1774)

HABITAT: In the northern portion of its range,
wooded canyons, often with sycamore, walnut, and
oaks; farther south, thorn forest and more complex,
layered tropical forest, plantations, and light woodland (A.O.U. 1983; Behrstock).

DISCUSSION: Every year Sulphur-bellied
Flycatchers vacate their extensive breeding range
(SE Arizona to central Costa Rica) and migrate to
South America, mainly east of the Andes in Peru and
Bolivia (A.O.U. 1983). This is one of only a handful of
species that leave Mexico during the boreal winter
and move even farther south. Given the length and
breadth of their travels, it is not too surprising that
we have three local records, albeit on either end of
the breeding season. In all three cases, the birds were
observed roosting and hunting from tall shrubs and
trees, such as live oak, sugar hackberry, Chinaberry,
Hercules'-club, and willows. Listen for this bird: it delivers a rather comical high-pitched call that is usually likened to a rubber squeeze toy.

If a silent Sulphur-belly is encountered, observers
should very carefully note the bill size, tail color, and
distribution of white and yellow on the face, chin,
and belly so as to eliminate the possibility of similar
species. Streaked Flycatcher (*Myiodynastes
maculatus*) is the most similar. It nests as far north as
southern San Luis Potosí and Tamaulipas, but migratory overshoots from the South American population
are probably more likely to occur than are the northern birds. The Variegated Flycatcher (*Empidonomus*

varius) is another South American species that may overshoot during migration. It has been recorded in the eastern and southeastern United States. Piratic Flycatcher (*Legatus leucophaius*), a small-billed edition of these birds, is another species to consider. It nests as close as southern San Luis Potosí, Mexico. Vagrants have occurred in southern and western Texas and southern New Mexico.

TROPICAL KINGBIRD
Tyrannus melancholicus

Very rare but possibly increasing spring visitor
27 Apr 1999 High Island, GAL
10 May 2000 Crystal Beach, GAL
12 May 2000 Bolivar Peninsula, GAL (heard by J. Stevenson; later found dead by another observer) (TCWC 13622)
25 Apr 2004 W Galveston Is., GAL (TCWC 14112)

HABITAT: Savannas, marshes, edges of light woodland. Locally, open areas including golf courses and football fields.

DISCUSSION: Because of the numerous and increasing records in the Lower Rio Grande Valley, where it nests, Tropical Kingbird was removed from the TBRC review list in Nov 1998. Since that time it has become locally common in the Lower Rio Grande Valley, and birds have been found as far upriver as Cottonwood Campground, Big Bend NP. Wanderers have been found throughout the United States and have reached both coasts (Mlodinow 1998). However, there were no reports on the UTC until 27 April 1999, when S. Komito heard a vocalizing bird in an oil field outside High Island. The next report came the following year when Jim Stevenson encountered a singing bird near Crystal Beach on 10 May. Amazingly, an observer found a dead Tropical Kingbird nearby just two days later and called Stevenson regarding her find (now a specimen at the TCWC, Texas A&M University). Finally, there is an Apr 2004 report of a bird heard and seen on Galveston Island.

Given the species' continuing expansion in South Texas and its similarity to Couch's Kingbird (see following account), UTC observers should listen carefully to all Couch's/Tropical Kingbirds. Telescope views may provide additional bill and primary length identification clues.

COUCH'S KINGBIRD
Tyrannus couchii

Rare to uncommon winter visitor

WINTER: (17–18, 20 Sep) **mid-Sep to early May** (9, 11–12 May; 10, 17 Jun)

HABITAT: Found in woodland edges throughout South Texas; typically in less open areas than the Tropical Kingbird; winter visitors inhabit brushy areas, occasionally more open fence lines.

DISCUSSION: The breeding range of Couch's Kingbird extends northeast to the Guadalupe River just a two-hour drive west of the UTC. Each fall, the species disperses northward and eastward and small numbers are detected along the UTC. Arriving individuals have been found as early as Sep, but most wintering birds are not detected until intense birding during the late Dec CBCs. Most have departed by early spring; a few have been found at coastal migrant traps as late as early June—well after breeding has started to our west. It is not clear whether these were lingerers or migrants that appeared from elsewhere. Because of the difficulty in separating nonvocalizing Couch's and Tropical kingbirds, and the rarity of the latter in Texas (until recently only a few pairs nested in the lower Rio Grande Valley), we assumed that all UTC records pertained to Couch's; however, as the last species account attests, this is no longer a safe assumption.

Note that some populations of Tropicals annually disperse northward and are regular fall visitors in N California and rarely to British Columbia. It is possible that the small population of Tropical Kingbirds present in South Texas could provide a source for vagrants appearing on the UTC. We would encourage birders to listen carefully to any Couch's/Tropical-type birds, even playing recordings of both species to elicit an identifiable vocal response.

CASSIN'S KINGBIRD
Tyrannus vociferans vociferans

Very rare visitor
11 Oct 1953 Galveston, GAL
24 Apr 1955 Galveston, GAL
21 Jun 1972 High Island, GAL

17 Oct 1981 CHA
5 Nov 1988 W HAS

HABITAT: Locally, tall shrubs, trees, utility or fence wires, mainly in open country along the coast.

DISCUSSION: Although common in the foothills of the Trans-Pecos, and readily identifiable by virtue of its lead-gray head, cottony white chin, and pale-tipped tail, Cassin's Kingbird is one of the rarest UTC flycatchers. We note just five sightings during the last 50 years: Apr (1), Jun (1), Oct (2), and Nov (1), the last photographed 5 Nov 1988 in W HAS (TPRF 1055) and our only report away from the immediate coast.

WESTERN KINGBIRD
Tyrannus verticalis

Uncommon but increasing spring transient migrant and summer terminal migrant, rare winter lingerer

SUMMER: (26, 30 Mar) **early Apr to late Nov** (22, 25, 29–30 Nov)

HABITAT: Prairie or agricultural land with trees or bushes for nesting and hunting sites. In Houston, commonly nests on electric power substations.

DISCUSSION: Oberholser (1974) notes the arrival of this western flycatcher in the eastern Hill Country as late as the 1950s. During subsequent years, it spread eastward to the UTC, where it had been no more than an extremely rare member of our breeding avifauna. This species profits from the availability of artificial structures that provide nesting or hunting sites where none were present (on prairies), or surrounding grassy sites in which to forage (in urbanized areas). Locally, its spread has been facilitated by the presence of Houston Light and Power Company substations that provide nesting, roosting, and foraging habitat (Honig 1992). By leapfrogging from one substation to the next, the species became a regular breeder in parts of the UTC. Along the coast the species is a bi-seasonal transient, mostly during spring.

Apparently it is becoming more common in winter; a few have been reported lingering in each of the last few years. One that was relocated intermittently from 28 Nov 2000 to 14 Feb 2001 at Sea Center Texas in Lake Jackson, BRA, represents our latest winter record.

EASTERN KINGBIRD
Tyrannus tyrannus

Common summer terminal migrant, abundant bi-seasonal transient migrant

SUMMER: (10, 15–16 Mar) **mid-Mar to the latter part of Sep** (29, 31 Oct; 5, 17, 25 Nov)

HABITAT: Breeds in brushy fields, fencerows, woodland edge; during migration large flocks roost on the tops of coastal mottes, in weedy fields, on utility lines, etc.

DISCUSSION: This species is by far the UTC's most common kingbird, both in migration and during the breeding season. It is a regular summertime sight in undeveloped agricultural land and along the tour loops of our local refuges (Anahuac, Brazoria, and San Bernard). Migrants return in mid- to late Mar, moving through in moderate numbers until the end of May. This was our 18th most common migrant during censused spring fallouts, comprising about 2 percent of all migrants. Huge numbers can be found moving through in early fall. Most are gone by early Oct, but a few birds linger into winter. The Freeport CBC has reported this species a surprising four times (1970, 1971, 1978, 1992), and we recognize other sightings from 2 and 22 Jan.

GRAY KINGBIRD
Tyrannus dominicensis

Accidental or very rare vagrant
24 April 1974 W. Galveston Is., GAL (TPRF 323) (AB 28:824)
10 Oct 2001 Quintana NBS, BRA (TPRF 2001-126)

HABITAT: Breeds throughout the Caribbean region, including south and peninsular Florida, and westward to Alabama and Mississippi, typically in beach or savanna habitats with low open tropical scrub, scattered trees, or mangroves; also in towns.

DISCUSSION: There are two documented records of Gray Kingbird on the UTC. H. G. Stevenson noted the first bird as it foraged in scrub/hedgerow along overgrazed pasture on Sportsman's Road, GAL. More than 27 years later, another was observed perched on a power line in Quintana (BRA). This species occurs more frequently on the eastern Gulf Coast; Louisiana records and its apparent spread in Florida (A.O.U. 1998) suggest the reasonable possibility of additional UTC sightings.

SCISSOR-TAILED FLYCATCHER
Tyrannus forficatus

Abundant bi-seasonal transient migrant, common summer terminal migrant, rare winter lingerer

SUMMER: (1, 10, 15 Mar) **late Mar to late Nov** (1, 17–18, 26 Jan; 2 Feb)

HABITAT: Open country, including prairie or marsh with scattered trees or parking lots with scattered utility poles.

DISCUSSION: Scissor-tailed Flycatcher, a kingbird with an attitude, is a target species for many birders who visit the UTC. It may be seen just minutes after a visiting birder's arrival, foraging acrobatically over the parking lot of a Houston airport. This familiar and uniquely plumaged flycatcher is found throughout the open fields of the UTC, often nesting on the cross arms of utility poles in both urban and rural areas.

Scissor-tails return to local territories in late Mar and early Apr. Prior to fall departure, this species stages in flocks of several to a hundred or more. Scissor-tails are known winter lingerers, occurring rarely on CBCs, but are absent or decidedly scarce during long cold spells. The Freeport CBC found this species on 11 of its 48 counts, with a high of three in 2000. Records after Dec are extremely rare; the most recent was a bird found along Harper's Church Road (WAR) on 26 Jan 2002.

FORK-TAILED FLYCATCHER
Tyrannus savana

Rare spring visitor

23–25 April 1991 Gilchrist, GAL (TBRC 1991-66; TPRF 1001) (AB 45:471)

25 April 1993 Sabine Pass, JEF (TBRC 1993-77)

17 May 1997 Near Anahuac NWR, CHA (TBRC 1997-154)

13 Sep 1997 CHA (TBRC 1997-144) (AFN 52:90)

9–10 Nov 2004 Anahuac NWR, CHA (TBRC 2004-90)

HABITAT: Nests in marshy to dry savanna or grazed land with fences, scattered trees, or shrubs from which the birds hunt; our records are all near or on the coast.

DISCUSSION: Fork-tailed is one of the most widespread members of its family, nesting from E Mexico (Veracruz) south at least to central Argentina (Ridgely and Tudor 1994). Despite its simple markings, this Neotropical visitor is one of the most attractive New World flycatchers. With its dark cap, white breast, long dark tail, and (frequently) horizontal stance, the bird suggests a miniature Long-tailed Jaeger.

Austral migrant Fork-tailed Flycatchers (those originating in South America) seem prone to overshooting their wintering grounds. They have occurred at many sites in North America, primarily in the East. Indeed, virtually all U.S. and Canadian specimens represent the subspecies *T. s. savana* of southern South America. However, two individuals photographed in South Texas were identified as the Middle American *T. s. monachus* (A.O.U. 1998). To date, Texas has about 14 accepted records, most from near the Gulf Coast.

Shrikes

LOGGERHEAD SHRIKE
Lanius ludovicianus

Common resident, common to abundant winter terminal migrant

HABITAT: Open areas with scattered trees, live oak and holly thickets, hedgerows, brushy land, frequently in residential areas.

DISCUSSION: The two North American shrikes are similar-appearing outliers of a large Old World family. Both species have become rare throughout much of their range. Loggerhead Shrikes still hold their own along the UTC, even breeding within our cities. Their nests have been noted along roads, jogging paths, and railroad tracks, in woodland edge, brushy fields, and occasionally residential yards.

Generally, nests are built not far above the ground, often in live oaks, yaupon, hawthorn, and other low, dense trees. A less usual site was a roll of garden wire where a nest was constructed only four feet up. These birds hunt from utility wires, fence lines and posts, and the tops of trees and bushes. Locally, shrikes proclaim their territories, cache their food, and impress females by decorating barbed wire fences with impaled small lizards and snakes, frogs, crawfish tails, and various insects. These macabre larders are not difficult to find as one walks along a fencerow.

During winter, the resident race *L. l. ludovicianus* is joined by the migratory *migrans*. After migrants arrive, a day's birding in agricultural land might produce more than 50 of these masked carnivores; the Freeport CBC averages 232 per count, with a high of 582 in 1975. Not far to our west (COL), the migratory, white-rumped race *excubitorides* has been noted W of the Brazos River and should be looked for on the UTC.

NORTHERN SHRIKE
Lanius excubitor

Hypothetical: Possible winter vagrant
13 Dec 1876 (2) Hempstead, WAR (TOS 1995)
Nov 1961 Galveston Is., GAL (AFN 16:57)

HABITAT: Open country such as prairie or agricultural land with scattered trees or tall shrubs.

DISCUSSION: Northern Shrike winters annually in the northernmost part of Texas. Our database contains only two records of this erratically occurring invader. An immature was present on Galveston Is. for five days during Nov 1961. Additionally, two were taken near Hempstead (WAR) 13 Dec 1876. Due to the species' extreme rarity in most of Texas, and the fact that we are uncertain whether either of these records was unequivocally separated from the preceding species, we include these records with some misgivings.

Vireos

Vireos are small, simply colored songbirds with a diet often focused on caterpillars. Similar to warblers, they are duller, with larger bodies and bills and less obvious differences between the sexes. Distant birds may often be recognized as vireos by the slow, methodical manner in which they forage, stopping frequently to peer into leaf clusters for their favorite prey. After a capture, caterpillars with long hairs or spines are often beaten against a branch for many minutes in order to dislodge their protective devices.

All twelve vireos occurring on the UTC have simple, rhythmic songs that may be mimicked with English phrases to serve as memory aids. Two or three species of vireos may be encountered on the UTC throughout the year, but the majority are migrants. Red-eyed Vireo is one of our most abundant Neotropical migrants, and White-eyed Vireo nests abundantly on the UTC, but several locally recorded species are great rarities from other regions. Black-whiskered Vireo is a widespread Caribbean species; Yellow-green Vireo occurs throughout much of Mexico to Panama and is one of the few birds that depart those warm climes to winter farther south. The

Yucatan Vireo has been seen only once in the United States, a vagrant from the low, limestone-adapted woodlands of the Yucatán Peninsula. Except for Red-eyed Vireo, which winters in South America, our regularly occurring species are short- to medium-distance migrants, wintering from Mexico to Costa Rica or Panama. In light of the distances traveled by some migrating vireos, it seems curious that the Black-capped Vireo, a reasonably common breeder in the Texas Hill Country, has never been documented on the UTC.

WHITE-EYED VIREO
Vireo griseus

Common summer terminal migrant, very common bi-seasonal transient migrant

SUMMER: **Early Mar through early Nov**
HABITAT: This species is a specialist of scrub and understory, foraging throughout the foliage of low-growing plants and the lower branches of trees (Barlow 1980). Before the beginning of the twentieth century, Nehrling (1882) found it to be a common breeder

in areas with arrow-wood and blackhaw viburnum, Carolina buckthorn, flowering dogwood, laurel oak, and elms, including the borders of woods, open thickets, and peach gardens. This vireo continues to be a familiar breeder in riparian thickets and woodland understory (such as yaupon holly or the introduced oriental privets). A 1978 survey by Eubanks and J. Morgan at Brazos Bend SP indicated this vireo to be the most common breeding species after Northern Cardinal within the Brazos River cedar elm/green ash/sugar hackberry thickets so well represented there.

DISCUSSION: Herbicides and insecticides, cats, cowbirds, and the propensity of suburban dwellers to clear their property of understory vegetation (so as to replicate an unthreatening, parklike environment) have diminished the population of this delightful bird. Fortunately, thickets and vine tangles along the Brazos and other local rivers and bayous still support a thriving population. Few vocalizations better embody the bottomlands of the UTC than the staccato, percussive strains of this vireo piercing the mist shrouding a tannin-stained bayou. Our more onomatopoeic cohorts have variously described the song as *Quick, get the beer, Chuck,* and *Gee, fix your brassiere, quick!* White-eyed is the only vireo other than the Solitary varieties that winters regularly along the coast, where its modest numbers fluctuate with the severity of the season. The Freeport CBC recorded the species on 41 of 48 counts, with a high of 29 in 1983. During winter, the locally breeding *V. g. griseus* may be joined by *V. g. novaboracensis,* which occurs to the coast (TOS 1995). Although limited to thickets while nesting, during migration this vireo may be seen in a variety of unexpected locations, including the tops of oak trees within coastal mottes and deep inside beds of the locally introduced common reed bordering freshwater ponds and swales along the coast.

Birders beware: young White-eyeds lack the characteristic white iris and might be confused with the rare Bell's Vireo.

BELL'S VIREO
Vireo bellii

Rare spring and fall transient migrant; formerly a common breeder

SPRING: (18, 25 Mar) **mid-Mar to early May** (11 May)

FALL: (9 Jul; 6, 20, 26–29 Aug) **early Sep to late Oct** (10–12, 30 Oct)

HABITAT: Understory of coastal mottes, isolated salt cedar groves, yaupon holly thickets, residential plantings; only one recent inland record.

DISCUSSION: The UTC now represents a hiatus in the expansive nesting range of the Eastern Bell's Vireo, *Vireo b. bellii,* which has "decreased dramatically . . . in the wooded parts of east Texas" (TOS 1995). In parts of N and S California, and in Arizona, the species has become extirpated or nearly so (Brown 1993). To the northeast, it nests uncommonly in the Texas Pineywoods. To the south, it reappears as a local breeder in the thorn-scrub woodlands inland of the central coast (i.e., Choke Canyon SP). The lack of breeding Bell's Vireos around Houston may reflect the impact of urbanization associated with the city's monumental growth. Nehrling (1882) considered the species to be a "common summer sojourner" near Houston, noting "a not quite finished nest, discovered April 15 on a horizontal branch of [arrow-wood viburnum] on the edge of a thicket, about five feet above the ground." As recently as the late 1930s, Arlie McKay found possible breeders lingering during spring near Cove, CHA.

Invariably, contemporary sightings are of single birds, and the infrequent reports of singing yet presumably nonbreeding birds probably represent late migrants. Our compilation reflects two Mar records; three for Apr, including a songster encountered 15 Apr 1989 by Will and Jan Risser on Nottingham Ranch Road near the west end of Galveston Is.; one in May, in addition to an extralimital singing bird in adjacent Matagorda Co. heard by Richard Uzar; one in Jul; four during Aug, including multiples in one yard (J. Stevenson); four from Sep; and ten from Oct (nine, possibly all ten from the coast; the 1937 report lacks an exact site, although one can assume that Arlie McKay observed it along upper Galveston Bay near Cove, CHA). Interestingly, fall records have increased over the past few years, with two to three reports annually; this may be the result of increased fall coverage of the UTC's westernmost migrant traps. Although the species was reported from the Freeport CBC in 1969 and 1970, confirmation of wintering awaits documentation.

YELLOW-THROATED VIREO
Vireo flavifrons

Uncommon (formerly abundant) summer terminal migrant, common bi-seasonal transient migrant

SUMMER: (10, 13 Mar) **mid-Mar to late Oct** (15 Nov)

HABITAT: Coastal oak and hackberry mottes during migration, mixed pine-hardwood forest and riparian woodlands during the breeding season; forages higher than White-eyed Vireo and closer to the trunk than Red-eyed and Warbling vireos.

DISCUSSION: This vireo has declined dramatically along the UTC since the turn of the twentieth century, when Nehrling (1882) described it as being "abundant and breeding." He found many nests "during the months of May and June, and many contained one or two eggs of the Cowbird." Today, Yellow-throated Vireo persists as a breeding species in remnant UTC forests, particularly the dense bottomland hardwoods along the Brazos River and the fingers of Pineywoods that touch northern JEF, CHA, and HAS cos. However, nowhere on the UTC does this vireo approach the abundance it exhibits in NE Texas.

Although the Yellow-throated is occasionally reported in winter, we fear that its superficial resemblance to the far more common Pine Warbler has seduced many an unsuspecting birder into an unfortunate identification error. Adding to the confusion is the Pine Warbler's proclivity to wander during late fall and winter into a variety of forested habitats that completely lack the pines they demand during the breeding season. Pine Warblers show up in numbers after strong fall cold fronts and later, in the depth of winter, it is not uncommon to find a few residing in live oak mottes along the coast and inland in suburban insectivore flocks. Quickly glimpsing one from below could lead a CBC participant into an understandable mistake. However, on 27 Dec 1973, Mike Hoke banded a Yellow-throated Vireo at High Island. Thus at least some of the CBC records (reported on nine of Freeport's 48 counts) may be correct. Although the species ranked fortieth during our censused fallouts, a dozen or more of these birds might be encountered during a day-long investigation of the coast between late Mar and mid-Apr, many in full if leisurely song.

PLUMBEOUS VIREO
Vireo plumbeus

Very rare winter terminal migrant
31 Mar 1985 High Island, GAL
18 Dec 1987 Freeport CBC, BRA
20 Dec 1998 Freeport CBC, BRA
19 Dec 2004 Freeport CBC, BRA

HABITAT: Locally, has occurred at an oak motte at High Island; an oak woodland bordering an oxbow lake near Oyster Creek in the Freeport CBC circle; and in residential Lake Jackson.

DISCUSSION: Only four times has this lead-gray vireo, a common breeder and migrant in the Trans-Pecos mountains of West Texas, wandered to the UTC. The 1987 Freeport stray—associating with a feeding flock of Carolina Chickadees, Ruby-crowned Kinglets, Blue-gray Gnatcatchers, and Yellow-rumped "Myrtle" Warblers—materialized in live oak woodland where a number of western and tropical vagrants have been seen on previous and subsequent CBCs. This isolated forest, bordering an oxbow lake, is situated within one mile of the Gulf. Surrounded by coastal marsh, during the winter such woodlands within the Freeport CBC circle are magnets for migrants and disoriented vagrants lingering adjacent to the coast. The other two Freeport CBC records were birds in similar woodlands along Oyster Creek. Unfortunately, birders' interest in these winter rarities dissipates after the CBC period, so we are unsure about the true status of these individuals and their ultimate fate.

UTC birders sorting out the difficult "Solitary" Vireo complex should be aware of how similar worn Cassin's Vireos can appear to Plumbeous. Observers would do well to photograph any suspected Cassin's or Plumbeous vireos.

CASSIN'S VIREO
Vireo cassinii

Very rare visitor (status unclear)
30 Nov 1995 W HAS
25 Sep 1999 High Island, GAL (M. Austin)
19 Dec 1999 Freeport CBC, BRA (R. and M. Braun, M. Crane)
27 Dec 1999 Bolivar CBC, GAL (D. Peake)

27 Dec 1999 Bolivar CBC, GAL (B. Graber), different location than preceding record

What may have been one of the Bolivar birds was reported at High Island on 11 Dec (per state hotline)

29 Dec 1999 Old River CBC, near CHA/Liberty county line

13 Oct 2000 High Island, GAL (R. Pinkston)

31 Oct and 10 Nov 2000 W Galveston Is., GAL (*J. Stevenson)

26 Nov 2000 Sugarland, FOB (M. Scheuerman)

17 Dec 2000 Freeport CBC, BRA (D. and D. Peake and others)

29 Apr 2004 Sea Rim SP, JEF (J. Hinson and H. Laidlaw, photo)

8 Nov 2004 W Galveston Island, GAL (J. Stevenson)

HABITAT: Woodland edge, dense low shrubs.

DISCUSSION: Cassin's Vireo is the westernmost representative of the three species that resulted from the split of the former Solitary Vireo. It has long been known as a migrant through West Texas. Only since it was elevated to species status has it been actively searched for on the UTC. Previous claims of its repeated winter occurrence in this area have been met with considerable skepticism, largely because of its similarity to some (worn) Blue-headed Vireos. We have no evidence to support the suggestion that this species has only recently begun to occur along the UTC, nor can we say whether local records originate in West Texas or the species' extensive range in Mexico.

Birders are advised to consult Matt Heindel's (1996) identification article on the complex, noting as well Don Roberson's (2002) comments on Cassin's more contrasting loral streak. UTC observers should carefully document any bird believed to be a Cassin's Vireo. Only with more solid evidence can this species' true Texas and UTC status be determined.

BLUE-HEADED VIREO
Vireo solitarius

Common bi-seasonal transient migrant, common winter terminal migrant

WINTER: (8, 10–11, 14 Sep) **late Sep to late Apr** (13, 15, 17 May)

HABITAT: Forages inside the canopy of bottomland hardwood forests, pine-oak woodlands, isolated coastal mottes, and urban woodlots, occasionally in huisache-mesquite scrub.

DISCUSSION: Blue-headed Vireo, the eastern member of the "Solitary" Vireo complex, is present along the UTC during spring and fall migration and as a winter species. During winter, it associates with the archetypal eastern woodland insectivorous feeding flocks, which include Ruby-crowned Kinglet, Blue-gray Gnatcatcher, and Orange-crowned, Yellow-rumped "Myrtle," and Pine warblers. This vireo's former name is fitting, for rarely will more than a single "Solitary" Vireo be affiliated with a flock. Although this vireo is an infrequent singer during winter, a warm spring morning may elicit a halfhearted attempt, and later migrants may sing aggressively. Often the raspy scold of this vireo is heard well before a feeding flock ranges within view.

Annual numbers vary, and during harsh winters with extended freezes this vireo, perhaps a bird that migrates only when it senses the need, virtually disappears from the region's forests. The Freeport CBC averages 49 birds per year, with a high of 161 in 1991. Of course, for most of the history of this count, the component species of the "Solitary" Vireo complex were not distinguished, so a few Cassin's or Plumbeous vireos may have slipped through.

Movements during both migration seasons are almost imperceptible; numbers of Blue-headed Vireos arrive and depart in gradual stages rather than the maddening rush that we experience with so many of the UTC's transients.

WARBLING VIREO
Vireo gilvus gilvus

Uncommon spring, common fall transient migrant

SPRING: (14, 26–27 Mar; 5 Apr) **mid-Apr to late May** (25 May)

FALL: (6, 18, 20 Aug) **early Sep to late Oct** (2, 15–24, 21 Nov)

HABITAT: Canopy of coastal oak mottes, willow groves; less common inland among migrant feeding flocks in residential woodlots and remnant forests.

DISCUSSION: Warbling Vireo is the most widespread North American member of its family; its breeding range overlaps those of all other the other vireos except Black-whiskered (Barlow 1980). In the late 1800s, Nehrling (1882) considered it to be a rare migrant around Houston, yet Strecker (1912) believed it to be a "summer resident" in the eastern section of the state "breeding south to San Antonio" (a remark he attributed to Dresser). Although the species is no longer nesting along the UTC, if it ever did so, a relict breeding population persists in woodlands along the Trinity River in nearby Polk Co.

Occasionally, Warbling Vireo is the most common vireo accompanying the waves of migrants riding autumnal cold fronts. During fall, its accentuated yellow underparts have led to frequent confusion between this species and Philadelphia Vireo (note the lores: dark in Philadelphia, light in Warbling). Although Warbling Vireo is seen most frequently during fall, small numbers appear in spring, usually in Apr before the bulk of the Philadelphia Vireos pass through. Never common even then, only 28 Warbling Vireos were counted during our censused spring fallouts. The latest physically documented fall record was an individual photographed by Brower while it spent 15–24 Nov at Quintana, BRA. The only winter report occurred, not surprisingly, on the Freeport CBC on 19 Dec 1982.

PHILADELPHIA VIREO
Vireo philadelphicus

Common spring, uncommon fall transient migrant

SPRING: (4, 14 Apr) **late Apr to mid-May** (20, 22, 28 May)

FALL: (13 Aug; 1 Sep) **early Sep to mid-Oct** (7, 14 Nov)

HABITAT: Canopy of coastal mottes, residential plantings, salt cedar and willow groves.

DISCUSSION: Philadelphia Vireo is primarily a spring migrant along the UTC. During peak movements of Neotropical migrants, significant numbers concentrate in the coastal oak mottes and willow groves. Although the species is relatively scarce in fall, frontal passage may produce noteworthy numbers (70 on 10 Oct 1992). During late spring, they may concentrate among pecan catkins (pecan is the last tree on the UTC to bud after the winter). This species lingers into late fall, peaking in Oct, and there even a few Dec records. The Freeport CBC reported it five times, although we regard the 1971 total of four birds as suspect. The most recent Freeport CBC record was on 16 Dec 2001, when Weeks observed one at close range for about 10 minutes as it ate Chinese tallow berries.

RED-EYED VIREO
Vireo olivaceus

Common bi-seasonal transient migrant; formerly a common, now uncommon summer terminal migrant

SUMMER: (1 Mar) **late Mar through late Oct** (13, 16, 22 Nov)

HABITAT: Canopy of mature bottomland hardwood forest, mature pine-oak woodlands of the eastern counties.

DISCUSSION: Those of us who began birding with Chandler Robbins's classic *Birds of North America* learned that Red-eyed Vireo was "the most abundant bird in eastern deciduous forests" (Robbins et al. 1966). Despite widespread population declines from cowbird parasitism and habitat losses on both the nesting and wintering grounds, this bird maintains a major local presence. Indeed, few Neotropical species migrate through the UTC over such an extended period or in numbers as great as the Red-eyed Vireo (Black-and-white Warbler would perhaps compare in both respects). For approximately half the year (Mar through May and Aug through Oct) the species is passing through the region, with fall numbers lower than those tallied in spring. During our censused fallouts, Red-Eyed Vireo ranked third among all Neotropical migrants, representing about 5.5 percent of the total. Impressive concentrations are seen in the isolated migrant traps of the coastal hiatus, and during peak passages few wooded tracts, parks, or well-vegetated residential areas anywhere within the UTC are devoid of at least a few migrants.

As a breeding species, this vireo has decreased with the gradual loss of bottomland hardwood forests, exacerbated by cowbird parasitism and the widespread use of insecticides. Nehrling (1882) described it as "a common summer resident in all the deciduous woods." Urbanization, timbering, and agriculture have fragmented the unbroken eastern forests that once extended from the Sabine River west to the prairies of Katy, and Red-eyed Vireo is now absent as a breeding bird from much of this region. It remains tolerably common within remaining old growth forests, such as those along the Trinity and Brazos rivers and bordering Taylor and Buffalo bayous.

YELLOW-GREEN VIREO
Vireo flavoviridis

Rare spring transient migrant (overshoot)
1 May 1992 Bolivar Peninsula, GAL (TBRC 1993-42)
15–23 Apr 1996 High Island, GAL (TBRC 1996-69)
1–10 Jun 1998 (1–3) Quintana, BRA (TBRC 1998-79)
  (AFN 52:478)
20–28 Apr 1999 Sabine Pass, JEF (TBRC 1999-53)
28 May 1999 Quintana, BRA (TBRC 1999-62)
8 May 2001 W Galveston Is., GAL (TBRC 2001-94)
12 May 2003 Quintana, BRA (TBRC 2003-50)

HABITAT: Coastal oak and hackberry mottes.
DISCUSSION: Sightings of this tropical vireo have increased dramatically since 1992, when the UTC's first occurrence was banded on the Bolivar Peninsula by J. and B. Massey. Imagine the surprise when local birders searching for one located at Quintana by Weeks on 1 June 1998 found not one but three in the area. Since that time reports have become an annual late spring event, and in Jun 2004, the TBRC removed this species from its review list.

This vireo is a common breeder along both coasts of Mexico. Its range extends northward to the very tip of South Texas, with breeding in Texas most recently at Laguna Atascosa NWR, Cameron Co. Earlier writers such as Strecker (1912) considered the bird to be an accidental, and throughout the twentieth century it remained no more than an extremely rare summer resident in the Lower Rio Grande Valley. In recent years, it has roamed in Texas as far north as the Hill Country (Travis Co.).

Yellow-green's head markings tend to be less pronounced than those of the Red-eyed, lacking the strikingly contrasting dark border to the cap. Note that young fall Red-eyed Vireos may, like Yellow-green, exhibit a generous yellow wash on the underparts, especially the under-tail coverts. Thus birders should be cautious when attempting to identify what is an extremely rare species anywhere in Texas.

BLACK-WHISKERED VIREO
Vireo altiloquus barbatulus

Rare spring and summer visitor
28–29 Apr 1965 Galveston Is., GAL (*USNM 566527)
  (AFN 19:496; Oberholser 1974)

30 Apr–3 May 1981 Galveston Is., GAL (TBRC
  1989-122) (AB 35:842)
4–5 Apr 1987 High Is., GAL (TBRC 1988-223) (AB
  41:460)
20 Aug–2 Oct 1989 (2) High Is., GAL (TBRC 1989-195;
  TPRF 784; TBSL 196-01) (AB 44:125–26)
23–24 Aug 1991 High Is., GAL (TBRC 1991-112) (AB
  46:122)
10 May 1997 High Is., GAL (TBRC 1997-95) (AFN
  51:895)
28 May 1998 Galveston, GAL (TBRC 1998-95) (AFN
  52:357)
8 May 1999 Bolivar Peninsula, GAL (TBRC 1999-55)
2–19 May 2000 Quintana NBS, BRA (TBRC 2000-26;
  TPRF 1800)
26 Jun–3 Jul 2001 W Galveston Is., GAL (TBRC
  2001-99; TPRF 1936)
14–15 Apr 2001 High Is., GAL (TBRC 2001-70)
30 Apr 2002 High Is., GAL (TBRC 2002-78; TPRF
  1974)
23 Apr, 14 and 19 May 2003 Galveston, GAL (TBRC
  2003-46)
23 May 2003 JEF (TBRC 2003-47)
28 Apr–4 May 2004 JEF (TBRC 2004-58)

HABITAT: Mangrove swamps; locally in isolated coastal woodlands.
DISCUSSION: In the United States the Black-whiskered Vireo, a Caribbean cousin of the Red-eyed Vireo, is largely restricted to the mangrove swamps of southern Florida. Occasionally it strays westward along the Gulf Coast as far as Texas, where it has been sighted from the UTC to Brownsville.

The first local records of Black-whiskered Vireo probably represented misguided spring migrants. In 1989, however, a male appeared during late Aug at Smith Oaks Sanctuary in High Island. Highly vocal and territorial, it remained through late Oct, to the delight of numerous birders and of another individual of the same species. Another vocalizing Black-whiskered Vireo appeared in Smith Oaks Sanctuary during late Aug of 1991, yet this bird (returning from 1989?) could not be relocated after a brief two-day stay. Subsequently, Black-whiskered Vireo has become an almost annual spring visitor to the UTC, like Yellow-green Vireo. There are now at least 15 sanctioned records, 12 of which were detected in Apr or May. One particularly cooperative bird spent over two weeks in May of 2000 in the tiny Quintana

Neotropical Bird Sanctuary. There, many birders from around the country were able to add this species to their state and life lists.

The UTC's first Black-whiskered Vireo, discovered in Apr 1965 on the west end of Galveston Is., left less than fond memories with local birders. As the state's first record, this individual provoked intense interest among the then rather loosely organized Texas birding community. As numerous birders rushed to Galveston on 29 Apr hoping for a glimpse of a new Texas species, a local birder, determined to document the record properly for future generations, collected it. Unfortunately for both bird and birder, the individual did not have the proper USFWS permit for collecting scientific specimens. The birding community erupted in outrage, tempers and passions flared, and the USFWS ultimately prosecuted the person for illegally shooting the bird. The immoderate birder, a lawbreaker for a brief period, came to reside in another state. The vireo, after a brief period as evidence, came to reside in the American Museum of Natural History.

YUCATAN VIREO
Vireo magister

Accidental in spring

28 Apr–27 May 1984 Bolivar Peninsula, GAL (TPRF 310) (AB 38:934 incorrectly gives a last date of 31 May) (Morgan et al. 1985)

HABITAT: Low, scrubby woodlands on limestone soils, deciduous forest, mangroves; locally in a coastal hackberry motte, and Hercules'-club thickets.

DISCUSSION: The morning of 29 Apr 1984 dawned with the hope of seeing a Curlew Sandpiper and concluded with the discovery of a new species for the United States. Jim Morgan, Ted and Virginia Eubanks, and dozens of birders gathered that morning on Bolivar Peninsula to enjoy a shorebird that most had only dreamed of seeing on the Texas coast. Satiated with their view, Morgan and the Eubankses decided to wander up the peninsula a few miles to a hackberry–Hercules'-club thicket, hoping a few migrants recently arrived after the trans-Gulf flight would be replenishing their energy stores before venturing inland to the forests of East Texas. Larry White joined them at the motte, where the foursome noticed a rather drab, heavy-billed vireo, superficially resembling a Red-eyed, as it fed in a Hercules'-club. Baffled as to the bird's identity, the four gradually maneuvered it into a mist net being operated at the site by James Massey. Numerous photos were taken of the captured bird, Eubanks collected a series of key measurements, and Massey banded the bird before releasing it. Back in Galveston Morgan checked *A Field Guide to Mexican Birds* (Peterson and Chalif 1973). Within seconds he had located the enigmatic bird—Yucatan Vireo. By the following day news of the vireo had circulated in the birding world, and in the month that the bird remained, more than 1,000 birders traveled to the Bolivar Peninsula to share a moment of discovery.

Jay, Nutcracker, Crows, and Ravens

The widespread family Corvidae is recognized for its diversity and the gregarious and seemingly cunning behavior of its members. A number of species are unusually confiding and will land on a picnicker's plate or outstretched hand. Additionally, the family contains some of the world's most beautiful birds.

Although they are not uniformly appreciated, it is hard to ignore our local species. Six kinds occur on the UTC, three of which are breeders: a jay and two crows. We are aware of Green Jays that have visited feeders in the area; however, for the time being, we choose to consider them as escapes. The Western Scrub-Jay comes tantalizingly close to the western

boundary of the UTC and may eventually occur in the region.

The colorful and noisy Blue Jay is both hated and admired. Unquestionably one of our more attractive birds, it possesses a large vocal repertoire and exhibits decidedly scrappy behavior. Unfortunately, like many corvids, it has earned a well-deserved reputation as a nest predator. Moreover, it is one of the first birds to show up at feeders. By providing Blue Jays with extra food, the bird-feeding public may inadvertently be responsible for the death of numerous chickadees, titmice, Northern Cardinals, and other neighborhood songbirds.

The UTC's two nesting crows are a confusing pair of similarly sized black birds that are (usually) separable by voice and distribution. American Crow is common in the region's woodlands. Along the coast in the eastern portion of the region, it is replaced by Fish Crow. In areas where overlap occurs (e.g., Beaumont), not all crows may be safely identified.

Two ravens have been sighted locally. The Common Raven, a species that occurs in much of the United States and around the world, is known locally from one CBC record. A more recent sighting seems to pertain to a tame bird. The smaller Chihuahuan Raven (formerly White-necked Raven) is a rare visitor from the southwest or west.

Clark's Nutcracker, a familiar bird of the western mountains, has occurred once on the UTC. Like many other western montane species, it undergoes irregular movements that cannot be classified as true migration. During irruption years, small numbers occur in West Texas. Local birders should at least be aware of the possibility of seeing one on the UTC.

BLUE JAY
Cyanocitta cristata cristata

Common resident

HABITAT: Resident from E British Columbia to Newfoundland, southward to Florida and extreme S Texas and west to the eastern slope of the Rocky Mountains (A.O.U. 1998; Brush 2000). Found in nearly all wooded UTC localities, including residential areas with mature vegetation, less common in more isolated coppices. Largely absent from the coastal prairies and wetlands but now present in Galveston Island's historically recent woodlands. Adaptable: nests in shrubs and both coniferous and deciduous trees. During migration, more widespread, frequently seen over unsuitable habitat such as rice fields.

DISCUSSION: Harsh scolding, mimicked raptor screams, or sweet bell-like notes proclaim the arrival of a mischievous flock of Blue Jays, one of the UTC's most universally recognized songbirds. Like sushi or SUVs, people either love or hate Blue Jays. Seeing a spanking new bird feeder adorned with these large, colorful, and crafty birds has warmed the heart of many a backyard naturalist. Nonetheless they are a mixed blessing, voracious predators of eggs and nestlings, taking a terrible toll on other songbirds, as jays must feed their multiple broods of up to seven perpetually begging youngsters. By providing additional food, feeding tables serve to augment jay numbers. In order to manage these predators, many people have now stopped feeding birds altogether or use feeders that exclude larger species such as jays and grackles. This strategy is liable to have little effect on their East Texas population, as the region's diverse fruiting plants and acorn-laden oaks provide a virtually limitless supply of food for these prolific birds.

During the last several years, West Nile Virus has killed numerous UTC Blue Jays, the disease organism packing the bird's bloodstream until the blood becomes too viscous to flow. In eastern states that have experienced similar mortality, overall populations are bouncing back and seem to be negligibly impacted, if at all.

Although UTC birds are probably resident, some proportion of the northern Blue Jay population is migratory. During Sep, flocks containing hundreds of birds move southward through the northern states. Occasionally these movements are noted on the UTC; three flocks of migrants moved through the Katy Prairie on 12 Oct 1980, and 65 to 70 birds were seen on 4 Oct 2002 at Smith Point, CHA. The Freeport CBC finds an average of 92 birds per year, noting a high of 636 in 1984.

CLARK'S NUTCRACKER
Nucifraga columbiana

Accidental
14 Oct 2002 Smith Point, CHA (TBRC 2000-90)

HABITAT: Widespread in montane coniferous forests from W Canada to N Mexico, often associated with limber (white) pine.

DISCUSSION: This noisy, flashy species is well known to campers and hikers who frequent the mountains of W North America. Irruptive in its movements, it has been reported in Texas many times, but there are only 20 TBRC-accepted records, the vast majority of which are from the Panhandle and the Trans-Pecos. However, on 14 Oct 2002, those present at the Smith Point Hawk Watch watched the UTC's first and only Clark's Nutcracker wing by.

AMERICAN CROW
Corvus brachyrhynchos paulus

Common resident

HABITAT: Occurs in forest, second growth, residential areas, farmland with scattered trees; very scarce along the coast.

DISCUSSION: American Crow is abundant in East Texas, although largely absent in the northern, western, and eastern extremities of the state. Neither it nor Fish Crow inhabits the coastal prairies, rendering the Gulf's shores essentially crowless. As its distribution suggests, this is a bird of the soft- and hardwood forests that extend into East Texas. Like Blue Jay, Carolina Chickadee, and Common Grackle, it respects the boundary separating the pine and oak forests from the brushy country to the southwest. As with those same three species, crows have prospered from such human activities as planting of windbreaks and fruit-bearing trees, provision of bird feeding devices, and careless spreading of edible refuse.

Nonvocalizing crows are a Christmas counter's nightmare; silent birds seen along the Gulf in far eastern Texas, occasionally in small flocks, may represent either this species or the next. We lack data indicating what percentage of our winter American Crows are residents versus migrants from the north.

FISH CROW
Corvus ossifragus

Common but very local resident

HABITAT: Bottomland forest, occasionally venturing to garbage dumps, beaches, picnic areas, or more open sites; on the UTC, restricted to E JEF.

DISCUSSION: Fish Crow, widespread coastally in the eastern United States, is one of the state's more localized birds. To a large extent, it replaces American Crow in forest adjacent to the coastal prairies and marshes of extreme East Texas, extending from there to the northeastern corner of the state.

Unfortunately, Fish Crow is virtually identical to American Crow. David Sibley (2000) illustrates the Fish Crow's longer tail and more pointed wings, but both are traits best appreciated after becoming thoroughly familiar with both species. As Sibley's field guide warns, vocalizations of young American Crows sound just like the higher-pitched *cah* or *cah cah* of their coastal cousins.

The picnic area of Tyrrell Park in southwestern Beaumont is one of the most predictable places to encounter this species. Rarely, Fish Crows stray as far west as High Island and Smith Point, but the species has not been reliably documented west of that area.

CHIHUAHUAN RAVEN
Corvus cryptoleucus

Rare winter visitor
3 Apr 1960 Galveston Is., GAL (*Wilson Bulletin* 73:384)
1 Apr 1962 W. Galveston Is., GAL
21 Nov 1963 corpse in Cove, CHA
5 Apr 1964 Galveston Is., GAL
2 Apr 1967 Galveston Is., GAL
21–22 Apr 1982 Rettilon Road, Bolivar Flats, GAL
7 May 1982 Galveston Is., GAL
10 Feb 1999 Texas Point, JEF

WINTER: 21 Nov to 7 May
HABITAT: Grassland and desert from sea level to at least 5,000 feet elevation; common in the Lower Rio Grande Valley, much of northern Mexico, and west to southern Arizona. In some areas, replaces Common Raven at lower elevations. Locally, recorded in coastal scrub over sandy soils.

DISCUSSION: Beginning in the 1960s, our database reveals eight records of this SW desert and grassland species, six of which are from GAL (five from the island and one from the Bolivar Peninsula), one from JEF, and one from Cove, CHA. Five of these occurred during Apr; only one was from the fall. Additionally, Oberholser (1974) mentions several birds that were shot during May 1890 along the W shore of Galveston Bay (cited as Harris Co.). Our most recent sighting was a bird seen 10 Feb 1999 at Texas Point, JEF. Although this bird found by R. and H. Davis was well within the range of wandering Fish Crows, voice and structural and plumage details seem to support the sighting. Kincaid suggests that N Texas (Panhandle) birds retreat somewhat during winter, and although their breeding range is well to the west of us, disoriented northbound individuals could provide the source of our spring strays.

COMMON RAVEN
Corvus corax sinuatus

Accidental
3 Jan 1976 Old River CBC, near CHA-Liberty county line (AB 1976:520)

HABITAT: One of the most widespread birds of the Northern Hemisphere, the Common Raven occurs from sea level to the high Himalayas and on several island groups. In the United States it is primarily a montane species, common along coastal lowlands of the West only. In Texas it inhabits mountains of the Trans-Pecos to the eastern edge of the Edwards Plateau, where it is a rare to uncommon resident; winters rarely in the northwest Panhandle (TOS 1995).

DISCUSSION: The only record of Common Raven in our historic database is a bird recorded 3 Jan 1976 on the Old River CBC, which includes portions of CHA and Liberty cos. A bird recently seen at Galveston from 6 Nov 1998 to 16 Jan 1999 by J. Stevenson, D. Peake, and others exhibited the characteristics of a confiding pet. Because ravens and other corvids are frequently kept in captivity, for the time being we consider this later record hypothetical.

Horned Lark

HORNED LARK
Eremophila alpestris

Locally common resident; more common and widespread winter terminal migrant

HABITAT: Widespread in the United States, nesting at nearly all elevations. Locally, nests on higher, drier portions of beaches; during winter, along beaches and on plowed fields.

DISCUSSION: Among the most widespread breeding birds in North America, various subspecies of Horned Lark nest at literally every elevation from salty shores to alpine tundra. Local nesters *E. a. giraudi* are easily encountered along the beach road leading to the Bolivar Flats. We assume these birds winter locally. During winter other subspecies, including apparently *E. a. leucolaema* (TOS 1995), join flocks of longspurs in agricultural land. At such times reasonably large numbers can be seen, as evidenced by 85 on Wolf Island, BRA, on 2 Feb 2001. During summer, Horned Larks are found almost exclusively along the immediate coast. Thus an individual singing in WAR on 4 Jun 1987, and another in a plowed field there on 2 Aug 1987, are noteworthy.

Swallows

For thousands of years, seeing flocks of migrating birds has drawn innumerable observers into nature's processes, whether inspiring lofty poetry or simply reminding farmers that harvest time approaches. Many kinds of birds migrate at night, their travels going undetected by all but the most curious, sharp-eared, or high-tech naturalists. Indeed, the movements of most birds are not detected until the species suddenly appears or vanishes. Fortunately, a few birds exhibit obvious daytime movements, lending a note of credibility to the concept of migration.

Raptors, Fulvous Whistling-Ducks, several herons, and a various swallows are some of the birds for which migrations may be observed during daylight hours. Among them, raptors and swallows seem less likely to venture out over open water and are especially visible along the coast. Locally, Barn and Tree swallows are two of the most obvious coastal migrants. During spring and fall, it is not uncommon to see tens of thousands flying low over coastal prairies and beaches or crowded side by side along telephone lines. At certain sites, Purple Martins stage year after year for their southbound flights, and they too may be present in prodigious numbers.

Apparently certain swallows no longer breed on the UTC. Bank Swallow seems to have nested locally, and supposedly, Northern Rough-winged Swallow—probably still a rare nester—was more common.

Balancing the loss, Cave Swallow recently became an abundant breeder across Texas and continues to increase along the coast. Historically, Purple Martins did not nest on the treeless prairies and marshes of the UTC, but they are now abundant due to the recent provision of nest boxes.

PURPLE MARTIN
Progne subis subis

Common summer terminal migrant

SPRING/SUMMER: (28 Dec; 7, 15, 23 Jan) **early Feb to early Nov** (25, 30 Nov)

HABITAT: Ponds, marshes and impoundments, residential neighborhoods, parks, edges of agricultural land and other open habitats, cutover forest. Locally, almost always nests in artificial nest boxes. Elsewhere, may nest in holes in trees or columnar cacti.

DISCUSSION: Prior to European settlement, Purple Martin was very locally distributed and restricted to forests that provided tree hole nest sites. Due to human intervention, including the suburbanization of vast stretches of coastal and inland marshes and prairies, this species is now well represented throughout the region.

Lauded as destroyers of mosquitoes and other potentially harmful insects (at least partly true), Purple Martins are encouraged by homeowners and park managers, who now erect nest box apartment houses and arrays of hanging gourds—both natural and plastic—that enhance the distribution and population of martins. For many people, simply sharing the day-to-day affairs of these attractive birds and hearing their cheery rolling songs is reason enough to provide them housing.

This species is one of the earliest returning Neotropical migrants; rarely during late Dec and more typically during the first or second week of Jan, some are found most years in parts of South Texas. Local nesters are often in place by the end of Feb, and many new families have departed by mid-Jun. Most leave by Sep, their departure preceded by the formation of communal roosts that may contain thousands of birds. Rarely, a few linger until late Nov. We are comfortable with the Jan return dates; our 28 Dec record is ambiguous and may represent a lingerer or a very early northbound migrant. Out-of-season

martins should be carefully diagnosed, as there are several tropical species that may occur as overshoots or disoriented migrants.

TREE SWALLOW
Tachycineta bicolor

Common bi-seasonal transient, uncommon winter resident

SPRING: **Mid-Feb to mid-May** (24 May; 13 Jun)
FALL: (4–6 Jul?) **early Aug to late Nov;** dates obscured by summering and wintering individuals; seasonal peaks from Lockwood and Freeman (2004)

HABITAT: Migrants use a variety of open habitats—especially those where fresh water supports airborne insects.

DISCUSSION: This common species has been recorded in every month of the year and is one of the relatively few Neotropical migrants that may be encountered in numbers during mild winters. Tree Swallows are quite rare from mid-May to early Aug, during which time the bulk of the population is present on their immense nesting area, which ranges from the states surrounding Texas to the Arctic.

Tree Swallow has been recorded on just over half of the Freeport CBCs, with an average of 34 per year and a high of 920 in 2004. Numbers build in early spring, when the birds occasionally stage at huge roosts. Charles Brower estimated 250,000 at Quintana (BRA) on 2 Apr 2000, describing multiple layers of swirling birds covering an area estimated as a "few city blocks."

Although there are summer records—Nehrling (1882) observed a few in summer on the borders of woods—no recent UTC breeding evidence is known. Some field guides do not represent this species as a Texas nester (Dunn 1999; Sibley 2000). However, recent breeding records from the eastern Hill Country (Bell Co.) and northeast Texas (as close to the UTC as Nacogdoches Co.) hint at future breeding possibilities along the UTC. Tree swallows become common again in fall, forming seemingly continuous strings along with other swallow species. Migrating Tree Swallows are known to eat fruits including those of the dwarf wax-myrtle. Bodies of fresh water are especially attractive to winter lingerers.

Occasionally Tree Swallows exhibit reverse migration. On 28 Mar 1980, after an evening of strong, northerly, cold winds and significant rain, Eubanks and Fred Collins tallied over 5,000 flying south along the dunes. During late afternoon, the north winds subsided and the birds resumed their northbound migration.

VIOLET-GREEN SWALLOW
Tachycineta thalassina

Spring vagrant

HABITAT: Abundant in the western United States, this species occurs from sea level to timberline. In Texas, Violet-green Swallow nests no closer to the UTC than the Trans-Pecos and is a rare migrant anywhere else in the state.

DISCUSSION: On the afternoon of 29 Apr 2005, Jeff Mundy detected the UTC's first Violet-green Swallow. The bird was part of a flock of several hundred migrating Tree Swallows. The sighting occurred at Cattail Marsh, Tyrrell Park, in Beaumont, JEF, a site that attracts large flocks of migrating swallows. Observers should familiarize themselves with the Violet-green's extensively white face and white "saddlebags" on either side of the rump. Although not yet recorded in the United States, the Mangrove Swallow, *Tachycineta albilinea*, is a long overdue Texas vagrant. A bit smaller than both Tree and Violet-green swallows, it nests as close as S Tamaulipas on Mexico's eastern slope. The Mangrove's face pattern is more like a Tree Swallow's; its easily seen all-white rump is distinctive.

NORTHERN ROUGH-WINGED SWALLOW
Stelgidopteryx serripennis serripennis

Common transient migrant, rare winter lingerer, possible rare breeder

SPRING: (27 Feb; 1, 4 Mar) **early Mar to mid-May** (5, 7, 17 Jun)
FALL: (6, 8, 13 Jul; 3 Aug) **early Aug through early Nov** (20, 29 Dec; 24 Jan–19 Feb)
HABITAT: Migrants concentrate over open areas: prairie, agricultural land, rivers, and reservoirs, feeding on aerial prey.

DISCUSSION: Swallow migration is most imposing and impressive immediately along the coast. Tens of thousands at a time assemble into a river of birds

that follows the dune line throughout the migration season. The fall movement of Rough-wings seems interminable, and it is not unusual to find a few tardy birds well into Dec. During the winter of 1998–99 the species was numerous in BRA (14 on 18 Dec and 12 on 24 Jan at San Bernard NWR, 11 on 17–18 Jan and 20 on 19 Feb along County Road 25). On 17 Dec 1999, the San Bernard NWR CBC tallied an impressive 59 individuals.

Nehrling (1882) considered this species a "very abundant summer resident. Often nests under the roofs of sidewalks and on old buildings in Houston, but is more a companion to the Bank Swallow on the high banks of Buffalo Bayou and Galveston Bay." Later Simmons (1914) commented: "Though I have heretofore recorded but few during the summer months, I am told by several competent observers that they occur quite regularly and breed in sand banks of Buffalo Bayou and Galveston Bay." The only recent nesting evidence is based upon two adults, four fledged juveniles, and a second active nest in a World War II ship docked in nearby Orange, ORA. Additional nesting records as close as Colorado Co. suggest that they may yet breed on the UTC.

BANK SWALLOW
Riparia riparia

Common transient migrant; formerly bred

SPRING: (20, 23 × 2, 28–29 Mar) **late Mar to mid-May** (13, 18, 26 May)
FALL: (26 Jul; 3 Aug) **mid-Aug through early Nov** (6, 13, 15 Nov)
HABITAT: Migrants utilize a variety of open habitats, perhaps most often over rivers or reservoirs, also agricultural land.

DISCUSSION: Bank Swallows join other swallows in the UTC's most spectacular migratory movement. They are given little attention by birders; an accurate estimate of the number of swallows passing along the coast during the spring and fall has not been attempted. Bottlenecks along their coastal flight path, such as San Luis Pass on West Galveston Island, force the birds into a narrow stream. Surveys at such constrictions of the flight path should permit a fairly accurate count of the birds passing within a predetermined period. Migrants linger into early Nov and are occasionally reported on local CBCs. However, owing to this species' similarity to Northern Rough-winged Swallow, winter records are questionable. As with Northern Rough-wings, Nehrling (1882) observed: "A few pairs remain to breed in such localities as the banks of Buffalo Bayou and Galveston Bay." The species was evidently never a common breeder within these parts, and no evidence exists that it still nests on the UTC. It does, however, still breed in the state, including in the lower reaches of the Rio Grande.

CLIFF SWALLOW
Petrochelidon pyrrhonota

Uncommon summer terminal migrant

SUMMER: (8, 14–16 Mar) **late Mar to early Nov** (5 × 2, 6, 15, 29 Nov)

HABITAT: Locally, restricted to artificial structures such as bridges and buildings that serve as cliffs.

DISCUSSION: Cliff Swallows are a local nester on the UTC, being common in some areas with numerous bridges. The subspecies *P. p. tachina* nests in East Texas; other races almost certainly occur during migration. Cliff Swallows are most common during migration, when large numbers move through the area. Local nesters arrive in mid- to late Mar; spring migrants are present into May. Fall migration begins in late summer, peaking in Sep. Nehrling (1882) noted them in great numbers during Sep, with only the latest lingerers still moving through in Nov. All winter and early spring individuals should be carefully examined, as the similar-looking Cave Swallow has colonized the area, regularly wintering in small numbers.

CAVE SWALLOW
Petrochelidon fulva pallida

Common summer terminal migrant and local winter resident

HABITAT: Throughout much of the state, occurs especially in culverts, under bridges, and on other artificial structures that mimic geological features; locally, in buildings as well.

DISCUSSION: The Cave Swallow's range, like that of the Western Kingbird, has been spectacularly altered by the placement of artificial structures. In this case, concrete culverts placed under various roads throughout Texas now serve as sites for new colonies. Cylindrical culverts are often used, but the new, improved model is square in cross section— many thousands of Cave Swallows now nest in the right angles at top of such culverts.

The first known UTC nest site was found in 1989 under the roof of a boat shed at Sea Rim SP, a site shared with Barn and the locally rare Cliff Swallow. In 1995, Brent Ortego found a nesting colony where Cedar Lake Creek crosses FM 2611 in BRA. This site also harbored the first overwintering birds, as Cliff Swallow was reported (and rejected) from there on the 1996 San Bernard CBC. It was not until 1999 that this site was confirmed as a wintering Cave Swallow roost site, with 35 birds that year. The Cave Swallow is now a common breeder and local winter resident in BRA and likely several other UTC counties. The arrival of migrants in early to mid-Mar is obvious to drivers, who note the birds' sudden appearance at bridges over roads such as Interstate 10.

BARN SWALLOW
Hirundo rustica erythrogaster

Common breeder, abundant bi-seasonal transient migrant

SUMMER: (1, 7–8 Feb) **early Mar to late Nov** (17, 19 × 2, 20 × 2 Dec; 1 Jan)

HABITAT: Breeds throughout most of the Northern Hemisphere, winters south to Tierra del Fuego and southern Africa. Locally, virtually throughout the region, absent only from extensively wooded areas.

DISCUSSION: Barn Swallow is one of our most familiar breeding birds. It utilizes a variety of nest sites, frequently in close association with human beings: barns, porches, eves, and garages. This swallow forages over prairie and marsh, over fresh and salt water, and in urban and suburban areas.

Although present for much of the year, Barn Swallows are most obvious during late summer and fall as huge flocks travel through the UTC, often occurring very close to the ground as they feed over weedy fields. These southbound migrants, en route to Latin America, stream through the UTC into Nov, when their numbers thin greatly. Occasionally a few hardy birds stay through the CBCs; in 2003, they were located on the Galveston (two birds) and San Bernard (six birds) counts, and one was tallied at nearby Attwater NWR. The Freeport count located them in seven of 48 years, with a high of eight in 1972, and the San Bernard CBC has detected them in at least eight years. Lingering birds are rarely seen after Dec, and to date none has been reported as overwintering. Spring migrants return early, rarely in early Feb a few days after the earliest Purple Martins arrive.

Chickadee, Titmouse, Nuthatches, and Creeper

CAROLINA CHICKADEE
Poecile carolinensis agilis

Common resident

HABITAT: Woodlands, mature residential plantings, and riparian corridors, scarce or absent on inland prairies and coastal wetlands; uncommon in the southernmost and westernmost parts of the region, where habitat becomes brushier.

DISCUSSION: Endemic to the southeastern United States, Carolina Chickadee replaces the more widespread Black-capped Chickadee. Carolina is similar to Black-capped but smaller, with a higher-pitched voice, and lacks bright white edging on its secondaries.

The Carolina Chickadee is a well-known yard visitor, capable of deftly removing a meal from the tiny aperture of a thistle or sunflower seed tube or joining the mixed mob attracted to a platform feeder. The UTC is near the western edge of its range, which continues along the coast only to the Guadalupe River delta, as does the range of so many forest birds.

Chickadees may be attracted with nest boxes; they also utilize old woodpecker holes or may peck their own cavity in a dead tree trunk or rotting fence post. Nehrling (1882) found a 16 Apr nest with six nearly fledged young. This species is a characteristic and often common component of mixed winter insectivore flocks. The Freeport CBC averages 537 per year but tallied 1,156 in 1971.

TUFTED TITMOUSE
Baeolophus bicolor

Common resident

HABITAT: Woodlands, second growth, mature residential plantings; occasionally in brushy fields but prefers a fairly dense canopy. Its numbers *peter peter peter* out near inland prairies, dry brushy country, and coastal marshes.

DISCUSSION: Tufted Titmouse may be found in virtually any forest east of the Great Plains. The species was formerly more widespread in Texas, its range once extending west of the UTC to San Antonio and southwest to Corpus Christi. Kincaid attributed its withdrawal to the activities of humans and to periodic droughts that thinned the margins of the fingers of forest this titmouse inhabited. Its more southerly and westerly counterpart, the recently split Black-crested Titmouse (*B. atricristatus*) is more tolerant of arid conditions. Tufted Titmouse is virtually absent from seemingly suitable habitat on the Bolivar Peninsula and Galveston Is.

Tufted Titmice nest in natural cavities and old woodpecker nest holes. They may be attracted to nest boxes designed for various species of chickadees. Being quite a bit larger than a Carolina Chickadee, they may require a slightly larger entrance hole. Nesting pairs may be encountered on the UTC at the beginning of Mar (Nehrling 1882).

During winter, Tufted Titmice, generally in the minority, often join bands of Carolina Chickadees. Like the chickadees, they are attracted to a wide variety of food and feeders. The Freeport CBC averages 283 per year with a high of 730 in 1984.

RED-BREASTED NUTHATCH
Sitta canadensis

Rare (irruptive) winter terminal migrant

WINTER: (12–15, 22 Sep) **mid-Sep to mid-Apr** (25, 28 Apr; 4, 15 May)

HABITAT: Usually in coniferous or mixed coniferous forest and often montane; in migration and winter, may utilize a variety of trees and habitats, including residential areas; they also come to feeders.

DISCUSSION: During favorable years, Red-breasted Nuthatches join flocks of chickadees, titmice, kinglets, and Yellow-rumped Warblers that roam the local forests and neighborhoods, each industrious band divesting the trees of their myriads of spiders, cocoons, insects, and insect eggs. This nuthatch's occurrence is sufficiently erratic to be noteworthy when more than one or two appear. Occasionally they show up in considerable numbers, often with the first waves of Pine Warblers and Brown Creepers. A larger than average presence is usually termed an "invasion," as during the winter of 1980–81, when on 30 Sep eight were seen in woods along the Bolivar Peninsula, GAL. The species also made a strong showing during the fall of 1995, when numbers of them began appearing on or slightly before 25 Sep and remained through the CBC period. Five were seen at Bear Creek Park, HAS, on 8 Nov 2004, but the ripple reached neither the Freeport nor the San Bernard NWR CBC. Freeport has recorded them on eight of 48 counts, with a high of six in 1997.

WHITE-BREASTED NUTHATCH
Sitta carolinensis carolinensis

Former resident, now extirpated

HABITAT: Deciduous and mixed forest, where nesting occurs in natural cavities in living trees, less often in holes in dead trees or abandoned woodpecker nest holes.

DISCUSSION: White-breasted Nuthatch inhabits a wide range of elevations and forest types from across southern Canada and much of the United States to central Mexico. Thus its absence from the UTC, even during the occasional very cold winter, seems curious. Formerly, it bred as far south as HAS (TOS 1995), but now the closest population is at Huntsville State Forest. During recent years, the species has also been noted at Martin Dies SP in Jasper Co. and twice in southern Liberty Co. The last convincing report of a bird on the UTC was 7 Aug 1970 in JEF.

BROWN-HEADED NUTHATCH
Sitta pusilla pusilla

Formerly locally common UTC resident; now largely extirpated

HABITAT: Mature pine forest and pines mixed with hardwoods; also pines in older neighborhoods.

DISCUSSION: From 1948 to 1966, Brown-headed Nuthatch was seen regularly on the Houston CBC, dwindling thereafter to virtually no records for the last several decades. As recently as the 1980s, it persisted in locations such as the Memorial region of west Houston and forest surrounding White Memorial Park, CHA. Unfortunately, nest sites (and often food resources) for small hole-nesting birds are most plentiful in mature or dead trees. Contributing to degradation or loss of this species' habitat have been timbering, thinning, or wholesale elimination of pine trees during real estate development; loss of trees in disease control and utility line right-of-way clearing; and destruction of older trees during recent hurricanes. Apparently the minimum density of suitable trees necessary to support a widespread population of these delightful little birds is no longer available. While a few may remain near previous strongholds such as White Memorial Park, CHA, the last UTC record known to us was one seen at High Island, GAL, on 11 Apr 1998. We suggest that birds seen outside the normal breeding range be carefully scrutinized, as one cannot totally discount the possibility of a Pygmy Nuthatch wandering northward out of eastern Mexico.

Visiting birders seeking Brown-headed Nuthatch are advised to visit the W. G. Jones State Forest about an hour north of George Bush Intercontinental Airport or, better yet, the Big Thicket region north of Beaumont, where this nuthatch is still tolerably common alongside Red-cockaded Woodpecker and Bachman's Sparrow.

BROWN CREEPER
Certhia americana americana

Irregularly common but thinly spread winter terminal migrant

WINTER: (20 Sep; 16–18 Oct) **mid-Oct to mid-Mar** (22, 25 Mar; 13 Apr; 12 May)

HABITAT: An especially wide-ranging species found from southern Alaska to Nicaragua. Locally, winters in wooded regions including residential areas with mature trees.

DISCUSSION: Winter flocks of mixed insectivores often include a Brown Creeper, although the species is never common. Like nuthatches, individuals scurry along the trunks of trees where their barklike plumage renders them nearly invisible. Sharp-eared birders often detect the birds by their high, thin call notes.

Creepers are irruptive visitors, their numbers fluctuating greatly from year to year. During the winter of 1980–81, they "invaded" along with Red-breasted Nuthatch, another irruptive northern species. The Freeport CBC recorded 59 creepers that year versus an average of 11 per year. Migrants usually arrive with the first fronts in mid- to late Oct and are often detected in the coastal migrant traps. Most birds then move to interior woodlands, where they spend the winter, the majority departing by late Mar, rarely Apr or May.

Wrens

Members of an immensely successful family of kinglet- to thrush-sized birds, wrens are the archetypal "little brown jobs," often pleasantly patterned but rarely colorful. The group includes some of the most accomplished singers in the avian world, well known for their complex duets and especially long or creative deliveries. They occur in a wide array of habitats including deserts, wetlands, prairies, wet and dry coniferous woodlands, lowland and montane tropical evergreen forests, and windswept mountaintops at 12,000 feet or higher. All except one are restricted to the New World, the exception being Winter Wren, a fairly recent invader into Asia, Europe, and the British Isles.

The family's stronghold is in the tropics (Mexico has 32 species, including eight of the large Cactustype wrens), but it is well represented in the United States.

A few wrens are not shy and may be easily viewed. Others skulk in the densest vine tangles or grass clumps where their cryptic coloration makes them that much harder to locate. Although wrens are common and occasionally abundant, only a fraction of those present in any area are likely to be observed. Successful birders will have spent some time becoming familiar with the wrens' distinctive songs and call notes; their voices reveal their presence and true numbers. Although some of the region's wrens are local or quite rare, any day's birding is likely to produce two or more species of these endearing birds.

Seven species of wrens occur on the UTC, three nesting locally: Carolina, Marsh, and (perhaps rarely) Sedge wrens. House and Bewick's wrens occur during winter. House Wren numbers fluctuate; they may be common, scolding from every hedgerow and brushy woodland margin visited during a day afield, or nearly impossible to locate. Bewick's Wren is a very local and apparently decreasing member of the UTC's winter avifauna. Most birds are the now uncommon foxy red eastern form, but a very few of the grayer western birds have been noted.

The tiny Winter Wren is an infrequently seen species that inhabits dense brush and woodland understory. It is the only wren living in the Old World; in Great Britain it is simply referred to as the Wren. Despite its diminutive size, its high-pitched song is one of the longest deliveries among North American birds.

UTC birders will be fortunate indeed to see the sandy colored Rock Wren bobbing up and down. This western vagrant nests in the Texas Hill Country but is no more than an accidental in East Texas. It could occur anywhere that mimics its rocky home, from a boulder jetty to a pile of construction rubble.

ROCK WREN
Salpinctes obsoletus obsoletus

Accidental
27 Oct–22 Dec 1972 Cove, CHA
20 Nov–23 Nov 1974 Cedar Bayou, CHA

HABITAT: Cliff faces and road cuts, quarries, ruined buildings, usually in dry regions; wanderers often show up on rocky structures such as jetties, and stone or concrete buildings. In Texas, breeds eastward to the Austin vicinity (Travis Co.).

DISCUSSION: Rock Wren nests from south-central British Columbia to NW Costa Rica. Although its U.S. breeding distribution is western, there are many eastern sightings. Interestingly, the A.O.U. (1983) attributes many or most of these records to birds riding boxcars to sites well beyond their normal range. Hobos or not, we have two records of this noteworthy wanderer. One bird was present in Cove, HAS, from 27 Oct to 22 Dec 1972. Another was at the Houston Light and Power Company's Cooling Ponds, CHA, from 20 to 23 Nov 1974. Arlie McKay, the legendary birder from Cove, first noticed the 1974 bird by sound. Toward the end of his life, Arlie had lost most of his sight, yet his curiosity and inquisitiveness did not fade with his vision. Birders visiting this area later confirmed Arlie's rarity.

CAROLINA WREN
Thryothorus ludovicianus ludovicianus

Common resident

HABITAT: Nehrling (1882) summed up this species' habitat as well as anyone has, finding it in thickets and "low wooded localities with dense underbrush." He noted its occurrence in laurel greenbrier (or similar vines), blackberry bushes, viburnum, Carolina buckthorn, and woollybucket bumelia, among a host of other understory species, intermixed with a few larger trees (oaks or elms), which were commonly overgrown with mustang grape and Alabama supplejack (we have changed some of his names to conform with modern use). This species is often common in well-vegetated residential areas, where it nests in both natural and artificial cavities.

DISCUSSION: Although widespread in the eastern United States, and at times abundant within the UTC's counties, Carolina Wrens occur in spotty concentrations within the coastal hiatus. The reason is obvious. Although the expansion of human habitation in certain areas near the Gulf has no doubt benefited this wren, the thickets and underbrush demanded by the species are limited along the coast, and this wren is now virtually extirpated on Galveston Is. (J. Stevenson). Away from the coast (e.g., in Houston) this is among the few species to be expected in everyone's yard and garden; individuals have been known to build a nest in garments left on the clothesline.

Nearly all Carolina Wrens deliver some version of the well-known *tea kettle-tea kettle-tea kettle* song. To express their individuality, males in adjacent territories may render it as an explosively fast slur or drag it out until each syllable glows with its own bell-like resonance. In favorable habitat where many birds may be heard at once, their genetically limited chorus might be called "Variations on a Spring Morning."

BEWICK'S WREN
Thryomanes bewickii

Very local winter terminal migrant, rare transient migrant

WINTER: (24 Sep; 10, 15 Oct) **early Oct to early May** (29 May; 2, 6 Jun)

HABITAT: Winters regularly in the western portion of the UTC, especially in stands of huisache in WAR. During migration (Oct), rare inland in residential plantings, but seen with some regularity in coastal salt cedars.

DISCUSSION: Nehrling (1882) apparently differentiated this species from Carolina Wren and considered it "abundant in all suitable localities … very familiar, breeding in bird-boxes, stables, corn-cribs … in houses … etc." Later, Bewick's Wren ceased breeding on the UTC. We wonder about Nehrling's identification and whether the bird was actually as widespread as he deemed it; we note perhaps four summer records during the last 40–45 years; the last confirmed nesting was recorded on 4 Jul 1916 near Beaumont.

At least two subspecies occur in our area. Most records pertain, presumably, to the rusty eastern subspecies, *T. b. bewickii*; however, Jim Morgan recorded a gray individual, probably representing the western subspecies *T. b. cryptus*. Locally, wintering birds exhibit high habitat specificity. On 25 Oct 1987, 27 individuals were seen in WAR (the UTC high count). Virtually all were seen in stands of huisache. Habitat managers and birders take note: these same huisache stands also attract and concentrate Ash-throated Flycatchers and significant numbers of Blue-gray Gnatcatchers and other small insectivores. However, most of this habitat in WAR is rapidly being cleared for house trailer sites and other forms of rural development.

HOUSE WREN
Troglodytes aedon aedon

Common to uncommon winter terminal migrant

WINTER: (29 Aug; 16 × 2, 17 × 2 Sep) **mid-Sep to early May** (8, 13 May)

HABITAT: Dense thickets and hedgerows, woodland edges, occasionally in residential plantings.

DISCUSSION: During winter, House Wren is the most widespread wren in the region (although Sedge Wren is likely the most abundant in absolute numbers). The Freeport count averages 64 per year, with a high of 184 in 1988. Yaupon thickets, fencerows, and abandoned farm fields all host the birds. It is hard to imagine a winter day's birding without these wrens scolding in accompaniment, but the population is variable, and occasionally they may be virtually absent. House Wren lingers rather late in the spring, and those remaining until the end of the season often tune up with short clips of their songs.

WINTER WREN
Troglodytes troglodytes

Rare winter terminal migrant

WINTER: (1 Sep; 10, 12 Oct) **mid-Oct to early Apr** (6, 28 Apr)

HABITAT: Wet forest and understory, most frequently in tangles, stumps, and fallen limbs adjacent to streams and bayous.

DISCUSSION: Winter Wrens are sly skulkers, rarely venturing out from the densest thickets and tangles in our bottomland forests. Besides being rather rare, the bird is most often heard before being seen. It may respond to spishing noises, but winter birders should focus on learning its melodic, paired call notes—rendered as *kelp-kelp* for eastern birds (Dunn 1999)—prior to venturing out along the bayous, or to parks such as Bear Creek (HAS) or Brazos Bend SP. Once spotted, this wren is engaging, with its stumpy tail smartly cocked upward as it energetically explores every notch and log for its insect prey.

SEDGE WREN
Cistothorus platensis stellaris

Locally common winter terminal migrant, perhaps a very rare summer resident

WINTER: (13, 24 Aug) **late Aug to mid-May** (11–12, 18 May)

HABITAT: Coastal and inland weedy fields and prairies, often with broom grass (*Andropogon*), also

cordgrass (*Spartina*) meadows near Galveston Bay, particularly those that have not been invaded by baccharis.

DISCUSSION: Sedge Wrens are common to abundant members of the winter avifauna, when their chittering calls are easily heard. However, unless some effort is made, the species can be missed during casual birding. Midwinter birds may skulk in dense grasses or shrubbery, but patient spishing or judicious use of tape may coax one into view. As spring progresses, birds become more responsive and may be seen singing from the top of a baccharis shrub or fence wire.

Recent observations suggest that Sedge Wren is a very rare breeder on the UTC. Summer records provided by Mike Austin include two on 21 Jun 1987 at Armand Bayou Nature Center (HAS) and one in CHA on a 13 Aug 1988 Piney Woods Wildlife Society field trip. More recently, David Poteet heard one singing on 8 Jun 2003 during a breeding bird survey on Katy Prairie Conservancy property.

A cautionary note: although distinctively small, vocal, and not difficult to identify once seen well, this wren often occurs with similarly colored sparrows. Inland, Sedge Wrens coexist with Le Conte's and Grasshopper sparrows; near the coast, they may be seen (especially during infrequently available marsh buggy rides) in cordgrass with Sharp-tailed Sparrows or in weedy fields with Le Conte's. Sedge Wrens tend not to occur at pond or ditch edges with the similar but black-mantled Marsh Wren. During spring, note their very different songs, the Sedge Wren's being more of a sputter. Productive sites include overgrown rice fields, the entrance road to Brazos Bend SP, along oil field roads at High Island, and at all of the coastal refuges.

MARSH WREN
Cistothorus palustris

Common permanent resident

HABITAT: Stands of introduced common reed (Anahuac NWR), also marshes thick with native reeds and cattails.

DISCUSSION: Marsh Wren inhabits freshwater and brackish marshes, where it may often be very common within its chosen milieu. Nehrling (1882) considered it only a "rare migrant," yet within proper habitats the bird is now known to be a common breeder, more common in the eastern portion of the region. Despite searching since 1996, Weeks has failed to find it breeding (or present during summer) anywhere in BRA. The currently known UTC locations are just north of High Island, at Anahuac NWR, and in the extensive marshes in JEF. The subspecies *C. p. thryophilus* is the common breeder along the coast. During winter, Marsh Wrens of the subspecies *iliacus, dissaeptus,* and *palustris* may occur in the region as well (TOS 1995).

Bulbul, Kinglets, and Gnatcatcher

RED-VENTED BULBUL
Pycnonotus cafer

Exotic: apparently an established resident in parts of Houston

HABITAT: Scrub and brushy areas, second growth and (where introduced) native forest, cities and suburbs (A.O.U. 1998).

DISCUSSION: As a result of cage bird releases, two Asian members of the family Pycnonotidae are established in the United States. Red-vented Bulbul and the closely related Red-whiskered Bulbul (*P. jocosus*) have been present in Hawaii since 1965 or earlier. The latter is a target species for many birders who visit Dade County, Florida, where it was inadvertently introduced in 1960 during Hurricane Donna (Florida Fish and Wildlife Conservation Commission 2003).

Between May 1999 and Mar 2004, there were at least 14 posts to TexBirds concerning sightings of Red-vented Bulbul in and around the city of Houston. Included were messages referring to undated sightings made years earlier. Graham Gips and Dennis Shepler summarized these posts, and Shepler (TexBirds: 21 Feb 2003) estimated the records to represent 32 birds (including nestlings and fledglings) at 10 sites in a triangle extending from Greenspoint to south of the Houston Ship Channel to the Houston Heights. This species visits bird feeders, eats fruit, nectar, and insects, and flourishes in a variety of habitats including residential areas. Red-vented Bulbul is the most common bulbul in India, where it thrives in cities (Israel and Sinclair 1987). Apparently a small and dispersed population is able to persist in Houston. Although Red-vented Bulbul is not included in the TBRC's list of accepted Texas species, its continuing presence suggests that it may one day become part of the state's recognized avifauna.

GOLDEN-CROWNED KINGLET
Regulus satrapa satrapa

Uncommon winter terminal migrant

WINTER: (6, 14, 22–23, 29 Oct) **mid-Oct to late Mar** (23, 25, 31 Mar; 28 Apr)

HABITAT: Pine and mixed forest, residential plantings, light woodland and second growth. Common during certain winters, and then may occur in salt cedar groves and baccharis along the immediate coast.

DISCUSSION: Birders visiting from Great Britain or Europe feel right at home when they see Golden-crowned and Ruby-crowned kinglets. The resemblance to their native birds is so great that they might even blurt out "Goldcrest!" or "Firecrest!" upon seeing one. Indeed kinglets, some of our tiniest and most energetic birds, are actually Old World warblers, a group of birds with minimal presence on this side of the Atlantic.

In mixed flocks, this species is always outnumbered by Ruby-crowned Kinglets. It is rarely a common visitor to the region, and its numbers suggest that its arrival coincides to only a limited extent with the severity of northern winters, as with Red-breasted Nuthatches, Brown Creepers, and other irregularly present insectivores. In flight years this kinglet may be discovered even in vegetated dunes bordering the Gulf. Heard more frequently than it is seen, the bird has an insectlike *pseet* that announces its presence in mixed flocks of treetop foragers. Although rarely remaining into Mar, late spring birds may be found more consistently in the nearby Pineywoods.

RUBY-CROWNED KINGLET
Regulus calendula calendula

Common winter terminal migrant

WINTER: (23 Aug; 7, 14 Sep) **mid-Sep to early May** (6, 9, 12 May)

HABITAT: Widespread in all but the very lowest strata of vegetation; various wooded situations including bottomland forest, coastal mottes, mixed conifer-hardwood forest, second growth, and residential areas with mature trees; also in tall brush such as huisache and various hollies; only infrequently at bird feeding stations and hummingbird feeders.

DISCUSSION: The Ruby-crowned's short-tailed, plump profile, nervous single wing twitching, and incessant hard chittering notes render it easily identifiable, often without the aid of binoculars. Its name pertains to its least distinctive feature: the red crown feathers that remain hidden unless the bird is agitated. This species is a faithful member of winter mixed-species flocks, often the first bird responding to a birder's spishing or squeaking noises. Before these kinglets depart the UTC, several dozen may be present in a mixed flock, their numbers presumably augmented by individuals returning from Mexico.

The bird's unusual song, a long, spirited, high-pitched jumble, is often heard prior to its spring departure; occasionally, a sunny winter day will motivate one to sing.

BLUE-GRAY GNATCATCHER
Polioptila caerulea caerulea

Common bi-seasonal transient migrant, common winter terminal migrant, previously a common breeder

WINTER: (29–30 Jul; 2 Aug) **late Jul to mid-May** (12, 15–16 May)

HABITAT: A casualty of our shrinking bottomland forests, where it was known to have nested in elms and various oaks; now found in all wooded areas as a nonbreeder. In migration, flocks are often found in the oak mottes along the immediate coast at sites such as High Island and Galveston Is.

DISCUSSION: During the late 1800s, Blue-gray Gnatcatcher was a common breeder in our area, beginning to nest in early May. Apparently clearing of the original forests that bordered our waterways (such as Buffalo Bayou) doomed this bird as a nester. However, Blue-gray Gnatcatcher remains a common migrant throughout the region. During migratory waves, flocks consisting of dozens to hundreds of individuals may be present in oaks, willows, and shrubs along the coast.

This gnatcatcher is among the earliest migrants to arrive in both spring and fall, although the presence of a wintering population tends to mask its spring movements. Wintering birds appear to be facultative migrants, remaining during mild winters but vacating the UTC during those rare harsh seasons when insect populations are radically reduced by extended freezes.

Thrushes

Ten thrushes have occurred on the UTC. Four of them nest locally, although the tropical Clay-colored Robin has only recently (and barely) become a member of the avifauna.

Eastern Bluebird and American Robin are two of our most widely recognized birds—the subjects of innumerable placemats, calendars, note cards, and teapots. The uncommonly attractive bluebirds are well known even among nonbirders. There are three species of these dainty thrushes; all inhabit the New World. At least one occurs in nearly any part of the United States, where they are the beneficiaries of nest boxes installed by scout troops and civic groups. On the UTC, Mountain Bluebird is locally rare, and to date, Western Bluebird has not been reliably documented. Bluebird species are much less numerous than related genera; unfortunately, their kind represents but a minor twig on the thrush family tree.

At the opposite end of the numbers spectrum is the American Robin. It belongs to the widespread genus *Turdus,* with about 65 species. The different robins are noted songsters, and their characteristic caroling is a feature of dawn choruses throughout much of the world. In summer, small nesting populations or colonies of American Robins are widely scattered through East Texas. During most winters they are more common, and in favorable years flocks of thousands descend upon the UTC to strip our fruit-bearing vines and shrubs.

Four birds in the genus *Catharus* appear locally. Migrant Swainson's Thrushes visit during their north- and southbound flights. During spring their sweet, upward-spiraling song is often heard in the coastal migrant traps. Veery and Gray-cheeked thrushes are primarily spring visitors; their fall southbound flight path swings toward the eastern seaboard. The Hermit Thrush is a familiar winter bird in woodland understory and dense residential plantings, especially where yaupon and other berries are available. Previously, all four of these were much more numerous on the UTC; Swainson's Thrushes were tallied in triple digits during several of our censused spring fallouts and were the sixth most abundant spring migrant encountered. Veery was the tenth most common species, also occurring now and then in triple digits—although newer birders may find that difficult to believe. All four of the local *Catharus* have been impacted by loss of habitat in their migratory corridors, on the wintering grounds, and where they nest (Gray-cheeked Thrush perhaps less so in the latter category), plus the usual ravages of insecticides, cats, and forest fragmentation that favors parasitic cowbirds. For example, "Thrush Woods," a private woodlot open to birders at High Island, would often literally seethe with spring migrant thrushes. One year, it lost its understory to a rigorous manicuring that favored the passage of horses and cattle rather than songbirds. Fortunately, land acquisition that led to new coastal sanctuaries has partially offset these losses, and the planting of additional trees (such as at the TOS Sabine Woods Sanctuary) continues to convert coastal pastures to migrant-friendly woodland.

The Wood Thrush's rich, fluty song has become an uncommon sound on the UTC and throughout much of its range. The bird's decline has been blamed on loss of nesting habitat in North America, loss of wintering habitat in the tropics, and cowbird parasitism in fragmented forests. However, in 2002, Wood Thrush became the first U.S. songbird for which population decline (1.7 percent per year between 1966 and 1999)

was linked to the effects of acid rain. Measurements taken in much of the bird's range demonstrated a strong correlation between acid rain, calcium-poor soils, and poor nesting performance. Apparently the acid rain makes calcium-rich terrestrial invertebrates (such as snails) less available to female thrushes during the critical period of eggshell formation (Chu and Hames 2002). Calcium deprivation has been responsible for widespread nesting failure of some Western European songbirds and may also be responsible for the decreases of various species that inhabit eastern North America.

The colorful Varied Thrush represents a group of often strikingly patterned Old World thrushes. Although the bird is common in conifer forests of the Pacific Northwest, its piercing, minor whistle is often the only indication of its presence. Locally it has been recorded about five times, in both wooded and open habitats.

EASTERN BLUEBIRD
Sialia sialis sialis

Uncommon local resident, common winter terminal migrant

HABITAT: Forest edges near the contiguous woodlands of the interior UTC (i.e., along the Brazos River), pastures or oak parkland with large trees; winter birds are more dispersed, and found in a variety of woodland edge, open, and scrub habitats.

DISCUSSION: Eastern Bluebirds are nowhere as common along the UTC as in the nearby Pineywoods. They become more numerous in winter as they spread from the interior woodlands toward the Gulf, some even reaching the coastal migrant traps. Winter gatherings may be sizable; at times, single flocks may consist of dozens of individuals. The pecan woodlands bordering the Brazos River appear to be prime habitat (e.g., Harper's Church Road, WAR), and calling birds may dominate the morning chorus. Look for them also at Brazos Bend SP and at coastal refuges such as Anahuac.

Most often, breeding birds are found well away from the coast; productive sites include the Brazos River bottomlands and along the Trinity River. Nesting has been noted as early as 15 Feb; Nehrling (1882) observed a nest with young 6 Mar and a nest with four eggs 29 Apr.

MOUNTAIN BLUEBIRD
Sialia currucoides

Accidental
18 Apr 1950 Houston, HAS
5 Feb 1951 Houston, HAS
3–4 Nov 1960 Cove, CHA (AFN 15:58)
21 Nov 1992 W HAS
6–7 Nov 1993 Galveston, GAL

HABITAT: Shrubland, thickets, and hedgerows.
DISCUSSION: Mountain Bluebird is a rarity in our region; we recognize only five records. Winter flocks spread into nonmontane habitats, and hundreds of birds are commonly found in West Texas mesquite (particularly those thickets infested with mistletoe) and in the Texas Panhandle. The number of Mountain Bluebirds present in Texas during winter fluctuates annually, and major flight years provide an increased chance of one appearing along the UTC. Mountain Bluebird is one of the most striking of the intensely blue birds to have occurred here; the sky-blue cast of the adult males is uncompromised by contrasting tones. We lament its absence.

VEERY
Catharus fuscescens fuscescens

Common to uncommon spring and rare fall transient migrant

SPRING: (26 Mar; 5, 10 Apr) **mid-Apr to late May** (18–19, 28 May)
FALL: (7, 9, 17 Sep) **mid-Sep to late Oct** (22, 28 Oct)
HABITAT: Understory and forest floor of coastal woodlands.
DISCUSSION: Four *Catharus* thrushes migrate through the coastal woodlands of the UTC; none of them remain to breed. Veery, one of the transients, is usually encountered only during spring migration. Along with that of the Gray-cheeked Thrush, another transient, the Veery's fall return to its tropical wintering areas is mainly via the eastern United States, bypassing the UTC. In fact, during many fall migrations, not a single Veery is seen. High counts are characteristic only of spring fallouts, although at any moment during the spring migratory window the larger woodlots (such as Smith Oaks or Sabine Woods) nor-

mally host a few individuals. On 7 May 1987, 905 were located along the coast. Although Veery is occasionally reported from area CBCs, we have no confidence in these sightings, and there is no evidence that they winter anywhere in the United States.

GRAY-CHEEKED THRUSH
Catharus minimus minimus

Largely mono-seasonal: uncommon spring, rare fall transient migrant

SPRING: (29 March; 5, 10 Apr) **mid-Apr to late May** (21 × 3, 26 × 2, 28 May)
FALL: (25–26 Sep; 6 Oct) **late Sep to late Oct** (28 Oct; 8, 13 Nov)
HABITAT: Understory and forest floor of coastal woodlands.
DISCUSSION: Gray-cheeked Thrush is found along the UTC predominantly in spring; fall migrants, the bulk of which migrate to the east, are absent most years. During spring, Sabine Woods, Boy Scout Woods, and Smith Oaks are good locations to encounter a variety (and occasionally an abundance) of thrushes, including Gray-cheeked. More important, observers are usually able to see these birds foraging or bathing shoulder to shoulder, offering a unique opportunity to study the subtle differences between the species (and subspecies, in some cases). Gray-cheeked Thrush is most likely to be confused with Swainson's; the latter's buffy eye-ring and buff facial speckling serve to distinguish it. While Wood and Swainson's thrushes frequently sing (at least halfheartedly) during spring movements, the more northerly nesting Gray-cheeked is generally silent as it slides through the UTC. Note that the recently split and confusingly similar Bicknell's Thrush (*Catharus bicknelli*) of the NE United States and maritime Canada has not been recorded from Texas (Lockwood and Freeman 2004).

SWAINSON'S THRUSH
Catharus ustulatus swainsoni

Common spring, uncommon fall transient migrant; rare winter terminal migrant

SPRING:(23–24, 29 Mar) **early Apr to mid-May** (28 May; 3, 7 Jun)

FALL: (2, 15–16 Sep) **mid-Sep to late Nov** (18, 27–28 Nov)

HABITAT: Understory and forest floor of coastal and inland woodlands, also mature vegetation in residential areas.

DISCUSSION: Of the four *Catharus* thrushes that occur in our region, Swainson's is the most commonly seen. Formerly, there were few spring days when this species was not present along the immediate coast in moderate to substantial numbers. Now, days may pass without a sighting; the possible contribution of climatic changes to this lack of birds has yet to be determined. This bird is often seen well away from the coast and, except for the American Robin, is the most likely migrant thrush to appear in urban settings.

Unlike Veery and Gray-cheeked Thrush, Swainson's is also present during fall migration. However, fall numbers pale beside those seen in spring, and by late Oct, the species can be quite difficult to find. A Swainson's Thrush in a coastal woodlot may announce its presence (even if only with a half-hearted delivery) prior to its arrival on the breeding grounds.

HERMIT THRUSH
Catharus guttatus

Common winter terminal migrant

WINTER: (15, 25 Sep; 1, 6 Oct) **early Oct to late Apr** (21 × 3, 22 Apr; 2 May)

HABITAT: Woodland understory, larger coastal mottes, extensive hedgerows; occasionally residential areas with dense ground cover.

DISCUSSION: Nine subspecies of Hermit Thrush are recognized in Texas, two or three of which may occur on the UTC (TOS 1995). During winter, the subspecies *C. g. faxoni,* widespread in the East, is the only member of its species (and genus) likely to be seen in Texas or the United States. Most northbound individuals depart by early Apr, prior to the passage of other *Catharus,* so late Apr Hermits warrant a close look. A gray-headed bird suggesting the Rocky Mountain *auduboni* was observed at High Island by Jon Dunn and David Sibley, and we suspect that a few of the early Mar Swainson's Thrush records from the

UTC may have been non-*faxoni* Hermits. Watch for a tinge of red in the tail to separate gray-headed Hermits from the potentially similar Gray-cheeked Thrush.

In winter, Hermit Thrush are among the first birds to respond to a birder's whistled screech-owl imitation. Listen for the low *chuck* note that signals its presence and watch for it to hop up on a low branch as it searches for the intruder.

WOOD THRUSH
Hylocichla mustelina

Common bi-seasonal transient migrant, uncommon and decreasing summer terminal migrant

SUMMER: (12, 15, 21 Mar) **mid-Mar to early Nov** (30 Oct; 5, 9 Nov)

HABITAT: Inhabits "swampy thickets and bottom woods" (Nehrling 1882), most common in the Pineywoods to the immediate east of the UTC.

DISCUSSION: Wood Thrush is one of the earliest thrushes to return from the tropics, and East Texas birds are singing on territory as Gray-cheeks are passing through High Island. Formerly, Wood Thrushes were hunted as "Grassets" and prized for their delicate flesh. During modern times their numbers have plummeted to a fraction of historical population levels as forested land in North America has been cleared and developed, and the species' wintering grounds continue to be impacted by agriculture. There are several records of birds lingering through winter, including 16 Nov–16 Mar 1973 in High Island and 26 Jan 1947 in Cove. Reports of Wood Thrushes before mid-Mar may represent wintering birds that have remained through early spring migration.

CLAY-COLORED ROBIN
Turdus grayi tamaulipensis

Very rare resident or summer terminal migrant

HABITAT: A familiar bird in Latin America, the national bird of Costa Rica, and found as far south as Colombia, this species inhabits forest, forest edges, and second growth, venturing out onto residential lawns or similar openings.

DISCUSSION: The only UTC record, and one of the northernmost in the United States, is one located 6 Jun 2003 by Tom Morris as it sang in his yard in Lake Jackson, BRA. The bird remained vocal and easy to relocate over the first week of its stay but was heard with decreasing frequency until it disappeared in late Jul. This bird appeared again at the same site and was heard singing on 17 Apr 2004. It was still singing in Aug, and one wonders whether it ever actually left Lake Jackson. Given the species' increasing nesting presence in the Lower Rio Grande Valley and extralimital records from Victoria, Walker, and Gonzales cos., UTC birders should be open to the possibility of more visits from this tropical species. During the spring and summer months, long, somewhat listless robinlike songs emanating from a tree's canopy should be tracked down. Also, listen for the bird's somewhat inflected, catlike mewing call.

AMERICAN ROBIN
Turdus migratorius

Common to abundant winter terminal migrant, uncommon summer resident

HABITAT: Widespread in winter, occurring in woodland edge and understory, second growth, abandoned fields, and the ornamental or shade trees of neighborhood yards. Breeds locally, favoring live oaks and mature urban woodlots. Large numbers are found seasonally in yaupon thickets as the fruits ripen.

DISCUSSION: The familiar American Robin is a common to abundant winter visitor. Occasionally, flocks of hundreds or more are encountered, often in overgrown fields or woodland edge and understory, where they strip the berries from yaupon and other holly bushes. Migrant birds belong to the subspecies *T. m. migratorius*. After they return north, small numbers of the subspecies *achrusterus* remain to breed locally. These birds occur at widely scattered locations and much seemingly suitable habitat is not utilized. They are common now in La Marque, GAL; in Houston, nesting pairs may be encountered on the Rice University campus, in adjoining parts of West University Place, in Bellaire, and in Garden Oaks.

VARIED THRUSH
Ixoreus naevius

Very rare winter visitor

Winter 1935 Cove, CHA (A. McKay)

Winter 1956 Galveston County Park, GAL (remained for one month)

27 Dec 1978–31 Jan 1979 Gilchrist, GAL (TPRF 142; TPRF 981; *LSUMZ 151912) (AB 33:296, 582)

15–16 Dec 1979 Baytown, CHA (notes submitted to Houston CBC)

22 Feb–3 Mar 91 Smith Point, CHA (TBRC 1991-25) (AB 45:293)

HABITAT: Coastal mottes, rural areas with scattered live oak and cypress.

DISCUSSION: Each winter, small numbers of Varied Thrushes appear far to the east of their normal range, often as far as the eastern seaboard. Their penchant for wandering is shared by Townsend's Solitaire, another western montane thrush. Although the marshes and isolated mottes along the UTC are hardly reminiscent of the dense coniferous forests of the Pacific Northwest preferred by this species, on a number of occasions Varied Thrushes have wandered to our region. Generally, they were present within isolated woodlots surrounded by an ocean of coastal prairie and marsh. Two of these locations were heavily grazed by cattle, and the thrushes, associating with small flocks of American Robins, were frequently seen foraging in leaf litter around the copious cow pies.

A bird present in Gilchrist, GAL, from late Dec 1978 until the end of Jan 1979 was the state's first in about 10 years, and probably the most observed of the UTC's Varied Thrushes. Found during the Bolivar CBC by Dennis Caputo and David Dauphin, it was seen subsequently by birders from all over Texas. Later in 1979, John Tveten found not one but two males during the Houston CBC. The birds were located late in the afternoon in a woodlot at the League of Women Voters Park in Baytown, CHA. The first bird was noisily foraging in leaf litter in a deep drainage ditch. It and then a second bird a short distance away hopped into view in response to spishing noises. At least one bird was relocated the next day and seen by other observers.

GRAY CATBIRD
Dumetella carolinensis

Uncommon winter resident, common bi-seasonal transient migrant, rare summer breeder

HABITAT: Dense understory of forest edge, hedgerows, coastal mottes, densely planted gardens.

DISCUSSION: Although Gray Catbird is present locally throughout the year, UTC migrants eclipse residents (both winter and summer) by orders of magnitude. Most birders see catbirds only during spring and fall migration. During the latter part of spring, migrant traps such as Sabine Woods and the High Island sanctuaries are often awash in this species, and their catlike *mew* calls permeate the understory. This was our second most common species in censused fallouts.

Nehrling (1882) discovered a nesting Gray Catbird on 5 May 1881 in the thick underbrush of woods along Spring Creek. Recent breeding has been reported from JEF and, in 2004, HAS. However, we note that early southbound migrants (unsuccessful nesters from nearby East Texas?) can arrive on the UTC as early as late Jun, so observers should be cautious when classifying any summer catbird as a nester.

NORTHERN MOCKINGBIRD
Mimus polyglottos polyglottos

Common resident

HABITAT: Woodland, hedgerow, open areas with scattered trees, well-planted neighborhoods.

DISCUSSION: Although they are now among our most familiar birds and abundant throughout the year, Nehrling (1882) noted only a few Northern Mockingbirds remaining to winter. In the intervening century prairies and marshes were turned into residential neighborhoods packed with fruit-bearing ornamental shrubs and trees. This conversion provides both food and nest sites and has modified the bird's summer and winter distribution as well as its absolute numbers. Now, from suitably exposed perches everywhere, mockingbirds deliver their repertoires of resident and migrant bird songs, periodically taking a moment to dive-bomb a cat or drop to a lawn for a choice bug. During spring, like Yellow-breasted Chats, mockingbirds may sing throughout the hours of darkness, as human neighbors toss and turn and reach for their earplugs. Besides a variety of insects, native foods include the berries of pokeberry, American elder (elderberry), American beautyberry, hollies, and American mistletoe.

SAGE THRASHER
Oreoscoptes montanus

Rare winter terminal migrant
17 Sep 1945 Cove, CHA (A. McKay)
30 Apr 1955 Cove, CHA (A. McKay)
25 Dec 1956–6 Jan 1957 W HAS (S. Williams)
22 Nov 1959 Cove, CHA (A. McKay)
24 Jan 1964 Cove (A. McKay) (AFN 18 : 370)
27 Feb 1966 W Houston, HAS (R. and
   M. A. Moore) (SB)
22 Sep 1966 GAL (C. E. Hall) (AFN 21 : 58)
15 Oct 1967 Anahuac (J. Tveten) (SB)
19 Dec 1971 Freeport, BRA (SB)
19 Nov 1972 W HAS (AB 27 : 85 & SB)
2 Nov 1973 Anahuac NWR, CHA (AB 28 : 78)
9 Apr 1976 GAL (V. Emanuel) (AB 30 : 864)
19 Nov 1977 Anahuac NWR, CHA (R. Clapper) (AB
   32 : 229)
18 Dec 1977 Freeport, BRA (R. and M. A. Moore,
   J. Morgan, others) (AB 32 : 775)
19 Dec 1977 BRA (AB); probably same as preceding
   record
26 Oct 1979 JEF (SB)
15 Nov 1991 W HAS (D. Bradford)
20 Dec 1998 Freeport, BRA (D. and D. Peake photo)

WINTER: (17, 22 Sep; 15, 26 Oct; 2, Nov) **early Nov to early Apr** (9, 30 Apr)

HABITAT: Nests in sagebrush and similar low vegetation; locally, in hedgerows and fencerows, abandoned farm fields, thickets.

DISCUSSION: Sage Thrasher is a rarity along the UTC, and in two out of three years there are no local sightings. Despite intense coverage since 1940, the

Freeport CBC has located singles only in 1971, 1977, and 1998. Most sightings occurred near the onset of winter with the expected spike during the CBC season: Sep (2), Oct (2), Nov (5), Dec (4), Jan (1), Feb (1), and Apr (2). The Sep records may seem anomalous; however, Lockwood and Freeman (2004) state that Sage Thrashers generally begin arriving in Texas in late Sep (and remain from early Apr to early May). There are sporadic records in the brush country to the southwest, but the Trans-Pecos region is the nearest area where these thrashers regularly winter.

BROWN THRASHER
Toxostoma rufum rufum

Common winter terminal migrant, rare summer nonbreeding resident

WINTER: (7, 20, 25–26 Aug) **late Aug to late May** (18 May)

HABITAT: Woods, generally with thick understory; also frequents densely planted gardens and parks.

DISCUSSION: Brown Thrasher is a relatively common winter inhabitant of coastal woodlands in our region. It is rather adaptive in its habitat requirements, as likely in urban backyards as in the contiguous Pineywoods to the east. In fall migration, significant numbers arrive with the first fronts (460 in High Island 30 Sep 1987, and 550 along the coast between Sabine Woods and High Island 1 Oct 1985). During some years, nonbreeders linger through summer and may be found in migrant traps such as High Island and Quintana NBS. Although breeding has been reported on several occasions, the simple presence of a Brown Thrasher in summer is not indicative of nesting activity. As yet, we have seen no evidence of documented nests, eggs, or young from those few nonbreeding individuals that apparently choose to remain along the coast rather than migrate to their traditional breeding haunts.

LONG-BILLED THRASHER
Toxostoma longirostre

Hypothetical (perhaps accidental) winter visitor, imperfectly documented

HABITAT: Coastal woodlots.

DISCUSSION: Although there are several UTC reports of Long-billed Thrasher (remaining as late as 29 Apr), we are uneasy about its local status. This bird is resident along the Texas coast as far northeast as Matagorda Co., and it is conceivable that one could wander as far north as the UTC. However, without photographs or specimens, we feel it is difficult if not impossible to eliminate Brown Thrasher from consideration. A Brown Thrasher recently added to the Florida Museum of Natural History collection had an especially long bill with an exposed culmen that measured 32 mm, compared to a normal length of 25 mm (A. Kratter data). A difference of that magnitude could mislead observers in the field. To be fair, the challenge is similar in northern Mexico, where birders often struggle to find the odd Brown Thrasher amid the numerous resident Long-billeds. Therefore we suggest waiting for more convincing documentation before Long-billed Thrasher is placed on any official list of accepted UTC species.

CURVE-BILLED THRASHER
Toxostoma curvirostre oberholseri

Rare winter terminal migrant; previously, very rare resident

WINTER: (31 Oct) to (23 Apr) rarely summers

HABITAT: Mainly hedgerows, open scrub on sandy soil, coastally and inland.

DISCUSSION: Mention of Curve-billed Thrasher generally stirs up visions of saguaro cactus or dense stands of mesquite and acacia; however, this southwestern species has occurred at four UTC locations. The first was discovered 25 Apr 1974 on Nottingham Ranch Road, West Galveston Is., and appeared to be resident until last observed 13 Oct 1979. On 23 Jul 1977, a possible second bird was observed there. The Freeport CBC logged one on 17 Dec 1978. One was seen 23 Apr 1981 five miles north of High Is. Finally; one was present in east WAR on 31 Oct 1993.

From counties to our immediate southwest and west where habitat is more suitable, there are at least nine additional records, some involving multiple birds. This species is resident along the Texas coast as far northeast as Matagorda Co., so the appearance of one in BRA (for example) is certainly understandable.

EUROPEAN STARLING
Sturnus vulgaris

Introduced and abundant resident

HABITAT: Nearly ubiquitous in the lowlands of North America. Locally, found in all urban, suburban, and rural areas.

DISCUSSION: In any plumage the European Starling is not an unattractive bird. Its vocal repertoire is diverse, and some individuals are accomplished mimics. Perhaps then, it is not surprising that in 1890 Eugene Scheffland introduced 100 European Starlings to New York City, part of his goal for the United States to host all the birds mentioned by Shakespeare. Within approximately 75 years, their progeny had colonized the United States from the Atlantic to the Pacific.

European Starlings saturated the UTC long ago, and our combination of agricultural land and developed areas continues to suit them. In settled areas, they are attracted to bird feeders, ornamental plantings, insect-rich lawns, and organic trash. Outside town, clouds of them descend on fields to eat unharvested rice and other crops or to scavenge at rice elevators, railroad sidings, farmyards, and other sites presenting spilled grain. Frequently they flock with icterids, such as Brown-headed Cowbird and Red-winged Blackbird, then occurring in truly awesome numbers.

Starlings are cavity nesters, utilizing holes in trees and all manner of artificial structures, including homes, highway billboards, traffic signals, and birdhouses. They are fierce competitors for nest spaces, evicting Purple Martins, Eastern Screech-Owls, Eastern Bluebirds, and various woodpeckers from their nesting cavities, occasionally maiming or killing them in the process.

Pipits

AMERICAN PIPIT
Anthus rubescens rubescens

Common winter terminal migrant

WINTER: (25 Sep; 1, 9 Oct) **mid-Oct to early Apr** (3, 8–9 May)

HABITAT: Wet or dry plowed fields, margins of temporary wetlands, overgrazed pasture, prairie, historically in the streets of Houston and residential yards.

DISCUSSION: American Pipit (formerly Water Pipit) is the familiar pipit of North America. Typically, this pipit is found in loose flocks, at times with 100 or more individuals. Flying birds frequently utter a sharp two-note flight call and land with an interrupted descent, as if going down a flight of stairs. Once on the ground they actually walk, methodically placing one foot in front of the other, as opposed to hopping.

Although American Pipit is a winter bird on the UTC, we are aware of several summer records: 30 Jun 1954, GAL; 30 Jun 1960, Cove; and 6 Aug 1960, GAL. These birds typically migrate south during Oct and Nov. Shortly thereafter they form large flocks, often on agricultural land. In 1965 the Freeport CBC had a high count of 6,350 birds.

SPRAGUE'S PIPIT
Anthus spragueii

Uncommon winter terminal migrant

WINTER: (3, 7–8 Oct) **mid-Oct to mid-Apr** (27 Apr; 2 May)

HABITAT: A species of the northern prairies, found locally on grazed or mowed habitats that mimic the nesting grounds.

DISCUSSION: During the spring of 1877, G. B. Sennett (1878) secured a specimen of this pipit in Galveston, a single bird consorting with a flock of McCown's Longspurs. Sennett wrote: "South of Galveston, just without the city limits, are lagoons and salt-marshes.

The low ridges dividing them are covered sparsely with grass, and, as in other sandy tracts, all of the tall grass grows in clumps, or hummocks. . . . By chance my eye caught sight of a bird darting into a hummock. I flushed and shot it. It was in soiled plumage, and gave me more study than any other bird of the collection before I ascertained that it was the Missouri Skylark." It was just a little over 30 years earlier that Audubon discovered Sprague's Pipit along the Missouri River. This pipit remains an uncommon visitor to the coast and inland, usually inhabiting extensive grazed or mowed grassy areas that approximate a winter shortgrass prairie. During recent years,

Skyland Drive adjacent to the Texas City Dike has been a productive place to search for them.

Like many species that occur on grasslands, including Upland and Buff-breasted sandpipers, Eastern and Western meadowlarks, and Grasshopper Sparrow, Sprague's Pipit is covered in a pleasing array of buffs and browns that render it virtually invisible on a carpet of dry grasses. In the air, these birds may be identified by their *squeet* flight call (Scott 1987) and their habit of plunging to the ground like a falling rock. The Freeport CBC, which usually records the species, produced 56 in 1983.

Waxwings

BOHEMIAN WAXWING
Bombycilla garrulus

Accidental winter vagrant
7 Feb 1997 8 miles N of Rosenberg, FOB
    (S. Williams) (TBRC 1997-30) (AFN 51:771)
11 Feb 2005 Humble, HAS (TBRC 2004-41)

HABITAT: Anywhere in the United States, this visitor from the northern forests will most often be found wintering with Cedar Waxwings. Flocks occur in residential or other areas with fruiting trees.

DISCUSSION: This larger rendition of the better-known Cedar Waxwing breeds throughout much of the Northern Hemisphere, nesting in both deciduous and coniferous forests. On this continent it breeds in Alaska, much of Canada, and the northwestern border states (A.O.U. 1998). One occurring just outside Houston seemed all the more astonishing for being so far south and so close to the coast. On 11 Feb 2005, J. Walls discovered four Bohemian Waxwings at the Jesse H. Jones Park and Nature Center in Humble, HAS. Other local sightings during that winter (inadequately documented) suggest a minor invasion of this northern species.

CEDAR WAXWING
Bombycilla cedrorum

Common winter terminal migrant

WINTER: (28 Sep; 9, 15, 21 Oct) **late Oct to late May** (28 × 2, 29 May; 1, 12 Jun)

HABITAT: Open woodland, second growth, residential areas; attracted to fruiting trees including loquat, palms, and various hollies.

DISCUSSION: Concentrations of dozens to 100 or more Cedar Waxwings occur irregularly throughout the region, even at ornamental plantings along urban sidewalks. These flocks linger long enough to denude a tree or shrub of its fruit and then move on. Occasionally, birds alight to feed on plants where fruits have fermented or are toxic to the birds, and "drunken" waxwings career off the sides of cars and buildings or flap helplessly on the sidewalk, where they fall prey to cats, bicycle tires, and preoccupied feet.

Although many observers think of this species as a winter bird that departs our yards in early spring, waxwings are one of the latest northbound migrants, occurring annually until the last week of May. We assume these are birds that have wintered well south of the UTC. During some winters, waxwings become very common on the UTC; for example, 2,717 were observed 17 Dec 2002 on the Galveston CBC. Coastal records include May and Oct records at Quintana NBS and frequent sightings at High Island.

The American Wood Warbler assemblage (subfamily Parulinae, or tribe Parulini) is one of the most widespread and charismatic groups of New World birds. Their bright plumage, diverse songs, and migratory behavior have made them a symbol for the plight of declining North American songbird populations. More than any other group of birds, they are responsible for attracting the thousands of birders who visit the UTC each spring.

About 45 species of these colorful and energetic travelers have been recorded locally. More than 30 appear regularly, but others are great rarities, and searching for them adds an aura of adventure and discovery to every spring outing. As each warbler species begins to pass through the UTC, its vanguard is composed of the often more colorful males, charging northward to secure nesting territories before the return of their usually drab mates.

Seeing many different warblers together in a coastal woodlot might suggest that they are all in the midst of the same activity; however, this is hardly the case. A Worm-eating Warbler searching a vine tangle may be making the short trip between eastern Mexico and northern Texas, whereas the Blackpoll feeding in the canopy above is refueling during its long and often perilous journey between the Amazon Basin and the boreal forests of Canada or Alaska.

Although locations such as Sabine Woods and Smith Oaks act as "migrant traps," they do not attract all warbler species with equal efficiency. Palm Warbler, for example, almost never associates with the coastal mottes, although it may be common in nearby salt cedars along the beach.

Birders who are afield during both north- and south-bound migrations notice that certain species, such as Nashville and Mourning warblers, fly an inland route during spring, becoming more common along the coast during fall. The spring migration of such species lacks the trans-Gulf component that puts so many birds on our coast. Instead, they move northward via a mainland route located west of the Gulf. These and other species exhibit a general eastward shift during their southbound migration, hence the increased likelihood of coastal sightings during fall. The migration of Canada Warbler is

unique and is discussed briefly in the account for that species.

Naturally, possessing some knowledge of the UTC's habitats and the birds that prefer them increases the number of all bird species a birder comes across. During migration though, be prepared for birds to show up in unusual locations. This is especially the case early in the morning, before late arrivals from the previous evening have gravitated to preferred habitats. In the mornings many warblers and other Neotropical migrants may be found in reed beds or perched on a strand of barbed wire crossing the coastal prairie miles from the nearest tree.

In other parts of the United States and in Canada, an important ritual of springtime birding is enjoying and unscrambling the dawn chorus of singing warblers. Many visitors comment on how quiet the northern species are when encountered locally. Even though a few northern breeders do vocalize at this latitude, the Gulf Coast cannot be considered a good site for learning the songs of most eastern warblers. The number and diversity of warblers and other species to be seen, however, compensate for the lack of song.

Although most warblers return to the Neotropics for the winter, substantial numbers remain in the United States. Most of these occur from southern California to Florida, where insects and nectar continue to be available. Every year a few of the less usual species linger on the UTC. Certainly some continue southward after the CBC period, but a few stay through the winter. Table 16 lists 27 species of warblers plus one form and one genus category detected on 30 Freeport CBCs between 1975 and 2004. Several other species were seen earlier, but this list is representative of the bulk of the occurrences. Most of the species were rarely or infrequently seen. Yellow-rumped Warbler comprised 74.6 percent of the 68,692 warblers tallied during those years; this species and (in descending order) Orange-crowned Warbler, Common Yellowthroat, and Pine and Wilson's warblers account for almost 99 percent of the total.

Not only migrant birds but also migrant birders have a significant impact on the UTC. To demonstrate

Table 16. *Warbler Totals Freeport Christmas Bird Count, 1975–2004*

Species	Avg.	Yrs. Seen	High	Total
Yellow-rumped Warbler	1709	30	3888	51262
Orange-crowned Warbler	306	30	687	9188
Common Yellowthroat	176	30	474	5273
Pine Warbler	45	30	183	1337
Wilson's Warbler	29	30	107	856
Palm Warbler	13	30	46	387
Black-and-white Warbler	6	29	14	168
Nashville Warbler	2	19	10	46
Northern Waterthrush	1	15	4	26
Ovenbird	1	11	6	22
Black-throated Green Warbler	1	11	4	22
American Redstart	1	17	2	21
Yellow-throated Warbler	1	8	5	16
Northern Parula	0	8	3	11
Tennessee Warbler	0	9	2	10
Yellow Warbler	0	8	3	10
Prairie Warbler	0	7	1	7
"Audubon's" Warbler	0	6	1	7
Yellow-breasted Chat	0	5	1	5
Bay-breasted Warbler	0	3	1	3
Oporornis species	0	3	1	3
Black-throated Gray Warbler	0	2	2	3
Magnolia Warbler	0	2	1	2
Waterthrush species	0	2	1	2
Tropical Parula	0	1	1	1
Blackburnian Warbler	0	1	1	1
Blackpoll Warbler	0	1	1	1
Worm-eating Warbler	0	1	1	1
Mourning Warbler	0	1	1	1
Lucy's Warbler	0	0	0	0
Prothonotary Warbler	0	0	0	0
Kentucky Warbler	0	0	0	0
Connecticut Warbler	0	0	0	0
Hooded Warbler	0	0	0	0

Note: The last five species were reported prior to 1975.

this, the dollar value of visiting birders was calculated (Eubanks et al. 1993). Each spring, from late Mar to mid-May, ecotourists visiting High Island to seek warblers and other migrants pump an estimated *three million* dollars into the economy of East Texas. This monetary windfall is reason enough for communities along the Gulf Coast to manage and enhance habitat that attracts birders as well as birds.

BLUE-WINGED WARBLER
Vermivora pinus

Common spring and fall transient migrant, rare winter lingerer

SPRING: (9, 14, 25 Mar) **late Mar to early May** (7–8, 25 May)

FALL: (29 Jul; 2, 7 × 3, 8 × 2 Aug) **late Aug to mid-Oct** (8 Nov, 25 Nov–7 Dec; 10, 19 Dec)

HABITAT: Coastally in oak or hackberry mottes, well-planted residential yards and parks, salt cedar or tall willow clumps; inland in residential areas, parks, live oak groves.

DISCUSSION: Blue-winged Warbler is a familiar UTC migrant. Of the Blue-winged/Golden-winged species pair, it is the one more likely to occur in large numbers and the first to arrive, often well represented in the migrant traps by late Mar. There, the Blue-winged usually forages among the upper and outer branches of oak or hackberry trees, frequently in the company of an ad hoc assemblage of Tennessees, Black-throated Greens, or other species that glean the same elevational strata. Generally a few are heard each spring, practicing their buzzy song while still far from the nesting grounds. During our censused fallouts, Blue-winged Warbler was the 36th most commonly encountered of the 68 species we considered, representing about 0.6 percent of all birds encountered.

Occasionally Blue-winged Warbler lingers into early winter: for example, one was present at Lafitte's Cove, GAL, at least until 10 Dec 2004, and Mike Austin and Steve Gast located one on 19 Dec during the 2004 Freeport CBC.

GOLDEN-WINGED WARBLER
Vermivora chrysoptera

Uncommon spring, occasional fall transient migrant

SPRING: (28 × 3, 31 Mar; 4–5 Apr) **mid-Apr to early May** (13, 14 × 2, 19 × 2 May)

FALL: (15, 28 Aug) **late Aug to mid-Oct** (22–29 Oct)

HABITAT: Nests in open, early succession woodlands and edges from the Appalachians to the southern portion of the eastern half of Canada. On the UTC, occurs coastally in oak or hackberry mottes, mature vegetation in residential yards and parks, salt cedar or tall willow clumps; inland in residential areas, parks, live oak groves, etc.

DISCUSSION: Each year, smaller and smaller numbers of Golden-wingeds appear during their flights between North America and their wintering grounds in the highlands of Central and South America. Never common, the species was only one quarter as common as Blue-winged Warbler during our censused fallouts. Because of its dwindling populations, mainly in the southern parts of its range, Golden-winged Warbler has been the object of considerable scrutiny. Studies suggest that its declining numbers are due to several factors, including: habitat loss from fire suppression and maturation of early succession woodlands, and competition from the similar and more numerous Blue-winged Warbler, with which it hybridizes. Identifiable hybrids of Golden-winged and Blue-winged warblers, broadly categorized as "Lawrence's" and "Brewster's" warblers, have been recorded in roughly equal numbers, but the more subtle forms of Brewster's are probably underreported. Our database contains 13 spring sightings of Lawrence's, ranging from 12 to 30 Apr. We (and the rest of Texas) have but one physically documented fall Lawrence's record, a bird photographed by Jim Morgan on 10 Oct 1992 at High Island. Additionally, Winnie Burkett reported two on 24 Sep 2001, also at High Island. Although Brewster's is primarily a spring migrant, we note two 1936 records from late Sep at Kemah and Cove. Northbound birds have been sighted from 28 Mar (three occasions) to 8 May, most during the latter half of Apr.

TENNESSEE WARBLER
Vermivora peregrina

Common spring and fall transient migrant, rare winter terminal migrant

SPRING: (15, 17, 20 Mar) **early Apr to mid-May** (25–26, 28 May)

FALL: (15, 27–28 Aug) **early Sep to late Oct** (28, 30 Nov; 2, 13 Dec)

HABITAT: Coastal oak and hackberry mottes, willow clumps, salt cedars; also commonly in inland forests and residential areas.

DISCUSSION: Tennessee Warbler is one of our most numerous spring migrants. It ranked fourth overall in our censused fallouts, representing just over 5 percent of the total. By the third week of Apr, these birds are common in the migrant traps and many are seen inland. Flocks of 10–20 or more pass with seemingly frenzied haste through the canopy foliage of coastal woodlots, temporarily picking up then losing other warbler species along the way. Although most migrant warblers that sing on the UTC are species that breed in the southern United States, the sputtering song of northern-breeding Tennessees is frequently heard.

There is danger of confusing this species with Red-eyed, Warbling, and Philadelphia vireos, Orange-crowned Warbler, or other similar birds that lack wing bars. Note the Tennessee's rather short, thin bill, well-defined narrow supercilium, white lower belly, lack of chest streaking, and (during spring) the male's contrasting gray crown. Few Tennessees linger into winter: correctly identified individuals may include one or two on Freeport CBCs and two on Attwater CBCs, but the species is not expected, even as a rarity, during our winters.

ORANGE-CROWNED WARBLER
Vermivora celata celata

Fairly common bi-seasonal transient migrant, common winter terminal migrant

SPRING: (4–5, 18 May)
FALL: (21, 25 Aug; 11–12 Sep) **early Oct to mid-Apr**
HABITAT: Coastal mottes, woodlands and hedge-rows, residential and urban plantings.
DISCUSSION: Orange-crowned is one of but a few warblers that winter commonly on the UTC. Being familiar with its sweet chip (thinner than a Cardinal's) makes clear its true abundance. Birds may be encountered in mixed insectivore flocks or foraging independently. During cold weather Orange-crowneds may take sugar water at hummingbird feeders. Although dense hedgerows, coastal mottes, or light woodland may be more attractive to the species in the long run, they are also present in parklike habitats such as the widely spaced oak trees planted along Houston's Brays Bayou bicycle path. The widespread subspecies *V. c. celata,* breeding across much of northern North America, winters along the UTC. It is perhaps the dullest of the four races of Orange-crowns and probably the one most likely to be confused with a Tennessee Warbler.

NASHVILLE WARBLER
Vermivora ruficapilla ruficapilla

Fairly common bi-seasonal transient migrant, rare winter terminal migrant

SPRING: (4, 14, 16 Mar) **late Mar to late Apr** (6, 19 May)
FALL: (29 Jul; 21, 25 Aug) **mid-Sep to early Nov** (15, 21, 30 Nov)
HABITAT: Coastal mottes; inland in light woodland, parks, and residential areas.
DISCUSSION: Eastern Nashville Warblers winter from South Texas to Guatemala (Curson et al. 1994). Their northbound migration path does not involve the trans-Gulf crossing so typical of many of our Neotropical visitors. Thus spring Nashvilles are more likely to be seen and heard inland at forested locations such as the Edith L. Moore Nature Sanctuary in Houston or within the canopy of Russ Pitman Park in Bellaire. Indeed, only nine of the nearly 62,500 migrants estimated to have occurred during our censused coastal spring fallouts were Nashvilles. During their southbound migration, this species covers a broader front and is more likely to appear along the coast in mottes, willows, or salt cedars. Rarely, Nashvilles winter along the UTC; our database contains at least six records from early Jan to mid-Mar, but mid-Mar birds could represent early migrants. The Freeport CBC has detected this species on 27 of 48 counts, with a high of 10 in 1980.

VIRGINIA'S WARBLER
Vermivora virginiae

Rare bi-seasonal transient migrant
12–13 Oct 1977 W Galveston Island, GAL (B. Harwell, photo)
27–29 Apr 1980 W Galveston Island, GAL
25 Oct 1981 Sabine Woods, JEF
11 Sep 1982 NE of High Island, GAL
24 Sep 1982 Anahuac NWR, CHA
15 Apr 1989 E of High Island, GAL
4 Sep 2000 Sabine Woods, JEF

HABITAT: Coastal mottes and thickets including salt cedars.
DISCUSSION: Despite the likelihood of confusing this western montane species with an Orange-crowned or Tennessee Warbler, or a female Common Yellowthroat, at least seven local observers have ventured to report Virginia's Warbler at coastal sites. Our first record was a bird found by Ben Feltner on 12 Oct 1977 and photographed the next day by Bill Harwell.

Dunn and Garrett (1997) consider it a casual migrant on the Texas coast.

LUCY'S WARBLER
Vermivora luciae

Accidental winter terminal migrant
20–27 Dec 1964 Freeport, BRA

HABITAT: Thin woodland such as stands of mesquite, where it is the only hole-nesting warbler in western North America.

DISCUSSION: The closest known breeding population of this species is located in the Cottonwood Campground area at Big Bend NP, Brewster Co., Texas. In the western United States it is known to wander northward, but there are few records in the East. Nonetheless, one located during a Freeport CBC was observed by Nancy and Jerry Strickling and others from 20 to 27 Dec 1964.

NORTHERN PARULA
Parula americana

Common summer terminal migrant, uncommon winter terminal migrant

SPRING: (13, 19, 21 Feb) **early Mar to late Oct**
FALL: (10, 12, 14 Nov)

HABITAT: Bottomland hardwood and bayou edge riparian forest, second growth or modified wooded tracts with a moist understory, generally in association with Spanish moss.

DISCUSSION: Because they are common breeders in the SE United States, Northern Parulas are well represented among the first waves of trans-Gulf migrants in early to mid-Mar. The earliest known migrant was detected on an offshore rig over 60 miles from shore on 19 Feb 2000. A second northbound wave occurs in mid-Apr as migrants move toward nesting grounds in the NE United States and S Canada. By this time "our" birds are already nesting just a few miles away alongside other early migrants such as Swainson's, Prothonotary, and Yellow-throated warblers. Although Northern Parulas are common along riparian corridors and extensive bottomland forests, stands of live oaks such as those planted in some older communities—Lake Jackson, for example—or even woodlots with taller second

growth provide nesting habitat for these attractive birds. Wherever they are found nesting in East Texas, there is sure to be Spanish moss in the canopy, for the Parula's nest is generally incorporated into strands of this air plant, a diminutive member of the pineapple family.

We note more than a dozen records of wintering birds, and there are probably a few in the area during all but the most severe winters. Males heard singing during Feb may represent individuals that lingered through the winter or may be very early migrants. In recent years small numbers of them have reappeared on territory and in coastal migrant traps during the last few days of Feb.

TROPICAL PARULA
Parula pitiayumi nigrilora

Very rare winter terminal migrant
19 Dec 1982 Freeport CBC, BRA
1 Feb 1988 Freeport, BRA
17–19 Sep 1993 Brazos Bend SP, FOB
16 May 1998 San Bernard NWR, BRA
12 Mar 2000 High Island, GAL
3 Jan 2003 Buffalo Bayou CBC, HAS

HABITAT: Coastal mottes or extensive mature live oak plantings in residential areas.

DISCUSSION: At least six times, this almost exclusively Neotropical resident has occurred along the UTC. Our earliest sightings consisted of single birds from the Freeport–Lake Jackson area. More recently they seem to have been occurring on the UTC with greater frequency. Very likely this is due to increased observer coverage, but it is too early to tell. However, territorial birds have been found in late spring as close as Aransas NWR and, in the future, may be found singing in UTC live oaks. In South Texas, Tropical Parula is an uncommon breeding and wintering bird, often occurring in Spanish moss–festooned evergreen oak woodlands not unlike those found along parts of the UTC. Although most races of this species are resident, the northernmost ones, including *P. p. nigrilora,* are prone to disperse (Curson et al. 1994). Thus postbreeding wanderers that reach the UTC may encounter very familiar habitat to attract and hold them, equipped as well with roving bands of many of the same small insectivores with which they associate farther south.

Great care should be taken in identifying any potential Tropical Parula. Recent studies show that some Texas birds have intermediate traits of Northern and Tropical parulas—particularly those along the Devil's River and in the nearby Hill Country (*fide* Tony Gallucci).

YELLOW WARBLER
Dendroica petechia

Common spring and fall transient migrant, formerly bred

SPRING: (11, 15, 30 Mar) **mid-Apr to late May** (1, 2 × 2, 3, 7 Jun)

FALL: (10, 15, 18 Jul) **early Aug to mid-Oct** (20 Oct; 8, 10–12 Nov)

HABITAT: Salt cedar, willow, huisache, and other shrubby growth, fallow fields with baccharis and rattlebox; much less common in closed-canopy woodland, thus uncommon in coastal mottes.

DISCUSSION: Yellow Warbler is one of our most common migrants, ranking 17th during our censused fallouts. Nonetheless, birders who favor the shady trails of our coastal sanctuaries are in danger of missing these charming birds altogether. To appreciate the abundance of this species, look for it in low, dense habitat such as salt cedars, overgrown fields, thickets around pools, or in willow-lined riparian corridors. Yellows migrate along a broad front, entering the UTC via both an open-water crossing and inland routes over the Mexican mainland. Thus numbers of them are likely to be scattered across the UTC even when weather conditions do not favor the presence of trans-Gulf migrants.

The abundant, widespread *D. p. aestiva* migrates through the UTC, and represents most if not all recent records (Nehrling 1882; Curson et al. 1994; TOS 1995).

During summer, the few Yellow Warblers that appear on the UTC may represent nonbreeding birds or very early or late migrants. There is no evidence of local nesting. Recent records that may represent summer wanderers rather than late spring migrants include 16 Jun 2002 and 30 Jun 2003, both at W. Galveston Is., GAL.

The winter status of this species is unclear. During recent years there have been consistent CBC reports (including an adult male reported in 2002), indicating that there are occasional lingerers. Nonetheless we are concerned that some or most CBC birds that were called Yellow Warblers may have been misidentified.

CHESTNUT-SIDED WARBLER
Dendroica pensylvanica

Common spring, uncommon fall transient migrant

SPRING: (31 Mar; 6 Apr) **mid-Apr to mid-May** (26, 28, 31 × 2 May)

FALL: (2, 30 Jul; 27–28 Aug) **mid-Sep to late Oct** (8, 11, 25 Nov)

HABITAT: Coastally in oak and hackberry mottes and salt cedars; inland in parks, woodlots, and residential plantings.

DISCUSSION: Chestnut-sided Warbler is a common although apparently no longer abundant migrant along the UTC. Frequently, the species is present in double digits; our censused high count of 141 occurred during a fallout on 7 May 1987. Prior to our censusing efforts, 356, 1,300, and 230 individuals were reported on 2 May 1972, 3 May 1973, and 13 May 1976 respectively, suggesting the richness of past fallouts during better times.

Look for this species as it forages in the outer or upper branches of the taller trees of our coastal mottes or mature residential plantings, often alongside Tennessee Warblers. Later migrants deliver their sweet, rather explosive song, often depicted as: *please please pleased to meetcha* (Scott 1987).

MAGNOLIA WARBLER
Dendroica magnolia

Common spring and fall transient migrant, rare terminal migrant

SPRING: (23 Feb; 20 Mar; 28 Mar; 2 Apr) **mid-late Apr to late May** (29, 31 × 2 May; 5 Jun)

FALL: (15, 21 Aug; 10 Sep) **mid-Sep to late Oct** (15–16, 24, 29 Nov)

HABITAT: Coastal oak and hackberry mottes, willows and salt cedars; inland in parks, residential plantings, and woodlands.

DISCUSSION: Magnolia Warbler, along with Bay-breasted, is one of the latest spring migrants that pass through the UTC. It still constitutes a major percentage of the late spring movement, although its numbers have decreased significantly. Newer bird-watchers may have trouble comprehending the estimated 3,000 found by Ben Feltner and Victor Emanuel between Sabine Pass and High Island on 3 May 1973. This species ranked fifth during our censused fallouts, representing slightly over 4 percent of the total number of birds censused.

Elsewhere on the coast, Magnolias also represent a major proportion of the later spring movement. On 7 May 1951, exceptional rains, a cold front, and north-easterly winds forced vast numbers of birds to the coast of Padre Island. The next day, James (1956) counted corpses of 1,109 Magnolias among a 2,421-bird sample of well over 10,000 birds killed during that storm.

Fall migrants are also late; a few birds often linger into Nov or Dec. The Freeport CBC has tallied this species on three of 48 counts.

CAPE MAY WARBLER
Dendroica tigrina

Occasional spring, rare fall transient migrant

SPRING: (26, 31 Mar) **mid-Apr to mid-May** (19–21, 22 May; 5–8 Jun)

FALL: (6 Sep-19 Oct) **early Sep to late Oct** (24, 27, 31 Oct)

HABITAT: Coastal migrant traps, oaks, salt cedars; often feeds in pecan catkins.

DISCUSSION: The UTC lies to the west of the Cape May's normal migratory path from its Caribbean wintering grounds through Florida and the eastern Gulf. Thus seeing one here is always an unexpected treat. Some springs may produce ten or more, and the next two or three years may yield virtually none. We presume the species has declined during recent years. Our censused fallouts yielded only one individual seen 30 Apr 1988, a day that produced nearly 7,600 Neotropical migrants. However, lacking an eastern or southeastern component, those weather conditions generating coastal fronts may not necessarily drive birds westward from the eastern Gulf. Previously certain coastal residents, including George and Jane Clayton on West Galveston Island, were known to produce Cape Mays seemingly on demand. However, during recent years this feat has become more difficult. Fall Cape Mays are few and far between, and when they do occur, there is great danger of confusing them with a Yellow-rumped, Blackburnian, Blackpoll (rare), or other streaky-breasted warbler. Although they winter occasionally in the southern United States, we suspect that our late records merely represent lingerers. We note two Dec records (25 Dec 1945 at Cove and 19 Dec 1972 at High Island) and a CBC sighting at nearby Attwater NWR.

BLACK-THROATED BLUE WARBLER
Dendroica caerulescens caerulescens

Rare spring, occasional fall transient migrant and rare winter lingerer

SPRING: (4, 10, 12 Apr) **mid-Apr to late May** (22, 24 May; 1 Jun)

FALL: (9, 14, 18 Sep) **mid-Sep to mid- to late Oct** (25 Oct; 9, 11 Nov)

WINTER: (28 Nov–7 Dec; 9 × 2, 21, 23 Dec; 23 Nov–approx. 7 Feb)

HABITAT: Understory (usually) or canopy of oak or hackberry mottes and residential yards, privet, salt cedars, ornamental plantings; generally inside the forest, occasionally in dense edges.

DISCUSSION: As with Cape May Warbler, the main migration of Black-throated Blues occurs east of the UTC. Each spring sees one or two recorded along the coast. During fall they are slightly more common. Migrants are decidedly nondemonstrative, generally skulking in the shadowy undergrowth, where the sharpest-eared birders hear them utter a soft flat *tack . . . tack* suggesting the flight notes of some blackbirds.

Probably our longest remaining bird, a confiding first-year male of the more northerly subspecies *caerulescens*, was present in Houston 23 Nov 1995 until about 7 Feb 1996 (W. and J. Risser; Behrstock photos), when it met an untimely death in traffic. It foraged in leaf litter and on tree trunks and both living and dead branches, fluttered at blooms of giant Turk's cap, fed in loquat blossoms, and drank at four hummingbird feeders (from which it was occasionally driven by male and female Rufous Hummingbirds).

It also took insects in and below gutters, at window frames and roof shingles, and off wooden fences. Along with a Ruby-crowned Kinglet and an Orange-crowned Warbler, it vigorously responded to imitations of an Eastern Screech-Owl. During many hours of observation, this individual gave its call note almost constantly.

Our database contains records of six Dec lingerers. Perhaps more typical timing for a migrant would be a female present 20 Oct–1 Nov 2003 at Sabine Woods.

YELLOW-RUMPED "MYRTLE" WARBLER
Dendroica coronata coronata

Common to abundant winter terminal migrant

SPRING: (19, 30 May; 9 Jun)
FALL: (14–15, 24 Sep) **early Oct to mid-Apr**
HABITAT: Virtually throughout the region where trees or tall shrubs exist; occurs occasionally at feeding tables, rarely at hummingbird feeders.

DISCUSSION: During winter, Yellow-rumps (nick-named butter-butts) are generally the commonest members of roving bands of small insect-eating birds, typically outnumbering the resident chick-adees and titmice and migrant kinglets with which they associate. Frequently, flocks contain several dozen or more of these drab though rather noisy and hyperactive birds; learn their flat chips to find such flocks. A favorable day's birding may produce a prodigious number. For example, 3,888 were tallied during the 1982 Freeport CBC. By gleaning trunks and branches, flycatching, and taking fruits such as wax-myrtle berries, Yellow-rumps exploit a broad feeding niche, lessening the competition among themselves as well as with flock mates of other species that have more narrowly defined food preferences.

YELLOW-RUMPED "AUDUBON'S" WARBLER
Dendroica coronata auduboni

Rare fall and spring transient migrant, probably rare terminal winter migrant

FALL: (5, 12 Oct) to SPRING: (21, 25, 27 Apr)
HABITAT: To be expected coastally in mottes or willow thickets; inland in residential plantings or light woodland.

DISCUSSION: Although frequently encountered as migrants or winter visitors in West Texas, and per-haps commoner at more southerly coastal sites such as Aransas NWR, this western subspecies of Yellow-rumped Warbler is an unusual sight on the UTC. Winter birds are subtle, and unfortunately most birders fail to search Yellow-rumped flocks for yellow-throated individuals since taxonomic lumping has rendered the subspecies "just another butter-butt." Thus its true status remains somewhat clouded. The UTC *Checklist* (Ornithology Group 1989) deems it rare but continuously present from mid-Oct through the first week of May, probably a realistic assessment. Perhaps individuals are more common in the inland portions of the region, as migrants are noted periodically on the Rice University campus in Houston (W. and J. Risser). They are decidedly sparse on the coast; an alternate plumaged male foraging in willows at Anahuac NWR on 21 Apr 1995 was Behrstock's only spring sighting. The Rissers and Claytons noted an aberrant bird on Galveston Island that exhibited a red, not yellow, throat, apparently due to erythristic feather coloration, not berry juice.

BLACK-THROATED GRAY WARBLER
Dendroica nigrescens

Uncommon to rare bi-seasonal transient migrant and winter lingerer

SPRING: (12, 21, 22–26, 24, 28 Apr)
FALL: (22 Aug; 9, 16–19, 18, 24 Sept; 18, 25, 31 Oct; 1 × 2, 6, 10–13, 30 Nov)
WINTER: (29 Nov–2 Jan; 4 Feb)
HABITAT: Most records are from salt cedars and oak or hackberry woods.

DISCUSSION: Black-throated Gray Warbler is rare but regular in West Texas, the Rio Grande Valley, the southern coast, and along the UTC. Many Texas sightings are from various species of shrubby or tall oaks, trees in which these warblers frequently occur on their breeding grounds. This species has been sighted at least 20 times on the UTC; all records were along or very close to the coast, and most occurred during fall migration. At least one lingered from late Nov to early Jan and we have an early Feb record. In 1984, two were detected during the Freeport CBC, and to our west, we are aware of a 23 Dec sighting from the 1980 Attwater CBC. None was seen during censused spring fallouts; westerly winds seem most likely to encourage their presence.

GOLDEN-CHEEKED WARBLER
Dendroica chrysoparia

Accidental fall transient migrant
3 Aug 1977 W Galveston Island, GAL

HABITAT: A common breeder in the Texas Hill Country; coastal migrant traps are the most likely sites for an additional local occurrence.

DISCUSSION: Golden-cheeked Warbler inhabits the brush covered limestone slopes of the Edwards Plateau. There, it incorporates strips of bark from the Ashe juniper into its nest. Away from its nesting grounds it is extremely rare and is not expected elsewhere in Texas.

On 3 Aug 1977, David and Mimi Wolf discovered our only Golden-cheeked Warbler at 13-Mile Road on West Galveston Is. Except at certain mountainous sites in E Mexico, this bird is infrequently reported during its migration from the Texas Hill Country to the mountains of Middle America. Because of its similarity to both Black-throated Green and Townsend's warblers, extralimital birds must be carefully documented.

BLACK-THROATED GREEN WARBLER
Dendroica virens virens

Common spring and fall transient migrant, rare winter terminal migrant

SPRING: (11, 15–16, 21 Mar) **early Apr to mid-May** (28 × 2, 31 May; 8 Jun)
FALL: (26 Jul; 7, 10 Aug) **mid-Sep to mid-Nov** (17, 21–23 Nov)
HABITAT: Coastally in oak and hackberry mottes, pecans, salt cedars and willows. As they move inland, occurring frequently in residential areas and parks. Most birds forage in the crowns or upper and outer branches of taller trees. They are usually seen at forest edge or gaps inside the forest, such as the Cathedral area of Boy Scout Woods at High Island.

DISCUSSION: Black-throated Greens are common and characteristic spring migrants. Ninety-five on 7 May 1987 was the highest day total contained in our

fallout data. Based on the numbers present on the wintering grounds, substantial double-digit counts remain a possibility. Locally, some males vigorously deliver their buzzy song as they move northward from their wintering grounds in Mexico and Central America. Fall birds occur commonly in the usual migrant traps and may be numerous into Nov. During winter, one occasionally turns up in a mixed insectivore flock, but such birds are not detected annually. The Freeport CBC has found them on 13 of 48 counts. The handful of records after Dec includes 2 Jan 2003 on W Galveston Is., 11 Jan 1985 in CHA, and 20 Jan 1983 and 20 Feb 1979, both at High Island.

TOWNSEND'S WARBLER
Dendroica townsendi

Rare bi-seasonal transient and winter lingerer

SPRING: (3, 8–9, 13–16, 18, 20–21, 24–25, 29 Apr; 27 May)
FALL: (3, 9–15, 18, 20–21, 25–27 Sep; 1, 10, Oct)
WINTER: (2 Jan)
HABITAT: Coastal oak mottes and ornamental plantings.

DISCUSSION: Townsend's Warbler visits the UTC only a little more frequently than the Black-throated Gray Warbler. The number of spring and fall records is balanced with about 10 from each season. The vast majority of these records are from the coastal migrant traps in Apr and Sep., a number of the sightings being birds seen in oaks and hackberry trees, loosely associating with other migrating warblers.

HERMIT WARBLER
Dendroica occidentalis

Rare bi-seasonal transient migrant
29–30 Mar 1972 High Island, GAL
12–13 Apr 1991 Pilot Road, JEF
21 Apr 1993 Peach Point, BRA
1 May 1994 Galveston Island, GAL (banded and
    photographed)
8 Apr 1997 Smith Oaks, GAL
10–12 Apr 1999 Sabine Woods, JEF (photographed)
31 Aug–1 Sep 2001 Quintana, BRA (videotaped)

HABITAT: Nests in coniferous forests of the Pacific Northwest south to S California. Locally, occurs in coastal woodlands.

DISCUSSION: This western vagrant has occurred at least six times during spring and once during summer. The first sighting was at High Island on 29–30 Mar 1972 (AB 26:782). However, the first physically documented record was not until 1 May 1994—a male netted and photographed at a banding station on Galveston Is. We recognize four other spring records that likely represent full-blooded Hermit Warblers.

Hybridization needs to be considered whenever a Hermit Warbler is seen locally, as they occasionally breed with Townsend's Warblers. A Hermit that wintered in Anzalduas County Park (Hidalgo Co.) exhibited hybrid characteristics (Greg Lasley TexBirds post).

The only fall record is a first-year female found and videotaped by Weeks and others during its 31 Aug–1 Sep 2001 stay at Quintana, BRA. Oddly, this was the first fall UTC record despite the species being rare but regular in the Trans-Pecos.

BLACKBURNIAN WARBLER
Dendroica fusca

Common spring, uncommon fall transient migrant

SPRING: (12, 21, 25, 28 Mar) **early Apr to mid-May** (31 × 2 May; 11–12 Jun)

FALL: (15, 30, 31 × 2 Aug) **early Sep to late Oct** (4, 17 Nov)

HABITAT: Coniferous, mixed coniferous, and deciduous forest. Locally in oak, hackberry, and other tall trees in coastal woodlots or neighborhoods with mature plantings.

DISCUSSION: The neck contortions required to search among the highest branches may be rewarded with views of one of North America's flashiest songbirds. The word *orange* scarcely does justice to the Blackburnian's fiery hues, and sighting a fine male invariably draws gasps and sometimes wildly imaginative oaths from appreciative viewers. The species' song, rarely heard locally, is one of the higher-pitched paruline deliveries; birders without acute hearing may not hear it at all. Migrating females present an identification challenge; they are most likely to be confused with a Cerulean Warbler.

Never abundant, Blackburnian ranked 33rd during our censused fallouts. Seventy in a fallout on 30 Apr 1988 and an estimated 100 at High Island on 13 May

1976 are noteworthy. Blackburnian Warbler, like other forest nesters, is impacted by changes in its habitat. Logging or acid rain can deplete or kill the conifers in which it nests; acid rain also kills the lichens it incorporates into its nest cup and may impact its prey base. Some surveys have noted small-scale dips in its population; elsewhere, its breeding range has expanded. Locally, this species has become hard to find during fall migration.

YELLOW-THROATED WARBLER
Dendroica dominica albilora

Uncommon summer terminal migrant, rare winter lingerer or visitor

SPRING: (28 Feb; 1–3 Mar) **mid-Mar to early Oct**

FALL: (21, 25 Jul; 7 Aug; 14–15, 17 × 2 Oct); present many years on at least one CBC

HABITAT: Yellow-throated Warbler occurs in the uppermost canopy of coastal mottes, bottomland forest, cypress-lined bayous, and natural or introduced stands of live oaks, generally in association with Spanish moss.

DISCUSSION: Because this species breeds in East Texas and winters there in small numbers, it is difficult to present exact arrival and departure dates. Usually, birds are present in the coastal mottes by mid-Mar and can be common by the third week of the month. Spring migrants trickle through into early May. Southbound birds can be found in the coastal migrant traps as early as late July (i.e., 21 Jul 1996 and 25 Jul 2003) or early Aug. Most breeders and migrants have moved out by late Sep, and Oct sightings are rather uncommon.

Wintering individuals are likely to be encountered at well-vegetated locations such as Lake Jackson or Clute, or on Galveston Is., where tall shade trees planted at the beginning of the last century provide food and cover for many species of lingering passerines. The highest winter count appears to be five recorded during the 1979 Freeport CBC. So far, nearly all UTC breeders and migrants represent the white-browed subspecies *D. d. albilora*; *D. d. dominica* is a very rare coastal migrant (TOS 1995) but could appear on the UTC. Neither the TOS (1995) nor Lockwood and Freeman (2004) recognize Texas specimens of the NE Gulf race *D. d. stoddardi*.

GRACE'S WARBLER
Dendroica graciae

Accidental fall transient migrant
16 Sep 1987 High Island, GAL (D. Muschalek)

HABITAT: Grace's Warbler nests in montane coniferous forest and lowland pine savanna from the southwestern United States to Nicaragua and as close to the UTC as the Davis Mountains. Additional records are most likely to be detected in the UTC's coastal migrant traps.

DISCUSSION: Derek Muschalek described in detail a Grace's Warbler he observed 16 Sep 1987 at High Island. Given the species' immense breeding range, it seems likely that close scrutiny of all Yellow-throated Warblers will produce additional sightings of this similar species.

PINE WARBLER
Dendroica pinus pinus

Locally common resident

HABITAT: Pine trees in coniferous or mixed forest with either dense or open parklike understory, mainly eastern and northern parts of the UTC; occasionally at bird feeders with shelled sunflower seeds or suet.

DISCUSSION: Pine Warblers—at least their southern populations—are among the few nonmigratory warblers that nest north of Mexico. During the nesting season, their sweet trills may be heard from treetops in the remnant mixed or softwood forests that dot the UTC, including long established pine-clad neighborhoods in and around Houston. After nesting, these birds join roving bands of chickadees, titmice, kinglets, and Yellow-rumped Warblers, often away from dense stands of pines. While members of mixed flocks, Pine Warblers utilize lower levels of the forest than during the breeding season and are more likely to be seen close to the ground.

A pitfall for the unwary (CBC counters take note): the underparts of winter individuals may vary from bright canary yellow to nearly white, and we have seen them identified as Yellow-throated Vireos and a variety of other warbler species.

The Pine Warbler's trill may be confused with that of Chipping Sparrow or Dark-eyed Junco; the latter

is unlikely to be heard singing on the UTC. During recent years, breeding Pine Warblers have become more difficult to find locally, as pines succumb to bark beetles and storm damage or are cleared for suburban development. Nonetheless, this is one of our most frequently observed winter warblers, although the 183 individuals tallied during the 2000 Freeport CBC appears to be exceptional.

PRAIRIE WARBLER
Dendroica discolor discolor

Rare spring and uncommon fall transient migrant, rare winter lingerer

SPRING: (13, 15 × 2 Mar) **late Mar to late Apr** (25, 27, 29 May)

FALL: (19, 25, 26 × 2 Jul; 5 Aug) **early Aug to early Oct** (7, 11 Oct; 7 × 2 Nov)

HABITAT: Salt cedar, oleander, stands of reed and cane, occasionally oaks or pecans in the outer edges of coastal mottes.

DISCUSSION: During spring, Prairie Warbler delivers its ascending, high-pitched song from atop saplings in younger stages of pine plantation and regenerating cutover woodland. Nesting birds are not too hard to find just outside our area—for example, in the Big Thicket region north of Beaumont. Nonetheless, Prairies are very uncommon UTC migrants. The single most productive location for encountering them has been the isolated salt cedar clumps along the beach between High Island and Sabine Pass. Unfortunately, most coastal salt cedars have now been washed away during storms. Where these trees have been planted on Galveston Island, especially toward the west end at or near Indian Beach, one should look for Prairies. When (rarely) seen at one of the coastal woodlands, they are encountered at the extreme periphery of the stand, not inside the forest. The Freeport CBC has noted them on twelve of 48 counts with a high of six in 1970. Individuals occasionally overwinter; one returned for two consecutive winters (1998–99 and 1999–2000) at Brazos Bend SP, FOB, and another wintered at the Texas Medical Center (Houston) in 1998–99. Perhaps the most interesting local sighting involved a male singing in the West University section of Houston on the late date of 27 May 1993 (Eubanks).

The streaky yellowish breast of fall birds may suggest the even rarer Cape May Warbler, but an examination of the face pattern and noting the Prairie's distinctive tail bobbing should clarify identification.

PALM WARBLER
Dendroica palmarum

Locally common bi-seasonal transient migrant, uncommon winter terminal migrant

SPRING: (8–10 May; 13 June *D. p. palmarum*) **mid-Apr to early Oct**

FALL: (10, 14, 26 Sep)

HABITAT: Coastally in salt cedars and brushy margins of salt marsh, occasionally in willow thickets, rattlebox, and outer edge of light woodland; inland, usually in stands of salt cedar, huisache, and rattlebox.

DISCUSSION: Palm Warbler is quite habitat-specific and likely to be missed unless sought out. The remaining salt cedar clumps growing along the beach between High Island and Sabine Pass have consistently acted as a magnet for this species; 53 were recorded there on 10 Oct 1993. Wintering birds are generally quite dispersed in appropriate habitat; the Freeport CBC has detected them 45 of 48 years with a peak count of 46 in 1988.

Two subspecies of Palm Warbler visit the UTC. Nearly all the coastal sightings represent the pale western *D. p. palmarum*, most of which winter at various sites on the margin of the Caribbean and in the West Indies. A few of the brightly colored eastern *D. p. hypochrysea* have been observed, and some have been photographed. This subspecies winters primarily on the Gulf Coast from N Florida, where it inhabits pine woods (J. Stevenson data), to SE Louisiana, and rarely to Texas (Dunn and Garrett 1997). The status of *hypochrysea* is not documented in Texas (TOS 1995). Based on our observations, it is most likely to occur inland during winter.

Small but predictable numbers of Palms (mostly *palmarum*) overwinter in the dwindling stands of huisache in WAR, where they are members of an insectivore guild that includes Ash-throated Flycatcher, the eastern form of Bewick's Wren, Blue-gray Gnatcatcher, Ruby-crowned Kinglet, and Orange-crowned Warbler. During recent years, up to a half-dozen have wintered at Indian Beach, GAL (J. Stevenson).

BAY-BREASTED WARBLER
Dendroica castanea

Common to uncommon spring, occasional fall transient migrant, rare winter lingerer

SPRING: (8, 16–17 Apr) **late Apr to late May** (24, 28 May; 1 Jun)

FALL: (15 × 2, 18 × 2 Sep; 3 Oct) **late Sep to late Oct** (6, 13–14, 23 Nov)

HABITAT: Coastal mottes, mature residential plantings, parks.

DISCUSSION: Bay-breasted is one of the latest UTC spring migrants, often frustratingly difficult to find until the last week of Apr when they suddenly show up, although rarely in large numbers. They usually forage in the crowns of live oak and hackberry trees but occasionally feed in outer branches close to the ground. During serious fallouts, numbers of them may even congregate to forage mouselike in short grass. Prior to the twentieth century, Nehrling (1882) considered Bay-breasted one of the UTC's most common spring migrants. Apparently holding its own, it was the eighth most abundant species during our censused fallouts, representing just over 3 percent of the estimated total. During fall, Bay-breasteds are decidedly uncommon; the few we see generally associate with other warblers or flocks of Blue-gray Gnatcatchers. Winter records are rare, but there are four records from the Freeport CBC. The only Jan records are of one banded by M. Hoke at High Island (present 29 Dec 1973–15 Jan 1974) and another seen by Behrstock in WAR 11 Jan 1989.

BLACKPOLL WARBLER
Dendroica striata

Uncommon spring, rare fall transient migrant

SPRING: (9, 12, 15 × 2 Apr) **mid-Apr to mid-May** (27 May; 3, 16, 24 Jun)

FALL: (19, 27 Aug) **early Sep to late Oct** (8, 22 Oct; 21 Nov)

HABITAT: Coastal mottes and salt cedars; away from the coast, parks or neighborhoods with tall trees.

DISCUSSION: Blackpoll Warbler's spring migration route is primarily along the Florida peninsula and the extreme eastern Gulf of Mexico. Nonetheless, this warbler is more common on the UTC than Cape May

Warbler, another eastern scarcity, and at least a few Blackpolls can be counted on every year.

During spring, the attractive males are readily identifiable, but females might be confused with a female Cerulean or a dull female Blackburnian. Fall Blackpolls are infrequently recorded, and even in the East where they are common, birders lacking experience with them can easily confuse one with a Bay-breasted, Cape May, Blackburnian, Cerulean, or Yellow-rumped warbler. Typically, Blackpolls forage in the upper and lower outer branches of oak, pecan, hackberry, and other tall trees; however, they also occur deep within the coastal mottes, foraging in the lower shrubby strata, occasionally at ground level.

Dunn and Garrett (1997) do not recognize the 21 Dec 1980 Freeport CBC record, nor do they mention *any* late records from the lower 48 states. Their absolute scarcity is, in large part, a function of this warbler's southbound migration being concentrated along or seaward of the eastern seaboard of the United States and Canada. Thus it is quite possible that some of the fall records we have listed may represent misidentified birds.

CERULEAN WARBLER
Dendroica cerulea

Uncommon spring, rare fall migrant

SPRING: (19, 22, 31 × 2 Mar; 2 Apr) **early Apr to early May** (13 × 2, 15, 17 May)

FALL: (15, 22, 31 × 2 Aug) **late Aug to mid-Oct** (21, 22 × 2 Oct; 2, 4 Nov)

HABITAT: Bottomland riparian and upland forests. Occurs locally in coastal mottes, infrequently in mature plantings inland.

DISCUSSION: Since 1966, thousands of volunteer participants in the United States and Canada have censused 24.5-mile routes known as Breeding Bird Surveys. The tremendous amounts of data generated by these surveys (now more than 4,100 routes) constitute a powerful tool for assessing the health of bird populations. Based upon its small total population size and rapidly declining Breeding Bird Survey trends, Cerulean Warbler is considered one of the most threatened songbirds in the United States. Similarly, it is ranked as "extremely high priority" on the national watchlist of Partners in Flight (Rosenberg et al. 2000). On the UTC, it is generally present in small numbers, sometimes early in migration and other times late, and can be unusually difficult to find. Once individuals are located, inexperienced observers may misidentify or simply ignore the subtle female; although during spring there are few very similar birds that present opportunities for confusion.

Cerulean Warblers were encountered on 12 of 19 censused spring fallouts. Unlike other migrants that occurred in substantial numbers, only 57 individuals were recorded (0.001 percent of all fallout associates), relegating the species to the bottom third of all birds censused.

BLACK-AND-WHITE WARBLER
Mniotilta varia

Common spring and fall transient migrant, rare winter terminal migrant, extirpated resident

SPRING: (20, 25 Feb) **early Mar to late May** (23, 25 × 2, 26 May; 10 Jun)

FALL: (28 Jun; 7, 9–10 Jul) **early Aug to late Oct** (6–8, 21 Nov; all from migrant traps)

HABITAT: Trunks and larger branches of trees within coastal mottes, parks, and mature neighborhoods; migrants may be seen in salt cedars, willows, etc.

DISCUSSION: The nuthatchlike Black-and-white Warbler is a favorite of many birders, allowing long, satisfying views as it industriously examines fissures in tree bark for spiders, insects, eggs, and pupae. In the forests of East Texas, it continues to be a common breeding species. However, it vanished as a nesting bird on the UTC. Its populations declined and finally disappeared as local forests were subjected to increased logging and clearing for development. Apparently, this trend was well under way late in the nineteenth century when Nehrling (1882) wrote: "only few remaining to breed." The species is still a reasonably common migrant; previously, it ranked seventh in our fallout compilation.

Clearly many Black-and-whites are trans-Gulf migrants, but a significant portion of the population circumnavigates the Gulf, moving north- and southward along its western and eastern margins. Additionally, many birds travel well inland. Stevenson (1957) stated that migration along both sides of the Gulf is "just as important."

This species exhibits a prolonged spring migration. As later migrants head for the northern latitudes, East Texas birds are already well under way with nesting activities. The southward movement also stretches over several months. Thus this species may be present as individuals move through the UTC for the last six months of the year. Weeks notes that they have become so regular in winter that he now struggles with separating late winter from early spring records.

AMERICAN REDSTART
Setophaga ruticilla

Common bi-seasonal transient migrant, rare winter resident, rare or extirpated summer terminal migrant

SPRING: (27, 30 Mar; 2 Apr) **mid-April to mid-May** (5 × 2, 6, 18, 7–24 Jun)

FALL: (2 × 3, 3, 6 Aug) **mid-Sep to late Oct** (7, 10, 29 Nov; latest migrant trap records); also several CBC dates

HABITAT: Coastal mottes, open woodland, salt cedars, parks, and residential plantings.

DISCUSSION: Although appreciated by all birders, the male American Redstart's colorful plumage, loud sweet chip, and attention-grabbing acrobatic flight that flashes its striking pattern hold special appeal for birders not yet adept at ferreting out the dull thicket skulkers. Because of this bird's flashy pattern, aerial foraging behavior, and frequently fanned tail, birders visiting from other parts of the world quickly note its resemblance to many of the Old World flycatchers (subfamily Musicapinae). The bird's broad-based bill, elongate rictal bristles, and weak legs all suggest a New World flycatcher (Curson et al. 1994).

During spring, this well-known species—logo of the international Partners in Flight program—is an abundant trans-Gulf migrant. Locally, it is one of our most numerous spring migrants, ranking ninth in our censused fallouts. Other observers have also encountered prodigious numbers. On 3 May 1973, Ben Feltner and Victor Emanuel estimated 1,500 between High Island (GAL) and Sabine Pass (JEF) (AB 27:793).

Although less common during fall migration (when it may occur well inland), American Redstart often outnumbers other southbound warblers. Occasional birds linger into or through winter (i.e., 5 Dec 1954–20 Feb 1955 and 21 Dec 1986–28 Mar 1987).

Birds singing 29 May 1977 at Brazos Bend SP suggest breeding; indeed, the TOS checklist (1995) considers the species a "rare to uncommon summer resident . . . west to Ft. Bend Co." Perhaps the most interesting summer record is a male that spent 7–24 Jun 1998 at Sabine Woods, JEF. If this bird is not found in the migrant traps, it (and many other nesting warblers) may be found at Martin Dies Jr. State Park north of U.S. Highway 190 along the shores of Steinhagen Reservoir (Jasper/Tyler cos.). Small numbers of American Redstarts have nested there during recent years.

Migrants and breeders in East Texas represent the eastern *S. r. ruticilla*. Specimens of *S. r. tricolora*, ranging into the Pacific Northwest, have been taken in GAL (TOS 1995). Curson and colleagues (1994) suggest that the subspecific designations are invalid but agree that some western breeders move through the W Gulf.

PROTHONOTARY WARBLER
Protonotaria citrea

Common bi-seasonal transient migrant, locally uncommon summer terminal migrant, very rare winter lingerer

SPRING: (8, 15–17 Mar) **late Mar to late Sep**
FALL: (23, 26–27 Oct; 9 Nov)
HABITAT: Understory, wooded bayous, forested lake edge, ponds inside forest. During migration in interior of dense coastal mottes, also mature residential plantings. Occasionally ascends to the canopy to feed.

DISCUSSION: Prothonotary Warbler, a trans-Gulf migrant, winters in the Yucatán, many Caribbean islands, Central America, and northern South America. It begins arriving during mid- to late Mar along with Northern Parula and Swainson's and Yellow-throated warblers. Shortly thereafter, its slightly ascending *sweet, sweet, sweet* song mingles with the dawn chorus along local bayou margins and in relict bottomland forest. Migrants are readily seen during early to mid-Apr; fallout counts from 14 and 15 Apr 1989 yielded 45 and 30 individuals respectively. By the third week of Apr, they are decidedly scarce along the coast. On rare occasions, birds occur in the coastal migrant traps into May, such as one seen at Quintana, BRA, on 26 May. In fall, they begin departing by early

Aug; we note one High Island record on 19 Jul and another at Sabine Woods on 21 Jul. Winter records (some possibly only lingerers) include 1, 6, and 16 Jan, 2 Feb (twice), and 11 Feb.

Many birders agree that Prothonotary Warbler is one of our most beautiful nesting birds. Devoid of plumage complexities, it is simply attired with blue-gray wings and tail and a white vent; but its piercing black eye and long black bill are surrounded by a rich golden-yellow hood and breast. To its describer, this shade of yellow suggested the robes of the College of Prothonotaries Apostolic of the Roman Catholic Church, after which it was named (Gruson 1972).

Despite being flamboyant in hue, the species is particularly well concealed at the nest. Prothonotary Warbler is one of only two hole-nesting warblers in North America, and the only one occurring in the East. Typically, it nests in cavities in trees or stumps projecting from or adjacent to water. Holes excavated by Downy Woodpeckers and chickadees are often used as nest sites. In one study, nest holes averaged five feet above the ground or water. Artificial structures including nest boxes are utilized as well; these are occasionally near buildings (Scott et al. 1977). One pair observed by Behrstock in a noisy residential yard along Taylor Bayou, JEF, nested in the end of a pipe that formed the top of a child's swing set.

WORM-EATING WARBLER
Helmitheros vermivorus

Common spring, occasional fall transient migrant

SPRING: (13 × 2, 15 × 3, 16 Mar) **late Mar to early May** (8, 10, 22, 24 May)

FALL: (8, 12–13 Aug) **early Sep to mid-Oct** (18, 27, 29 × 2 Oct, 27 Dec)

HABITAT: Understory of coastal mottes, occasionally willow or salt cedar thickets; inland in light woodland, parks, or mature neighborhood plantings.

DISCUSSION: During spring migration, a dry buzz heard in the Virginia creeper, poison ivy, or wild grape vines that are so prevalent in the dark, nonmanicured understory of the UTC's remnant forests is likely to emanate from a Worm-eating Warbler. There, this large and subtly attractive warbler is often seen as it prospects for insects inside dead curled leaves. Indeed, Worm-eating Warbler is one of very few North American breeders that feed more than casually in

this manner, a behavior more typical of certain tropical forest antbirds and ovenbirds. Occasional individuals are seen foraging among fallen leaves, a trait the species shares with the Swainson's Warbler, another notably large-billed species. During migration, the Audubon sanctuaries at High Island as well as the TOS Sabine Woods property are excellent places to observe this species. Southerly nesting birds pass through the UTC during the earlier weeks of spring migration and, like Northern Parulas and Louisiana Waterthrushes, are already on their nesting grounds by the time the Bay-breasteds begin appearing at High Island. Observers who miss Worm-eating Warbler during early spring migration may encounter nesting birds at sites north and east of the UTC, including the Azalea Canyon Trail (Newton Co.) and the Big Creek Scenic Area (San Jacinto Co.). Although this species is still reasonably common, recent fallouts have not generated the several dozen to 70 individuals per day that we encountered in past years. Our latest recent record was observed at High Island on 27 Dec 2004 (B. and L. Feltner). There are at least two CBC reports (we have not listed those). We are not aware of any other well-documented winter records.

SWAINSON'S WARBLER
Limnothlypis swainsonii

Uncommon bi-seasonal transient, uncommon summer terminal migrant

SPRING: (24, 26, 29 Mar) **late Mar to mid-Apr** (22, 25, 28 Apr); spring dates include migrants; breeders are on the nesting grounds by early to mid-Apr

FALL: (14, 19, 21 Aug) **early Sep to late Sep** (30 Sep; 3, 7, 11 Oct)

WINTER: (17 Nov–28 Dec)

HABITAT: Frequently in coastal mottes during spring migration, but rare to absent there during fall. Breeds in moist to wet bottomland forest—often with palmetto in the understory—and along cypress-lined bayous. Historically, if not presently, nested in canebrakes.

DISCUSSION: Mouselike in behavior, subdued in coloration, and passing through the UTC early in the spring, most arriving Swainson's Warblers go undetected as they return from their wintering grounds in Middle America and the Caribbean. Each spring the High Island sanctuaries and Sabine Woods host a few. There, by scanning well ahead in the darkened understory, quiet and patient observers may find them foraging through leaf litter or hopping among ground-level vine tangles. If approached quietly, some migrants are surprisingly confiding. Although breeding just a short distance inland, migrants are unusually quiet; since 1980, Behrstock has noted only three singing along the coast. However, on the nesting grounds nearby, their loud, sweet, emphatic song boldly announces their presence: *ooo, ooo stepped in POO* (the last syllable often doubled and always reminiscent of the song of Hooded Warbler). Birders who miss Swainson's Warbler in the coastal migrant traps may want to check the bayous in the bottomland forests north of Beaumont and Taylor Bayou northeast of High Island. By the second or third week of Apr, nearly all birds are on the nesting grounds. Only infrequently are southbound birds recorded in the coastal mottes where lingerers have been noted into late fall. One of these lingerers was tracked by M. Hoke at High Island from 17 Nov to 28 Dec 1973.

OVENBIRD
Seiurus aurocapilla aurocapilla

Uncommon to common spring and uncommon fall transient migrant, rare winter terminal migrant

SPRING: (21 Feb; 2, 10, 21, 28 Mar) **early Apr to late May** (23–24, 26 May; 1 Jun)

FALL: (10–11, 14–15 Aug) **early Sep to mid-Oct** (25 Oct; 14, 22 Nov; 11 Dec)

HABITAT: On or near the ground in coastal mottes, extensive stands of salt cedars, often in parks or densely planted residential yards with tall ground cover or shrubby areas from which they occasionally stroll into the open.

DISCUSSION: Most sightings of Ovenbird occur deep within the coastal migrant traps, where they share the forest floor with Kentucky, Hooded, and Swainson's warblers and several species of thrushes. Because of its breast spots, compact form, and terrestrial habits, the Ovenbird may suggest to different observers a tiny rail, an antthrush, or a miniature Wood Thrush. Often, a glimpse of its peculiar rhythmic walking gait is enough to permit a quick identification. Once discovered, the bird generally flies some distance and then perches on a fairly low branch, to

survey the intruder (often while chipping loudly) before dropping to the ground. Waterthrushes exhibit much the same behavior. Observers who make the effort to follow the bird visually to its perch may be rewarded with leisurely views as it agitatedly paces back and forth.

Ovenbird was the 16th most commonly sighted bird during our censused fallouts. Migrants are frequently present in double-digit figures, and during several fallouts, 100 or more were tallied. For example, Jim Morgan and Eubanks estimated 280 on 30 Apr 1988. The recent decrease in this bird's numbers may be attributable to acid rain, as was noted in the discussion of Wood Thrush.

Typically, Ovenbirds are gone from coastal migrant traps by late Oct, but occasionally they remain. One individual wintered in a residential yard adjacent to Brazos Bend SP, FOB, for eight consecutive winters. Others such as the six tallied during the 1980 Freeport CBC may represent overwintering birds or merely lingerers.

NORTHERN WATERTHRUSH
Seiurus noveboracensis

Common spring and fall transient migrant, rare winter terminal migrant

SPRING: (5–6, 14–15 Mar) **early Apr to late May** (27–29 May)

FALL: (15, 23 Jul, 5 Aug) **mid-Aug to mid-Oct** (7, 20, 25 Oct); many Nov and Dec birds occur in the coastal migrant traps

HABITAT: Occurs on or just above the ground, generally at pools, along wooded drainage ditches, or similar poorly drained areas; also found in salt cedars, parks, and residential plantings. Migrants occur inland in well-vegetated residential areas, parks, and various types of woodland.

DISCUSSION: Because Northern Waterthrush nests as far north as Alaska and northern Canada, numbers of them pass through the UTC with some of the latest northbound Neotropical migrants. By late Apr, when this is frequently the only waterthrush present, warbler-crazed birders combing the UTC's woodlots encounter the species in good numbers. The streaky throat, browner legs, smaller bill, and buffy eye-line tapering behind the eye serve to separate most individuals from Louisiana Waterthrush.

Occasionally, Northern Waterthrush overwinters in small numbers. Birds were seen at four locations at San Bernard NWR, BRA, from 18 Dec 1998 to 28 March 1999 and were also noted from 13 Dec to 10 Jan at Quintana, BRA.

LOUISIANA WATERTHRUSH
Seiurus motacilla

Common spring, regular early fall bi-seasonal transient migrant, rare summer terminal migrant

SPRING: (5, 10, 23 Feb) **early Mar to late Apr** (6–7 May)

FALL: (7, 11, 15, 17) **late Jul to late Sep** (6, 17 Oct; 4 Nov; 8–20 Jan)

HABITAT: Nests just outside the region along clear, shallow streams in bottomland forest. In migration, at standing or flowing water, wooded drainage ditches, poorly drained ground in coastal mottes, parks, and dense residential plantings; rare inland away from breeding areas.

DISCUSSION: Louisiana Waterthrush is an early UTC migrant, peaking in Mar. It becomes decidedly scarce during the third week of Apr and is often absent by the last week of the month. Early Feb sightings may constitute very early migrants, as records from other areas of the state have occurred during this same window. A few birds nest just outside the region (i.e., Big Creek Scenic Area, San Jacinto Co.), and breeding within the UTC (CHA) is suspected. Returning fall birds are also very early; our limited records suggest a peak in late Jul and early Aug.

At Jesse H. Jones Park and Nature Center (HAS), a Louisiana Waterthrush was present from 8 to at least 20 Jan 2005. This individual was photographed, recorded, and banded. In nearby Washington Co., an overwintering Louisiana Waterthrush was banded as well (D. Vollert). Because of the species' extreme rarity during winter, and frequent confusion with Northern Waterthrush, such out-of-season individuals must be very carefully documented.

KENTUCKY WARBLER
Oporornis formosus

Fairly common bi-seasonal transient migrant, uncommon and decreasing summer terminal migrant, rare winter terminal migrant

SPRING: (20, 22–23 Mar) **migrants from late Mar to late Apr** (7 × 2, 9, 12 × 2 May)

FALL: (4–5, 7, 10 × 2 Aug) **migrants from mid-Aug to mid-Oct** (17, 20, 25 Oct; 2 Nov)

HABITAT: Migrants usually occur on the ground or within three to six feet of it in densely vegetated portions of coastal mottes, parks, and well-planted residential yards; breeding occurs inland in understory thickets of mixed woodland.

DISCUSSION: Although its loud chip is frequently heard in the migrant traps, UTC birders will be fortunate indeed to hear the Kentucky Warbler's sweet song. Today this delivery, sometimes deceptively like that of the Carolina Wren, is heard only where thickety forest understory remains. Populations have plummeted with the loss of habitat, a proliferation of feral cats, and tree farming practices that favor a manicured forest floor. During the late 1800s, Nehrling (1882) deemed Kentucky Warbler a common nesting bird, outnumbering the Common Yellowthroats near which it often nested. They were common: "in wet fields with patches of low bushes, and in the dense undergrowth near water ... Very abundant on Spring Creek, in the northern part of Harris County." Even then, they were known to be parasitized by Brown-headed Cowbirds. We are aware of at least five winter records, four of which were from Freeport CBCs.

CONNECTICUT WARBLER
Oporornis agilis

Rare spring and fall transient migrant
16 Sep 1978 High Is., GAL (TPRF 140) (AB 33:195; Morgan and Eubanks 1979)
10 Oct 1979 Bolivar Peninsula, GAL (TBRC 1989-76)
29 Sep 1992 Crosby, HAS (TBRC 1992-118) (AB 47:120)
6 Oct 1996 Galveston Island, GAL (TBRC 1996-166)
6 May 2000 Quintana, BRA (TBRC 2000-29)

HABITAT: Coastal thickets, inland in residential plantings.

DISCUSSION: During the roundtrip between their northern nesting territories and the wintering grounds in South American forests, most Connecticut Warblers travel through the West Indies, Florida, and the eastern United States. During spring, some make a trans-Gulf flight and continue northward via the

Mississippi River Valley (Curson et al. 1994). Neither passage provides much opportunity for an occurrence along the UTC, and the species remains one of our rarest strays. There are more than 50 undocumented sightings for the state but only eight accepted records, five of which are from the UTC. There were no occurrences during any of our monitored spring fallouts.

MOURNING WARBLER
Oporornis philadelphia

Occasional spring, uncommon fall transient migrant

SPRING: (22, 26, 27 Apr) **late Apr to mid-May** (23, 25, 30 May)

FALL: (12, 14, 18, 20 Aug) **early Sep to late Oct** (12, 18, 22 Oct)

HABITAT: Coastal mottes and their borders; inland in well-vegetated residential yards, parks, and light woodland.

DISCUSSION: Like Nashville Warbler, northbound Mournings are circum-Gulf not trans-Gulf migrants. Many return from Middle America on routes that take them far inland. They are uncommon spring visitors to the coastal migrant traps, but some days may produce several. We observed none during our censused spring fallouts. Curson et al. (1994) suggest that spring birds migrate northward along the Gulf Coast. However, our observations suggest that the species is more likely to be seen inland at well-vegetated locations such as in Bellaire, where numbers of individuals have been observed and banded. Migrants avoid the tall canopy, occurring from ground level to perhaps 10 feet up in low shrubs, small trees, or vines, both within the woods and at the edge. During fall migration, Mournings move southward along a broader front and are both more common and somewhat more likely to be observed along the coast.

MACGILLIVRAY'S WARBLER
Oporornis tolmiei monticola

Rare spring transient migrant, very rare fall migrant and rare winter terminal migrant

SPRING: (15–16, 20 Apr) **mid-Apr to early May** (3, 12 May)

FALL: (12 Sep; 21–27 Oct)

HABITAT: Coastally, in mottes, salt cedars, and residential plantings; rarely inland.

DISCUSSION: MacGillivray's Warbler, a common migrant through the Trans-Pecos region of West Texas, has been detected at least 13 times on the UTC. Of those, several were winter occurrences. One bird spent nearly two months during the winter of 1987– 88 in Clute (BRA), and another was seen on West Galveston Is. 21 Jan 1989. Most recently, a bird was present on West Galveston Is. 26 Oct 2002–Feb 2003 and was relocated 28–29 Feb 2004; suspicious chip notes suggest that it may have been present as early as Nov 2003. The only true fall migrants were individuals detected 12 Sep 1999 at San Bernard NWR, BRA, and 21–27 Oct 2003 at Sabine Woods, JEF. The balance of the records are from mid-Apr to late May.

Although the skulking habits of this species often preclude visual detection, its loud chip, recognizable with experience, should at least alert the observer to the presence of some worthwhile *Oporornis* warbler. Along the coast, where spring Mourning Warblers are very scarce, the possibility of a MacGillivray's (or even a Connecticut) cannot be overlooked, and all bold chips should be tracked down. Although Connecticut Warbler also walks, the MacGillivray's split white eye ring (appearing as opposing crescents above and below the pupil), long under-tail coverts, and walking (not hopping) mode of foraging help distinguish it from similar species.

COMMON YELLOWTHROAT
Geothlypis trichas

Common summer terminal migrant, abundant bi-seasonal transient migrant, common winter terminal migrant

HABITAT: Often in wet fields or emergent vegetation such as reed, cane, and willow growing around ponds and along waterways. Nehrling (1882) found several pairs along a ditch where: "the whole ground is covered with high broom-grass (*Andropogon macrurus*) with briar patches, thickets of water-oak, *Viburnum dentatum*, black haw (*V. pruneifolium*), etc." Coastally, common to abundant in both fresh and brackish marshes. During migration, individuals also concentrate in salt cedars along the beach and are widespread in ornamental and/or residential plantings, especially along the coast. Although the birds are generally seen near the ground, migrants commonly forage (and sing) in the upper branches of trees.

DISCUSSION: Along the UTC, four species of warblers overwinter in appreciable numbers: Pine, Orange-crowned, and Yellow-rumped "Myrtle" warblers and Common Yellowthroat. The last two are often numerically important during winter censuses (learn their chips). In the UTC's extensive coastal wetlands, few wintering species approach the density exhibited by Common Yellowthroat, aside from certain blackbirds. Curson et al. (1994) illustrate and describe 13 subspecies of Common Yellowthroat, and the TOS checklist (1995) discusses 10 recognized in Texas. The widespread *G. t. trichas,* breeding from northern Ontario and New Brunswick to northern and East Texas, is the locally nesting subspecies and is a common migrant and uncommon wintering bird along the UTC. The subspecies *brachydactylus* and *minnesoticola* have been taken along the UTC, and at least four others might occur. The various forms differ in the amount of brown on the back and flanks, fore crown coloration, bill size, and the extent of the black mask.

In the late 1800s, Common Yellowthroats were known hosts of Brown-headed Cowbird; the large numbers we see today suggest they are holding their own. The species ranked 20th in our censused spring fallouts (although we probably spent little time in habitat that favors them), but they are part of the UTC's avifauna the entire year.

HOODED WARBLER
Wilsonia citrina

Common bi-seasonal transient migrant, local summer terminal migrant, and rare winter lingerer

SPRING: (4, 6, 10–11 Mar) **mid-Mar to late Apr** (13–14, 18 May; all at migrant traps)

FALL: (3–4, 7 × 3, 7–8 Aug; all at migrant traps) **mid-Aug to late Oct** (24, 25, 28 Nov)

HABITAT: Coastally, in the interior of mottes and other isolated woodlands, less frequently in salt cedars or similar thickets; migrants occur inland in well-planted residential yards, parks, and various types of forest. Nesting birds favor remnant moist to wet forest, either mixed or largely coniferous but always with a dense understory. They can be numerous in older managed pine plantations with a thickety understory of yaupon, briar, and other low-growing plants.

DISCUSSION: For many local birders, the sight of a Hooded Warbler signifies the return of spring. Few birds anywhere can compete with the beauty of the male as it flits about investigating the sun-dappled forest floor. First, it is part of a shadow. Then it turns and is transformed into a living sunbeam. Just as suddenly, it is gone, its glowing form lingering for a moment in the mind's eye. Fortunately, there are still many opportunities to enjoy Hoodeds on the UTC; they are common migrants, ranking 12th in our censused fallouts.

This species is a common nester in the southeastern United States. Frequently large numbers of males appear along the coast during the last week of Mar. They concentrate deep within the woodlots, foraging in the lower stratum of the foliage, often on the ground. In the darkness among the fallen branches and vine tangles, the first clue to their presence may be a behavioral one—a tiny flash of white seen as a foraging bird slightly fans its tail. Frequently too, their presence is indicated by a rather loud and not especially sweet chip.

Although most Hoodeds leave by Oct, we note two recent winter records. A young male was seen 16 Jan 2003 on W Galveston Is., and an adult male was present 20 Jan 2002 at Sabine Woods, JEF. There are Freeport CBC reports from 1969 and 1970. Reports from the last week of Feb (JEF) may pertain to unusually early migrants or birds that wintered; however, even early migrants are not expected until the first week of Mar.

WILSON'S WARBLER
Wilsonia pusilla pusilla

Fairly common bi-seasonal transient migrant, uncommon winter terminal migrant

SPRING: (17, 19, 22 May; 11–12 Jun)
FALL: (12, 25–26, 30 Aug) **early Sep to mid-Apr**
HABITAT: Wilson's Warbler is found in coastal mottes and woodlands, willow or salt cedar thickets, open mixed woodland, and densely planted yards. Individuals utilize both the interior of woodlands and the denser edges, usually keeping to the lower stratum of vegetation.

DISCUSSION: Curson et al. (1994) suggest that some Wilson's Warblers are trans-Gulf migrants, while others follow the coast to and from their winter quarters in Middle America. Although they are typically silent, except for their chips, an occasional migrant sings vigorously; rarely, multiples may be heard.

The first fall migrants reach the coastal woodlands beginning in late Aug and continue through Oct, after which a small percentage of those birds may remain to overwinter. Occasionally they are numerous during winter; the Freeport CBC reports an average of 21 birds per count and a maximum of 107 in 1984.

Interestingly, adult males make up the vast majority of wintering Wilson's Warblers. They begin to disappear in early Mar and are decidedly hard to find after then. These warblers are much more common in Central Texas, where their overland migration is more pronounced.

CANADA WARBLER
Wilsonia canadensis

Uncommon spring, common fall transient migrant

SPRING: (13, 15–17 Apr) **mid-Apr to late May** (23, 25 May; 3 Jun)

FALL: (2, 4–5, 7 × 3, 8 × 2 Aug) **mid-Aug to mid-Oct** (12 × 3, 18 Oct; 7 Nov)

HABITAT: Coastally in mottes and salt cedar clumps; inland in parks and residential areas with tall shade and ornamental plantings.

DISCUSSION: With its crisply marked breast, uncluttered back and wings, pink legs, and bright yellow spectacles, the Canada Warbler rates among the most attractive of our spring migrants. Canadas visit the UTC during the later part of spring migration and are often difficult to find prior to the last week of Apr. By then, the first males are generally present (only very rarely singing) at High Island, Sabine Woods, or the migrant traps on Galveston Is. They may be encountered working the outer branches of tall shade trees or deep inside the woods foraging in viney thickets a few feet above the ground. Although Canadas are rarely present in significant numbers, on 14 May 1981 Jim Morgan and Behrstock tallied 115 among the

day's estimated 1,134 migrants censused between Sabine Pass and High Island.

Northbound Canadas exhibit an unusual swing to the western Gulf and are infrequently present in the migrant traps of coastal Louisiana, not more than an hour's drive east of the UTC. The bulk of their spring passage is directed inland via E Mexico (but not the Yucatán Peninsula, from which trans-Gulf migrants usually depart) through the extreme western Gulf and South Texas coast (Dunn and Garrett 1997).

During fall, the species' southbound migration shifts eastward, and the birds occur more frequently in Florida and states bordering the central Gulf. Fall birds appear beginning in Aug; they are usually done migrating by mid-Oct. There is one winter report, a bird lingering in Houston from 22 Nov to 16 Dec 1950.

PAINTED REDSTART
Myioborus pictus

Very rare spring transient migrant or vagrant
19 Apr 1988 Sugarland, FOB (photographed)
30 Apr 1960 Galveston Island, GAL
5–11 May 1973 High Island, GAL
15 May 1981 High Island, GAL
23 Dec 2002–14 Mar 2003 Richmond, FOB (photographed)
returning 7 Dec 2003

SPRING: (19 Apr–15 May)
WINTER: (7 Dec–14 Mar)
HABITAT: Coastal mottes, residential plantings.
DISCUSSION: The red, black, and white Painted Redstart is one of North America's most striking wood warblers. Its loud chip, sweet song, flirty tail, and propensity to investigate pishing noises all render it easy to see. Unfortunately, it nests no closer than the mountains of the Trans-Pecos region of West Texas. We note five records of this species, including once inland at Sugarland, twice at High Island, and once at Galveston. Of particular interest, an adult discovered in Richmond, FOB, on 23 Dec 2002 by Wendy Hale-Erlich wintered through 14 Mar 2003. A 7 Dec 2003 record is presumed to have been this same bird. While present, it gleaned insects from trees in a residential neighborhood.

YELLOW-BREASTED CHAT
Icteria virens virens

Formerly a common summer terminal migrant, now much reduced; common bi-seasonal transient migrant, rare terminal winter migrant

SPRING: (1–2, 5 Apr) **mid-Apr to late May** (10–11, 25 May)

FALL: (7, 13, 15–16 Aug) **late Aug to early Oct** (20–22 Oct); both spring and fall records represent coastal migrant trap birds

HABITAT: Of the Yellow-breasted Chat, Nehrling (1882) stated: "Its most favorable resorts are brier-patches in fields, thickets on the edge of woods, myrtle-holly thickets overgrown with tangled *Smilax laurifolia,* and similar localities. Nest in the interior of thickets near the ground; it has some resemblance to the Catbird's, and is built of nearly the same material." Mixed pine woodlands with yaupon holly in the understory are utilized nearby.

DISCUSSION: For months, a male Yellow-breasted Chat may sing through the evening hours, frequently delivering its thrasherlike chorus in flight or performing from the top of a snag or tall shrub, where it is readily observed. Such behavior might lead one to suspect that the chat is a canopy dweller. It is actually a denizen of the thickest understory, where individuals find fruit and insect prey and where the females nest.

Migrants return in early Apr; they are still present into early May. Yellow-breasted Chats breed in scrubby areas of the UTC, including less than a mile from the Gulf (i.e., San Bernard NWR). Fall birds return in mid-Aug, and some linger until mid-Oct. A few likely winter each year, resulting in many Jan and Feb records. The Freeport CBC recorded chats on only seven of 48 counts, but during winter, the species tends to be found more often at inland sites. The nearby Mad Island CBC (Matagorda Co.) has detected one or two (exceptionally five) each year.

No specimen evidence indicates that the richly colored race *auricollis* of West Texas migrates through our area (TOS 1995). However, Curson et al. (1994) suggest that during their southbound migration, most North American breeders follow the Gulf Coast instead of making a trans-Gulf crossing. Thus, intensely golden-yellow migrants that are occasionally seen on the UTC could represent the western form.

Yellow-breasted Chat is built like a tanager, sings like a thrasher, and has an aerial display that suggests a Bobolink. Indeed, ornithologists have argued for more than 40 years against classifying this bird as a New World wood-warbler. Recent analysis of the chat's mitochondrial and nuclear DNA indicates that it is not a wood-warbler and appears to be most closely related to the orioles, blackbirds, and other members of the family Icteridae (Lovette and Bermingham 2002).

Tanagers

Among the world's most beautiful birds, the 260 or so tanagers stand out, their brilliant hues rivaling those of parrots, hummingbirds, and birds-of-paradise. Fruit and insect eaters, tanagers are confined to the New World and are most numerous in mountainous regions of the tropics. Their species diversity is similar to that of the doves, hummingbirds, and flycatchers, tropical families well represented in the United States. Perhaps then, it is curious that only six tanagers occur north of Mexico—one a very rare breeder, another a vagrant. Attesting to their tropical origin, most migrate southward each winter and only a few hardy strays are detected on CBCs.

Identifying the UTC's four tanagers is straightforward, with a little practice. Their thick bills, shorter tails, and chunkier proportions distinguish them from orioles. Of the four species recorded locally, Hepatic Tanager has been noted only once. Learn the male's liver-red plumage and the dark bill and cheeks of both sexes. The wing bars present in both males and females separate the locally uncommon Western Tanager from the other three UTC possibilities; orange-faced males are distinctive, and note the female's yellow head and gray wings and mantle. Summer and Scarlet tanagers are common migrants along the coast, especially in fruiting mulberry trees, and

Summer Tanagers nest locally where suitable woodlands still exist. Males pose little problem in identification; note that either species may exhibit confusing patches of yellow or orange. The female Scarlet has a small bill, dull green back, and pale yellow underparts. Female Summers are a distinctive mustard brown and have a conspicuously large bill. Birders profit from learning the distinctive call notes of all four species.

HEPATIC TANAGER
Piranga flava

Accidental winter visitor
19 Dec 1999 Freeport CBC, BRA

HABITAT: Northern populations nest in conifer forests in the SW United States east to W Texas and NE Mexico and south to Nicaragua. They winter from northern Mexico (including lowlands) southward through the balance of the breeding range and casually in California and Arizona (A.O.U. 1998).

DISCUSSION: There are at least four UTC reports of Hepatic Tanager. However, the only satisfactorily documented record is of a female or immature discovered 19 Dec 1999 by Weeks and Ron Braun during the Freeport CBC. The bird was studied and videotaped at close range for 30 minutes as it picked large insects from an old squirrel nest. The dark bill and gray mask and flanks were noted. Additionally, both observers heard the bird give its almost blackbirdlike *chuck* call notes as it flew off.

SUMMER TANAGER
Piranga rubra rubra

Common bi-seasonal transient migrant, common summer terminal migrant, rare winter terminal migrant

SPRING: (8, 28–30 Mar) **late Mar to mid-May** (22, 28 May; 12 Jun; all migrant trap birds)

FALL: (7, 29 Aug; 4 Sep; all migrant trap birds) **mid-Sep to mid-Oct** (3 Nov)

HABITAT: Migrants occur in the canopy of coastal and interior woodlands, parks, and older neighborhoods; nests in mixed pine and hardwood forest.

DISCUSSION: Summer Tanager is a common migrant and decreasingly common breeder in the UTC's more mature woodlands. It returns in early Apr,

occurring in the migrant traps into May. Migrants appear again in Sep and are found regularly into early Oct.

Rarely, Summer Tanagers linger through the winter; we are aware of records from Dec, Jan, and Feb. The winter of 2000–2001 was exceptional for the number of wintering Summer Tanagers. That year, the Freeport CBC counted an amazing six individuals and others were sighted elsewhere on the UTC during Jan, Feb, and Mar. Over the last three years, a Summer Tanager has taken winter residence at Russ Pitman Park in Bellaire (HAS), where it feeds extensively at bee hives.

SCARLET TANAGER
Piranga olivacea

Common spring, uncommon fall transient migrant, rare winter lingerer

SPRING: (6, 16, 20 Mar) **early Apr to late May** (25–26, 28–29, 31 May; 4, 22 Jun)

FALL: (4, 6, Aug) **early Sep to late Oct** (26 Oct; 2, 3, 6–12 Nov)

HABITAT: Nests as close as Oklahoma and Arkansas in deciduous forest, especially where oaks are prevalent. Not a Texas nester, but may have bred in the NE portion of the state. Locally, most often observed in the coastal migrant traps, especially those with fruiting red mulberry trees; at inland sites, usually noted in mature residential plantings.

DISCUSSION: Few sights make a birder as glad to be alive as the appearance of the spring's first male Scarlet Tanager. Like many of its cousins in Latin America, it is simply and tastefully adorned in rich red and black. Juxtaposed against a spray of fresh mulberry or hackberry leaves, it has few rivals in the bird world. Common locally, Scarlet Tanager was the 13th most abundant species during our censused fallouts.

Female Scarlets may be distinguished by their brighter greenish yellow underparts, more olive upper parts, and smaller bills. In common with a number of other passerines, first-year male Scarlets may be recognized by their brown, not black, primaries.

A few late migrants have lingered into Dec (Mike Hoke observed one at High Island on 15 Dec 1973) and have been noted on local CBCs. Two Feb records and the early spring dates listed suggest that the species occasionally overwinters.

WESTERN TANAGER
Piranga ludoviciana

Rare bi-seasonal transient migrant, very rare winter terminal migrant or visitor

SPRING: (29 Mar; 8, 10, 14 Apr; all migrant trap birds) **early Apr to early May** (7–8, 9 × 2, 12, 27 May; 3 Jun)

FALL: (22–23 Aug; 10 Sep) **early Sep to early Nov** (26 Oct; 9–10, 25–28 Nov; all migrant trap birds)

HABITAT: Coastally in mottes and isolated clumps of trees, frequently in fruiting red mulberry; inland (rarely) in residential yards with large trees and ornamental plantings.

DISCUSSION: Although rare, Western Tanager comes close to being an annual visitor to the UTC. A splendid male popping up at High Island—usually in a mulberry tree already full of Catbirds, Scarlet and Summer tanagers, Rose-breasted Grosbeaks, and Indigo Buntings—generally results in pandemonium among delighted birders. Females cause less of a stir and are readily misidentified as orioles. Conversely, we have seen a number of orioles misidentified as female Western Tanagers.

This species occurs most frequently along the coast and only occasionally inland. Most sightings are in spring, but birds have been sighted in the fall, and we are aware of several winter records. Thus this species may occur throughout its nonbreeding season.

Cardinals, Sparrows, and Allies

Those who began birding long ago learned bird songs from vinyl records, wrote in little notebooks, and bragged of seeing the Red Crossbill and three kinds of juncos. Now, our minidisk players hold an entire continent's bird songs, we record the day's sightings on palm-held computers, and we brag instead of seeing a junco and three kinds of red crossbills.

Mitochondrial DNA analysis and DNA-DNA hybridization studies have changed the face of avian taxonomy, rearranging our field guides to reflect a newer molecular view of bird relationships. Our present understanding stems largely from work done during the 1970s and 1980s when Charles Sibley, Jon Ahlquist, and other "gel jockeys" began using electrical current to sort out bands of egg white proteins.

Prior to this upheaval, bird guides featured a large section at the back called Fringillidae. It encompassed the cardinal-like birds, towhees, sparrows, buntings, juncos, longspurs, grosbeaks, Dickcissel, and birds like goldfinches, Purple Finch, and redpolls. Almost any bird with a thick, seed-crushing bill fell into that convenient category, and everyone knew what "winter finches" were.

Evidence published in the 1980s forced a division of the old family Fringillidae. The A.O.U. (1998) favors a separation that produces three families: Emberizidae, some of which may be more closely related to tanagers; Cardinalidae; and the remaining

Fringillidae, now including the Hawaiian Honeycreepers and their kin. Under the A.O.U. determination the family Emberizidae contains nearly all the birds discussed in this section. However, other authors include most of them in the Cardinalidae, a treatment found in David Sibley's *The Sibley Guide to Birds* (2000). Our discussion of the few remaining fringillids is placed after the blackbirds and orioles.

These changes are mentioned to encourage birders to keep at least one current field guide at hand. To rely on a familiar copy of *Birds of North America* (Robbins et al. 1966) is to do oneself a disservice by ignoring all that scientists are learning about bird relationships. Using an outdated guide also causes problems when following a checklist or conversing with the new generation of bird enthusiasts.

Here, we discuss 44 species variously considered emberizids and cardinalids—one of the largest groups of birds on the UTC. Perhaps seven of the species nest locally; until recently, several more did. Such numbers are indicative of the northern or western affinities of the group (only Blue Bunting is a visitor from the tropics) as well as of the UTC's importance in attracting and nourishing a large assemblage of winter birds that inhabit other parts of North America. Among them are some of our best known species (Savannah Sparrow, Northern Cardinal), our most attractive birds (Painted Bunting, Rose-breasted Grosbeak), and our least frequently observed species

(Henslow's and Black-throated sparrows, Chestnut-collared and Smith's longspurs).

During winter, the majority of these birds live on or close to the ground, where species such as Grasshopper Sparrow and the four longspurs are well camouflaged by their dead-grass browns and tans. Only a few, including Rose-breasted and Black-headed grosbeaks, are decidedly arboreal. Wintering sparrows are often encountered in mixed flocks, and the cautious birder who diagnoses every bird is rewarded with the occasional rarity. For prolonged studies, providing seed attracts a few of these species (as well as other seed-eating birds) into view; red mulberry trees are magnets for some of the more colorful migrants.

We begin with the towhees—a group of fairly large thicket dwellers with loud calls and lots of field marks. Two have received recent taxonomic scrutiny; all three may be encountered during a successful winter day afield.

Next, we consider 25 species of sparrows, which are almost as intimidating to birders as the winter plumage shorebirds. Few novices plunge right into either group, although a handful do embrace the challenge. The UTC has earned a reputation as an excellent place to study sparrows and their relatives, 15 or more of which may be encountered in a day. Several local clubs offer winter workshops designed to help birders conquer the identification of these often confusing birds (see appendix 1).

A successful day of sparrow finding can be exhilarating and relies on visiting a variety of habitats. The objects of pursuit inhabit weedy fields, grazed pastures, tangled briar thickets, brushy hedgerows, mucky coastal cordgrass flats, and the understory of pine and oak woodlands. New birders may find the activity bewildering; sizes and colors vary greatly, and field guide illustrations may perplex rather than help. Texas naturalist Gene Blacklock teaches that virtually any sparrow can be identified with a good look at its head. Having some knowledge of the species' chip notes and habitat can also ease identification.

The last 16 species include easily identified favorites such as Northern Cardinal and Painted Bunting, but they also include a number of identification challenges—the four longspurs, the grosbeak females, and several buntings with confusing immatures and females. Many of these birds are locally rare; time spent studying field guides can provide useful positioning before one is confronted with an unfamiliar bird.

GREEN-TAILED TOWHEE
Pipilo chlorurus

Rare and irregular winter terminal migrant

WINTER: (8, 21 Oct; 5 Nov) **late Oct to mid-Feb** (14, 25 Feb; 28 Apr)

HABITAT: Coastally and inland in the understory of salt cedar, oleander and baccharis thickets, occasionally residential plantings.

DISCUSSION: Green-tailed Towhee is a decidedly rare bird on the UTC; indeed, most local birders have not seen one. Remarkably few records have made it into our database. We are aware of about eight inland UTC records, including recent sightings at Brazos Bend SP. One or two inland birds are known to have wintered. We know of several more sightings to the west or southwest (Attwater NWR and Victoria), where the species is probably more common during winter in brushy habitats. The few coastal records include wintering birds at brushy sites such as Old House (near Galveston Is. SP) and San Bernard NWR, BRA.

SPOTTED TOWHEE
Pipilo maculatus

Uncommon winter terminal migrant

WINTER: (22, 28 Oct) **late Oct to early Apr** (15 Apr); see following species account for more extreme dates

HABITAT: Most predictably in the western portions of the region, frequenting old hedgerows and thickets of McCartney rose, yaupon holly, possum haw holly, and similar dense shrubs or low trees.

DISCUSSION: Spotted Towhee, the western counterpart of Eastern Towhee, is an uncommon visitor to the UTC, where two or three of its forms may occur (TOS 1995; P. DeBenedictis, pers. comm.). In west HAS or WAR, an individual will occasionally respond to pishing or a screech-owl imitation, popping up alongside such species as Fox, Song, White-crowned, and Harris's sparrows.

EASTERN TOWHEE
Pipilo erythrophthalmus

Rare winter terminal migrant, formerly bred

WINTER: (19, 23 Oct) **early Nov to early Apr** (27 Apr, 9 May)

HABITAT: Woodland edge, thickets.

DISCUSSION: Now little more than a winter curiosity, Eastern Towhee, formerly Rufous-sided Towhee, once bred in woods along Spring Creek (HAS) and presumably elsewhere in the region. A bird of understory thickets, it declined in population with habitat loss, complicated by insecticides, cats, and parasitism by Brown-headed Cowbirds (paralleling declines of Wood Thrush, Yellow-breasted Chat, and Kentucky Warbler). The Freeport CBC found Rufous-sided Towhee, now split into Spotted and Eastern, on 40 of 48 counts, with a high of 28 in 1984. Other extreme dates attributed to this species pair include 14 Sep 1947, 7 Oct 1972, and 4 May 1947; some of these older dates could represent sightings of resident Eastern Towhees.

CASSIN'S SPARROW
Aimophila cassinii

Very rare winter terminal migrant; previously bred

HABITAT: Prairies, grassy openings in agricultural land, high desert grasslands with scattered brush.

DISCUSSION: Nehrling (1882) believed this species to be a common summer resident in open grassy prairies around Houston. Presently it continues to breed in counties near the UTC, where recent sightings include 24 Apr 1988, Matagorda Co. (R. Uzar); 8–24 Jun 1988, Colorado Co. (M. Crane); and 27 May 1989, Calhoun Co. (R. Uzar). Our only recent records for the UTC are one bird seen by Tony Gallucci on 1 Jan 1986 during the Cypress Creek CBC (WAR) and an undoubtedly disoriented migrant found and photographed 3 Apr 1998 by Weeks and Charles Hill as it perched on a metal crossbar at the tip of the Quintana jetty (BRA). Although we cannot verify Nehrling's sightings, it is worth recalling that during the later part of the nineteenth century, much of the UTC was still undisturbed prairie not yet ravaged by agriculture or covered by a mantle of Chinese tallow trees. As late as 1914, Simmons commented that once he hiked beyond the wooded margin of Houston's Buffalo Bayou, he was confronted with "flat, uncultivated prairie, sprinkled with ponds or grassy marshes."

BACHMAN'S SPARROW
Aimophila aestivalis illinoensis

Extirpated resident, presumably rare winter terminal migrant or wanderer

SUMMER (FORMERLY): (5 Apr to 27 Aug)
WINTER: (24 Nov to 13 Feb; 9 Mar)
HABITAT: Breeds in fire-adapted, open pine woods with a sparsely vegetated understory of grasses and low shrubs. During winter, may move into more open habitat, such as brushy fields.

DISCUSSION: Bachman's Sparrow, formerly Pinewoods Sparrow, is an unusual endemic of southeastern North America. One of our few forest sparrows, it possesses both a beautiful, varied song, and an unusually patterned plumage graced with purple mantle streaks.

Unfortunately, this species no longer nests locally and winters only rarely. Several factors accounted for its disappearance. Most of the UTC's outlying fingers of eastern softwood forest were logged or cleared for commercial development. Later, much of the remainder was fragmented by residential developments that brought in insecticides and cats and encouraged cowbirds. Fire suppression in the remaining forest allowed formation of a hardwood understory, suitable neither for this species nor for the Red-cockaded Woodpecker, a frequent neighbor in fire-adapted pines.

Apr and May records from the early 1940s to 1960, and during the early 1970s, suggest that the last UTC breeders persisted in woods near Sheldon Reservoir (HAS), and perhaps near the junction of FM 562 and FM 1985 (CHA), where Paul Nimmons found two singing on 22 Jul 1972. During the past 60 years, only eight winter records were reported (HAS, CHA), suggesting that birds are very difficult to locate once they stop singing and that habitat they previously utilized may no longer be suitable. Very rarely, a wintering individual is seen in woodland, woodland edge, or a brushy field. The last UTC report was 26 Dec 1988–14 Jan 1989 in W HAS.

RUFOUS-CROWNED SPARROW
Aimophila ruficeps eremoeca

Accidental fall visitor
9 Sep 1950 Cove, CHA
15 Sep 1979 Houston, HAS

HABITAT: Wide-ranging, inhabiting dry, rocky slopes with grasses, cactus, or low shrubs, from N California to S Mexico.

DISCUSSION: The closest breeding populations of this western sparrow are near Austin and San Antonio on the eastern edge of the Edward's Plateau (TOS 1995). The soggy and largely slope-free UTC offers few attractions for the species, and not surprisingly, we have but two records: 9 Sep 1950 at Cove and 15 Sep 1979 at White Oak Bayou in Houston. Additionally, we are aware of a 21 Dec 1982 CBC record just west of the UTC at Attwater NWR.

AMERICAN TREE SPARROW
Spizella arborea

Accidental winter visitor
17 Dec 2001 Lake Jackson, BRA

HABITAT: Weedy fields, brushy edges.
DISCUSSION: American Tree Sparrow winters in the Texas Panhandle but is rarely noted farther south. The only local report of this northern species is one seen 17 Dec 2001 on the Freeport CBC. Written details failed to note the bill coloration; however, another American Tree Sparrow was reported the same day at San Antonio, lending credibility to the Freeport record.

CHIPPING SPARROW
Spizella passerina passerina

Scarce resident, common winter terminal migrant

WINTER: (27 Aug; 2–3, 3, 8 Sep) **mid-Oct to mid-Apr** (10, 15–16 May; 31 May–1 June)
HABITAT: Many woodland types, including coniferous forests and their borders, pine and pine-oak,

open woods, and parks (A.O.U. 1998). In Texas, breeds from the Edwards Plateau westward throughout the Trans-Pecos, and in forests in the far eastern part of the state. Not known to nest on the UTC, but may have done so in the past.

DISCUSSION: Audubon failed to find the "Chipping Bunting" in Texas, but he knew it well from his travels. He characterized it as one of the most common and widespread birds in the United States, nesting in orchards and gardens as well as in evergreen trees and shrubs, where, in the south, it raises two broods.

By late Aug or early Sep, Chipping Sparrows—including confusing immatures with streaked breasts—begin drifting into the UTC from nesting grounds to the north or east. Wintering flocks are a common sight; watch for them along woodland borders, in open pine woods, stands of live oaks, and mature residential plantings.

Late May and Jun records suggest the possibility of a breeding population, and indeed there is plenty of suitable nesting habitat on the UTC. These birds usually feed on the ground, often in the company of several other species of sparrows. Their rather dry trill may be a source of confusion, as it suggests that of other birds with which it may occur, including Dark-eyed Junco and Pine Warbler. Of the three subspecies found in Texas, *S. p. passerina* breeds in the state's eastern forests (TOS 1995). Chipping Sparrow can be frustratingly similar in appearance to both Clay-colored and Brewer's sparrows, and a combination of field marks should be used to diagnose any out-of-place individual.

CLAY-COLORED SPARROW
Spizella pallida

Uncommon to rare bi-seasonal transient migrant and winter lingerer

WINTER: (29 Aug; 4, 17, 23, 26 Sep) **mid-Oct to mid-Apr** (2–3, 9 May; 7 Jun)
HABITAT: Occurs at edges of coastal thickets and marsh, salt cedars, and densely planted yards; rather sparse inland, where it may be more common during winter.

DISCUSSION: Nehrling (1882) considered Clay-colored Sparrow "abundant in winter near thickets and in fields with brier-patches." Although this sparrow is a common migrant in the Hill Country and West Texas, regular in fall on the barrier islands, and still abundant on its Mexican wintering grounds, annual records for the UTC appear to be on the wane. This species is now a rarity; spring and fall migrants are recorded infrequently, and early winter may be the best time to seek them. However, it appears that the number of these birds, perhaps merely lingerers, diminishes after the CBCs. Christmas Counts at Attwater NWR have generated the most records close to the UTC; as many as 26 have been seen during recent counts. The highest tally on a UTC CBC was eight at Freeport in 2000; this marked one of just 11 times they had been seen during 48 counts.

BREWER'S SPARROW
Spizella breweri

Very rare fall vagrant
9–15 Oct 1950 Cove, CHA
10 Oct 1980 Crystal Beach, GAL

HABITAT: Grassland, grass with scattered brush.
DISCUSSION: The UTC has but two records of this western *Spizella*. Arlie McKay found one at Cove that remained from 9 to 15 Oct 1950. Ben Feltner found another at Crystal Beach on 10 Oct 1980. In winter, this species occurs regularly in West Texas. Recently it has been present along the coast as close as Indianola, Calhoun Co. We do not know which subspecies occurs in East Texas. Observers are cautioned to note the extreme similarity between this species and fall Chipping Sparrows.

FIELD SPARROW
Spizella pusilla pusilla

Common winter terminal migrant

WINTER: (25, 27 Sep) **late Oct to early Mar** (9, 19 Apr; 13 May)
HABITAT: Thickets including huisache, hollies, and shrubby oaks, old fence rows, woodland edge.
DISCUSSION: Although its common name evokes a bird sitting on a barbed wire fence surrounded by wide-open spaces, a wintering Field Sparrow is more likely to be seen perched atop an oak or yaupon among Chipping Sparrows and Yellow-rumped

Warblers. Field Sparrows nest as close as Goliad Co. but are only winter visitors to the UTC. The number wintering on the UTC varies greatly from year to year. The Freeport CBC averages 20 per year; a high of 130 occurred in 2000.

VESPER SPARROW
Pooecetes gramineus gramineus

Common winter terminal migrant

WINTER: (24, 27 Sep) **mid-Oct to mid-Apr** (30 Apr; 2, 6 May)
HABITAT: Harvested or fallow fields, prairie, road edge, and similar open land, occasionally around hedgerows, thickets, or woodland edge; avoids developed areas.
DISCUSSION: Never as abundant as the Savannah Sparrow, with which it frequently occurs, Vesper Sparrow is a readily encountered but not always identified winter visitor. Inland agricultural areas such as west HAS and WAR are good sites to search for Vespers; watch for them on fence wires among flocks of Savannah Sparrows. Vesper shares the Savannah's pink legs, dark cheek patch, and streaked breast. On perched individuals, note the white eye-ring and pale lower border to the cheek patch. When seen well, some winter birds show chestnut lesser wing coverts. In flight, pipitlike white outer tail feathers are visible. Vespers are less common immediately along the coast. Nevertheless, 186 were seen on the 1989 Freeport CBC.

LARK SPARROW
Chondestes grammacus grammacus

Uncommon winter terminal migrant, formerly bred, possibly still doing so

FALL: (7, 15, 19 Aug) **mid-Aug to late Oct** (5, 7, 13 Nov); both fall and spring dates represent birds seen in coastal migrant traps, largely from BRA.
SPRING: (19 Mar; 4–5 Apr) **early Apr to late Apr** (9–10, 24 May)
HABITAT: Prairies near woods (Nehrling 1882).
DISCUSSION: During the latter part of the nineteenth century, Nehrling (1882) deemed this boldly patterned bird the commonest sparrow of the region.

Between May and Jul, two or three broods were raised. The usual nest site was a Spanish moss–covered oak branch at the edge of a woodland. However, ground sites in cotton fields, mulberry trees in gardens, and the corners of rail fences were also utilized. Simmons (1915) noted the nesting of this species "six miles south of Houston" as late as 1914. The last 60 years have yielded only a handful of nesting records, although several Jun to Aug sightings suggest that a small and dispersed breeding population may still exist. Fred Collins and others made the most recent summer sighting on 11 Aug 2000 at Warren Lake Ranch, HAS.

Occasionally the species occurs in large numbers near the UTC; for example, 224 were tallied during the 1983 Attwater CBC. The eastern subspecies *C. g. grammacus* formerly nested south to FOB (TOS 1995).

Currently, this sparrow is considered an occasional migrant with only about 10 noted per year. The only recent large count was 50 seen 8 Apr 1998 at San Bernard NWR. Most are found during spring and fall migration; very few, if any, remain to be detected on local CBCs. Historically, a small number wintered on Galveston Is., but the known locations are rapidly being developed, and there are only a few recent winter occurrences.

BLACK-THROATED SPARROW
Amphispiza bilineata bilineata

Accidental terminal migrant and spring visitor
18 Apr 1965 High Island, GAL
7 Feb 1982 W HAS
8 Nov 1997 Anahuac NWR, CHA

HABITAT: Dry brushy or desert habitats in the Rio Grande Valley, West and Central Texas.

DISCUSSION: Although adults of this delightful bird are well marked with a black bib and boldly striped face, first-year birds with streaked breast and browner body plumage are liable to present identification problems.

Black-throated Sparrow has been detected three times on the UTC. John and Gloria Tveten found the first on 18 Apr 1965 at High Island. Bob Honig located one 7 Feb 1982 in W HAS, and most recently, Paul Sharp observed one on 8 Nov 1997 at Anahuac NWR. This species was also found just west of the UTC on 30 Mar 1980 at Attwater NWR, COL.

LARK BUNTING
Calamospiza melanocorys

Rare bi-seasonal transient migrant, rare winter terminal migrant

FALL: (20 Jul; 7, 29 Sep) to SPRING: (16, 19, 24 Apr)
HABITAT: Prairies, both inland and coastal, weedy fallow fields, dry harvested rice paddies.

DISCUSSION: Prior to the beginning of the twentieth century, Nehrling (1882) considered Lark Bunting "abundant in winter on the prairie." Subsequently, development made much of its habitat unsuitable, and the wintering population withdrew toward the Panhandle. Now, it is only infrequently sighted.

Recent occurrences have involved minor invasions, generally in the agricultural lands of W HAS and WAR; however, birds have appeared coastally in BRA and GAL and at least twice offshore. The last major incursion was during the winter of 1987–88, when 102 were tallied on the Attwater CBC, and small flocks were scattered through the agricultural land just west of Houston. There have been fewer than 10 records between 1994 and 2004. The sighting of an adult male on the early date of 20 Jul 1999 at Brazoria NWR corresponds to the beginning of the species' passage through West Texas.

SAVANNAH SPARROW
Passerculus sandwichensis

Common to abundant winter terminal migrant, rare summer resident

WINTER: (18, 21, 26 Sep) **early Oct to late Apr** (15, 22, 27 May)
HABITAT: Formerly a common breeder on low grassy prairies, Savannah Sparrow winters in low, open vegetation, including beach grasses, roadsides, cutover and fallow fields, and coastal and inland prairie.

DISCUSSION: The ubiquitous wintering sparrow of open habitats, Savannah Sparrow offers us plenty of opportunities to raise binoculars. Hundreds are seen during any winter day's birding in undeveloped land. Becoming comfortable identifying this species can facilitate recognizing less common sparrows, such as Vesper, Le Conte's, or Grasshopper. Savannahs often congregate on fence wires, occasionally with other species such as Vesper or (rarely) Grasshopper Sparrow, allowing prolonged views and valuable plumage comparisons. Spishing noises from a car window can often lure individuals within photo distance.

Of the six races that visit Texas, two or perhaps three may be expected on the UTC (TOS 1995). Savannahs exhibit almost as much variability as Red-tailed Hawks. Mixed flocks may contain both light and dark forms with little or much yellow in the lores. Learning the species' weak *seep* note assists with recognition.

GRASSHOPPER SPARROW
Ammodramus savannarum

Uncommon bi-seasonal transient migrant, uncommon winter terminal migrant, rare and decreasing permanent resident

WINTER: (31 Oct; 10, 15 Nov) **early Nov to early Apr** (23 × 2 Apr; 20 May)

HABITAT: Dry or moist grassy habitats, prairie or fallow fields with shrubs; occurs both coastally and inland.

DISCUSSION: Grasshopper Sparrows begin arriving in late Oct and early Nov; apparently some are still moving in early Dec as evidenced by a 7 Dec 2003 record from the Quintana jetty, BRA. Most local birds have departed by late Mar, but often a very few migrants are detected in mid- to late Apr. The subspecies *A. s. pratensis*, which breeds in northeast Texas, occurs both as a migrant and as a winter bird on the UTC.

Grasshopper Sparrows nested in the area ("six miles south of Houston") as late as 1914 (Simmons 1915). Confirmed breeding records after the early 1900s have been lacking, however. In recent years, local birders have suggested that Grasshopper Sparrow was still a rare breeder on the UTC or perhaps just to the west in COL. This supposition may have been clouded by the fact that many wintering and possibly migrant birds sing from appropriate habitat well into Apr. However, after many years in which reports were lacking, the wet winter of 2002–2003 apparently enticed a few to remain and breed. Several were heard singing 21 May 2003 on the east end of Porter Road, HAS, and another was heard singing 6 Jun near Barker Reservoir, HAS. An individual seen 1 Sep 2004 at Bear Creek Park, HAS, may have nested locally,

perhaps on the Katy Prairie. It is not known whether local records pertain to *pratensis* or the western *perpallidus*, which breeds east to Travis Co (TOS 1995).

HENSLOW'S SPARROW
Ammodramus henslowii

Rare winter terminal migrant, extirpated breeder

FALL: (16, 19, 26, 29 Nov) **late Nov to mid-Mar**
SPRING: (23 × 2 Mar; 30 Mar; 8 Apr)

HABITAT: Henslow's Sparrow occurs in grassy areas including damp coastal prairie, inland meadows, and openings inside pine woods. When these areas become overgrown with shrubs, the birds disappear. Most recent UTC sightings have occurred in coastal or inland prairies or weedy fields interspersed with shrubs or young pines; the presence of broom sedge or bluestem grasses (*Andropogon* spp.) is often noted.

DISCUSSION: Historically, two tiny endemic populations of Henslow's Sparrow nested in fields in Deer Park (HAS) and along Mykawa Road in southeast Houston (Oberholser 1974; Arnold 1983). These birds represented the only known breeding Henslow's Sparrows in Texas. The Mykawa Road population with 60 singing males was discovered 8 Apr 1973. The final sighting there occurred on 15 Aug 1981, suggesting that the last survivor of the subspecies *A. h. houstonensis* probably sang its final *tsilick* about two years before its formal description reached library shelves. A more hopeful but as yet unproven scenario is that these populations may have moved to more suitable habitat, where they remain undetected.

During winter, small numbers of Henslow's Sparrows representing the subspecies *henslowii* are rare visitors to the region. Root (1988) considered eastern Texas and especially the Galveston Bay vicinity to be one of the most regular areas for encountering them during CBCs. Frequently sedentary, some wintering Henslow's Sparrows have been relocated and documented during subsequent days or weeks; birds announced on the UTC's rare bird report are probably worth a chase. Efforts such as Christmas Bird Counts and the Gulf Coast Bird Observatory's Project Prairie Birds have shown this species to be regular in small numbers throughout the UTC. During recent years, areas such as Brazos Bend SP (FOB) and Smith Point (CHA) have harbored as many as half a dozen birds.

LE CONTE'S SPARROW
Ammodramus leconteii

Locally common winter terminal migrant

FALL: (26 Sep; 7, 20 Oct) **late Oct to late Apr**
SPRING: (2, 5, 9, 11 May)

HABITAT: Gulf cordgrass flats (rarely marshhay cordgrass), weedy fields, and coastal bluestem prairies; often found over soggy ground, both coastally and well inland.

DISCUSSION: Le Conte's Sparrow is a sought-after species for visitors to the UTC. Here, it often relies on habitats that are in a state of flux, as does the much rarer Henslow's Sparrow. Previously attractive sites may be vacated after several weeks, having become wetter or drier or been plowed, mowed, burned, or even developed.

Although Le Conte's Sparrow usually occurs farther inland, it and the similar-appearing Nelson's Sharp-tailed Sparrow are sometimes found together. This occurs most frequently in gulf and/or marshhay cordgrass on the inland portions of coastal marshes (marginal habitat for both species), especially when Nelson's are forced into or near this zone by high tides. In these cases, Le Conte's should be carefully separated from the abundant Sedge Wrens and Nelson's Sharp-tailed Sparrows (neither of the latter two shows the pale midcrown stripe of Le Conte's).

Inland concentrations in grassy fields can sometimes reach 50 or more birds. Although they can be walked up nearly any time of day, dawn or shortly thereafter is the best time to see birds perched on the still dew-covered grasses. In 1999, Don Verser made a regular check of such a field at San Bernard NWR (BRA); his data suggest optimal dates to search for the species. He tallied 75 (6 Mar), 41 (20 Mar), 20 (28 Mar), 3 (17 Apr), 4 (25 Apr), 4 (1 May), 1 (9 May), and none on 15 May. The Freeport CBC has found the species on 44 of 48 counts, with a high of 344 in 1994.

NELSON'S SHARP-TAILED SPARROW
Ammodramus nelsoni

Locally common winter terminal migrant

FALL: (25–26 Sep) **late Sep to early May** SPRING: (18, 20–21, 24 May)

HABITAT: Virtually restricted to extensive stands of smooth cordgrass. Despite the large number present each winter, the species remains essentially unrecorded inland.

DISCUSSION: Each Sep, this beautiful little sparrow joins its larger and drabber congener, the Seaside Sparrow, in stands of smooth cordgrass growing behind coastal dikes and along intertidal mudflats. It is one of very few songbirds living on tidally swept mudflats. Watch for the Nelson's broad white mantle streaks. These are absent in the recently split Saltmarsh Sharp-tailed Sparrow (*A. caudacutus*) of the Northeast. A possible Saltmarsh Sharp-tailed Sparrow (TOS 1995) was later determined to be a Nelson's (Lockwood and Freeman 2004). Before reporting a Saltmarsh Sharp-tailed Sparrow on the UTC, please note the difficulty in identifying worn *nelsoni*, the paucity of records of any form of *caudacutus* away from the East Coast, and the lack of any Texas specimens of the latter.

If it is not raining or very windy, birders not concerned about muddy shoes, rattlesnakes, cottonmouths, or embarrassment in front of strangers can usually coax a few to a dozen or more of these attractive birds into view by making vigorous spishing noises. At Bolivar it may not be possible to walk to the very end of the flats during late spring, owing to the presence of nesting Least Terns; the more circuitous (and muddier) inland route is suggested. Alternatively, birds may be observed at many other locations, including the roadside near Texas Point (JEF), Sportsman's Road (GAL), or along the Bolivar Peninsula at sites such as Yacht Basin Road, where drivable asphalt penetrates tidally inundated cordgrass beds. Birds reported prior to the last week of Sep need to be carefully separated from young Seaside Sparrows, which can exhibit an orange cast to the head and chest; consider their different bill shapes.

SEASIDE SPARROW
Ammodramus maritimus fisheri

Locally common resident

HABITAT: Virtually restricted to extensive stands of smooth cordgrass.

DISCUSSION: Seaside Sparrow is our only sparrow that nests over the muddy intertidal zone and one of the few North American songbirds that breeds in such habitat. Its rather uniform dark coloration, yellow lores, and large conical bill are all noteworthy. UTC birds and those nesting along the coast southwest to about Matagorda Co. belong to the subspecies *A. m. fisheri* (TOS 1995).

Because of the Seaside's restricted habitat, few birds are likely to be confused with it. In its habitat, any form of Sharp-tailed Sparrow has a smaller body and bill, shows a more contrasting face pattern, and is brighter orange. Savannah Sparrow, often present on the drier parts of the beach and infrequently on moist sand near the realm of the Seaside, also has yellow lores, but its paler coloration, more obvious breast streaking, bright pink legs, and smaller bill should preclude confusion. Female Red-winged Blackbirds are larger, with a longer and finer bill, and are more heavily streaked. Seasides may be observed in many local salt marshes, including those around Sabine Pass, Sportsman's Road (GAL), at the Bolivar Flats and Anahuac NWR, and along roads running northward off Highway 87 on the Bolivar Peninsula. During spring, they may be located by their explosive, high-pitched, and rather insectlike song, which sounds remarkably similar to that of a Red-winged Blackbird in miniature.

Seasides respond to pishing and squeaking, occasionally by venturing out onto open mud or up to a fence wire. Less often, they sit atop the cordgrass, but typically not for as long as a Nelson's Sharp-tailed Sparrow. When males are singing, this species seems numerous and is easily encountered in the coastal marshes. At other times birds are present but may be difficult to find. Nonetheless, with some effort, birders located 216 during the 1979 Freeport CBC.

FOX SPARROW
Passerella iliaca iliaca

Uncommon winter terminal migrant

WINTER: (31 Oct; 8, 10 × 2 Nov) **early Nov to early Mar** (11 Mar)

HABITAT: Infrequently seen very close to the coast; inland, inhabits understory of woody thickets such as yaupon holly or McCartney rose, margins of woodland, abandoned home sites, and extensive hedgerows, nearly always away from developed areas.

DISCUSSION: Small numbers of Fox Sparrows may be encountered among wintering flocks of seed-eating species such as White-crowned and White-throated sparrows. Most often located by their call, these timid birds usually appear briefly in response to spishing or squeaking, then quickly retire to the depths of a thicket where they are nearly impossible to see. Fox Sparrows are much less common immediately along the coast; rare fall overshoots hit the migrant traps only to disappear within a day or two. Virtually all UTC records pertain to foxy red northern or eastern *iliaca*-type individuals. However, Jim Morgan and Eubanks had one of their most unusual spring sightings ever, when they observed a western montane Fox Sparrow exhibiting a distinctly gray crown and back. Even stranger, it was present in a salt cedar clump along the Gulf between High Island and Sabine Pass.

SONG SPARROW
Melospiza melodia melodia

Common winter terminal migrant

FALL: (1, 13, 20 Oct) **late Oct to late Mar** SPRING: (13 Apr)

HABITAT: Brushy fields, woodland edge, fence rows, occasionally in freshwater marsh.

DISCUSSION: Song Sparrow is a common winter visitor. Individuals are unlikely to remain long in more settled areas and are best sought outside the city limits. They do not require the impenetrable habitat favored by towhees or Fox Sparrows and are more likely to occur in weedy fields, with Lincoln's and Swamp sparrows and Sedge Wrens, or perhaps in a hedgerow flock with White-crowneds. Of the five subspecies that winter in Texas, *M. m. melodia* is known from and most likely to occur in our region.

Song Sparrow does not occur in flocks, but areas of good habitat can hold multiple birds. They are more common inland; for example, the Cypress Creek CBC (W HAS) averaged 99 per year for 20 counts, with a high of 227 in 2001. Freeport recorded a high count of 162 in 1980, but from 1993 to 2002 averaged only 44 per yr. During that same period, the Galveston CBC, where the species was once more common, averaged only 13 per yr.

LINCOLN'S SPARROW
Melospiza lincolnii lincolnii

Common winter terminal migrant

WINTER: (26, 27 Sep; 1, 6 Oct) **early Oct to late Apr** (6, 11, 20 May)

HABITAT: Wintering birds inhabit thickety growth along borders of woods, hedgerows, and weedy fields with shrubs or saplings. Migrants occur in residential yards and urban parks as well.

DISCUSSION: A soft, typewriter-like ticking frequently indicates the presence of a Lincoln's Sparrow. This species is similar to the slightly larger Song Sparrow and may occur with it in various habitats. Formerly a less common wintering bird than Song Sparrow, in some areas Lincoln's Sparrow now seems to outnumber it. If uncertain of identification, note the buffy boomerang-shaped mark on the lower border of the face and the dark breast streaks surrounded by a buffy orange ground color, both lacking in Song Sparrow. Unlike Song Sparrow, individuals of this species sing only infrequently on the UTC. Lincoln's is common during winter, occasionally very much so; the high count at Freeport was 353 in 1964.

SWAMP SPARROW
Melospiza georgiana georgiana

Locally common winter terminal migrant

WINTER: (1, 7 × 2 Oct) **mid-Oct to mid-Apr** (10–11, 27 May)

HABITAT: Coastal marshes, both fresh- and saltwater, thickets of willow or baccharis along edges of channels or pools, inland in moist fields with low brush, edges of dikes, ditches, and ponds.

DISCUSSION: During winter and early spring, hundreds of birders drive the dikes at Anahuac NWR to enjoy the ducks, herons, and other waterbirds. Human visitors are likely to be unaware of the surrounding hordes of Swamp Sparrows unless someone spishes, squeaks, or makes other strange noises. Inland as well, moist fields hold large numbers of these handsome sparrows; yet here too, they go largely unobserved. Learning this bird's phoebelike chip note alerts birders to the presence of a surprising number of individuals.

These birds begin to arrive with the first cool fronts in mid- to late Oct, remaining to winter in large numbers; for example, Freeport recorded its highest CBC count of 1,309 in 1993. Typically most are gone by mid-Apr, but there are two summer records. One was seen and heard singing by Don Verser at High Island, GAL, on 24 and 30 Jun 2001. The other was found 18 Jul 1984 at Brazos Bend SP.

WHITE-THROATED SPARROW
Zonotrichia albicollis

Common winter terminal migrant

WINTER: (27 Sep; 11, 19 Oct) **late Oct to early Apr** (10, 11 × 2, 14 May)

HABITAT: Woodland, dense thickets and hedgerows, rural yards; usually not in open situations.

DISCUSSION: During winter, squeaking or imitating an owl inside a local woodland, or along its thickety edge, is likely to produce White-throated Sparrows. They are more often encountered inside the forest than is the similar White-crowned Sparrow, a denizen of hedgerows and brushy fields.

White-throated Sparrows become regular by late Oct, their numbers building into early winter. They can be found in large numbers during most winters even within the coastal woodlands, where a peak of 2,482 was reported on the 1964 Freeport CBC. While this number is higher than recent tallies, this species was recorded in triple digits or higher on 11 Freeport counts between 1990 and 2002.

Although most birds are gone by early to mid-Apr, during exceptional years a few can be found into early May. White-throated Sparrows frequently sing during the spring and may even tune up on a sunny winter day.

HARRIS'S SPARROW
Zonotrichia querula

Uncommon to fairly common winter terminal migrant

WINTER: (25 Oct; 11 Nov) **mid-Nov to late Feb** (3 May)

HABITAT: Woodland edge, stands of yaupon and McCartney rose, dense or abandoned residential plantings, hedgerows; rare in coastal migrant traps.

DISCUSSION: Very rarely recorded along the coast, Harris's Sparrow is most frequently encountered in the inland portions of the region, often in the company of other *Zonotrichia*. This sparrow is the largest member of its genus; its buffy head, black-dappled face, pink bill, and rather loud bell-like chip note all aid with its identification. Prior to departing for Canada (where all Harris's Sparrows nest), some birds begin to sing on the UTC.

Numbers vary greatly from year to year, as evidenced from the Freeport CBC results. The species has been reported on only 22 of 48 counts, but a noteworthy 74 birds were found in 1980. The coastal migrant traps sometimes offer a few of these birds, only to have them vanish within a day or two, presumably finding more suitable habitat inland.

WHITE-CROWNED SPARROW
Zonotrichia leucophrys leucophrys

Common winter terminal migrant

WINTER: (29 Sep; 13, 15 Oct) **late Oct to late Apr** (3, 10–11 May)

HABITAT: Thickety woodland edge, hedgerows, scrubby oaks, thickets of huisache, hollies, and McCartney rose, fallow fields.

DISCUSSION: A common wintering species in low, dense habitats, White-crowned Sparrow often occurs in mixed flocks with other members of its family. Occasionally, fall cold fronts push individuals to the coast, and small numbers may even be seen feeding in grassy vegetation bordering the dunes. Although a few are counted on coastal CBCs (they have been missed on at least six Freeport counts), they are much more numerous inland. For example, this sparrow was recorded on every Cypress Creek CBC (W HAS) between 1983 and 2003, with a recent high of 626 on 1 Jan 1990. The black-lored subspecies *Z. l. leucophrys* winters on the UTC.

Birders should be on the lookout for Golden-crowned Sparrow (*Zonotrichia atricapilla*). Although a rarity in Texas with about half of the 28 records from the Trans-Pecos, this northwestern visitor has occurred three times in Orange County adjacent to JEF.

DARK-EYED JUNCO
Junco hyemalis

Uncommon winter terminal migrant

FALL: (10, 12, 16 Oct) **mid-Nov to early Mar** SPRING: (4, 9, 27 Apr)

HABITAT: Inhabits woodland edge, thickets, weedy fields, hedgerows, generally inland, occasionally on the coast.

DISCUSSION: Previously an abundant winter visitor (Nehrling 1882), the Dark-eyed Junco is rarely present now in more than small numbers. Of the eight subspecies that occur in the state, virtually all birds seen on the UTC represent the eastern *J. h. hyemalis*, formerly called Slate-colored Junco. However, on 20 Apr 1987, Wes Cureton observed an "Oregon"-type junco, presumably *J. h. montanus*, in vegetation outside Houston City Hall. Another collided with a window at Indian Beach, GAL, on 22 Oct 1998 (J. Stevenson). These birds provide documentation of a locally rare western form.

Most junco sightings are made inland. The Cypress Creek CBC (W HAS) reported the species on 11 of 20 counts (often as singles), with a high of 93 on 1 Jan 2001. During productive years juncos can be seen in reasonable numbers all the way to the coast. The 1972 Freeport CBC produced an astonishing 324 individuals, but 10 recent counts have averaged less than two per year.

MCCOWN'S LONGSPUR
Calcarius mccownii

Rare winter terminal migrant
28 Feb 1977 GAL
1–26 Jan 1986 WAR
30 Nov 1986–8 Feb 1987 WAR
26 Feb 2002 San Luis Pass, GAL

HABITAT: Inland and coastal prairie or prairielike agricultural land, typically grazed or sparsely vegetated, also lake beds, dunes; formerly, and once recently, sandy areas near the coast.

DISCUSSION: In 1878, Sennett first mentioned the presence of McCown's Longspur on the UTC. He remarked that he often saw Horned Larks and McCown's Longspurs "on the dry, sandy ridges adjoining the salt marshes" at Galveston. In such habitat, at San Luis Pass, the most recent UTC record occurred. Previously, Eubanks and others found McCown's Longspurs during two winters in WAR. Watch for this species in flocks of Lapland Longspurs and Horned Larks in fields in western portions of the UTC.

LAPLAND LONGSPUR
Calcarius lapponicus lapponicus

Irregularly common winter terminal migrant

FALL: (18, 21 Oct) **mid-Nov to early Feb** SPRING: (23 Feb)

HABITAT: Wet or dry agricultural fields, plowed, or with residual stubble or short grass, rarely on sandy beaches.

DISCUSSION: This tundra breeder makes its way south to the UTC only occasionally. In some years, it is seen in small numbers on the Katy Prairie in WAR and W HAS; rarely it occurs in flocks numbering a hundred or more. Occasionally it reaches the coastal beaches, staying for only a short period.

SMITH'S LONGSPUR
Calcarius pictus

Accidental winter terminal migrant
5 Dec 2004 Galveston Is. SP, GAL (R. H. Peake,
    G. Nunn, and others)

HABITAT: Nests on dry, grassy tundra from N Alaska to N Ontario (A.O.U. 1998); in Texas rare to uncommon in some NE counties and (largely undocumented) at scattered sites elsewhere in most other regions of the state. Locally observed (once) in tussock grasses near bay edge.

DISCUSSION: Smith's Longspur is the most recent addition to the avifauna of the UTC. On 5 Dec 2004, Dick Peake, Gordon Nunn, and 10 very lucky field trip participants spent more than 15 minutes observing one at close range. The bird was located on the bay side of Galveston Is. SP, where it fed in tussock grasses with a Savannah Sparrow. A detailed description including body plumage, tail pattern, and call notes eliminated other possibilities.

CHESTNUT-COLLARED LONGSPUR
Calcarius ornatus

Rare winter terminal migrant
28 Feb 1965 Cove, CHA
4 Feb–10 Apr 1983 W Galveston Island, GAL
    (photographed)
4 Feb 1984 Bolivar Flats, GAL
14 Apr 1996 Texas City Prairie Preserve, GAL

HABITAT: Inland and coastal prairie or grazed prairielike and sparsely vegetated agricultural land, also lakebeds and dunes.

DISCUSSION: Despite being a regular winter resident in much of the northern half of Texas, this species has been detected only four times on the UTC. Arlie McKay found the first record at Cove on 28 Feb 1965. Eubanks found another that stayed for most of the spring of 1983 on W Galveston Is. One was detected by Bret Whitney on Bolivar Flats on 4 Feb 1984, and the most recent sighting was from the Nature Conservancy's Texas City Prairie Preserve in 1996.

NORTHERN CARDINAL
Cardinalis cardinalis magnirostris

Common resident, numbers increase during winter

HABITAT: Mixed and coniferous woodland, second growth, neighborhood plantings, coastal mottes, hedgerows.

DISCUSSION: Northern Cardinal was the most common breeder encountered by Eubanks and Jim Morgan at Brazos Bend SP during their 1978 survey of the avifauna of the Brazos River cedar elm/green ash/sugar hackberry thickets. Elsewhere, it is one of the UTC's best-known residents. Widely recognized as the redbird, it demands to be noticed, even by nonbirders. Its loud and highly variable song, heard throughout much of the year, consists of both rich and sweet notes and flat, rather mechanical ones. Male cardinals in adjacent yards may define their territories with anything from a few short pleasant phrases to a long machine-gun-like series. As if to flaunt their bright plumage, males deliver songs from conspicuous perches including utility wires, TV antennae, and treetops.

Cardinals often nest around houses, where fruiting ornamental shrubs provide nourishment and dense nesting habitat. Besides flourishing in suburbia, they inhabit the UTC's various woodlands, overgrown fields, thickets of yaupon and hawthorn, and hedgerows—indeed almost anywhere that seeds or fruit and cover are available. Cardinals are common at feeders, where, despite incessant cowbird parasitism, they appear with brood after brood of noisy, dull brown youngsters. During winter, the local population swells as UTC breeders are joined by the more northerly *C. c. cardinalis.* The 1971 Freeport CBC tallied an impressive 1,448 individuals.

PYRRHULOXIA
Cardinalis sinuatus sinuatus

Sporadic winter visitor

WINTER: (3–5, 14, 21, 27 Nov) **late Nov to late Mar** (4, 23 Apr; 30 May)

HABITAT: Occurs coastally and inland in hedgerows, fallow fields with shrubs, planted yards, or thickets of salt cedar, yaupon or McCartney rose.

DISCUSSION: Along the UTC, Pyrrhuloxia is not sighted annually. It is more regularly and more commonly seen in the brush country to the southwest. The TOS checklist considers it an irruptive wanderer that is spreading northward (Lockwood and Freeman 2004). When the species does occur locally, small numbers may appear at various sites. The last such minor invasion was in 1997, when two birds were found on both the Freeport and Galveston CBCs. The Freeport CBC also recorded them in 1992 (3 birds), 1982, 1977, and 1972. We are aware of at least 20 UTC occurrences, many from W of Houston in W HAS and WAR. Because 26 were tallied on the 1987 Victoria CBC, searching the southern UTC could be a productive strategy for finding them. The mid- to late Dec records (and others from Victoria and Attwater) reflect the CBC window when coverage is most intense. The 23 Apr 1978 record of five at Old House (GAL) is exceptional for both the late date and the number present. Very dry conditions during the spring of 2000 may have accounted for one seen on the extremely late date of 30 May 2000 at Quintana, BRA. Noting the bill shape and color on any pale cardinal-like bird will greatly enhance chances of discovering this species.

ROSE-BREASTED GROSBEAK
Pheucticus ludovicianus

Common spring, uncommon fall transient migrant, rare winter lingerer

SPRING: (12, 18, 21–22 Mar) early **Apr to mid-May** (23, 26 May; 14 Jun)

FALL: (4, 19 Aug) **late Aug to late Oct** (6–30 Nov; 13 Dec)

HABITAT: Coastal mottes, open woodland, residential areas.

DISCUSSION: Rose-breasted Grosbeak is a common trans-Gulf migrant, often congregating by the dozens in coastal woodlots, feeding in red mulberry trees beside catbirds, various tanagers, and buntings. Any yard that contains a female mulberry tree has probably hosted these attractive visitors. Occasionally the species appears in impressive numbers; on 3 May 1973 Ben Feltner and Victor Emanuel estimated 450 between High Island and Sabine Pass, JEF, and Eubanks and Fred Collins estimated 600 at Galveston Is. on 22 Apr 1979. The species ranked 11th in our censused fallouts, accounting for nearly 3 percent of the total. Because of their large size, loud *eek* call, and the ease with which they are usually seen, these grosbeaks may seem more common than they actually are.

As the TOS checklist suggests, this species is a rare UTC winter resident. Sightings include birds at Houston, Cove, and Indian Beach as well as lingerers from 8 Nov 2002 to 15 Dec 2003 at Quintana (BRA), 15 Dec 1973–13 Jan 1974 at High Island, and 6 Feb–16 Mar 1993 from a residential feeder in Clear Lake (HAS). Great care should be used in distinguishing this species from Black-headed Grosbeak, which sings a similar fluty, fast robinlike song; females and first-year birds can be especially difficult to identify correctly. During winter, both species occur roughly annually on the UTC.

BLACK-HEADED GROSBEAK
Pheucticus melanocephalus

Rare bi-seasonal transient migrant, rare winter lingerer

SPRING: (31 Mar; 5 Apr, 30 Apr–1 May, 25 May)
FALL: (26, 28–30 Sep; 11–19 Oct; 27 Nov)

HABITAT: Perhaps most frequent in coastal oak and hackberry mottes; often attracted to fruiting mulberry trees.

DISCUSSION: This western counterpart of the Rose-breasted Grosbeak is a scarce visitor to the UTC. Most individuals are located in the well-patrolled migrant traps. Female and immature grosbeaks should be carefully inspected for individuals with a lack of streaking in the center of the breast, as this species is very similar to the Rose-breasted Grosbeak. In most cases, other marks such as the wing lining and breast coloration can then be used to confirm identification.

The Freeport CBC found this species on 11 of 46 counts; a maximum of four was reported in 1980. Recent winter records after the CBC window include singles seen 14 Jan 1992 in HAS and 6 Feb 2001 at Richmond, FOB. Two birds visited a feeder 10–26 Feb 2001 in Lake Jackson, BRA.

BLUE BUNTING
Cyanocompsa parellina

Very rare winter vagrant

20 Dec 1987–12 Feb 1988 Clute (Freeport), BRA (TBRC 1988-153) (AB 42:291, 988)

20 Dec 1987–early Jan 1988 Lake Jackson (Freeport), BRA (TBRC 1988-154; TPRF 642) (AB 42:291, 988); different area and sex than preceding record

HABITAT: Occurred locally in much the same habitat it utilizes farther south: the interior of woodlands, frequently with vines, shrubs, or saplings forming a thicket in the understory.

DISCUSSION: Imagine smugly walking into the Freeport Christmas Bird Count dinner with a female Blue Bunting on your day list, only to hear that another party had a male, and both birds were playing second fiddle to the state's first live and photographed White-collared Swift! Such is birding on the UTC—from triumph to almost wanting to hang up one's binoculars.

During the early to mid-1980s, Blue Buntings were frequent visitors to the Lower Rio Grande Valley, several hours' drive to the north of their brushy haunts in Mexico. Occasionally, two or more were present. This trickle of birds, perhaps attributable to a few nesting pairs close to or on our side of the border, has all but dried up. Theories as to why they occurred there, and along the Gulf Coast as far as Louisiana, generally point toward loss of habitat in Mexico due to agricultural activity, and the resulting dispersal of birds seeking food and shelter. This species is similar to the locally rare Varied Bunting. The latter has a smaller beak and shows deep red accents on its hind

crown, whereas the Blue Bunting has pale blue on the fore crown.

BLUE GROSBEAK
Passerina caerulea

Common bi-seasonal transient migrant, very rare winter lingerer; formerly bred

SPRING: (28, 31 Mar; 4 Apr) **early April to mid-May** (19–20 May)

FALL: (7, 21, 26 Aug) **mid-Sep to mid-Oct** (16, 20, 21 Nov)

HABITAT: Widespread, breeding from Northern California and Pennsylvania to Costa Rica (A.O.U. 1998). Locally, migrants utilize edges of woodlands, thickets, salt cedars, and weedy fields.

DISCUSSION: Although a common enough migrant, Blue Grosbeak may no longer breed on the UTC. The local population, representing the subspecies *P. c. interfusa*, was severely impacted by loss of its nesting habitat, and we are aware of no recent breeders. Before the beginning of the last century, Nehrling (1882) found this grosbeak nesting in briar patches, fields, wooded borders, and roadsides, where it was a "regularly distributed summer resident, but nowhere abundant." During its spring and fall migrations, it is seen most often in fields and woodland edges. Although winter reports are rare, the Freeport CBC has turned up the species on four of 48 counts, with a high of two birds in 1984. These CBC records are likely very tardy migrants, as we know of no confirmed Jan records.

LAZULI BUNTING
Passerina amoena

Rare spring and fall transient migrant; rare winter visitor

SPRING: (24, 30 Apr) **late Apr to early May** (1, 10 May)

FALL: (7, 19 Oct) **mid-Oct to mid-Nov** (15 Nov)

HABITAT: Weedy, fallow fields, shrubby woodland edge.

DISCUSSION: We are aware of at least 15 sightings of this western visitor; most records are from late Apr to mid-May. The largest count was of three reported from High Island, on 25–26 Apr 1964. We are aware of two winter records: one was found 22 Dec 1985 on the Freeport CBC (also seen the following day), and the other was located 22 Dec 1977 just outside the UTC on the Attwater CBC.

INDIGO BUNTING
Passerina cyanea

Abundant spring and less common fall bi-seasonal transient migrant, locally common summer terminal migrant, rare but regular winter terminal migrant

SPRING: (20–21, 25 × 2 Mar) **late Mar to mid-May** (19 May)

FALL: (21 Aug) **mid-Sep to mid-Nov** (15, 20 Nov)

HABITAT: Brushy fields, salt cedars, willows, and eastern baccharis; less frequently in the canopy or edges of oak and hackberry mottes, residential areas; often attracted to feeders and bird baths.

DISCUSSION: Indigo Bunting was the most common species tallied during our censused spring fallouts, representing almost 18 percent of the estimated total. Prodigious numbers have been seen during one day, including an estimated 3,500 at Galveston Is. on 22 Apr 1979. Often a dozen or more may be seen in the coastal mottes, drawing *oohs* and *ahhs* as they feed in mulberry trees or bathe in front of the viewing stand at Boy Scout Woods. However, to truly appreciate their abundance, more open habitat must be sought. During fallout conditions the rattlebox, baccharis, salt cedars, willows, overgrown gardens, and other rank growth along the Bolivar Peninsula are literally dusted with Indigo Buntings as well as numerous Yellow Warblers, which are attracted to the same habitats. By no means, however, is their presence felt only along the coast; as migration progresses, they are frequently seen well inland at bird baths and feeders or in hedgerows and weedy fields.

This species' song, a pleasant series of paired notes very different from the Painted Bunting's delivery, is readily learned. The call note is a short, burry, fairly loud *jeeet*. Recognizing it allows birders to locate Indigo Buntings on their breeding and wintering grounds as well as to identify both day- and nighttime migrants as they fly over the UTC.

A few birds remain into summer to nest. They are not common anywhere on the UTC but are found most years at Brazos Bend SP (FOB). Local breeding

and the birds' propensity in recent years to linger into winter make defining their migration window quite difficult. They first begin appearing in coastal migrant traps in late Mar, and migrants are present into mid-May. Those seen on West Galveston Is. 16 Jun 2002 and 8 Jul 2000 may have represented local breeders as opposed to wandering summer birds.

Fall migrants begin showing up in late Sep–early Oct and are still present into early Dec. Winter birds may be found inland in brushy areas throughout the season; occasionally flocks are reported—17 birds at Lake Jackson (BRA) on 24 Jan 1999 and 16 birds at East Columbia (BRA) on 14 Feb 2001.

VARIED BUNTING
Passerina versicolor

Very rare or accidental visitor
7 Apr 1992 Freeport, BRA
Fall 1992 HAS
16 Apr 1999 High Island, GAL
21 Apr 2004 W Galveston Is., GAL

HABITAT: Brushy hillsides, washes, and canyons (none of which are present locally); thorn forest, woodland edge, occasionally overgrown fields.

DISCUSSION: We are aware of only four local records of this southwestern species: a male seen 7 Apr 1992 by W. Pruess and G. Brooks within the Dow Chemical facility at Freeport (BRA); one observed 16 Apr 1999 at High Island (GAL); a report from HAS in 1992; and most recently, on 21 Apr 2004, a male photographed by Brian Small on West Galveston Is., GAL. This species' uniformly brown female should not be confused with many other birds found on the UTC.

PAINTED BUNTING
Passerina ciris ciris

Locally common summer terminal migrant, common spring and uncommon fall bi-seasonal transient migrant, rare winter terminal migrant

SPRING: (13, 25 Mar; 4 × 2 Apr) **mid-Apr to late Oct** FALL: (15, 17, 9–19 Nov)

HABITAT: Open woodland with a brushy understory, overgrown fields with emergent shrubs or saplings, unmanicured hedgerows, overgrown gardens, young or thinned pine plantations.

DISCUSSION: For northern birders visiting the Gulf Coast, a male Painted Bunting is one of the most sought-after target species. This striking bird can be found in both spring and fall in the coastal migrant traps. Many stay to breed at locations such as the Bolivar Peninsula (GAL), Galveston Is., and especially San Bernard NWR (BRA), where males may be seen singing from atop tall shrubs or trees. Learning its harsher song, which lacks obvious paired notes, helps differentiate it from Indigo Buntings singing nearby. Among North American birds, the females and immature males are unique; their dull to bright yellowish green plumage cannot be mistaken for that of any other songbird.

During spring, most Painted Buntings arrive during the middle portion of Apr. Rarely, this species lingers into winter, having been found on eight of 48 Freeport CBCs. On several occasions, individuals have been noted overwintering. Recent records include two birds on feeders, 6–27 Feb 2001 at the Gulf Coast Bird Observatory in Lake Jackson, BRA (possibly one of these same birds was seen there on 22 Mar); 10 Jan–Feb 2002 at the same location; a male 31 Dec 2003 in Beaumont, JEF; a male 30 Jan 2004 in League City, GAL; and a male 7–20 Feb 2004 at Armand Bayou Nature Center, HAS. The presence of overwintering birds compromises our spring arrival dates; thus a 13 Mar singing male discovered by Victor Emanuel may have overwintered or simply been an early migrant.

DICKCISSEL
Spiza americana

Abundant bi-seasonal transient migrant, fairly common but decreasing summer terminal migrant, rare terminal winter migrant

FALL: (2, 4, 10, 29 Nov; 27 Dec)

SPRING: (6 Apr) **mid-Apr to mid-Oct**

HABITAT: Hedgerows, prairie grasses, weedy fields; large numbers of migrants may congregate in salt cedars and other coastal shrubs.

DISCUSSION: By the third week of Apr, the Dickcissels' buzzy song may be heard from fences, power lines, and weed stalks throughout the region's agricultural lands and less disturbed grasslands. Farther north, where endless prairies once blanketed the central portion of the continent, much of the Dickcissel's extensive habitat has been converted to the production of corn and cereal grains; this bird is yet another casualty of the land- and water-hungry beef and poultry industries. In Venezuela, where perhaps the bulk of Dickcissels winter, their habitat is also being converted for agricultural purposes, and they are more likely to come into contact with agricultural toxins. During the late 1800s, Nehrling (1882) considered them abundant breeders on local prairie, much of which has been lost to rice cultivation or subdivisions. Fortunately, they still breed on the UTC, and birders willing to brave the summer heat should find them in unmowed fields. The Dickcissel's abrupt call note is easily recognizable. Some liken it to the buzzing of high-tension power lines. Familiarity with the call reveals many flying over the UTC.

Dickcissel rarely winters in the region; we are aware of at least four older records between mid-Dec and mid-Feb as well as a 27 Dec 2004 sighting from High Island (B. and L. Feltner). During the winter of 1998–99, Dickcissel staged a minor invasion: birds were seen at feeders and sang all along the Texas coast, as if on territory. Records included 24–29 Jan 1999 Lake Jackson, BRA (at feeder); 19 Feb 1999 Danbury, BRA (singing); 17 Mar 1999 at Richmond, FOB; and 27 Mar–2 Apr 1999 Lake Jackson, BRA (one to two singing birds at a feeder). One seen 14 Mar at Cove, CHA, may also have overwintered.

Blackbirds, Orioles, and Allies

The family Icteridae contains mostly tropical birds that are confined to the New World. Among its 96 or so species, a dozen or more are endemic to certain islands, mountains, or forests. Others, however, are some of our most widespread birds, occurring in dense flocks that look like smoke drifting across the horizon. Many icterids are simply attired in black or steel blue, but even some blackbirds are splashed with crimson, yellow, or orange. The family is widely recognized for its vocalizations, which range from sweet songs to explosive renditions likened to crackling flames and waterfalls.

The orioles are well known for their pleasing songs, brilliant colors, and intricately woven nests. Mexico is the center of oriole diversity, but a number of species range northward into the United States. Of the six seen locally, two are commonly encountered. The colorful Baltimore Oriole is present only during migration, while the dainty Orchard Oriole continues to nest in the region. The latter's "extra" first year male plumage is the bane of inexperienced birders.

To date, the Texas fauna includes 22 kinds of icterids, 19 of which have been recorded on the UTC. Only the tropical Black-vented, Altamira, and Audubon's orioles have not strayed this far northeast. The balance includes several species of blackbirds, grackles, and cowbirds, which along with European Starlings become our most numerous winter birds, forming immense flocks and mesmerizing evening congregations that are among our ornithological spectacles.

Of the eight icterids that nest locally, perhaps the most widely recognized are Red-winged Blackbird, Eastern Meadowlark, and Great-tailed Grackle. All three are widespread and easily seen and possess commanding vocalizations.

Usually associated with the region's marshes, ponds, and roadside ditches, the Red-winged Blackbird is not averse to slipping into suburbia with its bounty of backyard feeders. Locally, as in many parts of the country, the bird has invaded residential neighborhoods, singing its strident *con-curEEEEE* from TV antennae instead of cattails. Our other three blackbirds—Yellow-headed, Rusty, and Brewer's—are all less numerous visitors, although the latter may be locally common during winter.

Eastern Meadowlark is found in drier habitats than the previous species and avoids areas that are more than lightly settled. During winter, the look-alike Western Meadowlark may inhabit the same fields, the two occasionally singing their very different songs side by side. The fact that Eastern Meadowlark is protected from hunters is of little consequence now that its habitat has become fair game for developers, a much greater threat. The bird's sweet song, roughly transcribed as *see you see heeere,* is still heard on the UTC, but its numbers plummet as agricultural land is converted to tract housing.

Is there another bird on the UTC with a presence more commanding (some would say obtrusive) than the Great-tailed Grackle's? Compressing a hundred dawn choruses into one and attaching this to a flock of birds that darkens the skies and whitewashes our cars gives some inkling of this bird's impact. The closely related Boat-tailed Grackle's grating song is a characteristic sound in our coastal marshes. This species lacks both the Great-tailed's vocal repertoire and its propensity to form vast flocks.

The most deviant of our icterids is certainly the Bobolink, a curious sparrowlike bird. Not only does it sing in midair during a sustained hovering display, but it is the only North American songbird that is white above and black below. Although most individuals migrate well east of the UTC, small numbers appear in most years. Males returning from their wintering grounds in southern South America are distinctive, even singing now and then in weedy coastal fields. Fall migrants are rare, and they resemble a female House Sparrow; it is a sharp-eyed birder who finds one on the UTC.

Brown-headed and Bronzed cowbirds breed on the UTC and the Shiny Cowbird has recently appeared here. They and the two other cowbirds are of special interest to biologists and habitat managers. Like certain ducks, cuckoos, and a few other birds, cowbirds have abandoned nest building and become brood parasites. The hows and whys that lead to nest parasitism and to being parasitized are the grist for countless theses and dissertations. Of more immediate importance, several cowbird populations are being aggressively controlled, as their presence has contributed to the depletion of populations of certain songbirds.

BOBOLINK
Dolichonyx oryzivorus

Uncommon to rare spring, rare fall transient migrant

SPRING: (5, 13, 19 Apr) **late Apr to mid-May** (13, 23, 26 May)

FALL: (13 Sep) **mid-Sep to mid-Oct** (17, 24 Oct)

HABITAT: Coastal prairie, weedy fields, agricultural land.

DISCUSSION: In some parts of the country this species is called rice bird, in reference to flocks descending on rice fields; indeed, its Latin name *oryzivorus* means "rice eater." Although encountering Bobolinks is hardly a sure thing, UTC birds are most readily seen during the last week of Apr and the first week of May. Small migrating flocks, often in the company of Dickcissels, Blue Grosbeaks and Indigo Buntings, share weedy fields along the Bolivar Peninsula, West Galveston Is., Pelican Is., and occasionally farther inland. Some sing as they pass through the region, and an unusual bubbly song may be the first clue to their presence.

During fall, Bobolinks are noted only rarely. Few are likely to be identified in their dull, basic plumage, and the bulk of the migrants occurs farther east. We hesitantly note a 31 Dec sighting from W Galveston Is.

RED-WINGED BLACKBIRD
Agelaius phoeniceus

Common summer terminal migrant, abundant winter terminal migrant

HABITAT: Marshes, wet fields and rice paddies, roadside ditches, dry plowed fields, hedgerows, and residential areas with mature vegetation; along the coast huge winter roosts occur in, but are by no means restricted to, beds of common reed.

DISCUSSION: Eight subspecies of the abundant and widespread Red-winged Blackbird occur in Texas; *A. p. littoralis* is resident along the coast. During winter, vast numbers of migrants, perhaps mainly the subspecies *phoeniceus* and *arctolegus* (TOS 1995), swell our local flocks. At that time, birders who appreciate avian spectacles may wish to be stationed near a historical roost site, such as the reed beds alongside Highway 124 (CHA), to watch tens of thousands of Red-wings and their icterid kin settle in for the night. Most birders perceive this species as a bird of marshes; however, large numbers nest in suburban settings, attracted by maturing vegetation and bird feeders. Although the male's red epaulets render him virtually unmistakable for most of the year, the heavily streaked females are often misidentified as sparrows. Noting the bill shape is helpful.

EASTERN MEADOWLARK
Sturnella magna argutula

Common but decreasing resident

HABITAT: Inland and coastal prairie, fallow agricultural land.

DISCUSSION: The Eastern Meadowlark—unrelated to Horned Lark, the New World's only true lark—was named for its resemblance to a European species. It is relatively common throughout the year and easily seen, either flaunting its brilliant yellow breast from a fence post or displaying its white outer tail feathers and triangular wings during its flap-and-glide flight. Birds on the ground are decidedly more cryptic; like pipits, longspurs, and certain shorebirds, meadowlarks have brown and buff streaked plumage that renders them nearly invisible in a field of brown grasses.

During winter the nesting population is greatly augmented by the many birds that migrate south to the UTC. Even though the species is more common then, individuals sing less frequently and are more difficult to locate. Although its preferred grassland habitat has declined considerably with development, Eastern Meadowlark can still be found in good numbers on local refuges and grasslands. The Freeport CBC recorded a high of 2,573 in 1972 but averages a more modest 691 per year. Four subspecies breed in Texas, *S. m. argutula* occurring in the SE part of the state (TOS 1995).

Formerly, many meadowlarks were killed for the pot. Today they are no longer hunted and will remain common wherever their prairie habitat is preserved.

WESTERN MEADOWLARK
Sturnella neglecta

Uncommon winter terminal migrant

FALL: (16–17, 24 Oct) **late Oct to mid-Mar** SPRING: (2 Mar; 10 May)

HABITAT: Inland prairie, agricultural land including harvested and fallow fields.

DISCUSSION: Western Meadowlark occurs most regularly and commonly in the inland portions of the UTC. Although it was reported near the coast on 13 of 48 Freeport CBCs, there have been no sightings since 1982. Suggested methods for separating this species from Eastern Meadowlark are almost as numerous as the people who have written about them. Cautious birders rely heavily on songs, and singing individuals may be heard during both winter and spring mornings. The Western's more oriole-like song is longer and richer than that of its eastern counterpart, and its *chuck* call note is also diagnostic.

YELLOW-HEADED BLACKBIRD
Xanthocephalus xanthocephalus

Occasional spring, rare fall transient migrant

SPRING: (19–20, 29 Mar) **early Apr to early May** (5–6, 19 May) FALL: (5–6, 11–12 Sep) **late Sep to late Oct** (30 Oct; 2, 4–5 Nov)

HABITAT: Marshy areas, rice paddies, pond margins, occasionally coastal lawns or dunes, plowed fields, occasionally at feeders.

DISCUSSION: Nehrling (1882) stated that this species was "very common in marshy localities from the latter part of October to March and April." Forty years later, its populations had declined to the point of Simmons (1914) remarking that it was "evidently quite rare in late years, for my only record for the past winter and spring is April 5, when three of these birds were noted in a small marshy spot near Webster." Although Nehrling thought May flocks might represent breeders, we suspect they were merely lingerers. Most sightings are along the coast during Apr, when thousands of binoculars are trained on rice fields, coastal prairies, or other habitats likely to produce this handsome species. Most sightings are of one or several birds, but rarely a flock of 20 or more may appear.

Fall records generally represent small numbers of birds seen foraging on their own. During winter, patiently sorting through a huge flock of mixed icterids occasionally yields a Yellow-head or two. Surprisingly, this conspicuous bird has been found on only two of 48 Freeport CBCs. Individuals seen 26 Jan and 1 and 15 Feb may have overwintered.

RUSTY BLACKBIRD
Euphagus carolinus

Locally uncommon to rare, sporadic winter terminal migrant

FALL: (1, 8 Nov) to SPRING: (28 Apr)

HABITAT: Inland and near the coast, generally in bottomland forest with a very wet to flooded understory.

DISCUSSION: Patiently scanning a plowed field containing 250,000 blackbirds may yield certain rewards, but is not likely to provide a sighting of Rusty Blackbird, a species for which the term "habitat specific" was created. Virtually all UTC sightings have occurred in the interior of flooded forest, where the birds may or may not associate with Red-winged Blackbirds or with other members of their family. Elsewhere in the country, their affinity for riparian corridors or bottomland forests is pronounced, and despite the odd bird that frequents a parking lot or actually does show up in a plowed field, they are difficult to find away from wet woods. During some years, small flocks of this northern breeder occur at inland sites such as Bear Creek Park or Barker Reservoir west of Houston, and there are a few records from closer to the coast (CHA, BRA). For example, a flock of between 30 and 40 Rusty Blackbirds wintered in a wet wooded area of Bear Creek Park during the winter of 2004–2005. The Freeport CBC data are worthy of note, as this species has been reported on 24 of 48 counts but only twice since 1982. These reduced numbers are likely due to birds wintering farther north and to declines in the overall population as evidenced by reduced CBC totals throughout the East (Niven et al. 2004).

BREWER'S BLACKBIRD
Euphagus cyanocephalus

Common winter terminal migrant; former summer status unclear

FALL: (14 Oct; 15 Nov) **mid-Nov to mid-Apr** SPRING: (25, 28 Apr; 5 May)

HABITAT: Typically in wet or dry plowed fields in the inland portion of the region, also frequents short grass (often heavily grazed fields) and stockyards; usually associates with other members of the family Icteridae.

DISCUSSION: Nehrling (1882) claimed to have found nests of this species in N HAS. They were located 10 to 12 feet above ground in the tops of densely growing trees that he referred to as post oaks. Given that there are only two confirmed nesting records in Texas, both well away from the UTC (Lockwood and Freeman 2004), we have reason to doubt Nehrling's record. He also described this species as the most common wintering icterid, outnumbering Red-winged Blackbird.

Today, Brewer's Blackbirds are local winter residents occurring most commonly well inland.

Previously, the Freeport CBC averaged nearly 1,000 birds per year, but recently numbers have fallen, and none was located in 2002. In part, this may be due to loss of field habitat within the count circle. Wintering Brewer's Blackbirds exhibit strong site fidelity and can be found reliably in certain farmyards year after year.

COMMON GRACKLE
Quiscalus quiscula quiscula

Common resident, common to abundant winter terminal migrant

HABITAT: Breeds in soft- and hardwood forest, open woodland, and well-wooded neighborhoods; winter concentrations, including many migrants, occur in agricultural land (especially plowed fields), at woodland edge, and in both urban and suburban areas.

DISCUSSION: Common Grackle is a familiar lawn and feeder bird throughout much of the inland portion of the region, nesting wherever suitable trees occur. Away from woodlands, these grackles are noticeably less common along the coast, and their numbers are variable. For example, they are abundant on Galveston Is. during some winters but virtually absent in other years (J. Stevenson). Breeding birds may be encountered south to near Rockport, where this bird's range terminates at the margin of the mesquite and huisache brush lands, like the ranges of so many of the eastern forest species. During the late 1800s, Nehrling (1882) considered this our most common breeding icterid, although perhaps that title now belongs to the aggressively spreading Great-tailed Grackle. The UTC checklist awards the two species equal status throughout the year, but in much of the area, Common Grackle is decidedly harder to find in late summer. During winter, large flocks move through residential neighborhoods. As evidence of their abundance, the 1992 Freeport CBC reported 33,849 Common Grackles. Besides the local *Q. q. quiscula*, the subspecies *stoni*, rare in East Texas during winter, may occur on the UTC (Arnold and Kutak 1974).

BOAT-TAILED GRACKLE
Quiscalus major major

Locally common resident

HABITAT: Fresh and brackish coastal marshes, ranging to adjacent farmland, occasionally around habitations; rarely occurring more than a short distance inland.

DISCUSSION: Boat-tailed Grackle, a United States endemic, is restricted to the Atlantic seaboard and Gulf Coast. It breeds in coastal marshes of the UTC, ranging southward regularly to Nueces Co., and is accidental in the Lower Rio Grande Valley (Lockwood and Freeman 2004). Although similar to and long considered conspecific with the Great-tailed Grackle, it may be distinguished by a suite of characteristics, including the Boat-tailed's rounder head, smaller size, coarser and less varied vocal repertoire, generally tawnier female, and brown iris. Birders familiar with the yellow-eyed Boat-taileds of the eastern United States note a switch in eye color. Here, in their zone of overlap, Boat-taileds are brown-eyed, as opposed to the yellow-eyed Great-taileds. This last character is slightly variable, as a very few pale-eyed Boat-taileds have been photographed and tape recorded (Eubanks and J. Morgan). Young of both species are dull-eyed.

Boat-tailed Grackles are loosely colonial, as is obvious at Shoveler Pond at Anahuac NWR, where dozens of males display from the reeds within which their nests are hidden. At such assemblages, their grating chorus frequently drowns out many of the other marsh singers. Unlike most U.S. icterids, Boat-tailed Grackles are decidedly sedentary. CBC totals do not reveal any particular winter influx of birds.

GREAT-TAILED GRACKLE
Quiscalus mexicanus prosopidicola

Abundant resident

HABITAT: Virtually throughout the region in urban and suburban settings; generally replaced in coastal marshes by Boat-tailed Grackle.

DISCUSSION: Although not always identified as such, Great-tailed Grackle is well known to the area's residents because it is present in large, occasionally awe-inspiring numbers. Certain roosts, such as the one on the Rice University campus, have developed special notoriety as a nuisance and have been subjected to control measures. Not far from there, few shoppers strolling at dawn or dusk along the sidewalks bordering Houston's Galleria shopping center can fail to be impressed by the cacophony arising from thousands of Great-taileds roosting in the surrounding trees.

This grackle is a Middle American species showing a northward increase and spread that is closely tied to human activities. Before global warming became a possible explanation for the northward spread of certain birds, Great-tailed Grackles were abundant around livestock operations and always present for a free lunch at feedlots, grain elevators, and railroad sidings where grain is spilled. Vast numbers visit residential lawns and are a plague at bird feeders, especially those of a platform type. There is some evidence that offering safflower in place of sunflower seeds may deter certain blackbirds and their kin. They are fond of dumps and seem equally happy scavenging the beach for maritime morsels or hopping into the dumpster at a fast-food restaurant for discarded fries.

At certain sites—for example, High Island and Brazoria NWR—Great-tailed and Boat-tailed Grackles may feed or roost together. However, Great-tailed is largely absent from the freshwater and brackish marshes so favored by Boat-taileds.

SHINY COWBIRD
Molothrus bonariensis

Accidental visitor
3 Feb 2000 Houston, HAS (TBRC 2000-9)
26 Apr 2003 JEF (TBRC 2003-36)

HABITAT: A widespread and spreading bird of South America and the Caribbean, inhabiting forest edge, fields, and disturbed habitats such as lawns and golf courses.

DISCUSSION: There are at least three reports of this species from the UTC, two of which have been accepted by the TBRC. On 3 Feb 2000, Will Risser observed one in a Houston neighborhood. It was part of a large icterid flock, apparently pausing en route to the roost site at Greenway Plaza. Plumage characteristics precluded other local cowbirds. Additionally, the bird uttered a few song phrases similar to those Risser had heard in Florida. In Apr 2003 Tony and Phyllis Frank located a male in JEF, not far from Winnie.

Like Brown-headed and Bronzed cowbirds, Shiny Cowbirds are nest parasites and their presence should be vigorously discouraged, as their spread into the SE United States would further imperil already threatened songbird populations.

BRONZED COWBIRD
Molothrus aeneus aeneus

Uncommon but increasing resident, presumed bi-seasonal transient migrant, some lingering into winter

HABITAT: Residential plantings, parklike areas with scattered shade trees, light woodland; like other icterids, attracted to feedlots, stables, spilled grain at railroad yards, and bird feeders.

DISCUSSION: Bronzed Cowbird, along with the innocuous Inca Dove, has reached us by spreading northward from the Lower Rio Grande Valley. Unlike the dove's, however, this brood parasite's path is marked by suppressed numbers of other songbirds.

The first report known to us was a bird observed on 2 Feb 1962. Subsequently, Bronzed Cowbird, once a local rarity, has come to be documented on the UTC for every month of the year. Territorial birds have been observed in many parts of Houston and the surrounding communities, and breeding almost certainly occurs in all counties of the region. The highest number observed was 110 present 22 Dec 1979 on Pelican Island, GAL. The Freeport CBC recorded the species on exactly half of 48 counts, with a high of 38 in 1972.

BROWN-HEADED COWBIRD
Molothrus ater obscurus

Common resident, abundant winter terminal migrant

HABITAT: Woodlands and well-planted residential areas.

DISCUSSION: Throughout the summer, Brown-headed Cowbird is a common UTC resident. Each fall huge numbers of additional birds descend upon the region. Vast flocks gather at sites such as harvested rice fields, where residual seed attracts them and a variety of other black icterids. These flocks are often prodigious; the 1964 Freeport CBC tallied 158,600 individuals, each one representing an unrealized White-eyed Vireo, Northern Parula, Northern Cardinal,

Painted Bunting, Orchard Oriole, or some other song-bird.

Recent studies suggest that fragmentation of wooded habitats enhances cowbird predation by bringing forest interior species closer to woodland margins, where cowbirds are more likely to parasitize them (see Robinson et al. 1992 for discussion of management and a bibliography). As in a number of other icterids, albino cowbirds are occasionally noted: Behrstock photographed an albino on 21 Nov 1987 (WAR). Presumably, UTC winter flocks also contain the more northerly subspecies *M. a. ater*.

ORCHARD ORIOLE
Icterus spurius spurius

Common bi-seasonal transient migrant, fairly common summer terminal migrant

SPRING: (20 Feb; 15, 25 × 2 Mar) **late Mar to late Sep**
FALL: (30 Sep; 23 × 2 Oct; 4–5 Nov)
HABITAT: Open woodland, stands of tall brush, orchards, hedgerows, and residential plantings.
DISCUSSION: Orchard Oriole is a common migrant on the UTC, the 15th most abundant bird encountered during our censused fallouts. Flocks containing many black-chinned, first-year males are readily seen as they assault the red mulberry trees at High Island or festoon the shrubbery along the Bolivar Peninsula. Spring migrants may also be encountered in salt cedars, willow thickets, reed beds, or various ornamental plantings. New arrivals are often full of song; their rather finchlike delivery is different from the Baltimore Oriole's sweet, jerky strains.

Previously very common, and breeding nearly anywhere trees were present, including gardens and around dwellings, this species is now relegated to the more rural portions of the region. The birds are still relatively common in willows along the immediate coast, such as at Anahuac and San Bernard NWRs.

Verified winter sightings are rare; we recognize records from 21, 25, and 27 Dec.

HOODED ORIOLE
Icterus cucullatus sennetti

Rare spring and visitor
22–23 Apr 1978 Mont Belvieu, HAS (TPRF 130)
11 Apr 1995 Sabine Woods, JEF

19 Jul 2000 W. Galveston Is., GAL
12 Mar 2001 Quintana NBS, BRA
12 Apr 2001 W. Galveston Is., GAL
18 Apr 2001 Sea Rim SP, JEF

HABITAT: A variety of woodlands and in residential areas, frequently with palm trees.
DISCUSSION: Various forms of Hooded Oriole are distributed to the west and southwest of our region, breeding at least from northern California to near the Mexico-Guatemala border. The subspecies *I. c. sennetti* is a common breeder in South Texas, ranging perhaps as far northward as Kerr and Gillespie cos. (TOS 1995), the same latitude as the UTC. This species has profited from the widespread planting of ornamental palm trees, in the leaves of which nests are often located.

The first UTC record was an individual photographed by Eubanks and present at Mont Belvieu (HAS) 22–23 Apr 1978. More recent sight reports include an adult male seen 11 Apr 1995 at Sabine Woods (JEF); a possible "yellow" male observed 19 Jul 2000 on West Galveston Is. (which may have been a postbreeding wanderer of the interior race); an adult male at the Quintana NBS (BRA) 12 Mar 2001; a female at west Galveston Island 12 Apr 2001; and an adult male at Sea Rim SP (JEF) 18 Apr 2001. The recent increase in records may be proportionate to an increased awareness of field marks.

Recent summer records from Refugio and Calhoun cos. and a bird that wintered in a palm plantation near Bay City, Matagorda Co., suggest that UTC birders should be on the lookout year-round for this expanding species.

STREAK-BACKED ORIOLE
Icterus pustulatus

Vagrant
12 Dec 2004–8 Apr 2005 Brazos Bend SP, FOB (TBRC 2005-32)

HABITAT: Streak-backed Oriole inhabits lowlands of the Pacific Slope from Sonora to NW Costa Rica. It is found in a variety of habitats from arid lowland scrub to tropical deciduous forest, occasionally ascending to lower subtropical elevations (A.O.U. 1998).
DISCUSSION: A party of birders located and photographed the UTC's first Streak-backed Oriole at Brazos Bend SP, FOB, on 12 Dec 2004 (B. Godley, B. Alprin, and

others). Additional photographs were obtained on 18 Dec (G. Lavaty, B. Ohmart, B. Godley, F. Gregg). Initially, the bird was identified as a Hooded Oriole and later as a Bullock's Oriole. Subsequently, the photos were posted to the Internet in early Feb 2005, when a consensus of experienced observers concluded that it was a young male Streak-backed Oriole—the state's first record! The bird overwintered and was observed on numerous occasions as late as 27 Apr 2005 (C. Whipple and others).

BULLOCK'S ORIOLE
Icterus bullockii

Uncommon winter terminal migrant, uncommon bi-seasonal transient migrant

FALL: (27–28 Aug; 3–4, 19 Sep) **mid-Sep to mid-Apr** SPRING: (15–17, 29 Apr)
HABITAT: Mature residential plantings, especially yards with fruit trees such as loquat and a variety of flowers; may be attracted to feeders.
DISCUSSION: Bullock's Oriole, the western counterpart of Baltimore Oriole, breeds about as far eastward as Austin (Travis Co., TOS 1995). Coastal and inland migrants occur infrequently during spring and fall and are usually observed at fruiting or flowering vegetation and feeding stations. The occasional wintering bird provides a splash of tropical intensity at our feeder assemblages. Observations at well-monitored yards reveal that birds visiting the region exhibit great site fidelity, returning to the same neighborhoods year after year. In Bellaire, for example, Gretchen Mueller reported what may have been the same individual returning for up to ten consecutive years. A high of four (two males and two females) was noted in a Bellaire yard 20 Sep 1995. Other known wintering sites include High Island and Lake Jackson. A few birds sing, but more often heard are their chatter and rather flat call notes. Most individuals followed did not associate with other icterids.

This species is attracted to sliced fruit and suet baskets but perhaps most consistently to sugar water feeders designed for hummingbirds and orioles. Feeders with attached perches are preferred. A well-planted yard almost certainly increases the likelihood of attracting this often shy species; a male observed many times during several winters often hid in dense shrubbery prior to emerging to drink at a hummingbird feeder.

BALTIMORE ORIOLE
Icterus galbula

Common spring and fall transient migrant; rare winter terminal migrant; formerly bred

SPRING: (31 Mar) **late Mar to mid-May** (14, 23 May)
FALL: (19, 26 Jul; 7 Aug) **late Aug to mid-Oct** (18 Oct; 15–16 Nov)
HABITAT: Coastal mottes, extensive stands of salt cedars, second growth and mature mixed woodland, orchards, shade trees, and gardens with nectar- or fruit-bearing plants.
DISCUSSION: Baltimore Oriole was the 19th most abundant bird during our censused fallouts, representing nearly 2 percent of all birds tallied. A rare breeder in East Texas, it was apparently extirpated from the forests of the UTC. This species is a crowd pleaser, bringing color to the migrant traps throughout the month of Apr. It is also a regular fall migrant, most abundant in late Aug; a few are still present in mid-Oct. In many years a small number of them remain to winter; the Freeport CBC reported the species on at least 12 of its 48 counts, including a record five in 1990. Some fortunate birders have this species as a guest at their hummingbird feeders through the winter; one such visitor was seen in Lake Jackson 5 Jan–18 Feb 2003.

Identifying orioles other than adult males is fraught with pitfalls. Females, immatures, out-of-range birds, and hybrids all pose their own problems and have confused many experts. For useful discussions of oriole identification, see Zimmer (1985) and Jaramillo (1999).

SCOTT'S ORIOLE
Icterus parisorum

Rare visitor
4 Nov 1988 San Bernard NWR, BRA (TPRF 288)
22–23 Dec 1985 near Oyster Creek BRA
31 Oct 1998 W Galveston Is., GAL
18–21 Oct 2000 W Galveston Is., GAL
18 April 2001 Bryan Beach, BRA

HABITAT: Drier foothills with yucca, agaves, oak, juniper, and various pines. Nests as close as the Texas Hill Country.

DISCUSSION: Although the brilliant black and yellow Scott's Oriole feeds on insects and fruit, it is perhaps most often encountered at nectar plants, when numbers of the birds are drawn to open hillsides with flowering agaves. After their nectar sources dry up, they show much interest in citrus slices and hummingbird feeders, two food sources provided by many UTC birders. Although the sweet, jerky songs of nesting birds may be heard just a few hours' drive away, this western species is a great rarity on the UTC.

We recognize only five records. The first two were fall and winter birds seen 4 Nov 1980 at San Bernard NWR and 22–23 Dec 1985 along Oyster Creek during the Freeport CBC. The three most recent records are a male seen 31 Oct 1998 and an immature male seen 18–21 Oct 2000, both from W Galveston Is., and a male seen 18 Apr 2001 at Bryan Beach, BRA. Observers are cautioned that the occasional Baltimore Oriole is yellow instead of the typical bright orange, but the Scott's Oriole is quite different in shape and pattern.

Finches and Allies

Of the eight fringillids we consider, House Finch is an increasing resident (apparently derived from the introduced eastern population), and Lesser Goldfinch is an uncommon visitor from the west or southwest. The remaining six are travelers from the north, each falling loosely into the category "winter finch." Occasionally, they undergo significant irruptions or invasions that may barely penetrate the northern border of the United States or may extend southward to the southernmost states. Unlike true migratory movements, the factors that initiate these invasions are imperfectly known, but at least some appear to be the result of poor cone crops. American Goldfinch, probably Pine Siskin, and possibly Purple Finch occur each year, but their numbers fluctuate greatly. Red Crossbill, Common Redpoll, and Evening Grosbeak are great rarities, and a decade or more may go by without a record. All except for the bizarre crossbills have conical bills, the siskin's being notably long and slender. Learning their call notes facilitates identification.

DISCUSSION: At best an invasive northern visitor, Purple Finch often goes unrecorded from year to year. It is now rare anywhere on the UTC, especially on the immediate coast. In the Northeast its decline has been attributed to competition with introduced House Sparrows, followed by competition with introduced House Finches.

Since 1990, the region has had only a handful of sporadic winter records. During late 2004, Jim Hinson noted two on 19 Nov at Bear Creek Park, HAS (the best modern location for the species), Jim Stevenson had three sightings on 7 Dec on Galveston Island (where the species is particularly uncommon), and Ben and Linda Feltner observed one on 27 Dec at High Island.

The apparent decline of this previously more common bird is supported by the Freeport CBC history; the species has been seen on only 12 of 48 counts, and only once since 1986. There is a single recent coastal record during spring migration: one or two birds observed on the surprising date of 2 May 2004 at Sea Rim SP, JEF, in grasses and willows along the boardwalk.

PURPLE FINCH
Carpodacus purpureus purpureus

Rare and possibly decreasing winter terminal migrant

FALL: (10 Oct) **late Oct to late Mar** SPRING: (2, 10 May)

HABITAT: Woodland edge and mature residential plantings, often at bird feeders.

HOUSE FINCH
Carpodacus mexicanus

Locally common and increasing resident

HABITAT: Residential and urban shade and ornamental plantings.

DISCUSSION: Previously, House Finch was unknown on the UTC. Introduced from the western United States to New York during the early 1950s (A.O.U. 1983), it has now successfully colonized East Texas in its relentless march westward toward its ancestral home. Locally, the bird was first photo-documented by Fred Collins 26–27 Mar 1988. Strongholds with breeding populations now include the Rice University campus, the nearby West University district, and parts of Bellaire; but the birds have been reported from much of the region. Preferred nest trees include the densely foliaged Italian cypress and arborvitae.

It is interesting to note that this species became common in parts of Houston but has yet to colonize the coast. Although birds are now being seen in the Beaumont area, as of this writing, they are absent as breeders along the Texas coast. Occasionally, coastal areas do get a few winter birds, and perhaps these individuals will eventually remain to nest in areas such as Galveston and Freeport.

RED CROSSBILL
Loxia curvirostra

Very rare winter terminal migrant
21 Nov 1900 Galveston, GAL
7 Jan 1973 Freeport, BRA (5–7 birds)
2–3 Sep 1984 Houston, HAS (TPRF 340)
12 Nov 2004 W Galveston Island, GAL

HABITAT: Notably sporadic in occurrence, nests in both sea level and montane forests that offer various cone-producing evergreens.

DISCUSSION: We are aware of four records of Red Crossbill on the UTC, three of which occurred coastally. The first record of this locally rare and irruptive species came from Galveston on 21 Nov 1900. Our only physically documented occurrence is one photographed in Houston 2–3 Sep 1984. There is a sight record of five to seven, including males and females/immatures, from Freeport on 7 Jan 1973, and another 12 Nov 2004 from W Galveston Island (J. Stevenson). The gaps between the records indicate the species' great rarity. We do not know which of the nine described types of Red Crossbill has occurred locally. Birders wishing to make a contribution to the literature are strongly urged to make every possible effort to tape record crossbills that occur on the UTC.

COMMON REDPOLL
Carduelis flammea

Vagrant
18–19 Jun 2002 Galveston, GAL (TBRC 2002-90, TPRF 2044)

HABITAT: Nests in N Canada and Alaska, continuing across Europe and Asia in arctic or subarctic habitats. Redpolls winters in light woodland and weedy fields, often frequenting thistle feeders.

DISCUSSION: Given that Texas had only five accepted records of Common Redpoll, the odds were slim that what some thought were two separate birds would show up on the Texas coast. Even longer than those odds were the chances that this would occur during the hot Texas summer. Yet that is just what happened in 2002, when a bird was seen at Laguna Vista (just east of Brownsville, Cameron Co.) from 28 to 31 May (TBRC 2002–66). Shortly after that bird left, a very similar appearing bird showed up at the home of Ian and Deirdre Becker in Galveston. This female spent 18–19 Jun 2002 eating seeds off their back patio. There is an additional report of one 2 Apr 1926 at Galveston attributed to R. A. Selle (Oberholser 1974).

PINE SISKIN
Carduelis pinus pinus

Sporadic, occasionally common winter terminal migrant

FALL: (19 Oct) **early Nov to mid-Apr** SPRING: (25 May)

HABITAT: Woodland edge, mature neighborhood plantings, fallow fields, bird feeders.

DISCUSSION: During most winters, small numbers of Pine Siskins occur in urbanized areas such as Houston; but they are present in somewhat greater numbers in the wilder parts of the UTC. Coastal records are less common; for example, the species has been found on less than half of the Freeport CBCs. However, during invasion years such as 1977–78 and during the late 1980s, when birds flee severe weather or food shortages to the north, dozens to hundreds may show up at feeders. These birds, usually in the company of American Goldfinches, send homeowners dashing to purchase large quantities of thistle seed. The subspecies *C. p. pinus* visits the UTC.

LESSER GOLDFINCH
Carduelis psaltria psaltria

Very rare visitor
17–18 Apr 1970 Galveston, GAL
20 Jan–25 Feb 1972 Cove, CHA
16 Dec 1979 Freeport CBC
18 Dec 1988 Freeport CBC
30 Jan–26 Feb 1993 Houston, HAS
4–12 May 1993 W Houston, HAS (TPRF 1181)
29 Nov 1993 Barker Reservoir, HAS
4 Feb 1995 Houston, HAS (photographed)
8 May 2000 Quintana NBS, BRA
10 Feb 2002 Hitchcock, GAL (photographed)

FALL: (29 Nov, 16, 18 Dec) to SPRING: (8, 4–12 May)
HABITAT: Brushy areas, neighborhoods with feeders.

DISCUSSION: Rarely, Lesser Goldfinch visits the UTC during winter or spring. It nests as close as Goliad Co. just W of Victoria, and may stray eastward when moving south.

This western species was first noted in the UTC at Galveston 17–18 April 1960. It was next located 20 Jan–25 Feb 1972 at Cove, CHA. Since that time it has been found twice on the Freeport CBC and a few times elsewhere, frequenting feeders. In some cases birds have remained for a while, such as 30 Jan–26 Feb 1993 at Houston and 4–12 May 1993 in W Houston (TPRF 1181),. The May 1993 record and a lone male seen 8 May 2000 at the Quintana NBS, BRA, may represent individuals that drifted eastward during migration.

AMERICAN GOLDFINCH
Carduelis tristis tristis

Common winter terminal migrant

FALL: (20, 23, 27 Oct; 1 Nov) to SPRING: (17 May; 5, 7, 13 Jun)
HABITAT: Woodland edge, mature neighborhood plantings, fallow fields, bird feeders.

DISCUSSION: Each year, numbers of American Goldfinches visit the UTC. During some years their flight is meager and thistle seed spoils in feeders. In other years, they are present by the thousands, devouring hundreds of pounds of seed. When they occur in prodigious numbers, it is often in the company of Pine Siskins.

Besides congregating at bird feeders, goldfinches feed heavily on various grasses, thistles, and sunflowers, button-bush, sycamore, sweetgum, and other seed-bearing plants. Band returns from birds ringed on the UTC indicate that individuals do not always winter in the same region. A record of approximately 10,000 at Cove on 18 Jan 1970 suggests a flock of near biblical proportions.

EVENING GROSBEAK
Coccothraustes vespertinus vespertinus

Sporadic and rare winter terminal migrant

FALL: (27 Dec) to SPRING: (12 May)
HABITAT: Boreal to tropical latitudes in isolated or continuous and extensive woodlands, usually at montane elevations or higher latitudes.

DISCUSSION: For a number of reasons, this handsome invader from the boreal forests is a great rarity on the UTC. Most eastern populations are not truly migratory, and their movements to find winter food are often wandering or nomadic. In fall, some birds move eastward or westward rather than south, perhaps in response to the availability of tree seeds or spruce budworms. Christmas Bird Counts reveal that high totals of wintering birds occur in alternate years, that large invading flocks do not visit the same area twice in succession, and that the eastern population has been in decline since about 1980. Suggested reasons for this decline include changing forest practices, global warming, and stabilization of the NE population after the species expanded east of the Great Lakes (Kelling 2002). Major invasions may occur at 20-year intervals; birders should plan on being patient.

The most recent influx occurred during the winter of 1977–78; more recently birds were present in Montgomery Co. Ron Braun banded and photographed a female at Sabine Woods on the very late date of 26 Apr 1986. It is not known which subspecies visits the UTC.

HOUSE SPARROW
Passer domesticus domesticus

Abundant introduced resident associated with human activity

HABITAT: Especially common near human dwellings, virtually throughout the region but absent from isolated beaches and the interior of extensive forest.

DISCUSSION: The House Sparrow is a member of the Old World weaver finch family, well known for the elaborate woven nests crafted by many species. In 1851 it was introduced into the United States when 100 were liberated in Brooklyn, New York. Since its introduction there and elsewhere, the House Sparrow (a.k.a. black-throated brown, slum weaver) has benefited mightily from the population growth and dispersal of humans, and it now breeds on six continents, typically in developed areas. Although the species is not often visible in huge numbers, it has been suggested that House Sparrows are the most abundant songbirds in North America. On Christmas Bird Counts their numbers often pale in comparison to those of other species, including various blackbirds; however, unlike the blackbirds, they do not congregate in huge wintering flocks.

Cavity nesters, and aggressive ones at that, House Sparrows often usurp artificial nest sites provided for more endearing species such as Eastern Bluebird and Purple Martin. On the UTC, they inhabit all manner of structures, nesting under eaves, bridges, and roof tiles, inside traffic signals, in or on old swallow nests, among shrubs, and in nest boxes meant for other birds. They are numerous at bird feeders but get nourishment wherever waste food is available, especially at feedlots, railroad sidings, or farmyards where spilled grain is available. During a typically warm year on the UTC, House Sparrows may raise four or more broods, making them one of the most fecund birds in the region. In Great Britain between 1972 and 1996, House Sparrow populations plummeted as much as 60 percent in both rural and urban areas. Changing agricultural practices may account for the decrease in rural birds and increased electromagnetic activity from cell phones may impact urban populations, but the actual reasons for the decline have yet to be determined.

APPENDIX 1
BIRDING AND ENVIRONMENTAL ORGANIZATIONS ON THE UPPER TEXAS COAST

The organizations listed offer field trips and informative programs that pertain to the birds of the Upper Texas Coast. Some have monthly meetings that may include identification workshops. A few sponsor Christmas Bird Counts or other activities that solicit participation from both new and advanced birders. Phone numbers are included if published on a Web site and serving an office rather than a club member.

Armand Bayou Nature Center (Pasadena)
Phone: (281) 474-2551
URL: http://www.abnc.org/

Friends of Anahuac Refuge (Anahuac)
Phone: (409) 267-3337
URL: http://www.friendsofanahuacnwr.org/index.html

Galveston Bay Foundation (Webster)
Phone: (281) 332-3381
URL: http://www.galvbay.org/

Golden Triangle Audubon Society (Beaumont and vicinity)
URL: http://www.goldentriangleaudubon.org/

Gulf Coast Bird Observatory (Lake Jackson)
Phone: (979) 480-0999
URL: http://www.gcbo.org/

Houston Audubon Society
(including Galveston County Group)
Phone: (713) 932-1639
URL: http://www.houstonaudubon.org/

Katy Prairie Conservancy (Houston)
Phone: (713) 523-6135
URL: http://www.katyprairie.org/home.html

Lower Trinity Valley Bird Club (Liberty and vicinity)
URL: http://www.ltvbc.org/

Ornithology Group of the Outdoor Nature Club of Houston
URL: http://www.outdoornatureclub.org/

Piney Woods Wildlife Society, Inc. (Spring and vicinity)
URL: http://www.cechouston.org/groups/pwws.html

Texas Ornithological Society (TOS, San Antonio)
URL: http://www.texasbirds.org/

APPENDIX 2 PLANTS MENTIONED IN THE TEXT

Many sources were used to attach a common or scientific name to plants discussed in the text. These sources included a number of people who possess expertise with local wild and cultivated plants (see acknowledgments); butterfly and hummingbird plant handouts from Houston Audubon Society and other environmental organizations; university, state, and federal Web sites with online floras, photographs, or discussions of such topics as aquatic plants or invasive weeds (not in the list that follows); and various texts. Authors we consulted included Ajilvsgi (1979, 1984, 1990), Britton and Morton (1989), Correll and Correll (1972), Correll and Johnson (1970), Gould (1975), McAlister and McAlister (1987), Miller (1991), Tveten and Tveten (1993), and Vines (1960). Despite our efforts some names will be unfamiliar, as plant names seem to be in a continuous state of flux.

Alabama supplejack	*Berchemia scandens*	Dallisgrass	*Paspalum dilitatum*
American beautyberry	*Callicarpa americana*	Dwarf palm (palmetto)	*Sabal minor*
American beech	*Fagus grandifolia*	Dwarf wax-myrtle	*Myrica pusilla*
American elder (or elderberry)	*Sambucus canadensis*	Eastern baccharis	*Baccharis halimifolia*
American mistletoe	*Phoradendron flavescens*	Eastern gamagrass	*Tripsacum dactyloides*
American wildcelery	*Vallisneria americana*	Eastern prickly pear cactus	*Opuntia compressa*
Arborvitae	*Thuja occidentalis*	Eastern redbud	*Cercis canadensis*
Ashe juniper	*Juniperus ashei*	Elms	*Ulmus* spp.
Bahiagrass	*Paspalum notatum*	Firecracker bush	*Russelia equisetiformis*
Beach evening primrose	*Oenothera drummondii*	Florida paspalum	*Paspalum floridanum*
Beach morning glory	*Ipomoea stolonifera*	Flowering dogwood	*Cornus florida*
Bermudagrass	*Cynodon dactylon* (and hybrids)	Giant cane	*Arundinaria gigantea*
Big bluestem	*Andropogon gerardii*	Giant Turk's cap	*Malvaviscus arboreus*
Blackberries (and dewberry)	*Rubus* spp.	Glasswort (or pickleweed)	*Salicornia* spp.
Broom (sedge) grass	*Andropogon* spp.	Green ash	*Fraxinus pennsylvanica*
Broomsedge bluestem	*Andropogon virginicus*	Gulfdune paspalum	*Paspalum monostachyum*
Brownseed paspalum	*Paspalum plicatulum*	Gum (woollybucket) bumelia	*Sideroxylon lanuginosum*
Buffelgrass	*Cenchrus ciliaris*	Firebush (or firecracker bush)	*Hamelia patens*
Bulrush	*Scirpus* spp.	Hercules'-club (or toothache tree)	*Zanthoxylum clava-herculis*
Bushy bluestem	*Andropogon glomeratus*	Hollies	*Ilex* spp.
Buttonbush	*Cephalanthus occidentalis*	Huisache	*Acacia farnesiana*
Cardinal flower	*Lobelia cardinalis*	Indiangrass	*Sorghastrum nutans*
Carolina buckthorn	*Rhamnus caroliniana*	Italian cypress	*Cupressus sempervirens*
Cattail	*Typha* spp.	Japanese honeysuckle	*Lonicera japonica*
Cedar elm	*Ulmus crassifolia*	Johnsongrass	*Sorghum halepense*
Chinaberry	*Melia azedarach*	King Ranch bluestem	*Bothrichloa ischaemum*
Chinese tallow	*Sapium sebiferum*	Laurel greenbrier	*Smilax laurifolia*
Cigar plant (or firecracker plant)	*Cuphea* spp., including *micropetala* and *ignea*	Little bluestem	*Schizachyrium scoparium*
		Loquat	*Eriobotyra japonica*
Common bald cypress	*Taxodium distichum*	Macartney rose	*Rosa bracteata*
Common lantana	*Lantana camara*	Maidencane	*Panicum hemitomon*
Common reed	*Phragmites australis* (= *P. communis*)	Manatee grass	*Syringodium filiforme*
		Mangrove	
Coral bean	*Erythrina* spp.	Black	*Avicennia nitida*
Coral vine	*Antigonon leptopus*	Red	*Rhizophora mangle*
Cordgrass		White	*Laguncularia racemosa*
Gulf	*Spartina spartinae*	Mesquite	*Prosopis* spp.
Marshhay (saltmeadow)	*Spartina patens*	Mustang grape	*Vitus candicans*
Smooth	*Spartina alterniflora*	Oak	
Cory rattlebush	*Sesbania drummondii*	Laurel (or swamp laurel)	*Quercus laurifolia*

Live	*Q. virginiana*	Southern magnolia	*Magnolia grandiflora*
Pin	*Q. palustris*	Southern wax-myrtle (or bayberry)	*Myrica cerifera*
Post	*Q. stellata*		
Water	*Q. nigra*	Spanish moss	*Tillandsia usneoides*
Oleander	*Nerium oleander*	Spatterdock	*Nuphar luteum*
Pecan	*Carya illinoinensis*	Sugar hackberry	*Celtis laevigata*
Pines		Sweetgum	*Liquidambar styraciflua*
Limber	*Pinus flexilis*	Switchgrass	*Panicum virgatum*
Loblolly	*P. taeda*	Sycamore (or American planetree)	*Platanus occidentalis*
Longleaf	*P. palustris*		
Shortleaf	*P. echinata*	Texas mallow (or Turk's cap)	*Malvaviscus arboreus* var. *drummondii*
Slash	*P. elliottii*		
Plains wild indigo	*Baptisia leucophaea*	Tropical sage (or scarlet sage)	*Salvia coccinea*
Poison ivy	*Toxicodendron radicans*		
Pokeberry	*Phytolacca americana*	Trumpetvine (or trumpetcreeper)	*Campsis radicans*
Possum haw	*Ilex decidua*		
Privet (several introduced species)	*Ligustrum* spp.	Turtle grass	*Thalassia testudinum*
		Viburnum	
Rattlebox	*Sesbania drummondii*	Arrow-wood	*Viburnum dentatum*
Red mulberry	*Morus rubra*	Blackhaw	*V. pruneifolium*
Rice	*Oryza sativa*	Vinemesquite	*Panicum obtusum*
Rushes	*Juncus* spp.	Virginia creeper	*Parthenocissus quinquefolia*
Salt cedar (tamarisk)	*Tamarix gallica*	Walnut	*Juglans* spp.
Saltgrass	*Distichlis spicata*	Water hyacinth	*Eichhornia crassipes*
Seacoast bluestem	*Schizachyrium scoparium* var. *littoralis*	Water lettuce	*Pistia stratiotes*
		Water lily	*Nymphaea odorata*
Sea lavender	*Limonium carolinianum*	Water tupelo	*Nyssa aquatica*
Seashore dropseed	*Sporobolus virginicus*	Weeping lovegrass	*Eragrostis curvula*
Shrimp plant	*Beloperone guttata* (also called *Justicia brandegeana*)	Widgeon grass	*Ruppia maritima*
		Willows (various)	*Salix* spp.
		Yaupon holly	*Ilex vomitoria*
Silver bluestem	*Bothriochloa longipaniculata*	Yellow lotus	*Nelumbo lutea*

BIBLIOGRAPHY

Ajilvsgi, G. 1979. *Wild Flowers of the Big Thicket, East Texas, and Western Louisiana.* College Station: Texas A&M University Press.

———. 1984. *Wildflowers of Texas.* Fredericksburg: Shearer Publishing.

———. 1990. *Butterfly Gardening for the South.* Dallas: Taylor Publishing.

Allen, R. P. 1942. *The Roseate Spoonbill.* Research Report 2. New York: National Audubon Society.

American Ornithologists' Union. 1983. *A.O.U. Check-list of North American Birds,* 6th ed. Lawrence: Allen Press.

———. 1997. Forty-first supplement to the American Ornithologists' Union *Check-list of North American Birds.* Auk 114(3):542–52.

———. 1998. *A.O.U. Check-list of North American Birds,* 7th ed. Washington, D.C.: American Ornithologists' Union.

———. 2000. Forty-second supplement to the American Ornithologists' Union *Check-list of North American Birds.* Auk 117:847–58.

Anon. 1994. *County-by-County Listings of Threatened and Endangered Species and Candidate Species within Clear Lake (Texas) Field Office Area of Responsibility.* Houston: U.S. Fish and Wildlife Service.

———. 1995. *The Texas Hummer: Spring 1995.* Austin: Texas Parks and Wildlife Department.

Arnold, K. A. 1975. First record of the Greater Shearwater from the Gulf of Mexico. *Auk* 92:394–95.

———. 1978. A Jabiru specimen from Texas. *Auk* 95:611–15.

———. 1983. A new subspecies of Henslow's Sparrow. *Auk* 100:504–505.

Arnold, K. A., and E. A. Kutac (eds.). 1974. *Check-list of the Birds of Texas.* Waco: Texas Ornithological Society.

Audubon, J. J. 1831–39. *Ornithological Biography, or an Account of the Habits of the Birds of the United States of America: Accompanied by Descriptions of the Objects Represented in the Work Entitled "The Birds of America," and Interspersed with Delineations of American Scenery and Manners.* 5 vols. Edinburgh: Adam Black.

———. 1840–44. *The Birds of America.* 7 vols. New York: Audubon and Chevalier.

Baker, M. C. 1979. Morphological correlates of habitat selection in a community of shorebirds (Charadriiformes). *Oikos* 33:121–26.

Baker, M. C., and A. E. M. Baker. 1973. Niche relationships among six species of shorebirds on their wintering and breeding ranges. *Ecological Monographs* 43:193–212.

Banks, R. C., C. Cicero, J. L. Dunn, A. W. Kratter, P. C. Rasmussen, J. V. Remsen Jr., J. D. Rising, and D. F. Stotz. 2002. Forty-third supplement to the American Ornithologists' Union *Check-list of North American Birds.* Auk 119(3):897–906.

———. 2004. Forty-fifth supplement to the American Ornithologists' Union *Check-list of North American Birds.* Auk 121:985–95.

Barlow, J. C. 1980. Patterns of ecological interactions among migrant and resident vireos on the wintering grounds. Pp. 79–107 in *Migrant Birds in the Neotropics: Ecology, Behavior, Distribution, and Conservation,* ed. A. Keast and E. S. Morton. Washington, D.C.: Smithsonian Institution Press.

Beavers, R. A. 1977. First specimen of Allen's Hummingbird from Texas. *Southwestern Naturalist* 22:285.

Behrstock, R. A. 2000. New records of Neotropical odonates on the Upper Texas Coast. *Argia* 12(1):8–11.

Bellrose, F. C. 1968. *Waterfowl Migration Corridors East of the Rocky Mountains in the United States.* Illinois Natural History Survey Biological Notes 61. Champaign: Illinois Natural History Survey.

———. 1976. *Ducks, Geese and Swans of North America.* 2nd. ed. Harrisburg: Stackpole Books.

Bent, A. C. 1921. *Life Histories of North American Gulls and Terns.* U.S. National Museum Bulletin 113. x + 345 pp.

———. 1929. *Life Histories of North American Shorebirds,* pt. 2. U.S. National Museum Bulletin 146. 412 pp.

Britton, J. C., and B. Morton. 1989. *Shore Ecology of the Gulf of Mexico.* Austin: University of Texas Press. 387 pp.

Brown, B. T. 1993. Bell's Vireo (*Vireo bellii*). In *The Birds of North America,* no. 35, ed. A. Poole, P. Stettenheim, and F. Gill. Philadelphia: Academy of Natural Sciences and Washington, D.C.: American Ornithologists' Union.

Brush, T. 2000. First nesting record of Blue Jay (*Cyanocitta cristata*) in Hidalgo County, Texas. *Bulletin of the Texas Ornithological Society.* 33:35–36.

Burkett, W. 1994. Productive summer in Galveston Bay. *Naturalist* (Houston Audubon Society) 13(3):3.

Chu, M., and S. Hames. 2002. Wood Thrush Declines Linked to Acid Rain. *Birdscope.* Cornell Laboratory of Ornithology, Autumn 2002. www.birds.cornell.edu

Clements, J. F. 2000. *Birds of the World: A Checklist.* Temecula, Calif.: Ibis Publishing Company.

Cooke, W. W. 1888. *Reports of Bird Migration in the Mississippi Valley in the Years 1884 and 1885.* Division of Economic Ornithology Bulletin 2. Washington, D.C.: U.S. Department of Agriculture. 313 pp.

Correll, D. S., and H. B. Correll. 1972. *Aquatic and Wetland Plants of Southwestern United States.* Washington, D.C.: U.S. Environmental Protection Agency, U.S. Government Printing Office.

Correll, D. S., and M. C. Johnson. 1970. *Manual of the Vascular Plants of Texas*. Renner: Texas Research Foundation.

Cramp, S. 1983. *Handbook of the Birds of Europe, the Middle East, and North Africa*. Oxford: Oxford University Press.

Craves, J. 2000. Eurasian Collared-Dove: The newest bird on many life lists is showing up at backyard feeders as it expands its range. *Birder's World* 14(1): 46–49.

Curson, J., D. Quinn, and D. Beadle. 1994. *Warblers of the Americas*. Boston: Houghton Mifflin.

Danforth, S. T. 1935. Leach's Petrel in the West Indies. *Auk* 52:74.

Dauphin, D. T., A. N. Pettingell, and E. R. Rozenburg. 1989. *A Birder's Checklist of the Upper Texas Coast*, 7th ed. Houston: Ornithology Group, Outdoor Nature Club.

Davie, O. 1889. *Nests and Eggs of North American Birds*. 4th ed. Columbus, Ohio: Hann and Adair.

Davis, W. B. 1974. *The Mammals of Texas*. Texas Parks and Wildlife Department Bulletin 41. Austin: Texas Parks and Wildlife Department.

DeBenedictis, P. 1994. Ringed Turtle-Dove vs. Eurasian Collared-Dove. ABAnswers. *Birding*. 26(3):133.

Delaware Riverkeeper Network. 2004. Fact Sheet: Horseshoe Crabs in the Delaware Bay. http://www.delawareriverkeeper.org/factsheets/horseshoe_crabs.html

Dennis, J. V. 1954. Meteorological analysis of occurrence of grounded migrants at Smith Point, Texas, April 17–May 17, 1951. *Wilson Bulletin* 66:102–11.

Dittman, D. L., and S. W. Cardiff. 1998. Kelp Gull and Herring × Kelp Gull hybrids: A new saga in gull ID problems. *LOS News: Newsletter of Louisiana Ornithological Society*, no. 181, July 1998.

———. 2002. Let's take a closer look—godwits. *LOS News: Newsletter of Louisiana Ornithological Society*, no. 198, July 2002.

———. 2005. The "Chandeleur" Gull: Origins and identification of Kelp X Herring Gull hybrids. *Birding* 37(3): 266–67.

Dunn, J. L. (ed.). 1999. *Field Guide to the Birds of North America*. 3rd ed. Washington, D.C.: National Geographic Society.

Dunn, J. L., and K. L. Garrett. 1997. *A Field Guide to Warblers of North America*. New York: Houghton Mifflin.

Elwonger, M. 1995. *Finding Birds on the Central Texas Coast*. Victoria, Tex.: Published by the author.

Emanuel, V. L. 1961. Another probable record of an Eskimo Curlew on Galveston Island, Texas. *Auk* 78:259–60.

———. 1962. Texans rediscover the nearly extinct Eskimo Curlew. *Audubon Magazine* 64:162–65.

Eubanks, T. L., Jr., 1977. Black-legged Kittiwake sightings on the Upper Texas Coast in winter of 1976–1977. *Bulletin of the Texas Ornithological Society* 10:42–43.

———. 1988. The changing seasons. *American Birds* 42:399–406.

———. 1994. The status and distribution of the Piping Plover in Texas. *Bulletin of the Texas Ornithological Society* 27:19–25.

Eubanks, T. L., Jr., and G. F. Collins. 1993. *The Status of the Eskimo Curlew along the Upper Texas Coast*. Unpublished report of the U.S. Fish and Wildlife Service, Division of Technical Services, Order #2018110522.

Eubanks, T. L., Jr., P. Kerlinger, and R. H. Payne. 1993. High Island, Texas: Case study in avitourism. *Birding* 25:6.

Eubanks, T. L., Jr., and J. G. Morgan. 1989. First photographic documentation of a live White-collared Swift from the United States. *American Birds* 43:258–59.

Fisher, W. L., J. H. McGowen, L. F. Brown, and C. G. Groat. 1972. *Environmental Geological Atlas of the Texas Coastal Zone: Houston-Galveston Area*. Bureau of Economic Geology. Austin: University of Texas.

Fisher, W. L., L. F. Brown Jr., J. H. McGowen, and C. G. Groat. 1973. *Environmental Geologic Atlas of the Texas Coastal Zone: Beaumont–Port Arthur Area*. Bureau of Economic Geology. Austin: University of Texas.

Flickinger, E. L., G. Juenger, T. J. Roffe, M.R. Smith, and R. J. Irwin. 1991. Poisoning of Canada geese in Texas by parathion sprayed for control of Russian wheat aphid. *Journal of Wildlife Diseases* 27(2): 265–68.

Fleetwood, R. J. 1973. Jacana breeding in Brazoria Co., Texas. *Auk* 90:422–23.

Florida Fish and Wildlife Conservation Commission. 2003. *Florida's Breeding Bird Atlas: A Collaborative Study of Florida's Birdlife*. Accessed 6 Jan 2003. http://www.wildflorida.org/bba/

Frederick, P. C. 1997. Tricolored heron, *Egretta tricolor*. In *The Birds of North America*, no. 306, ed. A. Poole and F. Gill. Philadelphia: Academy of Natural Sciences and Washington, D.C.: American Ornithologists' Union.

Fritts, Thomas H., A. B. Turner, R. D. Jennings, L. A. Collum, W. Hoffman, and M. A. McGehee. 1983. *Turtles, Birds and Mammals in the Northern Gulf of Mexico and Nearby Atlantic Waters*. Denver Wildlife Research Center. Contract no. 14-16-0009-81-949. Prepared for Division of Biological Services, U.S. Fish and Wildlife Service. Washington, D.C.: U.S. Department of Interior.

Gallucci, T., and J. G. Morgan. 1987. First Documented Record of the Mangrove Cuckoo for Texas. *Bulletin of the Texas Ornithological Society* 20:2–6.

Gauthreaux, S. A., Jr. 1971. A radar and direct visual study of passerine spring migration in southern Louisiana. *Auk* 88:343–65.

———. 1972. Behavioral responses of migrating birds to daylight and darkness. *Wilson Bulletin* 84:136–48.

Gehlbach, F. R. 1994. *The Eastern Screech Owl: Life History, Ecology, and Behavior in the Suburbs and Countryside*. College Station: Texas A&M University Press.

Graham, G. L. 1992. *Texas Wildlife Viewing Guide*. Helena: Falcon Press.

Gould, F. W. 1969. *Texas Plants: A Checklist and Ecological*

Summary. Texas Agricultural Experiment Station Misc.
Publ. no. 585 (revised). College Station: Texas Agricultural
Experiment Station.

———. 1975. *The Grasses of Texas.* College Station: Texas
A&M University Press.

———. 1978. *Common Texas Grasses: An Illustrated Guide.*
College Station: Texas A&M University Press.

Green, A., M. Osborn, P. Chai, J. Lin, C. Loeffler, A. Morgan,
P. Rubec, S. Spanyers, A. Walton, R. D. Slack, D. Gawlik,
D. Harpole, J. Thomas, E. Buskey, K. Schmidt, R. Zimmer-
man, D. Harper, D. Hinkley, T. Sager, and A. Walton. 1992.
*Status and Trends of Selected Living Resources in the
Galveston Bay System.* Publication 19. Webster, Tex.:
Galveston Bay National Estuary Program.

Gruson, E. S. 1972. *Words for Birds: A Lexicon of North
American Birds with Biographical Notes.* New York:
Quadrangle Books.

Haase, B. 1996. Kelp Gull *Larus dominicanus:* A new
breeding species for Ecuador. *Cotinga* 5:73–74.

Hagar, C. M., and F. M. Packard. 1952. *Check-list of the birds of
the Central Coast of Texas.* Rockport: Published by the
authors.

Haig, S. M. 1987. *The Population Biology and Life History
Patterns of the Piping Plover.* Ph.D. diss., University of
North Dakota, Grand Forks.

———. 1992. Piping Plover *Charadrius melodus.* In *The Birds
of North America,* no. 2, ed. A. Poole, P. Stettenheim, and
F. Gill. Philadelphia: Academy of Natural Sciences and
Washington, D.C.: American Ornithologists' Union.

Haig, S. M., and L. W. Oring. 1985. Distribution and status of
the Piping Plover throughout the annual cycle. *Journal of
Field Ornithology* 56:334–45.

———. 1988. Distribution and dispersal of the Piping Plover.
Auk 105:630–38.

Hall, C. E., J. E. Hildebrand, R. T. Binhammer, and O. Hall.
1959. The birds of Galveston Island. *Texas Journal of
Science* 11:93–109.

Hancock, J. A., and J. A. Kushlan. 1984. *The Herons Handbook.*
New York: Harper and Row.

Hancock, J. A., J. A. Kushlan, and M. P. Kahl. 1992. *Storks, Ibises
and Spoonbills of the World.* San Diego: Academic Press.

Hanowski, J., N. Danz, J. Lind, G. Niemi, and J. Sales. 2003.
Blue Jay species account in *Birds of Western Great Lakes
Forests.* http://www.nrri.umn.edu/mnbirds/accounts/
BLJAa2.htm

Hardin, G. 1960. The Competitive Exclusion Principle. *Science*
131:1292–97.

Harrison, P. 1983. *Seabirds: An Identification Guide.* Boston:
Houghton Mifflin.

Hayman, P., J. Marchant, and T. Prater. 1986. *Shorebirds: An
Identification Guide to the Waders of the World.* Boston:
Houghton Mifflin.

Heiser, J. M. 1945. Eskimo Curlew in Texas. *Auk* 62:635.

Heindel, M. T. 1996. Field identification of the Solitary Vireo
complex. *Birding* 28:458–71.

Hill, G. E., R. R. Sargent, and M. B. Sargent 1998. Recent
changes in the winter distribution of wintering Rufous
Hummingbirds. *Auk* 115(1):240–45.

Hilty, S. L., and W. L. Brown. 1986. *A Guide to the Birds of
Colombia.* Princeton: Princeton University Press.

Hoke, M. W. 1974. *A Census of the Avian Fauna of Smith
Woods (Brannan's Woods), High Island, Galveston County,
Texas.* M.S. thesis, Lamar University, Beaumont:

Holt, H. R. 1993. *A Birder's Guide to the Texas Coast.* Colorado
Springs: American Birding Association.

Honig, R. A. 1992. Western Kingbird (*Tyrannus verticalis*)
utilization of electric power substations in Houston
(Harris County), Texas, and vicinity. *Bulletin of the Texas
Ornithological Society* 25(1)13–19.

Howell, S. N. G. 1994. A new look at an old problem. *Birding*
26(6):400.

Howell, S. N. G., and B. M. de Montes. 1989. Status of the
Glossy Ibis in Mexico. *American Birds* 43(1):43–45.

Howell, S. N. G., S. J. Correa, and B. J. Garcia. 1993. First
records of the Kelp Gull in Mexico. *Euphonia* 2(4):71–80.

Howell, S. N. G., and S. Webb. 1995. *A Guide to the Birds of
Mexico and Northern Central America.* Oxford: Oxford
University Press.

Israel, S., and T. Sinclair (eds.). 1987. *Indian Wildlife.* Hong
Kong: APA Productions.

James, P. 1956. Destruction of warblers on Padre
Island, Texas in May, 1951. *Wilson Bulletin* 68(3):224–27.

Jaramillo, A. 1999. Identifying a mystery oriole. *Birding,* June
1999: 259–61.

Jehl, J. R., Jr. 1979. The autumnal migration of Baird's
Sandpiper. In *Studies in Avian Biology,* no. 2, pp. 55–68, ed.
F. A. Pitelka. Los Angeles: Cooper Ornithological Society.

Johnsgard, P. A. 1981. *The Plovers, Sandpipers, and Snipes of
the World.* Lincoln: University of Nebraska Press.

Kastner, J. 1986. *A World of Watchers.* New York: Alfred
A. Knopf.

Kaufman, K. 1996. *Lives of North American Birds.* Boston:
Houghton Mifflin.

Kelling, S. 2002. Population Trends in Evening Grosbeak.
BirdSource. Audubon and Cornel Laboratory of
Ornithology. http://www.birdsource.org/Features/
Evegro/

King, K. A. 1976. Bird mortality, Galveston Island, Texas.
Southwestern Naturalist 21:414.

König, C., F. Weick, and J. Becking. 1999. *Owls: A Guide to the
Owls of the World.* East Sussex: Pica Press.

Kutac, E. A. 1989. *Birder's Guide to Texas.* Houston: Gulf
Publishing.

Lack, D. 1960. The influence of weather on passerine
migration: A review. *Auk* 77:171–209.

Lammertink, M. 1995. No more hope for the Ivory-billed
Woodpecker *Campephilus principalis. Cotinga* 3:45–47.

Lasley, G. W. 1992. *Rare Birds of Texas Master List of Review
Species.* Austin: Texas Ornithological Society, Texas Rare
Birds Committee.

Leavens, W. 1979. *Habitat Selection in Shorebirds on Bolivar Peninsula, Texas.* M.S. thesis, Texas A&M University, College Station.

Lockwood, M. W. 1997. A closer look: Masked Duck. *Birding* 29(5):386–90.

———. Jul 2004. Public statement concerning the Canada/Cackling Goose Split. TBRC News. http://www.texasbirds.org/tbrc/Canadagooset.html

Lockwood, M. W., and B. Freeman. 2004. *The TOS Handbook of Texas Birds.* College Station: Texas A&M University Press.

Lovette, I. J., and E. Bermingham. 2002. What is a Wood-Warbler? Molecular characterization of a monophyletic Parulidae. *Auk* 119(3):695–714.

Lowery, G. H., Jr. 1945. Trans-Gulf spring migration of birds and the coastal hiatus. *Wilson Bulletin* 57: 92–121.

———. 1974. *Louisiana Birds.* 3rd ed. Baton Rouge: Louisiana State University Press.

Marshall, J. T., Jr. 1967. *Parallel Variation in North and Middle American Screech-Owls.* Monographs of the Western Foundation of Vertebrate Zoology 1. 72 pp.

Martin, C. 1990. *Eskimo Curlew Habitat Identification Status Survey.* Section 6 performance report. Austin: Texas Parks and Wildlife Department.

McAlister, W. H., and M. K. McAlister. 1987. *Guidebook to the Aransas National Wildlife Refuge.* Victoria, Tex.: Mince Country Press.

McGowen, J. H., L. F. Brown Jr., T. J. Evans, W. L. Fisher, and C. G. Groat. 1976. *Environmental Geologic Atlas of the Texas Coastal Zone: Bay City–Freeport Area.* Bureau of Economic Geology. Austin: University of Texas.

Meitzen, T. G. 1963. Additions to the known breeding range of several species in south Texas. *Auk* 80: 368–69.

Miller, G. O. 1991. *Landscaping with Native Plants of Texas and the Southwest.* Stillwater, Minn.: Voyageur Press.

Millington, R., and M. Reid. 1995. Photo-forum: Red-billed Royal Terns. *Birding World* 8: 89–99.

Mlodinow, S. G. 1998. The Tropical Kingbird north of Mexico. *North American Birds* 52: 6–11.

Moore, F. R. (ed). 2000. Stopover ecology of Nearctic-Neotropical landbird migrants: Habitat relations and conservation implications. *Studies in Avian Biology* 20: 34–42.

Moore, F. R., and D. A. Aborn. 2000. Mechanisms of en route habitat selection: How do migrants make habitat decisions during stopover? *Studies in Avian Biology* 20: 34–42.

Moore, F. R., S. A. Gauthreaux Jr., P. Kerlinger, and T. R. Simons. 1992. Stopover habitat: management implications and guidelines. Pp. 58–69 in *Status and Management of Neotropical Migratory Birds,* ed. D. M. Finch and P. W. Stangel. USDA Forest Service Gen. Tech. Rep. RM-229. Fort Collins: U.S. Forest Service.

Moore, F. R., and T. R. Simons. 1992. Habitat suitability and stopover ecology of Neotropical landbird migrants. Pp. 345–55 in *Ecology and Conservation of Neotropical Migrant Landbirds,* ed. J. M. Hagan, III, and D.W. Johnston. Washington, D.C.: Smithsonian Institution Press.

Morgan, J. G., and T. L. Eubanks. 1979. First documentation of Connecticut Warbler in Texas. *Bulletin of the Texas Ornithological Society* 12: 21–22.

Morgan, J. G., T. L. Eubanks, V. Eubanks, and L. N. White. 1985. Yucatan Vireo appears in Texas. *American Birds* 39: 244–46.

Morgan, J. G., and L. M. Feltner. 1985. A Neotropical bird flies north: The Greenish Elaenia. *American Birds* 39: 242–44.

Morrison, R. I. G., and J. P. Myers. 1987. *Wader Migration Systems in the New World.* Wader Study Group Bulletin 49, Suppl.: 57–69. Ottawa: Canadian Wildlife Service.

Mowbray, T. B., C. R. Ely, J. S. Sedinger, and R. E. Trost. 2002. Canada Goose, *Branta canadensis.* In *The Birds of North America,* no. 682, ed. A. Poole and F. Gill. Philadelphia: Birds of North America, Inc.

Myers, J. P. 1979. The Pampas shorebird community: Interactions between breeding and nonbreeding members. Pp. 37–49 in *Migrant Birds in the Neotropics: Ecology, Behavior, Distribution, and Conservation,* ed. J. A. Keast and E. S. Morton. Washington, D.C.: Smithsonian Institution Press.

Myers, J. P., R. I. G. Morrison, P. Z. Antas, B. A. Harrington, T. E. Lovejoy, M. Sallaberry, S. E. Senner, and A. Tarak. 1987. Conservation strategy for migratory species. *American Scientist* 75: 19–26.

Nehrling, H. 1882. List of birds observed at Houston, Harris Co., Texas and vicinity and in the cos. Montgomery, Galveston and Ford [*sic*] Bend. *Bulletin of the Nuttall Ornithological Club* 7: 6–13, 166–75, 222–25.

Newfield, N. L. 1985. Records of Allen's Hummingbird in Louisiana and possible Rufous × Allen's Hummingbird hybrids. *Condor* 85: 253–54.

Nicholls, J. L., and G. A. Baldassarre. 1990. Winter distribution of Piping Plovers along the Atlantic and Gulf coasts of the United States. *Wilson Bulletin* 102: 400–12.

Niven, D. K., J. R. Sauer, G. S. Butcher, and W. A. Link. 2004. Christmas Bird Count provides insights into population changes in landbirds that breed in the boreal forest. *American Birds* 58: 10–20.

Oberholser, H. C. 1918. The subspecies of *Larus hyperboreus. Auk* 35: 62–65.

———. 1930. The migration of North American birds. 2nd ser., 43: Ivory-billed Woodpecker. *Bird Lore* 32: 265.

———. 1974. *The Bird Life of Texas,* ed. E. Kincaid. Austin: University of Texas Press.

Ornithology Group, Outdoor Nature Club. 1953–2004. "Clearing House" column, *Spoonbill.* Houston: Outdoor Nature Club.

———. 1962. *Checklist of the Birds of the Upper Texas Coast.* Compiled by S. G. Williams. Houston: Outdoor Nature Club.

Packard, F. M. 1946. California Gull on the coast of Texas. *Auk* 63:545–46.

———. 1947. Notes on the occurrence of birds in the Gulf of Mexico. *Auk* 64:130–31.

Peake, D. E., and M. Elwonger. 1996. A new frontier: Pelagic birding in the Gulf of Mexico. *Winging It* 8(1):1–9.

Peterson, R. T. 1960. *A Field Guide to the Birds of Texas.* Boston: Houghton Mifflin.

Peterson, R. T., and E. Chalif. 1973. *A Field Guide to Mexican Birds.* Boston: Houghton Mifflin.

Peterson, R. T., and J. Fisher. 1955. *Wild America.* Boston: Houghton Mifflin.

Pettingell, N. 1967. Eskimo Curlew: Valid records since 1945. *Bulletin of the Texas Ornithological Society* 1(3, 4):14, 21.

Phillips, A. R. 1975. Semipalmated Sandpiper: Identification, migrations, summer and winter ranges. *American Birds* 29:799–806.

Post, P. W., and R. H. Lewis. 1995a. The Lesser Black-backed Gull in the Americas: Occurrence and subspecific identity, Part I: Taxonomy, distribution, and migration. *Birding* 27(4): 282–90.

———. 1995b. Lesser Black-backed Gull in the Americas: Occurrence and subspecific identity, Part II: Field identification. *Birding* 27(5): 370–81.

Poulin, R. G., S. D. Grindal, and R. M. Brigham. 1996. Common Nighthawk, *Chordeiles minor.* In *The Birds of North America,* no. 213, ed. A. Poole and F. Gill. Philadelphia: Academy of Natural Sciences and Washington D.C.: American Ornithologists' Union.

Pulich, W. M., Sr. 1988. *The Birds of North Central Texas.* College Station: Texas A&M University Press.

Ramos, M. G. (ed.). 1995. *1996–1997 Texas Almanac.* Dallas: Dallas Morning News.

Rappole, J. H., and G. W. Blacklock. 1985. *Birds of the Texas Coastal Bend.* College Station: Texas A&M University Press.

———. 1994. *Birds of Texas: A Field Guide.* College Station: Texas A&M University Press.

Remsen, J. V., Jr. 1986. Was Bachman's Warbler a bamboo specialist? *Auk* 103: 216–19.

Rich, T. D., C. J. Beardmore, H. Berlanga, P. J. Blancher, M. S. W. Bradstreet, G. S. Butcher, D. W. Demarest, E. H. Dunn, W. C. Hunter, E. E. Iñigo-Elias, J. A. Kennedy, A. M. Martell, A. O. Panjabi, D. N. Pashley, K. V. Rosenberg, C. M. Rustay, J. S. Wendt, and T. C. Will. 2004. *Partners in Flight North American Landbird Conservation Plan.* Ithaca: Cornell Laboratory of Ornithology.

Richardson, D., E. R. Rozenburg, and D. Sarkozi. 1998. *A Birder's Checklist of the Upper Texas Coast,* 8th ed. Houston: Ornithology Group, Outdoor Nature Club.

Richardson, W. J. 1978. Timing and amount of bird migration in relation to weather: A review. *Oikos* 30(2):224–72.

Ridgley, H. 2003. Backyard Habitat: Why curtailing your cat is for the birds. *National Wildlife* 31(3), Apr/May 2003.

http://www.nwf.org/nationalwildlife/article.cfm? articleId=768&issueId=61

Ridgely, R. S., and G. Tudor. 1994. *The Birds of South America,* vol. 2. Austin: University of Texas Press.

Robbins, C. S., B. Bruun, and H. S. Zim. 1966. *Birds of North America.* New York: Golden Press.

Roberson, D. 2002. Some thoughts on the 'Solitary Vireo' complex: Blue-headed Vireo *Vireo solitarius* v. Cassin's Vireo *V. cassinii.* Accessed 24 May 2002. http://www .montereybay.com/creagrus/sovi-id-comm.html

Robinson, J. A., and G. Aumann. 1997. An American Woodcock nest in Galveston County, Texas. *Bulletin of the Texas Ornithological Society* 30(1):20–22.

Robinson, S. K., J. A. Grzybowski, S. I. Rothstein, M. C. Brittingham, L. J. Petit, and F. R. Thompson. 1992. Management implications of cowbird parasitism on Neotropical migrant songbirds. Pp. 93–102 in *Status and Management of Neotropical Migratory Birds,* ed. D. M. Finch and P. W. Stangel. USDA Forest Service Gen. Tech. Rep. RM-229. Fort Collins: U.S. Forest Service.

Roemer, F. 1849. *Texas: With Particular Reference to German Immigration and the Physical Appearance of the Country.* Bonn. Translation by Oswald Mueller, 1935, San Antonio: Standard Printing Company.

Root, T. 1988. *Atlas of Wintering North American Birds.* Chicago: University Chicago Press.

Rosenberg, K. V., S. E. Barker, and R. W. Rohrbaugh. 2000. *An Atlas of Cerulean Warbler Populations, Final Report to USFWS: 1997–2000 Breeding Seasons.* Cornell Laboratory of Ornithology. http://birds.cornell.edu/cewap/ cwapresultsdec18.pdf

Sarkozi, D. 2004. *Birds of the Upper Texas Coast. Texas On-line Clearinghouse.* http://www.texasbirding.net/ txclrhouse/index.html

Sasser, R. 1997. Texas discovers HIP way to track gamebird numbers. *Dallas Morning News,* 21 Sep 1997, p. 6B.

Scott, S. L. (ed.). 1987. *Field Guide to the Birds of North America.* Washington, D.C.: National Geographic Society.

Scott, V. E., K. E. Evans, D. R. Patton, and C. P. Stone. 1977. *Cavity-Nesting Birds of North American Forests.* Agriculture Handbook 511. Washington, D.C.: Forest Service, U.S. Department of Agriculture.

Sennett, G. B. 1878. Notes on the ornithology of the lower Rio Grande of Texas, from observations made during the season of 1877. *Bulletin of the U.S. Geological and Geographical Survey of the Territories* 4(1): 1–66.

Seyffert, K. D. 2001. *Birds of the Texas Panhandle: Their Status, Distribution, and History.* College Station: Texas A&M University Press.

Seymour, F. 2004. Cats—An Annotated Bibliography. *Animals Australia.* Accessed 9 Oct 2004. http://www .animalsaustralia.org/default2.asp?idL1=1274&idL2=1311

Shackelford, C. E., and G. G. Simons. 2000. *A Two-year Report of the Swallow-tailed Kite in Texas: A Survey and*

Monitoring Project for 1998 and 1999. Austin: Texas Parks and Wildlife Department PWD BK W7000-496 (6/00).

Shelford, V. E. 1963. *The Ecology of North America.* Urbana: University of Illinois Press.

Shepler, D. 2003. Birding discussion list for Texas. Posted 18 Feb 2003. University of Houston. Texbirds@listserv.uh.edu.

Sibley, D. A. 2000. *The Sibley Guide to Birds.* New York: Alfred A. Knopf.

Simmons, G. F. 1914. Spring migration (1914) at Houston, Texas. *Wilson Bulletin* 26:128–40.

———. 1915. *With Rallus in the Texas Marsh.* Condor 17:3–8.

Singley, J. A. 1893. Notes on the birds of Galveston Island. Pp. 355–63 in *Fourth Annual Report of the Geological Survey of Texas for 1892.* Austin: Department of Agriculture, Insurance, Statistics and History, Geological Survey of Texas.

Smalley, A. E., G. B. Smalley, A. J. Mueller, and B. C. Thompson. 1991. Roof-nesting Gull-billed Terns in Louisiana and Texas. *Journal of Louisiana Ornithology* 2(1):18–20.

Spearing, D. 1991. *Roadside Geology of Texas.* Missoula: Mountain Press Publishing Company.

Stevenson, H. M. 1957. The relative magnitude of the trans-Gulf and circum-Gulf spring migrations. *Wilson Bulletin* 69(1):39–77.

Stevenson, H. M., and B. H. Anderson. 1994. *The Birdlife of Florida.* Gainesville: University Press of Florida.

Stiles, F. G. 1972. Age and sex determination in Rufous and Allen hummingbirds. *Condor* 74:25–32.

Stout, G. D. (ed.). 1967. *The Shorebirds of North America.* New York: Viking Press.

Strecker, J. K., Jr. 1912. The birds of Texas: An annotated checklist. *Baylor University Bulletin* 15(1):1–69.

Texas Ornithological Society, Bird Records Committee. 1984. *Check-list of the Birds of Texas,* 2nd ed. Austin: Texas Ornithological Society.

———. 1995. *Checklist of the Birds of Texas.* 3rd ed. Austin: Capital Printing.

Texas Parks and Wildlife Department. 1999. *The Great Texas Coastal Birding Trail: Upper Texas Coast* (map). Austin: Texas Parks and Wildlife Department.

———. 2004a. *Endangered Birds of Texas.* Accessed 15 August 2004. http://www.tpwd.state.tx.us/nature/endang/animals/birds/

———. 2004b. *Summary of 2004–2005 hunting regulations.* Accessed 15 Aug 2004. http://www.tpwd.state.tx.us/hunt/regs/2004/waterfowl/duck_limits/

Thompson, J. A. (chair). 2003. *Mute Swan (Cygnus olor) in the Chesapeake Bay: A Draft Bay-Wide Management Plan.* Chesapeake Bay Mute Swan Working Group. U.S. Fish and Wildlife Service, Chesapeake Bay Field Office. http://www.chesapeakebay.net/pubs/calendar/NISW_12–10–03_Report_6_5129.pdf

Tveten, J. L. 1993. *The Birds of Texas.* Fredericksburg, Tex.: Shearer Publishing.

Tveten, J. L., and G. A. Tveten. 1993. *Wildflowers of Houston and Southeast Texas.* Austin: University of Texas Press.

U.S. Census Bureau. 2003. United States Department of Commerce News. Texas county fastest-growing in nation. 17 April 2003. Washington, D.C.: Public Information Office. Accessed 8 Nov 2004. http://www.census.gov/Press-Release/www/2003/cb03–65.html

U.S. Department of Agriculture, National Agricultural Statistics Service. 2002 Census of Agriculture. http://www.nass.usda.gov/census/census02/profiles/tx/index.htm

U.S. Fish and Wildlife Service. 2004. News Release, 1 Dec 2004. *Whooping Crane Population Reaches Record High.* http://news.fws.gov/NewsReleases/R2/8F4A82F1-EE32-D71A-21F0F54EC683910C.html

Vines, R. A. 1960. *Trees, Shrubs and Woody Vines of the Southwest.* Austin: University of Texas Press.

Wauer, R. H. 1973. *Birds of Big Bend National Park and Vicinity.* Austin: University of Texas Press.

Weeks, R. J., and M. A. Patten 2000. First Texas record of a Yellow-footed Gull. *Texas Birds* 2(1):25–33.

Weller, M. W. 1994. Seasonal dynamics of bird assemblages in a Texas estuarine wetland. *Journal of Field Ornithology* 64(3):388–401.

Weniger, D. 1984. *The Explorer's Texas: The Lands and Waters.* Austin: Eakin Press.

White, M. 2002. *Birds of Northeast Texas.* College Station: Texas A&M University Press.

Wiedenfeld, D. A., and M. G. Wiedenfield. 1995. Large kill of Neotropical migrants by tornado and storm in Louisiana, April 1993. *Journal of Field Ornithology* 66:(1)70–80.

Williams, G. G. 1936–51. *Gulf Coast Migrant*, privately published newsletter, nos. 1–66. Houston, Tex.

———. 1938. Notes on the waterbirds of the Upper Texas Coast. *Auk* 55:62–70.

———. 1945. Do birds cross the Gulf of Mexico in spring? *Auk* 62:98–111.

———. 1950. Weather and spring migration. *Auk* 67 (3):52–65.

———. 1959. Probable Eskimo Curlew on Galveston Island, Texas. *Auk* 76:539–41.

Williamson, S. L. 2001. *Hummingbirds of North America.* Boston: Houghton Mifflin.

Wilson, E. O. 1992. *The Diversity of Life.* Cambridge, Mass.: Harvard University Press.

Winkler, H., D. A. Christie, and D. Nurney. 1995. *Woodpeckers: An Identification Guide to the Woodpeckers of the World.* New York: Houghton Mifflin.

Wolfe, L. R. 1956. *Check-list of the Birds of Texas.* Lancaster, Pa.: Intelligencer Printing Company.

Zimmer, K. J. 1985. *The Western Bird Watcher.* Englewood Cliffs, N.J.: Prentice-Hall.

INDEX

Major discussions of bird species are indicated by bold page numbers; references to photographs appear in italics.

Calamospiza melanocorys, **246**
Calcarius: lapponicus lapponicus, **252**; mccownii, **251**; ornatus, **252**; pictus, 252
Calidris: alba, 105, 107, 108, **123**; alpina, 105, 107, 108, **127–28**; bairdii, 105, 107, 108, 125, **126**; canutus, 105, 106, 107, 108, **122–23**; ferruginea, **128**; fuscollis, 105, 106, 107, 108, **125–26**; himantopus, 105, 107, 108, **128**; maritima, 105, **127**; mauri, 105, 107, 108, **124–25**, 127; melanotos, 105, 107, 108, **126–27**; minutilla, 103, 105, 107, 108, **125**; pusilla, 105, 107, 108, **123–24**
Calonectris diomedea, 62, **63**
Calypte: anna, 165, **170**; costae, 165, 170
Campephilus principalis, 174, **179–80**
canebrake habitat, 12, 13
Canvasback, 37, **47–48**
Caprimugidae, 161–64
Caprimulgus: carolinensis, 23, 25, 27, 161–62, **163**; vociferus vociferus, 161–62, **163–64**
Caracara, Crested, 82, 83, **94–95**, following p. 34
Caracara cheriway, 82, 83, **94–95**, following p. 34
Cardinal(s): about, 241–42; Northern, 242, **252–53**
Cardinalidae, 241
Cardinalis: cardinalis magnirostris, 242, **252–53**; sinuatus sinuatus, 253
Carduelis: flammea, **265**; pinus pinus, **265**; psaltria psaltria, **266**; tristis tristis, **266**
Carl, Prince of Solms-Braunfels, 12
Carpodacus: mexicanus, **264–65**; purpureus purpureus, **264**
Catbird, Gray, 13, 22, 24, 27, **215**
Cathartes aura, **81–82**, 83
Catharus: bicknelli, 211; fuscescens fuscescens, 22, 24, 211, **212**; guttatus, 211, **213**; minimus minimus, 23, 25, 211, **212**; ustulatus swainsoni, 22, 24, 211, **212–13**
Catoptrophorus semipalmatus, 104, 106, 107, 108, **117**
cats, and bird mortality, 30
cattail (Typha spp.), following p. 34
Central Flyway, 19
Certhia americana americana, **205–206**
Ceryle: alcyon alcyon, **173**; torquata torquata, **173**
Chaetura: pelagica, **164–65**; vauxii, 165
Charadriiformes, 103
Charadrius: alexandrinus, 104, 106, 107, 108, **110–11**; melodus, 2, 104, 108, **112**,

following p. 34; montanus, 15, **113**; semipalmatus, 103, 104, 107, 108, **111–12**; vociferus, 27, 104, 106, 107, 108, **112–13**; wilsonia, 104, 106, 107, 108, **111**
Chat, Yellow-breasted, 13, 23, 25, 27, 220, **239**
Checklist of Birds of the Upper Texas Coast (Williams), 1
Chen: caerulenscens, 19, 27, 37, **39–40**; rossii, **40**
Chickadee, Carolina, **204**
Chlidonias niger, 134, **148**
Chloroceryle americana, **173–74**
Chocolate Bayou, 15
Chondestes grammacus grammacus, 18, **245–46**
Chordeiles: acutipennis texensis, 161, **162**; gundlachii, 163; minor, 161, **162–63**
Christmas Bird Counts, 27
Chuck-will's-widow, 23, 25, 27, 161–62, **163**
Circus cyaneus, 82, 83, **87**
Cistothorus: palustris, 206, **208–209**; platensis stellaris, 206, **208**, 248
Clangula hyemalis, **51**
Clark, Ed, 30
Claybottom Pond rookery, 72
climate, 10. See also weather conditions
coastal habitats of shorebirds, 107–109
coastal marshland habitat, 10–12
coastal plain habitat, 14
coastal prairie habitat, 10–12, 14–15
Coccothraustes vespertinus vespertinus, **266**
Coccyzus: americanus americanus, 22, 24, 27, 154, **155**; erythropthalmus, 23, 25, 154, **154–55**; melacoryphus, 155; minor continentalis, 154, **155–56**
Colaptes: auratus auratus, 174, **178–79**; auratus collaris, 28, 174, **179**
Colibri thalassinus, **167**
Columba livia, 28, **150**
Columbidae, 149
Columbina: inca, **152**; passerina passerina, **152–53**
Conlinus virginianus, 55, **56**
Contopus: cooperi, 23, 25, **180–81**; sordidulus, **181**; virens, 22, 24, 27, **181**, following p. 34
Conuropsis carolinensis, **154**
Coot, American, 97, **101–102**
Coragyps atratus, **80–81**, 83
cordgrasses (Spartina spp.), following p. 34
Cormorant(s): about, 65; Double-crested,

65, 69, **70**; Neotropic, 65, **69–70**, following p. 34; Olivaceous (see Cormorant, Neotropic)
Corvidae, 197
Corvus: brachyrhynchos paulus, 198, **199**; corax sinuatus, 198, **200**; cryptoleucus, 198, **199**; ossifragus, 198, **199**
Coturnicops noveboracensis, 97, **97–98**
Cowbird(s): about, 257; Bronzed, 257, **261**; Brown-headed, 13, 257, **261–62**; Shiny, 257, **261**
Crane(s): Sandhill, 72, **102**; Whooping, 72, **102–103**
Creeper, Brown, **205–206**
Crossbill, Red, **265**
Crotophaga: ani, 157; sulcirostris sulcirostris, 154, **156–57**, following p. 34
Crow(s): about, 198; American, 198, **199**; Fish, 198, **199**; Rain (see Cuckoo, Yellow-billed)
Cuckoo(s): about, 154; Black-billed, 23, 25, 154, **154–55**; Dark-billed, 155; Mangrove, 154, **155–56**; Yellow-billed, 22, 24, 27, 154, **155**
Curlew(s): Eskimo, 2, 15, 30–31, 106, 110, **118–20**, following p. 34; Long-billed, 15, 104, 107, 108, **120**
Cyanocitta cristata cristata, 89, 197, **198**
Cyanocompsa parellina, **254**
Cygnus: buccinator, **42**; olor, 28, 37, **41–42**
Cynanthus latirostris magicus, **167–68**

Dendrocygna: autumnalis, 37, **38**; bicolor, **38–39**
Dendroica: caerulescens caerulescens, 20, 23, 25, 26, 27, **225–26**; castanea, 21, 22, 24, 27, 220, **230**; cerulea, 21, 23, 25, **231**; chrysoparia, **227**; coronata auduboni, 22, 24, 27, 219, 220, **226**; coronata coronata, **226**; discolor discolor, 23, 25, 27, 220, **229–30**; dominica albilora, 23, 25, 220, **228**; fusca, 23, 24, 27, 220, **228**; graciae, **229**; magnolia, 22, 24, 27, 220, **224–25**; nigrescens, 27, 220, **226–27**; occidentalis, 20, **227–28**; palmarum, 15, 23, 25, 26, 27, 219, 220, **230**, following p. 34; pensylvanica, 22, 24, 27, **224**; petechia, 22, 24, 27, 220, **224**; pinus pinus, 193, 219, 220, **229**; striata, 20, 23, 25, 219, **230–31**; tigrina, 20, 23, 25, **225**, 230; townsendi, 20, 27, **227**, 228; virens virens, 23, 25, 27, 220, **227**
Dickcissel, **256**

Gull(s): about, 133; Black-headed, 138; Bonaparte's, **137–38**; California, 133, **138–39**; Franklin's, 133, **136–37**; Glaucous, 133, 139, **141**; Great Black-backed, 140, **141**; Herring, **139**, 141; Kelp, 133, **141–42**; Laughing, 133, **135–36**, *following p. 34*; Lesser Black-backed, 140, *following p. 34*; Little, 133, **137**; Mew, 133, **138**; Ring-billed, **138**; Sabine's, 133, **142**; Thayer's, 133, **139–40**; Yellow-footed, 133, **140–41**

habitats: diversity of, and birdlife, 16–17; ecoregions, 4, 8; fragmentation of, 13–14, 29; grasslands, 14–15, 18–19, 55; loss of, and raptors, 82, 84; modification of, impact on birdlife, 14, 15, 18, 19, 21, 29; partitioning of, among shorebirds, 106–109; wetlands, 11–12, 37, 107–109; woodlands, 10–11, 12–14, 21. *See also* vegetation
Haematopus: ostralegus, 113; *palliatus*, 104, 106, 107, 108, **113–14**
Hagar, Connie, 1
Haliaeetus leucocephalus, 82, 83, **86–87**, 94
Harrier, Northern, 82, 83, **87**
Harvest Information Program, 131
Hawk(s): about, 82, 83; Broad-winged, 83, **89–91**; Cooper's, 82, 83, **88**; Ferruginous, 83, **93**; Fuertes Red-tailed, 92; Harlan's, 92–93; Harris's, 83, **89**; Krider's Red-tailed, 92; Marsh (*see* Harrier, Northern); Red-shouldered, 83, **89**, 90; Red-tailed, 82, 83, **92–93**, 94; Rough-legged, 83, **93–94**; Sharp-shinned, 83, **87–88**; Sparrow (*see* Kestrel, American); Swainson's, 83, **91**, *following p. 34*; White-tailed, 82, 83, **91–92**, 93, 94, *following p. 34*; Zone-tailed, **92**
hawk watch at Smith Point, 82–84
hazards for birds, 29–31
Helmitheros vermivorus, 21, 23, 25, 219, 220, **233**
herbicides, and bird mortality, 30
Heron(s): Black-crowned Night-, 72, **77**; Great Blue, **73**; Great White (*see* Heron, Great Blue); Green, **76–77**; Little Blue, 72, **74–75**; Louisiana (*see* Heron, Tricolored); Tricolored, 72, **75**; Yellow-crowned Night-, **77–78**
Heteroscelus incanus, **117**
High Island, 4–5, 72, *following p. 34*

Himantopus mexicanus, 104, 106, 107, 108, **114**, *following p. 34*
Hirundo rustica erythrogaster, 27, 200, **203–204**
history of Upper Texas Coast, 1–3
Houston Audubon Society, 21, 72, 269
Hummingbird(s): about, 165–67; Allen's, 165, **172–73**; Anna's, 165, **170**; Berylline, 168; Black-chinned, 165, 166, **170**; Blue-throated, 165, **169**; Broad-billed, **167–68**; Broad-tailed, 165, **171**; Buff-bellied, 165, **168**; Calliope, 165, **170–71**; Costa's, 165, 170; Ruby-throated, 22, 24, 27, 165, **169**, 170; Rufous-tailed, 168; Rufus, 165, 166, **171–72**, *following p. 34*; Violet Crowned, **168**; White-eared, 168
hunting: American Coot, 102; American Woodcock, 132; economic impact, 37; Mourning Dove, 152; for plumes, 16, 43, 74, 79; of waterfowl, 37, 40, 43, 48; Wilson's Snipe, 131
hurricanes, and bird mortality, 30
Hylocharis leucotis, 168
Hylocichla mustelina, 13, 18, 21, 22, 24, 211, **213**

Ibis(es): Glossy, 72, **78**; White, **78**; White-faced, **78–79**
Icteria virens virens, 13, 23, 25, 27, 220, **239**
Icteridae, 256–57
Icterus: bullockii, **263**, *following p. 34*; *cucullatus sennetti*, **262**; *galbula*, 22, 24, 27, 257, **263**; *parisorm*, **263–64**; *pustulatus*, **262–63**; *spurius spurious*, 22, 24, 257, **262**
Ictinia mississippiensis, 83, **86**
industrialization, impact on habitats, 29
introduced bird species, 28. *See also* names of specific birds
invasive plants, 15
Ixobrychus exilis, 72, **73**
Ixoreus naevius, 211, **214**

Jabiru, **79–80**
Jabiru mycteri, **79–80**
Jacana, Northern, 106, **115**
Jacana spinosa, 106, **115**
Jaeger(s): about, 133; Long-tailed, **135**; Parasitic, **135**; Pomarine, 133, **134–35**
Jay(s): about, 197; Blue, 89, 197, **198**; Green, 197; Western Scrub-, 197
journal articles on birdlife of Upper Texas Coast, 2

Junco(s): about, 241; Dark-eyed, **251**; Slate-colored (*see* Junco, Dark-eyed)
Junco hyemalis, **251**
Juncus spp., *following p. 34*

Katy Prairie, 14–15, 92, *following p. 34*
Katy Prairie Conservancy, 15, 269
Kestrel, American, 27, 83, 92, **95**
Killdeer, 27, 104, 106, 107, 108, **112–13**
Kincaid, Edward, 1
Kingbird(s): Cassin's, **188–89**; Couch's, **188**; Eastern, 22, 24, 27, **189**; Gray, **189–90**; Tropical, **188**; Western, 23, 25, 27, 180, **189**
Kingfisher(s): Belted, **173**; Green, **173–74**; Ringed, **173**
Kinglet(s): Golden-crowned, **209–10**; Ruby-crowned, 27, **210**
Kiskadee, Great, 180, **186–87**
Kite(s): Mississippi, 83, **86**; Swallow-tailed, 13, 18, 83, **84–85**; White-tailed, 82, 83, **85–86**
Kittiwake, Black-legged, 133, **142–43**
Knot, Red, 105, 106, 107, 108, **122–23**

Lampornis clemenciae clemenciae, 165, **169**
Lanius: excubitor, **191**; *ludovicianus*, **190–91**
large wading birds, 38, 71–79
Lark, Horned, **200**, *following p. 34*
Larus: argentatus, **139**, 141; *atricilla*, 133, **135–36**, *following p. 34*; *californicus*, 133, **138–39**; *canus*, 133, **138**; *delawarensis*, **138**; *dominicanus*, 133, **141–42**; *fuscus*, **140**, *following p. 34*; *hyperboreus*, 133, 139, **141**; *livens*, 133, **140–41**; *marinus*, 140, **141**; *minutus*, 133, **137**; *philadelphia*, **137–38**; *pipixcan*, 133, **136–37**; *ridibundus*, **138**; *thayeri*, 133, **139–40**
Laterallus jamaicensis, 97, **98–99**
lead poisoning, 48
Legatus leucophaius, 188
Limnodromus: griseus, 103, 105, 107, 108, **130**, *following p. 34*; *scolopaceus*, 105, 107, 108, **130–31**
Limnothlypis swainsonii, 13, 18, 23, 25, **233–34**
Limosa: fedoa, 105, 107, 108, **121**; *haemastica*, 104, 106, 107, 108, **120–21**; *lapponica*, 121; *limosa*, 121
Lonchura punctulata, 28
Longspur(s): about, 241, 242; Chestnut-

ISBN-13: 978-1-58544-510-3
ISBN-10: 1-58544-510-X